More praise for *American Judaism: A History*, by Jonathan D. Sarna

"As the distillation of Jonathan Sarna's lifetime of careful scholarship on Judaism and American Jews, this volume offers compelling reading for general readers, as well as university students. It is hardly possible to imagine a more satisfying interweaving of four compelling narratives: of the Jewish people as an ethnic story, of Judaism as a religious story, of the Jewish people as contributors to American history, and of American Jewish experiences in relation to the experience of Jews in Europe and the Middle East. This is a landmark book."—Mark A. Noll, author of *America's God, from Jonathan Edwards to Abraham Lincoln*

"There is no person more qualified than Jonathan Sarna to give us a fresh, important, and provocative perspective on American Judaism. In this book he has given us precisely that. We are the better for it." —Deborah E. Lipstadt, Emory University

"Informed by a sophisticated awareness of trends in American social and religious history, this magisterial study demonstrates how Jews in different eras have actively shaped distinctively American versions of Judaism during their 350-year sojourn on these shores."—Jack Wertheimer, Provost, Jewish Theological Seminary

"This outstanding book represents a major contribution to the historiography of American Judaism. The book is comprehensive, thorough, and a delight to read."—Steven Bayme, Director, Contemporary Jewish Life, American Jewish Committee

"This astonishingly comprehensive and detailed history of American Jewish life offers a fascinating analysis of the complex effects of pluralism upon Jewish continuity. A major contribution to American religious history."—Albert J. Raboteau, Henry W. Putnam Professor of Religion, Princeton University

"What a prodigious feat. Jonathan Sarna has captured, in one book, 350 years of the trends and challenges which confronted American Jewry and confront us yet today. He presents the communal responses as a prelude to today's diversity and fragmentation and encourages us to be optimistic about the future of American Jewry. Very informative and illuminating."—Shoshana S. Cardin, Chairman, JTA–The Global News Service of the Jewish People

"*American Judaism* provides a comprehensive and insightful portrait of the American Jewish experience. Sarna is magisterial as well as accessible in this work, and *American Judaism* will serve as the standard book in the field. *American Judaism* indicates why Sarna has earned his reputation as the premier American Jewish historian of his generation." —Rabbi David Ellenson, President, Hebrew Union College–Jewish Institute of Religion

"Jonathan Sarna has written what I believe will be seen as the definitive book on American Judaism as we prepare to celebrate our 350th year in residence on these shores. We are at a point in this history when the American Jewish community is turning inward. We have come to realize it is time to reinvigorate and replenish our own community while still maintaining interest and support of our people throughout the world. In order to do this effectively we must know our story here in America, know how our vibrant and successful community was born and grew to its current heights. Dr. Sarna has given us the tool we need."—Carolyn Starman Hessel, Jewish Book Council

"A masterfully contextualized synthesis with exactly the right focus, full of elegance, empathy and insight."—Ismar Schorsch, Chancellor, Jewish Theological Seminary of America

"Jonathan Sarna has given us a rich, comprehensive history of Judaism's story in America. It is a lucid, insightful, engaging narrative of Judaism's journey through the American experience. Professor Sarna dispassionately relates the development of a passionate people's struggle to adapt a timeless tradition to a bold new world. Even as he chronicles an array of challenges confronting Judaism in America, he points to successes and opportunities as we continue building an enduring history into the future."—Richard M. Joel, President, Yeshiva University

American Judaism

JONATHAN D. SARNA

American Judaism

A HISTORY

Yale University Press
New Haven & London

Published with assistance from the Mary Cady Tew Memorial Fund.

Designed by Nancy Ovedovitz and set in
Monotype Times New Roman by Duke & Company.
Printed in the United States of America by R. R. Donnelley & Sons.

Library of Congress Cataloging-in-Publication Data
Sarna, Jonathan D.
American Judaism : a new history / Jonathan D. Sarna.
p. cm.
Includes bibliographical references and index.
ISBN 0-300-10197-X
1. Judaism—United States—History. 2. Jews—United States—
History. I. Title.
BM205.S26 2004
296′.0973—dc21   2003014464

A catalogue record for this book is available from the British Library.

The paper in this book meets the guidelines for permanence and
durability of the Committee on Production Guidelines for Book
Longevity of the Council on Library Resources.

10 9 8 7 6 5 4 3 2 1

To Aaron Yehuda and Leah Livia
Our children shall be our sureties
Midrash Tanhuma, Vayigash, 2

Contents

Acknowledgments

The fact that this volume appears at all represents something of a miracle. In 1999, while the manuscript was in progress, I was diagnosed with esophageal cancer. Chemotherapy, radiation, and massive surgery followed, and in defiance of the odds, I survived. My first thanks, therefore, go to the doctors, nurses, relatives, friends, and colleagues who carried me through this ordeal, and especially to Drs. Michael Jaklitsch, David Kelson, Andrea Ng, Michael Rabin, Nahum Vishniavsky, the nursing staff at the Brigham & Women's hospital, the members of Congregation Shaarei Tefillah in Newton, my colleagues at Brandeis University, and the on-line esophageal cancer discussion list known as the "EC-Group." Their collective faith is borne out by this volume, which demonstrates, among many other things, that there is life after cancer.

Beyond this, the volume represents the culmination of over thirty years of sustained interest in the history of American Judaism, a subject that first aroused my curiosity as a senior in high school. Along the way, I had the great good fortune to study under leading scholars at Brandeis and Yale, including Marshall Sklare, Leon Jick, Ben Halpern, Morton Keller, Kathleen Neils Conzen, Sydney Ahlstrom, and David Brion Davis. In the summer of 1977, I met for the first time the dean of American Jewish historians, Jacob Rader Marcus, and from then until the last days of his long life in 1995 he served as my teacher and mentor. For much of that time we also sat as colleagues on the faculty of the Hebrew Union College–Jewish Institute of Religion in Cincinnati. Both Professors Ahlstrom and Marcus encouraged me to write this book; both felt that the religious history of the American Jew had been unduly neglected.

I approach the study of American Judaism from the perspective of an insider. I have spent my entire life involved in Orthodox, Conservative, and Reform Jewish institutions, and I maintain close friendships and family relationships across the full spectrum of Jewish life, from fervently Orthodox to radically secular. In writing about American Judaism, then, I am writing about a world that I know at first-hand. At the same time, my life has also been spent within the world of scholarship, a world that I was born into, as the son of a professor, and one that I happily continue to inhabit. In this book, as in all of my writing, I have endeavored to balance my passionate Jewish commitments with my dispassionate scholarly ones.

Numerous libraries and archives have assisted me with my research over the years. I single out for thanks the Brandeis University library, now home to the personal library of Jacob Rader Marcus; the Hebrew Union College libraries in Cincinnati and Jerusalem; the Jewish National Library at the Hebrew University in Jerusalem; the Jacob Rader Marcus Center of the American Jewish Archives in Cincinnati; the National Center for Jewish Film at Brandeis; and the American Jewish Historical Society, formerly at Brandeis and now part of the Center for Jewish History in New York.

Through the years I have received numerous grants and fellowships that have assisted me in my research. I am particularly grateful to the American Council of Learned Societies, the American Jewish Committee, the Lilly Endowment, the Memorial Foundation for Jewish Culture, the National Foundation for Jewish Culture, the Pew Trusts, and the Scheuer Foundation whose support (in some cases for projects with other objectives) made it possible for me to research aspects of American Jewish history that I would not otherwise have understood. The Joseph H. & Belle R. Braun Chair at Brandeis University, and especially a fund set up to accompany that chair by Larry and Nancy Glick, have been of immeasurable help to me through the years, and helped to finance the preparation of this volume for press, as well as the ordering of photographs. The actual writing began with support from a Fellowship for University Teachers awarded me by the National Endowment for the Humanities in 1996. I completed the bulk of the book in Jerusalem, where I was once again honored to receive a fellowship from the Lady Davis Fellowship Trust. More recently, generous grants from the Lucius N. Littauer Foundation and from the Dorothy and Julius Koppelman Institute on American Jewish-Israeli Relations of the American Jewish

Committee have made it possible for this volume to be published in Israel in a Hebrew translation simultaneously with its English-language appearance.

Several chapters of this volume were first delivered as lectures. It was a great thrill to be able to deliver parts of Chapter 1, dealing with colonial Judaism, from the pulpit of the Touro Synagogue in Newport, America's oldest surviving synagogue, during the John Carter Brown Library's conference on "The Jews and the Expansion of Europe to the West." Part of the chapter appeared in print in the conference volume, edited by Paolo Bernardini and Norman Fiering, and is reprinted here with permission and in revised form. Much of the chapter also appeared as an introductory essay to David L. Barquist's magnificent catalogue, published by Yale University Press, entitled *Myer Myers: Jewish Silversmith in Colonial New York* (2001). I delivered sections from several other chapters as the 2002 Samuel Paley lectures in American History at the Hebrew University, and as other lectures at the Hebrew University, Tel Aviv University, Bar Ilan University, and Haifa University. I appreciate the many helpful comments made to me by my hosts and by audience participants on those occasions.

A great many friends and colleagues generously took time away from their own scholarship in order to read and comment on mine. Dianne Ashton, Jon Butler, Kimmy Caplan, Naomi W. Cohen, Steven M. Cohen, Jay M. Eidelman, Eli Faber, Rosemary Farber, Sylvia Barack Fishman, Allison Fultz, Jane Kamensky, Eli Lederhendler, Riv-Ellen Prell, Uzi Rebhun, David Silberklang, Ellen Smith, Holly Snyder, Lance Sussman, and Beth Wenger all read one or more individual chapters and provided valuable criticism. Zahava Cohen and Susan Glazer assisted me with photographs, the bibliography, and editorial chores, thereby improving this volume in many ways. Ryan Arp helped with one of the maps. My son, Aaron Y. Sarna, expertly scanned many of the photographs, which might otherwise not have been able to appear at all. Steven Bayme, the late Charles Liebman, Pamela Nadell, Dale Rosengarten, Stephen Whitfield, and three anonymous readers for Yale University Press read and commented upon the entire manuscript, sparing me from many infelicities and errors. Any that remain, of course, are my responsibility alone.

Brandeis University has been my academic home for the entire life of this project. Its remarkable president, Jehuda Reinharz, and my distinguished colleagues in the Department of Near Eastern and Judaic Studies have been singularly supportive and encouraging. Special thanks to Anne Lawrence, our academic administrator, and to her assistant Jennifer Coveney. The

Jacob Rader Marcus Center of the American Jewish Archives, whose Academic Advisory and Editorial Board I have the honor to chair, has also been consistently helpful. I am especially grateful to its executive director, Gary P. Zola, and to its chief archivist, Kevin Proffitt, for extending themselves on innumerable occasions on my behalf. I am also indebted to the Institute of Contemporary Jewry at the Hebrew University, where I taught during my sabbatical, and to Jerusalem's Pardes Institute, where my wife and I served as Blaustein scholars.

Yale University Press proved exceptionally generous, patient, and helpful to me throughout the course of this book's development. Charles Grench acquired the manuscript for Yale and was the very model of forbearance and understanding when I needed both. Lara Heimert inherited the volume, encouraged it, and made numerous editorial suggestions that redounded to my benefit. Heidi Downey, Keith Condon, and others at the Press magically transformed raw manuscript into a handsomely published book.

Last but not least, I thank my family. My wife, Ruth Langer, read and commented on each chapter as it appeared, listened with feigned interest to my latest discoveries, and believed that I would live to see this work completed even when I was far less certain. My parents, in-laws, and extended family of Sarnas, Horowitzes, Aarons, and Langers provided moral support, a great deal of love, and much-needed distractions. My children, Aaron and Leah, understood how important this book was to me, assisted in countless ways, and remain mystified by my fascination with the topic. Whether they know it or not, Aaron and Leah actually represent my most tangible contribution to the future of American Judaism. It is to them that I dedicate this book, with love.

Introduction

Thirty years ago, when I first became interested in American Jewish history, I mentioned my interest to a scholar at a distinguished rabbinical seminary, and he was absolutely appalled. "American Jewish history," he growled, "I'll tell you all that you need to know about American Jewish history: the Jews came to America, they abandoned their faith, they began to live like *goyim* [Gentiles], and after a generation or two they intermarried and disappeared." "That," he said, "is American Jewish history; all the rest is commentary. Don't waste your time. Go and study Talmud."

I did not take this great sage's advice, but I have long remembered his analysis, for it reflects, as I now recognize, a long-standing fear that Jews in America are doomed to assimilate, that they simply cannot survive in an environment of religious freedom and church-state separation. In America, where religion is totally voluntary, where religious diversity is the norm, where everyone is free to choose his or her own rabbi and his or her own brand of Judaism—or, indeed, no Judaism at all—many, and not just rabbinical school scholars, have assumed that Judaism is fated sooner or later to disappear. Freedom, the same quality that made America so alluring for persecuted faiths, also brought with it the freedom to make religious choices: to modernize Judaism, to assimilate, to intermarry, to convert. American Jews, as a result, have never been able to assume that their future as Jews is guaranteed. Each generation has had to wrestle anew with the question of whether its own children and grandchildren would remain Jewish, whether Judaism as a living faith would end and carry on as ancestral memory alone.

The history of American Judaism, as I have come to understand it, is in many ways a response to this haunting fear that Judaism in the New World will wither away. Over and over again for 350 years one finds that Jews in America rose to meet the challenges both internal and external that threatened Jewish continuity—sometimes, paradoxically, by promoting radical discontinuities. Casting aside old paradigms, they transformed their faith, reinventing American Judaism in an attempt to make it more appealing, more meaningful, more sensitive to the concerns of the day. They did not always succeed, as the many well-publicized accounts of eminent Christians whose parents, grandparents, or great-grandparents turn out to have been Jews amply attest. But the story of American Judaism recounted in this book is not just a stereotypical tale of "linear descent," of people who start off Orthodox and end up intermarrying. It is, instead, a much more dynamic story of people struggling to be Americans and Jews, a story of people who lose their faith and a story of people who regain their faith, a story of assimilation, to be sure, but also a story of revitalization.

Fear for American Judaism's future certainly underlies many aspects of this story. But, in retrospect, the many creative responses to this fear, the innovations and revivals promoted by those determined to ensure that American Jewish life continues and thrives, seem of far greater historical significance.

For students of American religion, Judaism's ongoing fear of disappearing arouses little surprise. Faiths ranging from Armenian Christianity to Zoroastrianism have faced similar challenges in the American environment. In fact, the vast majority of America's approximately sixteen hundred religious and spiritual groups are substantially smaller than Judaism, and many of them have good reason to fear for their future. The experience of the Huguenots, members of the French Reformed church, serves as an object lesson here. The Huguenots immigrated to America in larger numbers than Jews did in the colonial era, but they failed to maintain their distinctive faith and culture, and large numbers of their descendants intermarried. As a result, they had disappeared as an independent religious community by the beginning of the nineteenth century. Many other American faiths have likewise disappeared. Between 1890 and 1906, fully 13.8 percent of the groups listed in the U.S. Census of Religious Bodies went out of existence; between 1916 and 1926 that rate jumped to 15.3 percent. Some of those religious bodies merged; others metamorphosed in one way or another. Still others vanished completely.[1]

What does render American Judaism unique from the perspective of American religion is not its survival-related fears, which are commonplace and well founded, but rather the fact that for the major part of American history it has been the nation's largest and most visible non-Christian faith. Every Jew, every synagogue, every Jewish organization, periodical, and philanthropy has served as a conspicuous challenge to those who sought to define the nation (or its soul) in restrictively Christian terms. From their very first steps on American soil, back in 1654, Jews extended the boundaries of American pluralism, serving as a model for other religious minorities and, in time, expanding the definition of American religious liberty so that they (and other minorities) might be included as equals. "Giving them [the Jews] liberty, we cannot refuse the Lutherans and Papists," proclaimed New Amsterdam's colonial governor, Peter Stuyvesant. The decision to admit Jews forced the colony as a whole to become more religiously accepting. George Washington, in a famous letter in 1790, assured Jews that "it is now no more that toleration is spoken of as if it were by the indulgence of one class of people that another enjoyed the exercise of their inherent natural rights." Echoing the fondest hopes of the Newport Jews who addressed him, he offered his personal guarantee that the government of the United States "gives to bigotry no sanction, to persecution no assistance."[2]

Bigotry and persecution, of course, did not thereafter miraculously disappear. American Jews continued to have to fight for their religious rights well into the twentieth century, and manifestations of anti-Jewish prejudice have continued to the present day. But important changes nevertheless took place. Slowly, America came to understand itself in broader and more inclusive religious terms that pushed beyond the perimeters of Christianity. Abraham Lincoln's memorable phrase in the Gettysburg Address, later incorporated into the Pledge of Allegiance, was this "nation under God." Thanks to the efforts of interfaith organizations active around World War II, terms like "Judeo-Christian" came into vogue. Will Herberg, in a bestselling book published in 1955, described a "tripartite scheme" of American religion: "Protestant-Catholic-Jew." All of these terms signified Jews' newfound acceptance in the world of American religion—their emergence, in less than two hundred years, from a curiosity into America's "third faith." No longer were they grouped with exotic religions and nonbelievers, as in the well-known colonial-era phrase "Jews, Turks, and infidels." Instead, by the late twentieth century, they emerged as acknowledged religious insiders.[3] Emblematically, one of their number, Senator Joseph Lieberman, a practicing Orthodox Jew, received the Democratic Party's nomination in the year 2000 to be the vice-president of the United States.

"Only in America," Senator Lieberman declared upon being nominated.

While something of an exaggeration—Jews have also attained high office in countries stretching from Austria to Singapore—his comment reflects a widely felt sense that the history of Judaism in the United States is both special and distinct ("America is different"). Discrimination and persecution, the foremost challenges confronting most diaspora Jews through the ages, have in America been less significant historical factors than have democracy, liberty of conscience, church-state separation, and voluntarism. Emancipation from legally imposed anti-Jewish restrictions, and the penetration of secular "enlightenment" ideas into Jews' traditional religious culture, central themes of Jewish history in Europe, have also been far less central to the history of the Jews in the United States. Expulsions, concentration camps, and extermination, of course, have never been part of American Jewish history. By contrast, in America, as nowhere else to the same degree, Judaism has had to adapt to a religious environment shaped by the denominational character of American Protestantism, the canons of free market competition, the ideals of freedom, and the reality of diversity. What is distinctive in American Judaism is largely a result of these factors.

In addition to being distinctive, the history of American Judaism is also far more complex and interesting than common wisdom would have us believe. It is a history replete with cyclical patterns and unpredictable ones, periods of religious decline and periods of religious revitalization, eras when Judaism was far weaker than before and eras when, by all measures, it was stronger. It is a history that deserves to be better known and more assiduously studied by students of American religion. It is also a history that commands the attention of contemporary Jews, for American Judaism's past, at least as I read it, sheds considerable light on its present-day challenges and its destiny.

Any attempt to capture within a single book 350 years of American Judaism—all religious streams, all regions of the country, all synagogues, all Jews—necessarily smacks of hubris. The very term "American Judaism" defies meaningful definition, for Jews as a people cannot be disentangled from Judaism as a faith. Traditionally, Judaism constitutes what is known as an ethnic church: its members distinguish themselves as much by their common "tribal" ancestry (real or imagined) as by their doctrines and practices.* In reality, however, as my father, an eminent Bible scholar, once ob-

*Converts to Judaism, as a result, formally adopt both the Jewish religion and Jewish ancestry. Jewish documents register them as children of the biblical patriarch Abraham and his wife, Sarah.

served in another context, the "variable, restless, frequently chaotic, and always kaleidoscopic configurations of American Jewish life do not easily yield to procrustean generalizations." Indeed, American Judaism cannot even be directly paralleled to Protestantism and Catholicism, since Judaism embraces many individuals who affiliate with no religious institutions whatsoever but nevertheless carry a strong sense of Jewish identity based upon their Jewish descent and their commitment to secular, cultural, philanthropic, or nationalist Jewish causes. Any effort to offer even a reasonably comprehensive and coherent account of American Judaism must, as a consequence, fall short.[4]

In this volume, I have nevertheless sought to adapt for the study of American Judaism four basic guidelines enumerated by Sydney Ahlstrom in his magisterial *A Religious History of the American People.* According to Ahlstrom, the study of any religion must properly be situated within its historical framework. For American Judaism, this means paying special attention to American history, Jewish history, and the history of American religion. Second, the term "religion" needs to be construed broadly, so as to include not only "secular" movements but also those opposed to religion altogether. Jewish secularism, communism, and what came to be known as "Jewishness," or *"Yiddishkeit,"* are, from the historian's perspective, religions ("agnosticism does not preclude religiosity and moral seriousness"). They fall within the purview of American Judaism. Third, diversity must be accepted as a fact and analyzed. Differences in belief and practice, gender differences, regional differences, differences rooted in Old World custom—all characterize American Judaism and all merit attention. Holistic interpretations, by contrast, must be employed with great caution. Finally, Ahlstrom reminds us that religion can never be understood in a vacuum. Social, economic, political, cultural, and psychological factors affecting religious life must constantly be borne in mind.[5]

Hewing, however imperfectly, to these guidelines, my interpretation diverges in numerous places from accepted scholarly wisdom. Many readers, for example, will find my emphasis on the early period in American Jewish history, prior to the arrival of East European Jewish immigrants in the 1880s, something of a surprise. Already in the late colonial period, I contend, American Judaism had begun to diverge from religious patterns that existed in Europe and the Caribbean. The American Revolution, the ratification of the Constitution, the passage of the Bill of Rights, and the nationwide democratization of religion that followed from these developments further transformed Jewish religious life. All of this culminated, in the 1820s, in the first dramatic turning point in the history of American Judaism: the collapse of the unified "synagogue-community" and its replacement by a more pluralistic and diverse "community of synagogues." During the mid-nineteenth century, a further development of immense importance took place, as American Jews formulated three competing strategies to develop and preserve American Judaism: one that called for upholding Judaism's sacred traditions, another that sought to adapt Judaism to new conditions of life in a new land, and a third that attempted to preserve above all a strong sense of Jewish peoplehood and communal unity. Tensions between these different strategies, all of which reflect important Jewish religious values, persist to this day.

My periodic discussions of "revivals" and "awakenings" in American Judaism, such as those that occurred in the late 1870s and late 1930s, may also surprise some readers. Terms such as "revival," "awakening," and "renaissance" play little part in the traditional religious vocabulary of Judaism, and they run counter to those interpretations that posit inevitable declension ("assimilation") as Judaism passes down from one generation to the next. Moreover, some scholars have questioned whether even in Protestantism "religious awakenings" ever truly existed. Were they merely "interpretive fictions," perhaps "more a cycle . . . in the attention of secular writers than in the extent of actual religious excitement?"[6]

My own use of the term "revival" borrows heavily from anthropology, where religious revitalization movements are linked to major cultural reorientations. The "revivalists" I describe responded to events like the late nineteenth-century rise of antisemitism, the menace of Nazism, and the impact of the Holocaust by searching for new meaning, order, and direction in a society where rapid change and unexpected intrusions had disrupted the order of life. While by no means all-encompassing, the innovative programs they stimulated resulted, at the very least, in Jewish institutional growth, increased involvement in ritual and worship, and a heightened interest in Jewish education and culture, particularly among young people. These new initiatives, in turn, produced unexpected bursts of religious life where American Jews least expected to find them: in their own backyards.[7]

A large number of other discoveries and new interpretations may be found in this volume, far more than can be summarized here. But three points of departure from standard presentations of American Judaism require notice. First, I resist the common practice of dividing American Jewish history into artificially constructed "generations" defined on the basis of when the majority of Jews immigrated (1881–1914). Not only do all such generational schemes inevitably distort the historical record, ignoring hundreds of thousands of Jews with deeper roots in American soil, as well as hundreds of thousands more who immigrated after World War I, but the whole artifice rests on the false and tunnel-visioned assumption that Jews are more influenced by their "generation in America" than by their surroundings and the events of their day.

Second, I deliberately use the term "assimilation" sparingly, more often as a description of what Jews feared would happen to them in America than as a depiction of what actually befell them. Through the years, "assimilation" has become so freighted with different meanings, modifiers, and cultural associations that for analytical purposes it has become virtually meaningless. In some Jewish circles, indeed, the term is regularly employed as an epithet. While scholars remind us that assimilation can entail the "healthy appropriation of new forms and ideas" and can actually be salutary, "a challenge and a goad to renewed creativity," that hardly comports with common usage. I prefer, therefore, to avoid the word whenever possible.[8]

Finally, I steer away from the term "denomination" except insofar as I am referring to one or another Protestant denomination. Denominationalism emerged in eighteenth-century Protestantism to define the new religious situation in countries like the United States where no single church was numerically dominant or legally established, but all stood as equals before the law and had to learn to coexist. Denominational doctrine repudiated the monolithic notion of one all-embracing "true church" and affirmed instead a more inclusive and pluralistic conception of Christendom, recognizing, in effect, many parallel paths to divine Truth.[9] This concept, we shall see, greatly influenced the course of Judaism in America, but well into the twentieth century Jews resisted the term "denomination" itself. Reform, Conservative, and Reconstructionist forms of Judaism always referred to themselves as movements, wings, or streams of Judaism, not as separate denominations. Even today, most Jews identify themselves outwardly as "Jews" and are so identified by their neighbors—unlike Protestants, who, if asked, identify themselves denominationally as "Episcopalians," "Lutherans," "Baptists," and so forth. Moreover, ethnic ties among Jews continue to transcend denominational boundaries, and many of the most powerful Jewish communal institutions, from Jewish community centers to Jewish philanthropies, eschew denominational identifications altogether. To be sure, the *American Jewish Year Book* has, in recent years, adopted the term "denomination" in discussing the different religious movements, and the term has also become normative in contemporary Jewish religious discourse.

But "denomination" does not carry precisely the same meaning for Judaism as it does for Protestantism, and applied to nineteenth- or early twentieth-century Judaism it is clearly anachronistic. The newfound popularity of the term tells us more about divisions in American Jewish life today than about relations among America's Jewish religious movements in the past.

The great Norwegian novelist Ole Edvart Rølvaag once wrote that "when a people becomes interested in its past life [and] seeks to acquire knowledge in order to better understand itself, it always experiences an awakening of new life."[10] This volume, coinciding as it does with the 350th anniversary of American Jewish life, provides a welcome opportunity to profit from Rølvaag's keen insight. To study the history of American Judaism is, among many other things, to be reminded anew of the theme of human potential; in our case, the ability of American Jews—young and old, men and women alike—to change the course of history and transform a piece of their world. This volume is not just a record of events, it is the story of how people *shaped* events: establishing and maintaining communities, responding to challenges, working for change. That, perhaps, is the greatest lesson that I can offer readers: the knowledge that they too can make a difference, that the future is theirs to create.

Colonial Beginnings

New Amsterdam, part of the remote Dutch colony of New Netherland in present-day New York State, was among the New World's most diverse and pluralistic towns. A French Jesuit missionary in 1643 reported that "eighteen different languages" were spoken by local inhabitants of different sects or nations. In addition to the legally protected Calvinist faith, he encountered Catholics, English Puritans, Lutherans, and Anabaptists. A large supplementary influx of dissenting Protestants (including Lutherans, Quakers, and Anabaptists) subsequently arrived from Europe. Then, on a late summer day in September 1654, a small French frigate named the *Ste. Catherine* sailed into the port.[1] Most of the ship's passengers—"twenty-three souls, big and little"—were bedraggled Jewish refugees from Recife, Brazil. Having been expelled from Recife when the Portuguese recaptured the colony from the Dutch, they were now seeking a new home.[2]

The refugees were not the first Jews to arrive in North America. Back in 1585, a Jew named Joachim Gaunse served as the metallurgist and mining engineer for the ill-fated English colony on Roanoke Island. He conducted soil experiments in Carolina, returned to England a year later, and in 1589 was indicted as a Jew for blasphemy. Thereafter a small number of other Jews, mostly intrepid merchants bent on trade, made brief stops at American ports to conduct business. One of them, Solomon Franco, agent for a Dutch Jewish merchant, arrived in Boston in 1649. A "stranger" unable to post the necessary bond, he was duly warned out of town and sailed off as soon as he could. In 1654 itself, several Jews came to New Amsterdam from Holland and Germany, also presumably to trade. The "big and little" refugees from Recife, however, differed from the Jews who came before them. Though economically ruined, they sought to settle down and form a permanent Jewish community in North America, to "navigate and trade near and in New Netherland, and to live and reside there."[3]

By the time these Jewish refugees arrived, the clergy of the dominant Dutch Reformed Church already felt deeply agitated, fearing that their legal prerogatives as the colony's only recognized faith were being usurped. Peter Stuyvesant, the dictatorial director-general of New Netherland and himself an elder of the Reformed Church and the son of a minister, sympathized with them. His mission was to establish order among the citizenry, to combat "drinking to excess, quarreling, fighting and smiting." He sought to promote morality and social cohesion by enforcing Calvinist orthodoxy while rooting out nonconformity. When Lutherans petitioned for permission to call for a minister and organize a congregation, he was relieved that his superiors in Amsterdam turned them down. He forced them to worship in private; some were even subjected to fines and imprisonment.[4]

When the Jews arrived, Stuyvesant sought permission from Amsterdam to keep them out altogether. The Jews, he explained, were "deceitful," "very repugnant," and "hateful enemies and blasphemers of the name of Christ." He asked the directors of the Dutch West India Company to "require them in a friendly way to depart" lest they "infect and trouble this new colony." He warned in a subsequent letter that "giving them liberty we cannot refuse the Lutherans and Papists." Decisions made concerning the Jews, he understood, would serve as precedents and determine the colony's religious character forever after.[5]

Forced to choose between their economic interests and their religious sensibilities, the directors of the Dutch West India Company back in Amsterdam voted with their pocketbooks. They had received a carefully worded petition from the "merchants of the Portuguese [Jewish] Nation" in Amsterdam that listed a number of reasons why Jews in New Netherland should be permitted to stay there. One argument doubtless stood out among all the others: the fact that "many of the Jewish nation are principal shareholders." Responding to Stuyvesant, the directors noted this fact and referred as well to the "considerable loss" that Jews had sustained in Brazil. They ordered Stuyvesant to permit Jews to "travel," "trade," "live," and "remain" in New Netherland, "provided the poor among them shall not become a burden to the company or to the community, but be supported by their own nation." After several more petitions, Jews secured the right to trade throughout the colony, serve guard duty, and own real estate. They also won the right to worship in the privacy of their homes, which seems to have been more than the Lutherans were permitted to do.[6]

Just as Stuyvesant had feared, the economic considerations that underlay these decisions regarding the Jews soon determined policy for members of the colony's other minority faiths. "We doubt very much whether we can proceed against [these faiths] rigorously without diminishing the population and stopping immigration which must be favored at a so tender stage of the country's existence," the directors admonished in 1663 after Stuyvesant banished a Quaker from the colony and spoke out against "sectarians." "You may therefore shut your eyes, at least not force people's consciences, but allow every one to have his own belief, as long as he behaves quietly and legally, gives no offense to his neighbor and does not oppose the government."[7]

Expedience thus became the watchword in cosmopolitan New Amsterdam, though it stood in constant tension with the established Dutch church. The priority of economics proved fortunate for the refugee Jews and the small group of immigrants from Holland who joined them. They benefited from their ties to powerful merchants of the "Hebrew Nation" back in Amsterdam and drew sustenance from the struggles of other minority faiths in the colony whose efforts were linked to their own. New Amsterdam's Jews, like those of Trieste, Bordeaux, Amsterdam, London, and the Caribbean, were port Jews; they lived in societies that placed a premium on commerce and trade. This helps to explain the extraordinary privileges that they came to enjoy and the many "modern" features that distinguished their lives from those of the far more traditional Jews in Germany and Eastern Europe. Everywhere, the rights that port Jews battled hardest to obtain were civil and economic rights, not religious ones. Public worship, while desirable and available to Jews in cities like Recife and Amsterdam, was not, they knew, an absolute religious requirement. Granted the right to settle and trade openly, the Jews of New Amsterdam conceded to worship in private, just as enterprising religious dissenters did throughout Early Modern Europe.[8]

REFUGEES FROM THE INQUISITION

The seeds of Judaism sown in mid-seventeenth-century colonial America fell from plants nurtured in the soil of the Iberian peninsula. There Jews had lived for more than a thousand years, climaxing in the Golden Age of the eleventh and twelfth centuries, an era characterized by unparalleled Muslim-Jewish symbiosis. With the Christian reconquest of Spain, however, reaction and repression set in, and by the late fourteenth century conditions for Jews had precipitously deteriorated. Hundreds were massacred in anti-Jewish rioting in 1391 and 1412–14, and thousands at that time converted to Catholicism: some forcibly, some voluntarily, some out of conviction, and some simply to avoid a grisly death. All of these converts, known as *conversos,* were forbidden by church law from ever returning to Judaism. Consequently, a number—how many is disputed—began to practice their ancestral faith in secret, abetted by Jews, often their own relatives, who remained unconverted. The Holy Inquisition, introduced in Spain in 1481, attempted to root out such Crypto-Judaism, charging its adherents (whom they derisively labeled *marranos,* meaning "swine") with "Judaizing," a form of heresy. Inquisitors employed torture to wring confessions from those alleged to have practiced Judaism in secret, and they burned hundreds at the stake. In 1492, in an effort to sever lines of communication between conversos and Jews, Spain's King Ferdinand and Queen Isabella expelled "all Jews and Jewesses of whatever age they may be" from their "kingdoms and seignories," warning them never to return "as dwellers, nor as travelers, nor in any other manner whatsoever." Just as Christopher Columbus went sailing off to the new world in the summer of 1492, Jewish life in Spain officially ended.[9]

Five years later, when the royal families of Spain and Portugal were united in marriage, refugees who thought they had found haven in Portugal, along with that country's native Jews, faced expulsion again. This time, however, they were forcibly baptized en masse and then forbidden to emigrate for many years in order to protect the state from economic losses. With its leadership intact, Judaism in Portugal fled underground. And there it survived, albeit in mutilated form, passed clandestinely from one generation to the next. From the inside, it was protected by pious women and men who sanctified domestic time and space in ways that recalled the Judaism of their past—through rituals such as lighting candles on Friday night, cleaning house at Passover time, and fasting on the Day of Atonement. From the outside, it was reinforced by ties of kinship, as well as by "Judaizers" who risked their lives to exhort their fellow "New Christians" to keep the embers of Judaism from burning out.[10]

Crypto-Jews took their faith with them when they crossed the ocean to Spanish and Portuguese colonies in the new world. There, far from the clutches of the Inquisition, they thought it would be easier to reconcile the public Catholic and private Jewish aspects of their lives, and to prosper. As so often before, however, the initial success that they achieved proved fleeting. Beginning in 1569, the Holy Inquisition pursued "Judaizing heretics" —real and imagined—into the new world. Fear, repression, torture, and death followed in the Inquisitors' wake.[11]

Wherever they lived, Jews who traced their roots to the Iberian peninsula came to be known as Sephardic Jews, or Sephardim, from the biblical name *Sepharad* (Obadiah 1:20), which they understood to mean Spain. They distinguished themselves from the Jews of the Germanic lands, known as Ashkenazic Jews or Ashkenazim, based on the biblical name *Ashkenaz* (Jeremiah 51:27), associated with Germany. Sephardim developed many distinct rites, practices, traditions, and foodways, and the language of their faith, including words for sacred objects and occasions, appropriated Spanish and Portuguese terms. Culturally, too, Sephardim stood apart from their northern coreligionists. Because there were no ghettos in Spain or Portugal, Sephardim had lived among non-Jews, absorbing Iberian values and learning to appreciate secular knowledge. Yet their collective consciousness had also been seared by memories of cruel expulsions and Inquisitional terror. These experiences shaped the worldview of the Sephardim, underscoring the instability of diaspora life and the fragility of worldly success.[12]

Sephardic Crypto-Jews, forced converts who were outwardly Christian but inwardly Jewish, along with those who escaped Iberia from the fifteenth century onward in order to resume the open practice of Judaism under more favorable regimes, identified as members of a somewhat vaguely defined "Portuguese Jewish Nation."[13] This nation, something of an imagined community, was nevertheless rooted in a common place and culture. Tangled webs of association and kinship, common memories of persecution, and a shared devotion to the maintenance of the Sephardic heritage and tradition bound its members together. Embracing practicing Christians of Jewish origin, as well as strict Jews, the nation emphasized the tribal aspects of Judaism, ties of blood and peoplehood; religion remained a secondary element in this collective identity. The seismic questions posed by this separation of religion from ethnicity—questions concerning the authority of religion in Jewish life, the definition and boundaries of Judaism, and whether Judaism, like post-Reformation Christianity, could be practiced in a multiplicity of ways—would continue to rattle Jews throughout the modern period.[14]

Amsterdam is where these questions first came to the fore. The young Calvinist republic of the Netherlands, newly independent of Spain and bitterly antagonistic toward the Holy Inquisition, emerged as a vibrant center of world trade in the seventeenth century and became a magnet for Crypto-Jews seeking economic opportunity in a more tolerant religious environment.

By the first third of the seventeenth century, synagogues, a Jewish school, and Jewish printing houses had opened in Amsterdam, where most Jews settled. Those who had previously practiced Jewish rituals underground were now able to embrace their ancestral faith openly and to resume living as Jews in the sunlight. But conflicts concerning Jewish religious authority, intellectual and spiritual freedom, and the relationship between practicing Jews and those who still preferred to keep their Jewish ancestry secret plagued the Jewish community. In some cases, they resulted in painful excommunications, such as that of the philosopher Baruch Spinoza in 1656. Economically, meanwhile, the community expanded and thrived. As early as the 1630s, one study shows, Jews of Iberian descent were responsible for as much as 8 percent of the Dutch Republic's total foreign trade.[15]

In 1630, when Holland captured the colony of Pernambuco in Brazil from the Portuguese (aided, it was alleged, by local Crypto-Jews seeking revenge on their former persecutors), Jewish communal life on the Amsterdam model became possible for the first time in the new world. The Dutch West India Company, which governed the colony as a profit-making venture for its investors, sought to attract enterprising Jews to its new dominion. The company had learned to value Jewish merchants as stimulators of industry and trade—not to mention that Jews already spoke the local language (Portuguese) and were connected through ties of kinship and trade with Portuguese conversos who had settled there. In secret instructions, the West India Company explicitly ordered the chief of its expedition to grant Jews liberty on a par with Roman Catholics: "No one will be permitted to molest them or subject them to inquiries in matters of conscience or in their private homes."[16]

Recognizing the region's great economic potential, Jews flocked to Pernambuco, establishing in the city of Recife and its environs a community that, at its peak in the 1640s, amounted to between 1,000 and 1,450 Jews—between a third and a half of Dutch Brazil's total civilian white population. The community included ordained rabbis, an active synagogue, and two Jewish schools—more than any North American Jewish community would be able to claim for another two hundred years. Most significantly, the Jews of Dutch Brazil enjoyed rights unmatched by any other seventeenth-century Jewish community in the world. "Treat and cause to be treated the Jewish nation on a basis of equality with all other residents and subjects in all treaties, negotiations and actions in and out of war without discrimination," the States General of the United Netherlands ordered, seeking to encourage Jewish settlement and trade. With Portugal bidding to recapture Dutch

Brazil, this kind of guarantee may also have been necessary to prevent nervous Jews from moving away. As it was, some six hundred Jews remained in Recife when Portuguese troops recaptured the province on January 26, 1654. Jews as well as Protestants lost everything they had with Holland's defeat, and the Portuguese gave them just three months to leave.[17]

Those Jews who could find safe passage set sail for Amsterdam. There they asked Dutch officials for protection and begged assistance from the city's well-organized community of Jews. Other refugees searched for new world havens, particularly in the Caribbean. By April 26, 1654, all openly professing Jews had left Brazil.

Short-lived as it was, lasting a mere twenty-four years, this first organized Jewish community in the new world was nevertheless of considerable significance. At a time when most of Europe's Jews still lived highly restricted and traditional lives—excluded from many areas, denied citizenship even where they were permitted to settle, and far removed from regular contact with non-Jews—Recife offered an alternative vision, one based on legal equality and commercial opportunity. Protestants, Catholics, and Jews coexisted in Recife, albeit somewhat uneasily, and Jews practiced their religion conspicuously and traded lustily. Long before the forces of enlightenment and emancipation brought about comparable changes in the lives of German and Eastern European Jews, market forces in the new world triumphed over traditional prejudices and created a climate where Jewish life could develop and thrive.[18]

With the fall of Dutch Brazil came a series of three events that transformed Jewish life on both sides of the Atlantic. First, Sephardic Jewish merchants in Holland, seeking to strengthen trade links with the Caribbean weakened by the loss of Recife, stimulated the return of Jews to England, abetted by Manasseh ben Israel, a leading rabbi, mystic, and scholar in Amsterdam. In 1655, Manasseh went to England to petition Oliver Cromwell for the readmission of Jews, who had been expelled in 1290. The rabbi, knowing of Puritan interest in the subject, may even have infused the return with millennial significance, seeing it as a harbinger of Israel's redemption. No formal readmission of Jews took place, but informally Jewish settlement was permitted. By 1695, London was home to eight hundred Jews and a vital center of Sephardic trade between Europe and the new world.[19]

Second came the establishment by Sephardic Jews of new Jewish settlements in the West Indies to replace Recife. The most significant of these, in the Dutch communities of Curaçao (1659), Cayenne (1659), and later Surinam (which passed to Dutch rule in 1667), beckoned Jews with promises

of religious liberty and civic equality that more than matched what Recife
had offered. Prospective Jewish settlers in the Jewish-sponsored colony in
Cayenne, for example, were promised "freedom of conscience with public
worship, and a synagogue and school," as well as "all Liberties and Exemp-
tions of our other colonists as long as they remain there." Given such induce-
ments (plus, in some cases, free one-way passage), poorer Jews, refugees
from Recife among them, agreed to depart Amsterdam, where they lived
on charity, to seek their fortune anew in the colonial world of trade and
commerce. The Jewish population of the Caribbean grew apace.[20]

Third, and surely in the eyes of contemporaries least important, was the
new Jewish settlement established in 1654 by the Jewish refugees who stepped
off the *Ste. Catherine* into the port of New Amsterdam. Later generations,
looking back, celebrated these refugees as the "Jewish Pilgrim Fathers,"
but they were in fact nothing of the sort. The English Pilgrims, who sailed
into the bay at Plymouth, Massachusetts, in 1620, had migrated voluntarily
as Puritan religious separatists seeking a colony of their own where they
could worship, work, and live together according to the tenets of their faith.
By contrast, the Jews who arrived in 1654 came involuntarily, penniless,
and in need of refuge. They did not want a colony of their own but, rather,
permission to reside among the local residents and conduct trade. Moreover, at least according to one historian, women and children dominated
the group; only four among them, he claims, were actually fathers. If they
were not Pilgrim Fathers, however, the refugees did initiate the first Jewish
communal settlement in North America. With their arrival, the history of
American Judaism properly begins.[21]

PRESERVING AND MAINTAINING JEWISH LIFE

The most difficult challenge facing New Amsterdam's nascent Jewish
community—one that American Jews would confront time and again
through the centuries—was how to preserve and maintain Judaism, particularly with their numbers being so small and Protestant pressure to conform
so great. From the earliest years of Jewish settlement, a range of responses
to this challenge developed. At one extreme stood Solomon Pietersen, a
merchant from Amsterdam who came to town in 1654, just prior to the
refugees from Recife, to seek his fortune. In 1656 he became the first known
Jew on American soil to marry a Christian. While it is not clear that he personally converted, the daughter that resulted from the marriage, named
Anna, was baptized in childhood. Like the descendants of many subsequent

Jewish immigrants to America's shores, she vanished into the Protestant mainstream.[22]

Asser Levy (d. 1680/1681) stood at the opposite end of this spectrum. An Ashkenazic Jew from Vilna who had briefly sojourned in Amsterdam and perhaps Brazil, he arrived in New Amsterdam in 1654 impoverished but committed to the maintenance of his faith. In 1655 he protested when Peter Stuyvesant and local officials required male Jews between sixteen and sixty to pay a tax in lieu of guard duty. Stuyvesant had cited the "disinclination and unwillingness" of local residents to serve as "fellow-soldiers" with the Jewish "nation" and "to be on guard with them in the same guard-house." Levy insisted, however, that as a manual laborer he should be able to stand guard just like everybody else. Although initially thwarted, within two years he had succeeded in standing "watch and ward like other Burghers," whereupon he promptly petitioned for burgher rights (citizenship). Again he was thwarted, but, backed by wealthy Jewish merchants who had immigrated months before from Amsterdam and recalled the promises made to them by "the Worshipful Lords" of the Dutch West India Company, the decision was reversed and the rights of Jews to "burghership" guaranteed. Of course, local records still denominated Levy as "a Jew," ensuring that this would be the characteristic that defined him. But he nevertheless enjoyed considerable success as a butcher ("excused from killing hogs, as his religion does not allow him to do it"), merchant, and real estate entrepreneur. Among the Jews who immigrated to New Amsterdam in 1654 he was the only one who stayed, maintaining a home in the city until his death in 1682. For long lonely stretches as Dutch rule waned and the rest of the Jews departed for colonies with more sun and promise, his was the only Jewish family in town. Yet the inventory of his estate suggests that he resolutely observed at least the principal rituals of his faith, including the Sabbath and Jewish dietary laws, within the precincts of his home. His life epitomized both the hardships entailed in being a Jew in early colonial America and the possibilities of surmounting them.[23]

One spur to the maintenance of Jewish communal life was the abiding fear of death. The small congregation of Jews, among them refugees from Recife, the Inquisition, and other calamities and persecutions, had learned from experience that life was fragile—even more fragile for them than for their Christian neighbors. They knew that religious hatred, as well as the diseases and misfortunes common to all humanity, might strike them down at any time. For this reason, in New Amsterdam as in so many communities where Jews later settled, the establishment of a burial ground became the first priority—fear of death, as it were, promoting a spirit of communal life. As early as July 1655, three Jews acting in the name of all others in New Amsterdam petitioned the "Worshipful Director General and Council . . . to be permitted to purchase a burying place for their nation." They certainly "did not wish to bury their dead . . . in the common burying ground," which was Christian. Jews and Christians in Europe (and for that matter in Recife) had regularly buried their followers apart, maintaining in death the separate religious identity so strongly felt in life. The petition to continue this hallowed practice, therefore, proved uncontroversial. The Jews received "a little hook of land" outside the city for a burial place. The location of that land has long since been forgotten, but not its significance as the Jews' first municipally recognized religious turf. It offered Jews the spiritual serenity of knowing that when they died they would be buried within their faith. It also encouraged group loyalty and discipline, since burial in the "little hook of land" could be denied those who violated Jewish communal norms. In 1682, Joseph Bueno de Mesquita purchased a different burial plot "for the Jewish nation in New York" that remained in use (once it was enlarged in 1729) for one hundred and fifty years. Throughout this period and long afterward, death would prove to be a powerful religious stimulus for American Jews. Time and again, the exigencies of life drew individuals away from their people and their faith, and the mystery of death brought them back.[24]

The second and even more important spur to the creation and maintenance of Jewish communal life in New Amsterdam was the arrival late in 1655 of Abraham de Lucena, a Sephardic merchant bearing a Torah scroll garbed in a "green veil, and cloak and band of India damask of dark purple color," borrowed from the synagogue in Amsterdam. The handwritten parchment text of the Pentateuch is Judaism's central and most sacred ritual object, and its reading forms a focal point of Jewish communal worship. In colonial North America, as elsewhere, the presence of a Torah scroll served as a defining symbol of Jewish communal life and culture, of Jewish law and lore. It created a sense of sacred space: the presence of a Torah elevated a profane parlor into a cherished place of holiness, and the private home in which Jews worshipped into a hallowed house of prayer. The return of the green veiled Torah to Amsterdam in about 1663 signified that the community had scattered: the *minyan,* the prayer quorum of ten males over the age of thirteen traditionally required for Jewish group worship, could no longer be maintained.[25]

The subsequent reappearance of Torah scrolls in the city, no later than the 1680s under the British, was a sign that the Jewish community had been reestablished; group worship in private resumed. Wherever Jews later created communities in North America, as in Savannah, they also brought Torah scrolls with them, or as was the case in Newport in 1760, they borrowed a Torah from a larger congregation. In smaller eighteenth-century colonial Jewish settlements, such as Lancaster and Reading, where Judaism was maintained for years by dedicated laymen without a salaried officiant or formal synagogue, the Torah scroll similarly functioned as something of a Jewish icon. It embodied the holy presence around which Jewish religious life revolved.[26]

The British, who took control of New Amsterdam in 1664 and renamed it New York, sought to promote tranquility and commerce. To this end, they scrupulously maintained the colony's religious status quo, initially according Jews the same rights (but no more) as they had enjoyed under the Dutch. The operative British principle, for Jews as for other social and religious deviants from the mainstream, was "quietness," akin to what the sixteenth-century English poet Barnabe Googe had described as "out of sight, out of mind." King Charles II permitted Jews to remain in London in 1664 "soe long as they demeane themselves peaceably & quietly," and the same stipulation was applied to the colonies. If Jews practiced their religion "in all quietness" and "within their houses," the authorities generally left them in peace, tolerating dissenting religious practices so long as they took place privately, outside of communal space. When in 1685 the approximately twenty Jewish families in New York petitioned for the right to worship in public, they were summarily refused; "publique Worship," the Common Council informed them, "is Tolerated . . . but to those that professe faith in Christ." Years later, long after these restrictions had been lifted, many Jews continued to look upon "quietness" as a principle conducive to Jewish group survival. Their instinct, rooted in a history most no longer recalled, was to keep their Judaism as private as possible lest they provoke their neighbors.[27]

Public worship became available to Jews without any fanfare or known change in the law around the turn of the eighteenth century, just about the time when New York's first Quaker meeting house was erected, and before the Baptists and Catholics had opened churches in the city. Based on assessment lists, one scholar believes that he can date with great precision the moment of transition from covert worship in a private home to overt worship in a rented house: "The renting of the synagogue must have taken place between December 28, 1703 . . . and February, 1704." Even if the real date was more like 1695, as other scholars insist, it was in the early eighteenth century that the synagogue drew up its constitution and commenced keeping records. For the next 125 years the synagogue dominated Jewish religious life in New York. Indeed, the synagogue and organized Jewish community became one and the same—a synagogue-community—and as such it assumed primary responsibility for preserving and maintaining local Jewish life.[28]

THE SYNAGOGUE-COMMUNITY

The synagogue-community descended from the *kehillah,* the distinctive form of communal self-government that characterized Jewish life in the Middle Ages. In much of Europe, Jews had lived for centuries as a "people apart," with special obligations and privileges as well as separate taxes, all carefully spelled out in a charter that formed the basis for Jewish group settlement. With the advent of modernity, as states consolidated their power over their citizens and individual rights gradually triumphed over group rights, this corporate Jewish community came to an end. Now in seventeenth-century Western Europe, the synagogue became the locus for Jewish self-government. Where multiple synagogues existed this resulted in communal fragmentation, and in response the Sephardic Jews of Amsterdam in 1638–39 merged their city's synagogues into one, "Kahal Kadosh Talmud Torah." Its leaders became the leaders of the city's Sephardic Jewish community as a whole. The new congregation drew upon Jewish communal patterns going back to Spain and Portugal, but it defined community in terms of the synagogue. It governed its members much like a church governed its parish, thereby promoting discipline while avoiding the appearance of a Jewish "state within a state." The synagogue-community model, akin to the prevailing Protestant model of the established church, spread quickly and widely, taking hold in Recife, Hamburg, London, the West Indies—and then New York.[29]

The synagogue established in New York was located in a small rented house on Mill Street, today South William Street but then popularly known as Jews' Alley. The congregation's official name became Kahal Kadosh Shearith Israel (Holy Congregation Remnant of Israel). Like most new world synagogues of the eighteenth century—including Mikveh Israel (Hope of Israel) in Curaçao and Philadelphia; Nidhe Israel (Dispersed of Israel) in Barbados; and Jeshuat Israel (Salvation of Israel) in Newport—its name hinted at the promise of redemption. "I will surely gather the remnant of Israel," said the prophet Micah (2:12). "I will put them together . . . as the flock in the midst of their fold." The name Shearith Israel thus recalled the widespread belief that the dispersion of Israel's remnant to the four corners of the world heralded the ingathering.[30]

Shearith Israel closely resembled its old and new world counterparts in assuming responsibility for all aspects of Jewish religious life: communal worship, dietary laws, life-cycle events, education, philanthropy, ties to Jews around the world, oversight of the cemetery and the ritual bath, even the baking of matzah and the distribution of Passover *haroset* (a mixture of ground nuts, fruits, spices, and wine used as part of the seder ritual). It saw itself and was seen by others as the representative body of the Jewish community; it acted in the name of all area Jews. In addition, it served as a meeting and gathering place for local Jews, a venue for exchanging "news and tatle."[31]

The advantages of this all-encompassing institution were, from a Jewish point of view, considerable: the synagogue-community proved an efficient means of meeting the needs of an outpost Jewish community. It promoted group solidarity and discipline; evoked a sense of tradition, as well as a feeling of kinship toward similarly organized synagogue-communities throughout the Jewish world; and improved the chances that even small clusters of Jews, remote from the wellsprings of Jewish learning, could survive from one generation to the next.

Looming large among the values espoused by the synagogue-community were tradition and deference. These values had stood Sephardic Jews in good stead for generations and were considered essential to Jewish survival itself. At Shearith Israel, various prayers, including part of the prayer for the government, continued to be recited in Portuguese. The congregation's original minutes were likewise written in Portuguese, even though only a minority of the members understood that language and most spoke English in their day-to-day lives. Portuguese represented tradition; it was the language of the community's founders and of the Portuguese Jewish Nation scattered around the world. (Ladino, or Judeo-Spanish, written in Hebrew characters, was spoken mainly by the Sephardim of the Ottoman Empire.[32]) In matters of worship, too, Shearith Israel closely conformed to the traditional *minhag* (ritual) as practiced by Portuguese Jews in Europe and the West Indies. Innovations were prohibited; "our duty," Sephardic Jews in England (writing in Portuguese) once explained, is "to imitate our forefathers." On a deeper level, Sephardic Jews believed, as did the Catholics among whom they had so long lived, that ritual could unite those whom life had dispersed. They wanted a member of their nation to feel at home in any Sephardic synagogue anywhere in the world: the same liturgy, the same customs, even the same tunes.[33]

This goal, it turned out, proved difficult to realize. One cynical observer, Manuel Josephson, writing in 1790, complained that "our North American Congregations . . . have no regular system . . . they have continually remained in a state of fluctuation." He blamed the small numbers and "frequent mutability" of local Jews, and grumbled that "every new comer introduced something new, either from his own conceit and fancy, or . . . from the Custom of the Congregation where he was bred, or the one he last came from." Even the readers who chanted the liturgy, he fumed, "collected some materials from one & another And patched up a system of ceremonies of his own, which will be followed during the time he remains in office, but no sooner another one succeeds, some new customs & formalities will be introduced." Yet in the end, Josephson too came down on the side of tradition. What American synagogues needed, he proclaimed, was to emulate "the large & old established Congregations abroad." There, he nostalgically recalled, "Custom & ceremonies even the most minute [are] reduced to a regular system, from which they do not deviate on any account."[34]

Deference formed part of the Sephardic mindset as well. Worshippers expected to submit to the officers and elders of the congregation, which were entirely lay-dominated. As in most religious and political institutions of the day, power was vested in men of means. At Shearith Israel, governing authority rested in the hands of the *parnas* (president or warden), assisted by a small number of officers and elders who constituted the *mahamad* or *adjunta* (standing committee). These were usually men of wealth and substance who took on the burden of communal leadership out of a sense of noblesse oblige. *Yehidim* (first-class members), generally men of status who materially supported the congregation, made most of the important decisions; they were the equivalent of "communicants" in Colonial Protestant churches. The rest of the worshippers, including all women, occupied seats at services but held no authority whatsoever.[35]

Even those without power agreed that disobedience to authority should be punished. In 1746, for example, the yehidim of Shearith Israel decreed that obstreperous worshippers be asked to leave the synagogue and not return until they paid a fine. They explicitly included themselves in the edict "if wee do not behave well." In 1760, they severely punished Judah Hays for disobeying the parnas, although he himself was a significant member. In enforcing discipline through such edicts, Jews were following both the teachings of their ancestors and the practices of their non-Jewish neighbors. Indeed, deference to those in authority and to those who held the largest "stake in society" was accepted by "the bulk of Americans" in the mid-eighteenth century. By contrast, the right to dissent, the right to challenge the leadership in a free election, the right to secede and establish a competing congregation, the right to practice Judaism independently and on a voluntary basis—these were unknown in colonial synagogues. Jews of that time would have viewed such revolutionary ideas as dangerous to Judaism and to the welfare of the Jewish community as a whole.[36]

No Jewish religious authority of any kind in colonial America possessed sufficient status to challenge the authority of the laity. Not Shearith Israel, not any of the synagogues subsequently established prior to the Revolution ever hired a *haham* ("sage," the title given to a rabbi in the Sephardic community). Rabbis did not regularly grace American pulpits until 1840. Sermons, when they were delivered at all, were offered by visitors or by the officiating (unordained) reader. London's Sephardic synagogue had considered it "necessary and imperative . . . to have a Haham," and it appointed one in 1664, just seven years after that congregation's founding, to "instruct us and teach the observance of the most Holy Law." In the New World, the Jewish communities of Recife, Curaçao, Surinam, Barbados, and Jamaica all enjoyed the religious leadership of a haham at various times in the seventeenth and eighteenth centuries. In New York, a dearth of members and funds partly explains why Shearith Israel did not follow suit: as late as 1750 the city's Jewish population did not exceed three hundred (sixty families). But the practice of local churches probably explains more. Only about a fourth of the Christian congregations in the province of New York enjoyed full-time pastors in 1750, and even the Anglicans failed to appoint a bishop to oversee their flock. The absence of a professional religious authority thus did not demean Jews in the eyes of their neighbors.[37]

The diversity of the city's Jewish community, which by the mid-eighteenth century embraced Sephardim and Ashkenazim from many different locales, would in any case have made the task of finding an appropriate haham difficult, if not impossible. To compensate, the officiating *hazan* (cantor-reader), in addition to chanting the liturgy, assumed many of the ceremonial functions that a haham might otherwise have performed, including on rare occasions public speaking. Non-Jews came to respect the hazan as "reader and notary," "rector," "minister," "reverend," "pastor," "Jew priest," and even "doctor." To insiders, however, he remained a religious functionary, subject to the whim of the parnas.[38]

Colonial American synagogues also differed from their European and West Indian counterparts in their relationship to the state. In Sephardic Jewish communities as diverse as Bayonne (France), Curaçao, and the Virgin

Islands, synagogue leaders looked to the government to buttress their authority. The leaders of Curaçao's congregation, for example, were constitutionally empowered under various circumstances to seek the "intermediation of the Honorable Governor should all other means fail." In other communities, fear of the state justified extraordinary extensions of Jewish communal power. Concern for "our preservation" led synagogue leaders in London, for example, to demand the right to have "revised and emended" any book written or printed by any local Jew in any language. No such clauses, however, appear in any known American synagogue constitution. In the religiously pluralistic colonial cities where Jews principally settled, local governments (at least in the eighteenth century) extended a great deal of autonomy to churches and synagogues and rarely intervened in their internal affairs. As a result, synagogue leaders, like their church counterparts, found it necessary to rely on their own authority. Under ordinary circumstances, they knew, local officials would not step in to help them.[39]

The ultimate authority available to the synagogue-community was the power of the *herem,* or excommunication, the "principal means of defining social deviance and of removing from the community wayward members whose actions and behavior offended its values." The anathematized person lost all rights within the Jewish community and was treated as if he were dead. Synagogues threatened this punishment far more often than they actually invoked it, for its effectiveness in a society where Jews and Christians mixed freely was highly dubious, and there was always the danger that it would backfire and bring the whole Jewish community into disrepute. More commonly, therefore, punishments consisted of fines, denial of synagogue honors, and, most effective of all, threatened exclusion from the Jewish cemetery—punishments limited to the religious sphere and thus parallel to church forms of discipline.[40]

Even these punishments required some degree of communal consensus. The leaders of Shearith Israel found this out the hard way in 1757 when they attempted to crack down on outlying members of the congregation who were known to "dayly violate the principles [of] our holy religion, such as Trading on the Sab[b]ath, Eating of forbidden Meats & other Henious Crimes." The adjunta darkly threatened these violators with loss of membership and benefits, including that "when Dead [they] will not be buried according to the manner of our brethren." But six months later, in the face of opposition from congregants (and, presumably, a drop in donations), they decided to "reconsider." Citing Isaiah's call to "open the gates" for a "nation that keeps faith" (Isaiah 26:2), they welcomed everybody back into the congregation's good graces. Synagogue-communities thus may be said to have patrolled the "edges" of irreligious behavior, much as New England congregational parishes of the time did. It was more important, they knew, to blazon the possibility of censure than to pursue every accusation.[41]

What really sustained the colonial synagogue-community was not so much discipline as a shared consensus concerning the importance of maintaining Judaism and its central values. Shearith Israel's new Mill Street Synagogue, consecrated in 1730, reflected this consensus in its very architecture and design. Never before had North American Jews built (or even owned) a synagogue, so this was their first opportunity to shape the urban landscape. Since the completion of Trinity Church by the Anglicans in 1696, a slew of competing houses of worship had been built in New York City, including a French church, a Dutch church, a Lutheran church, and a Presbyterian church. These opulently designed buildings, with large spires and towers, had transformed and sacralized the city's skyline, displaying for all to see the colonists' burgeoning material success. Jews had likewise achieved material success (the house of Lewis M. Gomez, for example, was assessed at nearly ten times the value of the frame building that Jews had previously rented as their house of worship), but the new synagogue building as finally constructed favored tradition over external display. It focused on the interior, designed in classical Sephardic style; the exterior was kept comparatively simple, on the scale of the modest New York churches built by the persecuted Baptists and Quakers. In this, local Jews emulated the pattern of clandestine churches *(schuilkerken)* in early modern Europe and of London's Sephardic synagogue, Bevis Marks, completed in 1701. They also anticipated what the Jews of Newport would do when they completed their synagogue, Jeshuat Israel (now known as the Touro Synagogue), in 1763. All of these houses of worship disguised themselves as domestic structures to visually distinguish themselves from established churches and avoid offending the majority faith. They projected an image of deference, offering neighbors the reassurance that Jews kept to themselves. In so doing, they reinforced for local Jews an important cultural lesson that centuries of diaspora experience had repeatedly taught them: to practice great discretion on the outside, not drawing excessive attention to themselves, while glorying in their faith on the inside, where tradition reigned supreme.[42]

Seating arrangements in the new synagogue underscored this message of deference. They mirrored social and gender inequalities within the community and reinforced religious discipline. The congregation assigned a "proper" place to every worshipper, and each seat was assessed a certain

Buildings of note depicted on a map of the city of New York as it was in 1742–44.
The synagogue (second from right, opposite) is included among other houses of
worship and compares to the modest churches of the Quakers and the Baptists.
David Grim, *Plan of the City and Environs of New York as They Were in 1742–1744*
(1813), negative number 3046, Collection of the New-York Historical Society.

membership tax in advance. Members of the wealthy Gomez family thus
enjoyed the most prestigious seats and paid the highest assessments. Others
paid less and sat much farther from the Holy Ark. Women, in accordance
with Jewish tradition, worshipped upstairs in the gallery, removed from the
center of ritual action below. In Amsterdam, Recife, and London, few
women attended synagogue services, so there was little need for designated
seating. In New York, however, where Protestant women frequented church,
Jewish women attended synagogue much more punctiliously, and seats had
to be assigned to them. Since the women's section was small, disputes over
status and deference abounded—so much so that a special area was eventually reserved just for the elite women of the Gomez clan.[43]

An additional source of tension at Shearith Israel and throughout colonial Judaism stemmed from the ever-growing number of Ashkenazic Jews
in North America, immigrants from Central and Eastern Europe whose
traditions, background, and worldview diverged markedly from those of
the founding Sephardim. In Europe and the West Indies, Sephardim and
Ashkenazim worshipped apart. They formed two Jewish communities, married among themselves, and coexisted uneasily. North American Jews, by
contrast, worshipped together, as they had in Recife, with the Sephardim
exercising religious and cultural hegemony. This practice continued even
though Ashkenazim formed a majority of the Jewish population in New
York as early as 1720. The fact that the Sephardim had arrived first and
enjoyed higher status partly explains this anomaly, but the threat on the
part of Curaçao's wealthy Sephardic congregation to stop assisting the New
Yorkers unless they agreed not to allow the German Jews "any More Votes
nor Authority than they have had hitherto" probably explains more. Never-

New Dutch Church | Old Dutch Church | Presbyterian Meeting Baptist M. | Quaker M. | Synagogue | Half Moon Batery

theless, Ashkenazim did come to exercise considerable authority within Shearith Israel's new synagogue, serving as officers slightly more often, according to one calculation, than the Sephardim. Jacob Franks, an Ashkenazic Jew, was a perennial leader of the congregation, and Gershom Mendes Seixas (1745/1746–1816), its most important and beloved colonial-era hazan, was the product of mixed Sephardic-Ashkenazic parentage—as were a growing number of other colonial Jews. Sephardic traditions still held, but Iberian blood ties carried less and less significance. Religion and Jewish peoplehood were becoming the dominant bonds among the Jews of diverse origins who worshipped together in New York, and power was slowly shifting to the Ashkenazim.[44]

The synagogue-community structure of Shearith Israel served as the model for other organized Jewish communities that took root in the American colonies: Savannah (1733), Charleston (1740s), Philadelphia (1740s), and Newport (1750s). All of these communities developed in port cities with mixed urban populations, where Jews found economic opportunity and a substantial measure of religious toleration. Savannah's colonial community was the earliest, the shortest-lived, and the most distinctive. There, in a bid to become self-supporting, forty-two Jews arrived from England on July 11, 1733, sponsored by London's Sephardic community as part of a colonization effort characterized by one historian as an "amalgam of patriotism, philanthropy, expediency, and concern for their fellow Jews." The colonists carried with them a Torah and other religious articles "for the use of the congregation that they intended to establish," won the right to settle and trade (thanks, in part, to the Jewish physician Dr. Samuel Nuñez, who stopped the spread of a ravaging disease), received generous land grants, and were soon joined by other Jews seeking their fortune in the new world —Sephardim as well as Ashkenazim. Group worship in a small hut began at once, the numerically superior Sephardim apparently dominating, and two years later, according to a surviving diary, Jews met "and agreed to

open a Synagouge [*sic*] . . . named K.-K. Mikva Israel," which was organized
on the model of a synagogue-community. In 1740, however, war with Spain
and the threat of a Spanish invasion from St. Augustine frightened the
Sephardic Jews away—they knew what awaited them if Spain won—and
a Torah that had been used in Savannah was forwarded to New York. Two
Ashkenazic Jewish families remained in town worshipping individually, but
the congregation only resumed meeting, at a private home, in 1774. Thereafter, while Sephardic tradition predominated, the lay leaders of Savannah's
community were Ashkenazim.[45]

Charleston, Philadelphia, and Newport developed along different lines.
All three had witnessed multiple attempts to organize as a community, dating back in Newport to the seventeenth century. Success came only in the
second half of the eighteenth century, however, as the number of Jews in
the American colonies increased, approaching one thousand, and colonial
cities prospered. Shearith Israel extended help to these fledgling congregations, and all three followed its lead in organizing as a synagogue-community,
embracing Sephardic tradition and welcoming Jews of diverse origin, including Ashkenazim, into their midst. Not until after the American Revolution
did Jews in Charleston and Philadelphia get beyond the stage of worshipping
in private homes or rented quarters. They lacked both the money and the
confidence to invest in a permanent house of worship. The wealthy Jews of
Newport, by contrast, with financial assistance from Jews in New York,
London, and the West Indies, built a beautiful synagogue, the oldest still
surviving in North America, which they dedicated in 1763, when there were
fifteen to twenty Jewish families in town. Ironically, and not for the last
time in Jewish history, the Newporters who placed much confidence in the
security of their surroundings would soon be disappointed, while the Philadelphia and Charleston Jews who placed little confidence in them were
pleasantly surprised.[46]

JEWISH AND WORLDLY DOMAINS

Synagogue-communities, as they developed in the major cities of colonial
America, bespoke the growing compartmentalization of eighteenth-century
American Jewish life into Jewish and worldly domains. This distinction was
unknown to medieval Jews or for that matter to most European Jews of
the day, but it was characteristic of American Judaism almost from the beginning. Colonial synagogue-communities did not tax commercial trans-
actions, censor what Jews wrote on the outside, or punish members for

The interior of Congregation Jeshuat Israel
in Newport, Rhode Island, now known as
the Touro Synagogue. Designed by the noted
colonial architect Peter Harrison and
dedicated in 1763, the synagogue's interior
resembles, in miniature, those of the Sephardic
synagogues in Amsterdam and London.
Women sit above the men in the balcony.
Courtesy of the Touro Synagogue, Newport.
Photograph by John T. Hopf.

lapses in individual or business morality, unlike synagogues in Amsterdam, London, and Recife. Instead, like the neighboring churches, they confined their activities to their own sphere, disciplining some religiously wayward congregants with fines and loss of religious privileges but leaving commercial and civil disputes, even those that pitted one Jew against another, to the municipal authorities. Some Sephardic Jews went so far as to employ different names in each realm, recalling their former double identities as Crypto-Jews. The renowned Newport merchant Aaron Lopez (1731–1782), for example, occasionally inscribed his business ledgers with his Portuguese baptismal name, Duarte. In the synagogue, he was always known as Aaron.[47]

The social club founded by Newport Jews in 1761 similarly reflected compartmentalization. "Conversation relating to synagogue affairs" was, if not totally prohibited, severely regulated within the club's portals. The very existence of such an institution, a place for low-stakes cardplaying, supper, and imbibing every Wednesday evening in winter, indicates that Jews led bifurcated lives, complete with rules, institutions, and customs that kept synagogue life and general life distinct.[48]

The problem for early American Jews was that central Jewish observances —maintaining the Sabbath on Saturday, celebrating Jewish holidays in the fall and the spring, and observing Jewish dietary laws—blurred the boundaries that the separation of realms sought so scrupulously to maintain. This engendered painful conflicts between the demands of Jewish law and the norms of the larger society in which Jews moved. Refusing to work on the Jewish Sabbath effectively meant working five days instead of six, since local "blue laws" prohibited work on Sunday, the Christian Sabbath. Jewish holidays similarly conflicted with the workaday world of early America. Jewish dietary laws—a complex system of forbidden foods, separation of milk and meat, and special laws for slaughtering and preparing ritually acceptable animals—made travel away from home and social interactions outside of Jewish homes both difficult and awkward.

Early American Jews found no easy solutions to these dilemmas. There was religious laxity aplenty, just as historians have found among English Jews of the time, but there were also those who managed to weave Judaism into the fabric of their daily existence. Indeed, the most striking feature of Jewish life in the colonial period was its diversity—a feature that continued to characterize American Judaism long after the uniformity of colonial synagogue life was forgotten. Within every community, even within many individual families, a full gamut of religious observances and attitudes could be found, from deep piety to total indifference.[49]

Ignorance of Jewish law and the absence of rabbinical authority partly account for this diversity. The small community of Jews in North America consisted of merchants, not scholars, and though some had studied traditional Jewish texts in Europe, none is known to have possessed even a rudimentary Jewish library. Adult Jewish education was not seriously promoted by the synagogue-community. Indeed, Isaac Pinto of Shearith Israel admitted in 1766 that Hebrew, the language of the Bible and the prayer book, was "imperfectly understood by many, by some, not at all." Precisely for this reason, he undertook to translate the Sabbath and High Holiday prayers into English. Dependent on translations and received traditions, rather than on thoroughgoing knowledge of Jewish law, colonial Jews negotiated the gap between Judaism and American life with a combination of intuition and expedience.[50]

When it came to the Sabbath, for example, the wealthy Aaron Lopez "rigidly observed . . . Saturday as holy time," closing his business from Friday afternoon to Monday morning. Over the three-year period for which we have records, none of his ships left port on a Saturday. Many surviving colonial Jewish letters also reflect strict Sabbath observance. One, for example, ends abruptly with the comment "Sabbath is coming on so fast," for once the sun set on Friday, writing was prohibited. Visiting New York in the middle of the eighteenth century, the Swedish naturalist Peter Kalm heard that the city's pious Jews "never boiled any meal for themselves on Saturday, but that they always did it the day before, and that in winter they kept a fire during the whole Saturday." (To avoid lighting a fire on the Sabbath, which was prohibited, fires were lit before sundown on Friday.)[51] On the other hand, Kalm also heard reports of Jewish ritual laxity. Indeed, evidence that Jews were trading on the Sabbath and traveling in violation of its commandment to rest abound—so much so that, as we have seen, Shearith Israel once threatened wayward members who violated the Sabbath with excommunication.[52]

The most revealing of all accounts of Jewish Sabbath observance in the colonial period, however, comes from a missionary to the Delaware Indians named David McClure. Sometime in 1772 he spent a weekend in Lancaster, Pennsylvania, and went with a business order on Saturday to the home of Joseph Simon, a prominent Jewish merchant:

> [Simon] said, "Gentlemen, today is my Sabbath, & I do not do business in it; if you will please to call tomorrow, I will wait on you." We observed that the same reasons which prevented his payment of the order on that day would prevent our troubling him the day following [Sunday]. We apologized for our intruding on his Sabbath, & told him we would wait until Monday. He replied, you are on a journey, & it may be inconvenient to you to wait. He went to call in his neighbor, Dr. Boyd, & took from his Desk a bag, laid it on the table & presented the order to the Dr. The Doctor counted out the money and we gave a recipt. The Jew sat looking on, to see that all was rightly transacted, but said nothing, & thus quieted his conscience against the rebuke of a violation of his Sabbath.

The dilemma of Simon, torn between his Sabbath, his business, and what he saw as common courtesy, very much reflected what many an observant American Jew of his day experienced. Simon's use of a surrogate to solve the problem, however, failed to impress: "He might as well have done the business himself," McClure groused. But what made Jewish life among the Gentiles so difficult was that every solution would likely have been wrong; often Jewish law and American life simply proved irreconcilable.[53]

Jewish holidays posed similar problems. In a traditional Jewish community, as in contemporary Israel, holidays defined the rhythm of the year. They marked the change of seasons, offered a welcome respite from work, and promoted conviviality, family togetherness, and communal religious renewal. America, of course, operated according to a totally different set of annual rhythms. When Jews abstained from work on their holidays they knew that their Christian neighbors, employers, and competitors did not. Nevertheless, the autumn holidays surrounding the Jewish New Year, especially the High Holidays of Rosh Hashanah and Yom Kippur, as well as the spring holiday of Passover, were widely observed—perhaps because they came but once a year and carried deep religious and social meaning. Colonial Jews living in outlying areas often visited communities with synagogues at these times in order to renew their ties with fellow Jews and to revitalize their faith. Isaac Solomon, although he had a Christian wife, traveled all the way from Halifax, Nova Scotia, to Shearith Israel in New York for the New Year's holidays in 1755, and some years later John Franks (likewise married to a Christian) paddled from Halifax to Montreal by canoe for the same purpose.[54]

As on the Sabbath, however, the demands of secular business sometimes clashed with the requirements of faith. On one occasion, the Philadelphia merchant Bernard Gratz was busy in western Pennsylvania negotiating a treaty with the Indians around the High Holidays. Although his brother hoped that he would be home "before Rosh Hashono," in fact he had to send for his High Holiday prayer book and worship alone. Two years earlier, Gratz had greatly distressed his non-Jewish partner, William Murray, by taking off from work on the Jewish holiday of Shavuot, which fell midweek. "Moses was upon the top of a mount in the month of May—consequently his followers must for a certain number of days cease to provide for their families," Murray complained in apparent exasperation. His sense of disbelief underscored the problems Jews faced in maintaining their rituals in an alien environment and explains why some compromised their rituals, or abandoned them altogether.[55]

Dietary laws, of course, presented even greater difficulties for colonial Jews. It was not always easy to find kosher-slaughtered meat, especially for Jews living in isolated communities. Moreover, the laws of *kashrut* were supposed to be observed at all times, even outside the home. They were intended to prevent precisely those kinds of social interactions with non-Jews that commerce and neighborly relations demanded. For those wishing to observe the dietary laws—to eat only kosher meat and avoid mixing dairy and meat products at the same meal—eating at the home of a Gentile friend or business associate posed an enormous challenge. Eighteen-year-old Naphtali Franks, who had recently moved from New York to London, faced this challenge in 1733. His mother, Abigail Franks, the highly intelligent and self-assured wife of the wealthy New York merchant Jacob Franks, "strictly injoyn[ed]" her son to follow the dietary laws faithfully. Assuming the voice of religious authority in her family—how common a role this was for a colonial Jewish woman is unclear—she warned him in a letter "Never [to] Eat Anything . . . Unless it be bread & butter" at any home, Jewish or non-Jewish, "where there is the Least doubt of things not done after our strict Judiacall Method." Some colonial Jews kept the faith by serving as their own ritual slaughterers. Wealthier Jews might hire immigrants to slaughter meat for them, and to teach their children the rudiments of Judaism on the side. Many, however, compromised their ritual observance when kosher food was unavailable. One report from New York claims that Jews on the road, especially if they were young, "did not hesitate the least" about eating pork "or any other meat that was put before them." A Lancaster Jew apologetically explained that he violated dietary laws because he was poor and could not "afford . . . to keep a Person to kill for me." Sephardic Jews in Savannah were particularly lax. Reputedly, they ate "the beef that comes from the warehouse or that is sold anywhere else." Whatever they did, Jews defined themselves religiously through their practice of these laws; they were what they ate. Many, probably the majority, maintained a double standard—one for home and one for outside—that effectively mirrored the bifurcated world which they inhabited.[56]

For all the diversity that characterized the ritual life of colonial American Jews, at least two bedrock principles continued to unite them: their commitment to Jewish peoplehood and their belief in one God. Peoplehood, the feeling of kinship that linked Jews one to another, obligated them to assist Jews around the world and set them apart from everybody else. Bonds of Jewish peoplehood were essentially tribal in nature, rooted in faith, history, and ties of blood. They began for males with circumcision, a rite of religious initiation that colonial Jews maintained (if not necessarily on the traditional eighth day of life) better than they did any other Jewish ritual with the possible exception of the rites connected to death. Ritual circumcision records demonstrate that even Jews far removed from major settlements and traditional Jewish life continued to circumcise their sons—and when necessary adult males too. In 1767, when Aaron Lopez spirited his half-brother and family out of Portugal, saving them "from the reach of Barbarous Inquisition," he arranged for them to obtain what he called, significantly, "the Covenant which happily Characterize us a peculiar Flock." Circumcision, he understood, defined Jews as "peculiar" by permanently distinguishing them from their uncircumcised neighbors. Whatever they might do later, once circumcised they bore forever the characteristic brand of their faith, the traditional sign of the covenant between God and Israel. Circumcision thus represented what one scholar has felicitously called "the cut that binds." It reminded even Jews remote from the wellsprings of Jewish life that they belonged to a worldwide community.[57]

The other bedrock principle that underlay colonial Jewish life was even more fundamental than the first: belief in one supernatural God—no Jesus, no Holy Spirit. References to the Divine power alone abound in colonial Jewish correspondence, from stock phrases like "whom God protect" to heartfelt prayers for life, health, and prosperity. Aaron Lopez once consoled the bankrupt Hayman Levy by referring to the "decrees of a just [and] wise Ruler, who directs all events for our own good." New York merchant Daniel Gomez expressed his belief in God through an original prayer, recorded in his ledger, beginning, "Be merciful to me, O Lord. Forgive my iniquities." Belief in God may also be inferred from mentions of weekday prayer with *tallit* (prayer shawl) and *tefillin* (phylacteries used in prayer), from calculations concerning the coming of the Messiah (anticipated dates included 1768 and 1783), and from the practice recorded in July 1769 by Newport's Reverend Ezra Stiles in which Jews during thunderstorms threw open doors and windows while "singing and repeating prayers . . . for meeting Messias" —a practice apparently inspired by the mystical belief that Jews were soon to be spirited away upon a cloud to Jerusalem. Some American Jews, to be sure, were less spiritually inclined. "I cant help Condemning the Many Supersti[ti]ons wee are Clog'd with & heartily wish a Calvin or Luther would rise amongst Us," Abigail Franks famously wrote in a 1739 letter to her son, Naphtali. But she remained a believing and observant woman. Eight years later, she consoled Naphtali upon the death of his firstborn child, terming it "the Will of that Divine Power to wich all must submit."[58]

While these private beliefs and practices defined Colonial Jews religiously and distinguished them from their Christian neighbors, social interactions in trade, on the street, and wherever else Jews and Christians gathered inevitably blurred these distinctions. The majority of American Jews resided in religiously pluralistic communities with people of diverse backgrounds and faiths, including many who had themselves experienced religious persecution. Perhaps for this reason, these Jews, like the port Jews of Europe, felt more comfortable interacting with Christians than most other Jews did—so much so that we know of Jews and Christians who joined forces in business, witnessed each other's documents, and socialized in each other's homes. Jews certainly faced continuing bouts of prejudice and persecution on account of their faith; legally speaking, in most American colonies they remained second-class citizens, barred from holding public office or even, in some cases, from voting. But from the very beginning of Jewish settlement, Jews and Christians also fell in love and married. This was an alarming development from the point of view of the Jewish community, which for religious and social reasons considered intermarriage anathema. But it was also a sure sign of Jewish acceptance—particularly since only a small number of the Jews who intermarried converted to Christianity in order to do so.[59]

Estimates of Jewish intermarriage in the colonial period range from 10 to 15 percent of all marriages, with men intermarrying more frequently than women, and those living far from their fellow Jews more likely to marry out than those who lived within or in proximity to a Jewish community. Available statistics leave many questions unanswered, chief among them whether the rate rose or fell over time. Still, the numbers are far lower than for some other religious groups of the day. New York City's French Huguenots, to take an extreme case, experienced an intermarriage rate between 1750 and 1769 that exceeded 86 percent.[60]

The subject of intermarriage raised thorny questions that would figure prominently later in the history of American Judaism. How to respond to intermarriages? How to respond to intermarrieds who sought to maintain their Jewish ties? How to promote in-group marriage without damaging social ties to non-Jews? How to survive in an American religious environment that was becoming increasingly open and competitive? Colonial Jews offered few firm answers to these questions and mostly dealt with intermarriages on an ad hoc basis. When, for example, Phila Franks married the wealthy Huguenot merchant Oliver DeLancey in 1742, her pious, grief-stricken mother, Abigail, withdrew from the city and in traditional Jewish fashion resolved never to see her daughter again, "nor Lett none of the Family Goe near her." Her more politic husband, however, demurred: "Wee live in a Small place & he is Related to the best family in the place," he explained, and tried to promote reconciliation.[61]

As a rule, intermarried Jews did sooner or later drift away from the Jewish community, but there were exceptions. David Franks, for example, continued to maintain close social and economic ties to Jews. Benjamin Moses Clava was buried as a Jew. Samson Levy and Michael Judah had their non-Jewish children ritually circumcised. Ezekiel Solomons, Heineman Pines, John Franks, Barnet Lyons, Uriah Judah, and David Franks, all of them intermarried, numbered among the twenty original founders of Shearith Israel in Montreal. In each of these cases, a Jewish tradition that was uncompromising on the subject of intermarriage clashed with colonial society's more indulgent social norms. Caught between two realms that they strove mightily to keep separate, colonial Jews vacillated. Once again, Jewish law and American life proved difficult to reconcile.[62]

ACCOMMODATION TO AMERICA

On the eve of the American Revolution, Judaism remained all but invisible to most colonists. No more than one American in a thousand was Jewish, only five cities had significant Jewish populations, and only New York and Newport boasted synagogue buildings; elsewhere Jews worshipped in rented quarters or private homes. America's Jewish communities paled in comparison with those of Curaçao, Surinam, and Jamaica. Each of those West Indies communities had more Jews in the mid-eighteenth century than all of the North American colonies combined. If Judaism was a statistically minor American religion, however, it was by no means inert. To the contrary, as it accommodated to its new American setting it underwent changes that mirrored in significant ways the transformations experienced by other American faiths far larger than itself.

First and foremost, American Judaism adapted—and contributed—to the pluralistic character of American religious life, already evident in major cities such as New York, Newport, and Philadelphia. Whereas in so many other diaspora settings Judaism stood all alone in religious dissent, Jews in America shared this status with members of other minority faiths—for example, Huguenots, Quakers, and Baptists. Jews formed the only organized non-Christian religious community, to be sure, but by no means the only one with a sad history of persecution and oppression. From the beginning, as we have seen, colonial leaders explicitly linked Jewish economic and religious rights in North America to those of other minority faiths; later Jews would seek parity in other ways as well. Indeed, the very term Jews used to define their community was influenced by American religious pluralism. If early on they were, in the Sephardic tradition, members of the Jewish or Portuguese "nation," by the eve of the American Revolution they more commonly spoke of themselves as members of a "religious society," on the model of parallel Christian religious societies, such as the Society of Friends (Quakers). When Ezekiel Levy was hired in 1774 to serve as ritual slaughterer, reader, and teacher in Philadelphia, his contract was thus with the "Jewish Society" of that city, not, as earlier contracts read, with the "Jewish Nation." Later, in 1783, when New York Jews wrote a formal letter of welcome to Governor George Clinton, they used the same term. Revealingly, they juxtaposed "the Society, we Belong to" with "other Religious Societies," as if to underscore that Judaism stood on an equal footing with all the rest.[63]

The second characteristic of American Judaism that reflected the larger population was that it too became increasingly diverse. The 1790 U.S. Census recorded Jews who had been born in England, France, Germany, Holland, Poland, Portugal, and the West Indies, as well as in the American colonies, a mix that mirrored the composition of the late colonial Jewish community.[64] The Sephardic form of Judaism predominated, as it always had in North America, but the preponderance of colonial Jews were actually Ashkenazim or of mixed background; "pure" Sephardim represented a vanishing breed. As a result, the synagogue-community functioned as something of a melting pot, its diversity echoing that of many a colonial city. This diversity carried over into congregational life. Notwithstanding the help and support that Shearith Israel, the "mother congregation" of America's synagogues, provided its more recent counterparts, it exercised no real authority over them, for even fledgling congregations jealously guarded their prerogatives. American Judaism thus developed along staunchly congregationalist lines, characterized by increasing multiformity, with each synagogue functioning as an autonomous entity.

Finally, Judaism on the eve of the revolution was largely confined to two settings, the synagogue and the home, leaving a large public space in between where Jews and Christians interacted. The effort to compartmentalize, as we have seen, caused severe strains—hardly a surprise, since Judaism, like Christianity, was designed to govern all aspects of life, not just selected spheres. The kind of communal discipline that the synagogue-community exercised elsewhere was no longer possible in the latter decades of the eighteenth century; the reach of its leadership was severely limited. Just how limited may be seen from a draft constitution proposed by Congregation Mikveh Israel of Philadelphia in 1798. Initially, the leadership proposed traditional language, warning any out-of-town Jew who came to the synagogue "occasionally or on holy days" and failed to contribute to the congregation's support that his name would be erased from its books; he would not be interred in its cemetery, and no officer or member would be allowed to assist at his burial. That draconian threat, however, must have met with stiff resistance, for it was crossed through in the original document. The amended text, more in keeping with the narrow sphere of the congregation's real authority, simply warned that such a person would "not be entitled to any mitzvas [religious honors], provided notice thereof be first given him."[65]

The great changes that Protestant churches experienced in the colonial period, the dramatic series of religious revivals and church controversies that historians refer to as the (First) Great Awakening, had no major impact on American Judaism, except insofar as they altered and further diversified the religious environment in which Judaism operated. Efforts in 1757 to revitalize Jewish religious life by strengthening discipline and cracking down on laxity, even if they were influenced by Protestant developments, came to naught. Theological changes, if any occurred, are not discernible at all, for sermons were not a regular part of Jewish religious worship in the colonial period, and the only full-scale sermon that survives in print was composed by a visitor from abroad. The Awakening may have influenced Judaism in more subtle ways, calling into question, for example, the power of mimetic tradition that earlier generations of colonial Jews held sacred. But whether anyone actually heard and internalized this message is a matter of speculation. Direct evidence of the Awakening's impact upon American Judaism has so far eluded historical detection.[66]

The American Revolution, by contrast, did transform American Judaism. Where colonial Judaism represented a modification of earlier patterns, an accommodation to a new setting, independence and the ensuing changes in society recast Judaism altogether. Elsewhere, in Jamaica and Barbados, Judaism developed along British lines, maintaining for as long as possible the traditions that characterized Anglo-Jewry in the eighteenth century. By contrast, in the wake of the American Revolution, Judaism in the United States, heavily influenced by democratization and American Protestantism, would develop during the half-century following independence a character all its own—one that had been anticipated in significant respects already in the colonial era.

The Revolution in American Judaism

"O Lord . . . may it please thee, to put it in the heart of our Sovereign Lord, George the Third, and in the hearts of his Councellors, Princes and Servants, to turn away their fierce Wrath from against North America," pleaded Congregation Shearith Israel on May 17, 1776, the "day of humiliation, fasting and prayer" called by the Second Continental Congress. More than a year after the Battles of Lexington and Concord, the congregation prayed for "an everlasting peace" between Great Britain and her colonies, "that . . . no more blood be shed in these Countries."[1]

Devoutly as they prayed for peace, American Jews separated in the face of war. New York's approximately four hundred Jews were reputedly "sharply divided on the lines of Tory and Patriot," and elsewhere, particularly in Newport, a "substantial minority . . . remained loyal to the mother country."[2] Many Jews vacillated and pledged allegiance to both sides in the dispute for as long as they could. Jews scarcely differed from their neighbors in this regard. Nativity, ties to Europe, and economic factors determined the loyalties of many colonists. When finally forced to choose, however, most of America's 1,000 to 2,500 Jews cast their lot for independence. They, like the Catholics, belie the generalization that minority groups that feared for their status sided with the British.[3]

THE SACRED ROAD TO LIBERTY

Much has been written concerning the Jewish contribution to the American Revolution. We know that up to one hundred Jews fought in the

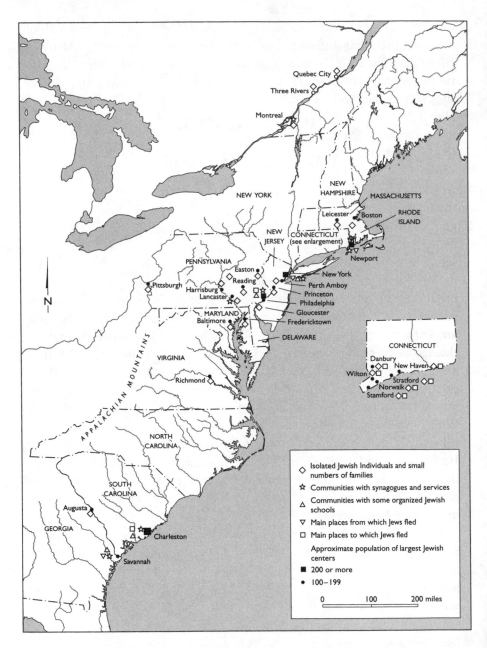

Jewish communities in America at the time of the Revolutionary War.
Courtesy of Prestel-Verlag and the Jewish Museum. Adapted from *Jews and the Founding of the Republic,* ed. Jonathan D. Sarna, Benny Kraut, and Samuel K. Joseph (New York: Markus Wiener, 1985). Copyright Hebrew Union College–Jewish Institute of Religion. Reprinted with permission.

revolution, one of whom was exempted from serving on the city watch on Friday nights; that three attained high office in the Continental Army (in Britain, no Jew could become an officer unless he took an oath as a Christian); and that other Jews served as "suppliers, bill brokers, moneylenders, shopkeepers, blockade-runners, and even 'manufacturers' on a small scale."[4] Haym Salomon, the best-known Jew of the revolutionary era, played a significant role as "Broker to the Office of Finance." His wartime generosity to Jew and Gentile alike is well documented. The contribution made by the several hundred Jews on the Dutch Caribbean island of St. Eustatius is less well known. In accordance with their government's pro-revolution policy, they successfully (and lucratively) ran the British blockade, smuggled vital goods and military supplies to the besieged Americans, and in 1781 paid a heavy price for their sympathies when Britain's Admiral George Rodney seized and despoiled the island, wreaking special vengeance upon its Jews.[5]

Prideful recitation of these Jewish contributions to the revolution, often in an exaggerated way, suited the needs of later generations of Jews who sought to legitimate their own presence in the United States and to rebut antisemites who questioned their loyalty. Jews who themselves lived through the revolution, however, tended to portray their experience more in personal and religious terms. They saw the divine hand working behind the scenes on the field of battle. This helped them to make sense of the events transpiring around them and imbued their struggle with transcendent meaning. Without going so far as some of their Protestant neighbors, who read Scripture typologically, comparing King George to Pharoah and themselves to Israel, revolutionary era Jews did evoke such themes as exile, loss, destruction, and redemption. Linking their experience to these classic Jewish religious motifs consecrated their wartime experience. It cast them as travelers on a sacred road to liberty.

The theme of exile emerged as early as August 1776, when Gershom Seixas, the native-born hazan of Congregation Shearith Israel, led patriotic members of his congregation out of New York City in the face of its impending occupation by British forces advancing from Long Island. Over the opposition of the congregation's Tories, Seixas took with him Torah scrolls and other religious "sundries" belonging to the congregation—a move likely justified by security concerns but freighted with deep symbolic significance. Armed with these sacred objects, Seixas and his followers felt secure that God accompanied them in their wanderings, first during their four-year sojourn in Stratford, Connecticut, and later, in 1780, when they moved to join a large congregation of Jewish war refugees in Philadelphia. Even

Gershom Mendes Seixas around the time of the
American Revolution. Nothing in this miniature
(artist unknown) identifies Seixas as a Jew,
but his collar does identify him as a cleric.
From the collection of Norman Flayderman.

as Jewish services continued intermittently in New York under the British,
the congregation's holiest objects remained with their patriotic protectors
in exile, reassuring them, as it were, that the Torah stood on their side of
the struggle.[6]

Jews living in other cities also experienced "exile" during the war years,
a sign that by the late eighteenth century they looked upon the American
cities where they regularly dwelt as "home." Levi Sheftall of Savannah recalled in his diary that the revolution occasioned "many Jews to be continually coming and going . . . there was nothing but warr talked of and Every
body had their hands and herts full." Aaron Lopez, the wealthy Jewish
merchant of Newport, compared himself to a nomad in a letter to a non-
Jewish friend. Seeking security in the face of the British invasion of Newport,
he reported that "I pitch'd my tent" in the "small inland township of Leicester, in the Massachusetts Bay." We know from other sources that this tent

was really a "large and elegant mansion" and that Lopez and his family were able to bring with them and maintain "their peculiar forms of faith and worship," including "keeping Saturday as holy time." Still, Leicester was exile. In 1779, two years after he had left Newport, Lopez still hoped to return, to "re-enjoy those injur'd habitations, we have so long been deprived of."[7]

The same sense of crushing loss that Lopez's letters expressed pervades other Jewish correspondence from this period. "We have had no less than six Jewish children buried since the sige [siege]," lamented Frances Sheftall, the wife of a recently released Jewish prisoner-of-war, in one of the few letters from a Jewish woman to survive from this period. Her concerns were primarily domestic: "How . . . to pay the doctor's bill and house rent." Faith sustained her in her husband's absence: "I still trust to Providence knowing that the Almighty never sends trouble but he sends some relife." Isaac Touro, the hazan of Newport's congregation and a Tory who followed the British out of Newport and subsequently left for Jamaica, also focused on his losses, reporting himself "so reduced in his circumstances" that had it not been for British assistance he would "have sunk under the weight of his affliction and distress." Michael Judah, an elderly merchant, lost almost his entire life savings on account of the war. "If I don't do something," he complained as he begged fellow Jews for credit, "I shall soon spend what little I have left."[8]

What was even worse than these personal losses was the wanton destruction that Jews experienced around them, reminiscent of so many earlier destructive episodes in their history. Newport, where Jews had so recently thrived, lay in shambles. From Leicester, Lopez thanked God for giving him the fortitude to escape in time, and he mourned that Jews less fortunate than himself were now unable to obtain kosher food and "were reduced to the alternative of leaving [living] upon chocolate and coffe[e]." He described a Newport dwelling that "sufer'd much," a former neighbor "found dead at his house," another neighbor whose wife "is crazy," and what he lamented most of all, "that the vertue of several of our reputable ladys has been attacked and sullied by our destructive enemys." Samson Mears, a New York merchant who with other Jews had taken refuge in Norwalk, Connecticut, personally experienced that city's destruction on July 11, 1779. The tragedy took place during the traditional three-week season of mourning leading up to Tisha B'Av, the fast day commemorating Jewish catastrophes since the destruction of the Temple in Jerusalem. Linking his present fate to that great chain of Jewish misery, he reported that local Jews "truly realized the Anniversary Season with all its gloom that our predecessors experienced."[9]

Against this background of exile, loss, and destruction, the peace that descended upon the new nation in 1783 seemed like nothing short of redemption, an ideal roughly parallel to the millennialism that pious Christians preached, and reinforced for Jews by the fact that Congress proclaimed the cessation of hostilities just prior to the start of Passover, the Jewish holiday of freedom. "Thanks to the Almighty, it is now at an end," an excited Mordecai Sheftall wrote to his son when he heard the news. "An intier new scene will open it self, and we have the world to begin againe." A similar sense of anticipation prevailed at the community level, as seen in the letter of welcome written by patriotic members of Shearith Israel to New York's Governor George Clinton in the final days of 1783. Recalling that they had themselves "lately returned from exile," they reminded the governor of Jews' "zealous attachment to the sacred cause of America," and looked forward "with Pleasure to the happy days we expect to enjoy under a Constitution, Wisely framed to preserve the inestimable Blessings of Civil, and Religious Liberty." A few months later, a Hebrew prayer composed for the congregation translated this redemptive message into the language of messianism, thereby linking America's divinely ordained fate to that of the Jews. "As Thou hast granted to these thirteen states of America everlasting freedom," the prayer concluded, "so mayst Thou bring us forth once again from bondage into freedom. . . . Hasten our deliverance . . . send us the priest of righteousness who will lead us upright to our land . . . may the redeemer come speedily to Zion in our days."[10]

"A GOVERNMENT WHERE ALL RELIGIOUS SOCIETIES ARE ON AN EQUAL FOOTING"

While the revolution did not ultimately usher in the messianic age for American Jews, it did effect changes in law and in the relationship of religion to the state that transformed American Jewish life forever after. Already in the first decade and a half of American independence, the parameters of religious liberty in the new nation steadily widened. New York, with its long tradition of de facto religious pluralism, became in 1777 the first state to extend the boundaries of "free exercise and enjoyment of religious profession and worship" to "all mankind," whether Christian or not (although it required those born abroad to subscribe to an anti-Catholic test oath). Virginia, in its 1785 Act for Religious Freedom (originally drafted by Thomas Jefferson in 1779), went even further, with a ringing declaration that "no man shall be compelled to frequent or support any religious worship, place or ministry whatsoever . . . but that all men shall be free to profess and by argument to maintain, their opinions in matters of religion, and that the same shall in no wise diminish, enlarge or affect their civil capacities." The Northwest Ordinance, adopted by the Continental Congress in 1787, extended guarantees of freedom of worship and belief into the territories north of the Ohio River. Finally, the Federal Constitution (1787) and the Bill of Rights (1791) outlawed religious tests "as a qualification to any office or public trust under the United States," and forbade Congress from making any law "respecting an establishment of religion, or prohibiting the free exercise thereof."[11]

America's two thousand or so Jews played no significant role in bringing about these epochal developments. Enlightenment thinkers and Protestant dissenters laid the groundwork for these new freedoms, and their interest in Jewish rights was limited. On a few occasions, however, Jews did speak up on their own behalf, justifying such extraordinary exceptions to their customary "quietness" by their contribution to the revolutionary cause. In 1783, for example, leaders of Philadelphia's new Mikveh Israel synagogue, dedicated in 1782 and temporarily home to as many as half of America's Jews, the bulk of them refugees, petitioned to amend the state's constitution requiring Pennsylvania office-holders to acknowledge the "divine inspiration" of the New Testament. The leaders argued, to no immediate avail, that this requirement unfairly deprived Jews (whose "conduct and behavior . . . always tallied with the great design of the Revolution") of their "most eminent rights of freemen." The German-Jewish immigrant merchant Jonas Phillips argued for a similar amendment to the state constitution in a petition he sent to the 1787 Federal Constitutional Convention meeting in Philadelphia, the only significant petition that it received concerning religious liberty. Jews "bravely fought and bled for liberty which they can not Enjoy," he complained. Blood, that most potent of religious substances, symbolizing sacrifice, covenant, and ritual cleansing, merited Jews a full measure of political and religious freedom, he believed. He promised that "the Israelites will think themself happy to live under a government where all Religious societies are on an Equal footing."[12]

Phillips notwithstanding, the Constitutional Convention, and most state discussions concerning the place of religion in American life, ignored Jews. The major American documents bearing on religious liberty do not mention them even once. Jews gained their religious rights in the United States (and in most but not all of the separate states) as individuals along with everybody else—not, as so often the case in Europe and the Caribbean, through a special privilege or "Jew Bill" that set them apart as a group. It did require a controversial "Jew Bill" to win Jews the right to hold public office in Maryland in 1826, and it took another fifty-one years before Jews achieved full legal equality in New Hampshire. Issues like Sunday laws, school prayer, and religious celebrations in the public square reminded Jews of their minority status long after that. Nevertheless, on the national level and in most of the American communities where Jews actually lived, they had achieved an unprecedented degree of "equal footing" by the end of the eighteenth century.[13]

A gala parade marking the ratification of the Constitution, held in Philadelphia on July 4, 1788, celebrated this achievement. It presented, marching together in one division, "the clergy of the different christian denominations, with the rabbi of the Jews [probably Jacob R. Cohen], walking arm in arm." The famed physician Dr. Benjamin Rush, who witnessed the unprecedented spectacle, wrote that this first-ever ecumenical parade "was a most delightful sight. There could not have been a more happy emblem contrived, of that section of the new constitution, which opens all its powers and offices alike, not only to every sect of christians, but to worthy men of *every* religion." Though it apparently escaped his notice, when the ceremony concluded, Jews ate separately at a special kosher table prepared on their behalf. Reflecting English custom, this public expression of Jewish ritual behavior (even, one assumes, on the part of those who were not always so scrupulous) effectively defined the boundaries of interreligious relations from the synagogue-community's official perspective. Much as Jewish leaders rejoiced at the "equal footing" that brought them politically into step with Christians under the banner of the Constitution, they exercised their right to eat apart, following the precepts of their faith, formulated to help preserve Jews as a group.[14]

The famed correspondence between Jews and George Washington went even further in defining the place of Judaism in the new nation. The address of the "Hebrew Congregation in Newport" to the president, composed for his visit to that city on August 17, 1790, following Rhode Island's ratification of the Constitution, paralleled other letters that Washington received from religious bodies of different denominations and followed a custom long associated with the ascension of kings. Redolent with biblical and liturgical language, the address noted past discrimination against Jews, praised the new government for "generously affording to all liberty of conscience and immunities of citizenship," and thanked God "for all of the blessings of civil and religious liberty" that Jews now enjoyed under the Constitution. Washington, in his oft-quoted reply, reassured the Jewish community about what he correctly saw as its central concern—religious liberty. Appropriating a phrase contained in the Hebrew congregation's original letter, he characterized the U.S. government as one that "gives to bigotry no sanction, to persecution no assistance." He described religious liberty, following Thomas Jefferson, as an inherent natural right, distinct from the indulgent religious "toleration" practiced by the British and much of enlightened Europe, where Jewish emancipation was so often linked with demands for Jewish "improvement." Finally, echoing the language of the prophet Micah (4:4), he hinted that America might itself prove something of a Promised Land for Jews, a place where they would "merit and enjoy the good will of the other inhabitants; while every one shall sit in safety under his own vine and fig tree and there shall be none to make him afraid."[15]

Washington's letter to the Jews of Newport was actually the second of three official exchanges between him and the American Jewish community. Two months earlier he had corresponded with the "Hebrew Congregation" of Savannah, and in December, fully twenty months into his administration, he received an embarrassingly late joint letter from the "Hebrew congregations" of Philadelphia, New York, Charleston, and Richmond. Later generations saw in this plethora of letters a reflection of Jewish communal disorganization and disunity, which we certainly know to have been the case.[16] But the episode also reveals anew the determined congregationalism of American Jews and their reluctance to cede authority to any single congregation, even the prestigious "mother" congregation, Shearith Israel of New York. In defining themselves vis-à-vis their neighbors, Jews in the new nation resisted the hierarchic model of organization that characterized the much-discredited Anglicans, and organized no Presbyterian-type synods to govern them. Instead, the congregational form of governance characteristic of Protestant dissenters from Anglicanism came to characterize American Judaism, sharply distinguishing it from Judaism as practiced in England, Europe, and the Middle East.

As the eighteenth century ended, the goal of "equal footing" seemed closer to realization. The burgeoning pluralism of American religion, the impact of new federal and state laws, and liberal pronouncements from political leaders all reassured Jews of their rights under the new regime and gave them a heightened sense of legitimation. Their numbers had scarcely grown; indeed, no more than three new synagogues were established in America between 1789 and 1824.[17] Their status, however, had improved immeasurably, particularly in those cities where organized communities of Jews existed.

Such was the case in Philadelphia. The city's Jewish community was actually much smaller after the war, as most of the refugees who had congregated there during the revolution had returned home, but ties between Jews and Christians in the Quaker city appeared stronger than ever before. Recognizing this, "the good People of the Hebrew Society" (as local Jews denominated themselves in addressing their neighbors) took the unprecedented step in 1788 of appealing to "their worthy fellow Citizens of every religious Denomination" to assist them in paying off large debts left over from the construction of their synagogue six years earlier. Before the revolution, Jews would reflexively have turned to their wealthy coreligionists with such a request, but now they sought the help of their Christian neighbors as well, knowing that local churches applied to the general public under similar circumstances. The printed appeal reflected, even if tentatively, a sense of shared identity and interests with the city's other faiths. It expressly hoped that Jews' "worshipping Almighty God in a way & manner different from other religious Societies" would not "deter the enlightened Citizens of Philadelphia from generously subscribing." An impressive array of Christian dignitaries did subscribe, including Thomas Fitzsimons, the city's leading Catholic layman, John Peter Gabriel Muhlenberg, its most prominent Lutheran minister (whose father had once battled to deny Jews political rights), and Benjamin Franklin, who proudly assisted "all sects . . . with subscriptions for building their new places of worship" and apparently considered Jews no different from the others. While the total sum raised proved insufficient, the symbolic significance of these contributions cannot be underestimated. In making them, Philadelphia's most prominent citizens had publicly declared Mikveh Israel worthy of support on a par with local churches. Two years later, still in need of money, Mikveh Israel borrowed yet another fundraising technique from its neighbors and received state permission to set up a lottery to retire its debt. Once again, Jews and Christians joined forces on the synagogue's behalf, and this time the "object so pious and meritorious" was temporarily achieved.[18]

In New York, Jews experienced a similar rise in status in relation to local Christians. In an unprecedented move, Hazan Gershom Seixas, upon his return to the city in 1784, was appointed to the board of regents of the newly rechartered Columbia College. The law required regents to be drawn from all of the *major* denominations; previously, Judaism had not been so recognized.[19] Partly in a bid for just such recognition, Seixas identified himself to non-Jews as "Minister to the Jewish Congregation in this City," a title they could understand. There were obvious legal reasons for this—

ministers were the only religious functionaries recognized under state law —but Seixas also cherished the status that accompanied this title. When press accounts, in 1789, listed him as one of just fourteen ministers serving the city upon the inauguration of George Washington, he knew he had succeeded. Though ranked at the very bottom of that list, below the Baptist minister, the fact that a "Jewish minister" was mentioned at all indicates a heightened degree of acceptance.[20] That same year, when Shearith Israel's cemetery experienced dangerous cave-ins, "Gentile and Jew vied with one another to save the burial ground from disaster," according to the cemetery's historian. Needing funds for emergency repairs, the congregation, likely influenced by the experience of Philadelphia Jews the year before, directly appealed to local Christian merchants, and they responded generously.[21]

All of this goes to show that the world of American religion, opened up with the leveling of restrictive colonial laws and monopolistic church establishments, extended the boundaries of legitimate faiths to embrace Jews in new ways. Neither prejudice nor legal restrictions completely disappeared, of course. Even supporters of Jewish rights, like Thomas Jefferson, poured scorn on what he believed Jews stood for—their theology, morality, and doctrine. Outside of the few cities where Jews and Christians dwelt side by side, most people had no direct knowledge of Jews at all.[22] Still, even where Jews had not yet settled, the principles underlying the Constitution inevitably affected their position. Privileges once accorded only to favored denominations of Protestants now applied far more broadly.

Five of these principles proved particularly important: (1) religious freedom, (2) church-state separation, (3) denominationalism ("the religious situation created in a land of many Christian churches and sects when none of them occupies a privileged situation and each has an equal claim to status"), (4) voluntaryism ("the principle that individuals are free to choose their religious beliefs and associations without political, ecclesiastical or communal coercion"), and (5) patriotism. Collectively known as "the great tradition of the American churches," these principles, even if sometimes honored in the breach, shaped the contours of American religion forever after; sooner or later every American faith adapted to them.[23] Judaism, as a minority non-Christian faith, especially benefited from this "great tradition." The question facing its adherents was how Judaism's own contours would now need to be reshaped and what the price of that adaptation would be.

THE CHALLENGE OF FREEDOM

As a diaspora people with a long history of persecution, Jews had accumulated centuries of experience in adapting themselves to new political situations and governments. The first step, they knew, was to ingratiate themselves to new leaders and to pray fervently for their wellbeing. Instinctively, then, one of the first known Jewish responses to the new American government was a traditional prayer. Recited by Gershom Seixas at the dedication of Philadelphia's new Mikveh Israel synagogue in 1782, the prayer replaced the old blessing for the royal family and substituted in its stead one for Congress, Commander-in-Chief George Washington, the General Assembly of Pennsylvania, and "all kings and potentates in alliance with North America." As if to underscore that the revolution represented a firm break with the past, Seixas, when he returned to New York, abandoned the venerable colonial tradition, widely followed throughout the Sephardic diaspora, of reciting in Portuguese the names of government officials to be blessed, and began reading them out in English, a gesture that symbolized independence, loyalty, and the congregation's new cultural affinities. Most revealingly of all, the congregants of Shearith Israel ceased to stand up for the prayer for the government. "The custom of sitting during this prayer," an oral tradition recalls, "was introduced to symbolize the American Revolution's abolition of subservience."[24]

While seemingly insignificant, the new prayer for the government served as a portent of more fundamental changes to come. It demonstrated that the revolution, far from being just another turn in Jews' political wheel of fortune, represented instead a massive cultural transformation. It challenged age-old traditions and demanded that revolutionary-era values be recognized within the synagogue's portals. The problem that Jews grappled with in the decades following the revolution was whether Judaism as they knew it *could* be reconciled with freedom and democracy. Could the traditional synagogue-community structure that bound Jews together and promoted group survival also accommodate new political and cultural realities?

In an initial effort to answer these questions affirmatively, each of America's synagogues rewrote their constitutions. The very word "constitution" is significant, for previously they had called their governing documents by the more traditional Jewish term of *askamot* (or *haskamot*), meaning agreements or covenants. Now, in an era when constitution writing was all the rage—some states rewrote theirs several times over—the more familiar American term was employed. The new documents broke from the old

Sephardic model, incorporated large dollops of republican rhetoric, and provided for a great deal more freedom and democracy—at least on paper. At New York's Congregation Shearith Israel, in 1790, an intriguing constitution was promulgated, the first that we know of to contain a formal "bill of rights." The new set of laws began with a ringing affirmation of popular sovereignty reminiscent of the American Constitution: "We the members of the K. K. Shearith Israel." Another paragraph explicitly linked Shearith Israel with the "state happily constituted upon the principles of equal liberty, civil and religious." Still a third paragraph, the introduction to the new bill of rights (which may have been written at a different time), justified synagogue laws in terms that Americans would immediately have understood:

> Whereas in free states all power originates and is derived from the people, who always retain every right necessary for their well being individually, and, for the better ascertaining those rights with more precision and explicitly, frequently from [form?] a declaration or bill of those rights. In like manner the individuals of every society in such state are entitled to and retain their several rights, which ought to be preserved inviolate.
>
> Therefore we, the profession [professors] of the Divine Laws, members of this holy congregation of Shearith Israel, in the city of New York, conceive it our duty to make this declaration of our rights and privileges.[25]

The new bill of rights explicitly ended many of the colonial-era distinctions between members and non-members, declaring that "every free person professing the Jewish religion, and who lives according to its holy precepts, is entitled to . . . be treated in all respect as a brother, and as such a subject of every fraternal duty."[26] It also made it easier for ordinary male members of the congregation to attain synagogue office. Leadership no longer rested, as it had for much of the colonial period, with a self-perpetuating elite.

The pace and extent of constitutional reforms differed from congregation to congregation, much as in America they did from state to state. Some of the most democratic and egalitarian tendencies within these documents were also in time reversed, especially as America's "contagion of liberty" gave way, in some quarters, to fear of the masses and concern for law and order. In slave-dominated Charleston, to take an extreme example, the synagogue constitution of 1820 returned "all the functions formerly exercised by the people at large" to a self-perpetuating "general adjunta."[27] Still, the experiment in constitution-writing in this era of American Jewish life bespeaks a profound attempt to reconstruct synagogue polity in accordance with new American norms. Just as revolutionary-era Episcopalians introduced a new constitution and a more democratic two-house General Convention in an effort to show that their church and the new nation were thoroughly compatible, so Jews too sought to harmonize the traditional hierarchic synagogue-community with the new democratic American state.

Effecting this harmony, however, proved easier said than done. Constitutional changes could not obscure the fact that democracy and personal freedom clashed with basic traditions of the synagogue-community, and in many cases also with Jewish law. Christians faced similar problems: "The American Revolution and the beliefs flowing from it created a cultural ferment over the meaning of freedom," proclaims a study of the democratization of American Christianity. "Turmoil swirled around the crucial issues of authority, organization, and leadership." For Jews and Christians alike in the United States, the tension between traditional religious values and new American values provoked a "period of religious ferment, chaos and originality unmatched in American history."[28]

Evidence of this ferment emerged as early as 1785, when leaders of Congregation Mikveh Israel of Philadelphia wrote to Rabbi Saul Halevi Loewenstamm, Ashkenazic chief rabbi of Amsterdam, seeking his advice and support in a battle against one of their most learned (and contentious) lay members, Mordecai M. Mordecai, a native of Telz, Lithuania. Writing in a combination of Hebrew and Yiddish and in the traditional idiom used when posing learned inquiries, they alleged that "Reb Mordecai" took the law into his own hands on two different occasions. Once, in an apparent attempt to reconcile members of his extended family, he allegedly performed an unauthorized Jewish marriage ceremony on a previously intermarried couple, his niece, Judith Hart, and her unconverted husband, Lieutenant James Pettigrew. On another occasion, they charged, he openly flouted synagogue authority by performing the traditional last rites on Benjamin Clava, an identifying but intermarried Jew whom the synagogue, as a warning to others, had ordered buried "without ritual ablution, without shrouds and without funeral rites." Since on both occasions Mordecai vigorously defended his actions, insisting that he knew Jewish law better than those who judged him, the congregation sought the "illuminating light" of the Dutch rabbi's opinion.[29]

While Rabbi Loewenstamm's opinion has not survived, the real question plainly had less to do with Jewish law than with Jewish religious authority in a democratic age. Mordecai, echoing the spirit of the American revolutionary tradition, and akin to many Protestant rebels of his day, challenged his religious superiors and claimed the right to interpret God's law as he personally understood it. Nor was he the only Jew to do so, according to the report that Mikveh Israel sent to Amsterdam: "In this country . . . everybody does as he pleases. Most deplorably, many of our people—including some *Kohanim* [priests]—marry gentile women. They consult so-called 'scholars,' thoroughly corrupt individuals, who flagrantly profane the name of Heaven and who contrive erroneous legalistic loopholes. . . . Yet the *Kahal* [community] has no authority to restrain or punish anyone, except for the nominal penalty of denying them synagogue honors, or of withholding from them sacred rites. However, these vicious people completely disregard such measures and continue to attend our synagogue, because under the laws of the country it is impossible to enjoin them from so doing."[30]

Mikveh Israel's problem was that Jews in post-revolutionary America made their own rules concerning how to live Jewishly, and there was little that the synagogue-community could do about it. Judith Hart and Benjamin Clava were hardly alone in intermarrying. Some 28.7 percent of all known marriages involving Jews between 1776 and 1840 were intermarriages, about twice the rate calculated for the colonial period.[31] As before, this was a sure sign of Jewish social acceptance, particularly since many Jews intermarried without themselves converting. Nor was intermarriage confined just to those remote from Judaism. In one remarkable case, in 1806, Abraham Hyam Cohen, the son of (and assistant to) Mikveh Israel's hazan, fell in love with a Christian woman. This was one of but twelve known cases of a mixed marriage that involved conversion to Judaism in this period, and it is all the more remarkable since the bride, Jane Picken, was converted without an ordained rabbi present and after only a brief period of preparation. (Years later, while suffering from a serious illness and after the death of her beloved youngest son, she returned to the Episcopal Church and separated from her husband.)[32] The marriage demonstrates that, even within the world of the synagogue-community, individual freedom was triumphing over the demands of Jewish tradition and law. Rabbis abroad may have been appalled, but as the immigrant Rebecca Samuel explained in a 1791 letter to her parents in Hamburg, here "anyone can do what he wants. There is no rabbi in all of America to excommunicate anyone."[33]

The freedom that produced this "anyone can do what he wants" attitude reinforced the diversity in Jewish ritual practice that, we know, already existed in colonial times. Haym Salomon, in an oft-recalled 1783 letter seeking to dissuade an uncle of his from moving to America, gave voice to one prevalent image of Judaism in this period. He summarized the "nature of this country" in two expressive Yiddish words: *vinig yidishkayt,* "little Jewishness."

Others made the same claim, none more colorfully than the aforementioned Rebecca Samuel, who having given birth to children now sought to guard their faith and was therefore less enamored of her new home than she had previously been. She described Jewishness as "pushed aside" in Petersburg, Virginia. The city's Jewish ritual slaughterer, she recounted, "goes to market and buys *terefah* [nonkosher] meat and then brings it home." With the exception of her husband and one sixty-year-old man from Holland, not one of the local Jewish worshippers prayed with a *tallit* (prayer shawl) on the High Holidays. "We do not know what the Sabbath and the holidays are," she lamented, hastening to reassure her pious parents that their own store remained shut on those days, and that "in our house we all live as Jews as much as we can." To prevent her children from becoming "like Gentiles," she planned to move to the larger Jewish community of Charleston. "The whole reason why we are leaving this place," she explained, "is because of [for the sake of] *Yehudishkeit* [Jewishness]."[34]

These accounts need to be balanced by other sources that paint an entirely different picture of American Jewish religious life at this time. Schoolmaster Jacob Mordecai, though his was the only Jewish family in Warrenton, North Carolina, scrupulously observed both the Sabbath and Jewish dietary laws. The merchant Moses Myers of New York, visiting London in 1783, found Judaism there very much "on the decline," and described himself, by contrast, as "religious," though he admitted that he "did not take the Methods of Shewing it, that others did." Aaron Hart, the leading Jewish merchant of Three Rivers, Canada, thought so highly of Jewish life in New York, in 1794, that he sent his sons there, "for them to learn to be good *Yehudim* [Jews]." Bankers Joseph and Solomon Joseph, having escaped a deadly theater fire in Richmond in 1811, vowed that they would "every year fast on that day" and then celebrate a "Frolick," an unusual fast-feast pairing known in Jewish tradition as a Special (or Family) Purim, and appropriately established in this case to commemorate the day on "which our Great God miraculously saved us." Philip Cohen, a leader of the Jewish community of Charleston, South Carolina, depicted Jewish life in his city, in a letter to the historian Hannah Adams in 1812, as socially liberal and unprejudiced but still rigorous: "The religious rites, customs, and festivals of the Jews are all strictly observed."[35]

Historian Jacob Rader Marcus, who spent half of his long career studying early American Jews, persuasively argued that a spectrum of Jews existed in America at this time, stretching from the "utterly devoted" to the "complete defector." He concluded that "there were almost as many Judaisms as there were individuals."[36] In matters of religious practice, as in so many other aspects of life during the early republic, individual freedom reigned supreme, setting a pattern that would govern American Jewish life forever after.

Women particularly benefited from this new spirit of freedom. At Shearith Israel, in measures aimed at democratization, the special bench reserved for the aristocratic women of the Gomez family was removed in 1786, and in 1805 the congregation abandoned its controversial status-based system of assigning and rating seats for both sexes. Instead, it rented them out on a first-come, first-served basis to all who could pay.[37]

In 1818, when the original Mill Street Synagogue was razed and a larger one built in its place, the women's gallery was transformed even more— new construction, as it were, serving as a spur to religious innovation. First of all, the number of seats available for women in the gallery was increased from about 65 to 133 (later 137), or 44 percent of the synagogue's total number of seats—a further indication that American Jewish women were expected to attend religious services, much as their Protestant counterparts did. In Philadelphia's synagogue, the percentage of seats available to women was an even higher 46 percent.[38] Second, women came down from the gallery to sing as part of a mixed choir at the new Mill Street Synagogue's dedication. The decision to form such a choir, heavily comprising unmarried women—fourteen of them, as compared to two married women and nine men—suggests that women were seeking new modes of expression within the synagogue. A mixed choir similarly sang at the dedication of Philadelphia's new Mikveh Israel synagogue building in 1825, and some hoped that this "very respectable class of singers in the synagogue" would become a regular feature of the congregation's life.[39] Third, and most portentous of all, women gained heightened visibility in the new 1818 synagogue. They now enjoyed an unobstructed view of the rituals performed by the men below, and they were in turn exposed to the men's gaze. They no longer sat, as in the old synagogue, behind a screen hidden by a "breast-work as high as their chins." This visibility created new problems of decorum—particularly "vertical flirting"—and some as a result sought to bar single women from the frontmost pews. Nevertheless, the open style became characteristic of American synagogues built at this time, probably in response to criticisms from non-Jews like Dr. Alexander Hamilton of Annapolis, who embarrassingly compared the old closed-off women's gallery to a "hen coop." Once Mikveh Israel introduced the same open-gallery style in 1825, the new tradition was confirmed. America now offered women more freedom to

Mikveh Israel Synagogue in Philadelphia,
dedicated in 1825. Like other early American
synagogues, its exterior was decidedly modest
and it did not outwardly identify itself as
a Jewish house of worship. Courtesy of the
Jacob Rader Marcus Center of the American
Jewish Archives.

feel part of general synagogue worship than they enjoyed almost anywhere else in the world.[40]

Protestant women, at this time, played a highly public role in American religion. In the revolution's wake, they integrated republican values into their lives, accepted religion as part of their sphere, and came to dominate church pews—so much so that in Philadelphia they outnumbered men in churches by anywhere from 2:1 to 4:1. Among Jews, women slightly outnumbered men for a brief period in the 1820s at Shearith Israel, where they occupied 108 seats and the men only 102, but there is no evidence that the synagogue became "feminized" or that men turned their attention elsewhere, as happened so frequently in Protestantism. Perhaps this is because Jewish law counted men and not women as part of the prayer quorum *(minyan)* and because the synagogue served communal as well as religious functions. Maybe there was simply nowhere else for Jewish men to turn. Whatever the case, in the era of religious revivals that American Protestants know as

Interior drawing reputed to be the interior of the 1825
Mikveh Israel Synagogue. The holy ark containing the
Torah scrolls is on the left. Note that the men wear prayer
shawls and that the women in the balcony have an
unobstructed view of the service below. From *The Jew at
Home and Abroad* (Philadelphia, 1845), courtesy of
Annenberg Rare Book and Manuscript Library,
University of Pennsylvania.

the Second Great Awakening, Jewish men and women *alike* experienced
new interest in their faith. Rebecca Gratz (1781–1869) of Philadelphia, the
foremost Jewish woman of her day and a perceptive observer, noticed this
in an 1825 letter to her (intermarried) brother Benjamin, living in Lexington,
Kentucky. "Our brothers have all become very attentive to shool [synagogue]
matters," she wrote. "They rarely omit attending worship. We all go Friday
evening as well as on Saturday morning—the [women's] gallery is as well
filled as the other portion of the house."[41]

Gratz also exemplifies other new currents within Jewish women's lives in
this period. The American-born daughter of a wealthy merchant, she mixed
in the highest circles of Philadelphia society, became well-acquainted with
the burgeoning religious vocations opening up to women, and brought
many of these ideas back to the Jewish community, where she carved out

new realms for women to explore. Thus, she participated in the establishment and ongoing work of Philadelphia's nondenominational (but largely Protestant) Female Association for the Relief of Women and Children in Reduced Circumstances, founded in 1801. She then used what she learned there to establish and oversee a parallel organization for Jewish women, the Female Hebrew Benevolent Society, founded in 1819. This was both the first Jewish women's benevolent organization and the first non-synagogal Jewish charitable society of any kind in Philadelphia, and it anticipated two significant nineteenth-century developments: the creation of independent, community-wide Jewish organizations outside of the synagogue, and the emergence of women—particularly single women like Gratz—into the world of Jewish philanthropy. As we shall see, Gratz later borrowed another idea from her surroundings and initiated the Jewish Sunday School movement, opening up yet another vocational role for Jewish women within their circumscribed religious sphere.[42]

Other Jewish women likewise pushed the boundaries of gender at this time, though not with equal success. In 1788, for example, two women applied for the position of *shammash* at Shearith Israel, apparently believing that they could fill this multi-purpose, general factotum position—often translated as sexton, beadle, or superintendent—as well as any man. Neither won the job, but in 1815, likely as an act of charity, Jennet Isaacs was elected "shammastress" to succeed her husband, and with the assistance of her son she held the post for six years, after which it reverted to the male domain. We also possess an 1821 account from the hinterland of Wilmington, North Carolina, concerning an informal service on Yom Kippur, the Day of Atonement, where two women served as "readers of the day," probably in the absence of a formal minyan, the traditional prayer quorum of ten men. As frontier communities became larger and more organized, women found these kinds of opportunities foreclosed to them; Jewish law reserved such privileges for men.[43] Finally, there are hints that many women rebelled against the traditional laws of Jewish purity requiring them to bathe in a ritual bath, or *mikveh,* seven days following their menstrual period so as to resume marital relations with their husbands. Manuel Josephson, who petitioned for the building of a mikveh in Philadelphia in 1784, complained that Jews "had been . . . neglectful of so important a matter," and felt sure that were one built, "evry married man" would "use the most persuasive and evry other means, to induce his wife to a strict compliance with that duty." The tone of his petition speaks volumes concerning his patriarchal view of marriage (he was divorced twice), and implies that women, if left to themselves, might not be so strict. In fact, once the mikveh was built, it was so little used that a visiting rabbi in 1844 lamented that "there is no ritual bath in Philadelphia about forty-nine years." In other cities, too, men carefully built the traditional mikveh, and many of their wives felt free to ignore it.[44]

As all of this indicates, America posed significant challenges to age-old Jewish practices. Even in Charleston, where, as we have seen, one observer described Judaism in 1812 as "strictly observed," he added the significant caveat that it was also "ameliorated with that social liberality, which pervades the minds and manners of the inhabitants of civilized countries."[45] Philadelphia Jews showed how important that "social liberality" was fourteen years later when they boldly rejected the rulings of London's chief rabbis and of the Jewish community of Jamaica, and voted to admit a man who was alleged to be a *mamzer* (bastard), the product of an impermissible sexual union, into membership at Mikveh Israel. Their reasons were in some respects technical, but what seems to have bothered them the most was that, as Americans, they viewed the earlier rulings as "utterly uncongenial to the liberal spirit of the constitutions and laws of this enlightened age and country."[46] Somewhat akin to the German-Jewish philosopher Moses Mendelssohn and other enlightened Jews in Central and Western Europe at this time, American Jewish leaders of the day optimistically believed that Judaism, "liberality," enlightenment, rationalism, and the demands of patriotism and citizenship could all be effectively harmonized.

Pride in America and a deeply felt gratitude for the privilege of living in a free and enlightened country nourished this optimism. Both publicly and privately, American Jews repeatedly expressed the conviction that they were uniquely favored. In his petition for a mikveh, for example, Manuel Josephson expressed gratitude to God for appointing "our lot in this country . . . whereby we enjoy every desireable priviledge and great preeminence far beyond many of our brethren dispersed in different countries and governments." In a public toast in 1788, the Jews of Richmond declared America to be a beacon of hope for their persecuted brethren. "May the Israelites throughout the world," they prayed, "enjoy the same religious rights and political advantages as their American brethren." Writing to the Jews of China, in 1795, Jewish leaders in New York boasted that "Jews act as judges beside Christians" and dwelt in great serenity. Most revealingly of all, Myer Moses, a leader of Congregation Beth Elohim of Charleston, in a published lecture delivered in 1806 to raise funds for the city's Hebrew Orphan Society, described "free and independent" America as a "second Jerusalem" and a "promised land." Picking up where George Washington left off in his letter to the Jews of Newport and echoing Protestant depictions of the country as "God's New Israel," he prayed for "Great Jehovah" to "collect together thy long scattered people of Israel, and let their gathering place be in this land of milk and honey." The idea of "Zion in America" implied that Judaism and Americanism, God and country, the synagogue-community and the larger community all were thoroughly compatible. In fact, however, tensions between Jewish tradition, American freedom, and the "great tradition of the American churches" were multiplying. As the nineteenth century dawned, the synagogue-community and the "liberal spirit of the age" stood on a collision course.[47]

FROM SYNAGOGUE-COMMUNITY TO COMMUNITY OF SYNAGOGUES

In Charleston and Philadelphia, the synagogue-community model—with one synagogue in each community that claimed overarching authority in Jewish life—had been challenged even before 1800. Recent evidence suggests that for a few years prior to 1791 Charleston Jews maintained two synagogues: Beth Elohim Unveh Shallom (which they translated as the "House of the Lord and Mansion of Peace") for the "Portuguese" who followed the Sephardic rite, and Beth Elohim ("House of God") for the "Germans" who followed the Ashkenazic one. The fact that the congregations carried similar names suggests that each claimed to be the legitimate heir of the original colonial-era synagogue-community. Communal divisions in Charleston ran along traditional old world lines—Sephardim in one synagogue, Ashkenazim in the other—but by 1791, in keeping with the American practice of having one congregation shared by all Jews in a community, the two had effected a somewhat uneasy reconciliation; centralized authority was restored.[48]

By contrast, in Philadelphia, where the Jewish community had fallen to fewer than fifty people, the "Hebrew German Society" began, in 1795, as an independent sick-burial society for immigrant German Jews, perhaps with a separate service that followed the Ashkenazic rite. It developed in 1802 into a separate "German Shul [Synagogue]" named Rodeph Shalom, Pursuit of Peace. Philadelphia's revolutionary-era synagogue, Mikveh Israel—small, impoverished, and internally divided at that time—had already forfeited most of its authority as its constituents left town. In the early 1790s it listed fewer than a dozen paying members, and in 1798 it stood in danger of "being totally dissolved." The rise of a new synagogue thus represented less a challenge to its authority than a response to its languid feebleness.[49] Perhaps appropriately, Philadelphia, the city where American freedom first took root, was also the city where the monolithic synagogue-community first withered away. The fact that the second synagogue, like the short-lived Charleston one, contained the word "shalom" in its name is also revealing. Whereas colonial synagogue names pointed toward the lofty promise of redemption, the scaled-down hope of nineteenth-century synagogues, faced with unprecedented challenges to their authority, was simply to pursue communal peace.

Two telling examples illustrate why peace so frequently proved elusive. In New York, in 1813, the *shohet* (ritual slaughterer) of Shearith Israel, Jacob Abrahams, decided to reject the congregation's terms of employment and to sell kosher meat independently. This served as a direct challenge to the authority of the congregation in a matter of critical religious concern, and the congregation, seeking to reassert its authority, promptly used its political connections with the New York Common Council to pass an ordinance that "no Butcher or other person shall hereafter expose for sale in the public Markets any Meat sealed as Jews Meat who shall not be engaged for that purpose by the Trustees of the congregation of Sheerith Israel." Once, that would have been the end of the story, except perhaps that the congregation might have disciplined the independent-minded shohet as well. Now, however, eight members of the congregation, supporters of Jacob Abrahams, protested to the New York Common Council that this Ordinance "impair[ed]" their "civil rights," was "an encroachment on our religious rites [*sic*] and a restriction of those general privileges to which we are entitled." They asked that the ordinance be "immediately abolished" and privately complained that it was an "infringement on the rights of the people." This language, resonant with the rhetoric of liberty and freedom that pervaded American life at that time, is extraordinarily revealing. The result was even more revealing, and it signaled a sharp diminution of the synagogue-community's authority. The Common Council, unwilling to enter into what it now understood to be an internal Jewish dispute, expunged its original ordinance and washed its hands of the whole matter. Henceforward, in New York, the synagogue-community's authority over kosher meat was purely voluntary; local Jews had established their right to select a shohet of their own. Though they did not immediately exercise that right, the challenge they posed to the ruling authorities was, as we shall see, a precursor of greater challenges to come.[50]

Meanwhile, in Charleston, whose port had boomed in the immediate post-revolutionary era and whose Jewish community had boomed with it, becoming for a time the largest in the United States, the authority of the synagogue-community was again being challenged—indeed, repeatedly. There were disputes over the synagogue's constitution, an ugly brawl in 1812 between "vagrant Jews" and congregational leaders over issues of authority, and, most revealingly, an unprecedented movement to establish private Jewish cemetery plots. The Tobias family established one, as did the da Costa family, and a larger private cemetery was established on Hanover Street in Hampstead by half a dozen Jewish dissidents, including Solomon Harby. Beth Elohim, Charleston's established synagogue, attempted to ban this practice, for it undermined a critical pillar of its authority: the threat of withholding Jewish burial from those who either defaulted on their obligations or were "rejected" by the congregation. "There shall be one Congregational Burial Ground only" proclaimed the congregation's 1820 constitution, although in the interests of peace it provided "that this law shall not extend to any family place of interment already established."[51] But like so many other efforts to reassert congregational authority, this one failed. Instead, in synagogues as in churches, we see in these post-revolutionary decades burgeoning religious ferment, challenges from below to established communal authority, and appeals to American values to legitimate expressions of religious dissent.

The result, in the 1820s, was a religious revolution that overthrew the synagogue-community and transformed American Judaism. The 1820s formed a remarkable decade in American Jewish history, paralleling the Second Great Awakening and the beginning of the Jacksonian age.[52] The Jewish community remained small—three thousand to six thousand—but more members than ever before were native-born, even as growing numbers of immigrants began trickling in from Western and Central Europe. This was a decade when Jews began moving in a serious way to the west, a decade that saw a few extraordinary Jews emerge in American cultural and political life, and a decade that witnessed the first serious writings by American Jews on Judaism, largely polemical and apologetic pieces by men like Abraham Collins and Solomon H. Jackson, designed to counter Christian missionaries. It was also a period when American Jews became seriously alarmed about what a later generation would call "Jewish continuity." In New York, Charleston, and Philadelphia, Jews expressed concern about Jewish religious indifference—what those in Charleston called the "apathy and neglect" manifested toward Judaism by young and old alike—and they worried about the future. "We are . . . fallen on evil times," Haym M. Salomon, son of the revolutionary-era financier, wrote to the parnas of Mikveh Israel.[53] While many of his complaints focused on religious laxity, the real question, not quite articulated, was how the tottering colonial system of Judaism— one established traditional Sephardic synagogue per community—could meet the needs of young Jews, born after the revolution and now inhaling the heady, early nineteenth-century atmosphere of freedom, democracy, and religious ferment.

Seeking their own answer to this question, highly motivated and creative young Jews in the two largest American communities where Jews lived, New York and Charleston, moved to transform and revitalize their faith, somewhat in the spirit of the Second Great Awakening, the great early nineteenth-century evangelical campaign to save the unchurched and Christianize the country. Jews hoped, in so doing, to thwart Protestant missionaries, who always insisted that in order to be modern one had to be Protestant, and they sought most of all to bring Jews back to active observance of their own religion. Chronologically, their efforts paralleled the emergence of the nascent Reform movement in Germany, where Jews "convinced of the necessity to restore public worship to its deserving dignity and importance" had in 1818 dedicated the innovative Hamburg Temple. They also paralleled developments in Curaçao, where in 1819 more than one hundred Jews, unhappy with their cantor and seeking a new communal constitution "in keeping with the enlightened age in which we live," had separated themselves from the organized Jewish community rather than submit to its authority. In both of those cases, however, government officials had intervened and effected compromise.[54] In America, where religion was voluntary and established religious leaders could not depend upon government to put down dissent, innovators faced far fewer hurdles. The young American Jews seeking to revitalize their faith, even if they knew of these other episodes, needed to chart their own course.

In New York, these young Jews, most of them from non-Sephardic families, petitioned Shearith Israel's leaders for the seemingly innocuous right to establish their own early worship service "on the Sabbath mornings during the summer months." The request brought out into the open a whole series of communal tensions—young versus old, Ashkenazim versus Sephardim, newcomers versus old-timers, innovators versus traditionalists—that had been simmering within the congregation since the death of Gershom Seixas in 1816. First, there was an ugly dispute concerning the pension rights due his widow. Then the synagogue was convulsed by the arrival of new immigrants who sought to revitalize the congregation and in the process threatened to transform its very character. Meanwhile, shifting residential patterns drove many members far from the synagogue; they wanted a congregation closer to where they lived. Sundry attempts to discipline members who violated congregational customs only added fuel to this volatile mix, and as passions rose synagogue attendance plummeted. With the proposed early morning service threatening to disrupt synagogue unity still further, the trustees "resolved unanimously . . . that this [petition] can not be granted." An accompanying "testimonial" warned that the proposed service would "destroy the well known and established rules and customs of our ancestors as have been practised . . . for upwards of one hundred years past."[55]

Rather than abandoning their plan for a new worship service, the young people "gathering with renewed arduor [*sic*] to promote the more strict keeping of their faith," and urged on by Seixas's own son-in-law, Israel B. Kursheedt, formed an independent society entitled Hebra Hinuch Nearim, dedicated to the education of Jewish young people. Their constitution and by-laws bespeak their spirit of revival, expressing "an ardent desire to promote the study of our Holy Law, and . . . to extend a knowledge of its divine precepts, ceremonies, and worship among our brethren generally, and the enquiring youth in particular." Worship, according to this document, was to be run much less formally than at Shearith Israel, with time set aside for explanations and instruction, without a permanent leader, and, revealingly, with no "distinctions" made among the members. The overall aim, leaders explained in an 1825 letter to Shearith Israel, was "to encrease [*sic*] the respect of the worship of our fathers."[56]

In these endeavors, we see all of the themes familiar to us from the general history of American religion in this era: revivalism, challenge to authority, a new form of organization, anti-elitism, and radical democratization. Given the spirit of the age and the fortunate availability of funding, it comes as no surprise that the young people plunged ahead, boldly announcing "their intention to erect a new Synagogue in this city" that would follow the "German and Polish minhag [rite]" and be located "in a more convenient situation for those residing uptown." On November 15 the new congregation applied for incorporation as B'nai Jeshurun, New York's first Ashkenazic congregation.[57]

As if conscious of the momentous step they were taking, B'nai Jeshurun's leaders took pains to justify their actions on both American and Jewish grounds. First, they observed that "the wise and republican laws of this

country are based upon universal toleration giving to every citizen and so-
journer the right to worship according to the dictate of his conscience."
Second, they recalled that "the mode of worship in the Established Synagogue"—the term is very revealing—"is not in accordance with the rites
and customs of the said German and Polish Jews."[58] Between them, these
two arguments undermined the whole basis for the synagogue-community,
and did so with such rhetorical power that, two full decades later, in Cincinnati and in Easton, Pennsylvania, Jews who likewise broke away from established synagogue-communities borrowed the identical wording employed
here to justify their own actions—without, of course, giving any credit to
the original.[59] The shared language demonstrates that we are dealing in this
period with a nationwide movement to transform and revitalize American
Judaism. What began in larger communities subsequently influenced developments in smaller ones.

In Charleston, where a far better-known schism within the Jewish community occurred, one finds several close parallels to the New York situation.
Again the challenge to the synagogue-community came initially from young
Jews, born after the revolution. Their average age was about thirty-two,
while the average age of the leaders of Charleston's Beth Elohim congregation approached sixty-two. Isaac Harby, the highly cultured editor, essayist,
and dramatist who became a leader of the dissidents, was thirty-six.[60] Dissatisfied with the "apathy and neglect which have been manifested towards
our holy religion," somewhat influenced by the spread of Unitarianism in
Charleston, fearful of Christian missionary activities which had begun to
be directed toward local Jews, and, above all, like their New York counterparts, passionately concerned about Jewish survival ("the future welfare
and respectability of the nation"), forty-seven men petitioned congregational leaders to break with tradition and institute change. The Charleston
reformers were about two-thirds native born—their city, hit by an economic
downturn in the 1820s, did not attract many new immigrants—and most
were people of comparatively modest means who participated in local civic
affairs. According to one account, almost three-quarters were not paying
members of the synagogue. The changes in traditional Jewish practice that
they sought were, from the beginning, far more radical than anything called
for in New York. They advocated, among other things, an abbreviated service, vernacular prayers, a weekly sermon, and an end to traditional free-
will offerings in the synagogue. When, early in 1825, their petition was dismissed out of hand, they, anticipating the New Yorkers by several months,

created an independent Jewish religious society, the Reformed Society of Israelites for Promoting True Principles of Judaism According to Its Purity and Spirit.[61]

The new society, initially modeled more on the local Bible Society than on the synagogue, and meeting monthly (later quarterly), aimed to replace "blind observance of the ceremonial law" with "true piety . . . the first great object of our Holy Religion." In an 1826 appeal to the public to help them erect a "new temple to the service of the Almighty," its members summarized their objectives in four paragraphs that illustrate the perfectionist, primitivist, and anti-rabbinic elements in their thinking:

> First: To introduce such a change in the mode of worship, that a considerable portion of the prayers be said in the English language, so that by being *understood,* they would be attended with that religious instruction in our particular faith, essential to the rising generation, and so generally neglected; and which, by promoting pious and elevated feelings, would also render the service solemn, impressive and dignified—such as should belong to all our addresses to the Divine power.
>
> Secondly: To discontinue the observance of such ceremonies as partake strongly of bigotry; as owe their origin only to *Rabbinical* institutions; as are not embraced in the *moral* laws of Moses; and in many instances are contrary to their spirit, to their beauty and sublimity and to that elevated piety and virtue which so highly distinguish them.
>
> Thirdly: To abolish the use of such portions of the Hebrew prayers as are superfluous and consist of mere *repetitions,* and to select such of them as are sufficient and appropriate to the occasion.
>
> Fourthly: To follow the portions of the *Pentateuch* which are to be said in the original Hebrew, with an English Discourse, in which the principles of the Jewish faith, and the force and beauty of the moral law, may be expounded to the rising generation, so that they, *and all others* may know how to cherish and venerate those sublime truths which emanated from the Almighty Father, and which are acknowledged as the first, and most hallowed principles of all religion.[62]

Like many Protestants of the day, the Charleston reformers thus argued for changes that would, simultaneously, improve their faith and restore it to what they understood to be its original pristine form, shorn of "foreign and unseemly ceremonies" introduced by subsequent generations. By renewing classical forms ("beautifying that simple Doric column, that primeval order of architecture")—the very forms venerated by contemporary American architects and educators—they thought to make Judaism more suitable to its new American setting. To this end, in 1830, they published a prayer book—*The Sabbath Service and Miscellaneous Prayers, Adopted by the Reformed Society of Israelites*—that is remembered as America's first published Reform Jewish prayer book and "the first radical liturgy produced in the Reform movement anywhere." Ultimately, though, the "new temple" remained unbuilt and the society failed to grow. Around 1838, after enduring a raft of criticism, much internal dissension, and the departure from Charleston of several key leaders, it ceased to meet at all. By then, many of its former members had returned to Beth Elohim, which they subsequently reformed and revitalized from within.[63]

Looking back, the strategies proposed for revitalizing American Judaism differed in New York and Charleston. The New Yorkers, influenced by contemporary revivalism, worked within the framework of Jewish law, stressing education as well as changes in the organization and aesthetics of Jewish religious life. The Charlestonites, influenced by Unitarianism, believed that Judaism itself needed to be reformed in order to bring Jews back to the synagogue. The former adumbrated Modern Orthodox Judaism; the latter Reform Judaism. Both explicitly rejected the traditionalist strategy of the "established" Sephardic congregations. But the issue was more than just strategic. Both secessions challenged the authority of the synagogue community, insisting that America recognize their right to withdraw and worship as they saw fit. All over the United States in the early decades of the nineteenth century, Protestant Americans were abandoning the "established" denominations in which they had been raised for ones that seemed to them more democratic, inspiring, and authentic; moving, for example, from Congregational, Presbyterian, and Episcopal churches to those of the Methodists, Baptists, and Disciples of Christ.[64] Jews now followed the same pattern.

Henceforward, in larger communities, dissenters no longer sought to compromise their principles for the sake of consensus; instead, they felt free to withdraw and start their own synagogues, which they did time and again. In New York, there were two synagogues in 1825, four in 1835, ten in 1845, and over twenty in 1855. By the Civil War, every major American Jewish community had at least two synagogues, and larger ones, like Philadelphia, Baltimore, and Cincinnati, had four or more. These were not satellite congregations created to meet the needs of dispersed or immigrant Jews, nor were they congregations sanctioned by any central Jewish authority. That continued to be the Western European pattern where church and synagogue hierarchies persisted. By contrast, in free and democratic America, congregational autonomy largely became the rule—in Judaism as in Protestantism.

Indeed, new congregations arose largely through a replication of the divisive process that had created B'nai Jeshurun and the Reformed Society of Israelites. Members dissatisfied for some reason with their home congregations resigned and created new ones more suited to their needs and desires. Some hard-to-please Jews founded several synagogues in succession.[65]

The result was nothing less than a new American Judaism—a Judaism that was diverse and pluralistic, whereas before it had been designedly monolithic. For the first time, American Jews could now choose from a number of congregations, most of them Ashkenazic in one form or another, reflecting a range of rites, ideologies, and regions of origin. Inevitably, these synagogues competed with one another for members and for status. As a result they had a new interest in minimizing dissent and keeping members satisfied. Indeed, more than anybody realized at the time, synagogue pluralism changed the balance of power between the synagogue and its members. Before, when there was but one synagogue in every community, it could take members for granted and discipline them; they had little option but to obey. Now American Jews did have an option; in fact, synagogues needed them more than they needed any particular synagogue. This led to the rapid demise of the system of disciplining congregants with fines and sanctions. Congregations became much more concerned with attracting congregants than with keeping them in line.[66]

Finally, synagogue pluralism brought to an end the intimate coupling of synagogue and community. Although into the twentieth century Shearith Israel (today the Spanish and Portuguese Synagogue) continued to demand, through its bylaws, that "all and every person or persons who shall have been considered of the Jewish persuasion, resident within the limits of the Corporation of the City of New York . . . shall be assessed and charged by the Board of Trustees ten dollars per annum,"[67] with the breakdown of the synagogue-community there was no incentive for anyone to pay. Instead, in every major city where Jews lived, the synagogue-community was replaced by a community of synagogues. No single synagogue was able any longer to represent the community as a whole. In fact, synagogues came increasingly to represent *diversity* in American Jewish life—they symbolized and promoted fragmentation. To bind the Jewish community together and carry out functions that the now privatized and functionally delimited synagogues could no longer handle required new communitywide organizations capable of transcending religious differences. Charitable organizations like the Hebrew Benevolent Society (incorporated 1832) and fraternal organizations like B'nai B'rith (founded 1843) soon moved in to fill the void.

By the 1840s, the structure of the American Jewish community mirrored in organization the federalist pattern of the nation as a whole, balanced precariously between unity and diversity. American Judaism had likewise come to resemble the American religious pattern. Jews, many of them young, dissatisfied with the American Jewish "establishment," influenced by the world around them, and fearful that Judaism would not continue unless it changed, had produced a religious revolution that overthrew the synagogue-communities and replaced a monolithic Judaism with one that was much more democratic, free, diverse, and competitive. American Judaism, as later generations knew it, was shaped by this revolution. Its impact and implications would continue to reverberate for the next half-century and beyond.

3

Union and Disunion

AN ASYLUM FOR THE JEWS

St. Paul's Episcopal Church in Buffalo must have seemed an unlikely setting for the dedication of a Jewish colony. But it was the city's only house
of worship and the only hall large enough for the huge anticipated crowd.
So on September 15, 1825, the day after Rosh Hashanah, the Jewish New
Year, crowds of (mostly non-Jewish) spectators, many of them women,
gathered at St. Paul's to witness an "impressive and unique" ceremony. Musicians, soldiers, politicians, Masons, and clergymen marched up from the
Masonic lodge in a long procession at whose center stood Mordecai Noah,
then America's best-known Jew and a prominent journalist, politician,
dramatist, and one-time consul to Tunis. Dressed up as a "Judge of Israel,"
resplendent "in black, wearing the judicial robes of crimson silk, trimmed
with ermine" (actually the costume of Richard III, borrowed from the Park
Theater), with a richly embossed gold medal suspended around his neck,
Noah entered the church and proceeded down the aisles. Following a short
nondenominational service led by the newly arrived rector of St. Paul's,
Addison Searle, Noah delivered a "proclamation" announcing to "Jews
throughout the world" that "an asylum" was being offered to them, a "City of
Refuge" located on Grand Island in the Niagara River, "to be called Ararat."[1]

Ararat, named for the mountain where the ark of the biblical Noah came
to rest after the flood (Gen. 8:4), was not meant for Jews already resident
in America. It aimed instead to draw persecuted foreign Jews to America's
shores and to settle them in a frontier outpost that the newly completed

Erie Canal promised to enrich. Reviewing the condition of Jews worldwide, Noah had concluded that "they suffer much, and are deprived of many valuable rights." What they needed, he believed, was a "period of regeneration" and the potential for "ample livelihood and corresponding happiness." He promised his audience that in America, "under the influence of perfect freedom," Jews would "cultivate their minds, acquire liberal principles," and qualify themselves to rule in the Land of the Patriarchs. While he did not view America itself as a Zion for the Jews, he looked to it as being a kind of Ararat, a temporary resting place between tribulation and redemption.[2]

Noah's colony plan was hardly a new one. At least four other plans for Jewish colonies in various parts of the United States had preceded his, and a plethora of other colony schemes—including the American Colonization Society's effort to create a colony for black Americans in Africa—circulated simultaneously and subsequently.[3] Nor was Ararat unique in its theatricality, its dream of an extraordinary role for America in the promotion of Jewish restoration, and its appeal to the overwrought religious imaginations of western New Yorkers, residents of the so-called "burnt-over district," whom religious visionaries of various sorts kept in a state of perennial ferment. What did make Ararat unique was its prescient anticipation of five themes that dominated American Judaism over the next fifty years: immigration, dispersion, concern for Jewish survival, the promise of "regeneration," and the dream of Jewish union. Long after Ararat was forgotten, these themes continued to engage American Jews wherever they lived.

Ararat never got past its dramatic dedication; it failed to attract foreign Jews. The plan met with ridicule in the European Jewish press, found little sympathy among American Jews, and occasioned a good deal of mirth among Noah's political opponents. Today, all that remains of the proposed colony is its three-hundred-pound cornerstone, inscribed in Hebrew and English. America, however, did become increasingly attractive to foreign Jews, and for the very reasons that Noah had understood: the persecutions and privations that Jews continued to experience abroad and the freedom and prosperity that they hoped to enjoy in the United States. Between 1820 and 1840, according to inexact estimates, America's Jewish population increased fivefold, from 3,000 to 15,000. Between 1840 and 1860 it increased another tenfold, to 150,000. By the time the first "official" census of the American Jewish community took place, in 1877, the American Jewish community's numbers had ballooned to about 250,000. Overall, during these years, the American Jewish population increased at a rate that was almost fifteen times greater than that of the nation as a whole.[4]

The estimated 150,000 Jews who emigrated to America during these years represented many corners of the Jewish diaspora. The 1830 national census enumerated Jews born in England, Holland, Germany, Poland, France, the West Indies, Ireland, Hungary, Bohemia, and Morocco, a mix not so different from that of forty years earlier.[5] Even the most prominent and influential American Jews boasted widely diverse roots. A compendium of the leading "Hebrews in America," published in 1888 and chronicling the achievements of those born many years earlier, included Jews who emigrated from no fewer than fourteen different countries.[6] During these years, Jews also began to trickle in from Eastern Europe. Just over 7,000 East European Jews, according to one source, are estimated to have settled in America between 1821 and 1870.[7]

The great majority of Jews who immigrated to the United States between the mid-1820s and the mid-1870s were Central European Jews from three specific regions: Bavaria, Western Prussia, and Posen (in addition, several thousand Jews from Alsace emigrated to the American South). These immigrants are traditionally described as having been young, unmarried, and poor, though recent scholarship has softened these generalizations somewhat. Close to 30 percent of the Jews, it turns out, came in the company of their wives and children. Most of the immigrants were not the poorest of the poor but, rather, lower-middle-class Jews stymied on the road to economic advancement.[8]

Jewish immigration, of course, formed part of a much larger stream of emigration from Germany and Poland that also deposited millions of Protestant and Catholic immigrants on America's shores, spurred particularly by famine, economic dislocation, and political discontent. All faced poverty as traditional village occupations disappeared and young people looked in vain for jobs. Jews, however, emigrated at a rate almost four times that of their non-Jewish counterparts, and often for reasons peculiar to their situation. Well into the nineteenth century, Jews in Germany and Poland faced severe restrictions on where they could live, what kind of work they could pursue, and even, in the case of Bavaria, whether they could marry. Only Jews listed on the official registry *(Matrikel)* could marry and settle down in Bavaria, according to a regulation passed in 1813, and except in extraordinary circumstances Matrikel numbers were transferable only to the oldest son. Younger children who wanted to marry had to move away, which Bavarian officials, seeking to "gradually decrease" the number of Jewish families in their midst, smilingly encouraged them to do.[9]

In addition to these social, economic, and legal "push factors" that stimulated Jews to emigrate from Central Europe, there were also, as Mordecai Noah understood, significant "pull factors" that drew them to far-off America—specifically, economic opportunity and religious freedom. Aaron Phillips of Charleston, an early immigrant from Germany, alluded to both of these themes in a gushing letter to his parents in Bavaria written just two months before Ararat's dedication: "How on earth is it possible to live under a government, where you can not even enjoy the simple privileges that correspond to a human being," he exclaimed. "Here we are all the same, all the religions are honored and respected and have the same rights. An Israelite with talent who does well, can like many others achieve the highest honors. . . . America the promised land, the free and glad America has all my heart's desire. . . . Dear parents, if only the Israelites knew how well you can live in this country, no one really would live in Germany any longer."[10]

Letters of this kind not only provided information and reassurance, they also served as an important spur for emigration. Indeed, Aaron's brother Joseph soon arrived to join him in "America the promised land." Sometimes such letters also made their way into old hometown newspapers, giving reports from America a much wider readership and influence. *Das Füllhorn* in Dinkelsbühl, for example, published in 1835 a family letter from a Jew living in New York who wrote back to his Bavarian relatives that he lived "quite happily . . . as part of a circle of many respectable Israelites." He reported that "in general the Israelites here live completely free and without restrictions like all the rest of the citizens." America, he concluded, is "much better than Europe."[11]

Letters from America, and the money that often accompanied them to assist relatives left behind, were described by the mid-nineteenth-century Jewish traveler I. J. Benjamin as "missionary tracts of freedom." In their wake, he observed, "immigration grew at an incredible rate."[12] Indeed, between 1830 and 1865, the small Bavarian village of Demmelsdorf, which in 1811 had a total Jewish population of only 136, saw no fewer than 30 of its Jews (28 men and 2 women) immigrate to Cincinnati, including virtually every young Jewish male in the community. In another Bavarian village, Unsleben, 48 out of its total Jewish population of 225 migrated to America between 1834 and 1853, mostly to Cleveland. In both communities, information concerning America spread quickly among the village folk, and emigrants literally followed in one another's footsteps, a phenomenon known as "chain migration." Still a third village, Jebenhausen in Württemberg, saw its Jewish population drop from 485 in 1830 to 127 in 1871. Fully

329 of its Jews had left for America during these years, while another few hundred moved to urban areas within Germany itself, a reminder that emigration and urbanization were often closely linked phenomena.[13]

Overall Jewish emigration from Central Europe peaked in the 1850s: partly in response to the failed liberal revolutions of 1848, partly in response to the antisemitism that followed them, and mostly because of a dramatic rise in food prices and a sharp decline in real wages throughout the region. By no coincidence, record numbers of non-Jewish Germans also immigrated to America at this time. But though immigration subsequently slackened, German-speaking Jews continued to arrive in America well into the twentieth century—250,000 of them, according to one estimate, by World War I alone.[14]

Immigration to America, for Jews as for non-Jews, kindled profoundly religious feelings and fears, and was often marked with appropriate ceremony. In one case, the religious teacher Lazarus Kohn of Unsleben presented Moses and Yetta Alsbacher, who set sail in 1839 for Cleveland, with an ethical testament that opened with a suitable Hebrew blessing, along with a translation into Judeo-German, presumably for family members who did not understand the holy tongue. "May God send His angel before you / May no ill befall you," it read. "In all your ways know Him / And he will make your paths straight." The testament carried the names of all the community's Jews whom the Alsbachers were leaving behind, and it included the "fervent wish" that these names be passed on to future generations in America—testimony to the concern that emigrants might forget their hometown roots. The document also carried a personal admonition from Kohn warning of the dangers that American freedom posed to Jewish religious life and tradition:

> Friends! You are traveling to a land of freedom where the opportunity will be presented to live without compulsory religious education.
>
> Resist and withstand this tempting freedom and do not turn away from the religion of our fathers. Do not throw away your holy religion for quickly lost earthly pleasures, for your religion brings you consolation and quiet in this life, and it will bring you happiness for certain in the other life.
>
> Don't tear yourself away from the laws in which your fathers and mothers searched for assurance and found it.
>
> The promise to remain good Jews must never and should never be broken during the trip, nor in your home life, nor when you go to sleep, nor when you rise again, nor in the rearing of your children.[15]

Kohn's warning reflected the haunting fear, already seen among native

Jews, that American freedom, for all of its benefits, would undermine traditional Judaism. Immigrants traveled to America in spite of this fear, and in some cases determined to surmount it. Many carried necessary religious objects with them, including prayer shawls, phylacteries, miniature ("travel-size") prayer books and Bibles, and even in some cases large-size Torah scrolls—an emblem, as we have seen, of communal migration. In one case, a group of almost one hundred Jews from Bavaria and Saxony set out in 1839 "to found a small Jewish community together in America." They assembled all the necessary religious accoutrements, including a Torah scroll, a Scroll of the Book of Esther for reading on Purim, and a shofar (ram's horn) for the High Holidays. They also carefully included among their number essential religious functionaries, such as a ritual slaughterer, a ritual circumciser, teachers, and cantors. They made all of these arrangements well in advance, a Jewish newspaper reported approvingly, "so that they may live during the voyage undisturbed in their religion." While this was unusual, the idea that Judaism was portable, that it could be conveyed on ship from the old world to the new, was not unusual at all. The "common man," one promoter of Jewish emigration reassured his readers, could "take with him the religion of his ancestors" and find in America "thousands with whom he can join in practicing his religion."[16] Like so many of the claims spouted by those who promised the poor and persecuted of Europe an asylum on America's shores, this claim turned out to be true only in part.

THE MARKET REVOLUTION
AND THE SPREAD OF JUDAISM

The America that Jewish immigrants from Central Europe encountered when they disembarked in coastal port cities was in the throes of economic change. What had been, outside of a few port cities, a largely subsistence economy, consisting of small farms and tiny workshops that satisfied local needs through barter and exchange, gave way during the first half of the nineteenth century to a market-driven economy in which farmers and manufacturers produced food and goods that they shipped for cash to sometimes distant places. Canals, turnpikes, and later railroad tracks linked far-separated points of the country, producing a vast national transportation network along which goods and commodities flowed. The result was what historians call a market revolution. Entrepreneurial values coupled with new economic and cultural resources enabled people "to make choices on a scale previously unparalleled: choices of goods to consume, choices of occupations to follow, educational choices, choices of lifestyles and identities." As we shall see, the market revolution also profoundly shaped the lives of America's growing community of Jews. They too now made choices on a scale previously unparalleled, ones that affected their patterns of settlement, their occupational preferences, their values and attitudes, and the practices of their faith.[17]

Peddlers were the foot soldiers of this far-reaching revolution. They were the proverbial middlemen who purchased goods (usually on credit) from producers and set forth to transport and market them to far-flung consumers, residents of America's rapidly expanding frontier. Peddling was a difficult and tiring occupation, but it required very little capital and promised substantial returns. As the desire for goods rose among those who once found most of what they needed close to home but now pined for luxuries from faraway places, young, vigorous, success-minded immigrants rushed in to meet the burgeoning demand. Many of these immigrants—indeed, most of the sixteen thousand peddlers listed by the 1860 census-taker, according to one source—were Jews.[18]

Peddling, of course, long predated the nineteenth century. The "Yankee peddler" was a familiar figure in eighteenth-century America, and Jewish peddlers roamed around Europe as early as the Middle Ages. For immigrants to America in the nineteenth century, however, peddling was less a career than a starting point; it served as the standard business apprenticeship for able-bodied young male Jews (Jewish women almost never engaged in peddling)[19] looking to ascend the economic ladder to success. Coming to America in their late teens or early twenties, these young men spent one to five years selling notions, dry goods, second-hand clothing, cheap jewelry, and similar products as they learned English and accumulated capital. Then they moved on to something better. Some succeeded handsomely: most of the great Jewish department store magnates began their lives as peddlers, and so did a large number of other Jewish businessmen. A typical rags-to-riches story went as follows:

> Philip Heidelbach . . . arrived in New York in 1837. A fellow Bavarian helped him invest all of his eight dollars in the small merchandise that bulged in a peddler's pack. At the end of three months the eight dollars had grown to an unencumbered capital of $150. Heartened by this splendid return Heidelbach headed for the western country, peddling overland and stopping at farm houses by night, where for the standard charge of twenty-five cents he could obtain supper, lodging and breakfast. In the spring of that year Heidelbach arrived in Cincinnati. He peddled the country within a radius of a hundred miles from the source of his supply of goods, frequently traveling

through Union and Liberty counties in Indiana. Before the year was out Heidelbach accumulated a capital of two thousand dollars. Stopping in Chillicothe to replenish his stock, Heidelbach met [Jacob] Seasongood and the two men, each twenty-five years old, formed a partnership. They pooled their resources and for the next two years labored at peddling. In the spring of 1840 they opened a dry goods store at Front and Sycamore Streets in the heart of commercial Cincinnati under the firm name of Heidelbach and Seasongood. The new firm became a center for peddlers' supplies at once, and as their business expanded they branched into the retail clothing trade.[20]

The majority of Jewish immigrants, of course, did not climb quite so high on the ladder to success. In Philip Heidelbach's own city of Cincinnati, for example, just over a third of a sample group of Jewish peddlers in the early 1840s moved up into more sedentary professions within three years; the other two-thirds took longer. A great many peddlers never rose above the level of small-town shopkeeper. An undetermined number failed completely: some committed suicide, others lived out lives of penury, a few returned disappointed to Europe.[21]

Yet however they ultimately fared, this army of Central European Jewish immigrant peddlers transformed American Jewish life. As they fanned out across the country, spreading the fruits of American commerce to the hinterland, building up new markets for producers, and chasing after opportunities to get rich, they also carried Judaism to frontier settings where Jews had never been seen before. By the Civil War, the number of organized Jewish communities with at least one established Jewish institution had reached 160, spread over thirty-one states and the District of Columbia (the 1860 U.S. Census listed synagogues in nineteen of these states, plus the District of Columbia). Jews spread through every region of the country, including the rapidly developing West. In the wake of the 1848–49 gold rush, there were some nineteen Jewish communities and five permanent congregations in California alone. Subscription lists printed in Jewish newspapers show that individual Jews, though not a sufficient number to form a community, also lived in more than one thousand other American locations during this period, wherever rivers, roads, or railroad tracks took them. That these solitary Jews subscribed to a Jewish newspaper indicates that maintaining ties to their kin remained important to them.[22]

Jews never distributed themselves evenly across the American landscape: over a quarter of all the nation's Jews in 1860 still lived in New York City. Still, the fact that as a group they had dispersed throughout the country by the Civil War remains deeply significant, securing Judaism's position as a national American faith. Adherents had voted with their feet (and their packs) neither to confine themselves to a few major port cities, as colonial Jews largely had done, nor to form Ararat-like enclaves, as proponents of Jewish colonies advocated and some other persecuted minority groups did. Instead, like the bulk of immigrants to America's shores, Jews pursued opportunities wherever they found them. In so doing, simply by taking up residence in a prospective boomtown, they legitimated Judaism, winning it a place among the panoply of accepted local faiths.

At the same time, however, dispersion also posed significant religious problems for Jews. Without a minyan, communal worship could not take place. Nor could peddlers and frontier settlers, living apart from their fellow Jews, easily conform to the rhythm of Jewish life, with its weekly Sabbath on Saturday and its holidays that fell on American workdays. "God of Israel," one such isolated peddler prayed into his diary in 1843, "Thou knowest my thoughts. Thou alone knowest my grief when, on the Sabbath's eve, I must retire [alone] to my lodging and on Saturday morning carry my pack on my back, profaning the holy day, God's gift to His people Israel. I can't live as a Jew." Another peddler kept careful track of his observances and calculated that over the course of three years he had been able to observe the Sabbath properly fewer than ten times.[23]

Settling down in a remote corner of the frontier did not necessarily make life easier. Joseph Jonas, the first permanent Jewish settler west of the Alleghenies and the founder of the Jewish community of Cincinnati, recalled that he remained "solitary and alone . . . for more than two years, and at the solemn festivals of our religion, in solitude was he obliged to commune with his Maker."[24] Some frontier Jews, in the absence of any available Jewish worship, went so far as to attend Sunday church services, thereby reassuring Christian neighbors of their piety. But this was hardly a satisfactory solution. More commonly, isolated Jews looked forward to the arrival in town of other Jews, enough to establish a community.

According to Max Lilienthal (1814?–1882), a perceptive observer who was also one of America's first rabbis, the transformation of an isolated settlement into a full-fledged Jewish community involved four factors: (1) achievement of a critical mass, at least the ten adult males necessary to form a minyan; (2) a revival of religious feeling, often brought on by the approach of the Jewish High Holidays in the fall; (3) the emergence of a committed leader who spurred others into action; and (4) support from an already well-established Jewish community, to provide guidance and to supply necessary religious provisions. In a lengthy communication to the German-Jewish newspaper *Allgemeine Zeitung des Judenthums,* published in Leipzig, Lilienthal, in 1847, described this process in terms of how a typical "small and isolated congregation" developed:

> Several years ago a Jew moves out to a small town and lives there at a distance and separated from everything relating to Jews and Judaism. It is not known that he is a Jew; he keeps no Jewish commandment, observes no Jewish ceremony. Some time afterwards one more Jew settles, then a second and a third; the holy season of our New Year and Day of Atonement comes, the people think of God and see in their prosperity how much they have to thank Him for, notice their irreligious life and are ashamed of it. The desire stirs in their hearts to return to God. They count themselves and are ten and are in a position to form a *minyan.* One proposes that they constitute themselves as a congregation, the others gladly agree and are enthusiastic. They deliberate, club up some resources, and then a letter arrives in New York or another large community. The people remit money to send them a *Sefer Torah* [Torah scroll], *Tefilin* [phylacteries], *Mezuzot* [parchment scroll affixed to the doorpost of rooms in the Jewish home], and *Zitzit* [fringed ritual undergarment worn by men], give particulars of a *hazan* [cantor or reader] and *shochet* [ritual slaughterer] and if five years later one comes to the kind of place where at one's first visit there had been no trace of a single Jew, one finds an independent, well-organized congregation with a nice synagogue and its own *Beth Hakvorot* [cemetery], and feels amazed at how quickly and how securely Judaism has taken root in the new Fatherland.[25]

In establishing these new synagogues, Jews felt that they were contributing to the "taming of the frontier," the triumph of civilization over the "wild son of nature." The founders of the new Jewish congregation in Cincinnati went so far as to portray themselves as trailblazers, "scattered through the wilds of America," doing all in their power to "promote Judaism" in a territory "where a few years before nothing was heard but the howling of wild Beasts, and the more hideous cry of savage man." Joseph Jonas of Cincinnati, in a subsequent account, applied the Puritan "errand into the wilderness" (itself a biblical motif) to the Jewish trek westward: "The fiat had gone forth that a new resting place for the scattered sons of Israel should be commenced, and that a sanctuary should be erected in the Great West, dedicated to the Lord of Hosts, to resound with praises to the ever-living God."[26] These potent symbols aside, however, the immediate importance of frontier synagogues revolved around the sense of ethnic kinship, religious fellowship, and caring community that they brought to lonely scattered Jews living thousands of miles away from their parental homes. These synagogues, like neighboring churches, came to function not just as houses of worship but also as "informal institutions of adult education, giving practice, counsel, and direction in a society where very few other institutions were available."[27]

One synagogue, as we have seen, rarely sufficed for long in a fast-growing Jewish community. The same marketplace values that promoted competition and choice in business also resulted in the creation and growth of new synagogues (and then sometimes in their disappearance). The primary issue underlying the establishment of these synagogues was not, as had been the case in Charleston and New York, an effort to reform Jewish worship or to wrest leadership from the hands of a superannuated elite. Instead, during this period, synagogue diversity more commonly reflected communal diversity: immigrant Jews sought to re-create in the new world the same religious practices and customs that they recalled from their old home towns. In Europe, each local and regional Jewish community jealously guarded its own traditions as the embodiment of its distinctive religious identity, and infused its particular rite, or minhag, with a high degree of sanctity. By re-establishing these old-world rites in America, immigrants both underscored their devotion to hometown practices, and sought to create for themselves an island of familiarity within a sea of change.

In St. Louis, for example, Jews in 1841 established the first synagogue west of the Mississippi. Its name, United Hebrew Congregation, bespoke the noble quest for unity among the city's small and diverse group of pioneer Jews, but the synagogue's constitution reflected the ritual origins and loyalties of the majority: "Prayers," it decreed, "shall never be said otherwise than among the Polish Jews." In the years leading up to the Civil War, as St. Louis's Jewish population rose, four competing congregations sprang up in town, each dedicated to a different old-world rite. Only one of these, however, proved economically viable: B'nai El Congregation, the product of an 1852 merger between the Bavarian Congregation, Emanu El, and the Bohemian Congregation, B'nai B'rith. As a result, by 1860, the city's diverse community of Jews had a choice between the Polish congregation and the German/Bohemian congregation, each of which had an ideological commitment to an old-world tradition but nevertheless competed with the other for members and prestige.[28]

Religious and cultural differences between German and Polish Jews, as well as social and economic prejudices rooted in Europe, help to explain why those divisions tended to linger in the United States, while others (like the Bavarian-Bohemian split) more easily lent themselves to compromise. For similar reasons, German and Polish Catholics also worshipped and lived apart in America. Among Jews, divisions between Germans and Poles came to characterize many communities, from Boston to San Francisco. In the latter, the westernmost outpost of the American Jewish community, young, newly arrived Jews fully intended to create one synagogue for all of the community's Jews, and met for that purpose in 1851. Dreams of harmony rapidly dissolved, however, and they ended up creating two synagogues: Emanu-El, which followed the German rite, and Sherith Israel, which followed the Polish one.[29]

Jewish leaders regularly expressed impatience with all these divisions and pressed for unity. They argued that what Jews held in common was far more important than the liturgical differences that divided them, and they condemned the situation in cities like New York, where five or more Jewish rites competed. But since similar divisions characterized any number of American religious groups—French Catholics and Irish Catholics worshipped apart, as did Lutherans of different backgrounds, and in one Cincinnati county there were four Baptist churches reflecting four points of origin—arguments for unity frequently fell on deaf ears. In some Jewish circles, in fact, the smorgasbord of worship choices even drew praise, perhaps a reflection of new marketplace values. "The Israelites living here come from various countries," one immigrant wrote back to his relatives in Bamberg approvingly. "Everybody can choose freely where or in which synagogue he wants to be enrolled."[30]

Even those who lamented the absence of a unifying ritual for American Jews understood that there were far more serious problems that the community had to contend with. For one thing, large numbers of immigrant Jews elected not to enroll in any synagogue whatsoever. In America, unlike in Germany, the state placed no pressure on Jews to affiliate with a religious community, and in any case, thousands of Jews had settled in remote areas where no synagogues could be found. Even in Cincinnati, where four synagogues did exist by mid-century, 22 percent of the city's Jews were estimated to be unaffiliated. Nationally that figure was much higher. According to the 1850 census, only 35 percent of America's Jews could even be accommodated within America's synagogues: there were but 17,688 seats for some 50,000 Jews (and some of those seats regularly were vacant).[31] Discounting the smaller congregations that the census missed, and the young children who would have been left at home, it seems reasonable to assume that as many as half of America's Jews were unaffiliated at mid-century. Jewish leaders took this to be a matter of grave concern.

A second problem facing the community was the formidable challenge posed by organized and self-styled Protestant missionaries. Missionary campaigns devoted to the conversion of Jews to Christianity multiplied during and after the Second Great Awakening. At different times, Elias Boudinot, former president of the Continental Congress; John Quincy Adams, a future president of the United States; the heads of Yale, Princeton, and Rutgers Universities; and army chief General Winfield Scott all associated themselves with these missionaries—much to the consternation of America's Jews. In addition, well-meaning evangelicals, particularly women, privately missionized their Jewish neighbors, encouraging them to convert and save their souls. Jews generally rebuffed such advances: the idea that as non-Protestants they were religiously deficient seemed to them insulting, even a violation of their religious liberty. Through private letters, published and unpublished defenses of their faith, Jewish schools, Jewish newspapers, and a variety of other means, they worked to parry missionary thrusts. Mordecai Noah once went so far as to attend an annual meeting of the society for "Meliorating the Condition of the Jews" and laced his published account of the event with caustic comments concerning the missionaries' misappropriation of funds, lack of success, false piety, and immoral tactics. Still, some Jews, like Joshua (James) Seixas (son of Gershom Seixas and teacher of the Mormon prophet, Joseph Smith) and the three Mordecai sisters, Caroline Mordecai Plunkett, Rachel Mordecai Lazarus, and Ellen Mordecai, did find in Christian spirituality a solace that they never knew in Judaism and embraced the church, much to the horror of their Jewish relatives.[32] The fact that in America all such conversions were voluntary, never coerced as they so often had been in Europe, reminded Jews that they operated within a competitive religious marketplace. Those dissatisfied for any reason with their own faith found a bountiful array of other religious options open for them to explore.

The gravest threat of all to the American Jewish community, however, stemmed not from apostasy but from love. As had been the case since colonial times, everyday social and economic interactions between Protestants and Jews resulted in intermarriages, usually without either side converting. No precise statistics from this period exist, but the Jewish physician Simeon Abrahams, writing from New York in 1845, described a "large number of persons who have contracted marriage with those not of our faith." In Louisiana, all three of the state's best-known Jews at mid-century—Senator Judah P. Benjamin, Lieutenant Governor Henry M. Hyams, and House Speaker Edwin Warren Moise—were married to Christian women who had not converted. Frontier marriages between Jews and Christians were reputedly even more common. Abrahams, who served on the side as a ritual circumciser *(mohel)* initiating Jewish male babies into the faith, expressed alarm at these developments and advocated strong countermeasures, even excommunication. "Desperate diseases," he wrote, "require desperate remedies," lest the Jewish name in America become "a matter of history, but not of reality." A more assimilated Jew like twenty-year-old Joseph Lyons of South Carolina shared Abrahams's pessimism but felt that Judaism itself was fated to change. "Certainly," he wrote in his diary in 1833, "a synagogue, as it exists under the present organization, will not be found in the U.S. fifty years hence."[33]

COMPETING STRATEGIES

Fear for the survival of Judaism in the United States served, as so often it would, as a potent stimulus for change. The question of what direction change should take, however, generated substantial communal controversy. Some argued that Jews themselves needed to be "regenerated" through greater emphasis on Jewish education and the strengthening of Jewish religious life. Others insisted that Judaism as a religion was at fault and needed to be "reformed." Still others felt that community and kinship, rather than rituals and faith, should form the new basis for Jewish life; they sought to unite Jews around ties of peoplehood, the "mission of uniting Israelites in the work of promoting their highest interests and those of humanity."[34]

All three of these competing and overlapping strategies, much as they differed in their emphases and tactics, shared a common underlying assumption. They presupposed that Jews through their *own* actions would determine the fate of American Judaism; the destiny of the Jewish religion had not been predetermined. "My faith does not rest wholly in miracles," Mordecai Noah characteristically announced in a widely publicized address in 1837. "Providence disposes of events, human agency must carry them out."[35] This emphasis on self-determination and free will—sometimes known as Arminianism, after the Dutch Protestant theologian Jakob Arminius (1560–1609), who articulated his ideas in opposition to John Calvin's emphasis on predestination—dominated antebellum American religion, popularized by Methodist preachers and promoters of the Second Great Awakening alike. Arminian ideas also nicely complemented the credo of the market revolution, which similarly emphasized human agency and the virtues of competition and choice.[36] Jews, heirs to a tradition that viewed free will much more favorably than Calvinism did, embraced this theological outlook. The strategies

that they developed in the middle decades of the nineteenth century pre-
sumed that Judaism's future in the United States would be decided by
American Jews themselves.

ISAAC LEESER AND THE
"REGENERATION" OF TRADITIONAL JUDAISM

The first strategy that Jews developed in response to threats to their survival aimed at the revitalization of American Jewish life. Nineteenth-century
Jews sometimes used the word "regeneration" to describe what they sought
to effect. They borrowed this term from their Protestant neighbors, who
employed it in an evangelical setting to describe the religious transformation
of an individual from "entire sinfulness to entire holiness." Jews, however,
used the word "regeneration" somewhat more loosely to refer to three different means of revitalizing Jews: (1) turning them away from sinful behavior,
(2) cultivating more refined habits and values among them, and (3) strengthening their Jewish education. As in France, "regeneration" was often a syno-
nym for "modernization."[37]

Isaac Leeser (1806–1868), the foremost Jewish traditionalist leader in
America for over three decades, was a primary proponent of Jewish "regeneration." Born in the Westphalian village of Neuenkirchen in 1806, and
orphaned at the age of fourteen, Leeser received both a Jewish and a general
education before immigrating to the United States in 1824 to join a maternal uncle in Richmond, Virginia. He quickly learned English and soon
developed a reputation as an eager scholar, an able defender of Judaism
against its adversaries, and a competent synagogue officiant. Although he
was German and not Sephardic, Philadelphia's Congregation Mikveh Israel hired him in 1829 to serve as its hazan. His obligations, he later recalled, were "to read the prayers in the original Hebrew according to the
custom of the Portuguese Jews . . . to attend all funerals and subsequent
mourning services," and, with the permission of the congregational officers,
to perform other life-cycle rituals.[38]

Leeser, however, had grander ambitions. Within a year, in an effort to
strengthen Jewish life through education and exhortation, he began preaching English-language sermons on selected Sabbath mornings. He credited
this innovation, in part, to the encouragement of "some intelligent ladies"
within the congregation—a reminder of the significant behind-the-scenes
role that women played in promoting Jewish "regeneration." It surely did
not escape his attention, however, that some of these "intelligent ladies"

Isaac Leeser, painted in Baltimore by the
Jewish artist Solomon Nunes Carvalho in
1857. Original in the collection of Norman
Flayderman. Photo courtesy of the Jacob Rader
Marcus Center of the American Jewish Archives.

learned to appreciate the virtues of preaching from neighboring Protestants.
Indeed, Rebecca Gratz frequented the Unitarian Church on Sunday to hear
the sermons of her "favorite orator" (and family friend), William Henry
Furness. Leeser, though unquestionably influenced by these same church
practices, and perhaps recalling the demand for an "English discourse" by
Charleston's Jewish reformers, had no trouble legitimating his introduction
of regular "discourses" based on longstanding Jewish tradition. Rabbis had
preached occasional vernacular sermons from the pulpits of European
synagogues for generations, and he had even heard his own pious teacher,
Rabbi Abraham Sutro, preach in the vernacular back in Germany. London's
Sephardic congregation, beginning in about 1833, heard one English-
language sermon a month. A few sermons in the vernacular had also been
preached in America, notably by Gershom Seixas in New York. Of course,
fixed prayers and the assigned weekly reading from the Torah and the

Prophets continued to serve as the centerpiece of Jewish worship. Like
Catholics, and unlike most Protestants, Jews looked upon sermons as ancil-
lary to the main liturgy. Perhaps to underscore Judaism's traditional religious
priorities, Leeser initially relegated his periodic sermons to the conclusion
of the service. That way, his message achieved its aim—"that the untaught
may learn and the learned be fortified in faith"—without unduly disrupting
the rhythm of Jewish prayer. The compromise effectively illustrated the
strategy that he would likewise employ in all of his other efforts aimed at
revitalizing American Jews: he borrowed selectively from a wide range of
sources, Jewish and Christian, in an effort to educate and reinvigorate his
community, but he carefully reshaped and adapted his innovations so as to
keep within the parameters of traditional Jewish practice and law.[39]

Several of Leeser's sermons dealt directly with the theme of "regeneration,"
most frequently in connection with calls for repentance, delivered on the
Sabbath of Repentance *(Shabbat Shuva)* prior to the Day of Atonement.
His message, appropriate to the occasion, exhorted his fellow Jews to step
back from their sinful ways. "Our community is contaminated by the iniq-
uity of unbelief, by the boldness of open sin," he thundered from Mikveh
Israel's pulpit in 1843. He blamed Jews for their "accursed love of money,
of pleasure, and of power," and he warned that the "whole regeneration of
Israel rests on the basis of the precepts and commandments which we have
received as the will of our Father in heaven."[40]

Yet even as he railed against sin and promoted a return to traditional
beliefs and practices, Leeser advocated the Americanization of Judaism.
He insisted, for example, that sermons be delivered in English, not in the
immigrant vernacular. He also employed English in all of his own publication and translation projects. "Although the new-comers are themselves
unacquainted with the English [language]," he explained, "still their children
will understand in all likelihood no other language; hence the necessity of
providing for the wants of the rising and coming generations."[41] Leeser also
refused to impose a ban of excommunication *(herem)* on an obstreperous
congregant, even when ordered to do so by his lay superiors; to his mind,
public excommunications ran contrary to American values. Most important
of all, Leeser reshaped the office of the hazan in America so that it more
closely resembled that of the American Protestant minister. "There is hardly
any Christian society which does not strain every nerve to have an intelligent
and virtuous ministry, composed of men who would honour any calling
by their acquisition and general conduct," he wrote in 1844. He urged his
fellow Jews to follow suit. In his own public conduct, in everything from

his clothing and demeanor to his writings, speeches, and pastoral work, he modeled himself on the practices of his high church Protestant counterparts. He also regularly described himself to Jews and Christians alike as a "minister." Indeed, his tombstone memorializes him in English not as a hazan or any English equivalent of that term (like "reader" or "cantor"), but rather as a "reverend," a "minister," and "for forty years a preacher of the word of God."[42]

In a similar vein, Leeser sought to reconcile traditional Judaism and aesthetics. He called on American Jews to embrace beauty, elegance, and refinement.[43] The German-Jewish ideal of *Bildung* ("self-cultivation"), rooted in German philosophy and ultimately embraced even by such leaders of German-Jewish Orthodoxy as Rabbi Samson Raphael Hirsch, likely influenced Leeser here. German Jews, as part of their effort to achieve political emancipation, cultural acceptance, and middle-class status, promoted both the acquisition of knowledge and a sharpened appreciation for everything "good, beautiful, and true." They sought to acquire the "knowledge, tastes, and manners of the educated middle class for themselves and their children," and they worked hard to eliminate "distinctively Jewish habits of speech, gesture, and emotional expressiveness."[44]

In America, Sephardic Jews had pursued related goals for many years. As early as 1805, the Sephardic congregation in New York, Shearith Israel, had introduced a series of rules "to promote solemnity and order." Such regulations became far more widespread with the immigration of German Jews. Some synagogues issued full-scale "rules of order" in an effort to uplift their congregants. At Congregation Bene Israel in Cincinnati, for example, the new proprieties introduced in the 1840s included a precise system for distributing in rotation such synagogue honors as the privilege of being called up before the Torah (previously, such honors had at times been auctioned); rules requiring men to wear their prayer shawls during divine services; resolutions designed to keep "poor boys" in "good order," so that they might recite their prayers in "proper order" and not wander into the women's section; and a decision to "put in force" an old decree that "no girl or boy under five years old shall be allowed to be in the Shool [synagogue], or any girl in the [Men's] Shool." Later resolutions asked individuals to recite their prayers "in a low tone of voice, so as not to interfere with the *Hazan* or Chorus," and mandated that "no person shall interrupt or correct either the *hazan* during the service or reading the Torah." Americans generally during this time cultivated the virtues of "refinement," seeking to improve themselves socially and culturally no less than economically.

Leeser, through his sermons, writings, and personal example, promoted these same kinds of improvements in Jewish religious life. Enhancing elegance and dignity, he believed, advanced the cause of Jewish "regeneration."[45]

Leeser devoted the bulk of his time and talents to improving the sorry state of Jewish education. Like leaders of the Jewish Enlightenment in Europe, who wrote and taught in the vernacular and also translated Jewish texts into western languages in an effort to modernize and uplift the Jewish masses, and like Rabbi Samson Raphael Hirsch in Germany, he assumed that education held the key to Judaism's advancement. His voluminous writings as well as the bulk of his organizational efforts aimed to strengthen Jewish learning at all levels. He particularly advocated all-day schools, parallel to Catholic parochial schools, that combined general and Jewish studies in a Jewish religious setting. Sending Jews to public schools, he argued, was dangerous: "The Jewish child soon observes, when mixing with others, that even in America his *religion* is ridiculed and heartily despised by the great majority around him."[46]

Nevertheless, he did lend his support to the Jewish Sunday School movement, influenced by the Protestant Sunday School movement, that supplemented the "universal morality" taught in the public schools with two hours a week of "particularistic" religious education, provided within a religious setting. Initiated for Jews by Rebecca Gratz in 1838, as "an attempt to improve the degenerate position of a once great people,"[47] the Jewish Sunday Schools, largely staffed by female volunteers, taught basic prayers, catechisms, and Bible stories while providing Jewish reinforcement for the same middle-class values preached to children during the week in public school and to their parents on Saturday in synagogue. Leeser, like many other Jewish traditionalists, considered these schools inadequate: they failed to teach any Hebrew, much less the ability to understand Jewish texts in the original. But he also understood that Sunday Schools strengthened American Jewish life. They educated children (especially girls) who might otherwise have received no Jewish education at all, promoted Americanization within a Jewish setting, and helped Jews to ward off missionaries. That was enough to win his support. Meanwhile, he labored to deepen Jewish education in other ways, helping, for example, in 1867, to establish Philadelphia's Maimonides College, a theological seminary "for the rearing of Jewish Divines." It collapsed a few years following his death in early 1868.

Leeser's most enduring and significant contribution to Jewish education and the cause of Jewish revitalization lay in his publications—more than one hundred volumes that he wrote, translated, and edited. Nobody in

American Jewish life grasped the religious and educational potential of the printing press sooner or more effectively than he did. Having witnessed how effectively Christian evangelicals harnessed the press to spread their gospel, and having experienced the joy as a young immigrant of seeing an article of his own in defense of the Jews widely distributed and reprinted, Leeser embraced the printed word with a vengeance. A broad array of Jewish religious literature in English, including textbooks, prayer books, polemics, sermons, the first Jewish translation of the Bible into English, and a wide-ranging monthly journal, the *Occident,* all flowed from his prolific pen. Thanks to these publications, even Jews who lived miles from their fellow Jews and failed to frequent the synagogue could now deepen their knowledge and faith and, as part of a shared culture of print, identify with Jews across the country.

Leeser's Bible translation, begun in 1838, with the Pentateuch (Torah) appearing in 1845 and the complete Bible in 1853, proved particularly significant. The average American Jew in his day did not read Hebrew, and those Jews who studied the Bible at all used the venerable King James version, obtained cheaply or at no charge from the American Bible Society or from missionaries. These Bibles, well known to Americans of the day, contained the Hebrew Scriptures and New Testament bound together in one volume, according to the Christian canon, and in a thoroughly christological format. Every page and every chapter of the Bible Society's Bible bore a brief summary heading, many of which read Christian interpretations into the text. The King James Bible also translated many verses in a manner that Jews found thoroughly objectionable, since they implied that Jesus was anticipated by the Hebrew prophets and psalmist. Rather than defer, as a subordinate, to a translation authorized by "a deceased king of England who certainly was no prophet," Leeser, following the example of the great Jewish philosopher Moses Mendelssohn in Germany, staked Jews' claim to the Bible in its original language. By publishing a translation "made by one of themselves," he freed Jews from dependence on Protestant translations, underscored Jews' "special relationship" to the Hebrew Scriptures, and reminded Jews of the many Scriptural-based differences that divided them from their Christian neighbors. He also complicated the Protestant theological principle of *sola scriptura* ("by Scripture alone") by demonstrating that, in some cases, the Jewish understanding of Scripture differed markedly from traditional Protestant teachings. The appearance of a new Catholic Bible translation at about the same time, along with a spate of other new Bible translations, underscored the growing fragmentation of

American religion, which the plethora of different English Bible translations both symbolized and promoted.[48]

The same year that *The Law of God* (1845), Leeser's five-volume, exquisitely produced Hebrew-English edition of the Pentateuch appeared, Leeser also founded America's first Jewish Publication Society, designed "to support the noble fabric of our faith." "The press is at our service," he announced in an address to the "Israelites of America." He hoped that the new society would solve the problem caused by the fact that "our people live dispersed over so wide a space of country that we are precluded from waiting upon all individually." The American Tract Society and the American Bible Society, he knew, had long since used the press to spread Protestantism's religious message. Now, showing that he too had assimilated the lessons of the market revolution, he sought to emulate "the plan adopted by our opponents" and to "profit by them." He proposed to "prepare and publish works to be placed in the hand of all Israelites" and listed two major religious objectives for his new society: first, to provide American Jews with a "knowledge of their faith," and second, to arm them with the "proper weapons to defend . . . against the assaults of proselyte-makers on the one side and of infidels on the other." The publication society produced fourteen small English-language volumes, each an approximately 125-page tract, but in 1851 a fire consumed its entire stock of undistributed books, and it went out of business.[49]

Yet even as the society's literary effort went up in smoke, Leeser's Bible, prayer books, monthly magazine, and textbooks remained in print, in some cases well into the twentieth century. His strategy for revitalizing American Jewish life—his use of print media, his willingness to borrow successful techniques from non-Jews, his focus on education and aesthetics, and his commitment to communal defense—proved equally long lasting. Years after he himself had passed from the scene, those whom he influenced continued to pursue the goal of an Americanized traditional Judaism, insisting that Judaism's future depended on the education and uplifting of American Jews rather than on any fundamental changes to Judaism itself.

THE REFORM STRATEGY FOR SAVING JUDAISM

Leeser's strategy for saving American Judaism did not go far enough for some Jews. They insisted that Judaism itself needed to change in order to survive. Influenced by Protestant theology, by the tenets of Freemasonry, and in many cases by the currents of Jewish religious reform in Europe, they urged Jews to abandon rituals that seemed incompatible with modernity and to adopt innovations that promised to make Judaism more appealing and spiritually uplifting. Privately, Jews like the Mordecais, who lived "among people unaccustomed to our religious rites," had worried for some time about rituals that "from their novelty" made Jews "appear ridiculous" to their neighbors.[50] Publicly, the Reformed Society of Israelites in Charleston also continued to agitate the issue, particularly at its well-publicized anniversary dinners. Isaac Cardozo, in his address to fellow reformers at the 1827 dinner, warned that "if we do not adapt things to the existing state of human feelings" then "our religion [will] suffer in the permanency of its sacred character, and future usefulness and renown." "Such Rabbinical interpolations as have no support in reason or truth," he predicted, would in the long run "fall of themselves" while the Reformed Society would "acquire power and durability." The optimistic rhetoric did not quite jibe with the Reformed Society's waning organizational fortunes. Financial problems aggravated by Charleston's economic slump, the departure of two significant lay leaders, widespread Jewish communal opposition, and personality disputes, among other things, spiraled the society into decline. In 1833, it abandoned efforts to construct a building of its own, and around 1838 it dispersed completely.[51]

By then, however, the cause of religious reform had been taken up elsewhere. In a controversial 1834 address at the consecration of Shearith Israel's new Crosby Street synagogue in New York, Mordecai Noah surprised his audience (and embarrassed his hosts) by promoting limited reforms in Jewish law. He advocated synagogue music and vernacular prayers, "descanted upon the burdensome nature of some . . . ceremonies," disapproved of redundancies in the service, and cited with approval the "improvements" that [Reform] Jews in Germany had introduced into their congregations.[52] Six years later, Rebecca Gratz of Philadelphia, in a private letter, described what she called a "spirit of enquiry abroad & around us." She reported that "reformations are talked about and some innovations made in different communities in England & America," and she noted approvingly that these "reformations" "awaken a spirit of enquiry & elicit knowledge," even if not sanctioned "by the orthodox."[53] The strategy that called for changing Judaism in order to save it would make much more headway later, with the arrival of German-trained rabbis. But even before they came on the scene, proposals for Jewish religious reform—some domestically inspired and some influenced by developments abroad—both attracted support and spawned controversy.

Revealingly, the most significant early controversy surrounding a synagogue reform, and the first to wind up in court, concerned an organ. Organs began to appear in American churches early in the eighteenth century. Their glorious tones promised to harmonize cacophonous congregational singers and to inspire worshippers with a reverential sense of awe, bestirring them to moral improvement. Jews traditionally eschewed instrumental music in the synagogue—just as English Puritans, early-American Lutherans, and Scottish Presbyterians barred it from their churches—and Jewish law strictly enjoined the playing of musical instruments of any kind, even at home, on the Sabbath and holidays. But in nineteenth-century Germany, based in part on Jewish precedents from Italy and Prague, the pioneers of Reform Judaism introduced the organ into their "temples," believing that the instrument could promote the kind of refined and uplifting spiritual experience that they associated with modern worship. On both sides of the Atlantic the organ became, in time, a visible and audible marker of Reform, dramatically distinguishing the new mode of Jewish worship from its traditional counterparts.[54]

The first known proposal to introduce an organ into an American synagogue came in 1840, just as the members of Charleston's Beth Elohim were completing a magnificent new building in the Greek revival style (the congregation's former building, on the same site, had burned to the ground in 1838).[55] Thirty-eight members, seeking to extend the spirit of innovation represented by the new building and, in their own words, "anxious to embrace every laudable and sacred mode by which the rising generation may be made to conform to and attend our holy worship," petitioned for a congregational meeting "to discuss the propriety of erecting an organ in the synagogue to assist the vocal part of the service." Ten old-time proponents of Jewish religious reform in Charleston, having rejoined Beth Elohim, supported this proposal, and so did the congregation's popular new minister, Gustavus Poznanski, a native of Prussian Poland and himself an able musician.

Poznanski had come to Charleston with impeccable Orthodox credentials: he had served as the ritual slaughterer and assistant hazan at Shearith Israel in New York, and he carried an enthusiastic recommendation from Isaac Leeser. But within a couple of years he had become a powerful advocate of reform. What changed his mind remains a mystery, but one suspects that he was swayed by his young Charleston-born wife, his encounter with many native-born congregants who understood no Hebrew and found the long, traditional Sabbath service "wholly uncongenial," and possibly by his memories of Reform Judaism back in Hamburg, where, for a time, he had studied.[56] Whatever the case, he proceeded to sanction the innovation of an organ on religious grounds, and with his blessing the congregation voted forty-six to forty in favor of installing one. The reformers having won the day—in contrast to their experience fifteen years before—it was now the traditionalists' turn to secede. Some, particularly those born abroad, left to form a new congregation, Shearith Israel. That name, which would subsequently be adopted by various other breakaway traditional congregations in the nineteenth century, established an eponymous link between the local traditionalists and New York's pioneering Sephardic synagogue. It also reflected the traditionalists' sense of themselves as a surviving "remnant of Israel."

For their part, the reformers—who now denominated themselves "the only open and avowed reformers in the United States"—proceeded both to change the congregation's constitution so as to exclude the traditionalists and to introduce additional reforms, including vernacular prayers, revisions to the traditional Maimonidean creed concerning the coming of the messiah and the resurrection of the dead, and the abolition of the second ("extra") day of Jewish festivals ordained for diaspora Jews by the ancient rabbis. This latter change, scarcely discussed in Germany at the time but prominent among the reforms advocated in 1840 by the founders of Reform Judaism in England, alienated moderate reformers at Beth Elohim, who must only have been further alarmed by Poznanski's open declaration that "he knew no stopping place to Reform in this enlightened age." In response, they joined forces with Shearith Israel's members and endeavored to recapture the leadership of Beth Elohim so as to check the "great and growing evil" of reform, abolish the organ, and thereby "restore concord and harmony." A complicated legal struggle ensued, with both groups claiming control of the synagogue. For the next three years the battle shifted to the courts.[57]

Judicial and government intervention, in Europe, generally spelled bad news for advocates of Jewish religious reform. In Berlin, for example, the government shut down a Reform temple in 1823, believing that it made Jews "even more dangerous to civil society than they were before." England's Reform Jews, prior to 1856, could not legally register their marriages.[58] But in Charleston the result was different. The legal precedent set forth in the so-called "Charleston organ case," and subsequently upheld on appeal, significantly affected the course of Judaism in America by establishing that "questions of theological doctrine, depending on speculative faith or ecclesiastical rites," should not be decided by the courts at all. Testimony concerning whether Beth Elohim's reforms violated the congregation's legal commitment to uphold the Sephardic tradition (minhag) was completely overruled, since the court claimed to have no possible basis for determining what Jewish law and practice mandate. "Matters of that kind," Judge A. P. Butler of the Court of Appeals declared in 1846, "must necessarily belong and should be committed to the jurisdiction of the body that has the right of conducting the religious concerns of ecclesiastical corporations"—meaning, in the case of Judaism, the individual synagogue's own board of trustees. The court also determined that "in a country where toleration is not only allowed, but where perfect freedom of conscience is guaranteed by constitutional provision," religious change was inevitable. No synagogue charter, the court declared, could establish "the exact kind of music that was to be used in all future time."[59]

Practically speaking, then, the court's ruling made it all but impossible to mount a successful legal challenge against a majority bent on reforming traditional Jewish practice. Proponents of Jewish religious reform could proceed virtually without fear of legal or governmental challenge, while proponents of Jewish tradition could win only by persuasion, not by appealing to courts of law. Henceforward, the question of how best to secure Judaism's future would be decided just as so much else was in America: by majority rule.

Proponents of Reform, taking their cue from Protestantism's remarkable record of success in the English-speaking world, insisted that the majority would soon be theirs. Abraham Moise of Charleston, a native-born Jewish layman, made this very claim in a letter to Isaac Leeser. He explained what set apart the Reform Jewish strategy:

> The Israelites of Charleston, South Carolina, be it said to their eternal honor, have seen in a proper light, the existence of . . . serious evils; and are now pursuing with firmness and zeal, the only proper and wholesome remedy. They are causing by degrees and with all due deference to the prejudice of age and habit, the mode of worship of their fathers to be understood and appreciated; they are rendering the service of the Synagogue acceptable to all by restoring it to its primitive beauty and simplicity—they are in fact, so improving it by the aid of instrumental music, and the removal of many of its defects and deformities, that so far from destroying their faith, or touching in the slightest degree its fundamental principles, as handed down to them by their great Lawgiver, or, as many of you suppose, *Christianising* it, they are daily giving it strength, beauty, stability and perpetuity. Under these circumstances, I regard it as next to impossible that we can fail in this noble and laudable enterprise.[60]

Moise was premature in his assessment, but the organ dispute did clearly separate Reform Jews from their opponents, who in response began to call themselves "Orthodox." "We may be said to belong to a party . . . we mean that called the orthodox party in Judaism," Isaac Leeser explained to readers of his monthly, the *Occident,* in April 1845. The terms "Orthodox" and "Orthodoxy," scarcely known in American Jewish life before then, now turn up repeatedly in that journal—almost one hundred times just between 1844 and 1850. "Orthodox" became the term of choice for Jews who opposed Reform in the 1840s, and it meant, according to the rabbi of the new "Orthodox" synagogue in Charleston, "true adherence to our holy religion in its ancient form."[61]

Meanwhile, the arrival of German-Jewish immigrants, a few of whom had already been influenced by the currents of religious change rippling across their old homeland, added strength to the forces of reform within Judaism. In Baltimore, for example, a group of German Jews broke away in 1842 from Baltimore Hebrew Congregation to protest its traditionalist policies and what members saw as the "establishment of a Jewish hierarchy" —a reference to the policies of the congregation's defender-of-the-faith rabbi, Abraham Rice (1800/1802–1862). Seeking "mutual improvement in moral and religious knowledge," they established the Har Sinai Verein Society; the name captured their "back-to-the-Bible" anti-rabbinic sentiments and declared theirs to be the true path rooted in the laws given to the Children of Israel on Mount Sinai. The new congregation initially worshipped from the German prayer and hymn books published in 1841 by the Hamburg Reform Temple in Germany, and it accompanied its modernized liturgy with music from a parlor organ. Within eight years Har Sinai had grown strong enough to erect its own building, a large Romanesque structure that proudly displayed the six-pointed star of David in its windows.[62]

In New York, Reform-minded Jews enjoyed similar success. A small group of young German immigrants, seeking to promote the reform of Jewish worship, established in 1844 a *Cultus-Verein* (worship association). They aimed to attract young people, heighten religious devotion, and help Jews to "occupy a position of greater respect" among their "fellow citizens." Named initially for the German-Jewish enlightenment philosopher Moses Mendelssohn, the association expanded in 1845 into a full-scale congregation called Emanu-El. That name, found in the Book of Isaiah (7:14), proclaimed a message that was at once defiant and subversive. Its literal meaning proudly proclaimed that "God is with us"—perhaps a slap at traditionalists like Isaac Leeser who felt confident that God was on *their* side. The prophetic context hinted that the path to redemption likewise lay with Reform. And the very spelling of Emanu-El tacitly challenged the Christian interpretation of Isaiah's message, which understood "Immanuel" to be a name referring to Jesus. To accompany its bold name, Emanu-El rapidly introduced a series of bold changes into its worship, including German hymns, a sermon, an abbreviated service, and organ music. Within ten years it occupied a thousand-seat Gothic building, formerly a Baptist church, and drew three hundred worshippers each Sabbath, including some of the wealthiest and most powerful Jews in the city.[63]

Notwithstanding this and other scattered successes, however, the Reform strategy remained highly controversial. It divided congregations as well as loving families; it came in for significant criticism from traditionalists; and, in the 1840s, it could not boast even a single nationwide leader of status to stand opposite Isaac Leeser. The main advocates of Reform tended to be young, urban, upwardly mobile lay worshippers, influenced by the liberal intellectual currents of their day, who primarily sought changes in the aesthetics of Jewish prayer. They believed that a refined and pleasing ritual would be more spiritually meaningful and uplifting, thereby elevating Judaism both in their own eyes and in those of their neighbors. By contrast, an Americanized traditional Judaism, the goal advocated by Leeser, to their mind did not go far enough. They advocated more thoroughgoing reforms —the removal of what they saw as Judaism's accumulated "defects and deformities"—to keep Judaism alive in America and to lure young Jews back to the synagogue.

TIES OF PEOPLEHOOD:
THE B'NAI B'RITH STRATEGY

Still a third strategy that aimed at preserving Judaism in America rejected the synagogue altogether and focused on ties of peoplehood as the unifying element in Jewish life. It recognized, as the reader of Shearith Israel of Charleston put it in an 1848 poem entitled "Israel's Union," that

> Some are reformed and wisdom boast
> Some orthodox, indifferent most.[64]

These so-called "indifferent" Jews—large in number, far removed from the synagogue, and seemingly uninterested in the practice of Judaism—continued, for the most part, to identify as Jews, and at least some of them turn out upon examination to have been anything but indifferent to the fate of the Jewish people. Joseph Lyons of Columbia, South Carolina, for example, stayed home from the synagogue on the Day of Atonement (Yom Kippur) in 1833 and described himself in his diary as "almost an atheist." Yet he longed to write "a complete history of the Jews," he associated and corresponded heavily with Jews, he read and studied about Jews, and he clearly thought a great deal about what being Jewish meant. In New York, a group of Jews unconnected with synagogues formed, in 1841, what they called the New Israelite Sick-Benefit and Burial Society, supposedly the first "overtly secular Jewish philanthropy in the United States." The society may have provided a "secular" alternative to synagogue-based burial rites, but as its name indicates, it very much concerned itself with "Israelites" and their needs. In Louisiana, business and family relationships linking Jews to one another actually provided "a substitute for institutional religious contact," according to one historian. Rituals and synagogue practices may not have been important to these dispersed and "unchurched" Jews, but they remained a "cohesive, definable group" that maintained close economic and social ties among themselves.[65]

Nationwide, this idea that the bonds of peoplehood—ethnic and communal rather than faith-based ties—could preserve Jewish life in the United States found its most important institutional expression in the Jewish fraternal organization B'nai B'rith (literally, "sons of the covenant"), established in 1843. American Jewish men had long participated as equals in fraternal organizations like the Freemasons, where they networked with peers, interacted with non-Jews, performed elaborate bonding rituals, and committed themselves to middle-class values, mutual aid, and universal brotherhood. B'nai B'rith promoted many of these same goals within an exclusively Jewish context, proclaiming as its motto "Benevolence, Brotherly Love, and Harmony." The preamble to the order's original constitution carefully avoided any mention of God, Torah, ritual commandments, or religious faith but stressed the importance of Jewish unity: "B'nai B'rith has taken upon itself the mission of uniting Israelites in the work of promoting their highest interests and those of humanity; of developing and elevating the mental and moral character of the people of our faith; of inculcating the purest principles of philanthropy, honor, and patriotism; of supporting science and art; alleviating the wants of the victims of persecution; providing for, protecting, and assisting the widow and orphan on the broadest principles of humanity."[66]

B'nai B'rith was by no means anti-religious. Indifferent as many of its members were to Judaism, others belonged to synagogues and even played active roles within them, including leaders from across the spectrum of

Jewish religious life (among them Isaac Leeser and numerous Reform Jewish leaders). Yet the organization's "emphatic" policy, officially articulated in 1859, was neither "to interfere with nor to influence" religious opinions; in fact, "questions of purely religious character" were officially banned from the order for fear that they would produce "serious trouble and disastrous effects."[67] To be sure, for some of its members, B'nai B'rith served as a surrogate synagogue (its historian calls it a "secular synagogue"), especially since it developed its own ritual, complete with Jewish symbols, secret ceremonies, and a prayer. The order's objectives, however, were overwhelmingly communal, designed to strengthen many of the "peoplehood" aspects of Jewish communal life that had declined in America with the collapse of the organized synagogue-community. It provided benefits to the sick, supported widows and orphans, and helped members visiting from out of town. It even created its own internal judicial system to try wayward members and to adjudicate intra-Jewish disputes (though on the basis of equity, not Jewish law). While synagogues divided Jews and alienated some of them altogether, B'nai B'rith argued that fraternal ties—the covenant *(b'rith)* that bound Jews together regardless of religious ideology—could bring about "union and harmony." A parallel organization known as the United Order of True Sisters, established in 1846, sought (with considerably less success) to organize Jewish women on the same communal basis.[68]

The three strategies put forth to save American Judaism, in addition to being three means of achieving a common preservationist end, also reflected deep uncertainty surrounding the central priorities of American Jewish religious life. Which of their core values, Jews wondered, should be the main priority: (1) to uphold and maintain Judaism's sacred religious traditions, (2) to adapt Judaism to new conditions of life in a new land, or (3) to preserve above all a strong sense of Jewish peoplehood and communal unity? Many Jews, traditionalists and reformers alike, actually cherished all three of these values, and on different occasions, depending on the circumstances, their priorities shifted. In the Charleston organ dispute, for example, we saw that Gustavus Poznanski, initially a thoroughgoing traditionalist, became an ardent advocate of adaptation and reform, while some of those who had supported the introduction of instrumental music into the synagogue soon found that they could not abide further changes and moved back in a traditional direction. The history of American Judaism is replete with similar oscillations back and forth, a reflection of tensions, deeply rooted within Judaism itself, between the forces of tradition and the forces of change, between those who supported compromise for the sake of unity and those who insisted upon firmness for the sake of principle. In retrospect, these tensions may be seen to have been highly beneficial. Proponents of different strategies and priorities in American Jewish life checked each other's excesses. But for those living at the time those benefits came at a steep price. Often their religious lives seethed with acrimonious contention, the unseemly specter of Jews battling Jews.

THE COMING OF THE RABBIS

The arrival of German-trained, highly articulate, and ideologically passionate rabbis, beginning in the 1840s, only heightened internal battles within the American Jewish community. Prior to 1840, as we have seen, no ordained rabbi graced an American synagogue pulpit. Authority rested with lay leaders who often mistreated the hazan hired to conduct the sacred worship. Even Isaac Leeser, who did so much to upgrade what he called the Jewish "ministry," was treated as a common subordinate by the parnas (president) of his congregation—so much so that he eventually resigned his position. Protestant ministers of the same era, of course, faced similar problems: "The laity," historian Sidney Mead once observed, "were in a position to wield decisive power in every denomination." The coming of the first properly ordained rabbis to America's shores did not immediately upset this long-standing imbalance of power, but it signified that changes were afoot.[69]

The first ordained rabbi to settle in America was Abraham Rice (originally Reiss), who arrived in 1840. Born in Gochsheim, Bavaria, and lame from a childhood accident, Rice studied in the famed Talmudic academies of Furth and Wurzburg and received his rabbinic ordination from the noted German Orthodox rabbis Abraham Benjamin ("Wolf") Hamburger and Abraham Bing. Forbidden to serve as a rabbi in Bavaria because he lacked a university education, he became a teacher and eventually head of the Talmudic academy in the village of Zell. From there, at the age of thirty-eight, he immigrated with his wife to America—driven, one suspects, by poverty, the death of their only child, and a fervent commitment, proclaimed in his very first American sermon, "to establish pure Orthodox belief in this land."[70]

Subsequently, a series of other ordained and not-quite-ordained rabbis migrated to the United States, at least eleven in the 1840s alone. Almost all possessed some kind of rabbinical training, but not more than four boasted the double credentials that would shortly become the hallmark of modern, professional rabbis: a secular university degree, as well as rabbinic

Abraham Rice. This portrait, preserved
by Baltimore Hebrew Congregation, shows
Rice with a beard and a traditional skullcap,
visible signs of his Orthodoxy. Courtesy of
the Jacob Rader Marcus Center of the
American Jewish Archives.

ordination. The rest possessed more limited training and experience; some
were largely self-educated. Medical doctors and lawyers at that time sported
a similar range of professional (and sometimes unprofessional) credentials;
their performance in office rather than their diplomas determined their
success. So it was with rabbis—and, for that matter, Protestant ministers.
Thus, James Koppel Gutheim, an able preacher and much beloved Reform
rabbi in New Orleans, who arrived in America in 1843, held no degrees
whatsoever. "I am plain Mr. Gutheim and no doctor," he told the son of a
rabbinic colleague. Most other rabbis of the era were less modest. The great
Reform Jewish leader Isaac Mayer Wise (1819–1900), who was orphaned
at a young age and grew up in poverty, possessed in all likelihood neither
a university degree nor formal ordination when he immigrated in 1846,
but nevertheless regularly published under the title "Reverend Doctor."

"The waters of the Atlantic," his biographer explains, "washed away many a defect."[71]

The new immigrant rabbis quickly found jobs in America, but just as quickly they came into conflict with the lay leaders of the congregations that employed them. The issues in contention differed from place to place, but every dispute eventually boiled down to the question of power. Would the parnas and trustees continue to wield ultimate authority within the synagogue, or would power now shift to the professionally trained, Jewishly learned rabbi? Wise recalled that the parnas, at that time, "was an autocrat in the congregation. . . . He was the law and the revelation, the lord and the glory, the majesty and the spiritual guardian of the congregation." As a result, when Rabbi Max Lilienthal of New York allegedly "offended" the parnas and board of his congregation by refusing to respond to the complaint of an aggrieved congregant, his position was declared vacant. Rabbi Leo Merzbacher reputedly lost his job over the question of whether a married woman might uncover her hair. The board found his ruling too permissive and fired him.[72] Wise himself experienced several dramatic confrontations with his parnas in Albany. He described this "war" at length in his *Reminiscences,* beginning with the opening battle:

> During the services on Sabbath morning the *parnass* sent the sexton to me with the message *ex-officio,* "The *parnass* serves notice on you not to preach today." I understood the declaration of war and the arbitrary assumption of power, and retorted briefly, "I shall preach to-day." I stepped to the pulpit at the regular time as the choir finished its hymn. The *parnass* now arose in front of me, and said threateningly, "I tell you, you shall not preach to-day." I paid no attention to him, and began to speak in a loud voice, which thoroughly drowned the voice of the *parnass,* so that the people did not know why he was standing in front of me. He repeated his threat. I paid no attention to it, and continued to speak quietly. The *parnass* and a few of his adherents left the synagogue; but their action caused no disturbance. . . . The gage of battle had thus been publicly thrown, and both sides took it up.[73]

In the end, as we shall see, Wise too lost his job—but only temporarily. Since the demand for first-rate rabbis greatly outstripped the supply, the marketplace soon restored substantial power to the rabbinate. Within a few years, rabbis like Lilienthal, Merzbacher, and Wise entertained multiple offers from congregations that sought their services. They demanded and won high salaries and even, in a few cases, lifetime tenure. Most rabbis who came to America over the ensuing decades reaped far smaller rewards: their salaries were poor, they enjoyed no job security, and they battled with their presidents and lay boards continuously. Still, the example set by their super-star colleagues provided all rabbis with a measure of hope. In the rabbinate, as in so many other facets of America's market economy, the success of the few fed the aspirations of the many.

High-visibility rabbis also defined the evolving spectrum of American Jewish religious life, a spectrum that extended by the Civil War from fervent Orthodoxy to radical Reform. Rabbi Rice stood at one end of this spectrum: he was unwavering in his commitment to Orthodoxy. His rabbinical credentials, Talmudic learning, and evident zeal failed to win him a job in New York; he lacked the modern education, outward displays of refinement, and oratorical eloquence that America's best churchmen exhibited and that New York's best synagogues coveted. Instead, thanks to a fortunate connection with a successful Gochsheim native who served as the president of the ten-year-old Baltimore Hebrew Congregation, he won appointment to that pulpit. There he became a symbol of tradition in the extreme, looked upon as a "defender of the faith" committed to preserving all aspects of Judaism in the face of outside pressure. He lashed out against those who violated the Sabbath, and sought to punish them. He expressed outrage at the "heathenish rites" performed by Masons and Odd Fellows at some Jewish funerals, and sought to ban them. And he railed against a wide variety of other sins, from intermarriage and dietary law violations to prayer abbreviation and mixed dancing. "The character of religious life in this land is on the lowest level," he complained in a letter back to his teacher, Rabbi Hamburger, in Germany. In the same letter, he wondered privately "whether a Jew may live in a land such as this."[74]

Rice represented a model of Jewish religious leadership not previously seen in the United States and only rarely emulated until the coming of East European rabbis forty years later. Rice took pride in his *lack* of accommodation to America. Though he appreciated America's free institutions and understood the importance of Isaac Leeser's Bible translation, he himself never mastered English and never made peace with the modern lifestyle that Jews in America had effected. "In my own home—thank God—I conduct myself as I did in days of old in my native country. I study Torah day and night," he reassured his teacher. Facing dissent from congregants who failed to appreciate what he called his "rabbinic responsibility . . . to teach the right path of our religion, regardless of the consequences," he resigned in 1849, promising to "fight the battle of the Lord" as a private citizen. He thought about settling in Palestine but became instead a small, independent merchant, assisted by his long-suffering wife. All the while, he continued to teach, hold services in his home, issue rabbinic opinions, and agitate on behalf of traditional Judaism. He briefly resumed the pulpit at Baltimore Hebrew Congregation in 1862 but died shortly thereafter. "Like a sturdy oak, he stood firm; nothing could move him from the inflexibility of his principles," his friend the Reverend Samuel M. Isaacs declared in tribute. "Although all around him was indifference and innovation, he was unchangeable."[75]

Rabbi Morris Raphall (1798–1868)—an ordained Orthodox rabbi with impressive university credentials and dazzling oratorical skills—stood to the left of Rice on the Jewish religious spectrum.[76] He was anything but a fervent Orthodox rabbi who resisted changes of any kind; instead, like Isaac Leeser and several other Jewish religious leaders of the day, he championed a modernized, accommodationist Orthodoxy that focused on preaching, education, and aesthetics but made no fundamental alterations to Judaism itself. Born in Stockholm, the son of a prosperous banker, Raphall received a doctorate from the University of Erlangen and settled in England, where he assisted Chief Rabbi Solomon Hirschel and served as "Rabbi and Preacher" in Birmingham. His "unsurpassed perfection" in English combined with his talents as a speaker, writer, editor, and scholar earned him a substantial reputation. Called to America and offered life tenure in 1849 by New York's Congregation B'nai Jeshurun, he reputedly became the first "glamour-rabbi in American Jewish history." He commanded the highest salary of any American rabbi of his day ($2,000);[77] his weekly sermons and well-publicized series of lectures attracted legions of listeners, Jews and non-Jews alike; and clad in a traditional prayer shawl and a velvet skull cap, he even delivered the first-ever prayer by a Jew at the opening of a session of Congress (February 1, 1860).

During his tenure, Raphall brought to B'nai Jeshurun the decorous model of "enlightened Orthodoxy" that was then developing in England. His congregation obligingly built him an expensive new synagogue modeled on English neo-Gothic lines, and in an effort to elevate that synagogue "to that high standard of respectability which the world has a right to expect," it introduced a whole series of changes aimed at promoting greater decorum within its portals. It banned the sale of synagogue honors, prohibited members from approaching the reading desk during the service, introduced greater order into the recitation of the priestly blessing from the platform (*dukhan*), required mourners to recite the Kaddish prayer "in unison with the Reader," created a mellifluous choir of male voices, and in the mid-1860s garbed its rabbi and cantor in formal clerical gowns. But at Raphall's insistence, it refused to countenance changes that were seen to violate Jewish law—there the rabbi drew the line. As we shall see, this unswerving commitment to Judaism as traditionally interpreted sparked controversy in 1861 when, in a widely publicized address, Raphall defended slaveholding on the basis of his literal reading of the biblical text. Arrogance, "a taciturnity and semblance of preoccupation which was an obstacle to familiarity," and personal tragedy—the death of his wife and his son—also cast a pall over his ministry. Although in the end his nationwide influence was far less than Leeser's, he nevertheless helped to define the modern wing of the American Orthodox rabbinate. He demonstrated, by example, that a rabbi could combine Jewish and general learning, matchless oratory, and a thoroughly modern demeanor while still adhering scrupulously to the strict demands of Jewish law.

Farther to the left on the rabbinical spectrum stood the great architect of Reform Judaism in America, Isaac Mayer Wise. The difference between Wise and Raphall was publicly displayed in 1850 when they met, for the first time, at a debate in Charleston between Raphall and Gustavus Poznanski on the question of Jewish religious reform. At a climactic moment in the debate, Raphall turned to the thirty-one-year-old Wise, who was in the audience, with a thrusting challenge: "Do you believe in the personal Messiah? Do you believe in bodily resurrection?" "No!" the young preacher replied loudly and decisively. With that public declaration, Wise distanced himself from Orthodox Jewish theology and planted his feet firmly within the Reform camp.[78]

Wise had arrived in America in 1846, having served for three years as a teacher in the small Bohemian community of Radnitz. At the time of the Charleston debate he was serving as the rabbi of Congregation Beth El in Albany. There he introduced a series of ritual modifications aimed at improving decorum; he also organized a mixed choir. But when asked whether he was a reformer, he explained that he was only a reformer "if the people long for it, but then I seek to direct the public mind on the path of the *Din* [Jewish law]; but I never urge my principles upon another, nor do I commence to start a reform in a Synagogue." His declaration in Charleston demonstrated that this was a considerable understatement, and after a series of disputes concerning this and other matters, Beth El's traditionalist president, Louis Spanier, dismissed Wise, just two days before Rosh Hashanah. Wise considered his firing illegal (a court eventually agreed), and on the Jewish New Year he defiantly appeared at Beth El, dressed in his official garb.

Isaac Mayer Wise soon after he arrived in Cincinnati
in the 1850s, dressed in traditional rabbinic garb.
Courtesy of the Jacob Rader Marcus Center of the
American Jewish Archives.

Years later he recalled the scene: "I step before the ark in order to take out
the scrolls of the law as usual, and to offer prayer. Spanier steps in my way,
and, without saying a word, smites me with his fist so that my cap falls from
my head. This was the terrible signal for an uproar the likes of which I have
never experienced." It took the sheriff, "accompanied by a strong force,"
to restore order, and on the second day of Rosh Hashanah Wise conducted
services in his own home. Thereafter his supporters seceded from Beth El
and formed a new congregation provocatively named Anshe Emeth, "men
of truth." This was a Reform congregation from the start, and Wise was
its rabbi.[79]

Wise at the time seems to have classified himself as an "Orthodox Reformer," a middle-ground position that he distinguished, in his writings,
from that of the "ultra-Orthodox" on the right and the "Radical Reformers"
on the left. Orthodox Reformers, he explained, "are inclined to moderate
reforms but not to violent transitions."[80] When he moved to Cincinnati's

Congregation Bene Yeshurun in 1854, with a life contract, his aim was similarly moderate. He had no intention of creating a separate movement or denomination within Judaism; his goal was to shape what he called *American* Judaism, a legitimate heir to the Judaism practiced by different waves of Jewish immigrants. He believed, in other words, that his moderate brand of Reform Judaism—the "forms, formulas, customs, and observances" that he modernized—would in time be recognized as the rite, or minhag, of *all* American Jews, displacing the many diverse European rites then practiced by different synagogues. To this end, he called the Reform prayer book that he published in 1857 *Minhag Amerika.* He optimistically believed that it might unify all American Jews around a common liturgy—his own. Jewish unity, indeed, served as a leitmotif of his rabbinate—it was far more important to him than consistency. Pragmatic, flexible, and politically savvy, he looked to forge an American Judaism that was harmonious and strong. Ultimately, the goal of unifying all American Jews eluded him, just as it did everybody else who pursued this holy grail. But he did succeed in advancing, institutionalizing, and orchestrating American Reform Judaism.[81]

To help achieve his goals, Wise, following the lead of Isaac Leeser, exploited the vast religious and educational potential of the printing press. He edited two lively Jewish weeklies—the *Israelite* (later *American Israelite*) in English and *Die Deborah* in German—as well as a shelf of educational, religious, and sometimes polemical Jewish books that carried his message to the far reaches of the land. He also traveled the length and breadth of the country, preaching, dedicating new synagogues, and spreading the gospel of Jewish religious reform wherever he went. Finally he established Cincinnati as the center of American Reform Judaism, home to the movement's premier newspaper and to its central institutions and organizations. His aim in all of this was twofold: to "reconcile Judaism with the age and its needs" and "to endear and preserve our religion." As such, he embodied the complementary and contradictory desires of many American Jews of his day, seeking simultaneously to sustain Judaism and to change it.[82]

Wise's longtime adversary, Rabbi David Einhorn (1808–1879), stood far to the left of him on many religious questions of the day, representing the most radical position on the American Jewish religious spectrum—what Einhorn himself called Radical Reform Judaism.[83] Born in a village near Furth, Bavaria, Einhorn achieved renown in his youth as a Talmudic prodigy and went on to study at the same rabbinical academy that Abraham Rice had attended; both were devoted disciples of Rabbi Wolf Hamburger. Against his teacher's wishes, however, Einhorn enrolled in university, and by the time he graduated he had abandoned Orthodoxy for what he called Mosaism—a Judaism "rooted in Sinai," purged of most ceremonies, focused on the "essence of God's word" (the doctrinal and moral law found in the Bible), and committed to the Jewish people's universalistic mission to the nations of the world. Einhorn participated eagerly in the heady intellectual life of German Reform Judaism, but his radicalism made it difficult for him to find or hold a job as a communal rabbi; he proved too controversial. In Pesth, Hungary, where he made waves as the rabbi of a radical Reform congregation, he lasted just two months before the authoritarian government closed down his congregation.

Einhorn immigrated to America in 1855, at the age of forty-six, to become the rabbi of Congregation Har Sinai in Baltimore. "Judaism," he announced in his inaugural sermon, "has arrived at the critical stage when it must part company with dead and obsolete ceremonies, if it means to keep the Jews within the fold or prevent their moral decay." He saw no value in compromising for the sake of Jewish unity, and he emphasized instead the centrality of principle. This immediately set him apart from Isaac Mayer Wise, whose priorities were precisely the reverse. Einhorn soon established his own highbrow Jewish periodical, *Sinai,* and produced his own highly innovative Reform Jewish prayer book, *Olat Tamid*—both serving to underscore his differences from Wise. He also demonstrated his unyielding commitment to principle by fearlessly attacking slavery from the pulpit—this in a border state with many southern sympathizers. Singled out for attack by a mob, he had to flee for his life once the Civil War began. In Philadelphia and later in New York, Einhorn continued to fight for the ideas that he held dear: "First Truth and then Peace" was his maxim. Though he cherished the freedom that America offered him, he remained rooted in German theology and scholarship. Absent the German spirit and language, he warned, the "lovely flower" of Reform Judaism would wilt.

As it turned out, many of Einhorn's ideas, as well as his inspiring liturgy, long outlived him. Indeed, his conception of a separatist Reform Judaism, committed to its own principles, proved much closer to the mark than the all-embracing Minhag Amerika that Wise dreamed of creating. But in his own day, the radical Einhorn, with his abstract universalism and uncompromising principles, felt as estranged and alienated in his adopted land as did his Bavarian schoolmate, the steadfastly Orthodox Rabbi Abraham Rice. Standing as they did at opposite ends of the American Jewish religious spectrum, the two leaders also unwittingly helped to define the broad religious center where the majority of Jews felt most comfortable.

Of course, none of America's rabbis on the eve of the Civil War spoke for all of America's Jews; the community was far too varied and diverse for that. As a group, however, the first generation of American rabbis did both lead and represent the community that they served. They clarified complicated theological and ritual issues, modeled a full range of religious alternatives, and created in their newspapers a Jewish public forum within which spirited communal debate took place. While rabbis never resolved the daunting religious questions that divided American Jews, they did set forth an alluring array of options for them to choose from. Then, by carefully monitoring the preferences that Jewish consumers displayed—the synagogues they joined, the kinds of rabbis they followed, and the religious rituals that they abandoned or retained—many rabbis (but not Rice and Einhorn!) adjusted their religious messages in hopes of gaining a larger share of the Jewish spiritual marketplace.

The result was a substantial degree of uncertainty, inconsistency, and fluidity in mid-nineteenth-century American Jewish religious life. Instead of proceeding along a fixed path, carefully regulated by age-old laws and traditions, Judaism had become filled with crossroads and byways, multiple options, and innumerable questions. These led in some congregations to frequent changes of leadership. Congregation Bene Yeshurun in Cincinnati, for example, experienced five different spiritual leaders of different stripes (including, temporarily, a member of the congregation) in just five years, between 1849 and 1854. "We . . . never had a minister who could gain sufficiently the confidence of the people," one of its officers explained.[84] Some rabbis proved equally unsettled: they never stayed for long in one job, even when their congregations sought to keep them. Bernard Illowy, for example, served six different pulpits during his sixteen years in the active rabbinate (1853–69). Isidor Kalisch served in eight pulpits in twenty-five years (1850–75).[85]

Some congregations spent years oscillating between Orthodoxy and Reform. On the High Holidays, when ancestral memories stirred and atonement was sought, they followed a traditional Hebrew liturgy; the rest of the year, when they preferred to be modern, they followed a heavily anglicized Reform one.[86] Individual Jews were no more consistent. On the Sabbath, according to one memoir from Chicago, "most of the women and many of the men were regular attendants." But the men then "left hurriedly for their places of business"—a reminder that women often kept the embers of Judaism glowing. Young people, meanwhile, scarcely attended synagogue at all.

Even where Jews were notoriously casual in their regular observances, however, illness and death reminded them of the power of their faith, turning
them back to traditions long since abandoned.[87]

Outside observers, like the traveler I. J. Benjamin (1818–1864), believed
that amid all this fluidity the Reform movement was advancing. "There
is no doubt," he predicted in 1862, "that in the next generation Reform
will gain the upper hand and that Judaism will be transformed."[88] Based
on several individual transformations that he knew about, this seemed like
a safe prediction. Thus Leo Merzbacher, ordained by the pillar of antimodernist Hungarian Orthodoxy, Moses Schreiber, began his American
career by serving two traditional congregations in New York. He concluded
it at Temple Emanu-El, where he promoted a series of far-reaching reforms,
including the introduction of his own new prayer book, remembered as
"the first American Reform liturgy compiled by a rabbi."[89] Max Lilienthal
followed a similar path. Educated at the University of Munich and ordained
by that city's chief rabbi, he epitomized enlightened German Orthodoxy,
and while still in his twenties he played a significant role in Russia's controversial effort to modernize Jewish education. Arriving in New York in 1845,
he was appointed "chief rabbi" of the city's three leading German Orthodox
synagogues. But after three years he withdrew from this position: he proved
neither obsequious enough for some synagogue trustees nor Orthodox
enough for certain members. Under the influence of a group of young radicals known as the Lichtfreunde ("friends of light"), he became increasingly
sympathetic to more thoroughgoing religious reforms, and in 1855 moved
to Cincinnati, where, as rabbi of the city's oldest congregation, he promised
"to go hand in hand, in all matters concerning reform, with his beloved
friend Dr. [Isaac Mayer] Wise."[90]

Less than a decade after Benjamin made his prediction, even Abraham
Rice's own son-in-law, Joseph Leucht, changed his religious convictions.
Though he had served as Rice's Orthodox cantor in Baltimore in the early
1860s, by the end of that decade "Rabbi" Leucht was steering Congregation
B'nai Jeshurun of Newark firmly into the Reform camp. He soon introduced
the prayer book of David Einhorn into the synagogue, and in the early
1880s ended the wearing of head coverings, which he described as a sin.[91]

Even as Reform was advancing, however, Orthodoxy had by no means
disappeared. To the contrary, in 1852 recently emigrated Jews, mostly from
Lithuania and Poland, established New York's first East European Orthodox
synagogue, the Beth Hamidrash, which, true to its name, "house of study,"

emphasized the traditional study of Jewish texts.[92] Rabbis associated with the new Beth Hamidrash—Abraham Joseph Ash, Judah Mittelman, Aaron Z. Friedman, and others—soon quarreled among themselves and split into competing synagogues, but along with rabbis like Abraham Rice, Bernard Illowy, and later Moshe Aaronsohn they developed a small, fervently *(haredi)* Orthodox subculture of their own, where they debated Jewish legal questions, maintained ties with leading European rabbinic figures, and even published erudite articles and religious tomes in Hebrew that brought them to the notice of their counterparts in Europe.

Many of their discussions revolved around issues of *kashrut,* the Jewish dietary laws: Did the American practice of bloodletting animals prior to slaughter violate Jewish law? Was the Muscovy duck a kosher bird? May one use the same set of gold false teeth for eating milk and meat, and also for Passover? Other questions concerned marriage, divorce, and questions of Jewish status. How should American cities be identified in traditional Jewish legal documents? May a man in America use the mails (rather than a personal representative) to send a writ of Jewish divorce *(get)* to his wife back in Europe, so that she might be free to marry again? Should ritual circumcisers be permitted to circumcise the non-Jewish children of intermarried couples? These and a wide range of other questions that applied traditional Jewish law to contemporary new world conditions found their way into Jewish legal writings, shaping images of America that endured in Orthodox circles in Europe.

The first American Hebrew books dealing with matters of traditional Jewish law and interpretation likewise served to demonstrate that fervent Orthodoxy had found a modest refuge in America. These were pamphlets like B. I. Hamburger's *Dine Nikur* (1859), a "manual designed to the acquisition of the knowledge of the vessels and membranes of a beast, which are considered as unlawful food for Israelites, and the way to remove them illustrated by anatomical engravings," and Joshua Falk's more substantial *Avne Yehoshu'a* (1860), a rabbinic commentary on the Ethics of the Fathers. The greatest significance of these rabbis and what they accomplished, however, lies in the beachhead they established for those who came later. Who could have imagined that one day this handful of Orthodox zealots would multiply, turning America into the largest center of fervent Orthodoxy in the entire Jewish diaspora?

UNION AND DISUNION

With so many different kinds of Jews, so many ways of practicing Judaism, so many competing synagogues, and now a burgeoning number of contending rabbis, calls for peace and unity among American Jews rang out from many quarters. Even the names of synagogues reflected this quest. There was Ohabei Shalom ("lovers of peace") in Boston, founded in 1843, and B'nai Shalom ("children of peace") in Huntsville, Alabama, founded in 1860. A Fort Wayne, Indiana, congregation, established in 1848, was called Achduth Vesholom ("unity and peace"). Other congregations, like one chartered in Lafayette, Indiana, in 1849, dedicated themselves to brotherly love (Ahavath Achim). There was also a congregation named Concord started in Syracuse in 1850, and even (somewhat to the amusement of later members) a congregation named House of Love (Beth Ahaba), organized in Richmond in 1841.[93]

Peace, unity, and brotherly love were, of course, always more dream than reality. Still, for centuries Jews in Europe had lived in organized communities *(kehillot)* of their own, where they enjoyed a substantial degree of self-government and where unity was to a considerable degree imposed upon them. Even most American Jewish communities, we have seen, had been united around a single consensus-oriented synagogue until the system collapsed in the second quarter of the nineteenth century. In the countries where the majority of immigrants were born, some kind of organized Jewish community remained the norm, albeit in modernized form. In England, for example, the chief rabbi served as the central Jewish religious leader— the Jewish equivalent of the Archbishop of Canterbury—and the Board of Deputies served as the community's officially recognized representative. In France, Jewish religious leadership was vested in central and regional consistories, modeled on their Protestant counterparts, where committees of rabbis and laymen, under government mandate, supervised all aspects of Jewish religious life, levied dues, and exercised monopoly power, since no public worship could take place without the consistory's approval. In Germany, the status and structure of Jewish communities varied widely, but all were territorially based, government recognized, hierarchic, overseen by communal boards that defined the limits of normative Judaism, and supported by funds that the government through its taxing power helped to collect. With these models before them, Jewish leaders in America proposed a whole series of plans aimed at regulating American Jewish life by imposing some form of ecclesiastical authority and promoting communal unity. Each one eventually failed. During the two decades prior to the Civil War, however, they did spark a significant communal debate over "union" that echoed in many respects the increasingly strident national debate over "The Union" taking place at the same time.

Isaac Leeser, in 1841, set forth the first major "plan for establishing a religious union among the Israelites of America." In response to what he called the "great downfall of religious observance and the want of proper religious education," he proposed a three-point program: (1) The establishment of a "competent ecclesiastical authority," defined as a Central Religious Council composed of "three gentlemen of undoubted moral and religious character," elected by the congregational union to exercise religious leadership over American Jewry; (2) the creation of a network of "schools for general and religious education under Jewish Superintendence"; and (3) the organization of a "union" composed of delegates from all "regularly organized congregations" to promote harmony and undertake concerted communal action when necessary. Leeser's timing suggests that he was responding to the leadership vacuum displayed by American Jews in 1840, when Jews around the world, including some in the United States, sought to help their brethren in Damascus, maliciously charged with committing ritual murder. New York Jews had petitioned President Martin Van Buren for help "in endeavoring to obtain a fair & impartial trial for our Brethren in Damascus"—the first petition on behalf of Jews abroad ever sent to an American president—and demonstrations on behalf of the persecuted Jews eventually took place in half a dozen American cities. But the American Jewish response came embarrassingly late, and even then local Jews displayed neither "harmony" nor "concerted communal action"—problems that Leeser was evidently trying to remedy.[94]

Even if the Damascus Affair was on his mind, however, Leeser's major aim, in the words of his biographer, was "to clamp down on Reform." Orthodox synagogues still predominated in the United States in 1841, and this plan, somewhat modeled on the French consistorial system, would have allowed their representatives to hold fast to the reins of communal power. The sharp-eyed Abraham Moise of Charleston saw a direct parallel here to northern efforts to promote the Union at the expense of states' rights. Any such plan, he warned, would "keep away all Jews south of the Potomac." For similar reasons, Moise's home congregation, Beth Elohim, condemned Leeser's plan as "wholly inconsistent with the spirit of American liberty."[95]

Another idea discussed during this era was the appointment of a chief rabbi. This too aimed to strengthen the bonds of traditional Jewish religious authority so as to thwart the nascent movement for Jewish religious reform. In England, Chief Rabbi Nathan Adler, elected in 1844, proved quite successful in this capacity. Modeling his authority, demeanor, and later even his vestments on those of the Anglican archbishop, he gained substantial respect, prevented the Reform movement from spreading within the British Empire, and created precisely the kind of disciplined and dignified modern Orthodoxy that Leeser himself championed in Philadelphia. Many other Jewish communities abroad likewise enjoyed the spiritual leadership of a chief rabbi. "It will not be long," Isaac Leeser predicted in response to Adler's election, "before the American Israelites will also demand the election of a chief with several associates to preside over our worship and education."[96]

Some considered Abraham Rice a suitable candidate. He himself admitted to his "interested motives" to Leeser in a letter, where he spoke of the "great importance of selecting a spiritual chief." Subsequently, he was described as "Chief Rabbi in the United States" in several newspapers, although no election ever took place. In 1846, Max Lilienthal did officially bear the title of chief rabbi, albeit only of New York, when he briefly served three German Orthodox congregations in the city. But since there was no parallel Christian religious authority in America—no chief Protestant minister, no archbishop, not even a Catholic cardinal with nationwide jurisdiction—it was easy for opponents to dismiss any Jewish effort to create a chief rabbinate as "ridiculous" and antithetical to American ideals. Nor, given church-state separation, could any chief rabbi expect government recognition, much less the kind of authority that some European chief rabbis wielded. Finally, many Americans of the day, Jews among them, were deeply suspicious of strong central authority. The "tyranny of the majority," they feared, would soon come trampling down on the rights of the minority, be they southerners or religious reformers. As a result, all efforts aimed at electing a chief rabbi ended in failure, and the decentralized congregationalist polity that had characterized American Judaism since the Revolution remained in place. "Jews," Leeser sadly confessed, "have no ecclesiastical authorities in America, other than the congregations themselves."[97]

If no ecclesiastical authorities united American Jews, however, the community did develop a series of powerful unifying symbols and markers. First and foremost among these, as we have seen, was the Torah scroll. It defined Jewish sacred space; without a Torah no synagogue could call itself complete. Precisely for this reason, Baltimore's two traditional congregations refused to lend a Torah scroll to the Har Sinai Verein when it was set up in 1842; they hoped to prevent the Reformers from conducting worship. The new congregation defiantly used a printed Hebrew Bible instead and went ahead with its services, but it soon acquired multiple Torah scrolls of its own. Indeed, hundreds of Torah scrolls were imported into America during the mid-nineteenth century; every new synagogue needed at least one and most sought to acquire more than one.[98]

In addition to housing the holy Torah, almost every synagogue exhibited the Ten Commandments, positioned on or above the holy ark and usually portrayed as the two tablets of the covenant with five commandments on each tablet. These familiar images of the "two tablets" date back no further than the fifteenth century in synagogues, and the form was apparently borrowed from Christian art. But in America the tablets became so important that the old Jewish synagogue of Newport, which seems not originally to have displayed them, was considered deficient. Consequently, Benjamin Howland's fine painting of the two tablets (complete with errors in Hebrew) was added above the ark in 1828 when the synagogue was rehabilitated. So recognized a marker of Jewish sacred space had the two tablets become that in 1850, when New York's Congregation Anshe Chesed deviated from familiar practice by arranging the commandments in a circle on a stained-glass window above its ark, the innovation provoked an outcry. Within a year a committee was appointed to have the traditional two tablets restored.[99]

A more modern but today far more familiar symbol that came to unite Jews during this period was the hexagram, the six-pointed star (or shield) of David known as the *Magen David*. The hexagram is now believed to have become an emblem of Jewishness in Prague around the year 1600. By no means, however, was its usage ever confined to Jews. Indeed, the symbol can still be found as part of the emblem of the Order of Franciscan Friars of the Atonement, on stained-glass windows in the (Anglican) Church of the Redeemer in Toronto, and of course on every American dollar bill and as the shape of the standard American sheriff's badge. It was only at the beginning of the nineteenth century in Germany that the shield of David became a distinguishing religious marker of Judaism. Scholars believe that newly emancipated German Jews adopted the symbol to stand opposite the cross that so visibly symbolized Christianity. German immigrants brought this new "symbol of Judaism" with them to America, and in 1845 the shield of David made its first architectural appearance, built into the windows of the new Baltimore Hebrew Congregation synagogue building.

The Magen David, six-pointed star or shield of David, in its first
American appearance (1845), in a stained-glass window on the eastern wall of the
Lloyd Street Synagogue of Baltimore Hebrew Congregation. The symbol identified
the synagogue to outsiders as a distinctively Jewish house of worship. Note the
Ten Commandments displayed in two tablets over the ark. The five Hebrew words
inscribed over the doors on the ark remind worshippers to "Know before Whom
you stand." Courtesy of the Jewish Museum of Maryland Institutional Archives.

Har Sinai carefully placed the same symbol in the windows of its new building in 1849, thereby demonstrating that however much they differed from
the Orthodox they too were proud Jews. Soon the symbol became common
not only inside and outside of synagogues but also on American Jewish
books, ceremonial objects, and tombstones. It became a visible proclamation
of Jewishness, a symbol that all Jews could rally around, and a shorthand
way of distinguishing Jewish objects from Christian ones.[100]

Still another unifying and distinguishing marker of Judaism was the
opening line of what Jews call the *Shema* (Deuteronomy 6:4–9): "Hear
[*Shema*] O Israel: the Lord our God, the Lord is one." The Shema was

reputedly recited in the ancient Temple of Jerusalem (along with the Ten Commandments), and generations of Jews pronounced it twice a day in their prayers, as well as nightly upon retiring, and for the final time upon their deathbed. Its text also forms part of the *mezuzah* (literally "doorpost"), the encased parchment scroll affixed to the doorpost of rooms in the Jewish home. The Shema's six opening Hebrew words, easily remembered and taught to children at a young age, became the "preeminent expression of monotheism in Judaism," as well as the quintessential expression of Judaism's "most fundamental belief and commitment." Because of their emphasis on God's oneness, these words also came to serve as a powerful Jewish response to Christianity, a daily reminder from the Bible that Jews believe in one God alone and not in the trinity. In America, the Shema continued to serve all of these functions, and even Jews who read no Hebrew knew its opening words by heart. Mordecai Noah, in 1825, had these words incised in Hebrew on the cornerstone of Ararat, his proposed "city of refuge for the Jews." Charleston's Beth Elohim carved the words both in Hebrew and in English above the entryway of its 1840 synagogue building. The provocative non-standard translation employed in Charleston—"Hear O Israel! The Lord Our God Is the Sole Eternal Being"—still stands as a mute challenge to the Christian churches nearby. Every Jewish liturgy, traditional and Reform alike, likewise highlighted the Shema, which became known in some Jewish circles as "the watchword of our faith." Traditionally, Jews cover their eyes with their right hand while reciting the prayer's opening words, as an aid to concentration. Reform Jews, by the end of the nineteenth century, had adopted the custom of rising to their feet to pronounce the Shema in unison. However it was said, the Shema reinforced for Jews the most fundamental belief linking them together: their faith in one God. In addition, just as Protestants in America were essentially united by a negative, that they were "not Catholic," so the Shema reminded Jews of what, in America, essentially united them—that they were "not Christian."[101]

Many Jewish leaders, understandably, aspired to create a higher level of unity among their followers, unifying Jews not just around common symbols but structurally as well. "Ecclesiastical authority," they had come to understand, was impossible to impose, but what about some kind of overarching ecclesiastical assembly (the term they used was "synod"), a common liturgy, and a plan for promoting Jewish education? Isaac Mayer Wise and Isaac Leeser, as well as fifteen other clergy and lay representatives, met in Cleveland in 1855 at a "national conference" initiated by Wise in order to discuss these issues—the first time that the leading figures closest to the center of

The words of the *Shema* in English and Hebrew carved
above the entryway of the 1840 synagogue building of K. K.
Beth Elohim in Charleston, South Carolina. Courtesy of
Mark Bloch and K. K. Beth Elohim, Charleston.

the American Jewish religious spectrum had ever formally met.[102] The hope,
articulated by Wise, was to promote *"Shalom Al Yisrael"* ("peace unto
Israel"), and for a time that seemed possible. After long hours of private
deliberations, the conference adopted two guiding resolutions:

1. The Bible as delivered to us by our fathers and as now in our possession is of immediate divine origin and the standard of our religion.
2. The Talmud contains the traditional, legal, and logical exposition of
the biblical laws which must be expounded and practiced according to the
comments of the Talmud.

Yet, like so many other attempts at compromise in the middle decades of the
nineteenth century, this one too failed to take hold. Questions of authority

and principle, particularly but not exclusively related to slavery, divided Presbyterians, Methodists, and Baptists during these years, and the nation as a whole seemed poised to divide as well; moderates were everywhere in retreat. Accordingly, both Wise and Leeser met with enormous criticism and backtracked. On the Orthodox side, Rabbis Rice, Raphall, and others boycotted the meeting. Any discussion with proponents of Reform, they felt, compromised Orthodox Judaism's integrity. Even Bernard Illowy, who had initially joined the call for the conference, stayed away from Cleveland and criticized Leeser for his civility toward Reformers: "Chastise those people in public . . . ," he admonished, "let them change their ways and say 'We have sinned.'"

On the Reform side, Rabbi David Einhorn, who just weeks before had arrived in the country, also boycotted the meeting. "A peace which necessarily degrades Judaism," he charged, "appears to us to be too dearly bought." Einhorn opposed compromises with Orthodoxy on principle and objected vehemently to the conference's resolution on the Talmud, whose binding authority he denied and which he considered morally narrow and frequently unsuited to contemporary times. He also found the whole notion of a synod repugnant to religious freedom and to the fundamental principles of Judaism as he understood them. Here, revealingly, his views were strongly seconded by Rabbi Maurice Mayer of Charleston. Echoing the views of many South Carolinians on the issue of centralized power versus states' rights, Mayer insisted that each synagogue should decide religious issues for itself. The very idea that a central synod should have the "right to decide upon some portions of our Divine service" was to him anathema. With the failure of the Cleveland conference, Leeser and Wise drew farther apart and Judaism polarized into Orthodox and Reform camps. In the end, the conference designed to unite America's Jews only underscored their deepening ideological divisions.

The establishment in 1859 of the Board of Delegates of American Israelites confirmed these divisions. The grandly named board sprang to life in response to the worldwide Jewish campaign to free Edgardo Mortara from the House of the Catechumens in Rome. The six-year-old Italian boy had been secretly baptized as an infant by his nursemaid in Bologna and, as a consequence, was torn from his home in 1858 and handed over to the Catholic Church; as a Catholic he could not legally be raised by Jewish parents. The case provided grist for the anti-Catholic mill in America and attracted enormous public attention, but when American Jewish leaders sought President Buchanan's help in freeing the youngster, they were rebuffed. Buchanan solemnly explained that the United States had "neither the right nor the duty . . . to express a moral censorship over the conduct of other independent governments." What really concerned him, it seems, was the possibility that foreign governments might link the Mortara affair to American slavery, which similarly turned a blind eye to the forcible separation of slave children from their parents.[103]

Whatever the president's motivation, Jewish leaders on both sides of the Atlantic believed that the approach to Buchanan had been mishandled and that a better organized and more unified American Jewry would have been more successful. In response, a group of twenty-four congregations led by Shaaray Tefilla of New York (with assistance from Isaac Leeser) organized the Board of Delegates, its name echoing that of London Jewry's influential Board of Deputies.

The new organization made no pretense at promoting religious unity; its principal goals were "to keep a watchful eye on all occurrences at home and abroad" and to collect statistics. Even so, it proved highly controversial. Reform Jewish leaders attacked the board with language drawn from the politics of the day, charging that it would "interfere with the internal affairs of the congregations" and promote "sectionalism" in Jewish life (since the board was so heavily eastern in composition). Supporters of the board responded in kind, attacking the Reformers as "separatists" and advocates of "disunion." Leeser, whose own sympathies lay with the South, suggested at one point that the Reformers "quietly withdraw and form an homogeneous society of their own, seeing that a peaceful continuance with their former associates would be a surrender of principle on their part. . . . Between the extremes an entire separation would thus be effected and if not a peaceful one even, it would still be the next best thing, a severance of discordant or jarring elements." Without separation but also without Reform representation, the board, on the eve of the Civil War, represented less than a fifth of America's synagogues. Even significant Orthodox synagogues stayed away; the country's two largest Sephardic synagogues, for example, refused to join, fearing that their freedom and independence might be challenged. Thus, while the board, for the most part, represented compromise and unity, the majority of Jews, like so many other Americans of the day, stood firm in defense of cherished principles, agonizing over the "irrepressible conflict" that lay at hand.[104]

CIVIL WAR

The Civil War divided American Jews much as it did the nation as a whole. The bulk of America's 150,000 Jews, most of them new immigrants, lived in the North and supported the Union. The rest, something over 25,000 Jews, lived in the South and supported the Confederacy. Some on both sides, including Isaac Leeser and Isaac Mayer Wise, would have compromised over slavery or acquiesced to secession, rather than going to war in defense of principle. They sought to promote peace.[105]

Rabbi Morris Raphall of New York, in a celebrated address delivered on the National Fast Day (January 4, 1861) at the request of the American Society for Promoting National Unity, concluded that even if southern slaveholders had acted wrongly, slaveholding as such was "no sin," for slave property was "expressly placed under the protection of the Ten Commandments." His address reinforced familiar Protestant arguments but nevertheless received wide circulation, coming as it did from a learned rabbi. It sparked fierce debate in both Jewish and non-Jewish circles concerning how the Bible should be interpreted and read. Opponents of slavery, significant Jewish leaders among them, condemned Raphall's literal reading of the biblical text and insisted on a more contextualized reading or one that focused on the spirit rather than on the letter of divine law. David Einhorn, for example, argued vehemently that it was "rebellion against God to enslave human beings created in His image." On the other hand, one enthusiastic Protestant minister was so convinced by Raphall's close textual reading, based on the Hebrew original, that he declared the rabbi's lecture to be "as true almost as the word of God itself." The controversy brought unprecedented publicity to the supposed "Jewish view" on the slavery issue, but only underscored, in the end, the difference between Judaism and hierarchically organized Christian denominations. On the issue of slavery, the question of how properly to understand the Bible, and on most other controversial issues through the years, the Jewish community did not speak with a single voice.[106]

Some at the time expressed surprise that given their long history of persecution and their enslavement in Egypt, recalled annually on the holiday of Passover, Jews did not come out more strongly for abolition. "The objects of so much mean prejudice and unrighteous oppression as the Jews have been for ages . . . ," the American and Foreign Anti-Slavery Society once declared, "more than any other denomination, ought to be the enemies of *caste* and the friends of *universal freedom.*" History, however, spoke to Jews in different voices, and Jews responded to controversial issues like slavery in myriad ways. Many, in the absence of any explicit religious prohibition against slavery, simply followed in the ways of their neighbors, for good and for ill. In a city like Charleston, most whites owned slaves, most Jews owned slaves, and a great many free blacks owned slaves as well. There as elsewhere, the overall role of Jews in slavery was negligible. Only about 300 out of Charleston's 19,532 slaves were owned by Jews. But as a rule, those southern Jews who could afford slaves owned them—that was the southern way.[107] As for the abolitionists, many of them were staunch evangelical Protestants who had been involved in missionary efforts to convert Jews. Some, like William Lloyd Garrison and Edmund Quincy, employed anti-Jewish imagery and invective when it suited them; Garrison once termed Mordecai Noah "that lineal descendant of the monsters who nailed Jesus to the cross between two thieves." Under these circumstances, even influential Jews who wholeheartedly opposed slavery, like Rabbis David Einhorn and Bernard Felsenthal, never identified themselves as abolitionists prior to the war. In most Jewish circles the abolitionists were intensely unpopular.[108]

Jews fought on both sides of the Civil War. Some eight thousand to ten thousand Jews, mostly recent immigrants, donned uniforms, and at least fifty thousand rose through the ranks to become officers; religion generally posed no barrier to military promotion. "I have now become a respected man in a respected position, one filled by very few Jews," a peddler named Louis Gratz wrote when he became a first lieutenant in the cavalry of the United States. "I move in the best and richest circles and am treated with utmost consideration by Jews and Christians." One Union officer actually won his position because he was a Jew. Observing that "we have not yet appointed a Hebrew," Abraham Lincoln in 1862 ordered the secretary of war to assign C. M. Levy, Rabbi Morris Raphall's son-in-law, to the post of assistant quartermaster, with the rank of captain.[109]

In the Confederacy, of course, one of the most brilliant and accomplished Jews of the nineteenth century, Judah P. Benjamin, reached the pinnacle of power. He served at different times as the Confederacy's attorney general, secretary of war, and secretary of state, and, despite his intermarriage and complete lack of personal religious observance, always acknowledged his Judaism and always was known as a Jew.[110]

On the home front, too, Jews actively supported their comrades in arms. While men contributed thousands of dollars to relief activities, women sewed clothes, prepared bandages, tended the wounded, staffed booths and tables at "sanitary fairs," and collected funds for the needy. Some Jewish support organizations emphasized that they provided help to all who required it, "irrespective to religious creed." Jews' Hospital in New York, for example, made its facilities available to the government and treated hundreds of soldiers, largely at the Jewish community's expense. Other Jewish organizations focused on the particular needs of the Jewish community, supporting the families of Jewish soldiers who were away fighting at the front. The tension reflected here between universalism and particularism, between assisting all those in need and paying special attention to the wants of fellow Jews, recurred frequently in American Jewish life. In the Civil War, as later, neither approach alone sufficed; both forms of charity were required.[111]

Whatever pride Jews took in the military and civilian achievements of their fellow Jews was offset by the sadness, anger, and bewilderment engendered by the sectional cleavage, especially as it pitted Jew against Jew and family members against one another. "Since you have discarded the Lord and taken up the Sword in defense of a Negro government, your picture that has occupied a place in our Southern home, we return herewith," one Jewish Confederate wrote to the popular Cincinnati rabbi Max Lilienthal. The soldier scrawled his angry words across the face of the rabbi's lithograph, thereby disfiguring it, and warned that he "should be happy to rid Israel of the disgrace of your life." A few sentences later, however, he had a change of heart. "Should you ever desire to cultivate any acquaintance with me," he concluded, "I affix my name and residence." The contradictory message—at once breaking off ties with the rabbi and reaching out to him —bespoke the extraordinary tensions of the day as sectional loyalties, religious loyalties, and family loyalties clashed.[112]

Even close relatives sometimes found themselves on opposite sides of the struggle. Four of the children of Abraham Jonas, for example, fought for the South, one for the North. Septima Levy Collis's brother died fighting for the South; her husband was wounded fighting for the North. Cary Gratz and his stepbrother/cousin Jo Shelby actually battled each other at Wilson's Creek. As the invading northern armies moved into the South, such problems multiplied. One southern Jew found his house guarded by two Jewish soldiers from Ohio. "They felt very sorry for us," he recalled, "but could afford us no help." Another memoirist related the stir that took place when northern soldiers attended worship services at the synagogue in Natchez, Mississippi. Still another account, this one in a contemporary letter, described how frightened some local Jews in Memphis became when Colonel Spiegel of Ohio, dressed in full northern military regalia, wished them a "Happy Sabbath" and asked where he might find a kosher lunch.[113]

Lithograph of Cincinnati's Rabbi Max Lilienthal
defaced and returned by a Jewish Confederate
(1861). The correspondent charged that the rabbi,
by supporting the Union, had "taken up the
Sword in defense of a Negro government."
Rabbi Max Lilienthal Collection (1996/0001),
Western Jewish History Center, Judah L. Magnes
Museum, Berkeley, California.

Some Jews, torn between sectional antipathy and religious fraternity,
took refuge in silence, muffling their political differences to highlight what
they continued to hold in common. Isaac Leeser advocated precisely this
strategy in 1861, promising not to discuss "any political theme" in his newspaper "but simply matters belonging to us as a religious community."
Women, who traditionally bore much of the responsibility for maintaining
ties of kinship through letter-writing, were especially likely to adopt this
strategy. Eighty-year-old Rebecca Gratz, for example, carefully crafted the
messages she sent to her far-flung family members, north and south, so as
to accentuate common interests, notwithstanding the war that divided them.
Where all around her "familiar friends [were] becoming bitter foes," she continued to cherish her ties with her "many dear [ones] scattered over the land."[114]

Even if they muffled their political differences, however, Jews, much like their non-Jewish counterparts, fervently believed that God was on their side. They prayed earnestly that he would support them in their struggle. "Shemang Yisroel, Adonoy Elohainoo, Adonoy Achod," the most widely distributed Jewish Civil War prayer began, the transliteration reflecting the Sephardic pronunciation of the all-important *Shema.* Written for southern Jewish soldiers by the Reverend Maxmilian J. Michelbacher of Richmond, the prayer carried an explicit statement of southern grievances:

> This once happy country is inflamed by the fury of war; a menacing enemy is arrayed against the rights, liberties, and freedom of this, our Confederacy; the ambition of this enemy has dissolved fraternal love, and the hand of fraternity has been broken asunder by the hands of those, who sit now in council and meditate our chastisement, with the chastisement of scorpions. Our firesides are threatened; the foe is before us, with the declared intention to desecrate our soil, to murder our people, and to deprive us of the glorious inheritance which was left to us by the immortal fathers of this once great Republic.
>
> Here I stand now with many thousands of the sons of the sunny South, to face the foe, to drive him back, and to defend our natural rights. O Lord, God of Israel, be with me in the hot season of the contending strife; protect and bless me with health and courage to bear cheerfully the hardships of war. . . . [115]

The Reverend James Koppel Gutheim, who closed the doors of his synagogue when New Orleans was recaptured by Union troops, likewise composed ardent prayers for the South. In the wake of southern military reverses in 1862 he prayed that "the breaches lately made in our lines soon be repaired, a series of glorious victories blot out our recent reverses, and the unrighteous invaders be repulsed on every side, abashed, confounded, and discomfited." Northern rabbis, of course, prayed for their side of the battle with equal fervor, though their prayers (at least those that survive) placed less emphasis on sectional grievances and pleas for victory than on simple restoration of the Union. A prayer composed by the Reverend Sabato Morais of Congregation Mikveh Israel in Philadelphia, and later forwarded to Abraham Lincoln, was typical. It called upon the Almighty to speak to the hearts of his "misguided . . . disaffected children" and to renew within them the loyalty that they had once felt for the United States.[116]

Beyond these formal prayers, individual Jewish soldiers also cried out for divine personal assistance during wartime. Faith provided them with a sense of religious continuity and the spiritual tools that helped them to

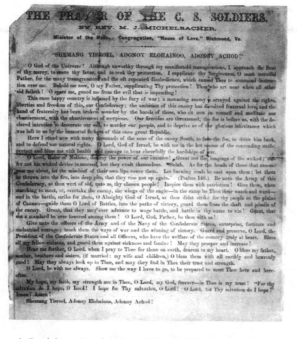

A Jewish prayer for the soldiers of the Confederacy
by the Reverend Maximilian J. Michelbacher
of Richmond's Congregation Beth Ahabah (House of
Love). Michelbacher, according to the historian
of Richmond's Jews, "was second to none in loyalty
to the Confederate cause." Courtesy of the Museum of
the Confederacy, Richmond, Virginia. Photography by
Katherine Wetzel.

survive in a world suffused with violence and mayhem. "Let us pray to the
Lord God of Israel for the deliverance of this once happy Country and the
Peaceful enjoyment of our family Circle at the End of this unhappy War,"
Colonel Marcus M. Spiegel of Ohio wrote to his wife on the eve of Rosh
Hashanah in 1862. A few months later he urged her to "keep up courage,
trust in God, and all will be right." Sadly, these prayers went unanswered:
Spiegel did not survive the war.[117] On the Confederate side, Captain Samuel
Yates Levy of Savannah penned "A Prayer for Peace." Like many of his
southern compatriots, he interpreted southern defeats as evidence of divine
wrath for having "wandered wildly" from God's word. Peace, for him, implied deliverance. He compared the North to the oppressive ancient Egyp-
tians, and the South to the Israelites seeking the Promised Land:

Roll back the clouds of War and give us Peace,
And as thou led'st thy chosen people forth
From Egypt's sullen wrath, oh King of Kings!
So smite the armies of the cruel North
And bear us to our hopes "on eagles' wings."[118]

A scribbled Hebrew manuscript blessing, however, may best preserve the fervent supplications of thousands of frightened Jewish soldiers who had only recently arrived from Europe. Written for a Jew in Titusville, Pennsylvania, apparently by a European "master of the divine name," a rabbi renowned for his "supernatural powers," this *kvitl* (a handwritten supplication that functioned as an amulet) embodied the hope that "Shlomo" would be "safeguarded from men of war [and] that God would help him return to his home"—to his wife, to his daughter, and to his three sons, "to raise them to a life of Torah."[119]

Maintaining traditional Jewish observances under wartime conditions proved immensely difficult though commensurately satisfying for those who lived up to the challenge. Two brothers named Levy who fought for the Confederacy reputedly "observed their religion faithfully . . . never even eating forbidden food." The awe with which this was recounted at the time that one of the brothers was killed suggests that such scrupulousness was extremely rare. The same was true of the northern soldier who described for readers of the *Jewish Messenger* how Jewish men in his outfit met for worship each Saturday on the outskirts of their camp in the Virginia forests. More commonly, Jewish soldiers strove to observe Judaism's major annual holidays, notably Rosh Hashanah and Yom Kippur in the fall, as well as Passover in the spring. One Jewish soldier planned to journey twelve miles to attend High Holiday services in Norfolk, then in Union hands. Two years later, Jews stationed near Vicksburg elected a young rabbi, Max del Banco, to conduct High Holiday services especially for them (the rabbi was killed in a steamboat accident on his way back home). Many other soldiers received passes for the holidays. General Robert E. Lee, himself a committed Christian, pledged in 1864 to do all in his power "to facilitate the observance of the duties of their religion by the Israelites in the army," and to allow them "every indulgence consistent with safety and discipline."[120]

We possess two lengthy accounts, one from the Union and one from the Confederacy, concerning the observance of Passover in 1862—a sure sign of how significant commemoration of the holiday of freedom was to Jews on both sides of the struggle. The southern soldiers purchased the requisite matzah (unleavened bread) in Charleston and cooked a fine traditional dinner, complete with "a pound and a half of fresh kosher beef." The northern soldiers, stationed in West Virginia, obtained from Cincinnati some of the supplies that they needed for their seder, the traditional ritual meal that accompanies the retelling of the Exodus story, and then went out and foraged for the rest. "We consecrated and offered up to the ever-loving God of Israel our prayers and sacrifice," one of the participants recalled four years later. "There is no occasion in my life that gives me more pleasure and satisfaction then when I remember the celebration of Passover of 1862."[121]

Given the strong evangelical character of some Civil War units and the rapidity with which some Jews had abandoned Jewish practices following their immigration, it comes as no surprise that the Civil War also found many Jews who, while serving as soldiers, hid their Jewish identities, maintaining no Jewish rituals whatsoever. Isaac Leeser, who in 1864 visited soldiers recovering from wounds, found that some "would scarcely confess their Jewish origin" and "even refused prayer-books when tendered to them." In the military as in civilian life, American Judaism thus covered a broad spectrum, embracing the meticulously observant, the totally non-observant, and all points in between.[122]

Two extraordinary episodes distinguished the northern Jewish experience during the Civil War, both of lasting significance. The first was the battle to amend the military chaplaincy law, passed in 1861, that stipulated that a regimental chaplain be a "regular ordained minister of some Christian denomination." An amendment to substitute the more inclusive phrase "of some religious society" had been voted down; significantly, the Confederate law, which employed the phrase "minister of religion," was more inclusive. Protestant chaplains, and, to the extent that they could, Catholic ones, made the most of their opportunity to influence warring troops. At their best, these chaplains tended to soldiers' spiritual needs, helped them to overcome personal and family problems, and modeled virtuous and courageous behavior under fire. Jewish chaplains, by contrast, were officially barred from the field, putting Jewish soldiers at a great disadvantage and, in effect, making the Jewish faith illegitimate. At least two elected Jewish chaplains (one of whom was not "regularly ordained") were rejected on account of the discriminatory law, setting off a national debate involving Christians and Jews alike. Although many supported a change in the law, one evangelical paper complained that if the law were changed, "one might despise and reject the Savior of men . . . and yet be a fit minister of religion." It warned that "Mormon debauchees, Chinese priests, and Indian conjurors" would stand next in line for government recognition—a tacit admission that the central issue under debate concerned the religious rights of non-Christians. To further the Jewish cause, one of the rejected chaplains, the Reverend Arnold Fischel, came to Washington at the behest of the Board of Delegates to lobby on behalf of a change in the chaplaincy law, and President Lincoln promised him support. After substantial wrangling, a revised bill that construed "some Christian denomination" in the original legislation to read "some religious denomination" became law on July 17, 1862. This represented a major political victory for the Jewish community and remains a landmark in the legal recognition of America's non-Christian faiths. In this case, as in so many others, American religious liberty was broadened by the demands of those who stood outside the American religious mainstream.[123]

The second episode involving Jews was far uglier. On December 17, 1862, a general order went out from Ulysses S. Grant's headquarters in Oxford, Mississippi, which read as follows:

> 1. The Jews, as a class, violating every regulation of trade established by the Treasury Department, and also Department orders, are hereby expelled from the Department.
>
> 2. Within twenty-four hours from the receipt of this order by Post Commanders, they will see that all of this class of people are furnished with passes and required to leave, and any one returning after such notification, will be arrested and held in confinement until an opportunity occurs of sending them out as prisoners unless furnished with permits from these Head Quarters.
>
> 3. No permits will be given these people to visit Head Quarters for the purpose of making personal application for trade permits.
>
> By Order of Maj. Gen. U.S. Grant[124]

Known as "the most sweeping anti-Jewish legislation in all American history," General Order #11, as it came to be called, blamed "Jews, as a class" for the widespread smuggling and cotton speculation that affected the entire area under Grant's command. Numbers of Jews in northern Mississippi and Paducah, Kentucky, were expelled as a result of the order; some were refused rail transportation and had to travel on foot, and at least one was briefly jailed. Historians have since determined that "Jews were neither the most numerous nor the most iniquitous of the legion of sharpers following the army: their peccadilloes were certainly no greater than the misdeeds of any number of crooked Yankees, Treasury agents and army officers." Indeed, a group of Cincinnati Jewish merchants formed a cotton speculating partnership with Grant's own father, Jesse Grant. At the time, however, Jews were "easily identifiable by their manners, accents, and surnames," and also stigmatized by age-old stereotypes, so that they came to symbolize *all* who were attempting to profit from wartime speculation and cross-border trading. The tensions and frustrations of war, which elsewhere found their outlet in persecutions of Catholics and African Americans, were directed in this case at "Jews, as a class."[125]

For their part, Jews lost no time in protesting Grant's order. Not only did they send letters and telegrams to the White House, but one of those expelled, Cesar Kaskel of Paducah, rushed to Washington and, accompanied by Cincinnati's Congressman John A. Gurley, went directly to President Lincoln's office. The president turned out to know nothing of the order, which he had never seen. According to a revealing but unverifiable later tradition, he resorted to biblical imagery in his interview with Kaskel, a reminder of how many nineteenth-century Americans linked Jews to Ancient Israel, and America to the Promised Land:

LINCOLN: And so the children of Israel were driven from the happy land of Canaan?
KASKEL: Yes, and that is why we have come unto Father Abraham's bosom, asking protection.
LINCOLN: And this protection they shall have at once.[126]

Even if no such conversation actually took place, Lincoln did instantly command the general-in-chief of the Army, Henry Halleck, to countermand General Order #11. "If such an order has been issued," Halleck telegraphed Grant on January 4, "it will be immediately revoked." In a follow-up meeting with Jewish leaders, including Rabbis Wise and Lilienthal, who had rushed to Washington to support Kaskel, Lincoln reiterated that "to condemn a class is, to say the least, to wrong the good with the bad. I do not like to hear a class or nationality condemned on account of a few sinners." After a few weeks of recriminations and a failed move by congressional opponents to censure Grant, the whole issue blew over. But its implications were profound. On the one hand, the episode reminded Jews that hoary prejudices against them remained alive—even in America. In fact, a dramatic surge in many forms of anti-Jewish intolerance, in the North as well as in the South, characterized the Civil War era, Grant's order being the most notorious but far from the only example. On the other hand, the episode also empowered Jews with the knowledge that they could fight back against bigotry and win—even against a prominent general. The overturning of

Grant's order, especially on top of the victory in the chaplaincy affair, appreciably strengthened the Jewish community and increased its self-confidence. The successes also validated an activist Jewish communal policy that based claims to equality on American law and values, while relying on help from public officials to combat prejudice and defend Jews' minority rights.[127]

The surrender of Confederate General-in-Chief Robert E. Lee at Appomattox Court House on April 9, 1865, coincided with final preparations for the eight-day Jewish holiday of Passover. According to a subsequent account, Isaac Leeser in Philadelphia "was so overcome" the next evening when news of the surrender reached him "that he had to stop the Service." Throughout the North that Passover, Jews gave thanks for the redemption of their ancestors from slavery in Egypt and for the restoration of peace to the inhabitants of the United States. The calendrical link between the anniversary of the biblical Exodus and the victory of the Union forces seemed to the faithful almost providential.[128]

The assassination of Abraham Lincoln five days after the surrender came on the eve of the fifth day of Passover (coinciding that year with Good Friday) and was harder for Jews to reconcile with the spirit of the holiday. Synagogues the next morning were filled with grief-stricken worshippers, and mournful melodies replaced the customary Passover ones. In subsequent sermons, delivered in Lincoln's memory by rabbis across the United States, the president was compared to the patriarch Abraham, to King David, and above all to Moses, who died without entering the Promised Land. Only the absence of parallels to Christ significantly distinguished the Jewish sermons from Christian ones. The critical point, for Jews, was that they be fully included in the memorials for Lincoln. The slain president's friendship with Jews and the gratitude Jews felt toward him made them especially eager to participate as equals in the rites of national mourning. In New York, some three thousand Jews marched in Lincoln's funeral pageant, at least half a dozen Jewish leaders sat on the dais, and one of the six speakers from among the clergy was Samuel Isaacs—granted coequal status with the others. Subsequently, for Jews as for Christians, Lincoln became something of an American saint. Hundreds of Jews contributed to the "holy national work" of memorializing the slain president. A contemporary Charleston-born Jewish artist, Solomon Nunes Carvalho, immortalized him as the "great emancipator" in a magnificent portrait, and his image continues to grace various Jewish homes to this day.[129]

While Lincoln was also memorialized by rabbis in the South, the quest to find meaning in the death and destruction that accompanied the Confederacy's collapse ultimately led elsewhere. The hundreds of dead and wounded soldiers, the burned and looted synagogues, the acres of despoiled property, and the loss of self-government recalled, to those who knew their Bible, the collapse of Jerusalem and the exile to Babylonia. "As Israelites, we are passing through another captivity which relives and reenacts all the troubles so pathetically poured forth by the inspired Jeremiah," Henry Hyams of Louisiana wrote in 1868. Like him, many southern Jews in the war's wake developed their own non-Christian version of the "Religion of the Lost Cause" that linked them to their white neighbors. They employed biblical metaphors of catastrophe, sanctified regional values and cultural symbols rooted in the old Confederacy, and imagined themselves to be divinely chosen as southerners *and* as Jews.[130]

The Hebrew Ladies' Memorial Association, founded in 1866 "for the purpose of caring for the graves of the Israelitish soldiers of the Confederate army," illustrates some of these themes. The ladies, in a published circular "to the Israelites of the South," spoke of "a brave people's struggle for independence," "hardships . . . nobly endured for Liberty's sake," and blood spilled in defense of a "glorious cause." Even as they explicitly linked their work to that of two non-Jewish associations with parallel aims, they declared that Jews had a special reason for commemorating "those who so nobly perished" in the South's defense. "When the malicious tongue of slander, ever so ready to assail Israel, shall be raised against us," they explained, thereby revealing the source of their angst, "then, with a feeling of mournful pride, will we point to this monument and say: '*There* is our reply.'"[131]

Bound up as it was in its own civil faith, southern Judaism thus became increasingly distinctive during the post–Civil War decades. As an example, Jews in southern cities turned out together as a community to celebrate Confederate Memorial Day and set aside special sections of their cemeteries for Confederate war victims. The distinguished Jewish sculptor Moses Ezekiel, himself a Confederate veteran and a loyal southerner (even though he lived in Rome), abetted this cult of martyrdom. He produced a series of "Lost Cause" monuments, including the "New South" monument to the Confederate war dead at Arlington National Cemetery, five busts of Robert E. Lee, a large bronze statue of Stonewall Jackson, and a monument entitled *Virginia Mourning Her Dead.* In his autobiography, Ezekiel described the latter in religious terms ("one of the most sacred duties in my life") and explains that he wanted it to serve as a memorial to his fallen comrades, "sounding their heroism and Virginia's memory down through all ages and forever." While northern Jews put the war behind them and moved on, southern Jews, like their neighbors, thus made the Lost Cause the center-piece of their faith. Focusing on the martyrdom of lost sons, they insisted that the cause for which so many had fought and died was right.[132]

THE VISION OF A NEW ERA

Outside of the South, the late 1860s and early 1870s were a period of confident optimism in American Jewish life. The immigrants of two decades before had by then established themselves securely. The Jewish community, thanks partly to the war, had grown in wealth and power. Now the nation was booming, liberal Jews and Protestants spoke warmly of universalism, at least eighteen leading Jews joined other religious progressives in the Free Religious Association, and beginning in 1867 rabbis and ministers even oc-casionally traded pulpits. Small wonder that many Jews looked forward with anticipation to the onset of a glorious "new era" in history. Isaac Mayer Wise predicted to his friends that within fifty years Judaism's teachings would become the "common property of the American people." He pointed out that on a whole range of issues—Providence, the Supreme Being, justice, wisdom, universal goodness, the immortality of the soul, the sanctity of virtue, the perfectibility of the human race, the Fatherhood of God, and the brotherhood of man—Jews, liberal Christians, and rationalists all basi-cally agreed. A liberal Jewish periodical entitled the *New Era,* initiated in 1870 by Rabbi Raphael De Cordova Lewin, promised to "advance mankind in true religious knowledge and to unite all God's children in a common bond of brotherhood." By its third volume, it claimed the second largest circulation "of any Jewish organ." Echoing the *New Era*'s themes, Rabbi Isidor Kalisch delivered a lecture entitled "Ancient and Modern Judaism" in "every important city east of the Mississippi River." The time is coming, Kalisch proclaimed, when "the whole human race shall be led to worship one Almighty God of righteousness and truth, goodness, and love." He pledged that Jews would stand in the forefront of those ushering in "the golden age of a true universal brotherhood."[133]

As if to echo these triumphant predictions, numerous congregations from New York to San Francisco built massive new synagogues in the immediate post–Civil War era. The seating capacity of America's synagogues more than doubled between 1860 and 1870, according to census figures, and the total dollar value of the community's synagogues increased by an astonishing 354 percent. One of the most famous synagogues built during these years was the Plum Street Temple in Cincinnati—today a National Historical Site—and it reveals much about developments within Judaism nationwide. The magnificent Moorish-style building was erected by Isaac Mayer Wise's congregation, then the second largest in America. The building was designed by one of Cincinnati's foremost architects, James Keys Wilson, and dedicated in 1866. Unlike the Newport synagogue of a century before, which demurely concealed its identity on the outside and was only identifiably Jewish within, the Cincinnati synagogue proudly proclaimed its faith to the world. Its Moorish architecture was the Jewish answer to Gothic architecture and visibly identified the edifice as sacred Jewish space. Its location, just opposite the city's leading Catholic and Unitarian churches and across from City Hall, announced that Judaism was no less a pillar of the city than the churches nearby. And by calling itself a "temple," complete with an organ, choir loft, and pews for the mixed seating of men and women, it underscored Reform Judaism's break with the past, its renunciation of any hope for messianic redemption. Rather than await the rebuilding of the Temple in Jerusalem, local Jews now declared that their synagogue was to be a temple unto itself.[134]

In Cincinnati and almost everywhere else where magnificent new temples and synagogues were constructed, including some more traditional congregations, their dedication was accompanied by the introduction of significant liturgical and aesthetic reforms into the worship service. Some of these had their roots in pre–Civil War days, but now they became far more widespread. The number of synagogues with organs, for example, leaped from eight to thirty, according to one estimate, just between 1860 and 1868. Many synagogues, as we shall see, also replaced gender-separated seating with mixed seating. The abolition of the second ("extra") day of Jewish festivals, seen as a "radical" reform when adopted by Charleston Jews back in 1840, also became commonplace during the 1860s and '70s. In an attempt to reduce the length of the worship service and to make time for sermons, vernacular readings, and organ music, many synagogues abbreviated the Torah reading and adopted shorter, non-Orthodox liturgies like Wise's *Minhag Amerika*. Finally, some congregations discarded the requirement that men wear prayer shawls when called for by Jewish law, and that they cover their heads during worship. Some of these changes were demanded by congregants, others inspired by rabbis, but all of them had the same four basic aims: (1) to attract younger, Americanized Jews into the synagogue; (2) to make non-Jewish friends and visitors feel welcome; (3) to improve Judaism's public image; and (4) to create the kind of solemn, formal, awe-

inspiring atmosphere that high-minded Jews and Christians alike during
this period considered conducive to moral reflection and effective devotional prayer.[135]

As a consequence of these reforms, Judaism in many large, formal congregations became an increasingly passive and vicarious experience, a performance. Worshippers watched and listened—they were sung to, spoken to,
told when to stand and when to sit—but they rarely participated themselves.
Over time, the gap between pulpit and pew widened, so much so that some
congregations required their rabbis and cantors to observe the Sabbath and
to retain skullcaps and prayer shawls even as congregants, especially men
and young people, openly abandoned them and more often than not stayed
home. Spiritual leaders thus found themselves transformed into representative Jews, "symbolic exemplars," guardians of their congregants' faith. What
Wise found in San Francisco in 1877 was true in many other places as well:
"the men keep no Sabbath, keep nothing besides Rosh Hashanah and Kippur . . . the same is the case with the churches. They are all in debt and
poorly attended." So long as leaders devoted themselves to the cause of
faith, ordinary members—albeit women less than men—felt increasingly
free to do as they pleased.[136]

Exterior (opposite) and interior of Cincinnati's Plum Street Temple (K. K. Bene
Jeshurun), dedicated in 1866. Its Moorish architecture immediately identified it
to passersby as a Jewish house of worship. Inside, men and women sat together
on the main floor and a large organ was played—visible and audible signs
of the synagogue's Reform Jewish identity. Courtesy of the Jacob Rader Marcus
Center of the American Jewish Archives.

Mixed seating—what critics called the "promiscuous seating" of women
with men—was the most contentious and also, in many ways, the most revealing of the reforms that became widespread during this period.[137] Traditionally, as we have seen, synagogues relegated women to the balcony and
separated them from the men with a partition, known as a *mehiza*. Reform
Jews in Germany brought women down from the balcony and abandoned
the partition, but still sat men and women separately, following the example
of Lutheran churches in Germany. In American churches, however, mixed-
gender seating had already become the norm in the eighteenth century as
part of church efforts to strengthen the family against the menacing forces
of industrialization. In time it became something of an American mantra
that "the family that prays together stays together." Synagogue practices

that "degraded" women by separating them from their families came in for significant criticism.

Mixed seating entered the synagogue in 1851, largely for pragmatic reasons. Wise's breakaway congregation in Albany, Anshe Emeth, purchased a church for its use that had been built with family pews, and the congregation "resolved unanimously to retain them," probably because changing the existing seats would have been highly expensive. Before long, however, mixed seating became a divisive ideological issue. To its Reform supporters, it represented the "religious equalization of women," as well as such positive values as family togetherness, conformity to local norms, a modern, progressive image, and saving the youth. To its Orthodox opponents, the same change implied abandonment of tradition, violation of Jewish law, assimilation, Christianization, and promiscuity. Synagogues in Cleveland and Cincinnati divided over the issue in the 1860s, and in 1875 the reform became the subject of a celebrated New York court case. The result echoed the earlier litigation in Charleston concerning the organ. Given opposing views concerning what Jewish law demanded, the judge left the matter "where it properly belongs, to the judicature of the church," and allowed the synagogue's majority to rule.

By the end of the nineteenth century, family pews had become ubiquitous in Reform congregations and common in middle-of-the-road congregations, like B'nai Jeshurun in New York. In these congregations, modern values like women's equality triumphed, while in opposing congregations separate seating was seen to impart just that sense of detached protest against modernity that traditionalists felt Judaism needed to express in order to survive. Seating—separate or mixed—thus became a highly visible marker of the difference between Orthodox and non-Orthodox synagogues during these years. Arguments over seating served as a shorthand way to debate differences on a host of fundamental issues concerning how best to respond to modernity's challenge.

Reform's passionate embrace of modernity looked like the wave of the future in the 1870s, empty pews notwithstanding. Prominent synagogues like Temple Israel in Boston and Rodeph Shalom in Philadelphia joined the Reform camp; B'nai Jeshurun upon the death of Morris Raphall appeared likely to follow; and there was substantial agitation for Reform even within the staunchly traditional Sephardic congregation of Mikveh Israel in Philadelphia. With Isaac Leeser dead, his alternative strategy aimed at regenerating Jews within the confines of Jewish law lacked a nationwide champion and lost ground.[138]

All Jews, to be sure, did not join the leftward swing. Every major American Jewish community continued to maintain one or more traditional congregations. In addition, some fifteen thousand to twenty thousand East European Jews migrated to America in the 1870s, many of them from Lithuania's famine-swept Suwalki province, thereby strengthening Orthodoxy's ranks still further. One immigrant to New York recalled finding in the city in 1870 "prominent individuals who were knowledgeable in Torah, God-fearing men of faith." In both Chicago and St. Louis, societies dedicated to the study of traditional Jewish texts met regularly. Yet the twenty-odd immigrant congregations in some seven cities that were established from the mid-1850s through 1879—congregations like Bet Tefillah in Cincinnati (1866), Beth Hamidrash Hagadol U'B'nai Jacob in Chicago (1867), the First Hungarian Congregation Ohab Zedek in New York (1873), and Congregation Shomre Shabbos in Boston (1870s)—scarcely appeared on the radar screen of most American Jews. Instead, observers took their cue from the practices of young native-born Jews and inferred, as one journalist did in the mid-1870s, that "the meager residues of Orthodoxy which one still finds in this land are insignificant." Understandably if incorrectly, Reform Jewish leaders concluded that the cause to which they had devoted their lives had triumphed.[139]

A strong signal of this triumph was the establishment in 1873 in Cincinnati of the Union of American Hebrew Congregations, the fulfillment of one of Wise's most cherished dreams. Wise had inspired the Union and gloried in its success, but the organization was actually created by lay leaders—in Jewish circles, as in Christian ones, lay leaders often had an easier time smoothing over ideological and doctrinal differences than the clergy did. The president of Wise's congregation, Moritz Loth, initiated the convention that established the Union, and it was he who ensured that a full spectrum of congregations participated, including several Orthodox synagogues. He also made sure that the goals of the new organization were suitably circumscribed: to establish a rabbinical seminary, to publish books appropriate for Jewish religious schools, and to prescribe a small number of rituals (he suggested three) that all Jews might consent to be bound by. The latter goal proved quixotic and was quickly abandoned. The new organization focused instead on issues that a broad range of Jews could easily agree upon: the need to "preserve . . . Jewish identity" and the importance of promoting Jewish education by training English-speaking rabbis and teachers—the era of German-speaking rabbis, lay leaders understood, was passing.[140]

Rabbi Bernard Illowy, one of the best-known and most learned Orthodox rabbis
of his day. Painted by the Jewish artist Henry Mosler (1841–1920) in 1869,
"Portrait of a Rabbi" captures Illowy's traditional Orthodox garb (skullcap, beard)
and his benevolent, aristocratic demeanor. Gift of the Skirball Foundation;
Courtesy of the Skirball Cultural Center. Photographer: John Reed Forsman.

This companion portrait, also by Mosler, is entitled "Portrait of a Rabbi's Wife" and is believed to depict Katherine Schiff Illowy. A rare portrait of an Orthodox rebbetzin, it shows her with the modest head covering typically worn by Orthodox Jewish women of the time. Gift of the Skirball Foundation; Courtesy of the Skirball Cultural Center. Photographer: John Reed Forsman.

To further these ends, the Union, amid considerable fanfare, established Hebrew Union College in 1875 under the presidency of Wise. Like its parent organization, the new college—which turned out to be the first successful rabbinical school in American Jewish history—took seriously its commitment to "union." Its nine young pupils focused on classical texts and avoided doctrinal issues. Even Sabato Morais of Mikveh Israel, no friend of Reform, described the school when he visited it in 1877 as "deserving of the support of all Israelites." Ever ready to compromise for the sake of union, Wise believed that a self-confident, appropriately moderate, and communally responsible Reform Judaism representing the majority of Jews could provide leadership on the European model for the entire American Jewish community. While similar attempts in the past had failed, foiled by those who advocated firmness for the sake of principle, now success seemed within reach. For a brief, exciting moment Cincinnati looked to become the capital of American Judaism and Wise its national leader. Two institutions committed to "union" and headed by Reform Jews promised to bind Jews together and lead them forward.[141]

Like Mordecai Noah's Ararat colony of fifty years before and so many other attempts to bring Jews together, however, the Cincinnati effort soon faltered. In fact, the whole hopeful scenario of the mid-1870s was undermined by a series of unanticipated crises that disrupted American Jewish life and called many of its guiding assumptions into question.[142] First, Reform Judaism as a whole was shaken by the defection of Felix Adler, one of the young men upon whom American Jews had pinned great hopes. The son of the rabbi at Temple Emanu-El of New York, Adler had been sent to study in Germany to prepare to follow in his father's footsteps. In 1876–77, however, he publicly abandoned Judaism in favor of what he called Ethical Culture. Renouncing belief in a theistic God and in the particularities of the Jewish religion, he advocated in their place a universalistic faith focused on ethics and the teachings of world religions. His critiques of Reform Judaism, and his growing Jewish following, especially among women and young people, unnerved many Jewish leaders—especially when he announced that "Judaism is dying." On the heels of this, some well-publicized cases of intermarriage, including that of Helen, the daughter of Isaac Mayer Wise, deepened Jewish nervousness. Helen eloped in 1878 with the Presbyterian attorney James Molony and was married by a Unitarian minister. Was Reform Judaism really the answer, some wondered? Had the effort to modernize Judaism gone too far? Would assimilation triumph?[143]

Developments within American Protestantism added yet another dimension to the mood of uneasiness within the American Jewish community. The spiritual crisis and internal divisions that plagued Protestant America during this era—one that confronted all American religious groups with the staggering implications of Darwinism and biblical criticism—drove evangelicals and liberals alike to renew their particularistic calls for a "Christian America." Visions of a liberal religious alliance and of close cooperation between Jews and Unitarians gradually evaporated. Although interfaith exchanges continued, Jews came to realize that many of their Christian friends continued to harbor hopes that one day Jews would "see the light." Much to the embarrassment of Jewish leaders, some Christian liberals looked to the Ethical Culture movement as a harbinger of Judaism's future course. Adler even became president of the Free Religious Association in 1878, over Jewish objections.[144]

Finally and most important, "antisemitism"—a word coined in Germany at the end of the 1870s to describe and justify ("scientifically") anti-Jewish propaganda and discrimination—unnerved American Jews. The rise of racially based anti-Jewish hatred in Germany, a land to which many American Jews had close ties and that they had previously revered for its liberal spirit and cultural advancement, came as a shock. Here Jews had assumed that emancipation, enlightenment, and human progress would diminish residual prejudice directed toward them, and suddenly they saw it espoused in the highest intellectual circles, and by people in whom they had placed great faith. What made this situation even worse was that antisemitism and particularly social discrimination soon spread to America's own shores. Anti-Jewish hatred was certainly not new to America, but Jews had previously considered it something of an anachronism, alien both to the modern temper and to American democracy. Like Jews in Germany, they optimistically assumed that prejudice against them in time would wither away. The two well-publicized incidents of the late 1870s—Judge Hilton's exclusion of banker Joseph Seligman from the Grand Union Hotel (1877) and Austin Corbin's public announcement that "Jews as a class" would be unwelcome at Coney Island (1879)—proved so shocking precisely because they challenged this assumption. "The highest social element . . . ," Corbin explained, "won't associate with Jews, and that's all there is about it." Antisemitic manifestations of every sort—from social discrimination to anti-Jewish propaganda to efforts to stem the tide of Jewish immigration —rose to new heights during the years that followed, and Jews experienced a substantial decline in their social status.[145]

In 1881, pogroms broke out against Jews in Russia, and mass East European

Jewish immigration to the United States began, adding fuel to the crisis of confidence that American Jews were experiencing. Even before then, however, it was clear that Utopia had proved far more distant than many Jews had expected. The universalistic prophecies of the 1860s and 1870s had failed, the hoped-for "new era" never materialized, and conditions for Jews in America and around the world grew worse instead of better. This posed a cultural crisis of the highest order for American Jews. As the hopes of Cincinnati's Reform Jews to unify and lead the community collapsed, developments elsewhere prepared to change the face of American Judaism forever.

Two Worlds of American Judaism

A GREAT AWAKENING

On the "fateful . . . night" of October 5, 1879, a group of earnest young Jews from Philadelphia and New York met at an undisclosed Philadelphia location and bound themselves together in a solemn covenant "for God and Judaism." They called themselves Keyam Dishmaya, an Aramaic term signifying their goal to uphold the dictates of heaven, and they pledged to do all in their power to bring Jews back "to the ancient faith." "The great question for contemporary Judaism," twenty-six-year-old Max Cohen, later librarian of New York's Maimonides Library, exclaimed in a letter to a friend, "is whether it will continue God's work or cease to be." His own conclusion, which the group as a whole shared, was unambiguous: "Israel must be whatever its children make it."[1]

A major goal of Keyam Dishmaya was to "recreate the ancient Hebrew Sabbath." Sabbath observance had declined markedly in the post–Civil War years, as surging business pressures combined with stricter Sunday closing laws to magnify the losses experienced by Jews who kept their stores and offices shuttered on Saturday. A public appeal to New York Jews in 1868 "to restore the Sabbath to its pristine sanctity" had fallen on deaf ears. Now the young people hoped that their efforts might enjoy greater success. They viewed revitalization of the Jewish Sabbath as a first step in promoting the observance of a wide range of neglected Jewish practices and the fostering of a "higher spiritual life."[2]

Beyond this, members of the group led adult Bible classes, taught Sunday

School, delivered lectures, promoted "the restoration of our people to the land of our inheritance," and—most surprisingly from the perspective of later generations—worked to revitalize the Jewish "national" holiday of Hanukkah. This winter holiday, which commemorates the Maccabean victory and the rededication of the ancient Temple, seemed in danger of falling into "oblivion" in post–Civil War America. The holiday's message of anti-assimilation and national renewal ran counter to Reform Judaism's universalistic ethos, and its comparatively minor status in the Jewish calendar made it an easy festival to neglect. For those seeking to revitalize Judaism, however, Hanukkah provided the perfect symbol. In addition, Hanukkah celebrations, complete with convivial pageants and extensive publicity (the custom of gift-giving came later), served to counteract the growing allure of Christmas. The Hanukkah festival sponsored in 1879 by Keyam Dishmaya proved particularly successful. "Every worker in the cause of a revived Judaism," one of the organizers wrote, "must have felt the inspiration exuded from the enthusiastic interest evinced by such a mass of Israel's people."[3]

To extend their message beyond those whom they personally touched, the young Jewish revivalists established in late 1879 a lively highbrow newspaper in New York entitled the *American Hebrew,* described by one of its founders as "our forcible instrument for the perpetuation and elevation of Judaism." "Our work," they explained to the public in their first issue, "shall consist of untiring endeavors to stir up our brethren to pride in our time-honored faith." Philip Cowen, the newspaper's publisher, recalled half a century later that "we were fully convinced that not only New York Judaism, but American Judaism, awaited its journalistic redeemers."[4]

The nine editors of the *American Hebrew,* some Philadelphians, some New Yorkers, were anonymous—understandably so, since their ages ranged from twenty-one to twenty-nine. As a group, they represented a new phenomenon on the American Jewish scene. Most were American-born Jews who were at once "strong for traditional Judaism" (two of the nine were rabbis) and at the same time eager to accommodate Judaism to American conditions. "Our proclivities . . . are toward 'reformed' Judaism and yet our disposition is toward orthodoxy," the editors admitted in their first issue. Years later, Max Cohen described his former associates as having been "a group of young American Jews who, while not inordinately addicted to Orthodoxy as a rigid standardization of thought and conduct, was yet opposed to the wholesale and reckless discarding of everything that was Jewish simply because it was inconvenient, oriental, or was not in conformity with Episcopalian customs."[5]

GRAND REVIVAL
OF THE
Jewish National Holiday of Chanucka,
ACADEMY OF MUSIC,
TUESDAY, DECEMBER 16th, 1879.

Members of Keyam Dishmaya in Philadelphia staged a "grand revival" of the Jewish Festival of Lights, Hanukkah. The emphasis on the "national" aspect of the holiday serves as a polemic against Reform Jews of the time who renounced Jewish nationhood, insisting that Judaism is only a religion. Collection of the author.

On the first anniversary of Keyam Dishmaya, twenty-two-year-old Cyrus L. Sulzberger (1858–1932), one of the group's leaders and later a prominent New York merchant and communal leader (as well as the grandfather of the distinguished *New York Times* columnist C. L. Sulzberger), set forth three cornerstones of the revival that he and his associates were trying to spawn. First, he explained, they sought to revitalize and deepen the religious and spiritual lives of American Jews; second, to strengthen Jewish education; and third, to promote the restoration of Jews as a people, including their ultimate restoration to the land of Israel. "Looking back . . . ," he concluded, "we have cause to be grateful to God for the successful manner in which we have begun our work. . . . May God grant us the ability to continue in the cause."[6]

While small in number and little recognized until later, the young people whom Sulzberger addressed represented the vanguard of a significant awakening within late nineteenth-century American Judaism. Concerned about the viability of Judaism and convinced that its post–Civil War assumptions and directions had been wrong, these young people, along with others around the country, promoted a new communal agenda characterized by a return to religion, a heightened sense of Jewish peoplehood and particularism, new opportunities and responsibilities for women, a renewed community-wide emphasis on education and culture, a burst of organizational energy, and, in time, the growth of two new movements in American Jewish life: Conservative Judaism and Zionism. By no means did *all* American Jews follow their lead; many Jews, as we shall see, resisted. The mass migration of East European Jews, however, would soon strengthen the hands of those who sought to transform American Judaism in more traditional ways and also lent new urgency to their efforts. As a result, by World War I, Jewish life in America looked entirely different from how it had looked forty years before. During the intervening decades, the basic contours of twentieth-century American Judaism had settled into place.[7]

Reports of an unexpected move back to tradition among American Jews began to circulate in Jewish newspapers as early as 1879 when, likely in response to the publication of the *American Hebrew,* a Chicago newspaper reported that "genuine Orthodox views are now becoming fashionable among Jewish young America." In 1887, the *London Jewish Chronicle* spoke of a "strong religious revival . . . among the Jews in the United States." In 1894, one of the young revivalists, Cyrus Adler, enumerated a whole series of Jewish cultural and intellectual achievements and declared that a "revival of Jewish learning" was in progress—he termed it an American Jewish "renaissance."[8]

As part of this renaissance, the number of Jewish publications published in America tripled between the 1870s and the 1890s. Thanks in part to the Jewish Publication Society, established in 1888, the quality of these publications rose apace. Heinrich Graetz's monumental six-volume *History of the Jews* appeared in a handsome, well-indexed American edition in 1891–98. The first best-selling Jewish novel in America, Israel Zangwill's *Children of the Ghetto,* came out in 1892. A still-unsurpassed dictionary of rabbinic literature by Rabbi Marcus Jastrow was published between 1886 and 1903. Throughout American Jewish life, emphasis shifted away from changing Judaism, the dominant Reform strategy, and back toward educating Jews about Judaism, the strategy earlier championed by Isaac Leeser. In 1893 alone, three significant new American Jewish institutions with strong educational aims were founded: Gratz College in Philadelphia, the first of a series of Hebrew teachers' colleges across the United States that trained women on an equal basis with men; the Jewish Chautauqua Society, modeled on its Protestant counterpart, which pursued the goal of wide-ranging adult Jewish education across the country; and the National Council of Jewish Women, devoted, among other things, to encouraging "the study of the underlying principles of Judaism."[9]

That women participated actively in all three of these institutions is no accident. In fact, women supplied a great deal of the energy behind the late nineteenth-century American Jewish awakening. As we have seen, back in 1838 Rebecca Gratz's Sunday School had transformed the role of women in American Judaism by making them responsible for the religious education and spiritual guidance of the young—as was the case among Protestants and Catholics. By the time Gratz died, in 1869, most American Jews who received any formal Jewish education at all likely learned most of what they knew from female teachers. These teachers, in turn, had to educate themselves in Judaism, which they did with the aid of new textbooks, some of them written by women as well. The three institutions founded in 1893 (one of them, Gratz College, funded by a legacy from Rebecca Gratz's brother, Hyman) looked to continue these efforts by extending the education of Jewish women still further.

Emma Lazarus (1849–1887), whose poem "The New Colossus" (1883) was composed to help raise funds for the pedestal upon which the Statue of Liberty rests, served as a role model for women caught up in the Jewish awakening. Lazarus was one of the most highly educated Jewish women of her day and the most prominent woman convert to the revival's cause. Born in New York to an aristocratic Jewish family of mixed Sephardic and Ashkenazic heritage, she had emerged at a young age as a sensitive poet (her first book was published when she was seventeen) but had never maintained close ties to the Jewish community; only a very small percentage of her early work bore on Jewish themes at all. Antisemitism and the first wave of East European Jewish immigration shocked Lazarus. In 1882, in a burst of creative energy, she emerged as a staunch defender of Jewish rights, the poet laureate of the Jewish awakening, and the foremost proponent of the "national-Jewish movement" aimed at "the establishment of a free Jewish state." Her often-quoted poem "The Banner of the Jew," composed in the spring of 1882, began with the words "Wake, Israel, wake!" and ended on a militant note:

> O deem not dead that martial fire,
> Say not the mystic flame is spent!
> With Moses' law and David's lyre,
> Your ancient strength remains unbent.
> Let but an Ezra rise anew,
> To lift the *Banner of the Jew!*

Meanwhile, her essays, notably her *An Epistle to the Hebrews* (1882–83), called for a "deepening and quickening of the sources of Jewish enthusiasm" in response to the "'storm-centre' in our history" that Jews were passing through.[10]

Lazarus herself soon became close with the publisher of the *American*

Hebrew, where much of her work now appeared, and began studying the Hebrew language. Her major interest, however, lay not in the religious re-vitalization of the Jews, as advocated by the members of Keyam Dishmaya. Instead, she placed her emphasis on Jewish peoplehood, stressing the virtues of unity, discipline, and organization in the service of Jewish national re-newal. Influenced by writers like George Eliot, Laurence Oliphant, and Leon Pinsker, she abandoned her former skepticism concerning Jewish na-tionalism—the "Re-Colonization of Palestine"—and became "one of the most devoted adherents to the new dogma." She embraced it as if it were a full-fledged religion, and in so doing recognized that she was not alone: "Under my own eyes I have seen equally rapid and thorough conversions to the same doctrine. In the minds of mature and thoughtful men, men of prudence and of earnest purpose, little apt to be swayed by the chance en-thusiasm of a popular agitation, it has taken profound root, and in some cases overturned the theories and intellectual habits of a life-time."[11]

With her untimely death from Hodgkins disease at the age of thirty-eight, Lazarus became something of a saint to Jews caught up in the late nine-teenth-century awakening. A special issue of the *American Hebrew* memorial-ized her with tributes "from the foremost literati of the age," and her *Epistles to the Hebrews,* published in pamphlet form in 1900, was kept in print for many years by the Federation of American Zionists. Her death deprived the movement of its most significant convert, its most inspiring and cosmo-politan intellectual figure, and its foremost advocate (to that time) of what would shortly become known as American Zionism.[12]

Yet another dimension of the effervescence of late nineteenth-century American Jewish religious life is suggested by the career of Ray Frank, known in her day as the "girl rabbi" and the "female messiah." While not of long-lasting significance, her stint as a charismatic Jewish revivalist dem-onstrates that the late nineteenth-century American Jewish crisis of expec-tations and faith was not confined to the East Coast, restricted to intellec-tual circles, or exclusively the preserve of traditionalists and proto-Zionists. It was, instead, a complex nationwide phenomenon that affected a range of Jews, men and women, in sometimes unpredictable ways.

Ray (Rachel) Frank (1861?–1948), born in San Francisco, was a school-teacher, writer, and lecturer.[13] Critical of the Judaism of her day, she pub-lished in 1890 a stinging critique of the American rabbinate in response to a New York Jewish newspaper's call for articles on the question, "What would you do if you were a rabbi?" What she "would *not* do," she empha-sized, was emulate the many abuses she considered characteristic of the pompously materialistic American rabbinate. She called on rabbis to don the "spiritual mantle of Elijah," and she implied that women ("were the high office not denied us") might do the job better. Shortly after this article appeared Frank achieved momentary fame when she traveled to Spokane, Washington, and became "the one Jewish woman in the world, maybe the first since the time of the prophets" to preach from a synagogue pulpit on the Jewish High Holidays. According to the story widely reported in her day and subsequently preserved by her husband:

> It happened to be on the eve of the High Holy Days and she made inquiries concerning the location of the synagogue as she wanted to attend services. When informed that there was no synagogue and there would be no services, she called on one of the wealthy Jews in town, to whom she had letters of introduction, and expressed surprise that a town containing many well-to-do Jews should be without a place of worship. The man, who knew Ray Frank by reputation, said, "If you will deliver a sermon we shall have services tonight." Ray acquiesced. At about five o'clock on that day special editions of Spokane Falls *Gazette* appeared on the streets announcing that a young lady would preach to the Jews that evening at the Opera House. The place was crowded. After the services were read, Ray spoke on the obligations of a Jew as a Jew and a citizen. In an impassioned appeal she asked her coreligionists to drop their dissensions with regard to ceremonials and join hands in a glorious cause, that of praying to the God of their fathers. She emphasized the fact that they shirked their duty if they did not form a permanent congregation and that by being without a place of worship and all that it stands for they were doing an incalculable harm to their children. After Ray finished her sermon, a "Christian gentleman" who was in the audience arose and said that he had been very much impressed by what he heard and if the Jews would undertake the building of a synagogue, he would present them with a site to be used for that purpose.[14]

Throughout the 1890s Frank delivered sermons and lectures, mostly in the West, and published articles extolling the virtues of Judaism, the Jewish family, and Jewish women. According to the memoir published by her husband after her death, people "flocked to listen" as she spoke on "Heart Throbs of Israel," "Moses," "Music and Its Revelations," "Nature as a Supreme Teacher," and related topics. In these lectures she attacked divisions in Jewish life, called for peace in the pulpit, and promoted spirituality, simplicity, earnestness, and righteousness: "Give us congregational singing which comes direct from the heart and ascends as a tribute to God. . . . Give us simplicity in our rabbi, sympathy with things which practically concern us, give us earnestness, and our synagogues will no longer mourn in their loneliness." On one occasion she disclosed a mystical vision, a call from God in which she herself was cast in the role of Moses. For the most part, though, hers was a conservative message. She opposed women's suffrage, spoke of motherhood as the culmination of womanhood, and reminded women "how all-important the home and the family are."[15]

Much like Protestant women revivalists of the day, Frank was described by those who heard her as a spellbinding preacher whose enthusiasm proved infectious. "Before she had finished," the *San Francisco Chronicle* wrote of one of her lectures, "her words were dropping like sparks into the souls of aroused people before her." So famous had she become that at the Jewish Women's Congress, held in Chicago in 1893, she was invited to deliver the opening prayer. Four years later, in 1897, seven thousand people reportedly turned out to hear her at the Chautauqua adult education gathering that took place at Gladstone Park in Portland, Oregon, on what was billed as "Ray Frank Day."[16]

In 1898, Ray Frank traveled to Europe, where she met and married an economist named Simon Litman. Her marriage and sojourn abroad (the couple did not return until 1902) effectively ended her public career.[17] The success that she demonstrated during her years on the lecture circuit, however, suggests that her message struck a meaningful chord. On the one hand she spoke to the spiritual concerns and traditional values of American Jews of her day; on the other hand, simply by virtue of her sex, she challenged Jews' religious and gender-based assumptions. In evoking, simultaneously, both new and old, she embodied, but in no way resolved, the cultural contradictions that underlay the religious ferment to which she herself contributed.

In raising the issue of women's role both in American society and in Judaism, Ray Frank had pointed to one of the central concerns of the late nineteenth-century American Jewish awakening. In response to the manifold crises of the day, particularly assimilation and immigration, responsibility for "saving Judaism" came increasingly to rest on the shoulders of women. Just as in Protestantism, so too in Judaism religion had become "feminized." The home, the synagogue, and philanthropic social work came increasingly to be seen as part of women's domain, especially among Reform Jews. As a result, women became significant players in the campaign to revitalize Judaism to meet the needs of a new era.[18]

The National Council of Jewish Women was the first national Jewish organization to take up this challenge. Its historian points out that "no one believed more strongly in woman's ability to save Judaism than did Council women themselves"—that is why it placed so much stress on the importance of women's education. Council rhetoric also frequently spoke of motherhood and the primacy of the home, but in most of those cases, as so often in women's history, "tone . . . concealed substance." Traditional symbols camouflaged and legitimated the new activist goals that council members proudly espoused as they took upon themselves the role of "savior of Jewish life in America."[19]

Through "sisterhoods of personal service," Jewish women extended the sphere of "motherhood" into new realms aimed at combating the social crisis within the Jewish community as a whole. Initiated at Temple Emanu-El of New York in 1887, sisterhoods offered Jewish women the opportunity to emulate the same kind of philanthropically directed urban missionary work performed by New York's Protestant and Catholic women, as well as the women of the Ethical Culture Society, but within a synagogue setting, from a staunchly Jewish perspective, and without conversionary aims. Outdoor relief, home visits, religious schooling, industrial and domestic education, day nurseries, kindergartens, employment bureaus—these and related efforts devoted "to the care of the needy and the distressed" harnessed the energies of Jewish women in ways that synagogues never had before. By 1896, practically every major uptown synagogue in New York had established a sisterhood—one had been established in San Francisco as well—and that same year a Federation of Sisterhoods was established in cooperation with the United Hebrew Charities.[20]

What distinguished these efforts from their more secular counterparts was their religious character. Indeed, Rabbi David de Sola Pool, recounting the activities undertaken by the Orthodox sisterhood established in 1896 at the venerable Shearith Israel Synagogue in New York, stressed the sisterhood's role in the "loyal conservation and transmission of Jewish religious values." Increasingly, in response to the perceived crisis of the day, women were fulfilling new roles within the Jewish community, expanding on those that they had formerly carried out largely within the home.[21]

All of these new themes—the cultural and educational work of young Jews in Philadelphia and New York, the Zionism of Emma Lazarus, the spirituality of Ray Frank, salvation through motherhood and activism as preached by the National Council of Jewish Women, and the charity work of the sisterhoods of personal service—eventually came together in what became, later in the twentieth century, the largest and strongest of the Jewish women's organizations created to revitalize American Jewish life: Hadassah, the Women's Zionist Organization of America. Henrietta Szold (1860–1945), who played the dominant role in the establishment of Hadassah in 1912, had been involved in the work of Jewish renewal since she was a teenager, first as an essayist and educator, later as secretary of the Publication Committee (that is, editor) of the Jewish Publication Society, and still later, in addition to her other work, as a leader of the Federation of American Zionists. She served as a role model to her peers and was respected as one of the most learned and accomplished Jewish women of her day. Now, in the wake of her first visit to Palestine (1909), she and a few like-minded Zionist women activists in the New York area met to form a new women's Zionist organization that, at Szold's insistence, would have both a general and a highly specific purpose: "In America, to foster Jewish ideals and make Zionist propaganda; in Palestine, to establish a system of District Visiting Nursing."[22]

In many ways, the new organization did for Jewish women what foreign missions did for Protestant women: it provided them with an opportunity to participate in the "holy work" of "salvation through social, medical, and educational agencies." Women, Szold believed, were interested in practical projects that appealed emotionally to their maternal and religious instincts. She was convinced, therefore, that "we [American Jewish women] need Zionism as much as those Jews do who need a physical home." By working to strengthen Jewish life in the Land of Israel, she hoped that women's own Judaism, and American Judaism generally, would be strengthened and renewed.[23]

REDEFINING REFORM JUDAISM

Reform Judaism maintained an uneasy relationship with all of these proponents of Jewish renewal. This was understandable: For half a century, young progressive American Jews had marched under the Reform banner and had viewed its program as the wave of the future, the only viable direction for Judaism in the New World to follow. Now, unexpectedly, Reform Jewish leaders found this and other long-cherished assumptions of theirs called into question. Indeed, some critics argued that Reform, far from being the solution to the crisis facing American Jews, was actually part of the problem. Others found the religious agenda of their day "entirely different" from what it had been before. "Then the struggle was to remove the dross," a confused young rabbi named David Stern remarked in a letter, "to-day it is to conserve the pearl beneath." Finding itself on the defensive, and shaken by the same crisis of confidence that transformed so much of American Jewish life during this period, the Reform Movement worked to redefine itself.[24]

The ordination of Hebrew Union College's initial class of four rabbis, grandly celebrated in Cincinnati on July 11, 1883, conveyed the two major options open to the Reform movement. The ordination itself, coinciding with the tenth anniversary of the Union of American Hebrew Congregations, was the first ever held on American soil. It drew more than one hundred rabbinic and lay leaders, representing seventy-six different congregations from around the country. Isaac Mayer Wise's Plum Street Temple "was filled to capacity and ablaze with lights. . . . There was resounding music and festive oratory." The broadly inclusive ceremony marked "the high point of Jewish religious unity in America" and symbolized Wise's long-standing goal: to lead a broad ideologically diverse coalition committed to strengthening American Judaism.[25]

The lavish nine-course banquet three hours after the ordination, however, unwittingly undid all of the unity and goodwill produced by the earlier ceremony and displayed a different, more narrowly defined strategy for Reform Judaism. Held at Cincinnati's posh Highland House and planned and sponsored by insensitive lay leaders, the banquet included four biblically forbidden foods (clams, crabs, shrimp, and frogs' legs), and also mixed meat and dairy products, another violation of the Jewish dietary code. Some of the guests were horrified; two stomped out in anger. The fiasco, known later as the *trefa* (unkosher) banquet, was reputedly the product of carelessness rather than malice. The Jewish caterer, Gus Lindeman, and most of his local clients, reflecting Reform Jewish tendencies of the day, had themselves long since abandoned the Jewish dietary laws and refrained only from serving pork products, which the meal carefully avoided. Traditionalists, however, viewed the banquet as a "public insult," particularly since Wise, instead of apologizing for the gaffe, took the offensive against what he called "kitchen Judaism" and insisted that the dietary laws had lost their validity. In so doing, he appeared to undermine the "union" which the Union of American Hebrew Congregations and Hebrew Union College had earlier pledged to uphold, and to cast his lot decisively with proponents of an exclusive strategy for Reform Judaism, concerned less with compromise for the sake of unity than with firmness for the sake of principle. Symbolically, the trefa banquet separated American Jews into two opposing camps that could no longer even break bread together. The incident both anticipated and stimulated further divisions.[26]

In the wake of the trefa banquet, several congregations resigned from the Union of American Hebrew Congregations. And calls rang out in the *American Hebrew* and in Philadelphia's *Jewish Record,* both edited by young Jews caught up in the American Jewish awakening, for the establishment

BANQUET

IN HONOR OF THE

DELEGATES TO THE COUNCIL

— OF THE —

UNION OF AMERICAN

Hebrew Congregations,

JULY 11, 1883.

HIGHLAND HOUSE,   CINCINNATI, O.
Frank Harff, Prop'r.

BLOCH & CO.

MUSIC BY CURRIER'S ORCHESTRA.
C. M. CURRIER,
Conductor.

MENU.

Little Neck Clams (Half Shell).
"Amontillado"
Sherry.

POTAGES.

Consomme Royal.
" Sauternes."

POISSONS.

Fillet de Boef, aux Champignons.
Soft Shell Crabs,
a l'Amerique, Pommes Duchesse.
Salade of Shrimp.
" St. Julien."

ENTREE.

Sweet Breads, a la Monglas.
Petits Pois, a la Francaise.
" Deidesheimer."

RELEVEE.

Poulets, a la Viennoise.
Asperges Sauce, Vinaigrette Pommes
" Punch Romain."   [Pate.
Grenouiles a la Creme and Cauliflower.

ROTI.

Vol au Vents de Pigeons, a la Tyrolienne.
Salade de Saitue.
" G. H. Mumm Extra Dry."

HORS-D'OEUVERS.

Bouchies de Volaille, a la Regeurs.
Olives Caviv, Sardelles de Hollande.
Brissotins au Supreme Tomatoe,
Mayonaise.

SUCRES.

Ice Cream.
Assorted and Ornamented Cakes.

ENTREMENTS.

Fromages Varies.   Fruits Varies.
" Martell Cognac."   Cafe Noir.

The official menu of the "trefa banquet" (1883), which violated the
Jewish dietary laws in multiple ways. Courtesy of the Jacob Rader Marcus
Center of the American Jewish Archives.

of a new and more religiously traditional seminary to compete with Hebrew Union College. The arrival in America, in May 1885, of one of Europe's leading Jewish scholars, the Hungarian rabbi Alexander Kohut (1842–1894), strengthened the hand of this traditionalist camp. The author of a multi-volume Talmudic dictionary known as the *Aruch Completum,* Kohut in Hungary had occupied "a middle ground between Orthodoxy and Reform" and followed the conservative traditions of the Jewish Theological Seminary of Breslau, where he himself had been ordained. He came to America at the invitation of Congregation Ahawath Chesed (later Central Synagogue), a congregation somewhat to the left of his own proclivities that had introduced a great many reforms into its worship and that belonged to the Union of American Hebrew Congregations. The combination "of his wife's illness, increased difficulties in publishing the *Aruch,* and political and Jewish conditions in Hungary" reportedly motivated Kohut's decision to emigrate, but whatever the reason, once in New York he came to champion a Judaism that he defined as "Conservative" rather than "Radical." "Progress," he insisted, "can only be effected within the limits of revealed law, always in harmonious connection with the entire community and ever true to historical continuity."[27]

In a celebrated series of public lectures on the rabbinic text known as the Ethics of the Fathers, Kohut threw down the gauntlet to Reform Judaism. "A Reform which seeks to progress without the Mosaic-rabbinical tradition," he thundered in German, "is a deformity—a skeleton without flesh and sinew, without spirit and heart. It is suicide; and suicide is not reform." David Einhorn's son-in-law, Kaufmann Kohler (1843–1926), rabbi of nearby Temple Beth El, took this as a personal challenge: "The gauntlet thrown in our faces," he declared, "must be taken up at once." In response, he delivered five discourses of his own entitled "Backwards or Forwards," quoting biblical and other sources to defend his own position and attack the "Conservative" one. "Which are we to espouse," he demanded, "the one that turns the dials of the time backward, or the one that proudly points to the forward move of history?"[28]

The Kohut-Kohler controversy, as it came to be called, received wide publicity in the Jewish press and helped to clarify for a new generation the differences between two longstanding strategies for securing Judaism's future: one that promoted far-reaching changes designed to accommodate Judaism to modernity, and the other that sought to uphold, as far as possible, Jewish religious law and tradition. Reform Jewish leaders who only a few short years before had thought that their brand of Judaism might become

Minhag Amerika, the custom of all American Jews, now, in the wake of resurgent traditionalism, understood that this was not to be. Instead, like American Catholicism and Protestantism, Judaism would factionally divide in the face of modernity's daunting challenges: liberals and conservatives would put forth competing statements of religious principles.[29]

Kaufmann Kohler, still smarting from his public clash with Kohut, lost no time in calling on "all such American rabbis as advocate reform and progress" to join him in formulating precisely such a statement. At a three-day conference held in Allegheny City's Concordia Hall just outside of Pittsburgh (November 16–18, 1885), eighteen rabbis, including Isaac Mayer Wise, joined Kohler in an attempt to formulate a "common platform" for Reform Judaism: a set of guiding principles that "in view of the wide divergence of opinions and the conflicting ideas prevailing in Judaism to-day," would "declare before the world *what Judaism is and what Reform Judaism means and aims at.*" Kohut and the Jewish revival movement were certainly on Kohler's mind when he addressed his colleagues. "We cannot afford to stand condemned as *law-breakers,* to be branded as frivolous and as *rebels and traitors* because we transgress these laws on principle," he told them. But even as he attacked Conservative Judaism and Orthodoxy (which he considered synonymous), he also took pains to distinguish Reform Judaism from Felix Adler's Ethical Culture movement and from the combined forces of assimilation, apostasy, "religious indifference," and "lethargy among the masses." He expressed particular concern that "our younger generation grows daily more estranged from our sacred heritage." All of these problems taken together, he believed, posed grave dangers to Reform Judaism. They constituted the multiple challenges, from the right and from the left, that the assembled rabbis needed to address.[30]

To start things off, Kohler set forth a wide range of specific proposals designed to "stem the growing tide of evil" and to "stir our people up from their lethargical slumber." He called for, among other things, the revitalization of Jewish religious life in the home, Jewish mission work among the poor, educational improvements and English-language publications about Judaism, women's equality "in the entire religious and moral sphere of life," and a variety of liturgical and ritual modifications. But rather than focusing on these "practical measures as seen demanded by the hour," many of which simply echoed what others were doing, Kohler's colleagues concentrated on what they knew to be his primary objective: "to unite on a platform . . . broad, comprehensive, enlightened, and liberal enough to impress and win all hearts, and also firm and positive enough to dispel suspicion and reproach

of agnostic tendencies, or of discontinuing the historical thread of the past."
Kohler submitted a ten-point draft, and in one night a committee worked
with him to revise it, returning the next morning with an eight-point platform
that speedily won conference approval.[31]

The platform began on a triumphalistic note, recognizing other religions
but insisting that "Judaism presents the highest conception of the God-
idea." This idea, taught in the Bible, developed historically, and "preserved
and defended, midst continual struggles and trials," remained, according
to the platform, the "central religious truth for the human race." The document then proceeded to the Bible, which it characterized not in traditional
terms as a revelation of divine truth, but rather as "the record of the consecration of the Jewish people to its mission as priest of the one God" and
as "the most potent instrument of religious and moral instruction." Indeed,
the Bible also reflected the "primitive ideas of its own age," according to
the platform, and, as such, modern scientific and historical research that
challenged biblical conceptions was "not antagonistic to the doctrines of
Judaism." Point three of the platform, probably written with the trefa banquet in mind, made clear that Reform Jews "accept as binding only the
moral laws, and maintain only such ceremonies as elevate and sanctify our
lives, but reject all such as are not adapted to the views and habits of modern
civilization." Laws regulating "diet, priestly purity, and dress," the next
point specified, were "altogether foreign to our present mental and spiritual
state" and it declared their observance "apt rather to obstruct than to further
modern spiritual elevation." Point five, perhaps the most famous of the
platform's planks, optimistically interpreted "the modern era of universal
culture of heart and intellect" as a signal of "the approaching of the realization of Israel's great Messianic hope for the establishment of the kingdom
of truth, justice, and peace among all men." It then continued, in a statement
that the movement would fifty years later partly retract, with a far-reaching
declaration: "We consider ourselves no longer a nation, but a religious community, and, therefore expect neither a return to Palestine, nor a sacrificial
worship under the sons of Aaron, nor the restoration of any of the laws
concerning the Jewish state." Continuing with the same emphasis on religion
over peoplehood, point six defined Judaism as a "progressive religion, ever
striving to be in accord with the postulates of reason," and in a bow to traditionalists also expressed "the utmost necessity of preserving the historical
identity with our great past." It allied Judaism with "the spirit of broad
humanity of our age" and extended "the hand of fellowship" to "daughter
religions of Judaism," Christianity and Islam, and "to all who cooperate

with us in the establishment of the reign of truth and righteousness among men." Point seven reasserted Judaism's belief in the immortality of the soul but rejected, as "ideas not rooted in Judaism," bodily resurrection and everlasting reward and punishment. Finally, at the behest of the great social justice advocate Rabbi Emil G. Hirsch (1851/2–1923), the platform's final plank associated Judaism with "the great task of modern times, to solve, on the basis of justice and righteousness, the problems presented by the contrasts and evils of the present organization of society."[32]

The Pittsburgh Platform, as this document came to be called, crisply distilled ideas that had been circulating in Reform Jewish circles for two generations. Parallels to many of its planks may be found in the writings of liberal Protestants and among the advocates of Free Religion and Masonry. Yet for Reform Judaism, the document constituted what Isaac Mayer Wise, who presided over the Pittsburgh conference, presciently described as a "Declaration of Independence." It not only spelled out what the movement considered to be "self-evident truths," it also marked its final break from Orthodoxy and from Wise's own exuberant dream of an American rite broad enough to encompass Jews of every stripe. While Reform Judaism never turned the platform into an ideological litmus test and always included members who disagreed with some of its planks (particularly the controversial fifth one concerning Zionism and Jewish peoplehood), the Pittsburgh Platform nevertheless remained the most important statement of Reform Jewish beliefs until it was superseded in 1937. Conservative critics of the Pittsburgh Platform, meanwhile, used the statement as a rallying cry to further their aim of establishing in New York a competing seminary to Cincinnati's Hebrew Union College, what became the Jewish Theological Seminary. As one of the participants in the Pittsburgh conference noted at the time: "The intended establishment of a *pious* seminary is the first consequence [of the conference], for which it has provided the desired occasion."[33]

Even as Reform distinguished itself from traditional Judaism, however, many Reform Jewish leaders joined the call for an American Jewish revival. In 1885, twenty-eight different rabbis offered suggestions to the Union of American Hebrew Congregations in response to the question "What measures seem to you practicable to assure to the rising generation of Jews such Jewish teaching as will more surely tend to create in them an active interest in Jewish affairs and an earnest participation in the intellectual and moral life of the Jewish community?" Two rabbis specifically called for a "revival" and others suggested practical measures "to revive and reawaken the spirit that animated the generations of the past." One rabbi, in calling on parents to set an example for their children, observed that too many Jewish men "consider their dues to the congregation as hush money, paid to be let alone for a year." Another complained that "our houses of worship are deserted, our divine services are conducted without any active participation of the public; an icy cold paralyzes the members of our religious body, our homes are no longer blessed with the benign influence of our religion." At the Pittsburgh Rabbinical Conference, Kaufmann Kohler himself spoke out for the need to "foster Jewish life, awaken Jewish sentiment, and train the Jewish minds and hearts." In addition, he and others at the conference called for educational reforms to counter the "appalling ignorance . . . which seems to constantly grow from year to year."[34]

During the seasons that followed, educational and cultural programs, measures to revitalize Jewish home life, expanded roles for women, and enhanced spirituality in worship all loomed large on the Reform Jewish agenda. In addition, the movement participated in a general return to Jewish forms, characterized not only by a revival of certain Jewish ceremonies, like Hanukkah and the synagogue celebration of Sukkot (Tabernacles), but also by a return to distinctive Jewish terminology, such as greater use of the word "Jew" as opposed to "Hebrew" and "Israelite," and the almost complete abandonment by World War I of such once commonly used terms, borrowed from Protestantism, as the Jewish "Church" (meaning synagogue), the Jewish "minister" (meaning rabbi), and the Jewish "Easter" (meaning Passover).[35]

Most important of all, Reform Judaism in this period offered those disaffected with synagogue life a new alternative means of actively expressing their faith. Following Emil G. Hirsch's lead, it called on Jews to help resolve the great social problems plaguing American life. This social justice motif —the Jewish equivalent of the Protestant Social Gospel—became, as we shall see, ever more influential within Reform circles over the ensuing decades, and provided an alternative road back to Judaism for those whose interests focused less on faith than on religiously inspired work.[36]

MASS MIGRATION

While all of these efforts worked to redefine, strengthen, and revitalize Judaism among native-born and assimilating Jews, American Judaism was being drastically transformed by one of the largest waves of immigration in all of Jewish history. Some 2 million East European Jews from Russia, Romania, and Austria-Hungary (largely Galicia) landed on America's shores between 1881 and 1914, part of an epochal migration during these

years that redistributed the world Jewish population, sent 35 million Europeans of different faiths and nationalities across international borders, and
brought almost 22 million newcomers to the United States. For Jews, violent
attacks known as pogroms sparked many a decision to risk life and fortune
in the new world, but the root causes of the mass migration lay deeper—
in overpopulation, oppressive legislation, economic dislocation, forced conscription, wretched poverty, and crushing despair, coupled with tales of wondrous opportunity in America and offers of cut-rate tickets from steamship
companies plying the Atlantic. Once again, Jews emigrated at a much higher
rate than their non-Jewish counterparts, an indication that they were especially oppressed. They were, for example, almost three times as likely to
leave Russia during these years as Poles, Lithuanians, and Finns.[37]

Although Jews had been emigrating from Eastern Europe to America
since colonial days, mass emigration began with the assassination of Tsar
Alexander II in 1881. In its wake, an orgy of anti-Jewish hatred swept over
Russia, abetted by the new tsar, and 169 Jewish communities were attacked
in a series of pogroms that destroyed twenty thousand Jewish homes and
left tens of thousands of individuals economically ruined. Thereafter, in
1882, a parade of oppressive laws were introduced in Russia, known as the
May Laws, that forced Jews back into the crowded towns and villages of
the historic Pale of Jewish Settlement. The laws banned Jews from settling
in Russia's economically burgeoning cities, severely restricted their economic
activities, and limited by quota their ability to enter secondary schools and
universities. In 1891, Jews were expelled from Moscow altogether.[38]

In nearby Romania, Jews also faced growing restrictions. The expatriate
historian Elias Schwarzfeld described his former homeland at the turn of
the twentieth century as a "hellish country in which life had become intoler-
able." He depicted it as a place where the Jew was "refused the rights of a
man and a citizen," was "robbed of the means of living," was "persecuted
by everybody," and was "without land and without protection." In Romania,
Russia, and elsewhere where comparable conditions developed, *worsening*
economic and social conditions, not the fact that they were low to begin
with, pushed Jews to emigrate en masse. The ongoing deterioration of East
European Jewish life, coupled with improved means of transportation and
the promise of a better economic and political future abroad, made emigration the best available option for young Jews seeking to improve their
own lives and those of their children.[39]

The central question that East European Jews faced was *where* to immigrate. The well-known Russian Hebrew newspaper *Ha-Melitz,* published

in St. Petersburg, declared in 1882 that there were but two options: "Every intelligent and far-seeing person realizes that in order to preserve the welfare of our people there are no other places in the world to which we can migrate other than the Holy Land or America."[40] Thousands of East European Jews discovered that additional options also existed: they migrated to countries from Argentina to South Africa and spread through six continents. Nevertheless, the two basic options set forth by *Ha-Melitz*—Holy Land (Land of Israel) or Golden Land (America)—served from then onward as the central options available to oppressed Jews around the world, and they reflected diametrically opposite readings of the Jewish situation. Proponents of immigration to the Holy Land, later known as Zionists, insisted that the Enlightenment's promise of equality for Jews was a chimera; that every diaspora land left Jews vulnerable to persecution; and that Jews could only truly be safe in their own historic home, the Land of Israel, which they promised to redeem and rebuild. Proponents of immigration to America, by contrast, believed that freedom and equality awaited Jews in the Golden Land; that America's unique history and liberal Constitution distinguished it from other diaspora havens where Jews had settled; and that in the United States Jews would finally be able to realize the great Enlightenment goals that had eluded them elsewhere: social and religious liberty, economic opportunity, cultural advancement, and the right to maintain Jewish identity intact.

The American option triumphed decisively during the era of mass migration, 1881–1914. Some 80 percent of all Jewish emigrants from Russia came to the rapidly industrializing United States during these years; only about 3 percent to the economically stagnant Land of Israel, tottering in the death throes of Turkish misrule.[41] After World War I, when immigration restrictions all but foreclosed the American option, the question of where persecuted Jews should immigrate took on renewed urgency, and immigration to the Land of Israel, by then progressing under British control, accelerated.

The vast bulk of immigrant Jews who elected to come to America—about 85 percent of them—passed through the port of New York. With the abundant economic opportunities available to Jewish immigrants in the city, especially in the fast-growing clothing trade, and with the comforting presence of tens of thousands of other Yiddish-speaking Jews nearby, large numbers of East European Jews saw no need to travel farther. They settled down in New York City, mushrooming its Jewish population from about eighty thousand in the 1870s to almost 1.4 million in 1915, nearly 28 percent of the city's total population. "In New York City there have come and remained more Jews than have been together at any one time and place, since the destruction of Jerusalem," B'nai B'rith's president, Leo N. Levi, pointed out as early as 1903. Of course, immigrant Jews also settled in hundreds of other communities from Maine to California, and also in rural areas like Devils Lake, North Dakota. In Charleston, South Carolina, the arrival of over one thousand Jews more than doubled the city's Jewish population in just five years, between 1907 and 1912. It was nevertheless New York that became, for the masses of immigrating East European Jews, the "promised city."[42]

Wherever they settled, most Jews who crossed the ocean to America came with the intention of staying. Between 1908 and 1914, the rate of return migration for Jews was a mere 7.1 percent (compared to 32.2 percent for non-Jews). Moreover, women and children formed a large percentage of the Jewish immigrant pool during these years—45.6 percent of the Jewish immigrants were female and 24 percent children, as compared to 32.1 percent and 11.6 percent for non-Jews. As a rule, only those who expected to settle permanently, like the Jews, encouraged their families to follow them to the new world; other immigrants left their wives and children behind. To be sure, statistics from the 1880s told a different story. A higher percentage of Jews returned to Europe back then (15 to 20 percent), fewer women and children immigrated, and the differences between Jews and non-Jews were considerably narrower. Over time, however, as social and economic conditions deteriorated in Eastern Europe, particularly during the early years of the twentieth century, those who once had dreamed of coming to America, making lots of money, and returning home had second thoughts, while numbers of those who earlier had returned to Russia turned around and came back.[43]

Some of Eastern Europe's leading Orthodox rabbis righteously opposed immigration to America. In the absence of rabbinic authority, they feared, Jews would fall away from their faith, or worse, fall prey to German "Reformers." Nobody expressed this opposition to immigration more forcefully than the saintly Rabbi Israel Meir ha-Kohen (Kagan) of Radun, known by the title of his popular, inspirational book as the *Hafez Hayyim*—"the seeker of life." In a different volume that he published for the guidance of immigrants in 1893–94, the rabbi advised readers "not to settle" in countries like America. "If because of hard circumstances" one is "compelled to journey there," he exhorted, "let him return home [as soon as possible] and trust to the Lord who provides for all." He particularly warned against tarrying "for the sake of riches in a land many of whose inhabitants have broken away from religion." The longer a person remained in such a land, he admonished, the more susceptible he became "to perdition of the soul," and the more "the souls of his children [were] exposed to extreme danger." Carrying

An immigrant reciting morning prayers alone aboard
ship (undated). The worshipper is wearing *tefillin*
(phylacteries) on his left arm and forehead and is wrapped
in a *tallit* (prayer shawl). The prayers are printed in
the *siddur* (prayer book), which he is reading from.
Courtesy of the Jacob Rader Marcus Center
of the American Jewish Archives.

this same message to the new world, Rabbi Jacob David Willowski (Ridbaz)
of Slutsk, on a visit to America to raise funds in 1900, was quoted as having
rebuked America's Orthodox Jews for continuing to live in a "*trefa* land
where even the stones are impure." Three years later, he himself settled for
a time in Chicago.[44]

Other rabbis, notwithstanding America's reputation as an "unkosher
land," viewed its burgeoning Jewish community more hopefully, perhaps
because the modernity that America represented did not seem to them quite
so threatening. The rabbi of Antopol, Rabbi Pinchas Michael, when queried
by poor Jews as to whether they should emigrate, reputedly replied, "Travel
to America, there you will make a living." And then he added a significant
admonition: "Preserve the Sabbath." Rabbi Israel Salanter, the founder of
the ethical *(mussar)* movement in Judaism, also is said to have sanctioned

emigration to America, though he preferred his followers to settle in the Land of Israel. Rabbi Isaac Elhanan Spektor of Kovno offered to send his own son, in 1887, to serve as New York's chief rabbi.[45]

Jewish intellectuals and radicals were perhaps the most positively inclined of all toward emigration. The very fears that led rabbis like the Hafez Hayyim to oppose moving to America prompted these progressives to encourage it. America, they believed, was the land where their utopian dreams might be realized. The writer Judah Leib Levin (known by his Hebrew acronym Yehalel), a socialist and Zionist, thought that America offered Jews even more opportunities to regenerate themselves than did the Land of Israel; in America, he argued, there was no Orthodox religious establishment to contend with. He hoped that Jews might come in numbers sufficient for them to colonize and form a state of their own in the American West. The Jewish historian Simon Dubnov similarly advocated emigration, as did many others. The writer Nahum Mayer Shaikevich, known by his pseudonym Shomer, heeded his own advice and settled in America in 1889. Writing to his Yiddish readers back in Europe, he described his new homeland in glowing terms. It was, he explained, a kind of Zion, a land where Jews had prospered and "discovered their abilities and vigor." In America, he concluded, "one can see just how much 'Yankele' [the typical Jew] can accomplish if he is granted complete freedom."[46]

This diversity of views concerning whether to immigrate to America, combined with the costs and hardships that leaving home entailed, made immigration a selective process. Those who departed were by no means a microcosm of those left behind. It is too much to claim, as one expert did in 1904, that "the most enterprising, the most robust, the better off or the least wretched, alone succeeded in leaving"; and it is likewise an exaggeration to assert, as a more recent scholar did, that "only the poor and the not very learned came." What can be said with certainty is that fervently religious Jews and those who sought to spend their days engaged in Jewish learning immigrated much less frequently than those more temperate in their beliefs and more enterprising in their ambitions. Young people eager to make a fresh start in life (and to avoid the tsar's army) were far more likely to immigrate than older ones rooted in their communities and set in their ways. Poorer folks (though not the poorest of the poor, who lacked all means) ventured forth more often than did richer folks.[47]

Some of the religious implications of these differences between emigrants and those who stayed behind were already apparent to contemporaries. Rabbi Isaac Margolis, who immigrated to America in 1885, reported in disgust that the boat that took him to America included many Jews who "defiled themselves with non-Jewish food." Rabbi Moshe Sivitz of Pittsburgh, who immigrated a year later, claimed that Jewish immigrants, while still aboard ship, abandoned their daily prayers and considered their prayer shawls and phylacteries excess baggage. Rabbi Willowski, in the twentieth century, recalled that hundreds of just-off-the-boat newcomers who dined at the Hebrew Immigrant Aid Society's kosher facility at Ellis Island failed to ritually wash their hands and recite a benediction before breaking bread, nor did they say the prescribed grace after their meal. These anecdotes, and many like them, have been interpreted to show that the process of immigration itself loosed East European Jews from their religious moorings, or, alternatively, that the immigrant stream included a disproportionate number of those who had abandoned their faith years earlier. Both propositions are likely correct.[48]

On the other hand, the Hebrew writer Ephraim Lisitzky, a student of Rabbi Willowski's in Slutsk who immigrated to Boston in 1900, recalled in his autobiography that "to all outward appearances" he was able to live in Boston just as he had in Slutsk. The synagogue where he "prayed daily" was "always packed." The congregants "gathered after the morning prayers to study," and then studied again "between the afternoon and evening prayers." One group even "stayed on after the evening prayers to study the daily page of Talmud." "Everything in Boston," at first glance, "was just as it had been in Slutsk." But, as he quickly discovered, there was one overriding difference. In Slutsk, "the learned and the pious had been in the vast majority." In Boston, by contrast, "they were a small minority." "Very few Jews" in the city even "observed the Sabbath." As a result, he soon "felt like an alien in Boston" and "was seized with a longing" to return to Slutsk.[49]

In addition to these religious issues dividing immigrant East European Jews from one another, social tensions rooted in old world geography likewise splintered them, much as they did so many of their non-Jewish immigrant neighbors. "The Russian hates the Lithuanian; the Lithuanian is an enemy of the Pole; they unite against the Rumanian, and all alike are contemptible in the eyes of the Galician," one Jewish immigrant to New York explained in a letter to his son back in Europe. He might have noted that Jews from these different communities tended to live slightly apart from one another as well. At least in New York, the Jewish immigrant community was subdivided into clearly demarcated sub-ethnic districts. It resembled, according to one immigrant, "a miniature federation of semi-independent allied states."[50]

At another level, one may distinguish three conflicting immigrant types among the teeming masses of Jews who encountered America at this time; parallels may once again be found among their non-Jewish neighbors.[51] The first type consisted of people like Lisitzky: learned and pious Jews who, upon their arrival, tried to transplant their East European practices and institutions to the new world, challenges notwithstanding. These Jews often differentiated themselves from others in the way they dressed—head coverings, beards, modest attire—and they attempted to regulate their lives according to the dictates of Jewish law and the rhythms of the Jewish calendar. They took less-well-paying jobs, like piecework or Hebrew teaching, in order to keep the Sabbath and the Jewish holidays sacred, and they championed plans to re-create in America the kinds of traditional religious institutions that they believed Jewish life demanded. Some of these Jews, like Lisitzky, changed as they grew older. Others, especially those who immigrated later in life, changed less. Yet even they did not expect their children, who attended public schools and played with non-observant Jews, to follow in their footsteps. Like the rabbis back home, they wondered whether Judaism in the new world would survive at all.

A second type of immigrant was the hustler, known as a *shvitser* in Yiddish, who came to America to make a fortune. Shvitsers allowed nothing to stand in the way of their getting ahead. They shamelessly abandoned elements of their faith and upbringing, sometimes they abandoned their families, and in a few cases they intermarried. Everything they did focused sharply on the goal of making money and achieving success—that, they believed, was what America was all about. In return, America's rough and tumble world of capitalism often lavished pecuniary rewards upon them. They became *allrightniks:* Americanized, self-satisfied, and materially comfortable. They worried less about Judaism than about themselves.

A third type of immigrant was the freethinking radical: steeped in underground tracts and clandestine writings, he or she came to America with a hardened political ideology and a predetermined social agenda. Raised under tyrannical regimes, these revolutionaries—socialists, anarchists, Communists, and the like—tended to view America and its political institutions through the distorting lens of East European politics. They advocated far-reaching social, political, and economic changes, and promised to transform all aspects of life for the better. They hated the very institutions that the hustlers and the pious Jews held most dear, and they professed not to care even if Judaism as a religion disappeared from the earth.

The bulk of the Jewish immigrants from Eastern Europe, of course, combined elements of each of these three types. They sought to hold fast to Judaism like the learned and pious, but they focused on what they saw as its major tenets and practices, allowing the rest to slip. They sought to make money and forge ahead like the hustler, but not in so single-minded and self-centered a way. And they subscribed to the secular messianism that the radicals preached, with its vision of a better future, but without sharing in their political extremism, their fierce anticlericalism, or their revolutionary methods. They struggled, in short, to find some balance between their ancient faith, their economic aspirations, and their utopian ideologies —a halfway covenant between tradition and change. In so doing, even without realizing it, they followed in the footsteps of generations of earlier immigrants to America's shores, from the Puritans onward.

SPIRITUAL CRISIS

In trying to strike this fine balance, East European Jews had to contend with a religious world radically different from the one they had known across the ocean. In Eastern Europe, Jews understood that for all of the difficulties that they faced, religion defined them; it was an inescapable element of their personhood. They were taxed as Jews and drafted as Jews. Religious affiliation was stamped into their passports and noted on their official documents. When they married or divorced it was done only according to Jewish law, by rabbis authorized by the state. Indeed, the state recognized Judaism as a legitimate minority faith. Those who sought to observe Jewish laws and customs faced almost no difficulty in doing so, while those who sought to cast off Jewish identity entirely could not do so unless they converted.

The situation in the United States was entirely different. Indeed, what made immigration so dangerous, from the perspective of traditional European Judaism, was that religion in America was a purely private and voluntary affair, totally outside of the state's purview. Nobody forced Jews to specify their religion; they were taxed and drafted as human beings only. When a Jew married or divorced in America, it was state law, not Jewish law, that governed the procedure; rabbinic involvement was optional. Indeed, rabbis enjoyed no official status whatsoever in the United States. As a result, Judaism proved easy enough to abandon, but, in the absence of state support, difficult to observe scrupulously.

Partly because of this situation, rabbis could provide immigrants with very little guidance in making the transition from old world to new. In fact, very few East European rabbis even immigrated to America in the 1880s and 1890s. Rabbi Moses Weinberger, one of these few, claimed in 1887 that in all of New York City there were no more than "three of four" rabbis with the highest level of ordination, allowing them to issue rabbinic decisions based on Jewish law—this in what was already the largest Jewish community in the world. According to another source, there were but two hundred rabbis of any kind (including Reform rabbis) nationwide in 1890—fewer than one for every two thousand Jews.[52]

From a rabbinic perspective, this was a disaster; one rabbi compared immigrants to "sheep without a shepherd." From the perspective of the immigrant "sheep," however, the absence of rabbinic "shepherds" seemed no more problematic than it was to rabbi-less American Jews of earlier eras. Indeed, the immigrants seem to have taken their newfound freedom in stride, which explains why they failed to pay or treat their all-too-scarce rabbis any better than they did. In New York City, Rabbi Weinberger reported (based in part on personal experience) that immigrant rabbis found positions "only after a great deal of trouble and effort," and even then they lived "penuriously," their small salaries "barely cover[ing] their basic human needs." He counseled Jews of his type to "stay home." Rabbi Abba Hayim Levinson's experience gave credence to this advice. The poor rabbi trudged all the way up to Rochester, New York, in 1883 to offer his services to the city's East European Orthodox community. Yet, although there was no Orthodox rabbi for miles around, Beth Israel Congregation elected him by only a single vote and then offered him a paltry salary of $150—far less (as many another rabbi also learned to his chagrin) than the $400 paid to the same congregation's cantor.[53]

In part, this mistreatment may be blamed on the fact that East European Jews were not used to paying for rabbis—back home that was the job of the government or of the organized Jewish community. Some immigrants also harbored longstanding grudges against rabbis based on bad experiences with coercive rabbinic authorities in their home countries. Even those with no personal ax to grind found that the East European model of the rabbinate was difficult to transplant to America. In Eastern Europe, rabbis tended to define their responsibilities communally; they looked to serve all Jews in a particular territory. In America, organized Jewish communities on the European model did not exist and congregationalism ruled supreme; rabbis were expected to meet the needs of the synagogue members who paid their salaries. Democracy, America's entrancing egalitarian ideal, also worked against rabbis' interests. It undermined the deferential social structure that Jews

had once accepted, and it subverted rabbis' time-honored scholarly prerogatives. Men devoid of learning and piety, even boorish hand laborers
who in their native lands would likely have received scant attention, now
felt themselves to be the rabbi's equal. Some went so far as to usurp rabbinic
prerogatives, setting themselves up as teachers, preachers, ritual circumcisers,
and (until a change in the law made this illegal) marriage officiators. Precisely
for this reason, many a rabbi and scholar described America as an "upside
down world" and recoiled from it. Even some rabbis who had come to
America prior to 1900, like Rabbi Weinberger himself, later abandoned the
rabbinate and went into business.[54]

The upshot was the collapse among immigrants of spiritual life as East
European Jews had traditionally known it, parallel to what had happened
in early nineteenth-century America when old religious structures gave way
in the face of revolutionary changes. Henceforward, latitudinarianism
reigned supreme in Jewish immigrant circles: Jews could practice their faith
or not, as they saw fit, without rabbinic intrusion. The best evidence of this
collapse may be seen in the astonishing number of immigrant Jews who
failed to attend synagogue. Numerous surveys between 1900 and 1917 found
that the number of "unsynagogued" Jews exceeded the number of "syna-
gogued" ones by a wide margin. "Out of the estimated Jewish population
of one million persons, or two hundred thousand families in the United
States, four-fifths are 'unchurched,'" the *American Jewish Year Book* calculated in 1900. Some of these, of course, were native-born Jews, but the overwhelming majority were not. The *Yiddish Velt* reported in 1904 that no
more than 25 percent of young Jewish men on the Lower East Side attended
synagogue on a regular basis, and, although not stated, the number of
young women who attended was undoubtedly lower still. According to the
1906 U.S. Census of Religious Bodies only 26 percent of America's Jews
could even be accommodated within America's synagogues: there were but
364,701 seats for about 1.4 million Jews (America's churches, by contrast,
could seat about 70 percent of the Christian population). Ten years later,
the census counted membership figures, not seats, and listed 357,125 synagogue members, including women—no more than 12 percent of America's
by then 3 million Jews. Even in New York City, where there were more synagogues than anywhere else in the United States, a careful Jewish communal
survey conducted in 1917 found that "out of 900,000 [adult] Jews only about
415,000 are synagogue Jews." None of these numbers is error-free, but together they leave little doubt that a large majority of East European immigrant Jews, in some cases 60 to 80 percent of them, failed to affiliate with

a synagogue. This does not mean, of course, that they *never* attended synagogue. To the contrary, the *Year Book* reported that "comparatively few Jews . . . never go to synagogue or to a Jewish service." More commonly, immigrants assumed that the more fervent among them would keep the synagogue alive by worshipping in it regularly, thereby maintaining the facilities that everybody else could use on those rare occasions when it suited them. Throughout the immigrant period, as a result, the total number of Jews in the United States far exceeded the number who either belonged to synagogues or could even have been seated within them.[55]

Similarly telling is the massive amount of fraud that took place in the selling of kosher meat, another indicator of spiritual crisis. Kosher meat, which must be specially slaughtered and prepared, is significantly more expensive than non-kosher meat, but the two are often indistinguishable to the naked eye. Therefore, tremendous temptation has always existed to substitute one for the other so as to reap attendant profits. In Europe piety and fear of disclosure, however, generally prevented widespread abuse, especially in small Jewish communities where "every stone had seven eyes." People (usually women) took care to purchase their meat from reliable suppliers whose religious standards they trusted. But in America, with the collapse of religious life and in the absence of community controls, cases of fraud multiplied. Ritual slaughterers and kosher butchers, no longer motivated by the fear of sin, abandoned piety for profit. According to a 1915 estimate, only 40 percent of the retail butchers in New York who claimed to sell kosher meat were in fact doing so; the rest sold non-kosher meat and pretended that it was kosher. Some butchers shamelessly justified their fraudulent activities by explaining that their customers were "not among the scrupulous and couldn't care less." Even Jews who attempted to keep "strictly kosher" found great difficulty in doing so, leading to a great deal of cynicism toward everyone involved in this holy work. One generation later, many children of immigrant Jews abandoned the dietary laws altogether.[56]

Finally, the decline of Sabbath observance serves as an indicator of spiritual collapse within the Jewish immigrant community. Many Jews, to be sure, felt that they had no choice when it came to Saturday work: numerous jobs in the clothing trade, the cigar trade, and even on farms and in peddling made working on the Jewish Sabbath a condition of employment. With the six-day work week commonplace and Sunday closing laws strictly enforced, unsympathetic employers decreed that "if you don't come in on Saturday, don't bother coming in on Monday." The percentage of Jewish immigrants who violated the Sabbath at some point in their lives is unknown, but undoubtedly it is large. Even a Boston Orthodox synagogue named Shomre Shabbos ("Observers of the Sabbath") was filled with Sabbath-violators! Some pious Jews, of course, continued to preserve their Sabbath at all costs. The courageous tales they told about themselves years later, however, strongly suggest that in an earlier day they stood forlornly in the minority.[57]

The wealthy Orthodox builder and communal leader Harry Fischel (1865–1948), for example, looked back on his "early struggles" over Sabbath observance as the defining "spiritual conflict" of his life. He recounted its climactic scene in words that suggest that his experience was as rare as it was life-changing. After weeks of searching for work as a new immigrant, Fischel recalled that he found the job of his dreams in an architecture firm. He worked happily for five days and then requested to take Saturday off at no pay so he could observe the Sabbath. His request was firmly denied, and he was ordered to come into work or lose his job. "It seemed," he recounted, "as though God had decided to give him another test of his devotion to his religious principles and his ability to withstand temptation." After a sleepless night, he resolved to compromise: "He would not give up his position, but before going to work he would attend services in the synagogue." The very existence of early-morning Sabbath services for those who needed to work is, of course, deeply revealing. His worship complete, Fischel prepared to go to his office, but the sight of other Jews observing the Sabbath and the shock that he knew his parents would experience "could they but know the step he contemplated" gave him pause: "Suddenly, although the day was in mid-August and the heat was stifling, he trembled as with the ague. A chill went through every fibre of his being, as though he were confronted with the biting winds of January. At the same time a strange sensation attacked his heart and he was unable to move. It seemed as though he were paralyzed and he would have fallen, had not his body been supported by a friendly wall. When with difficulty he recovered himself, his decision had been reached." Thanks to this "mysterious manifestation of the Divine Power," he felt able to resist what he described as "the greatest temptation he had ever known." In the clarity of the moment, "he knew that neither then nor later would it ever be possible for him to desecrate the Sabbath."[58]

Fischel lost his job but subsequently prospered—good fortune that he credited to his lifelong "principle" of Sabbath-observance. His resolve, however, gives every indication of being atypical. More commonly, men who needed to feed themselves and their families did compromise their Sabbath observance. Sixty percent of the stores located in the heart of New York's

Lower East Side, according to a 1913 survey, remained open on the Sabbath. A heartrending Yiddish prayer *(techinah)* written in America for women to recite privately when they lit their Sabbath candles, and printed in a widely distributed women's prayer book, explains why. Speaking in the first person to God, the prayer laments that in "this diaspora land" where the "burden of making a living is so great," resting on Sabbath and holidays had become impossible, and it pleads for divine compassion. "Grant a bountiful living to all Jewish children," it entreats, "that they should not . . . have to desecrate your holy day."[59]

The plaintive prayer notwithstanding, immigrant women did not make Sabbath observance their own responsibility when their husbands went off to work. Nor is there much evidence that one sex within the immigrant community was more likely to assimilate than the other. Instead, immigrant Jewish women served alternately as agents of assimilation and as shields against its disruptive influences. Through patterns of consumption they introduced wondrous innovations into their homes: new foods, new clothes, new luxuries. Sometimes, indeed, their elaborate Sabbath and holiday preparations proved more important to them than completing all of their work by sundown when, according to Jewish law, the new day begins. On the other hand, women also served as guardians of tradition within their homes, ensuring that sacred times were appropriately marked. Moses Weinberger, writing in 1887, described immigrant women both ways. One of his acquaintances, the wife of a grocery store owner, "felt most distressed" when her husband agreed to compromise his religious principles for the sake of his livelihood, and she "argued with him daily" until he repented. Others, by contrast, "bustle[d] about from store to store, large baskets on their arms," on days when work was enjoined, while their more traditional husbands were "joyfully sitting before God" and praying.[60]

The sexes did clearly diverge, following East European practice, concerning *where* they focused their religious energies. Women played a far more central role in maintaining the spirit of Judaism in the home through cooking, cleaning, and childrearing. Men were more likely to focus their religious activities within the synagogue, where they prayed, studied, and socialized. Probably for this reason, men in the 1916 U.S. religious census made up 60.7 percent of synagogue members, women only 39.3 percent. This, of course, was the reverse of the general pattern in American religion, where women outnumbered men in churches by 56.1 percent to 43.9 percent.[61]

Once Sabbath-observant Jews became employers themselves, conditions eased somewhat for both sexes. Fischel, for example, prided himself on never working his employees on the Sabbath. In cities like New York, Philadelphia, Baltimore, Cleveland, Milwaukee, and Indianapolis, some religiously devoted business owners, along with their pious workers, committed themselves to strict Sabbath observance, and either worked on Sunday (legally or illegally) or made do with less. In far-off Minnesota, an ex-yeshiva student named Jacob Barron established a farm near Hammond where no work at all was undertaken on the Sabbath (except for milking the cows, a permitted activity). Instead, the family prayed "intensely" every Sabbath and holiday, and the men worshipped with phylacteries every weekday morning. But these immigrants were in the minority. The more general rule concerning the practice of Judaism among immigrant Jews, especially in the late nineteenth century, was laconically expressed by a young immigrant named Max Ba[e]r in a letter that he sent back to his mother in Poland in 1890. "It is very difficult to make a good living in America for one who wants to keep the Jewish way of life," he told her. He advised his father "to return home and not to suffer here."[62]

JUDAISM AND YIDDISHKEIT

The spiritual crisis that pervaded the Jewish immigrant community posed the same dramatic challenge to Jewish survival that America had posed to Jews repeatedly since they first had arrived on American soil back in 1654. Without rabbis, without synagogue affiliation, without reliably kosher food, and without Sabbath observance would the majority of immigrants, and especially their children and grandchildren, continue to remain Jewish? Amid the urgent efforts made to Americanize the immigrants and to find them remunerative jobs, the goal of maintaining and strengthening Jewish life generally took second place. First, social workers believed, immigrants had to become loyal and productive citizens. But within the community of newcomers itself, important institutions began to take shape to meet Jews' burgeoning communal and religious needs. As so often the case among immigrants, the initial institutions they created built upon old-world ties.

Landsmanshaftn, associations of immigrants from the same hometown, were by far the most successful of these new institutions.[63] They focused on fraternal ties. Like B'nai B'rith, founded decades earlier, they sought to unite Jews on the basis of their shared ethnic and covenantal commitments to one another, regardless of political, cultural, and religious differences. Community had been a powerful and defining force for Jews in Eastern Europe, notwithstanding their many intractable internal disagreements, and landsmanshaftn helped to harness these communal feelings, uniting under one roof Jews who shared common old-world roots and memories. As cultural mediators, they helped Jews make the difficult transition from old world to new, and underscored for them the active role that they themselves could play as agents of change, shapers of their own destiny.

Landsmanshaftn emerged out of traditional Jewish voluntary associations *(hevrot)* devoted to study, worship, charity, tending the sick, burying the dead, and related communal obligations. They also generally bore the name of the old-world community from which members hailed, such as Anshei [People of] Timkowitz, the Bialystoker Young Men's Association, or the Ekaterinoslaw Ladies' Charity Society. But notwithstanding these old-world references, they were self-consciously *American* institutions that jealously guarded their independence, operated according to democratic principles, and focused on mutual aid as opposed to charity. Many of the societies even employed terms like "independent" and "progressive" in their titles to underscore their commitments and aspirations.

With their focus on peoplehood as the unifying element in Jewish life, landsmanshaftn promulgated a nonreligious model of Jewish unity, similar to the one that we saw in the mid-nineteenth century. They emphasized ethnic and communal ties—especially mutual aid and support—as the basis for Jewish unity; religion, they knew, had become divisive. Landsmanshaft leaders were not necessarily themselves anti-religious—some of them, indeed, played significant roles in their synagogues. Others, however, harbored deep-seated antipathies to rabbis and rituals, considered formal religion antithetical to the progressive goals that they cherished, or simply sought to practice Judaism selectively, picking and choosing among its many laws and customs. Whatever the case, they united in the belief that religious practice was less critical to Jewish preservation than shared experiences and values, the sense of being one interrelated family concerned with the welfare of fellow Jews wherever they might be. They looked to these common denominators—which collectively came to be known as *Yiddishkeit,* or Jewishness—to unify and preserve Jews, even as the formal practice of religion came more and more to divide them.

Landsmanshaftn embraced various religious symbols and practices and had no objection to initiating synagogues for those of their members who wanted them. Indeed, their religiously devout members created the vast majority of new synagogues for East European Jews in the United States —hundreds of them in New York alone. But whereas the bulk of the landsmanshaftn considered the practice of Judaism voluntary and the values underlying Yiddishkeit paramount, religious Jews generally held to a different set of priorities. Without denigrating Yiddishkeit, they considered the practice of Judaism and the maintenance of Jewish law uppermost. The tension between these two visions—the one focused on Judaism and faith, the other on Jewishness and peoplehood—would characterize American Jewish life throughout the twentieth century, inspiring a great deal of disputation but no permanent resolution.

The process by which landsmanshaftn established synagogues was described at the turn of the century by a careful observer, and resembles in some respects the creation of frontier synagogues years before:

> A few individuals, usually such as came from the same town or district, feeling the necessity of some concerted action, banded themselves together to form a beneficial society ordinarily bearing the name of the town or district whence most of the members came. The aim of such societies, in the first instance, was to assist financially any of the members who might be sick, to provide burial for the dead, and a death benefit for the widow or orphan of a deceased member. After the society became strengthened in numbers, a hall was hired for meeting purposes and was converted into a praying room. With the approach of the high holy days, a season when every Jew feels the need of a synagogue, a reader was engaged and seats sold to members or non-members. This brought a considerable revenue to the society and after a few years, in many cases, the organizations saved enough money to begin negotiations for a synagogue building.[64]

Synagogues established in this way, like those of the Central European immigrants, aimed initially to maintain unchanged the minhag—the customs, the practices, the tunes—lovingly remembered from worship services back home. Even if they attracted only a minority of the Jews who had emigrated from the "old home," those who did come to pray expected an authentic experience. At the Tshortkover Shul in New York, for example, the Hasidic Jews from the Galician community of Tshortkov (Chortkov), donned Galician *shtraymlekh* (round fur-trimmed hats) every Saturday and "prayed with enthusiasm, just like at the [Hasidic] rebbe's prayer house in the old home."[65] Usually, these congregations were led by devoted lay people. Some synagogues, though, seeking to strengthen the sense of verisimilitude between old and new, went so far as to import a religious functionary from their native community—an authentic cantor, preacher, or ritual slaughterer—who bore the old-world faith and was supposed to personify the migration of its traditions. The goal in all cases was to re-create within a synagogue setting the feel of the Jewish world left behind.

The landsmanshaft synagogue was, by design, a multipurpose institution
—the East European Jewish immigrant journalist and novelist Abraham
Cahan once compared it to an "institutional church." It generally organized
three worship services daily, as well as special lengthier services on the Sabbath and Jewish holidays; it offered regular classes in traditional Jewish
texts as well as occasional lectures and homilies; it made sure that members
were assisted in times of trouble—when they were out of money, when illness struck, when a family member died; it collected funds to assist the
needy at home and abroad, as well as Jewish institutions across the world;
and it provided members with numerous opportunities to socialize, sometimes as families, more often in sex-segregated settings. Unlike the old
Sephardic synagogues and some of their Central European successors, it
rarely described itself as a holy community *(kahal kadosh)*. East European
Jews brought with them a tradition of having multiple synagogues within
a single geographic community. Instead, the synagogue was understood to
be a society *(hevra)* of more-or-less like-minded people; it aimed first and
foremost to serve the needs of its members. In this respect, it was utterly
different from neighboring Catholic churches, each of which was assigned
to serve a unique, geographically well-demarcated parish.[66]

Hundreds of landsmanshaft synagogues sprang up across the United
States. At the turn of the century, when the *American Jewish Year Book* attempted to list them, it found that the names of these synagogues mirrored
the geographical span of the Jewish immigration itself and reflected an almost infinite range of Hebrew pronunciations, from Congregation Beth
Hamidrash Hagodel in Louisville, Kentucky, to Besh Hamedrus Hagodail
in Omaha, Nebraska, to Bet Hamidrosch Hagodol in Newark, New Jersey.
All told, the *Year Book* located about 650 "barely organized" congregations
"composed of the recently immigrated population"—a figure that amounted
to some 82.2 percent of all of America's 791 congregations. Using a different
method of gathering information, the U.S. Census of Religious Bodies in
1906 counted 1,769 Jewish religious "organizations." Of these, 753 (42.5
percent) were wealthy enough to boast "church edifices" of their own; another 13 percent worshiped in rented quarters; and the largest number,
fully 786 congregations nationwide (or 44.43 percent of all American synagogues), worshiped in places unknown—presumably in homes or store-
fronts or other ephemeral locations where immigrant congregations sprang
up. In New York City alone, in 1917, a comprehensive survey located 1,127
congregations of various sorts, the bulk of them landsmanshaft-created.
Considering that New York, by then, housed 1.5 million Jews, this was not

a large number. Far more of the city's Jews belonged to landsmanshaftn than to synagogues.[67]

"Unsynagogued Jews" who preferred the communal values of Yiddishkeit to the day-to-day practice of Judaism were by no means utterly removed from Jewish religious life. For one thing, the language they spoke—Yiddish —was written in Hebrew characters and resonated with words and expressions drawn from religious usage. Thus, Saturday was called *Shabbes,* the biblical day of rest, even by those who spent the day engaged in arduous labor. Yiddish writers and journalists similarly drew in their writings upon biblical and Talmudic allusions—the binding of Isaac, the ethical cries of the prophets, the moral teachings of the rabbis. Strikers invoked biblical passages to legitimate their demands for improved working conditions. "If I turn traitor to the cause I now pledge, may this hand wither from the arm I raise," workers proclaimed in unison at the commencement of an epic strike of the shirtwaist makers' union in 1909; the oath was based on Psalms 137:5. The radical Yiddish poet David Edelstadt, in a poem that he published five days before Yom Kippur in 1890, went so far as to employ traditional religious vocabulary ("Torah," "transgression," "prophet," "exile") in a bid to undermine religious tradition:

> Each era has its new Torah—
> Ours is one of freedom and justice:
> For us, the greatest transgression
> Is to be an obedient slave.
> We also have new prophets—
> Borne, Lasalle, Karl Marx;
> They will deliver us from exile
> But not with fasts and prayers![68]

In a similar vein, the great Yiddish journalist Abraham Cahan, writing in the avowedly nonreligious *Arbeiter Zeitung,* penned, for a time, a regular Yiddish column *("Sidra")* that drew socialist "lessons" from the Torah portion traditionally assigned to be read aloud each week in the synagogue. He signed himself "The Proletarian Preacher" *(Der Proletarishker Maggid).*[69] Yiddish, in short, perpetuated the language of faith even among those who had largely abandoned its tenets.

Beyond this, many "unsynagogued" Jews continued to uphold selected well-loved traditional rituals. Statistics are hard to come by, but the widespread publicity given to a 1902 women-led kosher meat boycott, which the Socialist newspaper the *Forward* strongly supported, suggests that the Jewish dietary laws continued to be broadly maintained by immigrants, at least within the home. Unscrupulous ritual slaughterers and butchers, as we have seen, caused Jewish consumers to violate the dietary laws unwittingly, but willful violations were infrequently noted and among first-generation immigrants probably uncommon. One million New York Jews, in 1917, reputedly consumed kosher meat.[70] There were at least three reasons for the survival of kashrut at home even among Jews who ate non-kosher food out and failed to observe so many other ritual commandments. First, traditional foodways recalled warm maternal memories of the world left behind. Second, having a non-kosher kitchen meant cutting social ties with friends and relatives who did keep kosher. And third, dietary laws effectively distinguished Jews from their non-Jewish neighbors—they served as a boundary marker of identity.

As for other rituals, the most widely observed by far were those that signaled annual and life cycle changes. The High Holidays, which always stirred ancestral memories, proved particularly important to immigrants. During these sacred days, Jews prayed "everywhere," even "in theaters, restaurants, and private apartments," according to the American correspondent of the Russian Jewish newspaper *Yevreiski Mir.* He observed "thousands and thousands" in 1909 who spent Yom Kippur, the day when according to Jewish tradition God decides who shall live and who shall die, "await[ing] the celestial verdict in awe." From this he shrewdly deduced that many immigrant Jews had fallen away only "from external religious practice, but not from religion." Indeed, the High Holidays served as an annual religious revival for American Jews, a time that brought them back, year after year, for a shot of religious revitalization. In North Dakota, immigrant Jewish farmers "came from far and near" to celebrate at the home of Abraham and Rachel Calof early in the twentieth century, "some traveling for days by horse and buggy and by horseback." In New York, every available hall in the area where Jews lived—even sexually suggestive dance halls and saloons—turned temporarily into a crowded house of worship during these days, and Jews who regularly absented themselves from synagogues now sat for hours at a stretch. One hall on New York's Rivington Street housed five separate congregations, each on a different floor, with services lasting for twelve hours straight on Yom Kippur day.[71]

A self-described freethinker, embarrassed by his sudden display of religiosity, explained that his heart grew "heavy and sad" when the High Holidays approached. Walking past the synagogue and hearing the cantor intone the special melodies associated with the Days of Awe recalled to him his "happy childhood years" and his "sweet childlike faith." Eventually, he apologetically confessed, he decided to go inside: "I went not in order to pray to God but to heal and refresh my aching soul with the cantor's sweet melodies, and this had an unusually good effect on me. Sitting in the synagogue among *landslayt* [people from my own hometown] and listening to the good cantor, I forgot my unhappy weekday life, the dirty shop, my boss, the bloodsucker, and my pale, sick wife, and my children. All of my America with its hurry-up life was forgotten."[72]

In the early years of East European Jewish immigration, it was common for freethinkers, socialists, and especially anarchists to mock the holiest day in the Jewish calendar with noisy demonstrations and insolent "Yom Kippur balls." An oft-recalled "grand" ball with theater, in 1890, promised "music, dancing, buffet, 'Marseillaise,' and other hymns against Satan" on Yom Kippur night and throughout the day. These crude attacks on "Jewish idols," however, fell largely on deaf ears in America, for in the absence of any religious coercion a live-and-let-live attitude toward private religious observance prevailed. Accordingly, in the twentieth century, most such provocations disappeared. "Every man has a right to live according to his beliefs," the socialist Abraham Cahan instructed his readers. "The pious man has as much right to his religion as the freethinker to his atheism."[73]

Synagogue and "unsynagogued" Jews also shared practices that later generations dismissed as "magic" and "superstition." In a far-off North Dakota homestead, miles from any synagogue, for example, Charadh Kalov took great precautions to protect her daughter-in-law and new grandchild "from the contrivings of the devil." She placed a prayer book in bed "to prevent devils from harming" the mother and baby, and she insisted that her daughter-in-law "carry a knife at all times" to ward off the "fiend." This was extreme, but many immigrant Jews carried out other rituals to fend off devils and demons, from tying red strings to wearing garlic to slapping their daughters in the face when they experienced their first menstrual period. This kind of folk Judaism, preserved especially but not exclusively by women, rarely survived into their children's generation, but it formed part of the religious life of many an immigrant home, lasting in some cases long after formal daily and weekly synagogue rituals had disappeared.[74]

Life cycle celebrations also enjoyed high levels of participation among religious and nonreligious Jews, though unsurprisingly those committed to Yiddishkeit tended to be somewhat less punctilious in their observances than their Orthodox counterparts. So, for example, during the busy season in the garment trades, many a circumcision ceremony that should have

And it shall be for a sign upon thy hand, and for frontlets between thy eyes; for—
—by strength of hand the Lord brought us forth out of Egypt.

תְּפִלָּה בְּכַוָּנָה.

וְהָיָה לְאוֹת עַל יָדְכָה וּלְטוֹטָפֹת בֵּין עֵינֶיךָ. כִּי בְּחֹזֶק יָד הוֹצִיאָנוּ יְיָ מִמִּצְרָיִם:

Instructions illustrating how to pray with proper intention. The pious young man of bar mitzvah age is portrayed wearing a grown-up hat, a silk tallit, and tefillin. The biblical verse surrounding the picture, from Exodus 13:16, is printed in Hebrew, Yiddish, German, Russian, and English, recalling the various languages that immigrant Jews spoke. From *Magil's Complete Linear Prayer Book,* 2nd ed. (Philadelphia, 1908). Collection of the author.

taken place, according to Jewish law, on the eighth day after the birth of a son was "postponed until the following Sunday"—albeit not without "secret sadness." The ritual circumcisers *(mohalim)* were also often far less scrupulous in their religious behavior than would have been permitted in Europe. Similarly, the bar mitzvah ceremony for a boy, which as early as the 1880s was celebrated "as the greatest of holidays" among immigrant Jews, featuring a "great reception" and many "wisdom-filled speeches," often did not include the presentation to the bar mitzvah boy of his own brand-new pair of phylacteries *(tefillin)*. Knowing that their children would be unlikely to wear the leather boxes with handwritten Scriptural passages that traditional Jews strap to their weaker arm and forehead during weekday morning prayers, many parents made do with well-worn pairs of phylacteries, which their children speedily discarded. (The female equivalent of the bar mitzvah, known as the bat mitzvah, began to be introduced only during the interwar years and was unknown earlier.) As for weddings, they always occasioned great religious celebrations among the immigrants. But many a marriage officiator who knew how to conduct a traditional Jewish wedding ceremony was untrained in the intricacies of Jewish law. He was more interested in receiving his fee than in prying too deeply to find out, for example, whether the bride was truly a virgin, whether she had dipped in the mikveh prior to the ceremony, and whether she might be a divorcée, in which case, according to Jewish law, she could not knowingly marry a descendant of priests *(kohen)*. As a result, marriages described as being in "accordance with the laws of Moses and Israel" sometimes turned out to be so only in outward appearances.[75]

Death rituals proved particularly important to immigrants, especially when the death involved a parent. Having left home young, often without hope of ever seeing their parents again, and knowing, in many cases, that their parents would disapprove of their religious choices, immigrants honored their parents in death more, sometimes, than they had in life. Even the non-religious usually observed the traditional mourning rites, including *shivah* ("memorial week") following the funeral, when they sat on low stools at home to be comforted by friends and relatives who also joined them in prayer. Knowing how critical these traditional observances were, landsmanshaftn often included "a proper Jewish funeral and burial" among the benefits they offered. Even otherwise secular societies ensured that members in mourning were visited, and some of them also oversaw the ritual washing and preparation of the body and the religious funeral and burial proceedings prior to shivah, though in the twentieth century less religious Jews abandoned

parts of these practices. By 1910, funeral directors had begun to play a significant role in shaping the rituals connected with death; synagogues, lodges,
and burial societies became more peripheral. But even as funeral directors
sanitized and professionalized this final stage in the life cycle, its religious
implications remained profound. "Death sustains the life of American Judaism," an observer of East European Jewish immigrant life suggested in
1895. When death struck and immigrants stood most in need of religious
support, the traditional rituals of their faith comforted them.[76]

As the example of the mourning rituals demonstrates, Judaism and Yiddishkeit did much between them to strengthen East European Jewish immigrant life. Their relationship even achieved a measure of symbiosis: those
who made religion their highest priority joined periodically with their nonreligious counterparts in support of community-wide goals and charities,
while those who emphasized communal values turned from time to time
to religious institutions and practices for spiritual sustenance. The broad
spectrum that stretched from "strictly Orthodox" to "loosely connected to
Jewish life" embraced the vast bulk of the immigrant population, and individuals found their own place along it. The Orthodox committed themselves
to the totality of Judaism's commandments, the radicals rejected religious
authority completely, and the majority—even some who worshipped regularly in Orthodox synagogues—picked their way through the labyrinth of
Judaism's religious regulations, adhering to them selectively. The resulting
diversity—a consistent feature of American Jewish religious life since colonial days—was moderated by numerous commonalities that, we have seen,
bound immigrant Jews together. These included ties of language, culture,
community, and memory, as well as lives shaped at least somewhat by the
rhythms of the Jewish calendar, its Sabbath, its holidays, and its life-cycle
ceremonies.

Looking ahead, however, the future appeared bleak. As immigrants
Americanized, their religious needs changed. Like Central European Jews
before them, they sought a more "refined" worship experience, more in
keeping with their rising status in society. Their children, raised in America
and educated in its public schools, found their parents' institutions completely
foreign. Eager for acceptance in the new world, they sought out American
institutions; they also preferred English to Yiddish. Moreover, the bulk of
these children had received only a tiny fraction of the Jewish education that
their parents possessed. As a result, they knew very little about Judaism,
and what they did know was not particularly appealing. Even the "faithful
Orthodox," Moses Weinberger complained, "unhesitatingly allow[ed] their

sons to grow up without Torah or faith." There was, to be sure, no dearth of impoverished (and often embittered) Jewish elementary school teachers who, for far less than a living wage, provided instruction in the rudiments of Hebrew reading and Bible stories—more often, as had also been true in Europe, to boys than to girls. But the vast majority of Jewish children in America never went beyond that point: they neither studied biblical texts in a sophisticated way, nor did they learn anything of postbiblical Judaism —the Talmud, Jewish legal codes, modern Jewish literature. Boys generally stopped their Jewish education altogether following their bar mitzvah at age thirteen. A widely publicized "Community Survey of Jewish Education in New York City," published in 1910, demonstrated that between 75 and 80 percent of New York's Jewish children (male and female) were receiving no formal Jewish education at all at the time the survey took place, and many of the rest endured conditions so poor as to be counterproductive. The spiritual crisis that affected the immigrant community—the dearth of religious leadership, the collapse of traditional piety, the widespread abandonment of the synagogue—thus threatened only to deepen over time, as Americanizing immigrants grew disaffected with traditional institutions and their children abandoned them entirely. Would the rabbis who had warned against immigration to the new world be proven correct? Could East European Jewish immigrants and their children be saved for Judaism? Beginning already in the 1880s, farsighted Jews began to focus on this challenge.[77]

ORTHODOXY: BETWEEN ACCOMMODATION AND RESISTANCE

Orthodox lay leaders within the East European Jewish community of New York were among the first to respond. The earliest representatives of their community to succeed financially, men like banker Sender Jarmulowsky and businessmen Dramin Jones, Jonas Weil, and Henry Chuck, the latter a German Orthodox Jew who associated with East Europeans, looked to improve the image and character of Jewish life to make it seem more orderly and refined. Like earlier generations of Jewish immigrants before them and like modernizing Jews throughout Europe, they concluded that a Judaism that stood in harmony with the middle-class values that they and their children espoused would be more likely to endure. To this end, they made it possible for the oldest and wealthiest East European synagogues in New York, notably Beth Hamedrash Hagodol, Ohab Zedek, and Khal Adas Jeshurun, to move into enormous new showpiece synagogues (some of them converted churches) in the mid-1880s, and in each case they saw to it that the lavish new buildings spurred greater attention to issues of decorum and appearance. At Beth Hamedrash Hagodol, this was demonstrated at the synagogue's dedication, in 1885, which featured choral music and vernacular addresses and was the very model of order and good taste. "The usual noise and hubbub," one Anglo-Jewish newspaper sniffed, "were conspicuous by their absence." The newspaper compared the "quiet, respectable" dedication to the "mode formerly . . . monopolized by the reformers." Other synagogues began to enforce strict rules of order, similar to those introduced years before in America's Sephardic and Central European synagogues, to prevent talking, spitting, or bustling around. They also assigned every member to a permanent seat. The comfortable, easygoing "prayer-room" atmosphere that characterized new immigrant synagogues thus gave way, at least among upwardly mobile Jews, to one that was more formal and awe-inspiring, more akin to what Christians called "high church" and what Jews themselves described as decorous and refined.[78]

To further enhance the atmosphere of their magnificent new synagogues, and in a bid to make Sabbath and holiday worship more inviting for themselves and their children, Americanized lay leaders (one contemporary described them, revealingly, as "young reformers") also imported expensive European-trained cantors to chant the traditional liturgy. This so-called "*hazzan* [cantor] craze" began in the 1880s when the first "thousand dollar" cantors were hired on the Lower East Side. It was greatly enhanced in 1886 when New York's Khal Adas Jeshurun "shocked downtown society by engaging Rev. [Pinchos] Minkowsky for the then-staggering sum of five thousand dollars per annum," and Beth Hamedrash Hagodol countered by hiring, also for a large salary, Cantor Israel Michalovsky from Paris. Subsequently, one East Side congregation after another followed suit, importing the most famous European cantors for ever higher sums. According to contemporary accounts, worshippers thronged to attend the services led by these cantors. The tickets sold more than covered the cantors' high salaries. Dressed in their flowing robes and professional caps, the cantors substituted for the organ music that shaped the rarefied atmosphere in formal churches and Reform temples; cantorial voices were permitted according to Jewish law, while organ music was not. The cantors also served as living bridges between the European Jewish musical tradition and the new world. Those who became cantorial superstars, like contemporary gospel music stars, may even be seen to have embodied the contradictory cultural ideals of their day: tradition, modernity, religious spirituality, worldly success.

Whatever the case, the arrival of the cantors inaugurated a shift from participation to performance in East European Jewish immigrant worship. Replacing the simple *baale tefilah*—congregational prayer leaders who knew the
appropriate chants and rejoiced at the opportunity to lead the congregation
in divine worship—the star cantors, often accompanied by male choirs,
"performed" the service. Congregants were expected to be quietly moved
by all that they heard, but to join in only for the occasional refrains.[79]

All of this signified an outward turn among successful East European
Jews in America, akin to what had taken place earlier when Central European Jews had built similar edifices. Like them, the advancing new immigrants bid for religious equality by making a grand entrance onto the American religious stage. Their great synagogues and cantors proclaimed their
Americanization, their heightened self-confidence, and their rising station
in society. They proudly showed off these accomplishments to political and
religious luminaries, as well as to the native-born Jews who previously had
viewed their East European cousins with disdain. They also sent reports
(and even pictures) of the synagogues back to Europe to boast of their
achievements and to allay their parents' fears that Judaism in America was
doomed. "East European Jews have arrived and plan on staying," the massive buildings and their accouterments announced. In a dramatically concrete
way the immigrants established a place for themselves within the American
religious landscape, and paved the way for their American-born children
to follow in their religious footsteps.

The large new buildings soon led synagogue officials to enlarge their own
frames of vision. They now had vast new expenses and required equally
vast memberships. No longer could they afford just to appeal to landslayt,
Jews from their own hometown, and their offspring. Instead, they had to
welcome Jews from different homelands into their midst, cater to more varied religious needs, and become more tolerant of different customs and traditions. The process was neither rapid nor all-encompassing, but over time
these synagogues became one more force, along with schools, newspapers,
and Jewish and Gentile outsiders, in promoting what might be called the
"ethnicization" of East European Jews. By joining Jews together under one
roof, "grand" synagogues helped immigrants to dampen the old European-
based rivalries that divided Lithuanian, Polish, Russian, Romanian, Hungarian, and Galician Jews from one another, uniting them instead into a
more cohesive religious community.[80]

In more ways than they cared to admit, the Americanized East European
leaders of these grand synagogues took their cues in much of what they

did to transform immigrant Judaism from their Central European Reform
Jewish cousins. Just as generations of Lutherans and Catholics looked to
their predecessors in America for guidance, so East European Jews looked
to Reform Jews: sometimes they quietly emulated them, sometimes they
explicitly rejected them, but never could they totally ignore them. Kasriel
Sarasohn, editor of the Orthodox-leaning New York *Yiddishes Tageblatt*
(Jewish Daily News), for instance, once held up the youth activities and
"enlightened methods" of the Reform congregation Rodeph Shalom of
Philadelphia as a "brilliant example for my orthodox brethren to emulate."
Zvi Hirsch Masliansky, the foremost Yiddish-language preacher on New
York's Lower East Side, similarly advised Orthodox Jews to learn from
their liberal colleagues "how to honor leaders, and how to give charity." In
addition, the Orthodox, as we have seen, emulated the Reformers' rules of
order, their concern for decorum and propriety.[81]

Leading Orthodox synagogues even copied the architectural styles favored
by Reform Jews. In the 1880s this meant Moorish architecture, as evidenced
in the Moorish details of New York's famed Eldridge Street Synagogue
(Khal Adas Jeshurun), built in 1886. Later, at the turn of the century, Kehilath Jeshurun in Yorkville proudly borrowed the Renaissance Revival design
of a prominent Reform temple, the West End Synagogue, and this same
design was in turn copied by status-seeking Orthodox synagogues elsewhere.
In Boston, at least four immigrant synagogues imitated the architectural
style of the city's leading Reform Congregation, Temple Israel. Even as
they learned from their Reform cousins, Orthodox leaders also explicitly
rejected what they saw as more radical and impermissible Reform innovations, such as the organ, mixed seating, bareheaded worship, and Reform's
greatly foreshortened and largely vernacular liturgy. Their goal was to
Americanize Orthodoxy, not to undermine it.[82]

Leaders of grand synagogues sometimes referred to their congregations
by the title *stadt shul,* implying that theirs were "community" or "central"
synagogues on the European model. In fact, the synagogues were nothing
of the sort. Instead, like all American synagogues, they were private membership organizations supported by private dues and donations. Most of them,
moreover, catered less to the community at large than to economically rising
East European Jews who craved (and could afford) the fashions, manners,
and mores of the cultivated elite, and who sought refinement, formality,
and display in their religious lives as well. By marrying the trappings of respectability—elaborate chandeliers, dark woods, marbled floors, high vaulted
ceilings, and lush velvet seats—to the traditional liturgy, grand synagogues

The Eldridge Street Synagogue (Khal Adas
Jeshurun) in New York. This was the first
new synagogue building erected on the
Lower East Side by East European Jews.
Designed by the architectural firm of
Herter Brothers and dedicated in 1887,
the building combines Moorish, Gothic,
and Romanesque elements. Its main
sanctuary features massive brass chandeliers
and a magnificent Torah ark carved in Italy.
From a postcard in the author's collection,
courtesy of the Eldridge Street Project.

resolved for their members the problem of how to reconcile Orthodox Judaism with modernity. Akin to what Isaac Leeser had advocated half a century
earlier, they attempted to synthesize modern sensibilities with the requirements of Jewish law. The aim was to produce a decorous Orthodoxy that
would appeal to the American-born children of immigrants and survive
on American soil.[83]

The problem of religious leadership, however, remained unsolved. As perceptive lay leaders realized, young people, besides wanting modern synagogues, also needed religious role models: rabbis who displayed the same combination of Orthodoxy and modernity that their synagogues projected through their ambiance. In Cincinnati, the Reform movement had begun training its own English-speaking rabbis and was achieving great success with them. Could the immigrant community produce a parallel group of rabbis, fully at home in America and at the same time thoroughly conversant with all that an Orthodox rabbi needed to know? A key stumbling block here was the Talmud, the great compendium of Jewish law, redacted around the sixth century and studied and commented upon by traditional Jews ever since. In Europe, Talmud was the sine qua non of Jewish religious leadership, and talented youngsters commenced studying its folio pages long before their bar mitzvah. In America, however, except at Hebrew Union College, no known Jewish school so much as taught Talmud in the early 1880s, let alone focused upon it. Even the Machzike Talmud Torah, a supplementary Jewish school supported by immigrants, never managed to introduce its students to these fundamental sources of Jewish law. Nor were copies of the Talmud and its commentaries—traditionally printed in twenty folio volumes—easy to find in America; they all had to be imported from Europe at significant cost. To help resolve this problem and to improve what the directors of the Talmud Torah called American Jewry's "terribly degenerate spiritual situation," several of the same lay leaders who had built the grand Lower East Side synagogues gathered funds in 1886 to open a yeshiva, an academy for Jewish studies akin to a Catholic parochial school. Named, significantly, Etz Chaim (Tree of Life), the yeshiva conceived itself as being just that—a tree of life for American Judaism, a tiny oasis of traditional Jewish learning in a vast desert of secular ignorance. It set Talmud study at the core of its curriculum and grudgingly taught state-mandated secular subjects from 4 P.M. onward.[84]

Meeting in a drab storefront, the yeshiva contrasted sharply with the grand synagogues that the same leaders had earlier created: it displayed none of the trappings of refinement, and its curriculum resisted modernity as much as possible. The fact that many of the same people supported both institutions demonstrates a revealing ambivalence among the upwardly mobile leaders of immigrant Jewish life: in the effort to save the next generation of Jews for Judaism, they sought simultaneously both to accommodate modernity and to resist it, perhaps in the hope that each extreme would check the excesses of the other. Nor were they alone in this ambivalence;

the same seeming two-facedness affected Jews across the spectrum of Jewish life, as well as many Catholics and Protestants. Rather than pigeonholing themselves into boxes stamped "accommodation" and "resistance" or "tradition" and "change," a great many religiously committed Americans kept one foot in each box and struggled to find a place for themselves somewhere in between.[85]

The second step in the effort to solve the problem of religious leadership for immigrant Jews—the appointment of Rabbi Jacob Joseph of Vilna as chief rabbi of New York—provides a good example of how the forces of accommodation and resistance operated in tandem "to keep the next generation faithful to Judaism." The idea of a chief rabbi, as we have seen, was anything but new. Already discussed in America back in Isaac Leeser's day, it was revived periodically thereafter, usually by immigrants who came from lands where the authority of the communal rabbi carried substantial religious weight. In 1879, for instance, Orthodox East European Jews in America issued a public call for an eminent rabbi "whose character will inspire respect, whose abilities will impart confidence and whose erudition and reputation will silence all disaffection and end all cavil and dispute." The plan was to invite one of the leading luminaries of Europe, Rabbi Meir Loeb Malbim, to serve in this capacity, but his refusal, followed almost immediately by his illness and death, ended the project. Whether it would otherwise have succeeded is dubious: the absence of state support for the institution of a chief rabbinate, and the visceral resistance many American Jews felt to anything that threatened to limit the freedom of individuals and congregations to practice Judaism as they saw fit, probably doomed a hierarchic model of religious authority from the start. Nor was there even a remote chance that such a leader would have succeeded in silencing "all disaffection," much less in producing harmony among American Jewry's widely disparate and religiously variegated members.[86]

Nevertheless, in 1887, following the death of Beth Hamedrash Hagodol's longtime spiritual leader, Abraham Joseph Ash, calls to appoint a chief rabbi rang out anew. The usual group of immigrant Orthodox lay leaders from upwardly mobile East European Orthodox congregations in New York took hold of the project, and together they raised $2,500 in pledges and created a grandly named organization (influenced, one suspects, by Cincinnati's Union of American Hebrew Congregations) called the Association of American Orthodox Hebrew Congregations. Its most specific object was "to designate, support, and maintain a Chief Rabbi." In a letter seeking recommendations for the post dispatched to eight prominent European rabbis, the leaders of the organization explained that "many improvements must be undertaken to raise the standard of Judaism in our own country, and if the Orthodox congregations do not unite, then there is no hope for the preservation and upbuilding of Judaism in our city." The parallelism here between "our country" and "our city" is revealing. New York's East European Orthodox Jews tended to view their city as a microcosm of the country as a whole, and as a result the question of the rabbi's responsibilities —local versus national—was left intentionally vague. The use of the word "improvements" in connection with the rabbi's mission is even more revealing, for as subsequent documents made clear it carried a double and somewhat contradictory meaning. On the one hand, the chief rabbi was supposed to "improve" the regulation of Jewish dietary, divorce, and marriage laws, and to lead the "battle" against the many "influences which, in America, are so powerful [as] to make our sons and daughters forget their duty to the religion in which their ancestors lived." On the other hand, the rabbi was also supposed to "improve" Orthodoxy—"to create an intelligent orthodoxy, and to prove that also in America can be combined honor, enlightenment, and culture, with a proper observance of religious duty." The chief rabbi, in short, was expected both to resist the forces of Americanization and to accommodate them; he was supposed to be as ambivalent as the lay leaders who appointed him.[87]

Rabbi Jacob Joseph of Vilna (1840–1902), the man selected for the position, was not the leaders' first choice, but on paper at least he was an interesting one.[88] Born into a poor family, he had made a name for himself as a champion of the Jewish masses. He also boasted ties with some of Europe's most notable rabbis, associated himself with Lithuanian traditions of learning, and subscribed to the new pietistic revival introduced, in a bid to make Judaism more appealing to young East European Jews, by his revered teacher, Rabbi Israel Salanter. In Vilna he enjoyed a reputation for being an authority on Jewish law as well as a popular preacher, and he was also an avowed Zionist. He even brought with him experience with a variegated Jewish community where a whole spectrum of Jews lived side by side. His associates in Europe (and later in America) included men who possessed secular education and had been deeply influenced by the Enlightenment. In short, he was no obscurantist.

For all this, however, he sorely disappointed those who imported him; as chief rabbi, beginning in 1888, he proved an utter failure. Knowing nothing of America's language and culture, and overly dependent on lay leaders for advice, direction, and funds, he found himself unable to initiate any "improvements" in Orthodoxy at all. He did enjoy some early success as a ceremonial figure, issuing statements that others wrote for him and making public appearances. But his sermons, which had been celebrated back in Vilna, sounded old-fashioned to his American listeners; he "was satirized as 'a greenhorn,' 'a back number,' 'a man who makes funny speeches.'"[89] The one major area where he did attempt to initiate change, the supervision of kosher products, ended disastrously when both consumers and producers balked at the extra charge that the Association of Orthodox Congregations sought to impose in return for his services. Soon, other rabbis entered into competition with Rabbi Joseph—some even assuming for themselves the title of chief rabbi—and the association, which had projected that income from the supervision of kosher food would underwrite Rabbi Joseph's munificent salary, defaulted on its obligations to him and went out of business. His health broken and his livelihood cut off, the unfortunate rabbi spent his last years as an impoverished invalid. Even his massive funeral in 1902 ended in tragedy. The long honorific procession that accompanied his casket to the cemetery was pelted by Irish workers, some of whom had been taunting local Jewish immigrants for years, and a riot ensued, abetted by the police, in which many Jews were brutally beaten. In death, as in life, the rabbi thus fell victim to the clash between traditional religious values and the more sordid realities of American society.[90]

The failure of Jacob Joseph ended all hope of establishing a single rabbinic authority over the Orthodox community of New York, much less that of America as a whole. A few Orthodox rabbis subsequently managed to function as unofficial (or self-proclaimed) chief rabbis in such Orthodox Jewish communities as Boston, Philadelphia, Pittsburgh, Cincinnati, and St. Louis, and one or two even pretended to the title "chief rabbi of the United States." More commonly, however, Orthodox rabbis competed with one another for status and power and deferred only grudgingly to rabbis with greater seniority and learning than themselves; that was the American way. As for lay leaders, they continued to chafe at the disorganization and religious laxity so manifest within the American Jewish community, but they no longer looked for a chief rabbi to resolve those problems. Nor did the lay leaders of New York's major East European Orthodox synagogues, who bore the brunt of the blame and the cost for the Jacob Joseph fiasco, renew their attempt to resolve communal problems on their own.

Instead, for a generation, two different strategies vied among the fast-growing community of America's non-Reform Jews: one looked to save the next generation by creating a broad-based *inclusive* coalition of traditional

Jews to stand in opposition to the Reform movement, the other favored a more narrowly defined *exclusive* Orthodoxy that would distinguish itself both from Reform and from the middle-of-the-road Jewish position that eventually became known as Conservative Judaism. Strictly speaking, neither of these strategies was new. We have seen that Reform Jews likewise vacillated between "inclusive" and "exclusive" strategies in the 1870s, reprising debates between "compromise for the sake of unity" and "firmness for the sake of principle" that went back two decades earlier. Among the Orthodox, both of these strategies had been anticipated in print in the 1870s, and schools reflecting each position were established in the 1880s. But in 1902, coincident with the death of Jacob Joseph, champions of these two opposing strategies moved decisively to strengthen their flanks.

INCLUSIVITY VERSUS EXCLUSIVITY

The broad inclusive strategy found its institutional home at the Jewish Theological Seminary, which had opened its doors in New York City on January 2, 1887. The first sentence of the new seminary's constitution defined the institution's constituency: "Jews of America faithful to Mosaic law and ancestral tradition." This embraced a much wider group of Jews than those totally committed to Jewish law *(halacha),* but it nevertheless distinguished the new institution from Hebrew Union College, which in the wake of the "trefa banquet" and the Pittsburgh Platform could make no similar claims. Indeed, the diverse and somewhat unstable coalition of early Seminary supporters might best be described as "non-Reform." It included prominent Sephardic Jews like the Reverend Sabato Morais of Mikveh Israel and the Reverend Henry Pereira Mendes of Shearith Israel, many of whose congregants loved tradition but did not themselves uphold it; self-styled "middle-ground" rabbis like Alexander Kohut and Marcus Jastrow, whose own synagogues had traveled much further down the road to Reform than they themselves thought prudent; young American-born and German-trained Orthodox rabbis like Henry Schneeberger and Bernard Drachman; prosperous laymen of Sephardic, German, and East European extraction; and the young editors of the *American Hebrew,* who viewed the seminary as one more instrument of the Jewish awakening that they so ardently sought to stimulate. These men of different ages, backgrounds, and temperaments strongly disagreed among themselves concerning critical issues of religious tradition and change—some, for example, made their peace with mixed seating and modifications to the traditional liturgy, while others never would. But in the wake of what they saw as Reform Judaism's "extreme radicalism" and in the face of burgeoning East European Jewish immigration, the goals that united the seminary's founders seemed far more weighty than the issues that divided them. The non-Reform Judaism that they espoused—what some, at the time, called "Orthodox," others "Conservative," still others "Historical," and some "purely Jewish"—could, they believed, stem the drift to assimilation, build a bridge to new immigrants, and, most important of all, keep the children of East European Jews firmly within the faith. "Here a new Zion has been established," Kohut declared when the Seminary opened its doors, "a Zion of Jewish learning for the regeneration of American Judaism."[91]

In the fifteen years following its opening, the new seminary operated on a shoestring budget and graduated a grand total of fourteen rabbis and three cantors. The optimistically named Alumni Association of the Jewish Theological Seminary was founded in 1901 by six of these graduates, meeting in a private home. A number of East European Jews contributed financially to the institution, including Chief Rabbi Jacob Joseph, and some also taught at the school. But the broadly inclusive coalition envisaged by some of the founders—"an actual union of the east side and downtown Jews with their uptown brethren"—never came to pass. Although Sabato Morais, the president of the seminary, was held in high esteem by East European Jews in Philadelphia (where he continued to live), and Alexander Kohut, the school's professor of Talmud, was broadly respected, the young seminary's relationship with the immigrant community prior to 1902 ranged from ambivalent to hostile. Critics considered the school aloof, paternalistic, and insufficiently Orthodox. An insensitively worded plan to use "English-speaking Seminary graduates" to bring about the "religious betterment of our poorer [immigrant] brethren" didn't help matters. Nor did the seminary's chronic lack of funds, which prevented it from providing impoverished immigrant students with adequate stipends. Kohut's death, in 1894, followed by Morais' death three years later, and the death of its chairman of the board of trustees, Joseph Blumenthal, in 1901, placed the institution's very existence in jeopardy. The hope for a broad coalition of traditionally oriented religious Jews opposed to Reform seemed likely to die aborning.[92]

In 1898, perhaps in an effort to strengthen the inclusive traditionalist coalition, some of the leaders of the Jewish Theological Seminary, including H. Pereira Mendes, Cyrus Adler, Bernard Drachman, and Max Cohen, joined forces with leading East European Jews, including Kasriel Sarasohn, the editor of New York's foremost Orthodox Yiddish newspaper, the *Yiddishes*

Tageblatt, and some forty-seven congregations spread over eleven states, Washington, D.C., and Montreal, to establish what they called the Orthodox Jewish Congregational Union of America. The word "Orthodox" featured prominently in the new organization's masthead and publicity, but like the seminary, the congregational union (later known as the O-U) came into existence largely "to protest against declarations of reform rabbis not in accord with the teachings of our Torah . . . and the accepted rulings of recognized sages of Israel." The union's platform comprised almost a point-by-point refutation of the Reform Pittsburgh Platform ("Ceremonial law is not optative; it is obligatory"), and some of the union's supporters, including the editors of the *American Hebrew,* clearly looked upon the organization as the new non-Reform counterpart to the Union of American Hebrew Congregations. They hoped that it would provide a steady stream of funding for the Jewish Theological Seminary, and they called for it to "stand to the Seminary of New York as the constituent congregations of the Hebrew Union [Union of American Hebrew Congregations] stand to the [Hebrew] Union College." To be sure, the Orthodox Union was slightly less inclusive than the seminary: it did not employ the word "Conservative" in its official publications (although it did pledge to advance the interests of "Historical Judaism"), and its founders included no known rabbis of Reform synagogues. But like the seminary, it did envisage an American Judaism composed of two broad wings—one traditional, the other Reform—and its goal was to strengthen the former.[93]

To this end, the Orthodox Union worked closely if tacitly with the Jewish Endeavor Society, founded in 1899 by seminary students to provide young Jews on the Lower East Side with English-language lectures and classes, social and recreational activities, and "orderly, dignified" religious services "accompanied by congregational singing and an English sermon." The students, many of whom went on to become influential rabbis, also served as important role models for the young people of the "Jewish ghetto," demonstrating by example how Jews of East European background could achieve an American university education while maintaining a firm commitment to Jewish religious traditionalism. Modeled in part on the Christian Endeavor Society, an interdenominational youth ministry founded in 1881 by the Congregationalist minister Francis E. Clark to incorporate young people into the life of the church and prepare them for future leadership, the Jewish Endeavor Society even initiated "young people's synagogues," a conscious imitation of the Christian Endeavorers' "young people's churches." But while it borrowed selectively from Protestant techniques and terminology,

Young Jews being introduced to "dignified" Jewish worship at
New York's Downtown Talmud Torah. Note that young girls participated
in the worship but were relegated to the back rows. From the *Jewish
Communal Register* (1918), in author's collection.

the Jewish Endeavor Society also labored energetically to combat the "pernicious" influence of Christian missionaries and settlement house workers on young immigrant Jews and to compete with the efforts of Temple Emanu-El's Brotherhood to win immigrant Jews over to their Reform Jewish "Social House." Christianity, Reform Judaism, "dignified" Orthodoxy, or nothing —these were the options that young "ghetto" Jews were assumed to be confronting. The Jewish Endeavor Society, during its decade of work, sought to further the third of these options as it struggled, in league with the seminary and the Orthodox Union, to fashion a broadly inclusive American Orthodoxy traditional enough to satisfy Jewish law and modern enough to attract young Jews of East European descent back to the synagogue.[94]

Solomon Schechter (1847–1915), whose well-publicized arrival on America's shores on April 17, 1902, was heralded as the beginning of a new era in American Jewish religious life, shared this same audacious goal. Considered the greatest English-speaking Jewish scholar of his day, and described as the "most wonderful combination of learning, wit, and spiritual magnetism," Schechter left Cambridge University in England, where he was woefully underpaid and spiritually lonely, to assume the helm of the Jewish

Theological Seminary, which he looked to transform into a "centre of Jewish *Wissenschaft,*" an academically rigorous "scientific" institution committed to the vigorous pursuit of Jewish scholarship. Wealthy native-born and German-born Jews, including several Reform Jews, had taken control of the seminary, reorganized it, and infused it with new funds in advance of Schechter's arrival. Their hope was that Schechter would revitalize and modernize immigrant Judaism and thereby elevate America to a new status among the Jewish communities of the world. "In the near future," the *American Jewish Year Book* confidently predicted in 1902 in the afterglow of Schechter's assumption of his duties, America would become "the centre and focus of Jewish religious activity and the chosen home of Jewish learning."[95]

The combination of skills that Schechter boasted—vast rabbinic learning, traditional ordination, the best secular training that European universities could provide, and an earned doctorate—seemed to him, and to those who worked so hard to attract him, precisely what traditional Judaism needed if it wanted to survive in a modern setting. Like the Jewish Endeavor Society members whom he would now teach, he also personally modeled that synthesis of tradition and modernity that he and his supporters hoped to bring about, with the added advantage that he was already old and famous. A large, lumbering man who exuded warmth with his grandfatherly white hair and long handsome beard, he united within himself the spiritual heritage of Eastern Europe, where he had been born, and the scholarly heritage of Western Europe, where he had studied and taught. He spoke Yiddish natively and retained warm memories of his Hasidic childhood, yet his scholarship and outlook were thoroughly modern; the leading luminaries of Cambridge were his friends. As a young man, he had built his scholarly reputation with important books in the field of early rabbinic Judaism. He then greatly enhanced his fame with a series of remarkable discoveries based on long-lost fragments that he identified and recovered from Cairo's Genizah, a storehouse for discarded Jewish sacred articles, some a thousand years old. Thanks in part to his wife, who wrote beautiful English, he also became known for his sprightly pen, which he used both to illumine little-known facets of Judaism and to comment, often bitingly, on Jewish events of his day. He impressed all who met him with his dramatic personality, vast erudition, and unswerving opposition to Reform Judaism. "Schechter has spoken and Judaism has triumphed," the *Yiddishes Tageblatt* informed its downtown readers within months of his arrival. "He takes his stand on the broad platform of the Torah, opposing with all the vigor of his master mind the shams, hypocrisies, and expediencies of Reform."[96]

Schechter quickly became both the symbol and the standard-bearer for this broadly inclusive "platform of the Torah." Like his predecessors, he associated a range of adjectives with the Judaism he advocated, including "Orthodox," "Historical," and "Conservative," but he preferred no adjective at all and, as the *Tageblatt* understood, really sought to embrace everything to the right of Reform. For this reason, the Orthodox Union for a time marched hand in hand with him: in 1904 its president, H. Pereira Mendes, described the seminary as a "bulwark against reform Judaism."[97] Several significant Reform Jewish lay leaders, including such pillars of Temple Emanu-El as Jacob Schiff and Louis Marshall, also now supported the new seminary. They viewed it as an instrument of Americanization, an institution whose graduates could save the children of immigrants for Judaism. No less important, they saw it as a vehicle for elevating New York Jewry and through it American Jewry as a whole to a position of cultural prominence, if not preeminence, among the Jews of the world.

Within a few years, the seminary (known in Europe as Schechter's Seminary) occupied a handsome new building in Morningside Heights, strategically close to Columbia University's new campus and the future home of the Union Theological Seminary—a bold statement of the fledgling institution's scholarly ambition and religious self-confidence. It also boasted America's finest Jewish library, a world-class scholarly faculty, and, in 1905, more than one hundred students. The school's message, encoded in the biblical story of the burning bush that Schechter selected as the seminary's symbol, declared that "the bush was not consumed" (Exodus 3:2). Jewish learning and wide-ranging scholarship, the symbol implied, would sustain American Judaism and reinvigorate Jewish tradition.[98]

Outsiders understood that Schechter's brand of traditional Judaism differed from other brands being simultaneously marketed to New York Jews. In a famous Passover sermon at Temple Emanu-El in New York, Judah Magnes sought to explain the difference: "There is an orthodoxy that is in principle fixed and immovable. Such orthodoxy does not admit the possibility of change and development in Judaism. But there is another kind of orthodoxy which, holding fast to Jewish tradition, admits the possibility of change and development, of accommodation to new surroundings. Such an orthodoxy is that of a . . . Solomon Schechter."[99] Schechter actually was no friend of Temple Emanu-El's style of Judaism (although he was, at the time, friendly with Magnes). In fact, he vigorously opposed most of what the Reform Movement in Judaism stood for, and privately worked to undermine it. Nevertheless, he believed in cooperating with Reform Jews

Solomon Schechter (left) and Kaufmann Kohler (right) on a country outing, 1910s.
Behind them stand Louis Ginzberg, the young professor of Talmud at the Jewish
Theological Seminary, and Emil G. Hirsch, the Radical Reform rabbi of Chicago
(who was Kohler's brother-in-law). For all of their differences, these rabbis and
scholars socialized together—and all of them went bareheaded in the countryside.
Courtesy of the Library of the Jewish Theological Seminary of America.

in areas connected with Jewish learning, communal welfare, and social justice, and he publicly championed Jewish consensus; he popularized and
may even have invented the term "Catholic Israel." His influential metaphor
for American Jewish life was drawn from English politics, where two parties

fought each other constantly, even as both agreed that "His Majesty's government, as well as His Majesty's opposition form one large community." Thus, he invited his Reform counterpart at Hebrew Union College, Kaufmann Kohler, to the dedication of the seminary's new headquarters in 1903, and when Kohler returned the favor by inviting him to the dedication of Hebrew Union College's new campus ten years later, he traveled to Cincinnati. The two men similarly worked side by side (if not always peacefully) on the *Jewish Encyclopedia* and the Jewish Publication Society's Bible translation. Outwardly, theirs was a "respectful rivalry"—a familiar one that pit reformers against traditionalists and paralleled, ideologically, the debate between liberals and conservatives in American Protestantism of the day.[100]

Schechter, Kohler, Magnes, and much of the organized Jewish community at that time assumed that American Judaism had bifurcated into exactly two major wings, each associated with its own seminary (Hebrew Union College and Jewish Theological Seminary), congregational union (Union of American Hebrew Congregations and Orthodox Jewish Congregational Union of America), and rabbinical association (the Central Conference of American Rabbis and the Alumni Association of the Jewish Theological Seminary). The voices farther to the Jewish religious right, which spoke mostly in Yiddish and propounded a much more exclusive definition of Orthodoxy, one that excluded the "conservative" Jewish Theological Seminary altogether, scarcely registered on their radar screens. They considered those Jews altogether foreign to the realities of American life and unworthy of attention.

In a bid to gain greater attention, sixty European-trained rabbis who most vocally represented Judaism's right wing convened on July 29, 1902, the very day of Rabbi Jacob Joseph's funeral and just over one hundred days following Solomon Schechter's arrival, to formalize the creation of what they called, carefully avoiding the profane English tongue, the Agudath ha-Rabbanim (United Orthodox Rabbis). Talking in Yiddish and writing in Hebrew, the rabbis expressed the same concern over the future of Judaism in America that English speakers did. They worried about low standards of Jewish education, inadequate observance of the Jewish Sabbath, improper supervision of kosher food, lax observance of Jewish marriage and divorce laws, and the like. Their solution, however, was to reinvigorate the authority of European-trained rabbis (like themselves), who would work to solve these problems collectively rather than through the failed mechanism of a chief rabbi. Their solutions, moreover, involved a far more exclusive definition of Orthodoxy than either Schechter or the Orthodox Union propounded.

In fact, the rabbis of the Agudath ha-Rabbanim excluded from membership not only graduates of the Jewish Theological Seminary (whom they
called "not fit for the position of rabbi on account of lack of proper and
sufficient learning"), but also graduates of Western European seminaries.
The only Orthodox rabbis they were prepared to recognize were those
trained in traditional Talmudic academies, known as *yeshivot,* and personally
ordained by an East European rabbinic luminary. They also promoted a
strategy of resistance to Americanization, opposing English-language sermons and advocating Yiddish as the preferred language of instruction in
Jewish schools. In a coldly written letter to the president of the Orthodox
Union, they made clear that they did not view the inclusive congregational
body as consisting of "real" Orthodox congregations.[101]

In place of the Jewish Theological Seminary, which they criticized for its
modernity and especially its critical approach to Jewish texts, the rabbis of
the Agudath ha-Rabbanim promoted the fledgling Rabbi Isaac Elchanan
Theological Seminary (RIETS), founded in 1897 by associates of Rabbi Jacob Joseph, to serve, in the words of its historian, "as an American counterpart of the finest yeshivas of Eastern Europe." The advanced study of the
Talmud and its commentaries served as the focus of this institution. Its students—graduates of Etz Chaim Yeshiva or one of its European counterparts—studied traditional texts in a traditional way and in traditional
Jewish languages; neither practical rabbinical training nor any significant
concessions to the American environment were permitted to intrude.[102]

The creation of so traditional a school on American soil represented
something of a watershed. Just a few years before nobody would have imagined that America, the "unkosher land," could have supported such an institution; even the necessary rabbinic books, none of them printed in America, were difficult to procure. Still, the "America Torah enclave" that the
school's founders and Agudath ha-Rabbanim supporters envisaged did not
quite develop as planned. Repeatedly, during the early years of the twentieth century, students at the school publicly protested against rules that
deprived them of their meager stipends if they pursued secular studies. Intermittently between 1906 and 1908 the students even led well-publicized
strikes over curricular issues, demanding not only a broader array of courses
but also training "in the art of the sermon so that graduates might compete against the graduates of Schechter's Seminary." Thereafter, enrollments fell alarmingly until, as we shall see, the school was reorganized and
transformed on more inclusivist lines by Bernard Revel, who became its
president in 1915.[103]

By World War I, the exclusivist strategy of the Agudath ha-Rabbanim seemed doomed. The quixotic battle against the English language had been lost. Rabbi Isaac Elchanan Theological Seminary was failing. Most of the young men of East European background interested in the active rabbinate, including several whose parents were active in the Agudath ha-Rabbanim and one (Israel Levinthal) whose father was its president, had become students and alumni of the Jewish Theological Seminary. Nevertheless, what seemed at the time like a failure helped in the long run to bring about two highly significant results. First, the rabbis of the Agudath ha-Rabbanim broadened the spectrum of Orthodoxy, and, consequently, of American Judaism as a whole. Their exclusive definition of what constituted an Orthodox rabbi, their resistance to Americanization, and their desire to build, metaphorically, a protective wall around the Torah, an enclave where traditional Judaism would be safe from encroachments, however extreme these seemed at the time, laid the foundation on which later rabbis built fervent or Haredi Orthodoxy, the movement's rightmost wing. Second, the Agudath ha-Rabbanim contributed to what might be called the parting of the ways in American Judaism, the separation of Orthodox and Conservative Judaism into two distinct movements. Agudath ha-Rabbanim's efforts to severely narrow the definition of Orthodoxy, coupled with its support for a yeshiva without any of the modern trappings of the Jewish Theological Seminary, raised fundamental questions concerning Orthodoxy's boundaries—questions that remained unanswered for years as the fault line separating Orthodox from Conservative Judaism creaked and settled into place. The definition of Orthodoxy that eventually emerged was not nearly so exclusive as Agudath ha-Rabbanim would have liked, but the separation of Conservative from Orthodox Judaism, largely effected during the interwar years and completed after World War II, owed a considerable amount to the Agudath's rabbis' uncompromising stance. In this case, as so often in the world of religion, the margin helped to redefine the mainstream.

THE WORLD OF CLASSICAL REFORM JUDAISM
AND THE QUEST FOR A UNITED COMMUNITY

While Orthodox Judaism struggled to redefine itself, Reform Judaism, in the wake of the Pittsburgh Platform, consolidated. Having lost all hope of becoming Minhag Amerika, the Judaism practiced by all American Jews, Reform responded to the rapidly changing American Jewish situation by becoming increasingly exclusive. During this era, often known as the period of Classical Reform Judaism, Reform positioned itself as the religion of American Jews of German descent—somewhat misleadingly, since, as we have seen, some Jews of German descent had become decidedly anti-Reform. Reform temples nevertheless perceived themselves as citadels of "American Judaism," the antithesis of the unruly Yiddish-speaking Orthodoxy that Reform Jews associated with their immigrant coreligionists from Eastern Europe. Socially, culturally, economically, religiously, and even geographically, Central European Reform Jews and Eastern European Orthodox Jews stood at a considerable remove from one another, as if in two separate Jewish worlds. Yet however much they diverged during the era of mass immigration, these two wings of American Judaism also found opportunities to work together. As we shall see, this set the stage for improved communication and cooperation between them, and ensured that they did not completely split asunder.[104]

Numerous visual and auditory markers instantly distinguished Classical Reform Judaism from its Orthodox counterparts. In a Reform Temple, men and women sat together in mixed pews, the men bareheaded and without prayer shawls. Music filled the air, usually from an organ, and often from a mixed choir that included women and sometimes non-Jews as well. The prayer book, at least following the publication of the *Union Prayer Book* in 1895, opened from left to right (rather than from right to left, as traditional Hebrew prayer books do) and contained only minimal amounts of Hebrew; the bulk of the service was in English. Even on the Sabbath (when traditional Jews do not kindle fire) cigarette and cigar smoke permeated the corridors. In addition, food served at congregational functions did not follow the Jewish dietary laws; seafood was commonly eaten. Finally, the major service of the week was not held on Saturday morning, as among traditional Jews, but rather on Friday night or (less commonly) on Sunday morning, to accommodate worshippers who worked on Saturday.

Modernity dominated the agenda of Classical Reform Judaism. Its leading thinkers and preachers—men like Rabbis Kaufmann Kohler and Emil G. Hirsch (both married to daughters of David Einhorn)—addressed such topics as "The Mission of Israel and Its Application to Modern Times" and "Judaism and Modern Religion." Rabbi Joseph Krauskopf once delivered a sermon entitled "To-Day—Better Than Yesterday." Like their liberal Protestant counterparts, these rabbis gloried in Western culture, which they often communicated to their congregants, and most of them accepted the optimistic premises of evolutionary thought. They depicted the Judaism of earlier times as "primitive" (the Bible, according to the Pittsburgh Platform, reflected the "primitive ideas of its own age"), and they viewed their own Judaism as the highest and most advanced form of all. They also accepted the tenets of German biblical criticism, even where these seemed to undermine the traditional Jewish belief in "Torah from Sinai." Finally, they argued that moral conduct and social justice, rather than faith, laws, and ritual practices, formed the essence of Judaism. What the Lord requires of man, they declared, echoing the prophet Micah (6:8), was "Only to do justly, and to love mercy, and to walk humbly with thy God."[105]

Prophetic Judaism, as this emphasis on universalism and social justice came to be called, stimulated a wide range of political and communal activities on the part of Classical Reform rabbis. While influenced by social progressivism and parallel to the Protestant Social Gospel movement, the Jewish movement based itself on selected passages in Amos, Isaiah, and Micah, not on the teachings of Jesus and the Gospels. Using these as their proof-texts, Reform rabbis railed against such social evils as child labor and "white slavery," and they lent support to striking workers. In 1918, the Central Conference of American Rabbis, founded as a regional rabbinical organization in 1889 by Isaac Mayer Wise and soon transformed into the rabbinical arm of the Reform movement as a whole, adopted a fourteen-plank social justice platform. Akin to ones earlier issued by the (Protestant) Federal Council of Churches and the Catholic bishops, it advocated everything from the minimum wage and the eight-hour day to a redistribution of wealth.[106]

Calls to apply modern standards of "justice, equality, and fraternity" also rang out internally within Reform temples. In 1904, for example, Detroit's Temple Beth El abandoned its longstanding system of selling, renting, and assigning seats, which tended to bestow the choicest places on the wealthiest members, in favor of a system of free seating, under which all pews were unassigned. Pragmatic considerations—many new members and a shortage of seats motivated this decision, but externally it was trumpeted as a social justice reform: "In God's house all must be equal," the temple's rabbi, Leo Franklin, declared. "There must be no aristocracy and no snobocracy." In 1907, Rabbi Stephen S. Wise, one of the foremost advocates of social justice, extended this experiment when he opened his Free Synagogue in New York. There, free seating on a first-come, first-served basis represented a "token and symbol" of other freedoms: freedom from fixed dues, freedom of the pulpit, and freedom of opportunity for all—women included—to become temple members and officeholders. The values he espoused in his synagogue, Wise declared, were the values he proclaimed to society at large: "freedom, hospitality, inclusiveness, brotherhood [and] the leveling of the anti-religious bars of caste." Few congregations followed Wise's lead to the letter (especially with respect to dues), but through the twentieth century the idea that the synagogue should both advance social justice outwardly and reflect the ideals of freedom inwardly became widely accepted in American Judaism, influencing synagogues across the spectrum of Jewish life.[107]

Classical Reform Judaism's social justice initiatives, by promoting philanthropic contacts between wealthier "uptown" Jews and poorer "downtown" ones, broke down barriers between the two worlds of American Judaism; each began to learn more about the other. We have already seen how the sisterhoods of personal service, which started as a Reform initiative at Temple Emanu-El of New York and then spread more widely, introduced Reform Jewish women to "the needy and the distressed" in the immigrant community. Subsequently, Temple Emanu-El's brotherhood, in 1903, initiated a settlement house on the Lower East Side "for the purpose of moral and religious uplift" and to counter the "mendacious activity of numerous missionaries, who employ various seductive methods to evangelize Jewish children." The temple also hoped, discreetly, to spread the message of Reform Judaism among the immigrants, although it understood that in order to succeed it would have to "proceed with delicate caution, no hint of our purpose to be given lest they, whom we are to reach, elude our quest."[108]

Over time, Reform Jewish leaders became less condescending and paternalistic in their social justice initiatives, and more accepting of religious and cultural differences. At Temple Emanu-El, they heard Rabbi Judah L. Magnes berate them for having too little social contact with "the living Jewish people . . . the bulk and body of the Jewish masses, the poor as well as the rich, the lowly as well as the learned, the immigrant as well as the native." At the Judaeans, an elite New York association formed in 1897 "for the purpose of promoting and furthering the intellectual and spiritual interests of Jews," descendants of German Jews interacted as equals with a select group of East European Jews who had risen in the professions. At the patrician-dominated American Jewish Committee, established in 1906 "to prevent infringement of the civil and religious rights of Jews, and to alleviate the consequences of persecution," three delegates of East European background mingled with the other founders. Two years earlier, the Central Conference of American Rabbis had invited Rabbi William Rosenau of Baltimore, a friend of many East European Jews, to lecture on "what the immigrant Jew can give to us."[109]

A growing number of Jews from East European background were even accepted into the Reform rabbinical program at Hebrew Union College.

Some 70 percent of its students from 1904–29 were of East European descent, according to one survey; 28 percent had themselves been born in Eastern Europe.[110] For many of these students, who came from poor households, this represented a life-changing opportunity. The Jewish Theological Seminary, which might have been closer to some of them religiously, insisted that rabbinical students already be college graduates, a requirement that put the school beyond the reach of many poverty-stricken immigrant youngsters. By contrast, Hebrew Union College accepted students beginning at high school age, supplied them with a free college education at the University of Cincinnati, and also assisted them with board and lodging. Naturally, the young East European Jewish students were transformed by their immersion in the world of Reform Judaism, but the change was by no means theirs alone. The cultural encounter transformed Reform Judaism as well, and it helped the two worlds of American Judaism to become better acquainted with each other.

The demands of patriotism also helped to acquaint the two worlds of American Judaism with each other. At least as early as Mordecai Noah, American Jews had linked their own destiny to that of the United States so as to legitimate their place in America and to demonstrate their sense of belonging. This "cult of synthesis," as it has been called, reached new heights toward the end of the nineteenth century, partly in response to growing Jewish insecurity and partly in an effort to subvert Protestant efforts to identify Americanism squarely with Christianity.[111] While evangelical leaders spoke of adding a "Christian Amendment" to the U.S. Constitution, Jews insisted that they, in fact, had starred in all of the central roles of American history: from the secret Jews in the Spanish Court who supposedly funded Christopher Columbus, to the "Jews" who accompanied him, to the Jewish "pilgrim fathers" who fought for religious freedom in New Amsterdam, to the patriotic Jewish heroes who contributed financially to the success of the American Revolution, to the "loyal and faithful [Jewish] citizens" who "shared willingly in all the trials our country has passed through . . . until the present time." All major movements and ideologies within American Judaism insisted that Americanism and Judaism reinforced each other, and annually, on days like Thanksgiving, this message was reinforced, as if in an effort to de-Christianize America's cultural boundaries so as to render Jews more welcome. Sabato Morais, for example, once told his Orthodox congregants that "with the spangled banner of liberty in one hand, and the law of Horeb in the other, we will continue faithful citizens of this glorious republic, and constant adorers of the living God." The noted Jewish educator Henry Leipziger, meanwhile, assured Reform Jews that the "Jewish form of government" was really "republican" and that "free America" was the place where "the dreams of the prophets of old" would be realized.

East European immigrants took their cue from this rhetoric and obediently echoed it. At the celebration of the centennial of George Washington's inauguration in 1889, for example, Chief Rabbi Jacob Joseph published a proclamation and prayer in which he noted the first president's respect for "our holy Torah" and depicted Jews as eager "to become like other citizens of the country." Three years later, at the celebration of the four hundredth anniversary of Christopher Columbus's voyage, he again spoke out, expressing gratitude not only for Columbus, whom he amusingly described as "the first man in the New World," but also for the two Jews who, he declared, accompanied him on his voyage. The early twentieth-century bookplate of Peter Wiernik, the Orthodox editor-in-chief of the well-known New York Yiddish daily *Jewish Morning Journal,* raised this "cult of synthesis" to a symbolic level. Designed by Joseph B. Abrahams, longtime secretary of the Jewish Theological Seminary, the bookplate depicts an open Torah ark with an American flag serving as the sacred traditional curtain *(parochet)* before it. Judaism in this portrayal forms the core of Jewish identity, while Americanism provides its outer protective garb. Symbolically and rhetorically, then, the two worlds of American Jewry joined in the optimistic hope that they could accomplish what Jews had not successfully achieved anywhere else in the diaspora. Instead of having to choose between competing national and religious allegiances—the great Enlightenment dilemma—they could be both American and Jewish, their dual identities complementing and mutually enhancing each other, much like the Torah and its protective curtain.

This same optimistic sense of what could be accomplished in America propelled Jews into a series of feverish political activities that allied Central and East European Jews, further narrowing the chasm between them. For example, the infamous 1903 Kishinev pogrom in Russia that saw 47 Jews killed and 424 wounded, and 700 houses burned and 600 looted, aroused protests from American Jews across the religious spectrum, along with numerous Christians, and united Jews in urgent political and humanitarian measures aimed at ameliorating the suffering of their oppressed brethren. At least in their own eyes, America's Jews emerged during this crisis to stand at the very center of world Jewish life—a signal of what they could accomplish through cooperation. *The Voice of America on Kishineff* (1904), the commemorative volume that recorded the meetings, sermons, resolutions,

The bookplate of journalist Peter
Wiernik (1865–1936) designed by
Joseph B. Abrahams. Wiernik
suggests that the Torah (Judaism) lies
at the core of his identity, while
America (the flag) forms its outer
protective curtain. The mailbox at the
bottom left alludes to Wiernik's
signature column, known as
Der Brief Kasten (The letter box).
Peter Wiernik and Bertha Wiernik
Collection, Box 12/21, Yeshiva
University Archives.

editorials, relief measures, and petitions that responded to the pogrom, also
served as an unmistakable statement to communities abroad that the Jews
of the United States had become a powerful force, one that they needed to
reckon with.[112]

The prolonged campaign to abrogate America's 1832 treaty of commerce
with Russia, where Jewish tourists and even visiting American Jewish dignitaries faced discrimination on religious grounds, promoted some of these
same cooperative efforts. Leaders of the campaign believed that Russia,
were it compelled to treat foreign Jews "upon a basis of equality," would
soon have to treat its own Jews the same way. They also sought to "punish"

the Russian regime for mistreating its Jewish subjects. Working behind the
scenes, and deftly exploiting the sinking political fortunes of President William Howard Taft, a united American Jewish community eventually succeeded in its goal. Termination of the treaty was announced on December
18, 1911.[113]

The long political battle to keep America's doors open to immigrants
provided yet another cause that brought together the two worlds of American Jewry. Although some Jews in the nineteenth century advocated
restrictions against immigrants, when it came to victims of persecution,
twentieth-century Jews remained stalwart in their commitment to the idea
of America as an immigrant haven. Jewish leaders, among them prominent
Reform Jews, testified before Congress in spirited defense of Jewish immigration from Eastern Europe, and they lobbied intensely behind the scenes
to put off and defeat laws aimed at restricting the immigrant flow, or, at the
very least, to exempt victims of religious persecution from their provisions.
Ultimately, as we shall see, the battle was lost. In 1917, Congress mandated
a literacy test for new immigrants, and subsequently it imposed and then
tightened highly restrictive anti-immigrant quotas that reduced Jewish immigration by more than 80 percent. Even in defeat, however, Central and
Eastern European Jews had the satisfaction of knowing that they had
worked hand in hand in support of a common aim. Religious and cultural
differences had not prevented them from speaking with one voice on an issue of shared communal concern.[114]

The boldest effort of all to bring the many segments of the Jewish community together built on political ties but extended far beyond them. On February 27, 1909, in response to New York City police commissioner Theodore
A. Bingham's charge (quickly disproved and retracted) that the "Hebrew
race" produced "perhaps half" of the city's criminals, and in an effort to
combat a wide range of social and religious ills within the city's Jewish community, three hundred delegates representing every element within Jewish
life met to form what became known, employing a Hebrew word of great
historical resonance, as the Kehillah—the organized Jewish community of
New York. The new organization combined elements of traditional Euro-
pean-Jewish communal structure with American-style Progressive-era
democracy. The Kehillah's sponsors, its historian explains, "envisioned a
democratically governed polity which would unite the city's multifarious
Jewish population, harness the group's intellectual and material resources,
and build a model ethnic community"—based, of course, on the principle
of voluntarism and without any formal ties to the state. Disagreements

between Orthodox Jews, Reform Jews, and anti-religious socialists nearly wrecked the Kehillah before it began. But thanks to the able leadership and chameleon-like qualities of Judah Magnes—who was, at one and the same time, trained in the Classical Reform tradition, enchanted by Orthodoxy, related to New York's best Jewish families, and sympathetic both to Zionism and to Socialism—an uneasy harmony prevailed. The elected twenty-five-member Kehillah executive board, although dominated by Central European patricians, represented a surprisingly wide range of community figures, including such East Europeans as Harry Fischel and Sender Jarmulowsky. Together, these leaders struggled mightily to contend with a number of daunting communal problems, including the supervision of kosher food and the chaotic condition of Jewish education. By promising to restore "to the Rabbis their authority in matters affecting Judaism as a religion," they succeeded in winning cooperation even from some distinguished members of the Agudath ha-Rabbanim, notably Rabbi Moses Z. Margolies. But though the Kehillah brought together "the most varied assemblage of Jews that can be imagined" and achieved several notable successes, including the creation of a vibrant and pioneering Bureau of Jewish Education, its reach quickly exceeded its grasp. Like many boldly conceived Progressive-era projects, it suffered from financial, organizational, and political problems, and it barely survived World War I; by 1922 it was dead.[115] Still, its dream of uniting and organizing Jews into a cohesive internally pluralistic community lived on. Even if forever unrealized, the dream helps to explain why, for all of their seemingly intractable disagreements, different wings of American Judaism never succumbed to the temptation to separate and break away. A deep-seated belief in the unity of the Jewish people held the perennial threat of communal schism in check.

ZIONISM

The movement that became known as Zionism threatened, periodically, to undermine that belief. Calls to establish a Jewish state in Palestine, partly as a haven for persecuted Jews and partly as a means of revitalizing Jewish life around the world, began to gather momentum in America, as we have seen, during the last third of the nineteenth century, coincident with the rise of antisemitism. Only the existence of a permanent home for the Jews, supporters believed, could solve the problems posed by Jews' minority status and thereby bring the persecution of Jews to an end. Young people like Emma Lazarus, Richard Gottheil, Judah Magnes, and Stephen S. Wise strongly associated themselves with this new movement, and it also attracted support from the venerable Reform rabbi Bernhard Felsenthal, who viewed Zionism both as an antidote to assimilation and as "the best method and the most rational way" to help the suffering Jewish masses whom no Western countries seemed eager to admit.[116]

Many East European Jews, even though they themselves had elected to immigrate to New York rather than to Jerusalem, sympathized with Zionism's goals. Adam Rosenberg, a German Orthodox lawyer who immigrated to America about 1886, encouraged these immigrants to purchase land in Palestine through the organization Shavei Zion ("Returning to Zion"), which he headed. Chief Rabbi Jacob Joseph and many of the leaders of the Agudath ha-Rabbanim were also avowed Zionist sympathizers. For all this, the Federation of American Zionists, founded in 1898, and other Zionist clubs and fraternities in America remained small and disorganized. Exuberant converts may have believed, with Henrietta Szold, that the future of American Jewry depended on the nationalist and cultural awakening that Zionism promised to advance, and that "if not Zionism then nothing —then extinction for the Jew." But many East European Jews viewed Zionism in somewhat more prosaic terms, as a response to antisemitism and an extension of the age-old Jewish longing to return to Zion. Either way, the movement provided its supporters with a unifying ideal, a future-oriented goal, and, paradoxically, a mission that for all of its nationalist eloquence actually ended up hastening Americanization, as Zion became for many Jews a utopian extension of the American dream.[117]

As for Reform Jews, their commitment to universalism, their sense of patriotism, and their privileging of religion over peoplehood led most of them to view Zionism as anathema, a negation of all that Jewish emancipation and enlightenment stood for. Notwithstanding the support that some individual Reform rabbis accorded the movement, the Pittsburgh Platform of 1885 forswore Zionism, and in 1898, a resolution of the Union of American Hebrew Congregations spelled out the Reform anti-Zionist position in detail: "We are unalterably opposed to political Zionism. The Jews are not a nation, but a religious community. Zion was a precious possession of the past. . . . As such it is a holy memory, but it is not our hope of the future. America is our Zion. Here in the home of religious liberty, we have aided in founding this new Zion, the fruition of the beginning laid in the old. The mission of Judaism is spiritual, not political. Its aim is not to establish a state, but to spread the truths of religion and humanity throughout the world."[118] One synagogue, San Francisco's Reform Congregation

Sherith Israel, so sought to emphasize the idea of America as "our Zion" that it installed a stained-glass window in 1904 which reinterpreted a biblical scene from the Book of Exodus to this end. According to its revised version, Moses, holding the two tablets of stone containing the Ten Commandments, descended from El Capitan straight into California's Yosemite Valley—the New Promised Land![119]

For years, no issue in Jewish life proved as divisive as Zionism. In 1907, the resignation of three pro-Zionist members of the Hebrew Union College faculty—brought about, allegedly, on ideological grounds—sparked a nationwide Jewish debate concerning Zionism and freedom of expression. Pettier issues of personality and collegiality turned out to have factored significantly in the resignations, but Hebrew Union College president Kaufmann Kohler made clear amid the ensuing uproar that the teachings of Zionism, in his view, held no place in a seminary committed to Reform Judaism. Zionist ideas, he charged, were "twisting and distorting the grand universal teachings of the prophets and sages of Israel." At the Jewish Theological Seminary, Solomon Schechter memorably defended Zionism "as the great bulwark against assimilation," yet many of his board members at the time, including the great Jewish philanthropist Jacob Schiff, vigorously disagreed, as did his "colleague and friend" Cyrus Adler. Indeed, arguments over Zionism raged throughout Jewish life for decades into the twentieth century, dividing organizations and even families. Over time, the conversion of several notable Reform rabbis and lay leaders to the cause produced some ideological reconciliation. American Zionists, for example, adapted Reform Jewish rhetoric concerning the Jewish "mission" to improve the world and argued that this very mission could best be accomplished by Jews living in a state of their own who would spread Israel's message to the far corners of the earth. Reform Zionists also helped to redefine Zionism in staunchly American terms, as a burden voluntarily assumed by Jews to help their persecuted brethren overseas find a home, thereby warding off charges that the movement promoted dual loyalty.[120]

Yet Zionism became a significant force in American Jewish life only on the eve of World War I, just as the problems facing Europe's Jews multiplied and immigration restrictions limited the chances that America's "golden door" would open wide enough to admit even a fraction of those clamoring to get in. The conversion of the nationally famous "people's lawyer" Louis Brandeis to Zionism and his subsequent promotion to the chairmanship of the Provisional Executive Committee for General Zionist Affairs in 1914 served as a prime catalyst for Zionism's growth. "Men! Money! Discipline!"

Moses descending from Yosemite's El Capitan into California's
Yosemite Valley, holding the Ten Commandments.
From a 1904 stained-glass window at Congregation Sherith Israel,
San Francisco. Ben Ailes Photography.

Brandeis famously demanded, and in good Progressive fashion he promoted
the virtues of organizational efficiency. Thanks to his persona, mystique,
charm, prestige, fluency, sincerity, and passion—the thrill of being part of
a movement that he headed—Zionism's ranks and treasury swelled as never
before. The fact that a person of his stature stamped Zionism with his seal
of approval also gave the movement instant legitimacy—the more so once
he became, in 1916, America's first Jewish Supreme Court justice. In addition, his conversion set off something of a chain reaction, bringing to Zionism a coterie of other distinguished American Jews who, like himself, were
far removed from Jewish religious life (Brandeis was an agnostic secularist)
and who found in Zionism a way of synthesizing their Progressive ideals
with their hitherto somewhat latent Jewish attachments. Zionism became,

in effect, a religion for these secular Jews—a form of civil religion, to be sure, but one that developed, over time, transcendent goals, sacred symbols, revered texts, holy days, pilgrimages, doctrinal debates, and even prophets and priests. Its central mission was to create what one of Brandeis' associates described as a "model state in the Holy Land—freed from the economic wrongs, the social injustices and the greed of modern-day industrialism." Drawing on American experience, taking advantage of the latest in social, economic, and political thinking, and conforming to prophetic teachings of justice, this utopian vision offered Jews who had become disenchanted with the traditional beliefs, rituals, and practices of Judaism a sacred task that both linked them to other Jews and infused their own personal lives with meaning—the lofty satisfaction that comes from pursuing work of transcendent importance. Zionism thus tapped precisely the same kind of religious energy that motivated those who embarked on other great American religious missions, from the Puritans' "errand into the wilderness" to their descendants' "errand to the world." It also mirrored in more ways than anyone recognized at the time the social justice ideals of Classical Reform Judaism and the socialist goals of the Jewish labor movement, with the important added ingredient of Jewish nationalism.[121]

Many of the Zionist masses, and especially the religious Zionists, did not view Zionism as the essence of their faith, but rather, in Schechter's term, as a "cherished dream."[122] For them, Zionism was an extension of Jewish messianism: it promised not only to revitalize the Jews as a people but also to secure them a better future. They were interested less in social engineering than in strengthening the fabric of Jewish life at home and abroad. A series of new synagogues established in the early twentieth century made it possible for those committed to these goals to worship and commune together as religious Zionists; they included synagogues named Chovevei Zion ("Lovers of Zion"), Herzl, Tel Abiv [*sic*], and Petach Tikvah. The Religious Zionist organization known as Mizrachi, which was established in Vilna in 1902 and held its first national convention in America in 1914, provided religious Zionists with an institutional home. Its aims were summed up in its motto: "The land of Israel for the people of Israel according to the Torah of Israel." It promoted the idea that the Torah should serve as a "spiritual center" for Zionism, and it attempted to synthesize the new movement with traditional Judaism.[123]

However Zionism was viewed—and from the beginning it meant different things to different people—it served as a prime leavening agent in twentieth-century American Judaism, affecting everything from education and culture to philanthropy and politics. For all of the divisiveness and controversy that the movement engendered, its broad inclusiveness and ideological diversity, coupled with its captivating solution to the steadily worsening problems of Europe's Jews, made Zionism the twentieth century's greatest Jewish success story. World War I in all its devastation set the stage for that success and marked a turning point in the history of American Judaism as well.

The American Jewish community on the eve of World War I looked dramatically different from when Max Cohen, thirty-five years earlier, had posed the "great question" of whether American Judaism "would continue God's work or cease to be." The community had grown more than tenfold since then, owing largely to East European Jewish immigration, and was now the world's next-to-largest Jewish community, second only to Russia. On account of the religious awakening that young native-born Jews like Cohen had stimulated, it was also a far stronger community, rich with cultural and institutional resources that had not previously existed. Books of international significance flowed from the country's Jewish presses; New York, Cincinnati, and Washington, D.C., boasted world-class Jewish libraries; Jewish scholarship had begun to proliferate; and Jewish education at all levels—for young and old, male and female alike—received unprecedented amounts of community attention.

American Judaism on the eve of World War I spanned the widest imaginable spectrum, from fervently Orthodox to Classical Reform, along with a great many Jews who professed no faith at all but still cared deeply about the life and destiny of the Jewish people. The two great religious "parties" within American Judaism—one centered institutionally in New York, the other in Cincinnati—each boasted its own training seminary, congregational union, and rabbinical association. Fervently Orthodox Jews, hardly visible back in 1879, were now sufficiently numerous to have organized a rabbinical organization of their own. Meanwhile, even the community's ideological emphases had changed from the 1870s, tending over time toward greater particularism as opposed to the earlier universalism; toward a heightened sense of Jewish peoplehood as opposed to the former stress on Judaism as a faith; toward a new emphasis on the spiritual and emotional aspects of Judaism as opposed to the former emphasis on rationalism; and toward the goal of a Jewish homeland as opposed to the "Zion-in-America" ideology that had predominated. Jews of Central European descent continued to hold disproportionate amounts of power within the American Jewish community, and Reform Judaism, modeling itself on Mainline Protestantism, still viewed itself as the ruling establishment's faith. But with almost 85 percent of the American Jewish community estimated to be East European in origin, the future clearly belonged to them.[124]

A "great question" remained to be answered on the eve of World War I, but it was no longer whether American Judaism would "continue" or "cease to be." That issue, for the time being, had been resolved. Instead, it was the question of what the nature of American Judaism would be, especially with the children of East European immigrants coming of age and beginning to make religious choices for themselves.

An Anxious Subculture

THE GREAT WAR

"The campaign to raise $5 million in New York for Jewish war relief and welfare work in the army and navy came to a triumphant close yesterday," the *New York Times* reported on December 16, 1917. Led by American Jewry's premier lay leader and philanthropist, Jacob Schiff, the campaign united the city's Jews as never before. "Jews of all ranks and classes; Jews from Wall Street banking houses and Fifth Avenue mansions . . . Jews from the East Side sweat shops and East Side tenements"; Orthodox, Reform, secular, and socialist Jews; men, women, children, even the indigents of the Hebrew Orphan Asylum—all joined forces under the slogan "New York will do its duty," and in a remarkable two-week campaign they collected "a sum equal to that which, in the previous year, had been given by the Jews of the whole United States." They also demonstrated New York Jewry's heightened significance on the world Jewish stage. This was graphically illustrated by a map bound into the New York *Jewish Communal Register* of 1918, which showed Germany, Great Britain, South America, Holland, Palestine, France, Canada, Italy, Switzerland, and Belgium, all scaled according to the size of their Jewish communities and all resting comfortably within the confines of New York City. With a Jewish population of 1.5 million, the map showed, the city alone was home to more Jews than all of those other lands combined.[1]

American Jews living outside of New York likewise raised unprecedented sums for their suffering kinfolk in war-torn Europe—all told, $63 million was collected between 1914 and 1924. Philanthropy, in a sense, became the

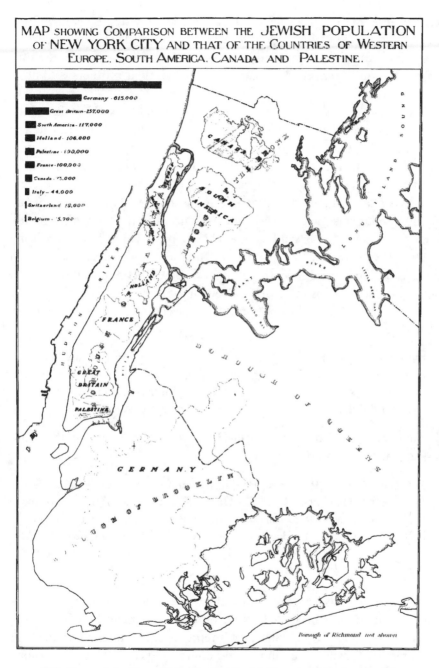

MAP SHOWING COMPARISON BETWEEN THE JEWISH POPULATION OF NEW YORK CITY AND THAT OF THE COUNTRIES OF WESTERN EUROPE, SOUTH AMERICA, CANADA AND PALESTINE.

Germany - 615,000
Great Britain - 257,000
South America - 117,000
Holland - 106,000
Palestine - 100,000
France - 100,000
Canada - 75,000
Italy - 44,000
Switzerland - 19,000
Belgium - 5,000

Borough of Richmond not shown

This map, originally published in the *Jewish Communal Register* (1918), graphically illustrates that the Jewish population of New York City had come to exceed that of Western Europe, South America, and Palestine combined. Collection of the author.

civil religion of American Jews during these bleak years. By contributing generously to feed, clothe, and house the suffering Jews of Europe and Palestine, American Jews found a collective mission—a way, in Schiff's words, to "prove ourselves Jews, prove ourselves their brothers, and postpone the end."[2]

The Great War, as it was called, broke out around the saddest day of the Jewish calendar, the Fast of Tisha B'Av, commemorating the destruction of the ancient Temple in Jerusalem, and unleashed what Jews of the time considered to be the "darkest tragedy of our race"—one rabbi, little anticipating that still worse lay ahead, eerily described it as a "holocaust of misery."[3] Over 1.5 million Jews were among the sufferers, including relatives, friends, and former neighbors of Jews who now lived in the United States. Newspaper reports, especially in the Yiddish press, carried the grim story, and it was subsequently preserved in the *American Jewish Year Book,* which chronicled the war's devastating impact on Jewish communities on both sides of the struggle, listing a series of Jewish towns as having been "partially or wholly destroyed" by invading armies. The section on Russia, for example, noted the following:

> SEPTEMBER 25 [1914]. Kalish: Seven hundred and fifty houses, mostly Jewish, burnt.—Dzevitza (Radom): Jewish quarter and synagogue burnt.—OCTOBER 16. Druskeniki burnt.— . . . [November] 25. Plotzk: Jewish townlet, and Blony and Bakalarzevo reported ruined by invaders. . . .

The news reported from Austria-Hungary, which fought on the other side of the war, was no better:

> NOVEMBER 6 [1914]. Podheitze, Husiatyn, and Temboole: Galician Jewish townlets burnt in course of battle.—Halicz: The Jewish quarter burnt by retreating Austrians.—13. Jewish quarters of Balshevitzi and Bolshabi, Galicia, burnt by Austrians.—27. Belsitz and Burgatch, Jewish townlets, Galicia, almost completely destroyed.—Brod: Fire set to town; twelve Jews and three hundred houses burnt.[4]

In the face of this tragedy, and with America still firmly pledged to neutrality in the European struggle, three different American Jewish relief organizations competed for funds, each representing a different segment of the American Jewish community and committed to a different ideology and worldview. The American Jewish Relief Committee, organized by the American Jewish Committee and chaired by its president, Louis Marshall, represented the community elite, most of them American born, of Central

European descent, and connected to Reform Judaism. The Central Committee for the Relief of Jews Suffering Through the War, organized by the Union of Orthodox Jewish Congregations, represented religious Jews outside of the Reform orbit, most of them East European in origin. The Jewish People's Relief Committee of America, organized by trade union leaders and East European–born Jewish socialists, represented "persons who can afford to give only very small amounts," the immigrant Jewish masses. All three of these organizations, for all of their social, economic, political, and religious differences, shared the same overriding goal: "to join hands in the work of immediate help and relief of the sufferers." To this end, and drawing on experiments in cooperation from the prewar period, they agreed to collect contributions from their respective constituencies, to pool the funds, and collectively dispense them through the organization that became the American Jewish Joint Distribution Committee (the "Joint"), established to apportion and send abroad money and supplies for Jewish war relief. Capitalists and socialists, Reform rabbis and Orthodox ones, Jews of widely different backgrounds and persuasions, including three women, all sat together at the Joint's meetings, reaching most decisions by consensus and others by majority vote. In so doing, they established a pattern of intra-communal cooperation that would soon reach beyond the realm of philanthropy and endure for many decades.[5]

Many of the leaders who cooperated at the Joint hoped initially that America would remain neutral in the European conflict. Some, like Jacob Schiff, retained a strong affinity for their old German homeland; in 1914, Schiff declared himself "pro-German," though not "anti-English." Others, German and Russian Jews alike, believed that the war justly punished Russia for the mistreatment of its Jewish subjects. "The bleeding of Russia rejoices my heart," the Yiddish proletarian poet Morris Rosenfeld sang out in 1915, "may the Devil do to her / What she did unto me." Still others, like the settlement house leader Lillian Wald, deeply believed in pacifism. As the war proceeded, however, German militarism, the collapse of the tsarist regime in March 1917 (an event described by some Jews as "a miracle" and widely celebrated a few weeks later at Passover seders across the nation), and, above all, America's declaration of war on April 6, 1917, turned the tide. Most leading Jews, including Schiff and a recent convert from pacifism, Rabbi Stephen S. Wise, spoke out in support of the war; numbers of German Jews (like their non-Jewish counterparts) Anglicized their names; and thousands of military-age Jews, immigrants and their children conspicuous among them, volunteered to fight. "This is a righteous war," Rabbi Mordecai

M. Kaplan of the Jewish Theological Seminary declared to a group of young Jews gathered at the Young Men's Hebrew Association on June 28, 1917. "The ideal for which we are fighting is to suppress the great bully and outlaw among the nations—the German government. . . . As Jews . . . we owe it to America to stand by her in her hour of trial." The few notable dissenters against America's entry into the war, like the unbowed pacifist Rabbi Judah L. Magnes and the Germanophile professor of Jewish history at Hebrew Union College, Gotthard Deutsch, found themselves marginalized, even persecuted.[6]

As in the Civil War, the age and sex distribution of the American Jewish community, skewed by immigration, meant that Jews contributed disproportionately to the war effort. They constituted 3.3 percent of the population and furnished 4 to 5 percent of its armed forces—200,000 to 250,000 Jewish soldiers and sailors in all. To thwart those who doubted their patriotism, Jews also carefully documented their contributions. Records were kept concerning every Jew in the military; an issue of the *American Jewish Year Book* painstakingly listed some fifteen hundred Jewish commissioned officers by name; and Jewish newspapers memorialized the thirty-five hundred American Jews who died in the struggle.[7]

The central communal challenge posed by the thousands of Jews in uniform, however, was a religious one: how to meet the diverse spiritual and welfare needs of American Jewish soldiers under wartime conditions. Among Protestant soldiers, these needs were met by the interdenominational Young Men's Christian Association, and among Catholics, by the Knights of Columbus. Anticipating a tripartite religious model that would later become commonplace in American society, the military now looked for a Jewish organization to stand alongside these Protestant and Catholic ones. Since existing organizations, like B'nai B'rith, were not geared to provide religious services and could not, in any case, command wall-to-wall support, a new body had to be created: the Jewish Welfare Board (JWB). Like the Joint, it reflected a once unimaginable level of intra-religious cooperation among American Jews, a further demonstration of how the exigencies of war forced leaders of radically different persuasions to work together.[8]

The JWB, more than any previous Jewish organization, imagined American Judaism to consist of "three distinct wings," which it described as "so-called Orthodox, Conservative, and Reform Jews." Respectful of all of these Jews, but aware that the military recognized only one Judaism, it brought together representatives of each "wing" to formulate a unified military prayer book (*Abridged Prayer Book for Jews in the Army and Navy of the*

United States [1917]), funded in part by the U.S. government. While the Orthodox found the final product inappropriately short and the Reform complained that it did "not reflect our particular theology," the widely distributed compromise prayer book, through its variant readings, taught Jews much about one another, introducing soldiers to diverse liturgies and to modes of Jewish worship that some had never before encountered.[9]

Perhaps no attempt to satisfy fourteen different national Jewish bodies, ranging from the Orthodox Agudath ha-Rabbanim to the Reform Central Conference of American Rabbis, could have been wholly successful. After various protests, Orthodox and Reform prayer books were made available, in place of the *Abridged Prayer Book,* to selected soldiers who requested them. But in this and everything else that it did the JWB prudently set "the morale of the Jewish soldiers" as its highest goal and declared itself Jewishly nonpartisan, committed to "no special -ism (except Judaism)" and permitting "none to be preached." Reporting on its work, it described how it sought to meet the religious needs of Jewish soldiers of every kind, "as these needs are . . . ascertained." "For Jews desiring an orthodox service it promotes orthodox services. For sons of Reform Jews it supplies reform services with the Union Prayer Book. For the preponderating group of soldiers of orthodox Jewish families, whose requirements are best met by what is called Conservative Judaism, appropriate services are conducted accordingly. Without standardizing any doctrine of its own, the Welfare Board endorses all degrees of doctrine, if soldiers of Jewish faith uphold them."[10]

The fact that the "preponderating group of soldiers" chose to attend Conservative services—a mixture of the traditional Hebrew liturgy, selected English readings, and an English-language sermon—proved, as we shall see, to be a harbinger of the future. For the next fifty years, thanks largely to Americanizing East European Jews and their children, Conservative Judaism would grow faster than any other American Jewish religious movement. At the same time, wartime conditions also introduced soldiers to other Jewish movements and practices, such as a "common Jewish service" for Passover, celebrated in France by three hundred frontline Jewish soldiers both "Orthodox and Reform"; and a weekday service "on the occasion of the anniversary of some departed relative of a soldier." Not all Jews participated, of course. Some Jewish chaplains complained about "camouflage Jews . . . who disclaim their Jewish origin" and about "the unwillingness of the assimilated Jew, especially of officer rank, to identify himself with [the] Jewish cause." The armed forces, just as it had back in the Civil War, constituted a microcosm of the American Jewish community in all of its pluralistic diversity. The "most striking aspect" of the JWB's work, however, at least in its own eyes, was "its unifying influence on Jewish communal life": the fact that "men and women representing every variety of Jewish opinion are found working together amicably and eagerly . . . theological differences are being laid aside, [and] class distinctions are being ignored."[11]

AT HOME IN AMERICA?

"This morning at 6 A.M. (New York Time)," Mordecai Kaplan recorded in his diary on November 11, 1918, "the Great World War came to an end." Even as he joined in the "general rejoicing," however, the ever-astute rabbi-scholar was filled with apprehension. "In place of wars of nations," he feared, "we shall now have wars of classes." "Social Revolution," he confided two months later, "is in the air nowadays." The contradictory feelings expressed by Kaplan—celebration on the one hand, trepidation on the other—anticipated the great paradox of the interwar years. There was much to be joyful about. Jews numbered among the many immigrants and their children who benefited from new opportunities in higher education and from the burst of wartime prosperity and postwar investment. As a consequence, they bounded into the broad middle class, where they worked in "white-collar" positions as professionals, clerks, shopkeepers, and salesmen and lived in new and better neighborhoods reflective of their improved economic circumstances. A few East European Jews, like Harry Fischel, even became millionaires. Only a minority remained wage laborers. The Jewish community also became increasingly native-born during the interwar years. American-born children of immigrants came to outnumber their parents during the 1930s, with the result that the majority of the American Jewish population, for the first time in more than a century, was not born abroad. Finally, American Jews came increasingly to feel "at home" in America during these years. Those born or raised in the country, and especially those who had served in the war, developed an American consciousness and identity; they came to feel "equally American and Jewish."[12]

Yet, simultaneously, American Jews also had much cause for apprehension. In response to the atmosphere of social revolution that Kaplan sensed, fear gripped many Americans: they lashed out at immigrants, "Bolsheviks," and those seen not to conform. Nativism, xenophobia, racism, anti-Catholicism, antisemitism—all characterized the "tribal twenties." Even Jews whose families had lived in the country for generations felt prejudice's sting. The 1930s added economic depression to this scalding brew, exacerbating social tensions still further. With Hitler rising in Germany and with domestic anti-semites like Father Charles Coughlin ranting on America's airwaves, Jews had good reason to be nervous. However much they personally felt at home in America, did America feel at home with them?[13]

The answer was by no means clear. Already in the immediate years following World War I attacks on radicals and immigrants filled Jews with foreboding. A small but disproportionate number of highly visible Jews stood among the avowed radicals who struck terror into the hearts of many Americans during the Red Scare of 1919–20; some were subsequently deported. "It is impossible to state whether or not these persons still adhere to the Jewish faith," explained Attorney General A. Mitchell Palmer in a private letter to the Jewish leader Simon Wolf, "for previous investigations by the [Justice] department have shown that many . . . while previously members of the Jewish faith, have renounced that faith and are at the present time in no way connected with any religion." Still, he and others classified them as "Russian Jews." Jews also figured disproportionately among the much-feared Bolsheviks who had seized power in Russia, and, it was alleged (not without reason) looked to provoke class struggle in the United States as well. Generalizing from the few to the many, undiscerning Americans perniciously concluded that because some radicals and Bolsheviks were Jews, all Jews were radicals and Bolsheviks.[14]

Immigration restrictions that sought to restore the nation's ethnic mix to its nineteenth-century white Protestant character also aimed directly (though by no means exclusively) at Jews. The House Committee on Immigration received a report prepared by Wilbur J. Carr, the director of the Consular Service, and approved by the secretary of state, that described Jews who desired to migrate to the United States as being, among other things, "undesirable," "of low physical and mental standards," "filthy," "un-American," and "often dangerous in their habits." Resulting legislation never mentioned Jews, and it restricted other "undesirable" immigrants like Italians and Slavs no less stringently, while Asians were barred entirely. "Chauvinistic nationalism is rampant," Louis Marshall, the foremost American Jewish leader of his day, recognized. "The hatred of everything foreign has become an obsession."[15]

The National Origins Immigration (Johnson-Reed) Act of 1924, strengthening an "emergency" measure passed three years earlier, confirmed Marshall's worst fears. It imposed country-by-country quotas set at 2 percent of each nation's contribution to the 1890 population of the United States —this in a vain attempt to restore America's ethnic make-up to what it had supposedly been before the bulk of the "new immigrants" had arrived. As a result, the legislation hit Jews especially hard. A rabbinic plea for those "victims of political oppression or religious persecution [who] come hither seeking an opportunity to live their lives . . . in freedom and under equal laws" fell on deaf ears. Over the next decade (1925–34), an average of only 8,270 Jews were annually admitted into the country, less than 7 percent of those welcomed when Jewish immigration stood at its peak. These draconian limitations caused great hardship, not just to Jewish victims of persecution but also to those who sought to bring their extended family members into the United States. Even parents, siblings, and grown children were compelled to await a scarce quota number. Later, when America faced economic crisis, the already reduced immigration flow was further limited by strict administrative measures, so that very few immigrants were admitted even from relatively high-quota countries such as Germany. As a result, when Jews most needed refuge, following Adolf Hitler's ascension to power in 1933, they found America's doors virtually barred.[16]

The debate over immigration took place against the background of heightened antisemitism in America, a development that further shook the Jewish community's confidence and strengthened its sense of unease and apartness. Anti-Jewish hatred had waxed and waned periodically in America since the seventeenth century, rising to a particular peak during the Civil War. It then reemerged during the last third of the nineteenth century in a burst of antisemitic rhetoric and imagery coupled with crass social discrimination designed to exclude upwardly mobile Jews from the society of the Protestant elite. An infamous incident took place in Atlanta, where, in 1913, a twenty-nine-year-old Jewish factory superintendent and local B'nai B'rith leader named Leo Frank was convicted of molesting and murdering one of his employees, thirteen-year-old Mary Phagan, and dumping her body in the basement of the pencil factory where they both worked. The case attracted a frenzy of publicity, and much attention centered on Frank's religion— the mark of his being an outsider to the South, a symbol of otherness and change. Crowds around the courthouse chanted "Hang the Jew!" When Georgia governor John Slaton, unconvinced that Frank was the murderer, commuted his sentence in 1915 from death to life in prison, a mob that included many leading local citizens broke into the jail, kidnapped Frank, and lynched him: the first known lynching of a Jew in American history. Years later an eyewitness confirmed what Frank's defenders had long believed —that Mary Phagan was murdered by the janitor of the pencil factory, the "star witness" against Frank. Frank himself was innocent.[17]

Social and religious tensions of many kinds rose higher during World War I, when the civil rights of numerous citizens were violated and innocent people fell prey to hysteria-driven mobs. Most hostility focused, initially, on German-Americans, as well as those deemed for one reason or another insufficiently patriotic. Before long, however, Catholics, "radicals," and Jews also felt the sting of popular animus. As Americans grew "disillusioned with internationalism, fearful of Bolshevik subversion, and frightened that foreigners would corrupt the nation's values and traditions," manifestations of antisemitism rose precipitously. "Within three years following the close of the war," the president of the Central Conference of American Rabbis gravely reported, "there was perhaps more antisemitic literature published and distributed in the United States than in any previous period of its history."[18]

What made this literature particularly insidious and incendiary was that so much of it bore the imprimatur of a national hero, automaker Henry Ford. For ninety-one straight issues beginning on May 22, 1920, Ford's weekly newspaper, the *Dearborn Independent,* purported to describe an international Jewish conspiracy based on the notorious antisemitic forgery known as *The Protocols of the Elders of Zion,* first published in Russia in 1905. Four volumes entitled *The International Jew,* drawn from the series, reprinted these scurrilous charges and disseminated them in hundreds of thousands of copies—including such fantastic claims as "Rule of the Jewish Kehillah Grips New York" and "Jewish Jazz Becomes Our National Music." Only in 1927, under intense economic and legal pressure, did Ford publicly apologize "for resurrecting exploded fictions, for giving currency to . . . gross forgeries, and for contending that the Jews have been engaged in a conspiracy." But by then the damage had been done.[19]

Jews, in the face of these and other accusations, felt less secure than they previously had in America, and many Christians wondered privately whether their Jewish neighbors could be trusted. In one case, the Federal Council of Churches of Christ sought from Rabbi Edward Calisch "an explanation regarding the *Kol Nidre* Prayer for Yom Kippur," having heard from some of its members that the prayer, recited at the beginning of the evening service on the Day of Atonement, offered Jews dispensation from swearing falsely. Others questioned Jews' loyalty, their contribution to America, even the humanity of their (kosher) method of slaughtering animals. Naturally, Jews attempted to rebut the manifold charges leveled against them. In the *American Jewish Year Book,* for example, five different articles in 1923 responded to critics who maligned and belittled the Jewish people and their faith. Yet many of these justifications fell on deaf ears. One of the apologists, the learned Professor Israel Davidson of the Jewish Theological Seminary, grimly warned against "too many explanations." "Friends do not need them," he pointed out, "and enemies would not believe them."[20]

The same issue of the *American Jewish Year Book* carried, in twenty-five pages of small print, a learned rabbinic disquisition by Professor Louis Ginzberg, America's foremost Talmudic scholar, on the question of "whether unfermented wine may be used in Jewish ceremonies." The Eighteenth Amendment to the Constitution, which went into effect on January 16, 1920, and barred the "manufacture, sale, or transportation of intoxicating liquors," provided the context for this question. Prohibition, like nativism and antisemitism, tapped into deeply rooted antimodernist trends in American life; it attempted to turn back the cultural clock so as to restore the nation to its earlier, pre-mass-immigration state of "purity." Even as it did so, however, it grudgingly recognized the rights of religious minorities. The National Prohibition (Volstead) Act granted a specific exemption to those who required wine "for sacramental purposes or like religious rites," including Catholics, whose church rituals demand wine, and Jews, who bless the "fruit of the vine" as part of Sabbath and holiday home rituals, as well as at circumcisions and marriages.

To the deep embarrassment of the Jewish community, however, the terms of this exemption, and particularly the fact that Jewish wine rituals largely entail home consumption, opened the door to widespread abuse. Impoverished immigrant rabbis, unscrupulous impostors, and mobsters found the temptation to sell wine on the side for nonritual purposes too lucrative to resist. "Ritual consumption" of wine on the part of Jews skyrocketed during these years as Prohibition created, in the words of one cynical inspector, "a remarkable increase in the thirst for religion." Judging from official records, in fact, "blessing the fruit of the vine" became during Prohibition the most widely and scrupulously observed of all Jewish religious practices. In response to this abuse and to the unsavory publicity that it generated, Reform rabbis decreed that their followers use only unfermented wine for their rituals: the law of the land demanded it, the rabbis declared, and Jewish law permitted it. Ginzberg's ruling, spread over seventy-one pages of rabbinic Hebrew (which the *Year Book* translated, edited, and abridged for English readers), provided a much more elaborate rationale for permitting grape juice for ritual purposes and was aimed at persuading readers concerned with the dialectics of Jewish law. Ginzberg urged "all Torah scholars" to agree with his findings, thereby "removing the ugly stain [of scandal] from our midst." That, of course, proved to be wishful thinking.[21]

What did end the scandals were stricter regulations introduced in 1926 and 1927, followed by the repeal of Prohibition in 1933. Meanwhile, the lurid publicity accompanying the disclosure of illicit activities permanently tarnished the reputation of several immigrant Orthodox rabbis, while well-publicized Jewish criminal involvement in bootlegging only confirmed, in the public's mind, the association of Jews with corrupt practices. The scandal surrounding the 1919 World Series that eight members of the Chicago White Sox ("Black Sox") conspired with gamblers to lose, blamed by Henry Ford on "too much Jew" and by the public, rightly or wrongly, on the Jewish gangster Arnold Rothstein, reinforced this stereotype. As late as 1940 more than half of the population, according to pollsters, declared the quality that they found most objectionable in Jews to be their "unscrupulousness."[22]

The massive damage inflicted on the Jewish image during the interwar years—some, as we have seen, self-inflicted—was compounded by the damage wrought by educational quotas, restrictive covenants, occupational discrimination, and physical attacks. During the 1920s, according to one incomplete list, Harvard, Yale, Princeton, Columbia, Duke, Rutgers, Barnard, Adelphi, Cornell, Johns Hopkins, Northwestern, Penn State, Ohio State, Washington and Lee, and the Universities of Cincinnati, Illinois, Kansas, Minnesota, Texas, Virginia, and Washington all found ways implicit and explicit to limit the number of their Jewish students, as did numerous private academies and preparatory schools. The extent of the restrictive quotas and the means used to achieve them differed from place to place, but what really mattered for Jews was that they were excluded not on the basis of merit but simply on account of their ancestry and faith.[23]

Even harsher restrictions faced Jews in various fraternities, clubs, hotels, resorts, and elite neighborhoods—there, in many cases, they were shut out completely. Clubs in fifteen different cities large and small are known to have barred Jews, while discrimination at luxury resorts was "near universal." One hotel described itself as being "exclusively for gentiles"; another announced in its advertising: "no Hebrews or tubercular guests received." In addition, bigoted practices and "restrictive covenants" excluded Jews from some of the most desirable neighborhoods in New York, Chicago, Washington, D.C., Los Angeles, Miami, Denver, Baltimore, Boston, Chattanooga, and Cleveland, as well as from many newly emerging suburbs. Some inviting apartments on Coney Island, for example, shamelessly advertised themselves as being "sensibly priced, sensibly built, [and] sensibly restricted."[24]

Physical violence against Jews likewise became all too common during this period. In the 1920s, the revived Ku Klux Klan badly frightened Jews, though it directed most of its animus against blacks and Catholics. Attacks increased in the 1930s, particularly in cities where German-Americans sympathetic to Hitler took to the streets, and where Catholic supporters of the increasingly pro-Nazi radio priest, Father Charles Coughlin, beat Jews mercilessly. "CHRISTIAN FRONT HOODLUMS TERRORIZE BOSTON JEWS," a headline in one newspaper screamed in 1943. By then, according to an official state investigation, reported incidents of violence against Boston Jews averaged two a month, and many more incidents apparently went unreported.[25]

Violence, like antisemitism generally during this period, affected Jews of every stripe, religious and irreligious, immigrant and native-born alike. No matter how strongly they differed in matters of faith, Jews, like many other persecuted minorities, found that when times were hard they all shared a common fate. This realization, in turn, succored a strong sense of group identity that transcended factional differences. Tensions between Central European and Eastern European Jews, Jews from Lithuania and Jews from Galicia, Radicals, Reform Jews, and Orthodox Jews—all diminished in the face of burgeoning antisemitism. Some, then and later, misunderstood this unity to mean that the "Russians defeat[ed] the Germans" in American Jewish life and that the majority had come to rule.[26] A closer look, however, discloses that Jews of German descent, like Felix Warburg, now worked alongside the rising East Europeans—a good thing since, by working together, Jews found themselves able to counter or circumvent the worst of the restrictions raised against them. Adversity thus promoted unity within the American Jewish community. Consequently, for all that they suffered during the interwar years, Jews as a group managed to advance remarkably.

Mutual assistance and simulation—the strategy of creating Jewish institutions parallel to the very ones that kept Jews out—help to explain why. The concept of mutual assistance formed part of the tool kit of cultural resources that Jews brought with them from Europe. A central Jewish religious precept, summed up in the rabbinic phrase "all Israel is responsible for one another," it remains widely practiced. During the era of mass immigration, mutual assistance translated into philanthropy, free loans, and employment help. Those longer in the country aided those who arrived more recently; wealthier Jews helped out poorer cousins. These patterns carried over to the interwar years. Jews who made it into the white-collar world helped those with aspirations and talent to follow in their footsteps. Jewish organizations, fraternities, and synagogues disseminated news of appropriate openings through their membership and kinship networks. Most important of all, Jews tended to hire and patronize other Jews, thereby transforming the faith and ancestry that antisemites considered a liability into a productive asset. The result may be characterized as a Jewish "sub-economy," linking employers, employees, consumers, and suppliers in one commercial web. Through their purchases of goods and services, Jews helped to sustain one another.[27]

Simulation proved no less important. Rather than capitulating to prejudice, Jews created "functional alternatives" to the institutions that excluded them. Those prevented by quota (or financial need) from attending Harvard, for example, frequently went off to study at what they called the "Jewish Harvard"—City College of New York. They also crowded into (and often improved) an array of other state-sponsored and Catholic colleges that remained open to them. Indeed, during the interwar years Jews attended college at a rate more than double that of Americans generally. When fraternities, sororities, country clubs, and resorts kept them out, Jews likewise responded by creating their own. During the interwar years, some twenty-two national Jewish college fraternities and sororities operated across the United States, with a membership, in 1945, estimated at 75,000. The extent of Jewish country club membership is unknown, but a listing in 1918 enumerated a total of 229 Jewish clubs, quite a number of them, with suggestive names like "Harmony" and "Concordia," clearly catering to wealthy Jews whom the gentile clubs summarily rejected. As for Jewish resorts, the Yiddish-language *Forward* reported that Jews who vacationed there "had their revenge on the Gentiles who didn't want to accept them." When, for example, members of the Straus family of department store magnates were refused admission to a Lakewood, New Jersey, hotel on account of their faith, Nathan Straus built the Lakewood Hotel "with no other policy than to throw it open to all, whether Jew or Gentile." Similarly, when the opulent Hotel Kaaterskill refused to accept Jews, Jewish entrepreneurs opened their own opulent hotels in the Catskills—and Jews came to summer in the area in large numbers. However much they emulated their non-Jewish counterparts in appearance and form, however, Jewish-owned resorts catered almost entirely to Jews; they stood firmly apart.[28]

In so doing, Jewish resorts effectively reinforced patterns of residential segregation that confined Jews across the country. Partly voluntary, partly encouraged, and partly imposed, this segregation had the effect of creating Jewish neighborhoods that simulated their non-Jewish counterparts—similar-style homes and streets and parks—while still remaining overwhelmingly Jewish. In New York City, where Jews considered themselves highly mobile, most Jews by 1930 "lived in sections significantly segregated from the Gentile population"—more markedly, indeed, than in 1920. Communities like

Brownsville, Far Rockaway, and Grand Concourse were fully 60 to 80 percent Jewish. In Cleveland, in 1926, seventy-one thousand of the city's seventy-eight thousand Jews—over 91 percent—resided "in three relatively limited neighborhoods." Even in the small community of Johnstown, Pennsylvania, with a Jewish population of no more than thirteen hundred, Jews in the 1930s "clustered side by side within particular blocks."[29]

The result was a Jewish population that gave every appearance of being "at home" in America but that actually inhabited a largely self-contained subculture, a parallel universe that shared many of the trappings of the larger society while standing apart from it. One student dubbed these Jewish communities "gilded ghettoes," defined as "closed communit[ies] of middle class Jews whose social life was carried on exclusively with Jews of appropriate status." Their "institutions paralleled those of the American middle class," but the gilded ghettoes' residents "were all Jews." As in late nineteenth-century Germany, where Jews also faced substantial antisemitism and incomplete acceptance, the American Jewish community, during the interwar years, "was both set apart without and held together within by secular factors—economic, demographic, [geographic], social, and cultural." Its distinctiveness remained largely "invisible to its members," but in retrospect it was a community where a "new sort of Jewish identity" had come to the fore, one characterized less by religious observance than by ethnicity, propinquity, and culture.[30]

The infrequency of Jewish-Christian intermarriage in America at that time—standard estimates range from 1.7 percent to "somewhere below seven percent"—underscores this relative insulation. Besides the religious taboo against intermarriage, young Jews and Christians did not interact enough to fall in love. Novels and films talked about intermarriage, but social conventions and the realities of domestic life ensured that it remained a highly unusual occurrence.[31]

The existence of sixty-two Jewish hospitals in twenty-five major cities where Jews lived likewise reinforced the culture of separatism. The earliest of these hospitals arose in the mid-nineteenth century in response to attempts on the part of well-meaning Christian nurses to convert Jews on their deathbeds. In the twentieth century, though, they provided a work place for Jewish doctors, excluded from employment at many another hospital, and also provided a refuge for Jewish patients who, when ill, sought to mingle with those who understood and respected their faith. Thus, when they were sick and when they were well, and even when they maintained superficial ties with the non-Jews in their community, Jews still largely lived and operated among their own kind. Even as they gloried in being part of the larger American culture they remained firmly rooted in a subculture that consisted largely of Jews.[32]

JEWISHNESS WITHOUT JUDAISM

The existence of this Jewish subculture helps to explain the widespread belief during the interwar years that Jewishness *(Yiddishkeit)* could thrive in America even in the absence of such standard components of religious life as synagogue attendance, ritual practice, and Jewish education. "The dominating characteristic of the streets on which I grew was Jewishness in all its rich variety," writer Vivian Gornick recalled. "We did not have to be 'observing' Jews to know that we were Jews."[33] Indeed, the very act of living in close proximity to other Jews gave a Jewish "feel" to the neighborhood. The Sabbath and holidays that Orthodox neighbors scrupulously maintained; the synagogues calling out for men to complete the minyan required before public prayers could begin; the kosher butcher, the Hebrew bookstore, the candy store, and the familiar restaurants; the Yiddish newspaper, music troupe, and theater; the vendors selling hot knishes and other Jewish delicacies on the street—these and countless other cues signaled to inhabitants that theirs was a Jewish community. Simply by living there they experienced, absorbed, and in many ways internalized that Jewishness. Even if they neither practiced it nor trained their children in its precepts, they assumed that it was well-nigh inescapable—as inescapable as the neighborhood atmosphere itself.

Jewish secularism provided the ideological justification for this emphasis on "Jewishness" rather than "Judaism." The concept meant different things to different people, but according to the formulation of its most profound thinker, the Russian-born and Swiss-educated Chaim Zhitlowsky (1865–1943), who first came to America in 1904, Jewish secularism had two major tenets: (1) it opposed all forms of religious coercion, insisting that both religion and anti-religion were "private affairs"; and (2) it demanded that education and culture not be held captive to any form of heresy-hunting. "Secularism," Zhitlowsky insisted, "denotes the exclusion of everything that comes in the name of any revealed superhuman, supernatural *authority,* [or] divinity."[34]

In place of religion, Jewish secularists advocated language (meaning, in Zhitlowsky's case, Yiddish; others stressed Hebrew) and a shared civilization as the binding elements in Jewish life. They sought "to foster Jewish concepts and ideals—ideals that are reflected in Jewish literature, in Jewish history, and in all emanations of the Jewish ethos." Following Zhitlowsky, they also worked to develop "a network of Yiddish cultural and educational institutions to serve as a basis for . . . a new Jewish culture grounded in democracy and humanistic values." While not opposed in principle to the observance of Jewish practices, particularly those, like Passover, which carried a strong humanistic message, they insisted that all observances and rituals be voluntarily assumed rather than mandated. In practice, most secularists considered radical causes and the battle for social justice the focal point of their Judaism. They assumed that their own deep Jewish commitments and the Jewishness of their milieu would inspire their children to follow in their footsteps.[35]

A popular radio program in the 1930s, *The Goldbergs,* reflected the world of secular Jews. Featuring Jewish names (Molly, Rosalie, Jake, and Sammy), Yiddish accents ("Molly, your soup is feet for a kink"), and popular wisdom ("every day a little is someday a lot"), as well as gentle humor, abundant nostalgia, and timeless tales of the immigrant upraised, it aired six evenings a week for three years, including Friday night, when it competed with the Jewish Sabbath. In various incarnations on radio and later on television, it played on for twenty-five years. Gertrude Berg, the matriarch-heroine who wrote each show and starred in it, had little in the way of formal religious training and generally avoided particularistic religious themes, except for annual shows on Passover and the High Holidays. Her major aim through the series was to disseminate "progressive ideas, tolerance, and understanding." She evoked pride in being Jewish and projected herself as the very embodiment of Jewish values and inter-religious goodwill. Her world, in show business as in life, centered far more on Jewishness than on Judaism.[36]

Meanwhile, synagogues, Jewish schools, and other Jewish institutions languished from neglect. The *American Jewish Year Book,* in 1919, estimated that only just over "three-quarters of a million of the Jewish population of the country [including women and children] are regularly affiliated with congregations"—less than 23 percent of the total Jewish population, which had grown to 3.3 million. The 1926 U.S. Census of Religious Bodies found only one synagogue per 1,309 Jews, while the comparable figure for Christian churches was one per 220. In San Francisco, in 1938, only 18 percent of Jewish families had one or more of its members affiliated with a synagogue.[37]

Weekly attendance figures were even worse. In the Brownsville section of Brooklyn, renowned at the time as the Jerusalem of America, only 8 percent of adult Jewish males, and even fewer females and children, regularly attended synagogue. Three-quarters of young Jews surveyed in New York in 1935 had not attended any religious services at all during the previous year—not even, apparently, on the High Holidays. A related study, particularly interesting because it was comparative, determined that among a sample of youth in New York City in 1935, only 10.8 percent of Jewish boys and 6.6 percent of Jewish girls attended synagogue in the week prior to the inquiry, while among Protestants the comparable figures were 37.8 percent and 42.2 percent, and among Catholics, 60.5 percent and 69.5 percent. Surveys of Jewish college students from New England to North Dakota, summarized in 1943, gave no cause for optimism concerning the future. They found that the students by and large considered synagogue attendance marginal to their lives as Jews and that they "observe[d] few of our customs." "The Jewish religion as a social institution is losing its influence for the perpetuation of the Jewish group," an article in the highly respected *American Journal of Sociology* concluded. It went on to predict the "total eclipse of the Jewish church in America."[38]

The situation concerning Jewish education was much the same. A study of 566 Jewish children in the immigrant section of East Baltimore, published in 1920, found that 65 percent of them "had received no Jewish education." The 1926 U.S. Census of Religious Bodies estimated "the average length of stay of a Jewish child in a Jewish school" at about two years total. Other nationwide figures vary widely, but in what was then America's most populous Jewish community, Brooklyn, only 12 percent of Jewish youngsters reputedly received any kind of Jewish education in the 1920s, notwithstanding the fact that the community was home to some of the most innovative and vibrant Jewish schools in the United States. In New York City as a whole, in 1924, 17 percent of Jewish children attended some kind of organized Jewish school (the number who studied privately with a tutor is unknown). Nationally, about a quarter of a million Jewish children were receiving a Jewish education in 1927—this out of a total Jewish population that numbered over 4 million. Reform Jews and rural Jews sent their children to religious school at a higher rate than their Orthodox and urban counterparts, but they did not stay there long enough to learn much. Students in Reform Jewish Sunday Schools received, on average, only an hour and twenty-seven minutes of classroom instruction per week. The situation in higher Jewish education, at least judging from its financial condition, was still more bleak. Cyrus Adler (1863–1940), who simultaneously headed both the Jewish Theological Seminary in New York and Dropsie College for Hebrew and Cognate Learning in Philadelphia, confided in 1920 that "practically every Jewish organization of higher learning or science" in America "was broke." Even the Jewish Publication Society, which had been publishing Jewish books for more than thirty years, stood deeply in debt.[39]

Jewish leaders were naturally alarmed by all these developments, particularly the decline in religious education and practice. At the Union of American Hebrew Congregations in 1923 "speaker after speaker . . . stressed the imminent danger of a religiously ignorant, untaught, and unbelieving generation, following upon the heels of an indifferent one." Three years later, at the convention of the fervently Orthodox Agudath ha-Rabbanim, the main speaker declared that "in recent times . . . the situation has grown progressively worse. The deficiencies in [Jewish religious] life have multiplied horribly." Reform and Conservative rabbis bewailed in 1930 that the American synagogue was "being invaded by secularism." The decline in synagogue attendance seemed so pronounced in the early 1930s that Judge Horace Stern of Pennsylvania devoted an entire article to the subject in the prestigious *American Jewish Year Book*. He blamed the problem on, among other things, the competition that synagogues faced from "automobiles, golf clubs, radios, bridge parties, extension lectures, and the proceedings of various learned and pseudo-learned societies."[40]

These problems were not confined to Jews, of course. The period from 1925–35 was an era of "religious depression" in America, marked by declining church attendance, as well as a deepening "secular" interest in universalism and the "cosmopolitan spirit." Statistics suggest that this religious depression affected Judaism more profoundly than it did other faiths. Nevertheless, Catholics and Protestants also lamented, as Judge Stern did in his article, that "religion, at least in its organized forms, has to an appreciable extent lost its hold upon the present generation." Particularly in the major urban areas, where most Jews had congregated, complaints about religious "indifference" and spiritual "unresponsiveness" abounded. Revealingly, one of the era's most famous films, *The Jazz Singer* (1927), inspired by the career of entertainer Al Jolson (Asa Yoelson), depicted a son's rebellion against the religion of his parents. "My songs mean as much to my audience as yours do to your congregation," the film's hero, a vaudeville performer named Jack Robin (born Jakie Rabinowitz), responded when accused of apostasy by his father, a traditional cantor. Samson Raphaelson, author of the story "The Day of Atonement," on which the movie was based, insisted that "jazz is prayer" and that the America that packed cabarets, musical revues, and dance halls was "praying with a fervor as intense as that of the America which goes sedately to church and synagogue."[41]

The fear, in Jewish religious circles, was that children like Al Jolson and

"Jack Robin" had abandoned God and the synagogue for one of the many "false gods" that preyed upon impressionable young minds: popular culture, atheistic materialism, socialism, communism, and more, each itself splintered into warring bands of devout followers. Some of these surrogate religions preached a universalistic or cosmopolitan ethic, akin to Felix Adler's Ethical Culture movement, which called upon Jews to renounce particularism for a universalistic faith dedicated to the betterment of humanity. Others offered adherents a new system of absolutes to substitute for the faith they had lost, complete with some of traditional Judaism's most familiar and beloved cultural patterns. Marxists, for example, encouraged their followers to master "sacred" Marxist-Leninist texts, revere selected Communist "prophets," dialectically debate questions of orthodoxy and heterodoxy, and above all to believe with a perfect faith in the coming of Marxian Socialism's secular messianic kingdom. In New York, many radicals even gathered regularly at a "temple"—the famed Labor Temple on Fourteenth Street. A "rich variety of ideological orthodoxies [stood] on display at the Labor Temple," the Yiddish journalist Judd Teller recalled. "Each of these radical faiths was an absolutist, possessive, jealous God, unforgiving of errancy."[42]

ORTHODOXY'S DILEMMA

Those who remained firmly committed to Judaism and Jewish life searched for ways to bring wayward Jews like these back into the fold. The bonds of secular Jewishness, they believed, even if temporarily secured by the antisemitism of non-Jewish neighbors and the reassuring presence of Jewish ones, would in the absence of strong religious institutions and commitments prove too weak to endure. Fearing once again for the future of their faith, they initiated bold measures to save it. No more than in the past, however, could adherents agree on how best to achieve this common preservationist aim: By upholding and maintaining Judaism's sacred religious traditions? By adapting Judaism to conditions of life in a new land? Or by preserving above all a strong sense of Jewish peoplehood and communal unity? As a result, no single solution emerged from the array of innovative programs put forth during this period—perhaps no surprise given the pragmatic and pluralistic approach to problems that characterized American domestic policy, and particularly Franklin Roosevelt's New Deal, at about the same time. Instead, the interwar years incubated a series of far-reaching developments and innovations in Judaism whose impact, for the most part, became apparent only later, after World War II.

Orthodox Judaism faced the greatest challenge during these years. With the end of immigration, its supply of pious newcomers was shut off at the very moment when the children of those who had immigrated years earlier seemed to be abandoning the movement's teachings. Even among some of the most fervently Orthodox of America's Jews the permissive social environment of the 1920s took its toll: "Clothing was selected for style and there was less concern for its modesty. There were new foods to taste, and acceptable ways for men to pass the time in the evening and on Shabbes [Sabbath] other than at Torah study. The line distinguishing the social behavior of Orthodox and secular Jews also became less distinct. Orthodox Jews and Hasidim attended the theater, and courting couples could go to the movies without stirring community gossip and disapproval."[43]

One of those who sought to stem this tide was Rabbi Shraga Feivel Mendlowitz (1886–1948),[44] an immigrant from Hungary who, in 1921, at the age of thirty-four, became the principal of what was then only the fifth Jewish all-day school in America, Brooklyn's Yeshivah Torah Vodaath. Founded initially as a Religious Zionist elementary school combining secular studies, Hebrew language instruction, and the study of traditional Jewish texts in Hebrew, the school under Mendlowitz's direction became an Orthodox citadel, combining Lithuanian-style learning and Hasidic fervor with limited secular study, Yiddish as the language of instruction, and a pronounced non-Zionist philosophy. Within eight years he had expanded Torah Vodaath to include both a high school *(Mesivta)* and a post–high school Talmudic academy. What set the school apart, in addition to its rapid growth, was that it consciously set out to train not rabbis and scholars but ordinary laymen who, Mendlowitz shrewdly intuited, would form the rank and file of a future American Orthodox Jewish community. Indeed, his goal and lifelong strategy was to create "a generation of *ba'ale-battim,* laymen, who are competent businessmen or professionals who have devoted years to intensive study of Torah and will continue to do so in their spare time." He even insisted on having himself called by the title "Mr." (rather than Rabbi), as if seeking personally to exemplify the type of Jewishly well-educated and deeply committed lay leader that he sought to produce through his school. By 1936, Torah Vodaath claimed 751 students and had spawned several imitators and competitors. Mendlowitz subsequently created an Orthodox Jewish educational camp, a teacher training institute named *Esh Das* (Fire of Faith [see Deuteronomy 33:2]), and, most significant, in 1944, Torah Umesorah, the National Society for Hebrew Day Schools. In the face of the destruction of European Jewry, Torah Umesorah worked "to disseminate

Max Weber's *The Talmudists* (1934), painted after the artist made a pilgrimage "to one of the oldest synagogues of New York's East Side," depicts a world that seemed to be disappearing. Weber was deeply impressed by the elders, "bent on and intent upon nothing but the eternal quest and interpretation of the ethical, significant, and religious content of . . . the Torah." There are no youngsters in his painting, however, and without them the old Lower East Side synagogues were dwindling in membership. Most would soon disappear. Oil on canvas. Gift of Mrs. Nathan Miller. Photograph by John Parnell. The Jewish Museum, New York/Art Resource, New York.

the true Torah spirit by establishing yeshivas . . . throughout the United States of America," its goal being "a day school in every community." During the postwar era it helped to create hundreds of these schools by unifying Orthodox leaders of different ideologies behind them. By then, the idea that native-born American Jews could be shaped into Torah-studying businessmen and professionals no longer seemed radical, and the seeds for Orthodoxy's late twentieth-century resurgence had been sown.[45]

Mendlowitz's strategy for saving American Judaism, though considered right-wing in much of the Orthodox world of his day, proved still too tame for some of his students. Under the influence of a man known as "The Malach" (Angel)—Rabbi Chaim Avraham Dov Ber Levine HaCohen, a recently immigrated charismatic spiritual leader who had been intimate with and later estranged from the Lubavitch Hasidic movement in Russia —some Torah Vodaath students in the late 1920s endeavored to sever themselves entirely from their secular surroundings and to live out their lives in devotion and holiness. They allowed their beards and sidecurls to grow long, gave up wearing neckties and "other frivolous and gentile attire," and dressed in long black kaftans, known as *kapotes,* as well as black derby hats and large protruding ritual fringes. They shunned secular culture completely —no radio, no newspapers, no movies. They even described their knowledge of English, their mother tongue, as not an advantage but a burden. Expelled by Torah Vodaath for extremism in 1931, they became M'lochim (followers of the Malach; literally, "angels"), a Hasidic sect that communicated only in Yiddish, prayed intensely, lived ascetically, and devoted all of its spare hours to study, in anticipation of a society-ending catastrophe followed by redemption.[46]

The M'lochim remained a tiny sect centered in the Williamsburg section of Brooklyn and reaching no more than a few hundred members around World War II. Its symbolic significance, however, loomed far larger. First of all, it demonstrated that assimilation among the American-born children of immigrants was by no means inevitable. Even the pietistic tenets of East European Hasidism, it showed, could become attractive to American youngsters under certain conditions. Second, the M'lochim stood in the vanguard of what would later become, following World War II, a significant and unanticipated Hasidic revival. Back in 1918, America's soil was described by a writer in the *Jewish Communal Register* as being "rather unfavorable for the seed of the Hasidic cult." Most Hasidic immigrants, the writer reported, were not interested in following a rebbe (Hasidic "grand rabbi") in America, and America's four Hasidic rebbes, as a consequence, had almost no Hasidic followers.[47] The M'lochim, in establishing a new Hasidic court composed mostly of native-born Jews, demonstrated that American soil offered Hasidism greater opportunities for growth than previously imagined. In this, as in so much else, they served as a harbinger of change, a sign that the "unkosher land" might nevertheless sustain pockets of fervent Orthodoxy. Finally, the M'lochim defined, for those who knew of their existence, the most extreme possible response to the perils facing American Judaism. Their strategy for maintaining traditional faith was to totally reject America's cultural mores and, insofar as possible, shut themselves off, like the Protestant Amish and Hutterites, in a pious enclave shielded from worldly contamination. Fewer than 5 percent of America's Jews would ever follow this zealous strategy of total separation. Yet as had earlier been true of Rabbi Abraham Rice and some rabbis of the Agudath ha-Rabbanim, those who did prescribe their Judaism in opposition to American culture helped to define the broad religious mainstream where many more Jews felt comfortable.

Rabbi Bernard (Dov) Revel (1885–1940), by contrast, sought to make American Orthodoxy part of the religious mainstream.[48] A child prodigy and the scion of distinguished rabbis, Revel studied at some of Lithuania's most distinguished centers of Jewish learning, earning ordination at age sixteen. On the side, he also undertook secular studies; he even associated himself with the socialist Bund, and in 1905 in Kovno he was arrested by the tsar as an agitator. Arriving in America in 1906, he continued simultaneously to pursue both traditional Talmudic learning and modern scholarship, studying both at Rabbi Isaac Elchanan Theological Seminary and at Temple University, New York University, and Dropsie College, where he earned his Ph.D. in 1911. Within five years of his arrival in America he had managed to impress both the traditional East European rabbis who led the Agudath ha-Rabbanim (in fact, he served as assistant to its president, Rabbi Bernard Levinthal) and the more modern Jewish scholars who taught him at Dropsie. He had also become financially independent, having married into one of America's wealthiest East European Orthodox immigrant families, the Travis family, which had founded the Oklahoma Petroleum and Gasoline Company and, following his marriage, brought him into the business. Uniquely, he thus united within himself traditional religious scholarship, modern secular scholarship, and business acumen. Recognizing his potential, the directors of Etz Chaim yeshiva and Rabbi Isaac Elchanan Theological Seminary invited him in 1915, though he was not yet thirty, to reorganize and lead their newly merged institution. His goal in accepting the position was to create "a bridge over which the Torah could be brought from Europe to America and without compromise be made meaningful in contemporary American life."[49]

Initially, the new institution, tentatively named the Rabbinical College of America, defined itself as a "Jewish parochial school, with elementary, high school, and collegiate courses." It emphasized that "both Jewish and secular studies" were taught in the first two levels, and thereafter students were "given the opportunity to attend at the same time one of the colleges of the city." This, in itself, distinguished the school from its Orthodox predecessors and competitors (including, a few years later, Torah Vodaath), which taught secular studies only grudgingly and discouraged college attendance. The fact that half of the Rabbinical College's Jewish Studies faculty in 1918 were practicing Orthodox Jews who boasted earned doctoral degrees from secular colleges and universities bespoke the institution's highest values.[50]

In 1923, following his return from four years in Tulsa, where he went to help save the family oil business, Revel developed plans to establish a "Yeshiva College" side by side with the elementary school, high school, teachers' institute, and theological seminary that already formed part of the institution. The goal, initially, was modest and in keeping with Revel's general philosophy: "to provide a general academic training to those who are also studying in the other departments of the Yeshiva, so that they may harmoniously combine the best of modern culture with the learning and the spirit of the Torah and the ideals of traditional Judaism." But the enthusiasm of the trustees, and subsequently of the larger East European Jewish community in New York, rapidly expanded the project, ballooning it into an unprecedented $5 million campaign to create a prominent campus in upper Manhattan's Washington Heights. The new institution would place Orthodox Judaism "conspicuously before American Jews as a challenge and an invitation," one supporter announced. Another described it as "a line of defense against the inroads of indifference and desertion, which is noticeable among our young in this country." Still a third thought that the new college would compete with its most famous non-Jewish counterparts and cater "to the Jews who have been barred from Christian schools for non-scholastic reasons." Inspired by so many starry-eyed hopes, and notwithstanding critics who considered the endeavor too expensive or parochial, the project (with the help of prodigious bank loans) met its ambitious goal—the largest, by far, ever announced to that time by an American Orthodox institution. When the massive Moorish-style structure was dedicated, in 1928, even the Agudath ha-Rabbanim, which perennially tormented Revel with complaints concerning heterodox tendencies within the Yeshiva, exulted that the new

Washington Heights campus "represent[ed] the pride and glory of Orthodox American Jewry . . . [and] the successful arrival of Orthodoxy in the mainstream of American Jewry."[51]

In fact, Yeshiva did increasingly become a "mainstream" institution, thanks in no small part to Revel's "uncanny mix of Talmudic erudition, knowledge of the ways of [the] country, and . . . political savvy," which allowed him to serve in a vital mediating capacity within the deeply conflicted school. He defended traditional learning against attacks from secularists and protected his more secular-minded faculty from attacks by traditionalists. He appeased his rabbinic colleagues at the Agudath ha-Rabbanim, and he advanced the careers of his own rabbinic alumni whom the Agudath ha-Rabbanim spurned. Most important of all, and notwithstanding the crippling financial problems that Yeshiva and Revel personally faced during the Depression, he guided Yeshiva as it created both a cadre of Americanized Orthodox rabbis and a large alumni of Jewishly educated Orthodox laymen —the nucleus of what would become known as Modern Orthodoxy. Beginning in 1948, under the administration of Revel's successor, Samuel Belkin, Yeshiva also assumed responsibility for educating Orthodox Jewish women. "Orthodoxy has been the great protagonist of the light of Jewish learning in modern times," a rising Conservative rabbi named Robert Gordis (who had earlier attended Yeshiva's Teachers Institute) wrote admiringly in 1941. "It insisted that learning was not the prerogative of a handful of rabbis, but the duty and privilege of every Jew."[52]

The M'lochim, Shraga Feivel Mendlowitz, and European luminaries like Rabbi Elchanan Wasserman remained highly critical of Yeshiva College and its embrace of modern culture. "Instead of insisting that [rabbis] should attend universities, you should insist that they shouldn't attend," Wasserman declared. He considered the Yeshiva "a center of *apikursus* [heresy] and *shmad* [apostasy]" and refused to cross its threshold when he visited New York in 1938. More Americanized Orthodox Jews, however, looked upon the college as a symbol that simultaneously reflected and legitimated their own quest to uphold and maintain Judaism and to adapt it to their new homeland. During the interwar years, these Americanized Orthodox Jews —they were sometimes referred to as the "cultured" or "reasonable" Orthodox—developed a form of Judaism that, they thought, could staunch the losses that traditional Judaism was experiencing and keep second-generation Jews within the fold.[53]

Americanized Orthodoxy, as we have seen, actually dated back to the 1880s, when some of New York's oldest and wealthiest East European synagogues moved into large showpiece synagogues and laid new stress on dignity and decorum. Over a century earlier, colonial Sephardic synagogues had promoted regulations to the same effect, and in the mid-nineteenth century Central European Jews, as they moved up the social ladder, likewise embraced the virtues of refinement and order. All alike sought, over time, to adapt their mode of worship to reflect their own newly awakened middle-class sensitivities, and all alike hoped that by improving the atmosphere of their synagogues they would impress their own children as well as visiting non-Jews, whose mainline churches generally reflected these same religious and social values. In 1913 the newly established Young Israel movement, backed by rabbinical students from the Jewish Theological Seminary, drew upon these precedents in seeking to "bring about a revival of Judaism among the thousands of young Jews and Jewesses . . . whose Judaism is at present dormant." Shortly thereafter, some of these young Jews established what became known as the Model Synagogue (later renamed the Young Israel Synagogue), "where, with the exception of prayer, English would be spoken in delivering sermons and otherwise, complete congregational singing instituted, *schnoddering* [publicly announced donations from those called up to the Torah] eliminated[,] and decorum . . . almost one hundred percent maintained." This basic formula—decorum, an English-language sermon, congregational singing, and a traditional liturgy ("every atom of our time honored traditions could be observed")—came to characterize Americanized Orthodoxy wherever it subsequently arose.[54]

Two basic types of Americanized Orthodox synagogues developed. One, influenced by the currents of modern Orthodoxy that had emerged in response to Reform in large German cities and also in England in the late nineteenth century, placed great emphasis on aesthetics and outward form. The synagogue became, as in Germany, a "veritable Temple of Devotion with shining pomp and ceremony requir[ing] great efforts in energy, time, and money." Formalized to a high degree, the service eschewed spontaneous spiritual outbursts and all forms of religious individualism. "Every unnecessary noise and every unnecessary movement were now prohibited, silent prayer was encouraged, overly ardent worship was to be avoided . . . nothing was left to improvisation. . . . Everything was highly organized and followed strict etiquette."[55]

In America, synagogues of this type developed only in particularly wealthy Orthodox communities. Manhattan's Jewish Center on the Upper West Side and Kehilath Jeshurun across Central Park in Yorkville became especially well known. There, rabbis and cantors, always meticulously groomed and bedecked in formal attire during worship, insisted that refinement and polish needed to underlie all aspects of religious life. The interior of these "high church" Orthodox synagogues conveyed the atmosphere that they sought to project. Light refracted through exquisite stained-glass windows. Red plush chairs adorned the dais. Chandeliers shone from high vaulted ceilings. Dark woods covered the walls and marble or thick carpeting the floors. Everything else, including the cushions and the sacred Torah scrolls, was covered in elegant, dark velvet. Members, most of them wealthy, clean-shaven, and well dressed, may have possessed only a minimal knowledge of Judaism. Yet they proudly identified with their synagogue and their religious movement, and they supported its institutions, including Yeshiva College, generously. One historian described theirs as an "American, religious, 'community of manners.'" [56]

Other Americanized Orthodox synagogues—whether they affiliated with the Young Israel movement or with the Union of Orthodox Jewish Congregations or remained unaffiliated—looked and felt poorer than Manhattan's Orthodox palaces. Their buildings were less grand, their services less formal, their members' homes and clothing far less elegant. These more modest congregations never hoped to compete with the ornate, formal "cathedral" synagogues of the Orthodox well-to-do; they catered to a different aesthetic. Yet like their wealthier counterparts, they symbolized internally the belief that modern American culture and Jewish religious tradition were inherently compatible. Their members dressed like other Americans, interacted in English, enjoyed sports, the radio, and the movies, and, much to the dismay of more right-wing rabbis, they even participated in mixed dancing, sometimes under congregational auspices. The synagogues also served as gathering grounds for young Orthodox Jews. The fourteen Young Israel synagogues in Brooklyn, for example, were reputedly "renowned central meeting places" for young people on the Sabbath and holidays. "There they met and discussed the compelling issues of contemporary Jewish life." There they also interacted with "members of the opposite sex at lectures, socials, and parties, all within the parameters of synagogue life."[57]

A short Yiddish film from 1931 captured the dilemma of Orthodox Jews during the interwar years, torn between those who embraced modernity, like the Americanized Orthodox, and those who resisted it, like the M'lochim and the faculty at Torah Vodaath. Entitled "Cantor on Trial," the spoof depicted the challenges that a search committee faced in selecting a new synagogue cantor for the High Holidays. One candidate from Galicia represented in his music, accent, and appearance the anti-modern East European

Cantor on Trial (1931). The three candidates trying out for the cantorial position are a traditional East European cantor; a formal German-style Orthodox cantor; and a cantor who is modern and hip. The latter alone excites the search committee. All three cantors were played in the film by Leibele Waldman. Courtesy of the National Center for Jewish Film.

alternative. While he offered a nostalgic reminder of the world left behind, most of the committee members knew instinctively that he was unsuitable. By his foreign manner alone, they recognized that he would never touch the souls of their own alienated children ("this won't please the public's will"). A second candidate embodied the formal qualities of a cantor at one of the German-style cathedral synagogues, complete with head gear, a German accent, and fancy trills. But his operatic performance left the committee members unmoved: they refused to accept the notion that cold formalism represented the wave of the future. The third candidate—youthful-looking, modern, and stylish—overcame general suspicions and won the day. His jazzy rendition of a sacred Sabbath prayer invigorated the committee members and brought them dancing into the aisles. The solution to Orthodoxy's problems, the film implied, lay in precisely that kind of synthesis between ancient texts and modern forms that the Americanized cantor represented. The fact that the film's star actor, the renowned Orthodox Cantor Liebele Waldman, actually played all three cantorial roles in the film both legitimated this message and hinted at a reassuring corollary: that the different parties in the Orthodox camp had more in common than they let on.[58]

THE PARTING OF THE WAYS

Many would have said the same concerning Conservative Judaism and Americanized Orthodoxy during these years. Indeed, contemporaries regularly made the claim, as one rabbi put it, that "modern Orthodox congregations are frequently indistinguishable in practice and spirit from avowedly Conservative synagogues and many of their rabbis frequently expound a similar philosophy of Judaism." Some synagogues, like the Brooklyn Jewish Center and Congregation Adath Israel in Cincinnati, were identified both as Conservative and as Orthodox, at least in the eyes of their members. In 1926, for this reason, a serious effort took place to effect a merger between the Jewish Theological Seminary and Yeshiva College. Even after that failed, numerous seminary students continued to boast a mix of Orthodox and Conservative training. In 1938, five of the seminary's eight ordainees had spent time at Yeshiva College. Well into the 1950s, 20 to 30 percent of the seminary's rabbinical students were Yeshiva graduates, and no less than 60 percent came from Orthodox backgrounds.[59]

The seeming congruence of goals between Conservative and Americanized Orthodox institutions helps to explain this. For example, the United Synagogue of America, founded in 1913 as the congregational arm of the seminary, listed among its objectives: "the maintenance of Jewish tradition in its historical continuity," "loyalty to the Torah and its historical exposition," "observance of the Sabbath and the dietary laws," preserving "the traditional character of the liturgy," and "the establishment of Jewish religious schools"—all goals to which every Orthodox Jew could heartily assent. In addition, members of the United Synagogue, like the Americanized Orthodox, "consciously strove to attract the Americanized children of immigrants from Eastern Europe." In 1926 the president of Young Israel, Moses Hoenig, addressed the Young People's League of the United Synagogue and described their "two outstanding organizations" in complementary terms as a portent of "the development of a youth movement in Jewish life."[60] The Conservative and the Orthodox even analyzed the problems of the American Jewish community in very similar language. "Unless something is done to check the indifference and apathy which is on the daily increase, particularly among our growing children and young folks, numberless of our people will be estranged and forever lost to the faith of their ancestry," a United Synagogue lay leader in Providence, Rhode Island, warned. His program mirrored that of his Modern Orthodox counterparts: "I have the firm conviction that an appeal in a tongue and under conditions which are more tasteful to our modern American life, yet not forgetting the fundamentals, the traditions and the ideals of Judaism, is the way to the solution to the problem."[61]

Nevertheless, Conservative Judaism and Americanized Orthodoxy increasingly diverged during the interwar years. As Yeshiva College became established and the United Synagogue ballooned from 22 member synagogues in 1913 to 229 synagogues in 1929 (making Conservative Judaism the fastest growing by far of America's Jewish religious movements),[62] institutional considerations and competitive pressures demanded clarification of the differences between the seminary and the Yeshiva, the United Synagogue and the Orthodox Union, Conservative Jews and Orthodox Jews. Conflict, painful as it was, helped the two movements to distinguish themselves from each other and to establish their own identities. Had the fervently Orthodox had their way, modernity and openness to secular culture would have determined the denominational boundary, much as *The Fundamentals: A Testimony to the Truth* (1909–15) sought to distinguish Evangelicals from modernists in Protestantism. In the absence of clear lines, however, symbols and rhetoric came to play as large a role as substance in differentiating the two groups. Over time, in a process as old as religion itself, small differences widened into large ones. What began as divergent tendencies within a single movement ended up as two movements, separate and increasingly distinct.

The creation of the United Synagogue did much to further this "parting of the ways."[63] The decision to initiate a new congregational union was made by Solomon Schechter, spurred on by economic, social, and ideological considerations. With the Jewish Theological Seminary's financial problems mounting, the arrangement within the Reform movement, where the Union of American Hebrew Congregations raised funds to support Hebrew Union College, began to look more and more practical. The Orthodox Union provided no comparable support to the Jewish Theological Seminary, and it seemed in any case increasingly reluctant to countenance the innovations that seminary-trained rabbis, in a bid to attract young people, sought to introduce into their congregations. There was, moreover, a growing social and ideological chasm between those member congregations of the Orthodox Union that were led by young seminary-trained rabbis and those that were not. Seminary alumni chafed under these difficulties and championed the creation of the new organization. It would, they thought, help both to fund their alma mater and to assist isolated colleagues. Some also thought that it would serve as a magnet for like-minded congregations, resulting in a "union of conservative forces in America," distinct in their eyes both from immigrant Orthodoxy and radical Reform.

Instead of ideological purity, however, the new organization, following the lead of Schechter and Cyrus Adler, broadly bid to embrace "all elements essentially loyal to traditional Judaism," and in a move fraught with symbolism adopted at the last minute the name of England's mainstream synagogue body, the United Synagogue. In fact, the hierarchic British model of Judaism, heavily influenced by Anglicanism, proved deeply alluring to the seminary's leaders. Just as England's newly elected chief rabbi, Joseph H. Hertz, himself the seminary's very first graduate, held authority over Great Britain's United Synagogue, representing the established faith of Anglo Jews, so the president of the seminary dreamed of seeing Conservative Judaism emerge as the established faith of American Jews. But if the hope was thereby to marginalize those to the right and to the left by co-opting the broad middle, that hope never was realized. Instead, the fast-growing United Synagogue became, over time, the synagogue body of a separate centrist movement, a status belatedly confirmed in 1991 when the organization was renamed the United Synagogue of Conservative Judaism.

Two issues involving women highlighted the controversies that helped to make Conservative Judaism a separate movement during these years—a fact less surprising than it seems since, as we have seen, Judaism's treatment of women had long been viewed as a test of its ability to parry modernity's challenges, and women actually attended Saturday morning services far more often than men (who had to work). One issue concerned the tragedy of the "anchored" wife *(agunah),* a woman whose husband had disappeared or proved recalcitrant and who could, therefore, not obtain the necessary certificate of Jewish divorce *(get),* permitting her to remarry under Jewish law. Immigration and particularly World War I with its large number of missing soldiers had greatly magnified this problem. Some placed the number of anchored Jewish wives in the tens of thousands. Critics observed sardonically that men, if their wives disappeared or were recalcitrant, faced no similar obstacles to remarriage under Jewish law; others noted that the Reform movement had solved the problem years before by abrogating Jewish laws concerning marriage and divorce, and relying on the provisions of state law. In response, Rabbi Louis M. Epstein (1887–1949), a graduate of the Jewish Theological Seminary who had previously studied at the famed Slobodka yeshiva in Europe and was an acknowledged expert in Jewish family law, put forth a proposal, tentatively approved by the Rabbinical Assembly in 1935, aimed at resolving this thorny problem by adding a codicil to the traditional wedding document *(ketubbah)* that would, under special circumstances, empower a wife to write her own bill of divorce in a manner that he hoped would prove acceptable to Orthodox rabbis worldwide. It wasn't. Instead, his proposal set off a firestorm of criticism aimed less at its content, which involved complex issues of textual interpretation, than at the "great insolence" of those (Conservative) rabbis who sought to advance it without prior approval from the foremost Orthodox sages of the day. The Agudath ha-Rabbanim, with Bernard Revel as a signatory, unanimously agreed to "excommunicate" anyone involved in a Jewish wedding ceremony performed according to the "misbegotten enactment." Agudath ha-Rabbanim President Joseph Konvitz, in a series of articles in the Yiddish press, went further, labeling seminary-trained rabbis as "ignorant" and "utterly unqualified to serve as teachers in Israel."[64]

The whole issue may have seemed like a tempest in a teapot to the vast majority of Jews who could scarcely understand the technical issues involved. But in many ways the long, ugly debate over how to resolve the problem of the anchored wife, which lasted long past World War II, highlighted issues that came to distinguish the Conservative strategy from its Orthodox counterpart and drew the movements farther and farther apart. Questions concerning rabbinic authority (did Orthodox sages always have the final word?), the place of the Talmud in the modern rabbinate, women's equality, and, most important, the extent to which Jewish law could be bent to meet the "progressive standards of American life" all underlay the controversy, and, increasingly, the two movements approached each of those questions differently. Ironically, while the agunah controversy helped to define distinctive features of the Conservative movement, it did little, in the end, to resolve the plight of the poor anchored women themselves. Neither Epstein's proposal, nor one put forth in 1953 by the preeminent Talmudist of the Jewish Theological Seminary, Saul Lieberman, fully resolved the problem.[65]

The other issue involving women that defined the Conservative movement during the interwar years and became, by the late 1950s, the most visible marker of its differences from Orthodoxy, was mixed seating. This, of course, was a familiar issue from the second half of the nineteenth century. As we have seen, reformers at that time abandoned the traditional separation of men and women in the synagogue as a demonstration of their commitment to women's equality and modernity, and in a bid to attract young people back to worship. Now, with Judaism again imperiled by massive numbers of unaffiliated and apathetic Jews, seminary-trained rabbis considered the same strategy. Although two seminary professors of Talmud, Louis Ginzberg and Moses Hyamson, expressed opposition to mixed seating on Jewish legal grounds, and the seminary's president, Cyrus Adler, made clear that he personally favored seating women up in the balcony, rabbis out in the field paid more heed to what they perceived as the "demands of the hour."[66] Mixed seating, sometimes with provisions made for those who still preferred to sit apart, became widespread. In 1922, for example, the Brooklyn Jewish Center debated the issue as it planned its new building: "[The] question . . . aroused a great deal of controversy. Should the men and women be seated together or should the strict orthodox rule of separating the sexes be enforced? The membership . . . consisted of men and women of various religious inclinations. . . . The committee wrestled with the problem at numerous meetings, where both sides of the question were argued. The majority recommendation was in favor of permitting men and women to sit together in the two center aisles, and of reserving the extreme left section for men who preferred their own section and the extreme right section for women who wanted to sit alone. This arrangement was adopted."[67]

In another case, at Adas Israel Congregation in Washington, D.C., bold young women forced the issue by daringly joining their husbands for worship on the ground floor, in violation of congregational policy. In still other cases, rabbis themselves promoted the change, hoping that it would draw new members and revitalize their congregations. By 1941, the Law Committee of the Conservative Rabbinical Assembly had recognized that the "prevailing attitude about the place of woman in modern society is making it increasingly difficult to maintain the traditional policy of isolation towards women in the synagogue." A 1947 survey of congregations led by seminary graduates confirmed that a "general practice in *nearly all of our congregations*" was that they permitted "mixed pews."[68]

To be sure, numerous rabbis ordained at Yeshiva's Rabbi Isaac Elchanan Theological Seminary likewise served mixed-seating congregations, especially as new suburban synagogues opened in the 1950s. One (possibly biased) source in 1961 counted "perhaps 250 Orthodox synagogues where family seating is practiced," while another estimate from 1954 reported that "ninety percent of the graduates of the Chicago Hebrew Theological Institution, which is Orthodox, and fifty percent of the graduates of the Yeshiva, the Orthodox institution in New York, have positions where family seating or optional family seating prevails." Orthodox leaders, however, never made their peace with the innovation. Yeshiva nominally revoked the ordination of graduates if they continued to serve mixed-seating congregations after having been warned to leave them. The Young Israel movement stipulated in its constitution that it would revoke the charter of any member congregation that failed to separate men and women. The Union of Orthodox Jewish Congregations and the Rabbinical Council of America also publicly denounced mixed seating as a violation of Jewish law (although they did not sanction individual members who behaved otherwise).[69]

Most important of all, a series of well-publicized court cases in the 1950s provided Orthodox sages with a forum for deprecating mixed seating as utterly incompatible with Orthodoxy. Courts, for the most part, refused to intervene in internal synagogue affairs and would not block moves from separate to mixed seating no matter what leading Orthodox rabbis said. But in the end that scarcely mattered. The widespread publicity generated by the court cases established in the public's mind the fact that "true" Orthodoxy and separate seating went hand in hand. As a result, those who tried to reconcile Orthodoxy and mixed seating found themselves increasingly isolated: some moved firmly into the ranks of the Conservative movement; others, particularly in the Midwest, began to worship under the label of Traditional Judaism. Seating—separate or mixed—soon became the most obvious visible boundary differentiating Orthodoxy from other branches of Judaism, even from Conservative synagogues that were otherwise largely traditional in their practice.[70]

RECONSTRUCTIONISM

Even as Conservative Judaism gained an identity separate from Orthodoxy, the nature of Conservative Judaism, and its strategy for luring Jews back to the synagogue, remained in considerable flux. At one extreme stood those who believed that Conservative Jews should "conserve" tradition to the fullest extent possible; they approached all changes with skepticism, especially those that seemed incompatible with Jewish legal codes. At the other extreme stood those who insisted that the only way to "conserve" Judaism at all was to "reconstruct" it, in the hope that by harmonizing Judaism and modernity young people would find it more compelling. A whole spectrum of views spanned these two extremes looking for a middle ground. All sides found themselves able to agree on innovations like the "late Friday night service," generally held in addition to the traditional evening service, which takes place at sundown. Group singing, an abbreviated liturgy, English readings, and a central sermon characterized this late Friday night service, which proved particularly popular with those who found Saturday morning services too long or in conflict with work, and who no longer celebrated Friday night traditionally in their own homes or among friends. Since the new service supplemented rather than replaced a traditional practice, it imparted just that sense of balance between tradition and change that Conservative Jews increasingly took as their ideal.[71]

But when it came to more substantive changes, Jews who denominated themselves as Conservative turned out to be of several minds. The arguments among them, like so many quarrels in the history of American Judaism, were not so much conclusive as defining. They helped individual Jews to negotiate their own place among the various contradictory values—secular and Jewish, traditional and modern—that simultaneously attracted them.[72]

The central figure behind many of these debates, and in the eyes of many the most significant American Jewish religious figure of his day, was Rabbi Mordecai M. Kaplan (1881–1983),[73] founder and leader of what is today known as Reconstructionist Judaism, the only full-fledged movement within American Judaism to have developed wholly within the United States. Born in Sventzian, Lithuania, about twenty-five miles from Vilna, Kaplan immigrated to the United States in 1889. His father, a traditional rabbi, had arrived the year before in the company of Rabbi Jacob Joseph and had subsequently become the ritual supervisor of kosher slaughterhouses on the Lower East Side. Young Mordecai studied with his father and also at Etz Chaim Yeshiva, City College, and Columbia University, where he specialized in sociology and philosophy and received a master's degree, and at the Jewish Theological Seminary, where he received a rabbinical diploma in 1902. On a visit to Europe in 1908 he acquired traditional ordination from Rabbi Isaac Jacob Reines, the founder of Religious Zionism. Kaplan thus united within himself a high level of both traditional and modern learning, as well as a firm commitment to Zionism. Yet, like many of his day, he was plagued with religious doubts and worried about whether Judaism and contemporary conditions could be reconciled. "The problem of Judaism," he wrote in his diary in 1913, "is inherently the problem of how it is to meet modern life."[74] He numbered among the first group of children of East European Jewish immigrants in the United States to understand, articulate, and even embody the dilemmas of the modern Jew.

Kaplan began his career in the world of Americanized Orthodoxy. He was a leader in the Jewish Endeavor Society, his first rabbinic position was at Congregation Kehilath Jeshurun of Yorkville, he played a role in the founding of the Young Israel movement, and he was the first rabbi of New York's Jewish Center. In 1909, after impressing Solomon Schechter with his "inspiring and stimulating personality," as well as his unaccented English, he rejoined the seminary to head its Teachers Institute; within a year he was also teaching homiletics to the rabbinical students. He remained at the seminary, influencing generations of its students, for the next fifty-four years, until his retirement in 1963. But during that time, like so many others of his generation, he found that he "could no longer preach and teach according to orthodox doctrine." Privately, he confided to his diary in 1914 that "Orthodoxy is the bane of Judaism" and that "the only hope . . . is in the introduction of radical and sweeping changes." He even claimed to have shared some of his "heterodoxical views" with the leaders of the Jewish Center when they first approached him, in 1916, about becoming the new congregation's rabbi. But it was actually only in 1920, in a widely discussed article entitled "A Program for the Reconstruction of Judaism," influenced by John Dewey's *Reconstructionism in Philosophy,* that readers heard him call for "new religious realism" and for a faith that was "both historic and progressive." Orthodoxy, he complained in the article, "precludes all conscious development in thought and practice, and deprives Judaism of the power to survive in an environment that permits of free contact with non-Jewish civilizations." "Any movement which aims at reconstructing Jewish life," he concluded, could not be Orthodox and would have to be willing to "revitalize the entire system of ceremonial observances by adjusting them to the spiritual needs of our day."[75]

With the publication of his "Program for the Reconstruction of Judaism," Kaplan by his own admission "crossed the Rubicon" of his career. In January 1922 he resigned from the Jewish Center and, along with thirty-five families who followed him, founded a new congregation, the Society for the Advancement of Judaism (SAJ). Following the example of Felix Adler and the Society for Ethical Culture, he agreed to serve SAJ as "leader for life," even as he continued to teach at the Jewish Theological Seminary. Within a few years, SAJ represented itself as the vanguard of a new movement—Reconstructionism—that aimed to "revitalize Judaism in America by making it function as a civilization in the everyday life of its adherents." In time, Kaplan hoped, Reconstructionism would become the guiding philosophy not only of Conservative Judaism but of all Judaism. "My version of Judaism," he boasted to his diary, "is at least in focus with the thinking of the day."[76]

The Judaism that Kaplan developed in his new pulpit, and then described in *Judaism as a Civilization: Toward a Reconstruction of American-Jewish Life* (1934) and other works, was a naturalistic and dynamic faith. The Jewish people, rather than God, stood at its center; there were no fixed beliefs, no divine revelations, no commandments. The Jewish religion, he insisted, existed for the Jewish people, not the other way around. Instead of focusing on Jewish law, as so many of his Orthodox and Conservative colleagues did, his "main concern," he once wrote, was "what innovations to introduce to render Judaism not only livable but a source of spiritual and moral creativity."[77] To this end, he focused on "Jewish civilization," which he defined as embracing every Jew and everything Jewish, including land (meaning Israel), history, language, literature, religious folkways, mores, laws, and art. Jews needed to "rediscover, reinterpret, and reconstruct" their civilization, he argued. He called upon Jews to reaffirm Jewish peoplehood, revitalize the Jewish religion, form a network of organic communities, strengthen Jewish life in the land of Israel, further Jewish cultural creativity, and cooperate with non-Jews in advancing freedom, justice, and peace.[78]

What made Kaplan's thought so controversial in Jewish circles was (1) his denial of supernaturalism and redefinition of God in terms of process ("the process that makes for salvation"); (2) his negation of Jewish chosenness ("modern-minded Jews can no longer believe, as did their fathers, that the Jews constitute a divinely chosen nation"); (3) his doctrinal latitudinarianism ("ideas or beliefs in conflict with what have come to be regarded as true or right should be eliminated"); and finally (4) his willingness to alter or discard commanded Jewish practices—what he called "folkways"—that had "outlived their usefulness."[79] Precisely these controversial elements,

however, appealed to those Conservative Jewish leaders who considered
the traditional Judaism of their youth out of touch with the needs of contemporary Jews and felt that Judaism, in order to survive, needed to be transformed. Like Kaplan, they were critical of "Orthodoxy because of its medi-
evalism and . . . Reform because of its un-Jewishness"—its negation of
Jewish peoplehood, its rejection of Zionism, and its spurning of the Hebrew
language.[80] By contrast, they found Reconstructionism's emphases—community, modernity, Zionism, freedom—"extraordinarily liberating," as one of
Kaplan's former students explained:

> [Kaplan resolved all of Conservative Judaism's] inner tensions and contra-
> dictions. Torah was not revealed from Sinai in words and letters. Judaism
> was in fact the creation of the Jewish people, very much a cultural document.
> Therefore, it could be studied critically, historically, and scientifically. The
> authority for what we do and believe as Jews lies not in the explicit will of
> a supernatural God but, rather, in the community that remains the instrument
> through which God reveals. Finally, since Judaism is whatever the Jewish
> people at its best would like it to be, we are completely free to redefine the
> content of Jewish religious belief and practice in the light of our own ongoing
> experience of God's revelation, and in doing so we ensure the survival of
> Judaism and the Jewish people.[81]

Kaplan's writings, read in retrospect, vividly portray the Judaism of the
interwar years. Kaplan's fears for the future reflected what he actually saw
in the present: thousands of children who had abandoned the immigrant
faith of their parents and neither practiced Judaism nor knew much about
it. His solution likewise reflected pragmatic considerations: he basically
provided a religious justification for ritual and ideological innovations that
a great many Jews had already adopted. Secular Jews too found many of
his ideas compatible, though where they understood religion to be part of
Jewish culture, he insisted that Jewish culture formed part of religion. Kaplan even understood that Jews, while fully American, still lived apart in a
subculture of their own. His discussion of "Jewish Civilization" and its relationship to "American Civilization" is, in many ways, as much description
as prescription. One scholar went so far as to speculate that Kaplan, in his
latitudinarian approach to theology and ritual as well as in his emphasis
on integration into America, church-state separation, Jewish peoplehood,
and Zionism, articulated the "major values or principles of *most* American
Jews, as gleaned from their behavior."[82]

Nevertheless, the vast bulk of American Jews did not become Reconstructionists, neither during the interwar years nor later, after 1968, when the movement established its own seminary, separated from Conservative Judaism, and struck out on its own as an independent branch of American Judaism. Reconstructionism's significance lies instead in the critical questions that it raised and the important debates that it stimulated within *all* movements of Judaism. Kaplan's liberal approach to tradition—his memorable claim that tradition should have a vote but not a veto—also served to further distinguish Conservative Judaism from Orthodoxy, especially after 1945, when the Agudath ha-Rabbanim publicly excommunicated him. Reconstructionism, as we shall see, influenced Reform Judaism as well, especially as it re-embraced Jewish peoplehood and some ritual practices.

Finally, two of the ideas that Kaplan vigorously championed became commonplace across the spectrum of American Jewish religious life. First was his claim that Judaism should be seen as a full-scale "religious civilization," not merely as a set of beliefs or a system of commandments. This emphasis on "the whole life of the Jew" stimulated greater attention to such previously neglected aspects of Jewish life as arts, crafts, music, drama, dance, and food—all of them, Kaplan insisted, no less intrinsic to Jewish civilization than doctrines and ceremonies. Over time, cultural programs became part of the life of almost every synagogue and Jewish community, even those utterly out of sympathy with Reconstructionism. Pageants, concerts, balls, dance recitals, art sales, the marketing of food products from Jewish farmers in the Holy Land, and similar activities became part of the "ritual calendar" of Jewish communal life throughout the United States.[83]

The second and related innovation that became widespread, partly in response to Kaplan's teachings, was the synagogue-center, the so-called "shul with a pool." The idea involved broadening the synagogue's mandate to embrace a range of social, educational, and even physical fitness activities designed to turn the house of worship into a seven-day-a-week multipurpose center, a hub of Jewish communal life. The synagogue, Kaplan explained in a 1916 article, "must become the Jew's second home. It must become his club, his theatre, and his forum." Jews who found religious worship unappealing might thereby be drawn into the synagogue through one of its other activities.[84]

Kaplan did not originate this idea. The synagogue-center drew upon earlier Jewish communal models as well as upon the institutional church movement that developed in the late nineteenth century to bring Protestantism and social services to the urban masses. Parallel to this, selected Reform temples, prior to Kaplan, had worked to broaden the mission of the synagogue by creating "temple centers" for the Jewish community at large. Synagogue-centers were also influenced by developments within the Young Men's Hebrew Associations, the Jewish settlement houses, community institutions for Jewish education, and the geographical movement out to wealthier streetcar suburbs. In 1917, for example, Rabbi Herbert Goldstein, a graduate of the Jewish Theological Seminary who was married to the daughter of Harry Fischel, opened what he called the Institutional Synagogue in the upscale Jewish community of Harlem, as part of his effort to bring Jews back to Orthodoxy (he even held "monster revival meetings" at the Regent Theatre, complete with bands and a rousing sermon in an effort to win over unaffiliated Jews). He proposed to build a synagogue that included "an auditorium, a Talmud Torah (Hebrew School—with twenty-one classrooms), club rooms, game rooms, a library, reading room, kindergarten, gymnasium, open air nursery, social rooms (one of which was to be equipped with a radio and a 'victrola'), a kitchen, a dining room, a roof garden, chess room, swimming pool, steam room, showers, bowling alleys, basketball courts, handball courts, and tennis courts." (The roof garden, tennis courts, and bowling alleys were later dropped from the plan.) These were the same features found in many a synagogue-center.[85]

Nevertheless, it was the multistory Jewish Center—part synagogue, part social hall, part athletic club—founded on Manhattan's West Side in 1918 under Kaplan's influence and with him as its initial leader that set the pattern for what became the synagogue-center movement as a whole. The Jewish Center, unlike its predecessors, was not aimed at philanthropic or missionary or uplift work: "For the first time, a Jewish recreational and educational center would serve the sponsors themselves, for they were in need of uplift themselves." It and its many imitators provided a full range of services—religious, social, cultural, educational, and recreational—to upwardly mobile middle-class Jews who were "ambitious and proud of their worldly accomplishments . . . devoted to their families and loyal to Judaism." Headed for the most part by Jewish Theological Seminary graduates whom Kaplan himself had helped to train and influence, synagogue-centers purported to subsume the functions of an entire Jewish community within the synagogue's portals. In Brooklyn alone, some thirty-three different congregations included the words "Jewish center" as part of their name.[86]

Other institutions, notably the more secular Jewish community center—heir to the Young Men's and Young Women's Hebrew Association, tied to no religious movement, and eager to welcome Jews of every kind into its facility—soon challenged the synagogue-center for communal supremacy.

Tensions between the two institutions, the one seeking to organize Jews on the basis of religious affiliation, the other on the basis of their ties to the Jewish people, became commonplace, especially in the post–World War II era, when Jews moved out to the more distant suburbs. But even when the Jewish community center became, in the end, the unifying *ethnic* institution of American Jews while synagogues became the *religious* institutions that divided them, the synagogue-center idea that Kaplan had so powerfully championed remained influential. In America, far more than elsewhere, synagogues across the spectrum of Jewish life came to assume that educational and recreational programs formed part of their mission. The functionally delimited "house of worship" largely passed from the scene.

THE METAMORPHOSIS OF REFORM JUDAISM

Mordecai Kaplan was deeply critical of Reform Judaism. He found it spiritually impoverished and sterile, "confined to one stratum of society— the so-called upper middle class," unrealistic in its effort to divorce Judaism from Jewish peoplehood, and unable "to check the process of gradual self-elimination of Jews from Jewish life." The signs, from his perspective, did "not point to Reformist power to hold the Jew very long." Indeed, mass East European immigration had, in many places, reduced Reform Judaism to a small minority position within the Jewish community, a kind of Jewish Episcopalianism. In New York, according to the *Jewish Communal Register* of 1918, just 2 percent of the city's synagogues were Reform. Among Reform rabbis nationwide, according to a survey published in 1926, there were "many expressions of dissatisfaction, that Reform is in need of resurrection, reformation, revitalization, that Reform must be reformed."[87]

What Kaplan failed to recognize was that during the interwar years, in response to criticisms such as his and perhaps out of fear that the movement would otherwise wither away, Reform Judaism began to transform itself. Many rabbis, directly influenced by Kaplan, placed increased "emphasis on Judaism as a civilization," focusing on "all the activities and relations of life." Even classical Reform congregations like Rockdale Temple in Cincinnati introduced sewing, music, dance, and drama into their program of activities. Others, in a bid to attract East European Jews, reintroduced once-discarded rituals such as the bar mitzvah. To be sure, half or more of all Reform Jewish families dissented. They did not observe even such occasional ceremonies as the Passover seder meal, the lighting of candles on Hanukkah, or fasting on Yom Kippur, and more than three-quarters did not kindle Sabbath candles in their homes on Friday night. But a survey indicated that attitudes were changing. Especially among young people and in those congregations that sought to attract East European Jews, traditional ritual practices had begun to return.[88]

Zionism too gained growing numbers of Reform adherents during the interwar years—not just for practical reasons, like the crisis facing European Jewry, but also in the hope that Jewish cultural and spiritual creativity in Zion would revitalize Jewish life everywhere, including the United States. Emblematically, a prominent Zionist, Rabbi James G. Heller, assumed the helm of one of the citadels of Reform Judaism, the congregation once headed by Isaac Mayer Wise in Cincinnati. Increasing numbers of faculty members at Hebrew Union College came to profess Zionism as well, including its leading exponents of Jewish theology and philosophy. In 1935, an avowed Zionist, Felix Levy, even assumed the presidency of the Central Conference of American Rabbis. A few years earlier, in 1930, a survey of Hebrew Union College students revealed that fully 91 percent of these future Reform rabbis either favored Zionism or were neutral on the subject; only 9 percent remained firmly opposed. So striking was the change sweeping through the Reform movement that the venerable David Philipson (1862–1949), a classical Reform rabbi who had been present at the conference that created the Pittsburgh Platform and who seemed to his Cincinnati congregants to be the very embodiment of Reform Judaism, now described himself as standing "in proud isolation" in his "universalistic advocacy of Judaism." Not only did his younger Reform colleagues disagree with his anti-Zionist interpretation of Judaism but, he confessed to his diary in 1927, he also felt himself "frequently laughed to scorn."[89]

As classical Reform Jews like Philipson found themselves marginalized, a new generation of Reform Jewish leaders, people like Rabbi Stephen S. Wise, Emanuel Gamoran, and Jane Evans, moved into the foreground. The changes that they introduced during the interwar years transformed the Reform movement and made it more inviting to East European Jews. This, in turn, paved the way for Reform's dramatic expansion in the postwar era.

Wise (1872–1949), born in Hungary and raised in New York, was the son of a New York rabbi associated with the "conservative" camp (no relation to Isaac Mayer Wise) and received private ordination in Europe. He moved firmly into the Reform orbit while serving a pulpit in Portland, Oregon, where he achieved renown as an eloquent speaker and advocate for social justice. He also dedicated himself from a young age to Zionism. Returning to New York in 1906, he peremptorily declined the rabbinate of the city's flagship Reform congregation, Temple Emanu-El, claiming that it would deny him complete freedom of the pulpit. The synagogue's trustees, following a long-established American practice, believed that their rabbi should be responsible to them. Instead, Wise defiantly founded and led what he called the Free Synagogue, under whose auspices he conducted brief services and addressed thousands every Sunday morning at Carnegie Hall. Becoming one of America's best-known rabbis, he reached out to East European Jews, forged alliances with liberal Christians, spoke out passionately for a Jewish state, and ardently advocated for the downtrodden and oppressed. In 1920 he helped reorganize the American Jewish Congress as a populist, democratic, and pro-Zionist alternative to the patrician-dominated and non-Zionist American Jewish Committee. He presided over the organization from 1923 until his death in 1949. In 1922, again marching to the beat of his own drummer, he opened a new rabbinical seminary, the Jewish Institute of Religion, in mid-Manhattan. Students at the new school held a variety of theological beliefs and affiliated with different branches of Judaism. All of them, however, identified with the three pillars that characterized Wise's own rabbinate: Zionism, social justice, and the task of serving *k'lal yisrael,* the Jewish people as a whole. This synthesis profoundly influenced generations of young Reform rabbis (and some Conservative and Orthodox ones as well), who continued to model their rabbinate on that of Wise even after the Jewish Institute of Religion merged with Hebrew Union College in 1950, following his death.[90]

Emanuel Gamoran (1895–1962) likewise influenced generations of rabbis (though he was not one himself), yet his influence on the Reform Jewish laity, particularly young Reform Jews studying in supplementary schools, was even stronger. Coming to the Reform movement in 1923 as an outsider, he assumed direction of its educational program and over the course of thirty-five years deepened and transformed it. Gamoran had immigrated to America at the age of twelve from Bessarabia, studied at Columbia University and the Jewish Theological Seminary, where he was particularly influenced by Mordecai Kaplan, and became one of the Jewish educational reformers, known as "Benderly boys," inspired by the creative work of the Jewish educational pioneer Samson Benderly. He brought to his new job a strong commitment to Zionism and to the Hebrew language, boundless energy, and an unswerving belief that young Jews should be trained in the customs, ceremonies, and language of the Jewish people—what Kaplan called its "civilization"—not just in matters of doctrine and belief. Where before the goal of Reform Jewish education was to turn Jewish young people

into better human beings, Gamoran looked to shape them into devoted adherents of the Jewish people as well. Indeed, one recent student claims that
Gamoran's aim was "no less than a re-injection of Jewishness into Reform
Judaism, a recovery of traditions and customs long ago set aside, [and]
reclamation of the very concept of peoplehood that Reformers parted with
in the nineteenth century as a price for citizenship." Gamoran taught Reform
Jews about Palestine and Zionism, introduced them to the practices of traditional Jews, encouraged them to learn Hebrew, and even provided them
with a wide range of arts and crafts projects designed to enhance their celebration of Jewish holidays within the home. Through a new generation of
beautifully produced textbooks, a thoroughgoing curricular reform, a professional journal, and personal exhortation, he managed to enhance Jewish
education at all levels within the Reform movement and to focus new attention on Judaism as a way of life. In so doing, he helped make Reform Judaism both more compatible with Zionism and more inviting to Jews, like
himself, with roots in Eastern Europe.[91]

Jane Evans (b. 1907) did the same for Reform Jewish sisterhoods. After
World War I, leaders in the field of Jewish philanthropy, following the general pattern in American social work, had forced sisterhoods of personal
service to cede their efforts aimed at relieving the plight of the urban poor
to professionally trained social workers, most of them men. No longer did
sisterhood women visit the poor in their homes. Now they were encouraged
to shift their energies "from the tumultuous streets of immigrant neighborhoods to the decorous pews and vestry rooms of their own synagogues."
There women initially assumed familiar domestic tasks: housekeeping, decorating, entertaining, and serving as hostesses; in addition, they helped to
raise funds for the synagogue through bake sales, the marketing of cards
and calendars, and the like. The National Federation of Temple Sisterhoods,
organized in 1913 by the Union of American Hebrew Congregations, coordi-
nated and promoted these sisterhood activities so successfully that, in 1926,
the union actually boasted more affiliated women's organizations than it
did congregations: 333 as compared to 280.[92]

With the appointment in 1933 of Evans as executive director of the National Federation of Temple Sisterhoods, the role of sisterhood expanded
in new directions. A woman of many talents, Evans, at the time, headed
the department of decoration at St. Louis's largest department store and
taught art courses to Jewish adults; she hoped to save enough money to
study medicine. Instead, she ended up devoting forty-three years to the
women of Reform Judaism. She brought to the job a Reform upbringing,

an abiding commitment to Zionism, a strong belief in Jewish education and social justice (indeed, she was a lifelong pacifist), and a religious sensibility influenced by the ideas of Mordecai Kaplan. She also was deeply committed to the advancement of women in Jewish life, a goal that she personally embodied through her wide-ranging communal activities and lectures. She helped to found the Jewish Braille Institute, played an active role in numerous Reform Jewish institutions, and chaired the Commission on Displaced Persons of the American Jewish Conference. In addition, she advocated the formal training of women for leadership and encouraged their participation in a plethora of synagogue activities. Finally, she encouraged women to become more active and knowledgeable as Jews and to strengthen the Jewishness of their households. "In our own homes, where we are in a sense custodian of . . . traditions, we Jewish women can do much to inculcate a love and reverence for Judaism through the observance of simple ceremonials," a report inspired by her and issued by the National Federation of Temple Sisterhoods declared in 1941. To this end, she encouraged diverse and innovative programs including, in the postwar era, the development of sisterhood-sponsored synagogue gift shops. By marketing Jewish ceremonial objects, including many from the new state of Israel; teaching women what these objects were and how to use them; and encouraging them to decorate their homes with Jewish symbols and artifacts, synagogue gift shops advanced some of her fondest goals. Through such activities, she, like Wise and Gamoran, contributed to the religious transformation of Reform Judaism, strengthening its ties to Zion and to the Jewish people as a whole.[93]

The new Guiding Principles of Reform Judaism, approved in 1937 at a tumultuous rabbinical convention held in Columbus, Ohio, and known thereafter as the Columbus Platform, granted this far-reaching religious transformation official sanction. Conscious of "the changes that have taken place in the modern world and the consequent need of stating anew the teachings of Reform Judaism," the controversial document pointedly devoted its two largest sections to "religious practice" and "Israel." Whereas classical Reform stressed that Judaism was a religion, the new document also spoke repeatedly of the "Jewish people," as if to stress that Judaism embraced both ethnicity and faith. Displaying the influence of Mordecai Kaplan, it also called for the "retention and development of such customs, symbols and ceremonies as possess inspirational value, the cultivation of distinctive forms of religious art and music[,] and the use of Hebrew, together with the vernacular, in our worship and instruction." Finally, and most strikingly in contrast with the Pittsburgh Platform of 1885, it described the "rehabilitation of Palestine, the land hallowed by memories and hopes" in positive and sympathetic terms. It "affirm[ed] the obligation of all Jewry to aid in its upbuilding as a Jewish homeland by endeavoring to make it not only a haven of refuge for the oppressed but also a center of Jewish culture and spiritual life." The carefully crafted language neither mentioned nor endorsed political Zionism by name. In 1942, a group of Reform rabbis and laymen publicly broke with their Reform colleagues over the volatile Zionism issue, and they established the hugely controversial American Council for Judaism, which opposed a Jewish state and sought to restore Reform Judaism to its classical moorings. But the rearguard action, for all of the emotion that it engendered, served in the end mainly to underscore the transformation that the Columbus Platform exemplified. By World War II, Reform Judaism had successfully reinvented itself, accommodating Zionism, a commitment to Jewish peoplehood, and many traditional customs and ceremonies as well.[94]

The spectrum of American Judaism during the interwar years, stretching from the antimodernist Orthodoxy of the M'lochim to the secular Judaism of some socialists and communists, mirrored, in many ways, the general picture of American religion at that time, characterized by what has been called the "noise of conflict." Religiously, America had never seemed less united. Conflict between faiths and among people of faith was the era's most characteristic religious tone. So it was among Jews. Conflict reigned within the different Jewish religious movements as well as between them; among Zionists, non-Zionists, and anti-Zionists; among natives, immigrants, and children of immigrants; among Jews of different political persuasions; among family; and among friends. While these conflicts also quietly attested to the richness of American Jewish life—testifying to the cornucopia of different religious options available—at least one outsider concluded that Jews had separated "into a number of competing camps."[95]

At a deeper level, however, significant commonalities continued to unite America's Jews. Indeed, in many respects the interwar years drew Jews of different backgrounds and beliefs closer together, particularly as cultural differences among them waned and antisemitic discrimination against them waxed. Feelings of peoplehood—the sense that Jews, whatever their background, ideology, and degree of religiosity form one "family of Israel"— provided the ties that bound together American Jews, the more so once Reform Jews recommitted themselves to peoplehood, and Jews of every stripe found themselves living within "gilded ghettoes" and a distinctively Jewish subculture. In addition, despite all the sound and fury of intra-religious conflict, many (though not all) Jews found themselves in agreement on a host of critical issues: they sought simultaneously to be both American and Jewish; they juggled parallel commitments to tradition and modernity; they understood Judaism to embrace much more than faith alone; they expected their synagogues to be multipurpose institutions; and, increasingly, they supported the creation of a Jewish national homeland in Palestine. Organizations as diverse as B'nai B'rith, the Jewish Publication Society, the Joint Distribution Committee, the National Jewish Welfare Board, the Synagogue Council of America, and the Zionist Organization of America all boasted representatives from across the spectrum of Jewish life during these years; their meetings drew Reform, Conservative, and Orthodox leaders to a common table. While the noise of conflict rumbled on relentlessly wherever Jews lived, something no less important worked to check it: the conviction that Jews as a people shared a common fate.

THE GREAT DEPRESSION

The events of the 1930s reminded Jews of that common fate. The decade opened with the toppling of a renowned symbol of Jewish economic success: the Jewish-owned and grandly named Bank of the United States, which failed on December 11, 1930. Some 20 percent of New York's Jews, or one out of every ten Jews nationwide, experienced losses from the debacle, and probably a higher percentage of Jewish businesses and communal institutions did so as well. Untold thousands, including spinsters, widows, and people who had scrimped for years to send their children to college, lost their entire life's savings—in part, some suspected, because non-Jewish bankers like the House of Morgan refused to rescue the "Pantspressers' Bank" from collapse.[96]

The impact of this disaster, added to the 1929 stock market crash, which had affected the wealthiest segments of the Jewish community, signaled for Jews the onset of the Great Depression. Beginning in 1930, according to the *American Jewish Year Book,* "every Jewish social service organization in the country" saw its facilities and services "in demand as never before, and yet, at the same time, their resources were drastically reduced." Practically every local Jewish federated charity in the country "was compelled to reduce its budget." Several Jewish organizations went out of existence altogether.[97]

Synagogues and Jewish educational institutions suffered particularly from the economic downturn. Historic congregations as well as brand new synagogue-centers found themselves "with shrinking memberships, expensive facilities, and large deficits." Temple Emanu-El of New York, one of the nation's oldest, wealthiest, and most prestigious Reform congregations, saw its membership plunge by 44 percent during the 1930s. Chicago's Rodfei Zedek congregation, a Conservative synagogue, suffered a membership decline of 52 percent (from 234 member families in 1929 to 113 in 1933)—this in a city where, in 1932, fifty thousand Jews were unemployed. Religious school enrollment at Rodfei Zedek dropped even farther, plummeting from 350 children to only 62. Jewish religious school enrollments declined almost everywhere during the Depression, falling about 18 percent over six years in New York and 16 percent in just six months in Chicago. Many teachers lost their jobs or took deep salary cuts.[98]

The situation was bleakest in the most intensive (and therefore most expensive) Jewish educational institutions. At the New Haven, Connecticut, yeshiva founded by Rabbi Judah Levenberg, one graduate later recalled, students regularly went hungry: "Every morning a fellow in the yeshivah would get up at 6:30 A.M. and go from butcher to butcher with a paper bag. And they would throw in scraps of meat. Some of the bakers gave us old bread and every Friday before *Shabbos* [Sabbath] some women would come around and donate a couple of chickens. I remember one Rosh Hashanah when all we had was a little *chalah* [braided bread] and two tomatoes and that was it."[99]

Bernard Revel's Yeshiva College also suffered disproportionately during the Depression. Even before the collapse of the Bank of the United States it found itself unable to meet its outsized obligations. At one point in late 1929 instructors went unpaid for sixteen straight weeks and all student support was cut off. By 1934, Revel described "actual starvation and acute suffering" among the faculty, at least one of whom also had his telephone disconnected.[100]

Jews at the time took pride in the fact that, despite their personal hardships, they participated in "all civic efforts to relieve suffering in general" and that, in addition, "Jewish organizations . . . established special agencies to help meet the crisis." The Hebrew Immigrant Aid Society opened its facilities to those needing food and shelter; synagogues welcomed the homeless; communities formed Jewish employment bureaus, particularly for those seeking jobs that permitted them to observe the Sabbath; and in many cities special fund-raising campaigns were initiated. Plum Street Temple in Cincinnati, the congregation once headed by Rabbi Isaac Mayer Wise, sheltered up to two hundred men a night in early 1931. "They have no work," a local Jewish newspaper explained, "they have no money, they need food and lodging."[101]

As these examples indicate, Jews turned primarily to one another during the 1930s, relying on ties of faith and kinship to carry them through the hard times. As so often before, traditions of self-help and mutual aid overcame religious, ideological, and generational differences within the Jewish community; Jews, like other close-knit groups, assumed responsibility for helping their own. This helps to explain why the Jewish unemployment rate stood at less than half the national average in major cities: Jews, when they could, helped one another find jobs. Moreover, bad as things were, few Jews recalled having to do without the basics of life, as so many other immigrants and their children did. But even if they suffered less than some of their neighbors, the combination of economic losses, stalled mobility, job discrimination, and rising antisemitism shook Jews' confidence in the American dream and transformed their lives. Indeed, the Great Depression constituted a "defining moment" for American Jews, "inaugurating alterations in Jewish families, occupational structures, political preferences, and communal organization that changed the face of Jewish life in the twentieth century."[102]

In terms of religion, the change that produced the longest-term impact on American Judaism during the Depression was the intensification of the movement toward the five-day work week. Unions with large concentrations of Jews among their members had been pressing for this reform since World War I, recognizing that the two-day weekend would promote workers' interest in "the progressive shortening of the hours of labor" while simultaneously aiding Jews who sought to observe their Sabbath as a solemn day of rest. Rabbi Bernard Drachman, the Orthodox head of the Jewish Sabbath Alliance, vigorously supported the five-day week, and the Agudath ha-Rabbanim even held a stormy debate on whether to cooperate with Reform Jews to advance the plan. During the 1920s the idea gathered steam, backed by an unusual coalition of labor and religious leaders who agreed, in the words of one rabbinic supporter, that the measure would "save the Sabbath for the Jew," "add health and strength to the American people," and "promote the home and home life," especially for men. Subsequently, the five-day week was also touted as a cure for the economic ills of overproduction and unemployment. As a result, the shortened work week became, during the 1930s, one of the chief goals of those seeking to stimulate industrial activity. President Franklin D. Roosevelt's New Deal embraced the idea in the National Industrial Recovery Act (1933), and many of the labor codes approved by the National Recovery Administration included forty-hour-week provisions. The Fair Labor Standards Act (1938) made it the law of the land in many industries. By 1939, countless workers enjoyed a two-day weekend, up from no more than half a million in 1929. The extra leisure did not immediately translate for most Jews into enhanced Sabbath-observance, but in the postwar era those who did seek to observe the Sabbath day strictly found it easier to do so than ever before. This brought to an end, particularly in some Reform Jewish circles, calls to shift the Sabbath to Sunday, and it deprived workers of what had once been their chief excuse for missing services on Saturday. Most important of all, the five-day week granted Judaism an enhanced measure of equality within American life. Instead of having to choose between the American pattern of work and the Jewish day of rest, now Jews could proudly embrace both.[103]

CONFRONTING THE HOLOCAUST

The domestic problems that plagued American Jewry in the wake of the Great Depression temporarily diverted the community's attention from the international arena. Even the *American Jewish Year Book* admitted in 1931 that "the Jews of the United States did not during the past years watch the situation of their overseas co-religionists with the same concentration as in the preceding twelve months."[104] Nevertheless, community leaders did continue to monitor unsettling developments in Germany, where Adolf Hitler was gaining in popularity. The ties between American and German Jewry had long been close: hundreds of thousands of American Jews had roots and relatives in Germany; thousands more had visited or studied there; some maintained regular scholarly, scientific, or business connections with Germany's Jews. All of these Jews followed developments in Germany with mounting concern.

Succeeding issues of the annual *American Jewish Year Book* chronicled the grim news from Germany as it unfolded. When Hitler's National Socialists became the second largest party in the Reichstag (German parliament) after winning 107 seats in the September 1930 elections, the *Year Book* reported the consequences: "street attacks against Jews, molestation of Jews in cafes and theatres, disturbance of religious services in synagogues and of Jewish meetings of all kinds, desecration of synagogues, and pollution of cemeteries." Two years later, it proclaimed the German-Jewish situation a "world-shocking catastrophe" of "momentous significance to Jews everywhere," and it devoted many pages to recounting all that it knew in frightening detail. The next year, it chillingly listed "the names of a number of distinguished German Jews who died by their own hands," as well as those "ousted from the laboratories and lecture halls of German colleges and universities," who, it said (with some exaggeration), were "cordially welcomed" in other countries. By 1935 it was warning of a "deliberate premeditated policy of a ruling clique ruthlessly to exterminate German Jewry— a policy springing from maniacal adherence to a fanatical dogma of race nationalism." Four years after that, it informed its American Jewish readers with singular finality "that the Nazi Government was bent upon annihilating the last vestiges of the German-Jewish community." The *Year Book's* dramatic conclusion—tragically prophetic and largely ignored in 1939—was that Germany would "not rest with the annihilation of the Jewish community within her own frontiers, but sought insofar as it was able, to visit the same fate upon Jews all over the world."[105]

How many readers read and internalized these fact-filled reports published in the small-print columns of the *Year Book's* annual review of events cannot be known. Elsewhere, the American press, and even some Jewish and Jewish-owned newspapers (like the *New York Times*), underreported German atrocities in the 1930s and 1940s and misinterpreted their significance; they considered the reports exaggerated, like the atrocity stories manufactured during World War I, and they feared charges of parochialism. Too many people, as a result, failed to assimilate the magnitude of the unfolding Holocaust facing European Jewry until it was practically complete. They dismissed the kind of horrific news that appeared in the *American Jewish Year Book* and the Yiddish press as being "beyond belief."[106]

Germany's Jews, of course, knew differently, and as conditions deteriorated, particularly after the burning and looting of German synagogues on the night of November 9, 1938, known as Kristallnacht ("crystal night"), they cast about desperately in search of refuge. What is astonishing, given the magnitude of American antisemitism and nativism, is that more than 100,000 Jews managed to gain entry into the United States during the 1930s. Overall, America accepted over 200,000 Jewish refugees between 1933 and 1945, more than any other country but still only a small fraction of those who could have been saved. Viewed in relation to size and capacity, the English, Dutch, French, and others in Western Europe were far more generous than was America in their acceptance of immigrants in the 1930s.[107]

For the most part, America's draconian immigration laws were stringently applied during the Depression. Consular officials were instructed to adhere closely to the ban on admitting persons "likely to become a public charge," and State Department officials responsible for issuing visas advocated a policy of "postpone and postpone and postpone." Since the Nazis stripped emigrating Jews of their wealth, permitting them to leave with no more than about four dollars to their name, American consuls had easy grounds to reject them. Immigrant quotas too proved inflexible. Congress knew that fewer than 5 percent of Americans, in a 1938 survey, expressed any willingness to raise quotas in order to accommodate refugees, while more than two-thirds insisted that "with conditions as they are we should try to keep them out." Surprisingly, 25.8 percent of American Jews admitted in a poll that they too would have voted against a bill to open the nation's doors to a larger number of European refugees. Though they did not explain why, they clearly feared that a new wave of Jewish immigration would only add to their economic burdens and further erode the position of American Jews, already battered by more than 120 organizations devoted to promoting anti-Jewish hatred. Not even the pitiful cries of refugee children sufficed to move American hearts. The Wagner-Rogers bill, which proposed to admit twenty thousand refugee children under the age of fourteen free of quota restrictions, failed to win presidential support ("File No Action," Roosevelt wrote) and then suffered "death by a thousand amendments" in the Senate.[108]

The fortunate Jews who made it to America's shores did so, for the most part, thanks to the hard work of friends, relatives, and supporters in the United States. Saving even one person required a blizzard of letters and telegrams, perhaps the intercession of a government official, and usually a guarantee that the individual concerned would be privately sponsored and not become a "public charge." Special efforts were made on behalf of rabbis, scholars, and prominent political and cultural figures whom immigration law and consular enforcers tended to treat more compassionately. The major rabbinical organizations and their seminaries, in spite of their own financial difficulties, also helped out by providing official affidavits and job offers. When immigrants at long last arrived, those who greeted them made extraordinary efforts to find them work within the Jewish sub-economy: in Jewish communal institutions, in the kosher food industry, or in Jewish-owned businesses. They knew that if immigrants were seen to be competing with non-Jews for jobs, pressure to bar new immigrants entirely would only increase. Ironically, the American Jewish community, and America generally, reaped the fruits of this refugee migration for years afterward. A disproportionate number of America's greatest scientists, social scientists, humanists, and artists, as well as many of its foremost rabbis and Jewish scholars, were people saved from the Nazi ovens. As we shall see, some of these Holocaust-era refugees would, in a few years, transform and reinvigorate American Jewish religious life.[109]

Could American Jewry have done more to rescue the Jews who fell under Nazi rule during the 1930s and early 1940s? The issue remains highly contentious. Some blame Jewish leaders for doing too little too late, some condemn Jewish organizations for their inability to unite in time of crisis, some argue that American Jews should have applied greater pressure on the government to help save Jews, and some point accusingly at missed opportunities—actions that if taken might have made a difference. Others conclude sadly that little more could have been accomplished given the realities of the day. Anti-immigrant sentiment within the United States, persistent isolationism, burgeoning antisemitism (in 1938, according to one poll, one-fifth of all Americans wanted to "drive Jews out of the United States"), and the politics of expediency, coupled later with the president's insistence that the best way to save Jews was to win the war, would have rendered even the most zealous Jewish rescue campaigns largely futile. By all accounts, Hitler's maniacal determination to annihilate the Jews greatly exceeded the American Jewish community's power to stop him. Yet nagging doubts remain, for Jews know that had they been even a little more successful in opening up America's gates, in bringing government pressure to bear on Great Britain to admit more Jews into Palestine, or in shaming the world to find some other haven for the Jews of Europe, many more of their brothers and sisters might have been saved.[110]

The problem of rescue took on new urgency on August 28, 1942, just before the Sabbath, when a telegram sent twenty days earlier by Gerhart Riegner, representative of the World Jewish Congress in Switzerland, finally reached Rabbi Stephen S. Wise from London. It conveyed "alarming reports" of "a plan . . . according to which . . . Jews in countries occupied [or] controlled by Germany[,] numbering three and half to four millions[,] should after deportation and concentration in east be at one blow exterminated in order to resolve once [and] for all [the] Jewish question in Europe." This was the first confirmation of a conscious German plan to annihilate the Jews, and to some diplomats it had all the "earmarks of a war rumor inspired by fear." But three months later, by which time many similar reports had surfaced, Secretary of State Sumner Welles confirmed to Wise that "there is no exaggeration. These documents are evidently correct." That same evening, November 24, 1942, Wise informed the press that 2 million Jews had been killed by the Nazis in an "extermination campaign" and that the news had been confirmed by the State Department.[111]

Some, like the editors of the *Christian Century,* continued to question the reports. But Jews, fearing the worst, organized a day of mourning and prayer on December 2, which received extensive attention. "New York City, summoned to prayer by Mayor Fiorello La Guardia, was the center of the day's solemn activities. Yiddish newspapers came out with black borders. Several radio stations were silent for two minutes. During the morning, half a million Jewish union laborers, joined by non-Jewish fellow workers, halted production for ten minutes. At noon, a one-hour radio program was broadcast. And special services were held at five o'clock in synagogues throughout the city. In many other American cities, the Day of Mourning was marked by religious services and local radio programs. Late in the afternoon, NBC broadcast a special quarter-hour memorial service across the nation."[112] Six days later, leaders representing every faction in American Jewish life, religious and secular alike, met with President Roosevelt, appealing to him to bring news of the extermination to the world "and to do all in your power to make an effort to stop it."[113]

There was no agreement, however, as to what Jews themselves might do to "make an effort to stop it." Should they work quietly behind the scenes or noisily through mass demonstrations and media events? Should they focus on saving Jews by winning the war, or risk delaying the war in order to rescue Jews from imminent destruction? Should they employ only legal means to save Jews, or, given the urgency of the situation, might illegal means also be employed, such as ransom payments to the Nazis and other violations of laws banning trade with the enemy? Should they explore every avenue of rescue, even temporary ones, or should they demand, above all else, throwing open the gates of Palestine so as to create a permanent home for the Jewish people? Finally, should they exert special efforts to save certain groups of Jews (rabbis? scholars? labor leaders?), or should all lives be considered equally valuable and holy? Given the moral and political complexity of these questions, it is easy to understand why individual Jews felt internally conflicted and why Jewish organizations and movements found it so difficult to reach consensus. On the other hand, it is also easy to understand why later critics faulted the community for doing too little, too late.

What did unite American Jews at the time was a sense of depression and sadness, even despair. The editor of the Jewish Publication Society, concerned about the "psychological effect" of so much bad news on the Jewish community's morale, decided in response to "call a halt to terrorizing the Jewish population in this country," and peremptorily rejected several manuscripts dealing with Jewish persecutions in Europe. In 1941, JPS actually published a joke book for its readers, the only one in its long history, with the significant title *Let Laughter Ring.* By 1943, however, there was nothing more to laugh about; the mood in Jewish circles had turned black. A controversial pageant entitled "We Will Never Die," created by some of Hollywood's finest Jewish talent as a "memorial" to the murdered Jews, captured the moment, reaching over 100,000 people who crowded into its performances and many thousands more on radio. "Remember us!" the actors pleaded, as groups of Jewish dead recounted their fate at the hands of the Nazis. Displaying the "corpse of a people," the narrator complained bitterly that "no voice is heard to cry halt to the slaughter, no government speaks to bid the murder of human millions end." Chillingly, the pageant closed with the chanting of the Jewish prayer for the dead, the Kaddish.[114]

In many ways, Kaddish was the appropriate prayer. The utter failure of the April 1943 Bermuda Conference on Refugees, which did nothing on Jews' behalf, coinciding with the liquidation and foredoomed uprising of the last remaining Jews in Warsaw, previously Europe's largest Jewish community, plunged American Jewry into despondency. One Jewish leader described his colleagues as being "more than desperate."[115]

Large numbers of Jews, in response, turned to Zionism, having witnessed first-hand the urgent need for a Jewish national homeland to which all Jews might freely immigrate. A short-lived democratically elected "parliament" of Jewish organizations, known as the American Jewish Conference, meeting on September 1, 1943, overwhelmingly endorsed "re-creation of the Jewish commonwealth," setting off a tumultuous demonstration and the rapturous singing of *Hatikvah,* (Hope), the Zionist anthem. Hope, indeed, is what the grassroots resolution offered the beleaguered community. Although a few prominent anti-Zionist dissenters soon abandoned the conference, the vast majority who stayed, among them Reform, Conservative, and Orthodox Jews, as well as militant secularists, found in Zionism the faith that united them. Amid the horrors of the unfolding Holocaust in Europe, the promise of an independent Jewish home in Palestine where all Jews would be warmly welcomed provided the only prospect of a brighter future.[116]

Thirty-five days later, some five hundred fervently Orthodox rabbis, spurred by organizations outside the American Jewish mainstream (several of them unsympathetic to Zionism), marched on Washington, three days before Yom Kippur, to plead for more immediate rescue efforts to save the surviving remnant of Europe's Jews, who were perishing by the thousands every day. "As the five hundred rabbis, wearing their *chassidic* garb of long silk gabardines and round plush hats, moved along Pennsylvania Avenue, they certainly presented a picture which for its exotic quality was unprecedented

Leaders of the Agudath ha-Rabbanim lead hundreds of fervently Orthodox rabbis
and other sympathizers on a march to the Capitol (October 6, 1943) demanding
"immediate action" to save the Jews of Europe. The three rabbis in long black coats at the
head of the march were, from left: Eliezer Silver, Israel Rosenberg, and Bernard Levinthal.
Orthodox Jewish Archives of the Agudath Israel of America.

even in such a cosmopolitan city as Washington," a Yiddish journalist reported. "There was something of the quality of a religious procession that
characterized the Rabbinical Pilgrimage and compelled the respect of every
passerby." Be this as it may, President Roosevelt failed to meet with the
group, and its efforts, at the time, received scant national attention. Years
later, however, the demonstration would proudly be recalled as the only
one of its kind in Washington on behalf of Europe's vanishing Jews. Though
condemned and in part thwarted by mainstream Jewish leaders, the color-
ful march anticipated two significant postwar trends: the growing political
sophistication of fervently Orthodox Jews and the increasing willingness
of Jews of all sorts to advocate publicly for what they believed.[117]

Even before their elders cried out for Zion and paraded down the streets
of Washington, young Jews had begun marching off to war. Some 550,000
Jewish men and women, 11 to 12 percent of the national Jewish population,
eventually served in America's armed forces during World War II; roughly
eight thousand were killed in action and thirty-six thousand received awards

for bravery. As before, the Jewish Welfare Board, the body charged with meeting the needs of American Jews in the armed forces, carefully compiled this information, documenting for posterity (and as a defense against anti-semitism) "that the percentage of Jews in uniform was always equal to and, in some instances, higher than the ratio of Jews to the general population." More than twelve hundred separate Jewish communities in the United States participated in the massive data-gathering operation, which had many of the earmarks of a vast religious undertaking and was remembered, proudly, as "perhaps the greatest voluntary Jewish record gathering effort ever orga-nized." The Welfare Board also continued its mission of meeting, on a broad, cooperative, and impartial basis, the social, cultural, and religious needs of "Jewish fighters for America." It supplied Jewish chaplains (311 in all) and organized Jewish religious services—including, in 1945, a memo-rable Passover seder held in the abandoned castle of Nazi Propaganda Min-ister Joseph Goebbels. It provided Jewish soldiers with prayerbooks (more than twice the size of the World War I version, but still "necessarily incom-plete"), Bibles, kosher food, and Jewish literature, understanding that it served a heterogeneous community, "men and women with Orthodox, Con-servative, and Reform backgrounds." And it offered Jews, under its banner, Jewish educational programs and the reassuring company of coreligionists. In short, it modeled in war a spirit of Jewish unity that so often eluded American Jews in times of peace.[118]

In the military and on the home front alike during World War II, Jews recited fervent prayers: for their country, for their president, for loved ones left behind in Europe, and above all for those risking their lives on the field of battle. "We beseech Thee, O God, to shield and protect our armed forces, in the air, on sea, and on land," one jointly agreed upon prayer declared. "May it be Thy will that the dominion of tyranny and cruelty speedily be brought to an end and the kingdom of righteousness be established on earth with liberty and freedom for all mankind." Participation in the war against Nazism represented for Jews the ultimate synthesis of patriotic alle-giance and religious duty. World War II, for all but the small number of Jews who remained pacifists, "was the quintessential just war."[119]

Their countrymen, Jews knew, did not all agree. In addition to the Chris-tian pacifists, who refused to bear arms on principle and considered all wars unjust, a prestigious group of isolationists also opposed America's entry into the war. Many members of the group belonged to the America First Committee, which claimed 15 million supporters at its height. Flying ace Charles A. Lindbergh, himself a prominent isolationist, blamed Jews explicitly for driving America into war with Germany, warning that their "greatest danger to this country" lay "in their large ownership and influence in our motion pictures, our press, our radio, and our Government." Antisemites of longer standing, including radio priest Father Charles Coughlin and the pro-Nazi German-American Bund, accused Jews of starting the war for their own benefit. The Pearl Harbor attack and America's entry into the war silenced some of these critics, but in 1943 an official government study found substantial amounts of Judeophobia in half of the forty-two states it surveyed, and as late as 1944 fully 60 percent of Americans claimed to have heard "criticism or talk against the Jews" in the previous six months.[120]

Notwithstanding a ban on the circulation of antisemitic publications at naval and military posts, anti-Jewish hostility within the armed forces also ran rampant. This is hardly a surprise since, until they met in the barracks, most Jews and Christians had never closely interacted with one another; they knew each other only as stereotypes. In fact, whole regions of the country where soldiers came to train, notably the South and the West, had only limited acquaintance with Jews. Eventually, wartime interactions and temporary Jewish geographic mobility during the war paved the way for important postwar social transformations, both in the relationship of Christians to Jews and in Jewish residential patterns across the country. In the short term, though, the military represented a microcosm of American society as a whole during World War II, beset by antisemitism as well as by many other forms of religious and racial prejudice. Slurs, harassment, and discriminatory promotion practices were legion. Even some battlefield commanders, like General George S. Patton, displayed their prejudices openly.[121]

In response to wartime antisemitism, liberal Jews and Christians joined together to promote "better understanding" and "goodwill." The institutional groundwork for this effort had been laid back in the 1920s when, in an effort to counter earlier explosions of social hatred, a series of goodwill committees and interfaith organizations had been established—notably what became the National Conference of Christians and Jews (NCCJ). The rise of Hitler added fresh urgency to these efforts. Under the auspices of the NCCJ, liberal-minded Protestants, Catholics, and Jews worked together to promote "brotherhood." They fashioned in the process a new and more religiously pluralistic image of America—not as a Protestant or Christian land, but rather as one nurtured by three ennobling spiritual traditions ("culture groups"): Protestantism, Catholicism, and Judaism. Representatives of these three great faiths—a minister, a priest, and a rabbi—barnstormed the country in an attempt to rout religious prejudice. In hundreds of local communities, "round tables" brought together Protestant, Catholic, and Jewish leaders to advance and symbolize interreligious cooperation. Brotherhood Day, a focus for these efforts, was first celebrated in 1934 (enlarged in 1947 to Brotherhood Week). Especially after the word "Christian" was appropriated by Fascist and antisemitic organizations, the phrase "Judeo-Christian" entered the lexicon as the standard liberal term for the idea that Western values rest on a religious consensus. In the face of worldwide antisemitic efforts to stigmatize and destroy Judaism, influential Christians and Jews in America labored to uphold it, pushing Judaism from the margins of American religious life toward its very center.[122]

The central military command, eager to promote religious harmony in the ranks during wartime, joined this earnest effort. Jewish chaplains in the military recalled participating "together with the Catholic and Protestant Chaplains in many a good will meeting." At basic training, "the Rabbi appeared in the same uniform as the Priest and the Minister," addressing servicemen who, in many cases "had never seen, much less heard, a Rabbi speak before." At funerals for the unknown soldier, "three Chaplains— Protestant, Catholic, and Jewish—[stood] at the grave of every unknown soldier and recite[d] a similar burial service in English, Latin, and Hebrew." Most famously, in 1943, the sinking of the USS *Dorchester* created an enduring interfaith legend. According to the oft-repeated and somewhat romanticized story, the ship's four chaplains—two Protestants, a Catholic, and a Jew—gave their own gloves and life belts to evacuating seamen and then stood together "arm and arm in prayer" as the damaged ship went down. A 1948 U.S. postage stamp summed up the heroism of the "immortal chaplains" in three evocative words: "interfaith in action." This icon of "Judeo-Christian" America, a land of Protestants, Catholics, and Jews, symbolized the model of American religion that rapidly gained ground in the postwar era. By 1952, "good Americans were supposed to be good Judeo-Christians. It was the new national creed."[123]

Even as interfaith ties strengthened, Jews also worked to reinvigorate their own faith, as if in response to those who labored to undermine it. Something of a spiritual and cultural revival washed over American Jewry as Hitlerism rose, paralleling in part developments within the German-Jewish community at the same time. Mordecai Kaplan's sensitive antennae quickly picked up the new phenomenon: "Jews . . . who had abandoned their people" were "returning like prodigal sons." "Because of the threat of annihilation," he hypothesized in 1934, the Jew was "impelled to rise to new heights of spiritual achievement."[124]

Jewish educators spearheaded this revival. In 1937 alone, three significant Orthodox Jewish all-day schools were founded: HILI (Hebrew Institute of Long Island), Ramaz School in Manhattan, and Maimonides School in Boston. In the ten years between 1940 and 1950, ninety-seven Jewish all-day schools were founded across the United States and Canada (as compared to twenty-eight that had been founded in the previous twenty-two years). Jewish educators also initiated intensive Jewish educational camps at this time, the most important of which were established between 1941 and 1952. Camp Massad, established in 1941, sought to create what its founder described as a "little Hebrew world," a kind of Hebrew utopia that was at once staunchly American in its activities and celebrations; profoundly Zionist in outlook; "positive" toward Jewish religious traditions; and fanatical (especially in the early years) about the Hebrew language. Brandeis Camp Institute, which opened that same year but focused more on leadership development, aimed, according to its historian, "to inspire [college-age] Jews to be Jews, to link them with Jewish peoplehood, to whet their appetite for more learning, and to encourage them to bring up their children as Jews." Both the Conservative and the Reform movements followed these up with Jewish educational summer camps of their own, Ramah (1947) and what became known as Olin-Sang-Ruby Union Institute (1952). The goal of training future Jewish leaders also underlay the Reform movement's National Federation of Temple Youth, established in 1939, and the Conservative movement's Leadership Training Fellowship in 1945. Meanwhile, the National Academy for Adult Jewish Studies, founded in 1940, promoted programs of Jewish learning in synagogues, spawning a small-scale Jewish education revival among adults. The Jewish Publication Society, which promoted Jewish education and culture through books rather than classroom instruction, also roared back to life at this time. Its total income increased fivefold between 1935 and 1945, and the number of books that it distributed tripled. Finally, Jewish organizational life as a whole surged during the war years. In 1945, the *American Jewish Year Book* reported that "a larger number of new organizations . . . formed during the past five years than in any previous five-year period, forty-seven new organizations having been established since 1940." "Interest in Jewish affairs," it explained, "has undoubtedly been heightened as a result of the catastrophe which befell the Jews of Europe under the Nazi onslaught."[125]

As before, women played a distinctively important role in this revival. "The future of American Jewry is directly conditioned on the education of its womanhood," Rose B. Goldstein, the wife of a leading Conservative

rabbi, reiterated in 1938. As if in response, Conservative sisterhoods organized a wide range of classes and workshops, many of them designed to
promote Sabbath observance and other Jewish home rituals. The most successful project by far was a pageant entitled "The Jewish Home Beautiful,"
subsequently published as a book (1941), designed to stimulate Jewish religious home life by inspiring modern Jewish women with the possibilities
inherent in Jewish material culture. "Beautify the Jewish home and ennoble
every Jewish life," the volume proclaimed. Echoing poet Grace Noll Crowell
while hinting at the mood of the times, it promised that:

> Although a people falter through the dark
> And nations grope,—
> With God Himself back of these little homes—
> We have sure hope.

As a guide to Jewish Sabbath and holiday home practices, complete with
background information, photographs, songs, recipes, and decorating suggestions, *The Jewish Home Beautiful* proved wildly popular among women
of every Jewish religious movement, going through eleven printings in
twenty years. Reputedly "hundreds of men and women in the armed services" also drew sustenance from it; presumably it reminded them of what
awaited them back home. The goal of the Home Beautiful movement, however, was avowedly revivalistic: it aimed to turn Jews away from the "non-
Jewish festive days [that] have won the hearts of many of our women" and
to help them "explore the possibilities of our own traditions," so as to "make
Judaism a thing of joy and beauty" for themselves and their children. Many
women, apparently, heeded the message and moved to mend their ways.
Delegates to a 1940 convention of the Conservative National Women's League,
for example, after viewing the narrative version of the pageant on which
the first part of the volume was based, vowed "to carefully observe our Jewish holidays, our Jewish ceremonies, and our Jewish tradition in the home,
thereby adding beauty and meaning to our religious and cultural life."[126]

Even secular Jews, a leading exponent later recalled, underwent something
of a religious revival in response to burgeoning antisemitism and the growing
Nazi threat: "On the eve of the Second World War—when it became apparent that the gains which the Emancipation had brought to European Jewry
were about to disappear, when many sensed that the Dark Ages were returning for European Jews, when the darkest recesses of human nature opened
up—it seemed that the pillars of Jewish secular culture were about to collapse. . . . Many Jews became disillusioned with their faith in progress and

Reform Jewish women at Mount Zion Hebrew Congregation in St. Paul, Minnesota,
perform "The Jewish Home Beautiful" pageant, demonstrating a
traditional Sabbath table setting and the lighting of the Sabbath candles (1940s).
Courtesy of the Jewish Historical Society of the Upper Midwest.

humanity, and sought comfort in the ancestral creed." The Yiddish poet
Jacob Glatstein published a widely discussed critique of Jewish universalism
in 1938 entitled "Good Night World." Re-embracing traditional Jewish life,
he declared: "I'm going back to the ghetto . . . I cry with the joy of coming
back." In a similar vein, leaders of the proudly secular Sholem Aleichem
Folk Institute decided, also in 1938, "to introduce the study of the Pentateuch
into the elementary schools, to emphasize the celebration of Jewish holidays,
and, in general, to establish a positive attitude towards all manner of Jewish
ways of life." The Workmen's Circle schools likewise began a process described as "inner Judaization" at that time, and the Yiddish secularist educator Leibush Lehrer reports that at the famous Yiddish secularist summer
camp named Boiberik, "a minimal degree of ritual along the lines of tradition
was introduced," protests notwithstanding.[127]

There were at least two reasons for all of these changes. One had to do with the rise of Hitler, which prodded secularists into becoming "warmer Jews." The second related to the decision of many Jewish Socialists to support the mainstream candidate, Franklin Delano Roosevelt—already something of a hero to Jews for his labor policies, opposition to Nazism, and appointment of Jews to high office—over the Socialist candidate in the 1936 election. These events, a Yiddish writer and educator who lived through the period theorized, wrought a "singular revolution" in the lives of secular American Jews, strengthening "their feeling for rootedness," for "accepting and perpetuating much more of our ancient legacy."[128]

Taken together, this Holocaust-era revival of American Jewish life represented both a defensive response to adversity and a form of cultural resistance, a resolve to maintain Judaism in the face of opposition and danger. It also promised to prepare the community for the new responsibilities that it faced in the wake of the European Jewish catastrophe. "American Jews," the *American Jewish Year Book* reported as early as 1941, "are realizing that they have been spared for a sacred task—to preserve Judaism and its cultural, social, and moral values." That same year, Hebrew Union College historian Jacob Rader Marcus, who would himself soon shift the central focus of his scholarship from Europe to America, also pointed to the American Jewish community's new historic role: "The burden is solely ours to carry," he declared. "Jewish culture and civilization and leadership are shifting rapidly to these shores."[129] As the Nazis reduced European Jewry to ashes, Judaism in America was gathering strength. Years of challenge and promise lay ahead.

6

Renewal

PEACE OF MIND

Rabbi Joshua Loth Liebman (1907–1948) understood, in 1946, how strange some would find it that he had written a book entitled *Peace of Mind*. Inspirational books in English aimed at a mass audience had always before been written by Christians. Would readers trust a Boston Reform rabbi to distill for them the "helpful insights about human nature that psychology has discovered" and to correlate these "with the truest religious insights and goals of the ages?" Would they heed one who drew upon the sources of his own "healthy-minded" faith, critiqued the Catholic confessional, and promoted a therapeutic culture of self-acceptance over a religious culture of self-denial? Would they even consider his "*reconstructed* God idea," influenced by Mordecai Kaplan, that defined God in naturalistic terms as "the Power for salvation"?

The answer to all of these questions, it turned out, was a resounding yes. *Peace of Mind* raced to the top of the *New York Times* bestseller list, sold well over 1 million copies, and was translated into ten languages. Never before had so many Americans of diverse faiths turned to a contemporary rabbi for help in meeting their own spiritual and psychological needs. Until Norman Vincent Peale's *The Power of Positive Thinking* supplanted it, *Peace of Mind* was the most successful American inspirational book of the twentieth century.[1]

Peace of Mind heralded Judaism's emergence as an intellectual, cultural, and theological force within postwar American society. Its success was one of many signs that Jews stood on the threshold of acceptance into the religious mainstream and anticipated the decline of domestic antisemitism, a trend that the volume's message of tolerance sought to advance. The book also gave expression to the shifting mood of American Jews in the wake of World War II. Its very title encapsulated the community's collective quest for happiness, tranquility, and self-fulfillment in the aftermath of more than a decade of unrelenting tragedy and horror. In passing, if not in depth, the book went on to touch upon many of the major themes of postwar American Judaism: interfaith relations, the Holocaust, Zionism, social justice, healing, and, most of all, the psychological and spiritual challenges, especially for Jewish women, of middle-class suburban life. In more ways than anyone at the time could have imagined, *Peace of Mind* signaled the onset of a new era in American Judaism.

Signs of that new era abounded. On September 8, 1945, judges in Atlantic City, New Jersey, crowned Bess Myerson "Miss America"—a title that would have been all but impossible for a daughter of impoverished New York Jewish immigrants to have held in prewar years. That very same month, the already widely respected Jewish baseball star Hank Greenberg gained national acclaim when his ninth-inning grand slam home run won the American League pennant for the Detroit Tigers; he then went on to lead his team to victory in the World Series. Both Myerson and Greenberg rapidly found themselves treated as "secular saints" within the Jewish community; they were looked up to as "symbols of sudden legitimacy . . . they had arrived."[2]

Soon Jews "arrived" in other circles as well. Arthur Miller's *Focus* (1945), Saul Bellow's *The Victim* (1947), Laura Z. Hobson's *Gentleman's Agreement* (1947), Norman Mailer's *The Naked and the Dead* (1948), and Irwin Shaw's *The Young Lions* (1948) broke into the mainstream book market, bringing fame to their authors and introducing the American reading public to Jewish themes and characters. In different ways, all of these works condemned antisemitism as un-American, presented Jews in a new and more sympathetic light, and promoted intergroup understanding and tolerance. *Gentleman's Agreement,* a courageous exposure of pervasive antisemitic discrimination in the United States, carried these objectives onto the silver screen. This 1947 film, based on Hobson's bestselling novel of the same title, won the Academy Award for best picture and, according to a contemporary sociological study, created among its viewers a "significantly more favorable attitude towards Jews." A year later, in 1948, the state of Israel came into being, a development that further improved the American Jewish image, especially as Americans came to view Israel as a "democracy similar in background and institutions to the United States." Eventually, as we shall see, the new Jewish state would become a central focus of American Jewish life.[3]

In the meanwhile, Jews understood all of these developments as signs of "affirmation" following the greatest tragedy in their history. Librarian Joshua Bloch, invoking a striking phrase from critic Van Wyck Brooks, spoke of a postwar Jewish "hunger for affirmations, for a world without confusions, waste, or groping, a world that is full of order and purpose." Elliot E. Cohen used a related phrase in late 1945 in the inaugural editorial of the Jewish intellectual magazine *Commentary,* which he described purposefully as "an act of affirmation." Following the publication of a spate of novels with Jewish themes, including Soma Morgenstern's *The Son of the Lost Son* (1946), depicting the return to Judaism of those who had denied their heritage, Cohen concluded in 1947 that so far as culture was concerned, "Jewish reaffirmation is the watchword."[4]

American Jews in the late 1940s felt a special responsibility to "reaffirm." With the destruction of so many of their European relatives, the major part of the world Jewish population resided for the first time on the North American continent. Whereas before, the Jews of Europe represented the demographic and cultural center of world Jewry, now that designation fell to America. Historians Oscar and Mary Handlin heralded this news on page one of the fiftieth volume of the *American Jewish Year Book,* published in 1949. "The events of the Second World War," they declared, "left the United States the center of world Judaism. The answers to the most critical questions as to the future of the Jews everywhere will be determined by the attitudes and the position of the five million Jews who are citizens of the American Republic."[5]

THE POSTWAR REVIVAL

American Judaism had actually been gaining strength since the late 1930s, partly, we have seen, as a form of spiritual resistance to Nazism and antisemitism. Now with the war over, the nation as a whole turned increasingly toward religion—a response, some believed, to wartime horrors and to the postwar threat from "godless" Communism. "One of the most significant tendencies of our time has been the turn to religion among intellectuals and the growing disfavor with which secular attitudes and perspectives are now regarded in not a few circles that lay claim to the leadership of culture," the left-wing *Partisan Review* reported in 1950. It predicted that "if the present tendency continues, the mid-century years may go down in history as the years of conversion and return." In 1954, Congress added the words "under God" to the Pledge of Allegiance, and in 1956 it made the phrase "In God We Trust," found on coins since the Civil War, the official national motto. "Never has religion been so institutionalized, so conspicuous, so public," journalist Claire Cox concluded in a 1961 book depicting the "new-time religion" that had taken shape in America since World War II. "Never has churchgoing been so acceptable, so much 'the thing to do.'"[6]

Judaism played a prominent part in this conspicuous "new-time religion." As antisemitism declined during the postwar decades, the religion of American Jews gained widespread recognition as America's "third faith" alongside Protestantism and Catholicism. Popular interest in Judaism burgeoned as Americans sought to learn more about this "unknown religion of our time."[7] Fueled by postwar prosperity, Judaism strengthened institutionally through the building of synagogues and religious schools and the development of new communal institutions, though whether Jews actually *became* more religious or only *affiliated* at a higher rate has long been disputed. Whatever the case, religion became the major vehicle for Jewish identity, while secular Judaism as an ideology largely collapsed. Judaism also began to adapt to new environmental conditions, accompanying Jews out to the suburbs and then to sunbelt cities like Miami and Los Angeles. Less noticeably but no less significantly, Holocaust-era immigrants began to affect American Judaism during these years. Their memories, commitments, and collective sense of obligation to those who had not survived set the stage for developments that would transform all of American Judaism, Orthodoxy in particular, for decades to come.

In the midst of these transformations, Judaism's status as an accepted American faith won striking confirmation in a 1955 bestseller entitled, memorably, *Protestant-Catholic-Jew*. Written by Will Herberg, a Jewish ex-Marxist intellectual, the book argued that America had become a "'triple melting pot,' restructured in three great communities with religious labels, defining three great 'communions' or 'faiths.'" To be an American, according to Herberg, meant defining oneself according to the new "tripartite scheme" of American religion: to be, in other words, a Protestant, a Catholic, or a Jew. To be anything else, he contended, "is somehow not to be an American." The argument, for all of its manifest inadequacies (for example, Herberg practically ignored Evangelical Protestants and blacks and seemed to write off non-believers, Muslims, Buddhists, and other minority faiths entirely), captured the national imagination and shaped subsequent religious discourse.

It provided a vocabulary, an explanation, and a new set of boundaries for the restructured American religion that had by then been developing for half a century. Carrying forward the achievements of the interfaith organizations, the military chaplains, Bess Myerson, Hank Greenberg, and Joshua Loth Liebman's *Peace of Mind*, *Protestant-Catholic-Jew* also reaffirmed the elevation of Jews to insider status within the hallowed halls of American religion. Though Jews constituted but 3.2 percent of the total American population, they found themselves, thanks to Herberg, "enfranchised as the guardians of one-third of the American religious heritage." *Time* magazine underscored that new status when it provided its readers with cover stories on Jewish Theological Seminary president Louis Finkelstein in 1951 and Hebrew Union College president Nelson Glueck in 1963.[8]

Antisemites, meanwhile, found themselves placed on the defensive as Judaism's status rose. Forced to justify their anti-Jewish prejudice in the face of America's increasingly tolerant norms, they beat a hasty retreat. "Organized anti-Semitic activity, which began to decline after the war, continued at a low ebb during the year under review," the *American Jewish Year Book* reported in 1950. Thirty-five antisemitic organizations folded completely (leaving fifty-seven others to keep the embers of hatred warm). Between 1946 and 1950, the percentage of Americans who claimed even to have heard "any criticism or talk against the Jews in the last six months" dropped from 64 percent to 24 percent. Thanks to federal and state legislation, pressure from returning veterans, government and media exposure (including films like *Gentleman's Agreement*), and the stigma of being compared to the Nazis, discrimination against Jews in employment, housing, and daily life also markedly declined. By the early 1960s, almost all resorts and housing developments had dropped their restrictive clauses; antisemitic college quotas had mostly ended; and professional fields like law, medicine, and banking proved more receptive to Jews than at any time in the twentieth century. Antisemitism by no means disappeared, of course, any more than nativism, anti-Catholicism, or racism did. Slurs, prejudice, and violence against Jews still occasionally flared; exclusive clubs and suburbs still attempted, in some places, to keep Jews out; and tensions, particularly involving school prayer, public celebrations of Christmas, and related issues, still managed to bring ancient animosities back to the fore. Looking back, however, Anti-Defamation League director Benjamin R. Epstein, who had spent much of his life battling anti-Jewish hatred, described the two decades following World War II as a "period of tremendous progress" and a "golden age." During those years, he recalled, American Jews "achieved a greater degree of economic and political security, and a broader social acceptance than had ever been known by any Jewish community since the [ancient] Dispersion."[9]

It was not just in terms of their security and social acceptance that contemporaries viewed the postwar era as a golden age for American Jews; prosperity characterized the period as well. By 1955, Jews of East European background had risen "more or less to the level previously achieved by the German Jews," and economic distinctions between the earlier and later immigrants had largely disappeared. Jews had become fundamentally middle class, their proportion in nonmanual occupations exceeding that of the general population. Jews had also moved up into the professions. One study discerned a particular increase in the number of Jewish journalists, authors, engineers, architects, and college teachers, and concluded that there had been a "rapid rise in the number of Jews engaged in all intellectual occupations in recent years." Another found that the number of Jews engaged in manual labor had markedly declined. "The Jewish worker in America," it turned out, "was typically a man of one generation. He was 'neither the son nor the father' of a proletarian."[10]

Religion, too, contributed to the characterization of the era as a golden age. In 1949–50, according to the *American Jewish Year Book,* "synagogue building continued," "membership in synagogues and affiliated associations was on the increase," "synagogue attendance was improving," "adult education was continuing to attract substantial enrollments," and "religious ceremonies were being observed in more homes with increasing regularity." Forty percent of America's 4.5 million Jews affiliated with synagogues, an improvement from the 1930s but still far below Catholic and Protestant affiliation rates. By the late 1950s, that figure would reach 60 percent, a figure never exceeded and the only time in the twentieth century that more than half of America's Jews were synagogue members. In Milwaukee, where about 65 percent of Jews affiliated in 1960, a survey found that in just twelve years, from 1945 to 1957, the number of families belonging to synagogues leapt from 2,169 to 3,600, with Conservative and Reform synagogues scoring the most impressive gains. "Judaism has changed," one respondent explained to researchers. "Nowadays people enjoy religion and going to synagogue." As late as 1962, surveys continued to describe the "flourishing state of the American Jewish community's religious bodies."[11]

Critics have claimed that the 1950s revival was more show than substance, that "what was revived was not so much religious belief as belief in the *value* of religion." For all that Jews may have professed to enjoy going to synagogue, for example, the number who actually attended on a regular basis (more than once a month) remained far smaller than among Catholics and Protestants. A comparative study from Detroit, where 69 percent of Catholics attended religious services weekly but only 26 percent of Jews did, concluded tartly that "Catholics are about as likely to go to church every week, as are Jews to attend synagogues a few times a year." Moreover, Orthodox Judaism was actually *losing* ground during these years. While in 1950 it still claimed more adherents than any other branch of Judaism, the bulk of its members were old, and even if they called themselves Orthodox, their level of observance was weak. Only 8 percent of Orthodox Jews in Milwaukee, for example, actually "sustain[ed] traditional Orthodoxy in theory and practice." Meanwhile, a widely publicized 1952 study found that "only twenty-three percent of the children of the Orthodox intend to remain Orthodox; a full half plan to turn Conservative." Within two decades that prediction was confirmed, and Orthodoxy's ranks diminished, falling far below those of Conservative and Reform Judaism. The movement's strength, by then, lay in the knowledge and commitment of its core membership, not in absolute numbers.[12]

Even among the non-Orthodox there was "every indication" in the 1950s that notwithstanding the supposed revival they were actually "becoming more lax in their religious practices." Occasional practices, like the lighting of candles on Hanukkah and the celebration of the Passover seder did find growing numbers of adherents, and the High Holidays continued to be widely maintained, but observance of the dietary laws *(kashrut)* declined markedly, and most Sabbath restrictions, except for the kindling of candles on Friday night, were observed in the breach.[13] The preeminent Jewish sociologist of the day, Marshall Sklare, seeking to understand the emerging pattern of ritual observance that he detected, spelled out five criteria "important in explaining retention of specific home rituals." His conclusion, still widely accepted, was that the highest degree of retention occurs when a ritual: "(1) is capable of effective redefinition in modern terms, (2) does not demand social isolation or the adoption of a unique life style, (3) accords with the religious culture of the larger community and provides a 'Jewish' alternative when such is felt to be needed, (4) is centered on the child, and (5) is performed annually or infrequently."[14]

Accordingly, the minor winter holiday of Hanukkah, with its stress on freedom, its easy-to-observe candle-lighting ritual, its child-pleasing gifts and games, and its convenient proximity to Christmas, became ever more widely observed among postwar Jews. The prohibition against carrying and using money on the Sabbath, by contrast, lost ground and was maintained only by the most scrupulous.

If belief, synagogue attendance, and the regular practice of Jewish rituals did not characterize the revival that so many discerned in Jewish religious life, what did?

First, the postwar decades witnessed the greatest synagogue-building boom in all of American Jewish history. Between 1945 and 1965, well over one thousand synagogues and temples were built or rebuilt, most of them, as we shall see, in suburbia (where Protestants and Catholics were similarly building churches in large numbers). The myriad details connected with these vast projects—planning, designing, fundraising, and furnishing—consumed vast quantities of time, energy, and money, and constituted the "central religious activity" of many American Jews. Each building campaign conveyed a message of life and hope. It projected an aura of religious self-confidence, especially where a synagogue crossed into the suburban frontier to display the symbols of Judaism where the Star of David had never previously penetrated. It aroused a spirit of religious activity, enthusiasm, and mission even among people who rarely attended worship services themselves. Whether as a supplement to regular religious work or as an alternative to it, the building of a synagogue excited a high level of religious energy.[15]

Second, the era produced a dramatic expansion of Jewish education on top of what had already been accomplished from the late 1930s. Between 1948 and 1958, the number of children attending Jewish schools more than doubled, jumping from 239,398 to 553,600. Whereas in the 1920s the majority of Jewish children received no Jewish education whatsoever, in 1959 the American Association for Jewish Education estimated that "more than eighty percent of Jewish children attended one or another type of Jewish school during the course of their elementary school years." To be sure, educators complained that as enrollment in Jewish schools *increased,* standards in Jewish education *decreased,* particularly since the average number of hours per week that supplementary schools met actually declined. This was balanced, however, by the continuing rise in Jewish all-day school education, which enrolled 42,651 students in 241 schools in 1958, as compared to 18,654 in 128 schools a decade earlier, a rate of growth more than double that found in Catholic and Protestant parochial education during the same years. Allocations to Jewish education from centralized Jewish philanthropies also rose dramatically, tripling from $14 million in 1943 to $42.2 million in 1959, a reflection of the community's new domestic priorities. Indeed, Jewish education at all levels found "increased community interest and support" across the United States. Hebrew Union College, the Jewish Theological Seminary, and the newly broadened and renamed Yeshiva University all announced far-reaching programs of expansion, spurred both by the "catastrophic extinction of Jewish centers of learning abroad" and by the "glaring need of the American community for religious direction and informed leadership."[16]

Third, a great wave of interest in Bible study overspread the Jewish community, paralleling the Christian back-to-the-Bible movement of the same period. In an effort "to reclaim the Bible for the Jews"—a reference to the spate of novels and films that presented the Bible in a Christian framework that Jews found thoroughly alienating—numerous synagogues organized Bible classes, and Jewish home Bible study programs proliferated. One writer, impressed by the work of the Gideons, a Christian voluntary organization devoted to the worldwide distribution of Scripture, even called for placing copies of the Jewish translation of the Bible in all kosher hotels. The Jewish Publication Society issued several new editions of its Jewish Bible translation in the 1950s, and the society marketed tens of thousands of copies of its Bible textbook, Mortimer J. Cohen's illustrated *Pathways Through the Bible* (1946), as well as a variety of other Bible-related works. Between 1952 and 1954, sales of its Bibles rose almost 40 percent—perhaps in response to the number one bestseller of these years, the Protestant *Revised Standard Version of the Bible*. In 1956, the Bible or books about it constituted almost half of the *total* number of books that the Jewish Publication Society distributed and sold. An up-to-date one-volume Jewish translation of the Bible commissioned by the society in 1953 finally appeared, after innumerable delays, in 1985.[17]

Fourth, postwar Jews evinced unprecedented interest in Jewish theology and religious thought. World War II challenged optimistic liberal beliefs concerning progress, reason, and human perfectibility, and raised profound questions concerning the problem of evil and the place of God. "Modernity itself was in crisis," one student recalled, "and with it the whole of modern Jewish thought." Members of the "postmodern generation" who looked to "return to religion" discovered, as Will Herberg put it, that "we have lost our direction and all but lost the ability to read the map that might show us how to regain it." Some looked for guidance from German-Jewish philosophers like Franz Rosenzweig and Martin Buber, whose teachings, translated into English, began to command a wide readership. Others turned to immigrant scholars like Rabbis Emil Fackenheim, Abraham Joshua Heschel, and Joseph Soloveitchik, who had started to synthesize traditional Jewish

learning with modern continental thought during their prewar days as doctoral students in Berlin and now brought the fruits of that creative encounter
to their American counterparts. Still others looked to American-born seekers
like Herberg or to an emerging younger generation of Jewish philosophers,
several of them German-born, who began their careers after World War II
in the universities and the rabbinate. All of these thinkers felt the impact
of neo-orthodox currents in Protestantism, best represented in America by
Reinhold Niebuhr, and they rebelled against the belief in naturalism (God
as experienced in nature) and human perfectibility that Mordecai Kaplan
and earlier Reform Jewish thinkers had taught. "The modern Jew has been
prone to forget that the world is unredeemed, and that God is in exile,"
Heschel thundered in an essay praising Niebuhr. "The present generation
is beginning to realize how monstrous an illusion it was to substitute faith
in man for faith in God." *Commentary* magazine opened its pages to theological articles in the late 1940s, and in 1952, *Judaism: A Quarterly Journal
of Jewish Life and Thought* published its first issue, the aim being to create
a "journal on Jewish theology transcending organizational barriers."[18]

The 1950s also witnessed a wave of book-length studies of Jewish theology—the most serious contributions written in America since the days of
Solomon Schechter and Kaufmann Kohler. Some of these works, like Herberg's *Judaism and Modern Man* and Heschel's *Man Is Not Alone* (both
published in 1951), focused on the predicament of human beings looking
for faith in a postwar age. Others, like Abba Hillel Silver's *Where Judaism
Differed* (1957) and Leo Baeck's *Judaism and Christianity* (1958), tried to
clarify Judaism's distinctiveness in a world where the term Judeo-Christian
had obscured critical differences between the two faiths. "We are in the
midst of a theological renaissance," a survey of "current theological trends"
happily concluded in 1959. The fact that so many serious thinkers now
thought seriously about Judaism provided yet another encouraging sign
that an American Jewish religious revival was under way.[19]

Finally, the postwar years coincided with the near collapse of Jewish
secularism as an organized movement, a development that heightened still
further the perception of a Jewish community restored to its religious moorings. The Nazis shook the pillars of Jewish secular culture, disillusioning
many who had come to believe with a perfect faith in progress, universal
justice, and human potential. News of Soviet purges, persecutions, and
deportations of Jews, beginning in the late 1940s, further undermined the
confidence of those who had come to see the Soviet Union as something
of a Jewish secular paradise. Meanwhile, persecutions of Communists,

suspected Communists, and former Communists in America during the opening years of the Cold War created a climate of fear in Jewish secularist circles. To call oneself secular (as but 1 percent of the national population did in 1952) was to declare oneself subversive, for religion was deemed an essential part of the "American way of life." Indeed, secularism even called into question an individual's mental health. In *Peace of Mind,* Rabbi Joshua Loth Liebman equated the denial of God's existence with "the denial of meaning in life" and "the distrust of the universe." In most cases, he warned, it was a sign of psychological illness, "built upon foundations of emotional conflict and disturbed human relationships in the early years of life." In this climate, many secularists prudently concluded that they were, in fact, not "completely divorce[d] from supernatural and fideistic presuppositions, but merely neglect[ful] of the orthodox ritual." To prove it, they proudly affiliated with Conservative and Reform synagogues, even if they rarely attended them.[20]

With the close-knit Jewish subculture of the interwar years on the decline, Yiddish losing its hold among the Jewish masses, and secularism under siege, the institutions that once buttressed the Jewish secularist movement closed their doors. In 1958, fewer than 2 percent of American Jewish children were studying in Jewish secular ("Yiddishist") schools, a decline of more than 50 percent in just a dozen years. Much like the Jewish working class itself, "unadulterated secularism" in the American Jewish community became largely a "one-generation phenomenon." It was replaced in the religiously revitalized 1950s by the Judaism of the suburbs.[21]

TO THE SUBURBS AND BEYOND

"The marked influx of Jewish families into the suburbs of the larger cities" came to the notice of the *American Jewish Year Book* in 1952 and served as the subject of a celebrated article in *Commentary* a year earlier. By 1959, "vast numbers" of Jews, especially young middle-class couples ("seekers of the good life"), were said to be living in America's suburbs. One study listed eighty-nine suburban Jewish communities spread over ten states. Another estimated that America's suburban Jewish population more than doubled in the 1950s, with Jews suburbanizing at a rate almost four times that of their non-Jewish neighbors. Still a third found that "between 1945 and 1965, about a third of all American Jews left the big cities and established themselves in suburbs." For Jews and non-Jews alike, suburbia during these years became the "symbol of Utopia"—a sign of success, prestige, money, power, and security—the "middle-class Shangri-La."[22]

Reasons for this outward migration were not far to seek: the alluring new homes obtainable in the suburbs; the great shortage of available housing in the city; government-assisted mortgage programs; changing neighborhoods; spiraling urban crime rates; the falling price of automobiles; the wide new roads that shortened commuting distances; and, of course, rising affluence. In addition, the suburban style of life became, especially for erstwhile religious outsiders like Jews and Catholics, a "symbol of Americanization," a sign of "acceptance in the culture of the United States." As suburbia came to house more Americans than either center cities or rural communities, suburban values like conspicuous consumption, the dominance of the automobile, the centrality of the nuclear family, and the widening division between work and leisure became, to a large extent, the values of the nation as a whole.[23]

For Jews, the migration to the suburbs posed particular challenges. Outside the protective womb of the urban Jewish subculture, Judaism could no longer be absorbed, like sunshine, from the surrounding atmosphere. Instead, in suburbs like Park Forest, Illinois, "the Jewish families were scattered at random, and only rarely were two Jewish families to be found in adjacent houses." "The environment is strange," a sociologist reported. "The Jewish residents are no longer the majority or plurality which they were, or felt themselves to be, in the urban neighborhoods or blocks from which they came." Moreover, many suburban Jews faced what they called the "five o'clock shadow." Although they did business with non-Jewish neighbors and exchanged pleasantries with them, in the evening, after five o'clock, social contacts ceased: "no parties, no home visits, no golf clubs—no nothing."[24] In response, following a pattern that dated back to America's earliest Jewish pioneers, the scattered and isolated suburbanites moved to establish a sense of community:

Young married couples, recently settled in a suburb, look first for fellowship and friendship. They decide that they "ought to have some kind of a Jewish club, maybe even a Jewish center, like a Young Men's and Young Women's Hebrew Association." Enthusiastically they set out to establish the center, only to discover that soon the religious educational needs of their very young children will have to be met. And "how can that be done without a Rabbi or a teacher?" After much cogitation and self-examination, they agree that they really need an institution that will provide for their children's religious needs, as well as for their own social and fellowship interests. They conclude that a religious institution can provide for social as well as education needs. Hence they expand their original concept to include a synagogue.[25]

Deciding what kind of a synagogue to create—Orthodox, Conservative, or Reform—proved no easy task. The young married couples who first moved out to the suburbs had often themselves abandoned synagogue life years before. Fully 90 percent of the founders of the first synagogue in Levittown, according to its president, had "not been in a synagogue since they were Bar Mitzvah!" Unwilling to re-create the kinds of immigrant Orthodox synagogues that they had long since rejected, but unsure how to proceed, suburban pioneers did what they would have done in business or politics when faced with a comparable dilemma. They invited representatives from different movements, sometimes in the same room and on the same night, "to explain why and how their movement could best help them live as Jews and see their children grow up Jewishly and still fit in with their new affluent and accepting surroundings." Following a spirited "debate and argument," participants would then decide by majority vote what kind of synagogue they would look to create and what kind of rabbi to hire.[26]

More often than not, the Conservative movement won out. Between 1945 and 1965, it increased the number of its congregational affiliates by 450, more than the number of new Reform and Orthodox synagogues combined.[27] Positioning itself as the "centrist wing" in Judaism, it proved attractive to those who could "not accept Orthodox traditionalism, but who at the same time [found] themselves alienated by Reform radicalism." Actually, as we shall see, Reform Judaism also grew substantially during this period, more than doubling the number of its congregations between 1943 and 1964 and more than tripling its family memberships. But Conservative Judaism grew still faster, capturing the allegiance of a clear plurality of America's Jews and becoming the largest of the Jewish religious movements. America as a whole was moving toward the center during this era. A widely publicized book by historian Arthur Schlesinger, Jr., bore the title *The Vital Center* (1949), and "consensus" became the watchword of the day in religion as well as in many other aspects of life. Conservative Judaism's middle-of-the-road message, at once religiously authentic and amiably inoffensive, seemed well suited to this cultural moment and felt in touch with the times.[28]

Conservative Judaism introduced important innovations in the 1950s that enhanced its claims to modernity, strengthening its attractiveness to suburbanizing Jews still further. In 1950, the Rabbinical Assembly's newly reorganized Committee on Jewish Law and Standards, noting "that the Sabbath observers among our people constitute but a tiny minority and a dwindling minority at that," and concerned that "the number of people who find themselves living in widely scattered suburbs is increasing," issued by a majority vote an enactment *(takkanah)* declaring that: "Where a family resides beyond reasonable walking distance from the synagogue, the use of a motor vehicle for the purpose of synagogue attendance shall in no wise be construed as a violation of the Sabbath but, on the contrary, such attendance shall be deemed an expression of loyalty to our faith."[29]

Another decision, issued that same year, permitted limited use of electricity on the Sabbath for such activities as "turning on lights, telephoning, refrigeration [and] using a radio and television." Together these opinions (labeled a "revolutionary step" even by supporters) provided Conservative rabbinic sanction for the basic lifestyle changes adopted by the majority of suburban Jews and represented a dramatic break with Orthodoxy, which (save for permitting refrigerators) granted its faithful no similar concessions. In debates with Orthodox representatives, Conservative Jews highlighted their suitability for the up-to-date lifestyle of modern Jews, and projected their Orthodox opponents as being out of touch socially as well as theologically. As they did so they evoked the noise and disorder of immigrant Orthodoxy —"the smell of herring and the sight of spitoons"—to remind the audience of all that the Conservative movement had put behind it.[30]

The Conservative movement also appealed to suburbanites on the basis of its youth programming. The postwar baby boom, affecting Jews no less than their neighbors, made its most pronounced impact on the suburbs, where those with young children tended to settle. Suburban Jewish families, as a result, often had more young children at home than their urban Jewish counterparts, and they looked to the synagogue to help them raise those children as Jews. One observer of suburbia went so far as to describe "the ascendance of a new type of formal Jewish community, the *child-oriented* one" in contrast with the "traditional Jewish community, which may be described as *adult-oriented.*" Conservative Sunday and afternoon Hebrew schools, which were often free to members; the Leadership Training Fellowship (1946) for high school students; Conservative ("Ramah") summer overnight camps (1947); United Synagogue Youth (1951); "junior congregations" for children and high school age youngsters; and related youth-oriented programs responded to these parental demands and contributed to the Conservative movement's success. Though Reform and Orthodox congregations soon emulated many of these programs, during the early postwar years the Conservative movement's youth programming set the new suburban standard.[31]

Finally, the Conservative movement appealed to the needs of suburban Jewish women. Overwhelmingly, these women, following middle-class cultural norms of the day, remained at home during the years that they bore and raised children, while their husbands spent long days commuting back and forth to jobs in the city. Almost 80 percent of Jewish women aged twenty-five to thirty-four stayed home, and many of them, paralleling the church work of their Christian neighbors, became deeply involved with their synagogue: its sisterhood, its Hadassah group (a popular women's Zionist organization), its Jewish education classes, its social and cultural activities, its fundraising, its newsletter, its library, its gift shop. In Park Forest, Illinois, a "sexual role shift" reportedly took place, women replacing men as the dominant presence within the synagogue's portals. While men continued "to monopolize political and financial leadership," women "car-r[ied] out most of the other activities not handled by the rabbi." In synagogues across the United States, the Conservative rabbi Albert Gordon declared, "the Jewish suburban wife . . . plays a prominent role" and "in large degree shapes the religious pattern of her congregation"—a situation he found somewhat unhealthy. Gordon also saw suburban Jewish women assuming responsibility for religious life in the home. "Whether the home will include Jewish ritual and ceremony; the extent of religious worship on the Sabbath and festivals; whether the children will be expected to observe the traditional ritual, and to what degree—these matters, regarded a generation ago as the direct responsibility of the Jewish husband, are now," he lamented, "increasingly the responsibility of the wife." The irony of the analysis, lost on him but not on subsequent feminists, was that suburban Jewish men faced rabbinic censure "because they were *not* present." But Jewish women were criticized "because they *were.*"[32]

Women not only made their presence felt within Conservative synagogues, they also experienced a heightened sense of religious status within them, principally as a result of mixed seating. In debates with the Orthodox, indeed, many a Conservative rabbi scored points by dramatically insisting that "the time has come for you women to come down from the balcony and take the place that you deserve down here among the men." In Conservative synagogues of suburbia, mixed ("family") seating represented the norm, distinguishing them from most of their Orthodox counterparts and symbolizing women's emancipation. But the emancipation remained limited. The handling and reading of the Torah scrolls, for example, was "still generally reserved for males," and during the High Holidays, when more men came to pray, "the exclusion of females from the pulpit [was] almost complete."[33]

In a sign of change, some Conservative synagogues in the 1940s began to call women en masse to the Torah on the festival of Simhat Torah, when

Jews traditionally complete and recommence the reading of the Pentateuch and every male is called to make a blessing over the Torah scroll. In 1954, the Conservative Rabbinical Assembly resolved itself in favor of regulations "leading to the complete equalization of the status of women in Jewish law." A year later, its Committee on Jewish Law and Standards accepted as a legitimate minority view the calling of women to the Torah *(aliyot)* on a regular basis.[34] The most portentous change of all, however, came about without any formal Law Committee ruling or Rabbinical Assembly vote; it was a grassroots development. Nevertheless, it became a well-established ceremony in Conservative Judaism, later spreading throughout American Judaism and then to Israel. This ceremony, the rite of passage for girls entering womanhood, bore the Hebrew name bat mitzvah ("daughter of the commandments").

A Jewish boy in America traditionally celebrated his bar mitzvah ("son of the commandments") at thirteen, when he became obligated to fulfill the commandments. Wealthy parents, even in the immigrant period, made a fabulous celebration to mark the event. No similar celebration, however, accompanied the religious maturity of a girl, which occurs, per tradition, at age twelve. Confirmation, which Reform Judaism had introduced in the nineteenth century as a group initiation ceremony for boys and girls, on the model of parallel Christian ceremonies, generally took place later in the teenage years. In Germany, Poland, and especially Italy, a few synagogues in the nineteenth and early twentieth centuries did introduce individualized Jewish coming-of-age ceremonies for their daughters. Possibly influenced by these experiments, Rabbi Mordecai Kaplan performed a bat mitzvah for his daughter, Judith, in 1922, the first known bat mitzvah on American soil.

The new ritual spread slowly at first, mainly among rabbis sympathetic to Reconstructionism. In 1932, only six Conservative synagogues had adopted it. More rapid growth took place during the 1940s largely as an educational spur—"a means of bringing girls into the serious study of Hebrew and Jewish texts"—though for some also as a symbol of equality. By 1948, one-third of Conservative synagogues had introduced the bat mitzvah; by the early 1950s more than one-half (though the number of girls in each synagogue who chose to celebrate their bat mitzvah was initially far smaller than the number of boys who celebrated their bar mitzvah). In the 1960s and 1970s the ceremony became virtually ubiquitous in Conservative synagogues, observed by most girls who came of age. Bat mitzvah girls generally chanted the Prophetic portion *(haftarah)* assigned for their week; sometimes they also read from the Torah scroll and led other recitations—

all of which subtly legitimated female participation in such rites. When they were older, some of these same girls, now women, stood in the vanguard of those pushing for further changes in the status of women within their synagogues, recalling their stint on the pulpit at their bat mitzvah and drawing upon what they had learned from it. More than anybody recognized at the time, therefore, the bat mitzvah ceremony opened the door to women's greater participation in Jewish religious life, in tandem with their changing place in society generally.[35]

Reform and Orthodox Judaism did not sit idly by while Conservative Judaism "captured" the suburbs with all of these innovations, appealing to women, children, the suburban lifestyle, and the centrist temper of the times. The Union of American Hebrew Congregations, the congregational arm of the Reform movement, appointed a dynamic new president in 1946, Rabbi Maurice N. Eisendrath (1902–1973), who called on his leadership to come out of its "provincial shell and accept this challenge." At his behest and in a bid to achieve closer proximity to the "vibrant multitudes of our people," the union, in a move fraught with symbolism and bitterly opposed by old-line Reform Jews, shifted its headquarters from Cincinnati to New York. It invested in new synagogues, opened regional administrative offices to help support them, and developed a traveling revival program called the American Jewish Cavalcade to spread the message of Reform to Jews who never had been exposed to it. As if to reinforce these initiatives, three presidents of the Central Conference of American Rabbis between 1945 and 1952 were noted Zionists of East European ancestry.[36]

"Neo-Reform" Judaism, as some called the movement's new direction, consciously aimed to appeal to the children and grandchildren of East European Jews with indissoluble ties to Zionism. Following Conservative Judaism, the movement positioned itself close to the center of the American Jewish religious spectrum, extending developments initiated during the interwar years. A new Reform temple that opened in the Boston suburb of Newton in 1956 went so far as to advertise itself as "traditionally Jewish in content." Throughout suburbia and in many East and West Coast cities as well, Reform Judaism displayed new interest in the Hebrew language, Zionism, the new state of Israel, and "ceremonials," including the bar mitzvah and, once it became popular, the bat mitzvah, which by 1953 was celebrated in 35 percent of Reform temples. The role of women expanded, especially thanks to the efforts of Jane Evans and the National Federation of Temple Sisterhoods. New attention was also focused on children and teenagers through the National Federation of Temple Youth and, beginning in 1952, a summer camping program.[37]

Classical Reform Jews opposed many of these innovations, especially those that focused on Jewish peoplehood and that re-embraced rituals rejected in the nineteenth century as "primitive." They considered neo-Reform a violation of the movement's historic traditions and charged that their cherished faith had been "hijacked" by newcomers. Some joined the anti-Zionist American Council for Judaism and dedicated themselves to the "immutable values of Judaism as a universal faith," rather than to practices that they saw as "nationalistic, racist, self-segregated, secular, or otherwise non-American." But as so often before, the religious marketplace had the final say. Religious innovations that proved popular and attracted legions of newcomers to Reform Judaism's ranks won acceptance as "meaningful" ceremonies and survived. Success in recruiting new members overruled objections from old-timers.[38]

More than Conservative Judaism did, Reform also focused on social action, maintaining the "prophetic" legacy of such venerated Reform rabbis as Emil G. Hirsch and Stephen S. Wise. Declaring that the "heart of religion concerns itself with man's relation to man," Eisendrath, for one, placed particular emphasis on issues like world peace, civil rights, and the population explosion. Following the lead of the national Jewish defense organizations, like the American Jewish Committee, the Reform movement also sought to combat prejudice and discrimination nationwide, believing that prejudice was a unitary phenomenon, so that by making America a better place for all of its citizens, black and white alike, Jews would inevitably benefit. By thus embracing and legitimating a wide range of Reform Jewish options from Classical Reform to neo-Reform, and from ritual action to social action, Reform Judaism expanded exponentially. In the postwar era it welcomed a growing number of Jews of East European descent, recognized diverse modes of practicing Judaism, and mounted a direct challenge to the Conservative movement in the major centers and suburban areas where most Jews lived.[39]

Orthodoxy, meanwhile, faced greater difficulties in the suburbs. The suburban ethos, with its dependence on the automobile, its sprawling and widely spaced nuclear-family homes, its religiously mixed residential patterns, and its embrace of modernity and personal freedom, ran counter to Orthodoxy's traditional emphases on fidelity to Jewish law and maintenance of a close-knit community. Strict preservation of the Sabbath (including its ban on driving), strict observance of the dietary laws, and strictly enforced inequalities between men and women in the synagogue seemed to many incompatible with the freewheeling suburban lifestyle. Orthodox Jews who moved out to the suburbs tended, as a result, to gravitate toward Conservative synagogues. Those Orthodox synagogues that did strike roots in the suburbs in the 1950s accepted the fact that many of their members would be less than fully scrupulous in their ritual observance. "What you [personally] do is unimportant," one spokesman for Orthodoxy explained, "but the shul [synagogue] should stand for Torah." Suburban Orthodoxy thus concerned itself far more with public religious norms, the example set by the synagogue and its rabbi, than with the behavior of individual members. Meanwhile, many of those members, like so many traditional Jews since colonial days, lived lives compartmentalized into Jewish and worldly domains.[40]

During the postwar years Orthodoxy did manage to tame selected suburban frontiers. In places like Riverdale, New York, Teaneck, New Jersey, Brookline, Massachusetts, Oak Park, Michigan, and Silver Spring, Maryland, a critical mass of Orthodox Jews committed simultaneously to strict Jewish tradition, and the suburban lifestyle shaped an environment often described as Modern Orthodox. By carefully choosing residences in walking distance of an Orthodox synagogue, by encouraging businesses that catered to their special religious needs (kosher butchers, bakers, and restaurants, Jewish bookstores, and the like), and by establishing strong social ties reinforced by regular interactions in the synagogue, these Orthodox Jews succeeded in faithfully observing Jewish law and in re-creating under suburban conditions the characteristics of a faith-based caring community familiar to them from previous areas of settlement. During the Sabbath and holidays, "sacred time," they transformed their suburbs, as if by magic, into walking communities where Jews bedecked in Sabbath finery greeted one another on the street, telephones went unanswered, and friends exchanged home hospitality. Later, at nightfall, when "ordinary time" returned, everyone reentered the workaday world of suburbia; driving and telephone use resumed. Even during the week the patterns and practices of daily life often reflected Orthodox commitments, including, for example, modesty in dress, the maintenance of daily morning and evening prayers in the synagogue, visiting the sick, comforting the mourning, studying Jewish religious texts, making advance Sabbath and holiday preparations, and observing traditional laws of female purity. To be sure, the Orthodox lifestyle never attracted more than a small minority of suburban Jews, less than 10 percent. But as a symbol of Orthodoxy's ability simultaneously to resist and to accommodate modernity's blandishments, suburban Modern Orthodox Jewish communities were deeply significant. Their very existence suggested that Orthodoxy and modernity might indeed be reconcilable, just as suburbia and close-knit community had proved to be.[41]

Orthodoxy was not alone in trying to tame the suburban frontier. The new suburban synagogues that all three major Jewish religious movements erected aimed in the same direction. They formed the major part of the great synagogue building boom that, we have seen, characterized the first two postwar decades. The new synagogues, some of them grand palaces of Judaism ornamenting the suburban landscape, others more modest and nestled in the woods, served educational, cultural, social, and recreational functions in addition to worship. On the outside, the sleek lines, the light wood facings, the well-kept grounds, the symbols, and sometimes the very shape of these synagogues, modeled on Mount Sinai or the Star of David rather than on an elaborate Moorish temple, displayed suburban Judaism for all to see, demonstrating that Jews valued religion and nature no less than their Christian neighbors. On the inside, architects like Percival Goodman made certain that the synagogues were multifunctional and flexible in design; many were built in an "accordion" style. For ordinary Sabbaths, the synagogue might be relatively small and intimate, reflecting the expectation of low attendance. For special occasions like the High Holidays, movable walls folded away, merging the sanctuary with the social hall or side rooms to create a greatly enlarged worship space. Modern public address systems, increasingly incorporated into synagogues and sanctioned in 1948 even by the Orthodox Rabbinical Council of America (which in 1954 reversed itself), made possible these new designs; acoustical considerations were no longer a dominant architectural consideration. In part for the same reason, some synagogues that once read the Torah in the midst of the congregation, where everyone could hear, now moved all functions to the raised pulpit up front, thereby relegating the congregants to distant observers. Large kitchen facilities, social halls, meeting rooms, an educational wing, a central professional office, a gift shop, and, except in selected Orthodox synagogues fearful of Sabbath desecration, a huge parking lot, sought to make the synagogue the "hub of all cultural, religious, social, and recreational life in the Jewish community"—a true synagogue-center. Thus, in its style, its emphasis on light and modernity, its accommodation to the automobile, and its orientation toward women and youth the postwar synagogue became more than just a Jewish house of worship. It symbolized the suburbanization of Judaism itself.[42]

Tens of thousands of Jews moved beyond the suburbs. As soldiers, tourists,

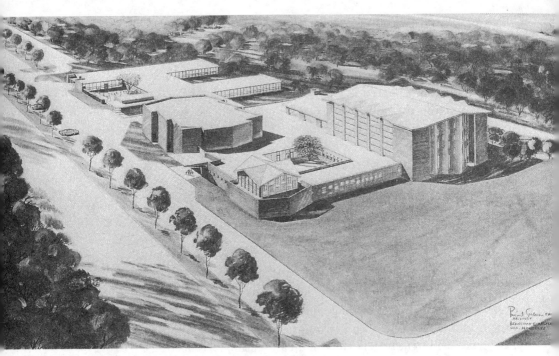

Aerial rendering of Percival Goodman's suburban Fairmount Temple in Beachwood, Ohio, completed in 1955. Note the natural wooded setting and the large parking area. As he often did, Goodman distinguished architecturally between the different functional areas within the synagogue. One wing was designed for worship, the second for social functions, the third for education, and the fourth for administrative offices. Courtesy of Anshe Chesed Fairmount Temple, Beachwood, Ohio.

or opportunity seekers, they had discovered sunnier climes—places like Miami and Los Angeles—and, beckoned by the good life that these "golden cities" promised, they decided to set down roots, often calling on relatives to join them. Miami's Jewish population ballooned from 13,500 to 140,000 between 1945 and 1965, reaching almost 250,000 in 1975. Los Angeles, a much larger Jewish community during the prewar era, tripled in size between 1945 and 1965, from about 160,000 to 500,000. The two mushrooming metropolises differed in significant ways, including the fact that they attracted Jews from dissimilar regions and age cohorts, and offered them disparate sets of economic opportunities. Together, however, they produced a significant geographic shift within the American Jewish community. In 1937, 71 percent of American Jews lived in the Northeast; 42 percent in New York City alone. Only 4.8 percent lived in the South and 4.6 percent in the West.

By 2000, the percentage of Jews living in the Northeast had fallen to 46 percent (36 percent in the New York area), while the percentage living in the South and West had more than quadrupled, reaching 21 percent and 22 percent, respectively.[43]

The new communities also reinforced the trend away from the distinctive Jewish subcultures of the inner cities and toward communities where Jews were less concentrated and more dispersed, at a further remove both from other Jews and from extended kin. Emphasizing privatism (symbolized by the private family home) and individual choice (exemplified by the many neighborhoods now open to Jews), these sunbelt communities heralded a new individualistic emphasis within Judaism: a "search for personal meaning to be found through experience and an emphasis on an individual's voluntary affirmation." Particularly in Los Angeles, denominational lines blurred and "an easy eclecticism took hold," influenced by the religious culture of the American West. "Rabbis mixed old and new, invented and restored to see what would work, what would attract other Jews, what would bring people into the fold." In short, the move to the sunbelt, paralleling as it did the move to the suburbs, set the stage for the growing diversification of American Judaism during the postwar years. As it emerged into the mainstream, American Judaism took root in new locations, addressed new communal needs, reached out to new constituencies, experimented with new ways of drawing in members, and, in the process, became ever more variegated and multiform.[44]

REMNANTS FROM THE HOLOCAUST

American Judaism also experienced deep and lasting effects from the more than 300,000 refugees, survivors, and "displaced persons" from Europe who found refuge in the United States between 1933 and 1950. These immigrants, some from Germany, some from Eastern Europe, included a number of Judaism's most illustrious rabbis and scholars. Grand Hasidic masters known as *rebbes,* the spiritual leaders of thousands of European Jews, arrived, among them the Lubavitcher rebbe, Rabbi Joseph I. Schneersohn (1880–1950), who immigrated in 1940; his son-in-law and successor, Rabbi Menahem Mendel Schneerson (1902–1993), who followed a year later; and the Satmar rebbe, Rabbi Yoel Teitelbaum (1887–1979), ransomed from the Bergen-Belsen concentration camp, who came to Brooklyn via Jerusalem in 1946. Fervently Orthodox scholars from prestigious European Talmudic academies *(yeshivot)* likewise found refuge in America at this time, people like Rabbi Moshe Feinstein (1895–1986), who escaped Communist threats to his life in 1936 and became in time the supreme rabbinic decisor *(posek)* of his generation, penning answers to thousands of rabbinic questions posed to him from around the world; and Rabbi Aaron Kotler, one of Europe's greatest students of the Talmud and a leading Orthodox political figure, who made it to America in 1941. The German Reform rabbi Leo Baeck, incarcerated in the Theresienstadt concentration camp, became a visiting professor at Hebrew Union College in Cincinnati in 1948, following his courageous young colleague Rabbi Joachim Prinz, who settled in America in 1937 and became a rabbi in Newark in 1939. Theologian Abraham Joshua Heschel, one of a group of refugee scholars who had studied and taught in German rabbinical seminaries, arrived in 1940.

Besides these towering figures, scores of future leaders and shapers of American Judaism settled in America during these years as children and teens, "embers plucked from the fires of the Holocaust," eager to complete their education and start life anew. These included three of the most influential figures in late twentieth-century American Reform Judaism, Alfred Gottschalk, W. Gunther Plaut, and Alexander Schindler; the future chancellor of the Jewish Theological Seminary, Ismar Schorsch; the charismatic Orthodox Jewish female "evangelist" Esther Jungreis; the influential composer, singer, and spiritual revivalist Shlomo Carlebach; and the founder of the Jewish renewal movement, Zalman Schachter. All of these men and women, notwithstanding the vast ideological chasms that divided them, stood united in their abiding commitment to Judaism and its future in the wake of the European catastrophe. They had survived, they came to believe, for a transcendent purpose and, albeit in utterly different ways, each worked to fulfill that purpose by strengthening and revitalizing American Jewish religious life.[45]

Like so many immigrants before them, the Jewish refugees from Europe (with the exception of celebrities like Albert Einstein) tended initially to live among their own kind. They preferred, understandably, to associate with those who shared their language, experiences, memories, and horrific sense of loss. The German-Jewish refugee community of Washington Heights, New York, for example, served as home to 22,401 German Jews in 1940. "They moved into the brick apartment buildings that covered the neighborhood and began to reconstruct both their economic and their communal lives. . . . [T]hey started social clubs and mutual aid societies. Within a few years they founded a dozen large synagogues, opened countless small shops . . . and tried to regain their bearings after the traumas of what they had suffered in Germany." Some Washington Heights Jews, led by Rabbi Joseph Breuer, attempted to re-create the world of German separationist Orthodoxy once associated with Rabbi Samson Raphael Hirsch. They established their own organic community (K'hal Adas Jeshurun), complete with a "ramified network of . . . institutions from the cradle to the grave." Other area Jews struggled to preserve the religious customs and traditions of their now destroyed rural hometowns. Still others, highly educated urban liberals back in Germany, displayed more interest in high culture than in religion yet took comfort in the *gemütlich* familiarity of their immigrant milieu. Whatever religious choices they made, German-Jewish refugees expressed their determination to remember and rebuild. The very names that they bestowed on their immigrant synagogues reflected this determination: Gates of Hope, New Hope, Habonim (The Builders). For German Jews and other Jewish refugees of the era, keeping memories and hopes alive formed a centerpiece of their faith.[46]

During the immediate postwar years, refugees stood almost alone in this determination to memorialize what they had lost. As early as 1946, the immigrant artist Arthur Szyk introduced a popular volume containing his Bible illustrations with the following full-page epitaph:

> In March 1943 my beloved seventy-year-old mother, was taken from the ghetto of Lodz to the Nazi furnaces of Maidanek. With her, voluntarily went her faithful servant, the good Christian, Josefa, a Polish peasant. Together, hand in hand, they were burned alive. In memory of the two noble martyrs I dedicate my pictures of the Bible as an eternal Kaddish for these great souls.

The YIVO Institute, destroyed by the Nazis in Vilna and re-created in New York by survivors, became the institutional center for memorializing the European catastrophe; it labored to preserve the very culture that the Nazis had sought to exterminate. Consequently it was there, in 1949, that Abraham Joshua Heschel of the Jewish Theological Seminary, who lost most of his own Hasidic family to the Nazis, delivered his poignant elegy for the world that was lost, subsequently published, complete with vivid woodcut illustrations, as *The Earth Is the Lord's: The Inner World of the Jew in East Europe.* Heschel also proposed the creation of a Hasidic Archive to preserve the history and teachings of the Hasidic masters lest they be forgotten completely. YIVO itself published an English-language *Guide to Jewish History Under Nazi Impact* (1960), summing up what was known and setting forth an agenda for research. That same year, Elie Wiesel, a survivor of Auschwitz, issued in English his memoir *Night,* the first of his many books written to keep the memory of the European destruction alive.[47]

The mainstream American Jewish community, to be sure, had not yet awakened to the significance of what would become known in the 1960s as the Holocaust. The Jewish Publication Society offered its readers exactly one book on the subject between 1950 and 1965. A planned memorial in New York's Riverside Park "to the heroes of the Warsaw Ghetto . . . and to the six million Jews of Europe martyred in the cause of human liberty," though dedicated in 1947, never was built. Neither was a memorial designed in 1967 for the city's Battery Park. Survivors themselves did annually recall the Holocaust around the anniversary of the Warsaw Ghetto uprising, and a committee of pious souls produced a plaintive "ritual of remembrance" for recitation at the Passover seder. "On this night of the Seder," it began "we remember with reverence and love the six millions of our people of the European exile who perished at the hands of a tyrant more wicked than the Pharaoh who enslaved our fathers in Egypt." But as we shall see, almost a full generation passed before the Holocaust, like so many other issues that transformed American Judaism through the years, moved from the periphery of American Jewish life to the center. Committed immigrants, spurred by painful recollections of those not fortunate enough to have survived, played a central role in that transformation. They were determined to ensure that the 6 million murdered Jews would not be forgotten.[48]

Some Orthodox immigrants went further, seeking to re-create in America what the Nazis had attempted utterly to exterminate. For example, Hasidic survivors from Hungary, which the Nazis invaded only in 1944, making it possible for more Jews to survive than in Poland, transformed the Brooklyn neighborhoods of Williamsburg, Crown Heights, and then Borough Park into citadels of faith on the model of East European Hasidic courts. They set up more than twenty-five Hasidic communities, each fiercely loyal to its own particular rebbe. They introduced a more stringent standard of kosher meat, known as *glatt* ("smooth") kosher, which eventually became the Orthodox norm. They also introduced Hasidic intensity into worship, with far more singing, dancing, and swaying than had hitherto been accepted. "Almost against my will I was drawn to the services . . . with their catchy melodies and the fervor that somehow imbued every moment of the prayers," one community old-timer recalled. A newspaper reporter discovered to his surprise in 1951 that "there were as many American youths singing along, dancing along, and swaying back and forth in the sacred rhythm of religious ecstasy . . . as there were refugees."[49]

The Satmar rebbe, Rabbi Yoel Teitelbaum, formerly of the Hungarian city of Satu-Mare (Szatmarnemeti), led what became one of the largest of Brooklyn's Hasidic courts, with over forty-five hundred devoted followers in 1961. Notwithstanding his advanced age—he was sixty-one when he arrived in America—he consciously set out to re-create in the new world as much as possible of the Hasidic old world that he and his followers had lost. Like his fellow refugee rebbes, he carefully transplanted not only the name and Yiddish vernacular of his former community but also its central institutions: the synagogue, the Jewish school system, the ritual bath, the free loan society, and so forth. He restored Satmar's unique customs, melodies, and modes of prayer, its zealous adherence to its own interpretation of the Jewish dietary laws, its fierce anti-modernism (no films, no television, no "inappropriate literature"), its militant anti-Zionism (soon translated into opposition to the state of Israel), and, most conspicuously of all, its distinctive style of Orthodox dress. For men, that meant full beards, shaved heads, dangling earlocks, a fringed four-cornered garment *(talit-katan)* worn over the shirt, kaftans, and black hats. For women, it meant long sleeves, heavy stockings, high necklines, below-the-knee dresses, and shorn heads covered by wigs or kerchiefs. In effect, the Satmar Rebbe brought back to life that which the Nazis had attempted to destroy. It was an act of audacious spiritual revenge that simultaneously paid homage to those who had perished and proclaimed victory over those who had murdered them.[50]

The goals of the Satmar community, and indeed of most of the reconstructed Hasidic enclave communities of the postwar period, were to resist acculturation, to distinguish themselves from the American mainstream, and to perpetuate their commitment to their own sacred path. The Amish, Hutterites, and Mennonites, among others, had been pursuing parallel goals in rural American communities for generations. The Hasidim, however, established their enclaves in Brooklyn in the very midst of those from whom they sought to keep apart. Based on their European diaspora experience, they believed that they could maintain a fervent religious community by erecting invisible walls between themselves and their neighbors: dressing differently, eating strictly kosher food, socializing among themselves, and living their lives according to the rhythms of the Jewish calendar. In 1954, Rabbi Yaakov Yosef Twersky, the Skverer rebbe, diverged from this pattern, acquiring land for his followers two miles from Spring Valley, New York, where his Hasidim established a "self-governing Torah community" with the revealing name of New Square, for the Hungarian community of Skvira where the rebbe's court had formerly stood. Separately incorporated in

1961, the village became a legally bounded Hasidic enclave composed exclusively of adherents—the Hasidic equivalent of the Puritan city upon a hill. Satmar Hasidim followed suit in 1974, when they established Kiryas Joel in Monroe County, New York, named for their spiritual leader. For the most part, though, Hasidic immigrants and their descendants upheld their distinctive ways within a more socially diverse urban or suburban setting. Even if they worked within the larger society and had occasional dealings with less religious Jews, they avoided extensive contact with them, preferring, as the Massachusetts Puritans had, to insulate themselves socially in order to protect the sanctity of their distinctive way of life.[51]

Lubavitch followed a different path. Scion of a late eighteenth-century Hasidic movement dedicated to "wisdom, understanding, and knowledge" (the acronym for which, in Hebrew, transliterates as *Chabad,* the name by which its adherents are frequently known), the movement was centered until World War I in the Belorussian city of Lubavitch. Later, in the face of Communist persecution, its followers worked underground to maintain and strengthen Judaism throughout the Soviet Union. On account of these activities, the sixth Lubavitcher ("of Lubavitch") rebbe, Rabbi Joseph I. Schneersohn, was reputedly condemned to death in 1927—a sentence that brought his name to the attention of the world, aroused international protests, and was eventually commuted to expulsion. Resuming his activities from a new base in Riga, Latvia, the rebbe paid a triumphant visit to America in 1929. There he raised funds and renewed ties with former followers who had immigrated years before. Eleven years later, confined to a wheelchair, he managed, thanks to a presidential visa, to escape the clutches of the Nazi invaders and settle permanently in the Crown Heights section of Brooklyn, establishing his movement's headquarters at 770 Eastern Parkway. In the midst of war, and working from the premise that America was "no different" from other diaspora Jewish communities, he began organizing a yeshiva, a network of supplementary Jewish religious schools, a publishing house, and other institutions aimed at transforming America into the "new center for Torah and Judaism," replacing Europe. Where other Hasidic leaders followed an enclave strategy, securing their followers against outside influences, he embraced a missionary strategy, reaching out to all Jews, affiliated and unaffiliated alike, in an effort to strengthen their religious consciousness and commitments in the face of the European catastrophe.[52]

Lubavitch (now known as Chabad-Lubavitch) became the most influential and visible Hasidic group, and one of the fastest growing of all American Jewish religious movements, under the leadership of Rabbi Menahem

Mendel Schneerson, the seventh Lubavitcher rebbe. He formally succeeded his father-in-law (and distant cousin) in 1951, a year after the elder Schneersohn died. Rabbi Menahem Mendel had arrived in America in 1941, following years of study at the University of Berlin and the Sorbonne. His secular university education, which focused on mathematics and engineering; the fact that his wife (the rebbe's daughter) had likewise studied in the university; and the short jacket that he wore during his father-in-law's lifetime in place of the traditional long Hasidic caftan all set him apart: he appreciated modernity. At the same time, he also possessed the deep Jewish learning, native brilliance, personal charisma, boundless energy, extraordinary administrative skills, and intimate family connections that equipped him to succeed in his job. Last but not least, he shared the Lubavitch movement's fervent messianism: its empowering belief, parallel to Protestant Arminianism, that Jews through their own active efforts could induce the coming of the messiah.[53]

Many Lubavitch faithful had understood the catastrophe of World War II to be the "last labors prior to the arrival of our Messiah" and took solace in the movement's counsel to "be ready for redemption soon!" When that prophecy failed, they experienced grave disappointment. The rebbe, through his lectures and outreach efforts to Jews around the world, his widely publicized prophecies, and his interpretation of modern Israel's role in the divine plan, rekindled messianic hopes, spurring his followers to years of selfless commitment as foot soldiers in campaigns to "force" redemption, to bring "*Moshiach* [messiah] now." Many of these efforts focused on the observance by Jews of a single commandment, such as the lighting of weekly Sabbath candles by women, the strapping on of leather phylacteries by men, or the giving of charity by everyone. At Hanukkah time, the rebbe promoted mass candlelighting ceremonies in outdoor public places, flouting the beliefs of Jews who felt that religion should be confined to the private sphere—the home and the synagogue. Personal emissaries *(shluchim)*, dispatched by the rebbe to set up institutions around the world wherever Jews lived or visited, served, in effect, as lifelong missionaries for his cause. They established Chabad centers in communities large and small and modeled a Hasidic Orthodox lifestyle, often at great personal sacrifice, so as to strengthen Jewish religious consciousness and hasten the messiah's coming. The rebbe also encouraged his followers to master new technologies, like satellite communications and computers, which they harnessed for religious purposes, to reach out to Jews wherever they lived and to further advance the movement's message.[54]

Substantial numbers of Lubavitch followers concluded, as time passed, that the rebbe himself was the not-yet-revealed messiah, a belief fostered by his childlessness, by the rapid worldwide growth of the movement he headed, and, according to some, by hints concealed in his public utterances. Rather than dampening these speculations, the rebbe's death, in 1994, only heightened them, with believers insisting that "our Master, Teacher and Rebbe, King Messiah" remained spiritually alive, that his portrait should be venerated, that he would miraculously respond to letters and petitions, that he would in time be physically resurrected, and even, in an extreme case, that he had become one with God himself. While Orthodox critics condemned these beliefs as alien to Judaism, the Lubavitch movement as a whole continued to thrive, boasting thirty-eight hundred emissary couples in forty-five states and sixty-five foreign countries in 2002, as well as twenty-six hundred institutions and hundreds of thousands of supporters. This success, reminiscent of that of the Mormons, highlighted the power and potential of a centrally driven, highly organized, fiercely independent proselytizing movement, even as the controversy and opposition it engendered indicated some of the perils.[55]

Hasidic Jews were not the only ones who sought to re-create in America what Hitler had attempted to destroy. Immigrant Jews from Lithuania, traditional opponents of Hasidism, championed the creation in America of advanced Talmudic academies on the model of those demolished in their homeland. These yeshivot and *kollelim* (singular, *kolel*), the latter being organized communities of advanced and usually married yeshiva students granted fellowships (like university graduate students) so that they might totally devote themselves to their learning, catered to the most serious of students. They were not like the American yeshiva all-day schools, geared to elementary or high school students of both sexes; nor did they merge religious and secular studies like Yeshiva University; nor did they set as their ultimate goal the training of rabbis and teachers. Instead, following the model established in 1803 with the founding of Lithuania's Volozhin yeshiva, they pursued Jewish learning "for its own sake," seeking to inoculate impressionable "college-age" Jewish males against modernity and its attendant evils:

The yeshiva socializes . . . students into a powerful Orthodox atmosphere, and during this critical stage in the development of personal identity and sense of self, seeks to isolate them from the perceived dangers of the outside. It inculcates Orthodox attitudes and patterns of behavior, which many stu-

A wallet-sized card (front and back) proclaiming
the Lubavitcher Rebbe, pictured here in front of
his Brooklyn headquarters, the long-awaited
messiah ("King Moshiach"). Collection of
the author.

dents take with them when they leave, and which they may then pass along
to their own children and students. The yeshiva education grants students
competence in the vast and highly complex world of Talmud and Rabbinic
literature. . . . Yeshiva graduates are likely to be Orthodox and remain Orthodox their entire lives.[56]

During the 1930s, several Lithuanian-style yeshivot of this sort had been
founded by immigrant rabbis, including Ner Israel Rabbinical College in
Baltimore, founded in 1933 by Rabbi Jacob Ruderman; Heichal Rabbenu
Hayyim HaLevi in Boston, founded in 1939 by Rabbi Joseph D. Soloveitchik;
and the Rabbi Chaim Berlin Yeshiva in New York, which became an advanced yeshiva under Rabbi Isaac Hutner in 1939. In 1941, America became
home to a genuine Lithuanian yeshiva when the famed Talmudic academy of the city of Telsiai (Telz) immigrated with its surviving students to

Cleveland following its leaders' harrowing escape through Siberia and Japan. While the Nazis occupied the original Telsiai, joining local Fascists in butchering its Jewish citizens and destroying all that they had sanctified, the name and spirit of the community's foremost Jewish institution lived on in the new world where, in a powerful symbol of continuity and resistance, the transplanted yeshiva set down new roots and eventually flourished.[57]

The year 1941 also witnessed the arrival in America of Rabbi Aharon Kotler, the man who would become known as the father of advanced Talmudic education in the United States and its foremost champion of fervent Orthodoxy. Kotler (1892–1962), descendant of a long line of distinguished rabbis, was recognized in his youth as a Talmudic prodigy, studied in the famed Lithuanian yeshiva of Slobodka, married the daughter of the head of the Slutsk yeshiva, opened a branch of that yeshiva over the border in Kletzk (Poland) to escape the Communists, and, ten years later, after his father-in-law settled in Palestine, succeeded him at the yeshiva's helm. While building up his yeshiva, Kotler immersed himself in the fervent Orthodoxy of the Agudath Israel political party and pursued a fiercely isolationist Jewish agenda, opposing Zionism, Jewish enlightenment (Haskalah), any form of secular education, and of course any deviation from the strictest Orthodoxy. In 1935 he traveled to America for the first time to raise funds, met Shraga Feivel Mendlowitz, and advocated for advanced Talmud study. But he discouraged his own students from settling either in America or in the Land of Israel, believing as he did that the insular European yeshiva, where students emulated their teachers' fidelity to Jewish tradition and devoted themselves single-mindedly to the study of Jewish texts as an end in itself, secured the survival of Jews everywhere. During the war, the Kletzk yeshiva moved east, seeking to escape both the Nazis and the Communists. Seeing the writing on the wall, Kotler took advantage of a special visa issued by President Roosevelt and immigrated with his family to America, hoping to work from there to save his students, whom he had earlier discouraged from immigrating. "I did not come here to save myself," he explained soon after his arrival, as some wondered at his abandonment of his charges. "I came to save, with your help . . . the ancient centers of Torah." He threw himself into rescue work through the Va'ad Hatzalah, the rescue committee of the Agudath Ha-Rabbanim.[58]

Within a year Kotler had also agreed to oversee and teach (mostly on weekends) a group of yeshiva students who had informally gathered around him to study. He insisted that they isolate themselves from the atmosphere of New York City, devote themselves to Torah, and treat him as their sole and central authority. From this nucleus, and aided by American supporters attracted by his zealous commitment to the traditional yeshiva way of life, he established in 1943 what would become known in time as the Harvard of American advanced Talmudic academies, the Beth Medrash Govoha in Lakewood, New Jersey. His goal, in the wake of the European destruction, was to re-create in America a yeshiva devoted to the same high standards as its European counterpart: committed to Torah study as an end rather than as a means, conducted in "an atmosphere of [total] dedication to the Torah . . . without involvement in any external and tangential things," and dwelling in even greater cultural and social isolation than back in Kletzk (hence the choice of the small resort town of Lakewood). Only under such conditions, he explained, would it be possible to raise a new generation of fervently religious elite: men untainted by secular studies and on the highest plane of Jewish learning and spirituality. The yeshiva grew from 13 students at its founding to 160 students by Kotler's death in 1962 to almost 1,500 students and 37 branches by its fiftieth anniversary, making it one of the largest institutions of its kind in the world.[59]

Kotler's uncompromising elitism of learning, coupled with his zealous commitment to truth as he understood it, transformed not only fervent Orthodoxy in the postwar era but also the Orthodox mainstream, whose concessions to modernity and willingness to cooperate with non-Orthodox Jews he openly scorned. In a celebrated episode in 1956 he led a group of eleven leaders of yeshivot, most of them fervently Orthodox Holocaust-era immigrants, in banning any official contacts between Orthodox rabbis and their Reform and Conservative counterparts through such organizations as the New York Board of Rabbis and the Synagogue Council of America. "It is forbidden by the law of our sacred Torah to participate with them either as an individual or as an organized communal body," the widely publicized ruling declared. At first, only a minority of Modern Orthodox rabbis deferred to the ruling; the majority within the Rabbinical Council of America and the Union of Orthodox Jewish Congregations cooperated with their non-Orthodox colleagues as before. But the awe in which Kotler and the others were held, the breadth of their rabbinic learning, and the respect that their European heritage commanded, along with the religious politics of Israel, where the Orthodox denied Conservative and Reform Judaism legitimacy, eventually turned the tide. Orthodox participation in interdenominational Jewish bodies declined, and in 1994 the Synagogue Council of America disbanded. Kotler likewise opened the door to Orthodoxy's shift on the issue of federal aid to parochial schools. While Modern Orthodox rabbis and the Synagogue Council had opposed such aid as a violation of church-state separation, he advocated for it in his final years as a means of funding Jewish education. More than anyone else, Kotler elevated the status and power of the "Torah sage" (the head of a yeshiva) in American Orthodox life and paved the way for the great expansion of traditional Jewish learning on American soil. Like so many of the great Orthodox rabbis who migrated to America's shores around World War II, he changed American Jewry far more than it changed him. His response to the Holocaust was to remake American Jewry in his image of prewar Eastern Europe.[60]

Rabbi Joseph D. Soloveitchik (1903–1993) was the exception among these great Orthodox rabbis and sages in *not* seeking to re-create the East European world of his youth in America. Nor was he, strictly speaking, a Holocaust refugee, having immigrated to America in 1932. Nor was he any stranger to secular learning, having studied at the University of Berlin, where he embraced neo-Kantian philosophy, wrote his doctorate on the liberal Jewish thinker Hermann Cohen, and undertook what became lifelong interests in such subjects as mathematics, the philosophy of science, Christian religious thought, and literature. His own father, scion of a distinguished rabbinic family, had come to appreciate the significance of secular learning and taught in Warsaw's Tahkemoni rabbinical seminary, where modern disciplines formed part of the curriculum. He then immigrated to America to serve as the senior Talmudic scholar at Yeshiva College, which likewise assumed that Orthodox Jews needed training in both traditional religious and modern secular studies. Rabbi Joseph Soloveitchik followed his father to the United States, settling in Boston. There he briefly and unhappily involved himself in reforming kosher poultry slaughtering in the city, and he began his life's work as a master Jewish educator. He oversaw, beginning in 1934, a coeducational supplementary school named Yeshivat Torat Yisrael for elementary and high school students, established a pioneering coeducational Jewish all-day school named Maimonides School in 1937, and, in 1939, in conjunction with Yeshiva College, opened a short-lived yeshiva named Heichal Rabbenu Hayyim HaLevi for "erudite yeshiva students who were reaching American shores" from Europe. In 1941, following his father's death, he succeeded him as the senior Talmudic scholar at Yeshiva College, commuting there weekly from Boston, and soon became the central religious authority for Modern Orthodox Jews in the United States, ordaining more Orthodox rabbis, reputedly, than any man in history. Dubbed "The Rav" by his followers, he seemed to them the very model of what an Orthodox rabbi in America should be.[61]

Like other immigrant Orthodox rabbis of his day, Rabbi Soloveitchik was deeply and personally affected by the destruction of East European Jewry. Among Hitler's victims were numerous friends and relatives. But while so many of his European-trained contemporaries responded by opposing modernity and religious Zionism, advocating physical isolation in an enclave or a yeshiva to keep the embers of traditional Jewish religiosity glowing, he considered immersion in the world of Jewish law *(halakhah)* compatible with a more open cultural stance. He dressed in modern clothes, addressed university audiences, began in 1960 to teach and lecture in English, quoted secular philosophers and theologians in his writings, and defended religious Zionism. "Halakhic man reflects two opposing selves," he argued in the opening words of his first published article, and this same sense of inner tension suffused much of his life. Casting himself as the "lonely man of faith," striving to be at home in two incompatible worlds, he symbolized and seemed to embody the modern Orthodox quest "to combine a commitment to traditional Jewish law with an openness to modern secular culture and society." On the one hand, he was an old-fashioned Talmudist, heir to the traditions of his Lithuanian forebears. On the other, he was a creative modern Jewish thinker, wrestling with the existential problems of contemporary Jewish religious belief. He defended Orthodox Judaism, warning his followers away from theological dialogues with other faiths and religious worship in non-Orthodox synagogues, yet he also found ways to interact with leaders of other faiths and disagreed with those who banned *all* contact with non-Orthodox rabbis and lay leaders; he did not sign Rabbi Kotler's ban on the Synagogue Council. Religious consciousness "is exceptionally complex, rigorous, and tortuous," he once explained, speaking, one suspects, from personal experience. For him, religious truth and sincere faith emerged "out of the straits of inner oppositions and incongruities, spiritual doubts and uncertainties, out of the depths of a psyche rent with antinomies and contradictions, out of the bottomless pit of a soul that struggles with its own torments."[62]

The debate between the Modern Orthodox, who looked up to Rabbi Soloveitchik, and the fervently Orthodox, who shunned the worldliness and religious Zionism that he held dear, echoed in some respects the prewar debate between the M'lochim, Shraga Feivel Mendlowitz, and Bernard Revel. On a larger scale, it also reflected arguments found within many a faith community between "fundamentalists" and "modernists," or more precisely among (1) those who sought to protect their world by withdrawing into a religious cocoon; (2) those, like Lubavitch, who ventured out into the larger world in a bid to proselytize and redeem it; and (3) those who struggled simultaneously to live in two worlds, believing that modernity and tradition could somehow be reconciled.

For American Orthodox Jews of the post-Holocaust era, however, the stakes in this debate had multiplied. With the destruction of European centers of Jewry, some felt that they could take no chances with modernity; the specter of further losses to the Jewish faith brought on by assimilation overwhelmed them. Others, as we have seen, considered the maintenance of tradition part of their responsibility to those who had perished. Far from being a "retreat" into a religious enclave, their distinctive lifestyle represented to them miraculous survival, even spiritual vindication. Still others lost confidence in their own ability to navigate the shoals between Orthodox Judaism and contemporary culture. The upheavals of mid-twentieth-century Jewish life, coupled with the new stringencies proclaimed by esteemed sages from abroad, left them feeling religiously insecure and fearful; they craved certainty and reassurance. The result in all three cases was a turn to authority. Where once ancestral custom passed down mimetically through the generations governed a good deal of traditional religious practice—from how to set up a kosher kitchen to how much unleavened bread (matzah) to eat at the Passover seder—now Orthodox Jews turned for direction to rabbis, teachers, and above all to codes and manuals that told them what to do and how to act. Ancestral customs, especially those deemed lax, lenient, or difficult to reconcile with Jewish law, fell into disuse, their authenticity questioned. Stricter "by-the-book" practices, some rarely seen in America (like the ban on any physical contact, including shaking hands, between unrelated members of the opposite sex), replaced them. This so-called swing to the right in Orthodox Jewish religious life, what one participant described as a radical change in the "very texture of [its] religious life and the entire religious atmosphere," weakened Modern Orthodoxy in the 1970s, the more so after the aged and ailing Rabbi Soloveitchik withdrew in 1984 from public engagements. By the time the post-Holocaust generation had grown up, much of Orthodoxy had veered away from its engagement with modernity. Shifting its attention inward, it concerned itself above all else with Jewish education, Jewish observance, and the needs of the Jewish state.[63]

FROM UNIVERSALISM TO PARTICULARISM

It was not just the Orthodox who turned inward during the latter part of the twentieth century. Throughout American Judaism a parallel shift took place. Whereas during the 1950s and 1960s universal causes like world peace, civil rights, interfaith relations, and opposition to the war in Vietnam dominated the American Jewish agenda, subsequent decades saw greater emphasis on issues of particularistic Jewish concern. Two symposia tell the tale. The first, entitled "Jewishness and the Younger Intellectuals," published by *Commentary* magazine in 1961, found alienation rife among its sophisticated participants. The overwhelming majority of those queried felt that "they properly belong to a much wider world than is encompassed by the Jewish community." The second, entitled "People of the Book," published thirty-five years later, found "thoughtful, engaged, Jewish intellectuals probing their disciplines, their past, and their beliefs in an attempt to locate themselves more fully on the map of Jewish subjectivity." A contributor to the first symposium argued that the modern Jew should be the "spokesman for a rationally organized, democratic world society, unfettered by parochial traditions and superstitions." A contributor to the second disclosed that his "effort to grapple with the Holocaust, intellectually and emotionally," enhanced his "own sense of Jewish tradition and all it includes." The first symposium included a writer who confessed the "hope" that "my children will have no need for any 'religion,' Judaism included." The second saw a scholar confide that he had "reembraced some of the central rituals of Judaism . . . and [was] anticipating with emotions more powerful than [he] could ever have imagined [his] own son's bar mitzvah."[64]

Skewed and subjective as these symposia may have been, they bespeak a striking cultural and religious transformation. In the early postwar decades, "social action" aimed at improving ("repairing") the larger world played a significant role in American Jewish religious life, much as it did among mainline Protestants. Following the Six Day War in 1967 and the subsequent Jewish religious revival stimulated by the counterculture and the upheavals of the 1960s, themes like "Jewish renewal," "Jewish continuity," and "Jewish renaissance" increasingly moved to the fore. Judaism, like much of American religion, reevaluated its mission. By the end of the twentieth century, many of the faithful focused less on the whole world than on the Jewish world, or even more narrowly on their own Jewish souls. Their ideology shifted from universalism to particularism or personalism. They became less concerned with social action and more concerned with self-fulfillment.

In the immediate postwar years, by contrast, Judaism had focused outwardly. In 1949–50, for example, the Synagogue Council of America, acting "on behalf of all of organized American religious Jewry," issued statements promoting international peace and American democracy. The following year, the Conservative movement's Rabbinical Assembly "supported the repeal of the Taft-Hartley Law [which limited the rights of organized labor, as well as the], strengthening [of] the United Nations, and the ratification of the Convention on Genocide." The year after that, the Orthodox Rabbinical Council of America "appealed to Jewry to support the North Atlantic Treaty Organization." The Reform movement, as we have seen, went the farthest in elevating social action into a cardinal principle of Judaism. "A synagogue which isolates itself from the fundamental issues of social justice confronting the community and the nation is false to the deepest traditions and values of the Jewish heritage," declared the directors of the Union of American Hebrew Congregation's Commission on Social Action in their widely distributed book, *Justice and Judaism* (1956). In pursuit of what Reform Jews called Prophetic Judaism, recalling the social justice proclamations of the biblical prophets Isaiah, Amos, and Micah, some 310 Reform congregations established social action groups by 1960, and the Union of American Hebrew Congregations, during the 1950s, promulgated forty-two different social action resolutions. Seeking to advance its agenda still further, and over the objection of those who insisted that religion and politics should not be mixed, the Reform movement, in 1962, opened the Religious Action Center in Washington, D.C. Dedicated to the pursuit of "social justice and religious liberty," it sought to mobilize the American Jewish community and to serve "as its advocate in the nation's capital."[65]

The issue of civil rights for black Americans soon forced its way to the top of the Jewish social action agenda. This was not a new concern. Notwithstanding evidence of prejudice and animosity extending back to the nineteenth century, Jews and blacks had long found common cause. "Blacks saw Jews as models whom they would do well to emulate; Jews saw Blacks as fellow victims whose protection and advancement had some bearing on their own." Jewish patricians loomed large in the financial, legal, political, and administrative work of the National Association for the Advancement of Colored People (NAACP) and the National Urban League. Radical Jewish secularists embraced blacks in their general effort to promote universal ethical values, transcending racial, ethnic, and religious boundaries. While Jewish religious organizations, lay and rabbinic, did not become deeply involved in civil rights issues prior to World War II, some of their leading members did, including at least three distinguished southern Reform rabbis: Max Heller, Morris Newfield, and William Fineshriber. At the behest of concerned members, the Union of American Hebrew Congregations as early as 1935 took time out from Jewish issues to protest the "injustice and cruelty" of "the lynching evil" and to "commend the Rabbis and lay leaders who . . . have taken a courageous position on this question."[66]

Civil rights became a central religious issue for American Jews in the postwar era. The National Council of Churches and the National Conference of Christians and Jews encouraged this trend, which also seemed to comport with Jewish self-interest. There "is the closest relation," the American Jewish Committee declared in 1947, "between the protection of the civil rights of all citizens and the protection of the civil rights of the members of particular groups." All three Jewish religious movements concurred. In 1953, the Central Conference of American Rabbis recognized Race Relations Day and issued a pronouncement entitled, following the biblical injunction in Deuteronomy 16:20, *Justice, Justice Shalt Thou Pursue.* A year later the distinguished New York Orthodox rabbi Leo Jung praised the Supreme Court ruling ending segregation in the public schools as "a red-letter day in American history." In 1956, a leading Conservative rabbi, Israel Goldstein, proclaimed while serving as president of the American Jewish Congress that "we must defend the rights of the Negro as zealously as we would defend our rights as Jews whenever and wherever these might be threatened." A less articulate but unknown number of Jews, to be sure, felt that racial integration did not comport with their interests. They feared that it would cause Jews social, economic, or physical harm, disrupting peace and social order. Counseling silence in the face of the black struggle, they considered Jewish organizational involvement in civil rights "not an advantage but a liability."[67]

In the South, some rabbis courageously spoke out in favor of civil rights notwithstanding pressure from those concerned that their actions threatened Jewish security. Other rabbis did not. A prominent Birmingham rabbi, who later modified his views, told a meeting of the southeast region of the Union of American Hebrew Congregations in 1956 that he "wouldn't risk one hair on the head of one of my members for the life of every *shvartzeh* [black] in this state." The challenge for southern Jewish leaders was to balance "prophetic" moral commitments against "pragmatic" Jewish interests, a calculation made more difficult as the South erupted in white-led racist violence. Some 10 percent of the terrorist bombings that racked the South between 1954 and 1959 were directed against Jewish targets—this in a region where Jews made up considerably less than 1 percent of the population. One twelve-month period witnessed bombings or attempted bombings of Jewish institutions (synagogues, rabbis' homes, and Jewish community centers) in Birmingham, Charlotte, Gastonia, Jacksonville, Miami, and Nashville, capped by the infamous bombing of Atlanta's oldest and richest temple on October 12, 1958.[68]

Jewish support for civil rights peaked in the early 1960s, its moral thrust amplified by two rabbis who came to America as refugees from the Holocaust. Joachim Prinz (1902–1988), a prominent rabbi in Newark, began his career in Berlin, where he was a much sought-after preacher and attracted hordes of young people to his Peace Synagogue (Friedenstempel). An early and vocal critic of the Nazis, he courageously urged Jews to leave Germany and endured arrest and harassment by the Gestapo before being expelled from Germany in 1937. Resuming his career in America, he became active in Jewish affairs and, from 1958–66, in addition to his rabbinate, presided over the American Jewish Congress. He became particularly involved in the civil rights movement, the plight of blacks recalling for him the plight of Jews in Germany, and he was one of the organizers of the much-publicized march on Washington in August 1963. His address on that occasion, "The Issue Is Silence," immediately preceded the unforgettable "I Have a Dream" speech of Martin Luther King, Jr., and attracted wide notice. "I speak to you as an American Jew," Prinz began, as if seeking to link his entire people to the African-American cause. Then, recalling his own experience in Germany, he uttered what became the most famous words of his career, an oblique comparison of American racism and German Nazism: "When I was the rabbi of the Jewish community in Berlin under the Hitler regime, I learned many things. The most important thing that I learned under those tragic circumstances was that bigotry and hatred are not the most urgent problem. The most urgent, the most disgraceful, the most shameful and the most tragic problem is silence. . . . America must not become a nation of onlookers. America must not remain silent." For Prinz and for those who followed in his footsteps, the Holocaust served not only as a universal reference point "that underscored the moral righteousness of antiracist activism" but also as a Jewish reference point, providing a specifically Jewish rationale for involvement in the civil rights movement. His attack on silence in the face of evil challenged the strategy of Jews who proposed to work quietly behind the scenes to effect change, and it helped to promote more vigorous Jewish communal action.[69]

Rabbi Abraham Joshua Heschel (1907–1972) soon emerged as the central prophet of civil rights activism within the Jewish community. Born into a distinguished Hasidic family in Warsaw, he was educated at the University of Berlin, expelled by the Nazis, rescued by Hebrew Union College in Cincinnati, and ultimately employed by the Jewish Theological Seminary, where he served as professor of ethics and mysticism. His very appearance commanded respect—long, flowing hair, a black skullcap, and an impressive patriarchal beard—and he maintained ties across the Jewish spectrum; he was at once traditional and modern. His theological emphasis on wonder ("radical astonishment"), awe, transcendence, holiness, the "need to be needed," and on the dialectical interaction between God and Man, all deeply influenced by his background in Hasidic piety and classical Jewish texts, had a pronounced impact upon Jews and Christians alike.[70]

Heschel delivered his first major address on civil rights as the keynote speaker to the National Conference on Religion and Race on January 14, 1963, where he met Martin Luther King, Jr., and electrified his audience by linking the black struggle to the biblical Exodus: "At the first conference on religion and race, the main participants were Pharaoh and Moses. . . . The outcome of that summit meeting has not come to an end. Pharaoh is not ready to capitulate. The exodus began, but is far from having been completed. In fact, it was easier for the children of Israel to cross the Red Sea than for a Negro to cross certain university campuses."[71] He soon befriended King, in whom he found a kindred spirit. They had similar theological positions: for both, "the theological was intimately intertwined with the political"; and each described the other as a modern-day heir to the Prophets. In 1965, Heschel (dubbed "Father Abraham" by his black associates) joined King, Ralph Bunche, and Ralph Abernathy for the great civil rights march from Selma to Montgomery, Alabama. "I felt a sense of the Holy in what I was doing," he wrote in his diary. During the march, he recalled, "our legs uttered songs. Even without words, our march was worship. I felt my legs were praying." A famous photograph from that time captured Heschel marching arm in arm with the black activists. It subsequently became an "icon of American Jewish life, and of black-Jewish relations," a visual symbol of Jewish religious commitment to the civil rights struggle. Ironically, Heschel himself considered his community's commitment to that struggle grossly inadequate.[72]

Heschel's own commitment to human rights, improved intergroup relations, and religious activism led him into two other areas that, along with the African-American struggle for freedom, dominated the universalistic Jewish social action agenda of the 1960s. First, he became involved in ecumenism. A series of publications in the postwar era called attention to Christian antisemitism, charged that church teachings unwittingly helped to create the atmosphere that made the Holocaust possible, and sought to change what became known as Christianity's "teaching of contempt."

Abraham Joshua Heschel (second from right) marching with black activists,
including Ralph Abernathy, Martin Luther King, Jr., and Ralph Bunche,
in the 1965 civil rights march through Selma, Alabama.

Vatican Council II, an ecumenical council of Catholic cardinals and bishops
announced by Pope John XXIII in 1959, provided a forum for considering
these issues within the framework of *aggiornamento,* an Italian word meaning modernization or adaptation. The papal objective was to harmonize
tradition "with the new conditions and needs of the time," and it included
plans for a revised Catholic statement on the church's relationship with the
Jewish people. As a theologian, Heschel was invited by the American Jewish
Committee to participate in its lobbying on this subject, and in 1961 he held
preliminary discussions in Rome with Germany's Augustin Cardinal Bea,
a papal friend and confidant. Heschel proposed to Bea that the council focus on three goals: (1) "to reject and condemn those who assert that the
Jews as a people are responsible for the crucifixion," (2) to "acknowledge
the integrity and permanent preciousness of Jews and Judaism," rather
than seeing Jews as potential converts and objects of mission, and (3) "to

eliminate abuses and derogatory stereotypes," by promoting scholarly co-operation and combating religious prejudice.[73]

As finally approved, *Nostra Aetate,* issued as part of Vatican II's "Declaration on the Relationship of the Church to Non-Christian Religions" (1965), did not quite live up to initial hopes. Whereas early drafts, for example, carried the admonition "do not teach anything that could give rise to hatred or contempt of Jews in the heart of Christians," that language was watered down in the final version to "do not teach anything that does not conform to the truth of the Gospel and the spirit of Christ." Similarly, the injunction "May Christians never present the Jewish people as one rejected, cursed, or guilty of deicide" was weakened to read "The Jews should not be presented as rejected or accursed by God, as if this followed from the Holy Scriptures." Heschel expressed particular disappointment at the fact that the collective charge of "deicide" (the act of killing a god) leveled against Jews was never specifically renounced. Nevertheless, the 1965 declaration marked a turning point in Catholic-Jewish relations and in Heschel's view opened the way for a new era of better understanding and mutual respect.[74] As interfaith dialogues between Jews and Christians proliferated across the United States, he welcomed them, reminding non-Jewish colleagues that "no religion is an island. We are all involved with one another." His poetic definition of "the purpose of interreligious cooperation" both shaped and echoed the universalistic and increasingly ecumenical spirit of the times:

> [The purpose of interreligious cooperation] is neither to flatter nor to refute one another, but to help one another; to share insight and learning, to co-operate in academic ventures on the highest scholarly level and, what is even more important, to search in the wilderness for wellsprings of devotion, for treasures of stillness, for the power of love and care for man. What is urgently needed are ways of helping one another in the terrible predicament of here and now by the courage to believe that the word of the Lord endures for ever as well as here and now; to cooperate in trying to bring about a resurrection of sensitivity, a revival of conscience; to keep alive the divine sparks in our souls, to nurture openness to the spirit of the Psalms, reverence for the words of the prophets, and faithfulness to the Living God.[75]

Heschel's position placed him in open conflict with the Orthodox. Rabbi Moshe Feinstein, president of the fervently Orthodox Agudath Ha-Rabbanim and the community's leading rabbinic decisor, explicitly banned attendance at interfaith gatherings and "any connections" with Christian officials, "even on ostensibly social-political matters." The "only intent" of such interactions, he warned, "is to cause all the Jews to abandon their pure and holy faith so that they will accept Christianity." Rabbi Joseph Solo-veitchik, speaking on behalf of the Rabbinical Council of America, was more welcoming of "communication among the various faith communities," but, in a veiled criticism of Heschel and others involved in interreligious dialogue, he insisted that such interactions "should occur not at a theological, but at a mundane human level . . . not in the realm of faith, but in that of the secular orders." Unlike Feinstein, he sanctioned interfaith dialogues concerning matters of general ethical and social concern, but in contradistinction to Heschel and most non-Orthodox leaders he prohibited theological exchanges, including "any public debate, dialogue, or symposium concerning the doctrinal, dogmatic, or ritual aspects of our faith vis-à-vis 'similar' aspects of another faith community."[76]

Troubled but unbowed by criticisms of his stance, Heschel soon moved to address an even more controversial issue: America's involvement in the war in Vietnam. This became the third focal point of the Jewish social action agenda of the period. In 1965, in response to the nation's escalating involvement in the conflict, Heschel, along with Richard J. Neuhaus, then a Protestant minister, and Daniel Berrigan, a Catholic priest, co-founded the moderate interfaith organization known as Clergy Concerned About Vietnam (later Clergy and Laymen Concerned About Vietnam). Several prominent Reform rabbis, including Maurice Eisendrath, immediately joined the new organization. "We transgress every tenet of our faith when we fight on another's soil, scorch the earth of another's beloved homeland, slay multitudes of innocent villagers," Eisendrath declared that year at the biennial meeting of the Union of American Hebrew Congregations. In response, the organization of Reform congregations pressed for a cease-fire in Vietnam followed by a negotiated settlement. By early 1966, the Synagogue Council also had come out in favor of American troop withdrawal, and leaders across the Jewish religious spectrum, Reform Jews in particular, had added their voices to the chorus of war protesters appalled by the death and destruction that the war left in its wake. President Lyndon Johnson expressed puzzlement and anger at Jewish antiwar rhetoric. He thought that as staunch supporters of Israel's right to exist, Jews should be more sympathetic to South Vietnam's struggle, and he reputedly hinted that his Jewish critics placed America's support of Israel at risk. Perhaps with this in mind, the Union of Orthodox Jewish Congregations in 1966 voted to endorse the war, praising America's determination to resist Communist aggression anywhere in the world. Others more explicitly cited Israel's security ("'No more

Vietnams' means no more Israel") in justifying their support for the president's policy, and trumpeted a not fully persuasive Gallup Poll that showed Jewish opinion to be almost evenly divided on the war, little different from the split among Americans as a whole and Protestants in particular. But Heschel, a fervent supporter of Israel, would have none of it: "To speak about God and remain silent on Vietnam," he thundered, "is blasphemous." The war, no less than civil rights and the interfaith movement, seemed to him a religious cause to which all the faithful, Jews and Christians alike, dare not fail to respond.[77]

The fateful period before, during, and immediately following the Six Day War in June 1967 jolted the American Jewish community from this universalistic agenda. "The great hour has come," Cairo radio announced on May 16, 1967. "The battle has come in which we shall destroy Israel." Expelling U.N. peacekeeping forces, Egypt blockaded the Strait of Tiran, and hundreds of thousands of Arab troops massed on Israel's borders, promising to drive the Jews into the sea. The specter of the Holocaust, the abandonment of the Jews in their time of need, loomed afresh. "Will God permit our people to perish?" Abraham Joshua Heschel wondered. "Will there be another Auschwitz, another Dachau, another Treblinka?" He felt particularly betrayed by some of his allies in the civil rights, interfaith, and anti-Vietnam movements who remained silent as Israel's fate seemed to hang in the balance.[78]

Following three weeks of fear and trembling, war erupted early on June 5, and in six days the Arab armies were routed, leaving Israel in control of the Sinai Peninsula, the west bank of the Jordan River, the Golan Heights, and, most important of all for Jews, the Old City of Jerusalem. Throughout the United States, Jews flocked to synagogues to express relief and give thanks; some talked of having witnessed a "miracle," a signal from God. More tangibly, Jews donated unprecedented sums of money to help Israel and to express solidarity with its goals: "Jews lined up at Federation offices throughout the country to donate; at times it was difficult to handle the stream of money. Five Boston families together donated $2,500,000; in Cleveland, three million dollars were raised in one day, and in St. Louis— one million in one evening. . . . One Holocaust survivor, the tattooed number visible on her arm, donated $5,000, her entire savings. Another person, who had gone bankrupt just a few days earlier, borrowed $10,000 from a friend to give to the campaign."[79]

All told, American Jews raised $240 million for Israel in 1967 and bought

$190 million in Israel bonds; the total, $430 million, being more than double what they had raised the previous year. American public opinion likewise favored the Jewish state, the lone democracy in the Middle East. As the U.S. military stumbled in Vietnam and Communism exerted itself in Eastern Europe, Israel's smashing triumph offered a sense of reassurance: its victory was widely perceived as a victory for America itself. "If the national press offers any guide to American attitudes, then Jews emerged as popular heroes in the Six-Day War," a study of journalistic representations of Jews confirms. "Americans elided Israelis and American Jews, rooted for David to triumph over the contemporary Philistines, and cheered when David became the new Goliath of the Middle East because they knew that he stood like Super-man for truth, justice, and the American way."[80]

For many Jews, Israel's victory meant more than Superman-like heroism. Temple University professor of political science Daniel Elazar defined the Six Day War in 1969 as a "watershed in contemporary Jewish public affairs." To him, Israel's victory marked "the climax of a generation, the sealing of an era, and the culmination of a 1900-year cycle." It made Jews both old and young "deeply aware of the shared fate of all Jews, and of the way that fate is now bound up with the political entity that is the State of Israel." Elazar himself would soon settle in Israel, as would thousands of other American Jews. *Aliyah,* the Hebrew word for immigration ("ascent") to the Land of Israel, rose more than 500 percent among American Jews in the immediate postwar years, while Jewish tourism from North America doubled in just one year. The Six Day War also marked for some "a turning point in American Jewish consciousness," changing the way American Jews thought "not only about Israel but about themselves." A volume of contemporary Jewish fiction, published in 1992, actually used 1967 to demarcate when the contemporary era for American Jews began. With the war's end, it explained, "Israel . . . became the religion of American Jews, the transcendent object of their politics and philanthropy and pilgrimages and as such a new source of loyalty and solidarity, and in time of dogma and controversy."[81]

Scholars have subsequently debated the extent to which the Six Day War actually transformed contemporary American Jewish life. They find that some of the changes attributed to the war, such as the greater communal focus on Israel and the Holocaust, began earlier; the war intensified rather than initiated these trends. Other changes in the war's wake chiefly affected the most engaged members of the community, not the periphery. Still others, like the spike in immigration from the United States, dissipated after a few years. Finally, America as a whole was undergoing a sobering metamorphosis in the face of the Vietnam debacle, black militancy, the 1968 assassinations of Martin Luther King, Jr., and Robert Kennedy, and the ascension of Richard Nixon. The politics of consensus was giving way to the politics of identity; Americans of all kinds came to focus on roots, race, ethnicity, and gender. Jews ascribed to the Six Day War the identity changes that they experienced, but they may actually have been more influenced by these domestic developments, which affected Jews and non-Jews alike. They attributed the many far-reaching changes that followed the Six Day War to the war itself, remembering it forever after as a turning point in American Jewish life.[82]

The Soviet Jewry movement illustrated the heightened political activism and new sense of communal empowerment that developed in the war's wake.[83] The fate of the Soviet Union's more than 2 million Jews had aroused concern almost as soon as World War II ended, as reports spread of purges, deportations, imprisonments, and widespread deprivations of religious and human rights—all spearheaded, we now know, by Soviet Communist leader Joseph Stalin himself. In 1952, the four-year-old state of Israel established a clandestine Liaison Bureau *(Lishkat ha-Kesher)* to maintain contact with Soviet Jews. It alerted the West to their plight and worked for the amelioration of their condition. Thanks to the bureau's behind-the-scenes efforts, news of Soviet antisemitism appeared periodically in the American press; public appeals and protests took place; and U.S. government officials formally raised the issue with their Soviet counterparts. Gradually, the plight of Soviet Jews came to be seen as a Jewish civil rights struggle, parallel to the black struggle for freedom in the United States. During the years leading up to the Six Day War, Abraham Joshua Heschel enlisted civil rights activists in the cause; Holocaust survivor Elie Wiesel traveled to Russia and wrote poignantly of *The Jews of Silence* (1967); mainstream organizations launched the American Jewish Conference on Soviet Jewry (1964); and college students, organized as the Student Struggle for Soviet Jewry (1964), took to the streets proclaiming "Let My People Go," a slogan that recalled both the biblical Exodus and a well-known Negro spiritual.

Only in the aftermath of the Six Day War, however, did the cause of Soviet Jews turn into a mass movement, overshadowing these earlier developments. Russian Jews themselves experienced a cultural and political awakening after Israel's victory, some openly challenging their government's ban on religious and Hebrew training. Growing numbers of Jews of all ages petitioned to emigrate, braving persecution when their petitions were denied and they became "refuseniks." "Suddenly the Jews of silence have discovered their voice," Abraham Joshua Heschel proclaimed. "Suddenly Soviet Jews have begun to write letters to the Soviet leaders and to the outside world, demanding their right to leave, proudly identifying themselves with the Jewish people and with Israel."[84]

For the next quarter-century, American Jews, sensitized to their failings during the Holocaust era, schooled by the sixties in political activism, and deftly exploiting Cold War politics, made the cause of Russian Jewry their own; it became the centerpiece of their "religious action" programming. Some set aside a "matzah of hope" for Russian Jews at their Passover seders and "twinned" their bar or bat mitzvah celebrations with Russian Jewish children who could not celebrate such milestones in synagogue. Others picketed, demonstrated, and promoted legislation to punish the Soviet Union for its misdeeds. Still others traveled to Russia on clandestine "missions"—a word pregnant with religious meaning—to strengthen persecuted Jews in their resolve and to assure them that they were not forgotten. Even as organizations seeking freedom for Russian Jews fought bitterly among themselves, unable to agree on tactics, goals, discipline, ties to the "established" Jewish community, and the role of Israel, the movement as a whole proved greater than the sum of its parts. The totality of "Soviet Jewry" activities—overt and covert, religious and secular, politically cautious and zealously militant—produced in the end one of the largest mass exoduses in Jewish history, as over 1.5 million Soviet Jews left for Israel, the United States, and Western Europe. For American Jews who helped make this happen, the movement was deeply empowering. It demonstrated how much they could do to assist their fellow Jews in need, and it justified, in their own eyes, the community's inward turn, its sharpening focus on the problems facing Jews.

In the years following 1967, the American Jewish communal agenda as a whole shifted inward, moving "from universalistic concerns to a preoccupation with Jewish particularism."[85] Domestic causes like civil rights and interfaith cooperation lost ground, particularly as concerns mounted over antisemitism and militancy in the black community, as well as anti-Israel sentiments among liberal Christians. In their place, Jews took up causes like Soviet Jewry and Israel, where the objects of assistance were fellow Jews. Influenced by the same "anti-establishment" restiveness ("don't trust anyone over thirty") and expressions of minority group liberation and pride ("Black is beautiful") that suffused America as a whole during this time, Jews—especially baby boomers born after the war and now coming to maturity—also channeled their feelings of rebelliousness, assertiveness, and alienation into domestic programs aimed at transforming and strengthening American Jewish life. They worried, as so many had before them, about the future of American Judaism, fearing that it would not survive unless it changed. In response, they sought to revitalize their own Judaism, developing bold new initiatives to show that their faith could be timely, "with-it," meaningful, and in harmony with the countercultural ideas of their day.

Some of the most exciting and enduring of these new initiatives emerged from within the "*havurah* movement," named for the separatist religious fellowships that radical Jewish pietists, mystics, and scholars had formed back in the days of the Pharisees during the late Second Temple period. The Reconstructionist movement had appropriated this term in the early 1960s in an effort to promote the creation of small fellowship circles consisting of Jews who were partial to the ideas of Mordecai Kaplan and gathered on a regular basis for study, discussion, and prayer.[86] Later that decade, in 1968, socially active, politically liberal students concerned with "the quality of Jewish living and the desire for an integrated lifestyle" appropriated the same term for a new institution established in Somerville, Massachusetts, called Havurat Shalom Community Seminary, devoted to fellowship, peace, community, and a "new model of serious Jewish study." Disdaining "self-satisfied, rich suburbanites" and "smug institutions," the new seminary, besides helping students to avoid the military draft, sought to meet the needs of "serious young Jews . . . deeply involved in honest religious search, who are quite fully alienated from Judaism by all the contacts that they have had to date." The idea, borrowed in part from Theodore Roszak's *The Making of a Counter Culture* (1968), was to jettison the bourgeois middle-class values of suburbia and to re-imagine Judaism "as a revolutionary force . . . [that works] toward liberation, toward greater freedom for the individual and the society."

Havurat Shalom soon abandoned the trappings of a seminary and became a "commune congregation." Its members enjoyed praying by candlelight and sat on cushions on the floor. Group singing and slow wordless melodies (*nigunnim*) borrowed from Hasidic chants punctuated their prayers. Relevant texts, particularly those that spoke to contemporary ideals, received particular emphasis. Along with like-minded "new Jews" who studied and prayed in companion institutions in major communities like New York, Washington, and Los Angeles, they spoke of "religious renewal," disdained Judaism's "established" movements and organizations (including the Conservative movement in which most of them had been raised), and believed that through

The prayer hall of Havurat Shalom (c. 1968).
The young, countercultural worshippers sat
on cushions on the floor rather than on chairs.
A modest Torah ark with a macramé curtain
displaying a Magen David, as well as an eternal
light hanging from the ceiling, defined the room
as sacred space. Courtesy of Arthur Green.

diligent efforts they could themselves "redeem the current bleakness of American Jewish religious life." Their aim was to re-create Judaism in their own generation's image.[87]

The ideals and values that the Jewish counterculture and the havurah movement embodied soon moved from margin to mainstream. The text responsible for this remarkable transformation was *The Jewish Catalog* (1973), a happy mixture of Jewish law and lore, apt quotations, well-chosen photographs, whimsical cartoons, and general irreverence that billed itself as a Jewish "do-it-yourself kit," a guide to how to become "*personally* involved in aspects of Jewish ritual life, customs, cooking, crafts, and creation." It served as the Jewish religious counterpart to the counterculture classic known as *The Whole Earth Catalogue*, a massive compendium of information, tools, and resources, and it also served as a popular, basic introduction to the practice of Judaism. No book published by the Jewish Publication Society, except for the Bible, ever sold so many copies. Eventually expanded to three volumes, *The Jewish Catalog* served as the vehicle for transmitting the innovations pioneered by the creative young Jews of the havurah movement to Jews throughout North America and beyond. The widespread return to ritual that soon became evident across the spectrum of American Jewish life, the renewed interest throughout the community in neglected forms of Jewish music and art, the awakening of record numbers of Jews to the wellsprings of their tradition—these and other manifestations of Jewish religious revival in America all received significant impetus from *The Jewish Catalog.* It spawned a whole library of competitors and sequels, brought fame to Havurat Shalom, to whom the book was dedicated, and helped to transform the Jewish counterculture into an influential mass movement.[88]

Havurah-style worship spread through Jewish communities across the land. Influenced by the Reconstructionist fellowship circles, by Havurat Shalom and its counterparts, and by *The Jewish Catalog,* independent *havurot* (plural of havurah) sprang up in cities large and small, while some Reform and Conservative synagogues put the havurah idea to work within their own institutions to promote the "humanization and personalization" of worship and the democratization of synagogue life. In place of the large formal synagogue service, these havurot adopted sixties-era ideals, including egalitarianism, informality, cohesive community, active participatory prayer, group discussion, and unconventional forms of governance. Participants met weekly, biweekly, or monthly; sat in circles; dressed casually; took turns leading worship and study; ate, talked, and celebrated together; and participated in the happy and sad moments of one another's lives—one rabbi perceptively described the havurah as a "surrogate for the eroded extended family." To be sure, havurot never replaced synagogues for the majority of American Jews. Most havurot, in time, either disappeared, evolved into larger and more formal prayer groups, or became attached to neighborhood synagogues. But the havurah movement's countercultural ideals, counteraesthetic values, and relaxed decorum lived on. In moderated form, they became part of mainstream Judaism, which as a result became more informal, more focused on promoting fellowship and community among members, and more open to discussion-based learning, group singing, and participatory prayer. "I think the notion of creating empowered engaged Jews who live in intensely participatory, vivid, vital Jewish communities is what we sought to create in the New York Havurah and is what many of us are now seeking to do in [mainstream] Jewish life," one anti-establishment havurah leader, who later became executive director of New York's Jewish federation, explained. "Many of the things that I have tried to do as a Jewish professional . . . are still motivated by those commitments." In the end, the havurah movement, like so many previous attempts to radically transform Judaism, produced evolution, not revolution.[89]

The havurah movement was by no means the only evidence of restiveness in the late 1960s. In 1968, the same year that Havurat Shalom began, the Reconstructionist Rabbinical College in Philadelphia also opened its doors, signaling Reconstructionism's willingness to institutionalize itself as an independent force in Jewish life. It denominated itself the "fourth movement" in American Judaism. Hebrew Union College, the Jewish Theological Seminary, and Yeshiva University, the major Reform, Conservative, and Orthodox rabbinical seminaries, had come under attack in 1968 for their stodginess: among other things, critics charged, they stressed "tradition and continuity" over "renewal and change" and failed to prepare rabbis adequately for the realities of the American pulpit. The Reconstructionist Rabbinical College, which featured a new approach to rabbinical education, offered an alternative vision. Its first students were avowedly radical: "They questioned all inherited values and concepts" and allegedly wanted the school to "function like a commune—no structured curriculum, no requirements, no examinations." The institution's sixty-two-year-old president, Rabbi Ira Eisenstein (Mordecai Kaplan's son-in-law) demurred, refusing to allow the school to become what he called "a 'hippie' institution." But the school did from the start admit women, something that no other American rabbinical school at the time permitted. This was a harbinger of greater changes to come.[90]

The Reconstructionist movement in 1968 also recognized as Jewish the offspring of a Jewish father and non-Jewish mother, so long as the parents "rear[ed] the child as a Jew"—a radical change in Jewish practice that became known as "patrilineal descent." According to Jewish law, Judaism passes matrilineally, meaning that the offspring of a Jewish mother and non-Jewish father is automatically Jewish, while the offspring of a Jewish father and a non-Jewish mother requires conversion. Reconstructionists found this law discriminatory. They argued, among other things, that a child's faith depended on how it was raised, and they insisted that in an egalitarian world the question of which of its two parents was Jewish made no difference, so long as the child was brought up as a Jew. In 1983, Reform Judaism likewise adopted the principle of patrilineal descent, at which time the change provoked tremendous controversy throughout Jewish life since it created two different definitions of who is a Jew.[91]

By then, the Reconstructionist movement, in its effort to revitalize Judaism, had come to embrace many features and ideals of the havurah movement and Jewish counterculture—so much so that the founder of Havurat Shalom, Rabbi Arthur Green, became president of the Reconstructionist Rabbinical College; Arthur Waskow, the founder of the Washington havurah, joined its faculty; and leaders of Reconstructionism boasted that their movement stood "on the cutting edge of Jewish ritual and practice." Some innovators, in an effort to update ("reconstruct") ideas set forth years before by Mordecai Kaplan, experimented with radical feminist liturgies and new forms of spirituality; others re-embraced supernaturalism and the concept of Jewish chosenness. In 1993, the movement triumphantly voted to become the first in Judaism to declare homosexuality and heterosexuality "normal expressions of human diversity." Setting aside biblical and rabbinic proscriptions against homosexuality (as well as the Victorian sexual mores of its founder), Reconstructionism embraced contemporary teachings and sanctioned heterosexual and homosexual lifestyles equally as "ways of being which offer fulfillment."[92]

Politically, Reconstructionism in the final decades of the twentieth century had become the most radical of Judaism's religious movements; it stood in the vanguard of those seeking to adapt their faith to comport with the values of liberal America. While it remained tiny, embracing less than 2 percent of the American Jewish population, its members often anticipated and articulated issues in advance of the Jewish mainstream. So it seemed particularly significant that the central concern of Reconstructionist congregants, according to a 1996 survey, had become "personal growth and spirituality." No longer "deeply concerned with . . . social action programming," Reconstructionist Jews now focused more on their own religious lives. In the process, along with the leaders of the havurah movement and the authors of *The Jewish Catalog,* they contributed to a new spirit that came to characterize late twentieth-century American Judaism: a pronounced "awakening" of Jewish ritual observances, learning, and culture.[93]

THE LATE TWENTIETH-CENTURY AWAKENING

Talk of a "Jewish revival," a "reawakening of American Jewish life," and a "revitalization of Jewish tradition" began in the 1970s across the spectrum of American Judaism.[94] This was no mere throwback to the 1950s, when affiliation, suburban institution-building, and a new interest in theology had cheered the hearts of rabbis. Now the emphasis was more on ritual and spirituality. Moreover, the movement of religious revitalization coincided with rapidly rising rates of intermarriage and assimilation. But even as the awakening left countless individual Jews unmoved, and had no appreciable effect on the size of the American Jewish community, the changes it wrought on the synagogue, on Jewish education, and on Jewish culture affected Jewish religious movements of every kind. By the year 2000, the look and feel of American Judaism had changed, and many aspects of Jewish religious life were revitalized and transformed.

The havurah movement and *The Jewish Catalog* anticipated and spurred many of these changes. Both focused on intimacy and worship in family-like settings, as opposed to large impersonal "sanctuaries," helping to break down the formality that had for so long characterized the American syna-gogue. Whereas an earlier generation concerned itself with decorum and solemnity, postwar children, influenced by new cultural surroundings, sought cozier religious settings where they could come to worship far less formally attired and feel right at home. The American synagogue, as a result, became less performance-oriented in the late twentieth century. Where once congre-gants expected to sit back passively to watch a service choreographed by the rabbi and the cantor, perhaps with the assistance of the choir and the organist, now more of them expected to participate in the service actively: praying aloud, singing, and even dancing in the aisles. Formal sermons in many synagogues became less frequent, replaced by interactive discussions and "words of Torah" prepared by lay members. Synagogue music also changed, becoming less operatic and more participatory; organs, in some synagogues, gave way to pianos and guitars. Even the very focus of the synagogue seemed subtly to shift: for decades social action had stood at the center of synagogue activities, but now emphasis leaned toward per-sonal and spiritual growth. Many a fiery rabbinic-prophet who battled pub-licly for justice and righteousness was succeeded, upon retirement, by a more modest and congenial rabbinic-pastor, the embodiment of personal and religious values that congregants sought to emulate in their private lives.

Among Reform Jews, these changes were accompanied by a visible return to once-discarded Jewish customs and practices—an extension of the neo-Reform trend of the 1950s. Growing numbers of men and women chose to don head coverings and prayer shawls in their temples, reversing the late nineteenth-century move to spurn these practices as "Oriental," and provid-ing women, for the first time, the opportunity to wear the same religious garb as men (traditionally, women covered their hair with scarves, hats, or wigs, but not with skullcaps, and they did not wear prayer shawls at all). A series of Reform publications also encouraged "Jewish living" in the home. Some Reform Jews jumped at this chance to deepen their ritual lives: they took up Jewish dietary laws, deepened their Sabbath observance, and even, in a few cases, re-embraced such traditional practices as *tefillin,* the wearing of phylacteries for weekday morning prayers, and *tashlikh,* the ceremonial casting of sins "into the depths of the sea" (following Micah 7:19) on Rosh Hashanah. Observers discerned a "revival among many Reform Jews of previously rejected practices and the desire for active participation in congregational worship and home observances." A 1989 survey confirmed the trend, showing that more than half of all Reform congregations provided skullcaps for their members and a third observed the Jewish dietary laws in a serious way, either keeping "strictly kosher" or not mixing milk and meat. "Customs and ceremonies," the survey concluded, "now play a larger role in the worship practices of Reform congregations than ever before."[95]

Dissident Reform Jews criticized this return to ritual and tradition as an abandonment of Reform Judaism's central message and teachings, and a "surrender to Orthodoxy." Leaders, however, recognized that Reform was becoming more diverse: embodying and even engendering pluralism and opening itself to liberal Jews of every sort. The movement's "Centenary Perspective," adopted in San Francisco in 1976, went so far as to describe "diversity within unity" as the "hallmark of Reform." The more controversial "Statement of Principles for Reform Judaism," adopted in 1999 in Pittsburgh (where, 114 years earlier, Reform rabbis had contemptuously rejected ceremonies "not adapted to the views and habits of modern civilization"), went further, serving notice that the majority of Reform rabbis were now sympathetic to the recovery of ritual. "Through Torah study we are called to *mitzvot* [sacred obligations], the means by which we make our lives holy," the statement declared. "Some of these *mitzvot* . . . have long been observed by Reform Jews; others, both ancient and modern, demand renewed attention."[96]

Conservative Jews likewise experienced renewed interest in ritual observance. *The Jewish Catalog* was largely (but not exclusively) the product of Conservative Jews, and the havurah movement as a whole made its largest impact in Conservative Jewish circles. The Conservative movement also produced a traditional *Guide to Jewish Religious Practice* in 1979, aimed at Conservative Jews, and issued a statement of principles that called on the Conservative community "to maintain the law and practices of the past as much as possible," although it recognized "variations of practice" and a "vibrant, healthy pluralism" within the movement. ("The ideal of complete observance is clearly honored," a perceptive outsider observed of Conservative Judaism in the 1990s, "but imperfection and individual variation are taken as the norm.") Most revealingly, a 1995 survey of Conservative synagogue members found that "younger Conservative Jewish adults are . . . more Jewishly active than their older counterparts, even when taking family life stage and the presence of children into account." In fact, the younger Conservative Jews, proved "more ritually active than older congregants despite having been raised by less observant parents."[97]

Orthodoxy, unsurprisingly, benefited the most from the end-of-century revitalization of Judaism. Some of its leaders trumpeted the other movements' rediscovery of Jewish ritual as a vindication, a sign that Orthodoxy had been on the right track all along. Others looked forward with anticipation to Orthodoxy's eventual triumph in the Jewish religious marketplace. One widely discussed book proclaimed that "in the struggle for the soul of American Jewry" the "Orthodox model" had triumphed already. In fact, Orthodoxy remained by far the smallest of American Judaism's major branches, with less than half a million adherents. But in the last decades of the twentieth century it added thousands of young new members who, while not born Orthodox, became known as *ba'ale teshuva,* penitent or returning Jews, parallel in some respects to "born again" Christians in Evangelicalism. Many of these new recruits—"the 'big story' of our time," according to one Orthodox Jewish periodical—were former members of the counterculture, "world-traveled college students . . . who had experienced everything the big world had to offer" and now sought meaning in the texts, trappings, and rituals of traditional Judaism. Published accounts described the "return" of people like "Arnold," whose "previous experience in Jewish education was limited to a three year stint at a Talmud Torah [Hebrew School] prior to his bar mitzvah. His mother is Jewish and . . . his father is not." There were also people like "Beth," a twenty-nine-year-old woman from a nonobservant Jewish background "who had spent most of her twenties in a community of 'born-again' Christians," but was now studying at Bais Chana, a Lubavitch Hasidic learning center for women. Indeed, ba'ale teshuva of both sexes came to Orthodoxy from all branches of Judaism, as well as from Jews for Jesus, the drug culture, and Buddhism. Some were actively recruited by outreach experts, who were adept at finding lost or troubled Jewish souls in need of warm embracing. Others came to Orthodoxy on their own, having become disaffected with other Jewish movements. Either way, Orthodoxy received an infusion of new blood and an injection of youthful self-confidence. While it continued to lose many veteran members to other Jewish movements (even among the younger and supposedly more committed Orthodox, according to one survey, Orthodoxy retained only 42 percent of those born into its fold), large numbers of exuberant newcomers made the community feel stronger.[98]

At the same time, Jews born and educated within the Orthodox community displayed new levels of outward piety and identification. Previous generations of Orthodox males had for the most part considered the skullcap (which they called a yarmulke or kippah) to be an "indoor garment"; on the street they either wore hats or went bareheaded. Now, Orthodox males, even doctors, lawyers, and Wall Street brokers, felt comfortable wearing skullcaps not only in the street but at work. A full-page ad found in major newspapers in August 2000 went so far as to depict young, well-dressed, business-types wearing skullcaps and expressing interest in "technology, politics, baseball, bad movies, fancy restaurants, and hip-hop." Orthodox Jewish naming patterns reflected a parallel move. Previous generations of Orthodox Jews had assumed American-style English names, reserving their Hebrew or Yiddish "Jewish names" for the synagogue and intimate friends. Now, Orthodox Jews tended to give their children only Jewish and Hebrew names. In one revealing case, preserved on the *New York Times* obituary page, "Fred . . . beloved husband of Edith" left children named "Thomas, Linda, and Steven," and was the "devoted grandfather of Simcha, Yonatan, Elisheva, Avigayil, Elayna, Benjamin, and Yael." The same general trend, reflecting a new level of comfort in overt displays of ethnicity and faith, characterized the "swing to the right" in Orthodox Jewish life, discussed above, and the public displays of Jewish ritual orchestrated by Chabad-Lubavitch, notably the candlelighting ceremonies that they held in public squares during Hanukkah. In an era when so many other racial and ethnic groups were taking public pride in what made them distinctive, and when Evangelical Protestantism, Buddhism, and Islam were emerging into public consciousness, the revival of Orthodoxy seemed consonant with the times.[99]

So too did the widespread return to ritual observance. For many Jews, ritual became "the single most important way in which [to] . . . express their Jewish commitments" in the late twentieth century, replacing such public activities as synagogue attendance, participation in Jewish organizations, and social action work. Family connections partly explain this. "Jews value ritual," a study of "moderately affiliated Jews" concluded, "because it brings them closer to grandparents, parents, partners, spouses, children, and grandchildren." The study also showed that rituals infused Jewish life with meaning, "usually in a highly personal way," and that Jews chose for themselves

"what to observe and what not to observe," updating and reinterpreting rituals in an effort to make them more personally meaningful. Spiritual leaders
and books like *The Jewish Catalog* encouraged the revival of ritual behavior,
but religious authority ultimately rested "with each individual or family."
For American Jews, as for Americans generally, faith had become a matter
of personal choice and preference. Selected Passover, Hanukkah, and Sabbath rituals, celebrated with family and friends, helped Jews feel connected,
and engaged them far more than hoary theological beliefs.[100]

The rediscovery of ritual, the continuing focus on the individual (the
"sovereign self"), and the recognition that the pursuit of faith is a lifelong
quest, a "journey of ongoing questioning and development . . . no final answers, no irrevocable commitments" all characterized the late twentieth-
century American Jewish "awakening." Whereas a previous generation had
rejected Jewish commitments in the name of modernity and universalism,
now, increasingly, Jews defined themselves through those elements of Jewish
tradition that they *chose* to embrace. They felt free to explore many options
in search of meaning, and they picked their way "cafeteria style" among
the diverse laws and customs that govern Jewish life. Seeking to make more
informed decisions and to explore Judaism more thoroughly, many Jews
also deepened their commitment to Jewish learning for themselves and their
children—another facet of the Jewish awakening that shaped Jewish life at
the end of the twentieth century.[101]

According to best estimates, American Jews in the late 1990s spent more
than $1.5 billion annually on Jewish education (about $300 for every Jewish
man, woman, and child) to cover the costs of "nearly three thousand schools
and thousands more educational programs held in a wide variety of institutional settings." Jewish day care centers, nursery schools, all-day schools, supplementary schools, Sunday Schools, high schools, colleges, university-based
Jewish studies programs, Talmudic academies, rabbinical schools, and adult
Jewish education programs, as well as a wide range of informal programs,
from summer camps to youth groups to Jewish Community Center activities to synagogue retreats, all fell under the rubric of Jewish education, and
almost all displayed dramatic growth. "Perhaps never before," historian
Jack Wertheimer concluded, "has a Jewish community pinned so much of
its hopes for 'continuity'—for the transmission of a strong Jewish identity
to the next generation—on programs of formal and informal education."[102]

The proliferation of Jewish all-day schools attracted the most notice. By
1998–99 there were at least 670 such schools with a total of 184,333 students,
more than double the number of thirty years before. In metropolitan New

York, America's largest Jewish community, a study showed that "roughly twice as many Jewish children attend day schools as supplementary schools (88,000 versus 37,000)." Greater Boston, even with its fabled public school systems, boasted thirteen Jewish all-day schools in 2002 and experienced a 60 percent growth in enrollment just between 1994 and 2001. Nationwide, Jewish all-day schools were found in thirty-eight states plus the District of Columbia. Every community of more than seventy-five hundred Jews in the 1990s boasted at least one such school; a community without one felt deficient. As in the past, the vast majority of these schools (95 percent in New York and about 80 percent nationwide) were Orthodox; the number of Conservative, Reform, and "transdenominational" schools, while growing, was far smaller. On the other hand, resistance to these schools by proponents of public school education largely collapsed in the late twentieth century. As Christian schools and private and parochial schools of many other kinds increased in number in the United States, and the overall quality of public schools declined, many Jewish parents sought a "more rigorous Jewish education for their children than they received themselves." They looked to all-day schools to promote Jewish identity and stem the tide of assimilation and intermarriage. Spurred by studies demonstrating that "extensive Jewish education is definitively associated with every measure of adult Jewish identification," those interested in revitalizing American Judaism considered the Jewish all-day school a keystone of their efforts.[103]

University-based Jewish studies programs likewise proliferated. An expansive listing published in 1995 found over seven hundred American institutions of higher learning "in which Jewish civilization is taught or researched." In 2003, the Association for Jewish Studies (founded in 1969) boasted some sixteen hundred members. By contrast, only about twelve positions had existed in the entire field in 1945; sixty in 1965. Whereas once the American college campus had been described as a "disaster area for Judaism, Jewish loyalty and Jewish identity," now many college campuses offered Jews the opportunity to explore their heritage in an intensive, scholarly way. Some students found their Jewish religious lives transformed by this experience. "Away from a home and a community which were 'automatically' Jewish . . . I made a conscious choice to pursue Jewish life as I never had before," an undergraduate who decided to become a rabbi explained. A revitalized campus organization known as Hillel: The Foundation for Jewish Campus Life (founded in 1923 and reorganized in 1988), promised to help America's estimated 400,000 collegiate Jews "to explore and celebrate their Jewish identity . . . to provoke a renaissance of Jewish life." In addition, thanks to the rapid growth in the number of academic positions in Jewish studies, scholarship concerning every conceivable aspect of Judaism and Jewish life mushroomed. The field as a whole emerged into the academic mainstream.[104]

Finally, adult Jewish education flourished during this time. The success of *The Jewish Catalog* and Barry Holtz's *Back to the Sources* (1984)—"the first complete modern guide to the great books of the Jewish tradition: what they are and how to read them"—demonstrated a hungering for adult Jewish learning, reaffirming the observation that "the most active periods in the history of adult education have always been those in which there has been the greatest rapidity of change." Three nationwide programs of adult Jewish education took off in their wake—the Wexner Heritage Program (1985), the Florence Melton Adult Mini-Schools (1986), and the Me'ah ("one hundred [hours]") Program (1994)—each of which attracted thousands of committed Jewish adults, women in particular, interested in learning more about the history, texts, ideas, and practices of their faith. New rituals like the adult bar/bat mitzvah reinforced these efforts, which synagogues, private foundations, and Jewish communal organizations all supported. By strengthening adult Jewish education, leaders believed, Jewish religious and communal life would likewise be strengthened.[105]

Thanks to the many varied institutions and settings that provided Jewish education formally and informally to Jews of all ages at the end of the twentieth century, more Jews received more Jewish education on American soil than ever before in American history. Indeed, Jewish learning for some became the essence of Judaism, an alternative mode of worship. For women, long denied access to Judaism's sacred texts, Jewish learning also served as a form of empowerment, a means of acquiring knowledge that was once the exclusive province of men. But for all its significance, education was not the only route back to Jewish identity for newly awakened late twentieth-century Jews. Culture—everything from fiction to film and from comedy routines to klezmer music—beckoned them as well.

Jews sometimes like to claim that they created contemporary culture. One scholar boasts that they taught Americans "how to dance (Arthur Murray), how to behave (Dear Abby and Ann Landers), how to dress (Ralph Lauren), what to read (Irving Howe, Alfred Kazin, and Lionel Trilling), and what to sing (Barry Manilow and Barbra Streisand)." Another reports that Jews "invented Hollywood." Still another invokes the authority of Marlon Brando, who once told an interviewer that, per capita, "Jews have contributed more to American . . . culture than any other single group." Without them, the actor claimed, "we wouldn't have music," "we wouldn't have much theater," and we wouldn't have "all the songs that you love to sing."[106] Dispropor-tionate as these contributions to American culture may be, for years the array of arts in which Jews participated actually bore little relationship to Judaism, and were, in many cases, an effective means of escaping it. Fearing that if their work were "too Jewish" it would remain provincial, the most creative Jews in America hid or sublimated their faith. They changed their names and universalized the products of their creative genius in a bid to attract a wide audience.

The late twentieth century witnessed a shift in this pattern, a veritable explosion in America of self-consciously Jewish culture of every sort. "We are in the midst of a Jewish cultural renaissance in America," the National Foundation for Jewish Culture triumphantly proclaimed. "When you see feature films reflecting the Jewish experience in your local cineplex, attend readings of new Jewish writing in your local bookstore, listen to new Jewish music in downtown jazz clubs, visit thousands of Jewish websites on the Internet, take courses in Jewish Studies on college campuses across the country—there can be little doubt that we are in a Golden Age of Jewish Culture unlike any in the four thousand year history of the Jewish people." Performing arts, media arts, visual arts, literary arts—all of them, the foun-dation found, explored Jewish themes with fresh urgency and renewed vigor, in many cases thanks to artists who had found their way back to Judaism after years of restless wandering through the desert of alienation.[107]

American Jewish fiction writers during the late twentieth century exempli-fied this trend. Whereas earlier American Jewish writing "was characterized by a universalistic orientation," now writers like Arthur Cohen, Nathan Englander, Jonathan Safran Foer, Rebecca Goldstein, Allegra Goodman, Cynthia Ozick, Chaim Potok, Philip Roth, and Elie Wiesel wrestled in their novels with weighty spiritual matters. In the process, they "produced a new, inward-turning genre of contemporary American Jewish fiction which ex-plores the individual Jew's connection to the Jewish people, to Jewish religion, culture, and tradition, and to the chain of Jewish history."[108] Jewish artists similarly discovered that they could "succeed in theater, dance, music, etc., with their Jewish sensibilities intact and positively asserted." All forms of Jewish art, literature, and music in late twentieth-century America found new practitioners and experienced dramatic renewal. "Despite dark talk in the American Jewish community about a crisis of Jewish 'continuity,'" the *American Jewish Year Book* reported in 1999, "American Jewish culture . . . continue[s] to flourish."[109]

The result, across the United States, was an outpouring of Jewish book,

film, and folk festivals, "annual cultural events, celebrated at approximately
the same time in communities coast to coast." The *Year Book* described
these events as "an analogue in cultural terms to the expectations and regularity of the religious holidays." A rabbi involved in Jewish music went so
far as to proclaim the cultural festivals "a uniquely American way to celebrate
Judaism." More than fifty museums, spread over twenty-two states, likewise
devoted themselves to the preservation, exploration, and celebration of
Jewish culture—up from just two major Jewish museums in the United
States in 1950. The "growth of a body of Jewish art, the existence of a pool
of wealthy collectors willing to purchase and donate such works, education,
artistic sophistication, emotions aroused by the Holocaust and events in
Israel, curiosity about Jewishness and Jewish identity—combined with the
general popularity of museums in American culture and the special qualities
of the museum experience"—all contributed to this development. Some of
the new museums focused on art, some on Holocaust commemoration,
some on the American Jewish experience, some on children, but all of them,
according to the writer Nessa Rapoport, shared a common responsibility:
"to translate and explain what has come before us to those who will carry
it on after us."[110]

Proponents, taking stock of the museums, the festivals, and the general
Jewish artistic efflorescence in America, viewed them as means of fostering
Jewish unity, continuity, and education while furthering "Jewish pride and
identity." Arts and culture, they believed, could "help renew Jewish life because their dynamic, spiritual, and emotional nature can inspire individuals,
create a sense of community, and provoke radically new ideas." Like B'nai
B'rith and the various forms of secular Judaism that had arisen in America
since the nineteenth century, culture embraced even those disaffected with
formal religion, offering them an alternative means of identifying with the
Jewish people and its achievements. Critics, meanwhile, saw the spread of
Jewish cultural institutions not as a sign of "renaissance," but as one more
indicator of assimilation. "As many Jews become more distant from their
roots and heritage—growing numbers of them becoming, through intermarriage, part of extensive family networks of non-Jews"—museums, festivals, and related cultural venues provided them with neutral, socially acceptable meeting places. Less threatening than the synagogue, these meeting
places demanded nothing in the way of practice or commitment, no proclamations of identity, no symbols of affiliation. They simply exposed visitors,
whatever their background or faith, "to the richness and variety of the
Jewish heritage."[111]

The late twentieth-century American Jewish awakening was thus something less than an unmixed blessing in the eyes of those who worried about the Jewish future. Welcome signs of revitalization mingled with disturbing evidence of assimilation, and sometimes the same phenomena could be read both ways. However much Jewish religious life, education, and culture seemed to be experiencing a "renaissance," the corrosive effects of intermarriage and demographic contraction seemed to portend decline. Could the grand themes of late twentieth-century American Judaism—the Holocaust, Israel, feminism, and spirituality—inspire Jews to remain Jews?

THE GRAND THEMES OF LATE
TWENTIETH-CENTURY AMERICAN JUDAISM

In surveys of American Jewish opinion conducted annually from 1993 by the American Jewish Committee, two themes always emerged as paramount. About three-quarters of American Jews agreed that "caring about Israel is a very important part of my being a Jew." The same number considered "remembrance of the Holocaust" to be either "extremely important" or "very important." By contrast, only about a third of those surveyed listed participation in synagogue services, Jewish study, or Jewish organizational activity as extremely or very important. Even "celebration of Jewish holidays" ranked below caring about Israel and remembering the Holocaust as central components of Jewish identity.[112]

The themes of Israel and the Holocaust developed together in the consciousness of American Jews; they were, in many ways, fraternal twins. Both emerged from the wreckage of the 1940s, when 6 million Jews perished in Europe and the tiny state of Israel won its independence. They incubated during the following decade, nourished by engaged subgroups like Holocaust survivors and Zionist activists, and reinforced by Jewish educators. They then moved onto the center stage of Jewish public life during the 1960s, becoming mass causes following the Six Day War.

In the case of the Holocaust, it was Israel's capture of Nazi leader Adolf Eichmann in 1960, his trial in Jerusalem about a year later, and Hannah Arendt's disturbing book on the trial published in 1963 that thrust the destruction of the Jews into public consciousness. All three developments, particularly the nationally televised trial, received widespread media attention. So did the "Auschwitz trials" of more than twenty former Nazis in West Germany in 1963, and, in 1964, the opening of Rolf Hochhuth's play *The Deputy,* a blistering and controversial indictment by a German Protestant of Pope Pius XII's inaction in the face of Nazi atrocities. The very word *Holocaust* as a shorthand term for what happened to the Jews during World War II entered popular usage at this time; it became the preferred translation of the Hebrew *Shoah.* In the days preceding the 1967 Six Day War, we have seen, the specter of "another Holocaust" filled Jews with dread.

Thereafter, the Holocaust became central not only in Jewish life, through museums, memorials, courses, cultural events, annual commemorations, and bulging libraries of books, it also became part of general American memory. Arthur Morse's widely publicized indictment entitled *While 6 Million Died: A Chronicle of American Apathy,* published in 1968 (and serialized a year earlier in *Look* magazine), showed Americans that they were not totally blameless for what happened; America, the book proclaimed on its cover, "ducked chance after chance to save the Jews." Subsequently, the television miniseries *Holocaust* in 1978, the establishment of the President's Commission on the Holocaust that same year, annual Holocaust commemorations in the Capitol Rotunda beginning in 1979, Holocaust curricula in public schools, and two epochal developments in 1993, the opening of the United States Holocaust Memorial Museum and the release of the film *Schindler's List,* heightened public awareness of the tragedy. Today, most Americans know more about the Holocaust than about any other single event in the entire history of the Jewish people. Ensuring that everyone continues to remember the Holocaust and its lessons is, for many Jews, a central tenet of their faith.[113]

Consciousness of Israel followed a similar trajectory. Although the establishment of the state was heralded—the *American Jewish Year Book* described it as "the most dramatic and perhaps most significant event in post-exilic Jewish history"—it by no means came to preoccupy American Jews in the 1950s. The *Year Book* itself, during those years, devoted far more attention to Germany than to Israel. Many American Jews, particularly the leaders of the American Jewish Committee, worried that Israel might interfere with the "internal affairs" of the American Jewish community and provoke charges of "dual loyalty."[114] A historic exchange in 1950 between Israel's prime minister, David Ben-Gurion, and the president of the American Jewish Committee, Jacob Blaustein (later known as the Blaustein–Ben Gurion agreement), sought to allay these fears. As summarized by the committee, the agreement stipulated: "(1) that Jews of the United States, as a community and as individuals, have only one political attachment, namely, to the United States of America; (2) that the Government and people of Israel respect the integrity of Jewish life in the democratic countries and

The Blaustein–Ben Gurion agreement (August 23, 1950). Present at the
historic exchange in Jerusalem's King David Hotel were Israel's Prime Minister
David Ben Gurion, American Jewish Committee president Jacob Blaustein,
and future prime ministers Golda Meir and Moshe Sharett. Courtesy of the
American Jewish Committee photo archives.

the right of the Jewish communities to develop their indigenous social, economic, and cultural aspirations, in accordance with their own needs and
institutions; and (3) that Israel fully accepts the fact that the Jews in the
United States do not live 'in exile,' and that America is home for them."[115]

Israel remained largely peripheral to American Judaism in the 1950s. A
survey of Jewish education in the United States at the end of that decade
found to its surprise that only forty-eight out of over a thousand teachers
"reported teaching Israel as a subject of study." Another survey, in 1951,
concluded with dismay that "not a single book has been published since
the establishment of the Jewish State which deals with any of the numerous
social aspects of the great events taking place at present in the country."[116]
Israel did influence American Jewish life in more subtle ways, some of them
rooted in pre-state developments; for example, "the introduction of regular
prayers for Israel" in some synagogues, "the normalcy of the appearance
of the Zionist or Israeli flag at Jewish gatherings," the sale of Israeli products
in synagogue gift shops (according to one survey in 1957–58, more American Jews had an Israeli-made object in their home than had Sabbath candle-
sticks), the adoption of the Israeli pronunciation of Hebrew among educators,
and the spread of Israeli dances among young people. Israel also played a

significant role in American Jewish philanthropy. But even though most American Jews described themselves as pro-Israel and 90 percent in one survey told researchers that they would feel a "sense of loss" if it were destroyed, few had visited Israel, and only highly committed Zionists considered it central to their lives or their faith.[117]

Israel began to play a heightened role in American Jewish consciousness in the 1960s, in tandem with the rise of Holocaust awareness. The wildly popular epic film *Exodus* (1960), based on Leon Uris' 1958 bestselling novel of the same name, "contributed mightily to the visibility of Israel on the American Jewish communal agenda," rivaling *Gone with the Wind* in its box office appeal and cultural influence. The film's highly sympathetic portrayal of Israel's birth and the conscious links it drew between brawny Zionist pioneers and the heroes of traditional American westerns (*Exodus,* according to one account, was "a tale of brave men overcoming the dangers of a wild frontier to bring law, order and civilization to a new land") fostered identification with the Jewish state among Jews and Christians alike. Lesser known films and a score of novels, as well as television programs and magazine articles, likewise portrayed Israel in a sympathetic light, particularly as Cold War tensions carved the world into friends and foes. More than ever, during the 1960s, Americans came to view Israel positively, as an oasis of democracy, a microcosm of America itself.[118]

The early 1960s also witnessed the beginning of a conscious effort on the part of the United Jewish Appeal, the central communal philanthropy, to train young Jewish leaders to be "proud of being Jews and of being connected to Israel." Thousands of future Jewish leaders along with hundreds of rabbis representing every stream of Judaism learned about Israel, met Israeli government officials, and toured Israel under the United Jewish Appeal's auspices. The characterization of these tours as "missions" or "pilgrimages" underscored their deep religious significance. For participants, they often proved to be life-changing experiences, initiating them into lives dedicated to Israel's aid and support.[119]

The Six Day War, as we have seen, heightened Israel consciousness among all sectors of the American Jewish community. In the years that followed, Israel became the dominant focus of American Jewish life. Philanthropy, political activity, education, religious life, and culture all became "Israel-centered"—so much so that critics charged American Jews with using Israel for "vicarious fulfillment of their Jewish identity." The Jewish Publication Society, to take just one example, published twenty-eight Israel-related books in the decade following the Six Day War, more than in the previous two decades put together. In fact, it published more books about Israel than about American Jewish life; more, indeed, than it did about all of the rest of Jewish history, ancient, medieval, and modern combined. "Diaspora Jewry . . . is doomed; Jewish life has a future, if at all, only in Israel," proclaimed its most widely discussed book, Hillel Halkin's *Letters to an American Jewish Friend: A Zionist's Polemic* (1977). Insisting that the diaspora was "historically played out," Halkin, who had himself migrated from America to Israel in 1970, concluded that to properly live as a Jew one had but one choice, "coming from the Diaspora to here."[120]

American Jews mostly rejected Halkin's call to migrate. For them, the prime justification for Israel's existence was not the declining state of the Jewish diaspora but the memory of the Holocaust. The destruction of 6 million Jews, followed by the "miraculous" creation of the Jewish state, constituted for them a modern-day reenactment of an ancient tale of death and rebirth. Taking their cue from Israel, where the creation of the Jewish state had long been seen as the "answer" to the Holocaust, American Jews too came to see an indissoluble bond between these two defining events of twentieth-century Jewish history. They developed the motif of "Holocaust and redemption"—"the generative myth," according to the well-known Judaic scholar Jacob Neusner, "by which the generality of American Jews make sense of themselves." Modern Jewish liturgies reinforced this motif. "Even in our age of orphans and survivors," a prayer in the Reconstructionist Prayer Book reads, "God's loving acts have not abandoned us, and God has brought together our scattered kin from the distant corners of the earth." Reform Jews likewise linked the Holocaust with the renewal of life in the Land of Israel, transferring this idea to the high point of their afternoon Day of Atonement liturgy, recalling the biblical prophet Ezekiel's vision of the "dry bones" that live again.[121]

"From Holocaust to Rebirth" became central to what has been called the "civil religion" of American Jews, the broadly shared faith articulated by Jewish communal and political institutions:

> Like the great speeches of Moses in the final chapters of Deuteronomy, the myth of "Holocaust to rebirth" presents the Jew with a fundamental choice: submit to the forces of death and destruction, or join with those who are fighting for life. Both are ever-present, yet the struggle is not vain, because Judaism insists—and the history/myth of the past forty years confirms— that life must eventually win out. The activity of the polity itself becomes part of this historic struggle between the forces of life and death. Both its achievements and its challenges are often framed precisely in these terms:

"We are the bridge between years of terror and persecution and new lives in freedom; between the agony of Jewishness denied and the joy of renewed Jewish identity." "It is our chosen responsibility—as one people—to renew life time and again."[122]

Two new holidays, commemorated just a week apart, underscored this message: Yom HaShoah (Holocaust Memorial Day) and Israel Independence Day. The former, established by Israel's parliament in 1951 and widely observed by American Jews beginning in the 1970s, is a day of mourning and remembrance. The latter, marking Israel's 1948 rebirth as a modern independent state, is a day of joy and thanksgiving. The connection between them extends far beyond their temporal proximity. According to *Gates of the Seasons,* the Reform Jewish guide to the Jewish year, "on Yom HaShoah, we mourn the death of six million Jews slaughtered by the Nazis, but our grief gives way to rejoicing when we join in the celebration of Israel's rebirth on Yom Ha-Atsma-ut [Israel Independence Day]." The two holidays are thematically linked: "The rebirth of Israel from the ashes of the *Sho-ah* is a symbol of hope against despair, of redemption against devastation."[123] The March of the Living, a carefully orchestrated pageant involving thousands of Jewish teenagers from around the world, re-enacts this motif on the ground. "Within a compressed period of time, participants 'relive' the Jewish past, moving from sites of death in Eastern Europe," including a silent procession at Auschwitz, "to sites of life and vitality in Israel." Through the march and the lectures that accompany it, a new generation is supposed to experience for itself the two dominant themes of late twentieth-century American Judaism: death in the Holocaust and rebirth in the Jewish national home.[124]

While the "Holocaust-Israel" motif reoriented late twentieth-century American Judaism, two other themes—feminism and spirituality—transformed its character. Feminism's "second wave" (the "first wave" had won women the right to the vote) burst upon the American scene in the 1960s. Rebelling against the idea that men should dominate society, governing a woman's place and body, feminists spoke of the need for equality and liberation. They argued that women "belong to a subordinate group; that they have suffered wrongs as a group; that their condition of subordination is not natural, but societally determined; that they must join with other women to remedy these wrongs; and finally, that they must and can provide an alternate vision of societal organization in which women as well as men will enjoy autonomy and self-determination."[125]

Jewish women played a disproportionate role among the leaders and theorists of the feminist movement, and some of them extended their criticism to Judaism itself. "Down through the generations in history my ancestors prayed, 'I thank Thee, Lord, I was not created a woman,'" Betty Friedan, bestselling author of *The Feminine Mystique* and founder of the National Organization for Women, lamented in a 1970 address. "From this day forward," she continued, "I trust women all over the world will be able to say, 'I thank Thee, Lord, I *was* created a woman.'"[126] Feminists "deeply rooted in Judaism and Jewish culture" extended this critique. Ezrat Nashim, a cleverly named organization of young Conservative Jewish women knowledgeable enough to appreciate that *ezrat nashim,* in Hebrew, could refer both to the "women's section" of the synagogue and to "assistance of women," called "for an end to the second-class status of women in Jewish life." In 1972, a year after its founding, its members appeared uninvited at the annual Rabbinical Assembly convention to present a series of emphatic demands:

> It is time that:
> women be granted membership in synagogues
> women be counted in the *minyan*
> women be allowed full participation in religious observances . . . [including being called up to the Torah, reading the Torah, and chanting the prayers]
> women be recognized as witnesses before Jewish law
> women be allowed to initiate divorce
> women be permitted and encouraged to attend Rabbinical and Cantorial schools, and to perform Rabbinical and Cantorial functions in synagogues
> women be encouraged to join decision-making bodies, and to assume professional leadership roles, in synagogues and in the general Jewish community
> women be considered as bound to fulfill all *mitzvot* equally with men.[127]

Equality for women was anything but a new issue for American Judaism. Beginning in the colonial era, we have seen, women had begun to frequent synagogues. Thereafter, debates over how visible women should be, where they should sit, what roles they should play, how much power they should wield, and how their status under Jewish law should be improved, including the issue of the agunah, the "anchored" wife who could not remarry because her husband could not (or would not) grant her a Jewish divorce, had flared repeatedly, affecting at some point every synagogue, temple, and movement in Judaism. The fact that American culture considered the treatment of women to be a gauge of modernity heightened the stakes in these debates.

Beyond their effect on the religious lives of women, the debates also pitted the conflicting values of tradition and modernity against one another and shaped Judaism's image within the larger American community.

Women's ordination became the focus and symbol of feminist demands for change in the late twentieth century. Traditionally, the rabbinate had always been a male preserve. As teachers, preachers, and community leaders —part prophet, part priest, part judge—rabbis considered themselves links in an unbroken chain of tradition handed down from one great man to the next, beginning with Moses ("our rabbi"), who had himself received the Torah from God. A few exceptional women became learned in Torah through the years, and some even became teachers and lay leaders revered for their piety and wisdom, but none until the twentieth century ever held the title of rabbi. More often, rabbinically inclined women became *rebbetzins,* the wives of rabbis. They married what they wanted to be.[128]

The question of whether women might themselves become ordained rabbis titillated readers of late nineteenth-century American Jewish newspapers and provoked a clamorous debate among Reform Jewish leaders in the early 1920s when a female student, Martha Neumark, whose father served on the Hebrew Union College faculty, petitioned for the right to serve a High Holiday congregation. The Central Conference of American Rabbis voted in her case that a woman "cannot justly be denied the privilege of ordination," notwithstanding Professor Jacob Lauterbach's rabbinic responsum to the contrary, but Hebrew Union College's Board of Governors reserved for itself the final word: "No change," it decided, "should be made in the present practice." Though at least four other women attended American rabbinical schools during the interwar years, not one of them was ordained, and only one actually completed the course. Some twenty-six Protestant denominations had agreed to ordain women by that time—the first woman minister, Antoinette Brown (Blackwell), had been ordained back in 1853. In Germany in 1935, the world's first woman Reform rabbi, Regina Jonas, received private ordination after completing a full course of study at the Berlin Reform seminary known as the Hochschule (she perished at Auschwitz in 1944). But in the absence of any groundswell of support for the ordination of women from within the American Jewish community, and with no reason to fear that Judaism's image in the wider world would suffer should the rabbinate remain exclusively male, even Reform rabbinical seminaries in America decided to play it safe. The question of women's ordination in Judaism remained theoretical until women in the late twentieth century thrust the issue to the forefront.[129]

Reform Jewish sisterhood women, led by the redoubtable Jane Evans, were the first to act, calling for the ordination of women early in the 1960s, just as women activists were renewing their demands for the equality of women in all the professions. Growing numbers of women were becoming leaders in Reform Jewish youth activities during the 1960s, some attended Hebrew Union College classes as undergraduates, and a few dreamed of being rabbis. One of those few, Sally Jane Priesand, entered the rabbinical track of the Hebrew Union College–Jewish Institute of Religion (Cincinnati) in 1968 and, in the face of numerous obstacles, stayed the course. She drew media attention and, more important, support from the college's president, Nelson Glueck, and then from Alfred Gottschalk and the Reform movement's top leadership. Ordained amid great fanfare in 1972, she became America's first woman rabbi, followed two years later by the first Reconstructionist woman rabbi, Sandy Eisenberg Sasso. By the year 2000, the Reform movement in the United States had ordained 335 women rabbis, the Reconstructionist movement, 98. Half or more of both schools' ordination classes every year consisted of women.[130]

The Conservative movement's path to women's ordination proved far more tortuous. Committed simultaneously to Jewish tradition and to change, the movement found itself split. Some, like its world-renowned Talmudist, Professor Saul Lieberman, insisted that Jewish law was unshakable: "Since a woman is not fit to judge [issues of Jewish law], and she cannot become qualified for this," he wrote, "she cannot be ordained." Others, like the distinguished Conservative rabbi and scholar Robert Gordis, countered that "both on ethical and on pragmatic grounds, taking into account the crying needs of Jewish life and the call for equal opportunity . . . their ordination is highly desirable." Plaintive letters from young, well-educated Conservative Jewish women eager to enter the rabbinate, as well as a perceptible movement of such women to Reform and Reconstructionist seminaries, led to worries about a "real loss in (WO)man power for our movement." Yet the chancellor of the Jewish Theological Seminary, Gerson Cohen, feared with good reason that "an outright policy" of ordination for women would mean "tearing our Movement apart."[131]

For just over a decade (1972–83) Conservative Jewish leaders "engaged in an intricate political dance of shifting alliances, studies undertaken, commissions formed, hearings held, motions tabled, and votes counted." Meanwhile, revolutionary changes in the status of women rocked Conservative synagogues across the country. Following a Rabbinical Assembly Law Committee decision in 1973, growing numbers of Conservative synagogues began to include women equally with men as part of the minyan required for prayer—some 59 percent of all Conservative synagogues did so by 1983. The number of synagogues calling women up to the Torah rose even faster, more than tripling (from thirty to ninety-four) in just two years, and reaching 76.6 percent of all Conservative congregations in 1983.[132] Many women also donned prayer shawls as men did, and some synagogues elected women presidents. These changes appealed to younger Conservative Jews, who agitated for women's equality in all aspects of Jewish life and helped set the stage for the decision to ordain women. But some older and more traditional Conservative congregants felt betrayed. Changes in the status of women, to them, cast doubt on Conservative Judaism's continuing fidelity to Jewish law and tradition. The lay-dominated synagogue arm of the Conservative movement, the United Synagogue, reflecting the views of its members, sided with the advocates of change. It promulgated three resolutions described as "the strongest statement for the equal participation of women in public ritual ever to be issued by any body in the Conservative movement." By the late 1970s, seminary chancellor Cohen, swayed by a commission on women's ordination that he chaired, had shifted his views and likewise came to advocate change. Concerned that the seminary's status would suffer if it became an obstacle to women's advancement in Judaism, and convinced that the whole future of his movement depended on its response to demands in this area, he became, in his own words, "passionately in favor of ordination of women."[133]

In May 1983, faced with the threat that the Rabbinical Assembly would preempt the seminary and admit women to the ranks of the Conservative rabbinate on its own, and following the death of Professor Lieberman, Cohen called the question. Five months later, on October 24, 1983, the seminary faculty voted thirty-four to eight, with one abstention, "that Jewish women be admitted to the Rabbinical School of [the] Jewish Theological Seminary as candidates for ordination as rabbis." Several opponents boycotted the session, objecting to the very notion of a faculty vote on matters of divinely inspired Jewish law. One distinguished faculty member left the institution for Columbia University. A group of Conservative traditionalists broke away, forming a small Union for Traditional Conservative Judaism (it later dropped the word "Conservative" from its name) that in 1990 established its own seminary. But though it was shaken by the struggle and lost members to Orthodox and Reform Judaism, the Conservative movement largely weathered the storm. Following Amy Eilberg, ordained as the first Conservative woman rabbi in May 1985, almost one hundred and fifty other women became Conservative rabbis over the next fifteen years, and gender equality, now dubbed "traditional egalitarianism," became an accepted part of the Conservative movement's ethos.[134]

The emergence of women rabbis in Conservative, Reconstructionist, and Reform Judaism both symbolized and advanced feminism's impact on late twentieth-century American Jewish life. In their synagogues, women now led worship services and read from the Torah on a par with men, and having had their consciousness raised by the women's movement, they became newly sensitized to language issues, such as prayers that addressed God in male ("Our Father, Our King") rather than neutral (or feminine) terms, petitions that invoked the biblical patriarchs but ignored the corresponding matriarchs, and supplications that left women out altogether. Many synagogues, as a result, introduced "gender-sensitive" prayer books for worship and some called for gender-sensitive Bible translations as well. Life-cycle ceremonies celebrating coming of age, marriage, and mourning also became egalitarian during these years, and where female equivalent ceremonies did not commonly exist, as in the lack of any religious initiation rite for girls parallel to circumcision, rituals were either formulated from scratch or laboriously recovered from the recesses of Jewish tradition. Even the most intimate turning points of a woman's life, such as menarche, childbirth, weaning, and the onset of menopause, now became subjects for prayers and rituals; and so, likewise, did such traumas as rape, miscarriage, abortion, and infertility.[135]

To be sure, women themselves disagreed as to whether equality alone sufficed for them, or whether women also needed periodically to worship apart from men, "in a different voice" beyond the male range. Feminist seders to celebrate Passover and monthly gatherings of women to mark the new moon *(rosh hodesh)* became popular in some communities, and women's mikveh (ritual bath) rituals of various sorts also gained new popularity. These and other ceremonies and traditions, some recovered, some invented, all evidenced the myriad ways in which the women's movement changed American Judaism in the late twentieth century, stirring controversy but also bringing new excitement and involvement on the part of women to diverse aspects of Jewish religious life.[136]

Orthodoxy stood firm against many of these innovations, particularly the ordination of women as rabbis. That issue, like separate seating before it, became a symbol of fidelity to tradition in the face of cultural pressure to change. But the women's movement by no means skipped over Orthodoxy; it only affected it in different ways. "Women's issues"—whether, for example, women might organize separate prayer groups on a regular basis, read and be called up to the Torah in the company of other women, don prayer shawls, dance with the Torah on the holiday of Simhat Torah, celebrate ritually the bat mitzvah of their daughters, or recite the traditional mourner's kaddish prayer for their deceased relatives—divided Orthodox synagogues one from another in many of the major communities where Orthodox Jews lived, and divided many Orthodox synagogues internally as well. As part of a 1998 symposium, *Jewish Action,* the magazine published by the Union of Orthodox Jewish Congregations in America, described "the feminist issue" as "perhaps the most explosive issue facing Orthodoxy." "How," it wondered, "can we preserve the special quality of the traditional Jewish woman in the face of the incessant demands of the American feminist agenda? How can we distinguish . . . legitimate requests for improvement and change?" Fearing that debates over women's issues might "estrange feminists and their supporters from the rest of Orthodoxy," it appealed for ways "to heal the developing breach between the opposing factions."[137]

Some looked to education to heal this breach. Indeed, every participant in one survey, without exception, cited "high-level Jewish education for women" as a major area of change in contemporary Orthodox life, brought about by "feminism and related social trends." Where once Orthodox women had largely been excluded from the study of the Talmud and had received far less Jewish education, on average, than their brothers, data from 1990 showed that Orthodox boys and girls now attended Jewish schools for about the same number of hours and years. Even in some fervently Orthodox circles Talmud study for women began to win approval, and in more Modern Orthodox circles it became almost ubiquitous, with hundreds of women going on, past high school, to study at newly created advanced Talmudic academies for women in Israel and the United States, as well as at university-level Jewish studies programs. As a result, Orthodox women no longer had to rely upon men to expound Jewish law for them; a growing number could study the primary sources of their faith for themselves. Some women, indeed, achieved great renown for their religious scholarship, becoming role models for their peers and silently challenging men, who for so long had held a monopoly in this area. Though they never carried the title of "rabbi" and in many cases eschewed the controversial "f-word" (feminism) altogether, these Orthodox women produced no less a revolution in the late twentieth century than women did in so many other realms, religious and secular alike. By challenging Judaism, they ended up strengthening Judaism. The discontinuities that they introduced into Jewish life worked to promote religious continuity.[138]

This same paradox, a discontinuity that worked to promote Jewish continuity, may also be seen in the late twentieth-century renewal of spirituality across the spectrum of American Jewish religious life. Like Americans generally, many Jews during these years shifted the emphasis of their faith from moralism to aesthetics and devotion. They sought to complement social justice and rationally oriented teachings that appealed to the mind with spiritual and emotive religious experiences that appealed to the heart and the soul, incorporating music, dance, mystical teachings, and healing.

Judaism, of course, boasted a long and varied spiritual tradition, summed up by Professor Arthur Green in two phrases: "a striving for the presence of God," and "the fashioning of a life of holiness appropriate to such striving." Modernizing Jews, in America as in Europe, had jettisoned central elements of this spiritual tradition as incompatible with scientific teachings and contemporary religious norms. They emphasized rational elements of their faith, eschewing spiritual practices that they found embarrassing. Meditation, theosophy, ecstasy—indeed, the whole corpus of Jewish mystical teachings, known as Kabbalah—scarcely featured in the literature of American Judaism until the second half of the twentieth century, when the term "spirituality" emerged in ecumenical circles "as a means of representing the common ground of religious experience and feeling." For religiously inclined Jews, as for their Christian counterparts, spirituality provided an alternative to the secularity that they found in so many interreligious political initiatives devoted simply to justice and peace.[139]

The writings of such scholars as Martin Buber, Abraham Joshua Heschel, and Gershom Scholem reacquainted American Jews with their spiritual past. The renewal of traditional spiritual practices, however, owed a much greater debt to charismatic figures, several of them Holocaust refugees with ties to the Lubavitch movement, who ministered to Jewish religious seekers and became, in the process, Jewish spiritual revivalists whose influence spread from the counterculture to the mainstream. Taking advantage of a newfound interest in spiritual teachings, brought about by the emergence in America of Eastern religions like Buddhism, these "Jewish gurus" focused on music, meditation, and the power of prayer. They attracted legions of followers and paved the way for a full-scale renewal of Jewish spirituality across the spectrum of Jewish religious life.

Rabbi Shlomo Carlebach (1925–1994)[140] was a prime mover behind these new trends. Known as the Dancing Rabbi, the Singing Rabbi, and even the Hippie Rabbi, he descended from a prominent German-Jewish rabbinical family that included a martyred uncle, Joseph Carlebach, chief rabbi of

Hamburg, who perished in the Holocaust. Shlomo, his parents, and his siblings escaped Berlin in 1938 and settled in New York, where Shlomo studied at Shraga Feivel Mendlowitz's Yeshiva Torah Vodaath and was accepted in 1943 as one of the early students of Aharon Kotler at his advanced Talmudic academy at Lakewood. There he won respect for his learning and was personally ordained by Kotler, who reputedly viewed him as a potential successor. Instead, however, Carlebach joined his twin brother in the court of Lubavitch, abandoning his German and Lithuanian training and allying himself with the more emotionally fervent and messianic-leaning Hasidim. "Lakewood," he reputedly declared, "grooms scholars, but Lubavitch grooms outreach workers . . . at Lubavitch, I'll learn how to expand the souls of thousands." In 1949, at the behest of his newfound rebbe, Rabbi Joseph I. Schneersohn, he, along with another Holocaust refugee named Zalman Schachter, became Lubavitch's traveling emissaries to college campuses. The goal, as in all Lubavitch outreach activities, was to bring Jews nearer to Judaism and to promote both Jewish education and the observance of the commandments. As a means to this goal, Carlebach, like so many others touched by Lubavitch, became confident of his own personal power to save Jews and bring on the messiah; he became a man with a mission.[141]

"Worship God through joy!" Carlebach proclaimed to audiences in the 1950s, echoing early Hasidic teachings. Guitar in hand and a fund of Hasidic stories on his lips, he developed a pioneering Orthodox ministry through song. On one occasion, in 1958, he kept hundreds of young people "awake all night" at a Young Israel convention, "singing along with him in virtually a trance-like ecstasy."[142] He also frequented Greenwich Village coffeehouses, where he not only composed and performed music but also reached out, as he would for the rest of his life, to help awaken "lost souls."

Carlebach released his first record album in 1959. A synthesis of traditional Hasidic and popular American folk music, it proved to be an instant hit and created a new genre: neo-Hasidic Orthodox folk music. Though he could not read music and had no formal technical training, he became, over the next thirty-five years, the most influential and prolific composer of Jewish religious music in the twentieth century. Many of his songs became popular "traditional melodies," several became staples of synagogue music, and one, "The People of Israel Lives" *(Am Yisrael Chai!),* composed in 1964, became the anthem of the Soviet Jewry movement. But Carlebach's spiritual influence extended much further. "Traveling across the world in search of lost souls," Elie Wiesel recalled, "he would sing of the love that everyone should have for his fellow man, for all of creation, and naturally

Shlomo Carlebach (center) leading worshippers in song at a crowded
1994 Purim service in the Carlebach synagogue of New York.
Used with the permission of the estate of Rabbi Shlomo Carlebach.

for the Creator Himself. He attracted young people most of all and they
adored him. He made them laugh, dance, dream. He would help them overcome the bleak intoxications of daily life by modeling for them the spellbinding and mysterious worlds that every human being carries within himself.
He would tell the hasidic tales, giving wings to their imagination. He would
show them how to discover the beauty of prayer."[143]

Invited to perform at the prestigious Berkeley Folk Festival in California
in 1966, along with such stars as Pete Seeger, Peter, Paul, and Mary, and
Joan Baez, Carlebach encountered for the first time "thousands of Jewish
hippies wandering the streets of San Francisco in search of nirvana." He
became a spiritual father to these faith-seeking young people (many of
whom were also being targeted by Moshe Rosen's Jews for Jesus campaign)
and within a year opened the House of Love and Prayer in San Francisco's
Haight-Ashbury district to serve them. Reaching out to the neighborhood's
"holy little brothers and sisters"—Jewish runaways, drug addicts, and the
spiritually adrift in particular—he provided the "holy *hippalach*" (the

Yiddish term of endearment that he invented for them) with a much-needed
haven, a combination synagogue, yeshiva, crash pad, and sanctuary, a place
where they could experiment with meditation, yoga, vegetarianism, Eastern
religions, even drugs and sex, while finding their way back to Judaism under
his loving tutelage. A published account captured the scene:

> His eyes rolling and crying "Gewalt" [Yiddish equivalent of "For heaven's
> sake!"] . . . he leads his disciples in celebrations of the Divine composed of
> chanting, storytelling and dancing that create a mood of overwhelming unity
> between Jew and Jew, between Jew and God. The yearning for ecstasy, for
> "experience" . . . he seeks to harness in God's service, acting, in fact, as a
> missionary with music as his medium. Full of an undifferentiating type of
> love for all Jews, he himself has described the type of harmony that he seeks
> to implement in his music: "To you, young people . . . who are so near to
> me. Your striving is my striving. Your struggle is my struggle. Together let
> us find our way to the *Ribono Shel Olam,* our Father in Heaven, to study
> His Torah, to keep His commandments and, above all, to be His friends."[144]

Carlebach closed the House of Love and Prayer in 1977 and brought his
hippie disciples to an Israeli settlement near Tel Aviv named Moshav Me'or
Modi'in. There many of them remain, perpetuating his teachings.

Carlebach defined Judaism as a religion of happiness and love. To the
chagrin of his Orthodox associates, he warmly embraced men and women
alike—hugging, kissing, but also, according to one posthumously published
exposé, harassing and committing sexual indiscretions with some women.[145]
Eschewing the traditional separation of the sexes, he accepted mixed dancing, mixed learning, even mixed praying. Indeed, he became a consistent
supporter of feminist causes—so much so that he privately ordained several
women and was the only male rabbi to join the crusading Women of the
Wall in 1989 when, in defiance of the Orthodox establishment, they read
from their own Torah scroll before the Western Wall, the surviving remnant
of Jerusalem's holy Temple. Carlebach also reached out beyond the Jewish
community, associating himself with a wide range of liberal causes, from
the plight of blacks in South Africa to the rebellion of the Sandinistas in
Nicaragua.

Taken together, Carlebach's work reflected, embodied, and advanced
many of the central tenets of Jewish spirituality: a stress on the inner life
and experiential religion; love for all human beings, particularly the oppressed
and the downtrodden; gender egalitarianism; and the embrace of Hasidic
and mystical forms of wisdom and worship, with a heavy emphasis on

singing and dancing. Carlebach also maintained ties, as so many spiritual figures in Judaism and Christianity did, with the leaders of Eastern religions, participating in the 1984 East meet West conference in Bombay, along with Swami Muktananda; finding his way into ashrams, New Age centers, and yoga retreats; and associating with Buddhists—not a few of them lapsed Jews. Yet he never severed his ties to Orthodoxy, and following his death in 1994 groups of fervently Orthodox Jews re-embraced him, turning him into a latter-day Hasidic saint. In Los Angeles, in 1995, a group that met in a Modern Orthodox synagogue and called itself the Happy Minyan like-wise perpetuated his memory, with lengthy prayers sung to his melodies and punctuated by fervent dancing. "Happy-clappy" services conducted at least partially according to the "Carlebach tradition" soon spread through-out North America and Israel, moving from the margin to the mainstream and across the spectrum of Jewish religious life.[146]

Carlebach served as a model for younger Jewish musicians, Orthodox, Conservative, and Reform, and also influenced two other independent Jewish spiritual movements of the late twentieth century, the transdenomina-tional Jewish Renewal movement, pioneered by his former associate Rabbi Zalman Schachter, and Hineni, the Orthodox outreach program run by Rebbitzen Esther Jungreis. Jewish Renewal, a catchphrase for a range of Jewish experiments aimed at "building community, enhancing spirituality, encouraging lay participation, and instituting gender equality," emerged from the havurah movement of the 1960s and focuses on the spiritual and experiential elements within Judaism: prayer, meditation, feminism, sexuality, and ecology; it features "dim lights, bare feet, lots of music and silence." Love rather than law dominates the movement, and its God, often addressed by the monosyllable "Yah," represents not the powerful masculine King and Master of so much traditional Jewish liturgy but rather a more per-sonal and feminine God, experienced physically, emotionally, and intellectu-ally "as the underlying oneness of all there is." Many in the movement speak of the four worlds or realms of God, as found in Jewish mysticism, roughly translated as "doing" (action), "formation" (feeling), "creation" (knowledge), and "nearness" (spirit). These four worlds, believers explain, "represent the great cosmic moments of creation and creativity, the slide show of God's inwardness . . . that bring an action from on high into this world."[147]

Rabbi Zalman Schachter-Shalomi (b. 1924), known to his followers as Reb Zalman, serves as the "granddaddy of the Jewish Spiritual Renewal movement," its founder and central thinker. Born in Poland and raised in Vienna in a family that was Hasidic in orientation but open to Western ways and ideas, he fled to France during the Holocaust, made his way to the United States, and studied along with Shlomo Carlebach in the court of Lubavitch. The two men toured the college circuit together, reaching out to lost Jewish souls, and Schachter (he added "Shalomi" to his name later, to counterbalance the name Schachter, which means slaughterer) then went on to an eclectic career serving as a rabbi, furrier, kosher butcher, Hillel director, and professor of Jewish studies. Most of all, he was a teacher and religious seeker, pursuing courses in chaplaincy and pastoral psychology, spending time with Trappist monks in Kentucky and at the Reform movement's Hebrew Union College in Cincinnati, experimenting with psychedelic drugs and moving on to explore Native American and Eastern religions. In his seventies, he was appointed to the Wisdom Chair at the Naropa Institute, a Buddhist teaching center.[148]

Reb Zalman described himself as a "davenner," from a Yiddish word meaning to worship or pray. *Davvenen,* he explained, means "living the liturgical life in the presence of God," and much of his life he spent exploring what he called "davvenology," the "science" of davvenen. Through the organization he founded in 1963, *B'nai Or* ("sons of light"), later renamed under the influence of feminism *P'nai Or* ("faces of light"), and also through his writings, particularly his influential devotional guide entitled "A First Step," partially reprinted in *The Jewish Catalog,* he worked to "renew" Jewish prayer, pioneering innovations that ranged from the handmade, multicolored prayer shawl to prayer "experiments" designed to "transform consciousness." Seekers of all kinds, "among them artists, dancers, singers, poets, and rock musicians," flocked to him, and, as one of his thousands of devotees explained, he changed them unalterably, teaching them to pray in new ways: "He was the one who taught us how to rehydrate the freeze-dried prayers of the prayer book, tie the words on the page to the experiences of our life of spirit, soul, heart, mind, body. He gave us access to our *siddur,* the book of prayer, brought it to life for us, showed us its intricacies and intimacies, the rhythms of its rungs ascending and descending. He reminded us that merely to recite is not to pray, that the words are a reminder, that the body, too, is holy, that the bombast of poor translation does not elevate the soul, that intention of the heart is the true ground of prayer."[149]

By 1996, Jewish Renewal boasted twenty-six "communities" spread over fifteen states, "with seven more in Canada, England, Israel, Switzerland, and Brazil." Reb Zalman's students and ordinees led most of these communities, which were affiliated in 1993 under an umbrella organization named ALEPH: Alliance for Jewish Renewal, a "non-denominational organization

Zalman Schachter-Shalomi (right) greeting the
Dalai Lama in Denver (June 1, 1997). Reb Zalman's
lifelong interest in worship and spirituality brought
him into contact with Tibetan Buddhism
in the early 1960s. In October 1990 he had been part
of a group of Jews who conducted a religious
dialogue with the Dalai Lama in Dharamsala, India.
"When I think of the job you have to do . . . I want
you to know that I feel with you from heart to
heart," he told the exiled Tibetan leader. The two
men discussed Jewish mysticism, rituals,
commandments, even their understanding
of God and the angels. They subsequently
maintained close ties. See Roger Kamenetz,
The Jew in the Lotus (New York: HarperCollins,
1995). Credit: Helen H. Davis/The Denver Post.

dedicated to advancing vital, relevant Judaism that is deeply spiritual, en-
vironmentally conscious, and politically engaged." Its spiritual retreat center,
Elat Chayyim, "a center for healing and renewal" in the Catskills, featured
"*davvening,* daily meditation, and a variety of special workshops," "the

spirit of liberation and renewal," and the promise of "transformation and rebirth." ALEPH's larger mission involved organizing and nurturing communities, training lay and rabbinic leaders, creating new liturgy and adult learning resources, sponsoring conferences, retreats, and seminars, and working for social and environmental justice.[150]

While Reb Zalman's followers sought to save lost Jewish souls by inspiring them with the vision and practice of Jewish Renewal, another revitalization movement inspired by Shlomo Carlebach sought to win back lost souls via more traditional means, through preaching, teaching, and the embrace of a warm community. The leader of the new movement, like so many others in late twentieth-century American Judaism, passed through the fires of the Holocaust, losing friends and relatives and starting life anew as a youngster in America. What distinguished the new movement was that its leader was an Orthodox woman. Her name was Esther Jungreis (b. 1936), scion "of a long chain of devoted servants of God dating back to King David," and she proudly denominated herself Rebbetzin Jungreis, the wife of the rabbi, though to some of her followers she functioned as a full-fledged rabbi in almost everything but name. Born in Szegad, Hungary, and a survivor of the Bergen-Belsen concentration camp, Jungreis grew up on miracle tales: one of her ancestors, she boasted, was "the *Tzaddik,* the righteous one of Csenger, who made miracles come about for his people." Her family had survived, her father taught her, to pursue a sacred task: "to teach our people to kindle the Sabbath lights." Pursuing outreach work from a young age, she initiated her own column in the Orthodox *Jewish Press* at the age of twenty-seven and honed her talents as a dynamic teacher and speaker. What Judaism needed, she concluded, was a Jewish version of the highly popular evangelical preacher and master of the media, Billy Graham. Jews, she intuited, could learn from the majority religion how to strengthen their own. With this in mind, she issued a call at the Young Israel Collegiate Youth Convention in 1972 for "a rally for *neshomas* (souls) at Madison Square Garden, a mass spiritual gathering where you teach people what it means to be a Jew."[151]

Shlomo Carlebach seized upon the idea. Speaking the next day at the bar mitzvah reception for Jungreis's son, he declared that "the *Heilege* (Holy) Reb[b]etzin is going to go to Madison Square Garden and change the Jewish world." Boldly, he encouraged the guests to go directly to the Rebbetzin's house after the bar mitzvah "and start planning the Madison Square Garden event immediately." The movement, named Hineni, was reputedly born that night. The name is revealing: pregnant with prophetic and even messianic symbolism, as if Mrs. Jungreis, like the biblical prophet Elijah, believed she had heard the voice of the Lord call out in a vision and had replied, "*Hineni,* here am I; send me."[152] Just over a year later, on November 18, 1973, thousands thronged Madison Square Garden's Felt Forum for Jungreis's first great Hineni "awakening." Elegantly dressed and modestly bewigged, her voice rising and falling, she reminded the assembled crowd that they were first and foremost Jews, "given the unique mission of proclaiming the One-ness of God." She captured them with stories and parables, reminded them of simple truths, and electrified them with the traditional prayer of *Shema Yisrael*—"Hear, O Israel, the Lord our God, the Lord is One!" Having proved her abilities in the very forum where Billy Graham had earlier launched his "international crusade," her career took off. Billed as "the Jewish Billy Graham" (one follower dubbed her "the most trustworthy spiritual guide in this generation"), she commenced her mission: succoring the spiritually needy; "rescuing" Jews from conversionists, cults, and drugs; opening Hineni centers in New York and Jerusalem; and through the medium of cable television, becoming America's first Jewish female televangelist.[153]

Hineni and every one of the Jewish spiritual movements of the late twentieth century employed the metaphors of illness. Minds, bodies, spirits, synagogues—all stood in dire need of healing, these spiritual diagnosticians proclaimed. To them, Judaism appeared desperately unwell, racked by assimilation, emptiness, and an epidemic of tormented souls. The loss of 6 million Jews in the Holocaust made it especially imperative, they thought, to nurture every spark and save every Jew who survived. While their precise prescriptions for how to do this varied, they generally recommended some mix of emotive prayer, ritual observance, textual learning, singing, dancing, the embrace of community, forays into Jewish mysticism, and carefully planned experiences in Israel. Reaching out to women as well as to men, they portrayed themselves as fully egalitarian. In the case of Carlebach and Reb Zalman, that, over time, is what they became.

The central features of this spiritual program soon made their way from the margins to the mainstream, taken up by Reform, Reconstructionist, Conservative, and Orthodox synagogues alike. Indeed, synagogues of all kinds added "spiritual dimensions" to their agenda. Moving beyond their prior emphasis on rationalism and the pursuit of social justice, they encouraged congregants to experiment with rituals, to explore Jewish texts, to close their eyes and meditate, to dance, to sing. A Reform Jewish folksinger named Debbie Friedman ("the Joan Baez of Jewish song") gave voice to

Rebbetzin Esther Jungreis in a
contemporary publicity photo.
On her website, www.hineni.org, the
rebbetzin is portrayed as a "dynamic
spiritual leader." She teaches "the world's
biggest Torah class," offers solutions to
personal problems, and provides "timeless
wisdom" on Jewish and family issues.
Courtesy of Rebbetzin Esther Jungreis,
founder and president of Hineni, the Jewish
outreach organization founded in 1973.

this movement. Her Jewish "soul music"—sung in hundreds of synagogues,
performed to packed concert halls, and preserved on albums like *Renewal
of Spirit* (1995)—offered seekers, in Friedman's words, "a sense of spiritual
connectedness." On one memorable occasion she moved even staid conven-
tiongoers at the General Assembly of the Council of Jewish Federations
to tears. Standing together in their business suits and high heels, they swayed
arm-in-arm to her melodies and lyrics.[154]

Revealingly, Friedman's best-known song, widely introduced into non-
Orthodox liturgies, was *Mi Sheberach* ("May the One who blessed"), a song

of healing. This and other prayers for healing, innovative and traditional alike, acquired new centrality among all manner of Jews in the late twentieth century, women in particular. Some synagogues went so far as to introduce separate healing services into their worship calendars, complete with the laying on of hands. At least twenty Jewish communities around the United States developed Jewish healing centers, most of them affiliated with a new National Center for Jewish Healing. The goal, clearly influenced by New Age religious movements, was to help Jews achieve a "sense of spiritual well-being, wholeness, perspective, fulfillment or comfort, especially around issues of illness, suffering and loss."[155]

A larger goal, expressed by numerous late twentieth-century Jews in their writings and teaching, was "renewal." Debbie Friedman, in *Mi Sheberach,* called for "renewal of body" and "renewal of spirit." An organization promoting the transformation of congregational life dedicated itself to "synagogue renewal." Reb Zalman, as we have seen, characterized his whole movement as one of Jewish Renewal. The Holocaust, Israel, feminism, and spirituality all played into these latter-day calls for American Jewish "renewal," but the actual meaning of the term proved elusive—as elusive as "peace of mind" had been half a century earlier. The only certainty as calls for renewal escalated and the twentieth century receded was that Jewish religious life remained vibrant enough to change. What those changes portended—whether they would strengthen American Judaism or weaken it —only time would tell.

Conclusion: American Judaism
at a Crossroads

Enter a traditional Jewish worship service just as prayers are commencing, and you may behold a curious sight. The people in charge will be searching for a minyan, a prayer quorum. Counting up those in attendance, they will pretend *not* to count them, calling out "not one, not two, not three, not four." When "not ten" finally arrives, the service may begin.[1]

Rooted in a Talmudic teaching ("Whoever counts the people of Israel transgresses a negative commandment"), this practice also reflects an ancient taboo, exemplified in the Bible, against communal censuses, so often the portents of taxation and conscription. Throughout history, and not only among Jews, head counts engendered tremendous communal anxiety, even popular resistance, particularly when the censor who counted people was also a moral censor looking to combat alleged evils. Yet however ominous, hateful, and dehumanizing head counts may once have seemed, the modern world considers them essential. In America, especially, census numbers came to be celebrated "because they were genuinely useful, because they were thought to discipline the mind, because they marked the progress of the era, and because they were reputedly objective and precise and hence tantamount to truth."[2]

At the dawn of the twenty-first century, no religious group in America is more number-conscious than Jews. Three times in three decades the Jewish community has sponsored expensive nationwide "population studies" to gather data about itself. Hundreds of smaller-scale and locally sponsored surveys have also appeared, taking the community's pulse on everything from demography to religiosity and from political preferences to marital preferences. Whatever Jews think truly counts in American Jewish life they have attempted quite literally to count and to quantify.

Two interrelated and highly contentious statistics count for Jews above all the rest: their absolute numbers in America and their rate of intermarriage.* Measures of survival on the one hand and of assimilation on the other, these numbers have fostered anew the great fear that has accompanied Jews throughout their American sojourn: the fear that the melting pot would subsume them, that they would disappear as a people. Reenacting on a communal level the same ambivalence toward numbers displayed at a Jewish worship service, Jews both obsess over these statistics and berate themselves for doing so. Even those who stress quality over quantity and point to indisputable evidence of religious revitalization and renewal can scarcely ignore the numbers' doleful message: accelerating demographic decline.

Two surveys completed at the beginning of the twenty-first century confirmed that America's core Jewish population—self-identifying Jews by either religion or ethnicity who adhere to no other religion—is shrinking. The 2001 National Jewish Population Survey (so fraught with methodological problems that some consider it worthless) pegged the ten-year decline at about 5 percent, from 5.5 million to 5.2 million. The American Jewish Identity Survey of 2001 placed that decline closer to 3 percent.[3] While hardly unprecedented—the Episcopal Church, United Church of Christ, and Christian Science church all declined far more over the second half of the twentieth century in the United States, and England's Jewish population between 1945 and 1995 fell, according to some accounts, by as much as 36 percent—the decline is nonetheless historic, marking the first time since colonial days that the total number of Jews in America has ever gone down. As a percentage of America's total population, moreover, Jews have been declining for decades. Having peaked in the 1940s, when they formed 3.7 percent of the population, they constituted less than 2 percent of America's overall population at the turn of the twenty-first century, the first time the numbers have fallen that low since 1910. Coming on the heels of reports showing that greater New York has fallen from its perch as the "greatest Jewish city in the world" and now ranks second to greater Tel Aviv, and that Israel's total Jewish population is about to eclipse that of the United States, American Judaism's demographic decline cries out for attention.[4]

---

*Unless otherwise specified, intermarriage refers to marriages between Jews and unconverted non-Jews. Marriages between born Jews and converts to Judaism, according to Jewish law, are *not* intermarriages.

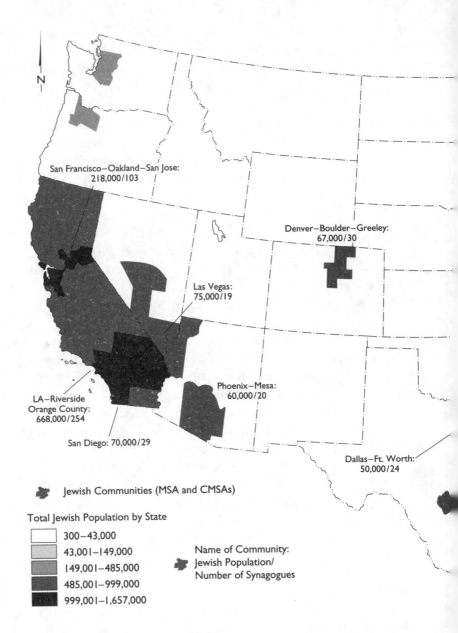

N

San Francisco–Oakland–San Jose:
218,000/103

Denver–Boulder–Greeley:
67,000/30

Las Vegas:
75,000/19

LA–Riverside
Orange County:
668,000/254

Phoenix–Mesa:
60,000/20

San Diego: 70,000/29

Dallas–Ft. Worth:
50,000/24

🔹 Jewish Communities (MSA and CMSAs)

Total Jewish Population by State

☐ 300–43,000
☐ 43,001–149,000
☐ 149,001–485,000
☐ 485,001–999,000
☐ 999,001–1,657,000

Name of Community:
🔹 Jewish Population/
Number of Synagogues

The Jewish population of the United States (2000). Jews are among the most densely concentrated of America's religions, with a large majority residing in coastal states. Almost 85 percent of America's Jews and 71 percent of its synagogues are located in the twenty metropolitan areas highlighted on the map. *Sources: American Jewish Year Book* (2002), 1996 ESRI MSA/MCA Data

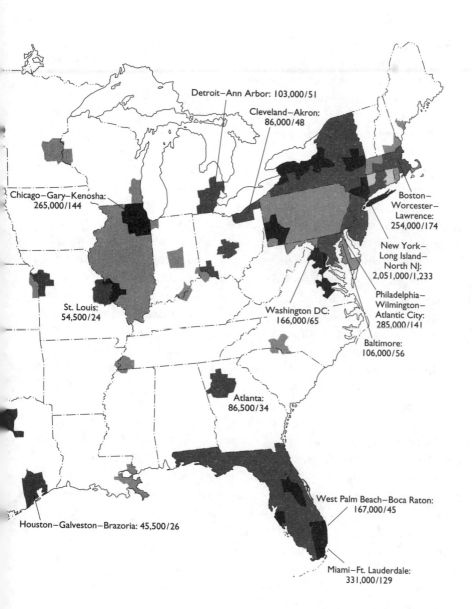

Detroit–Ann Arbor: 103,000/51

Cleveland–Akron:
86,000/48

Chicago–Gary–Kenosha:
265,000/144

Boston–
Worcester–
Lawrence:
254,000/174

New York–
Long Island–
North NJ:
2,051,000/1,233

St. Louis:
54,500/24

Washington DC:
166,000/65

Philadelphia–
Wilmington–
Atlantic City:
285,000/141

Baltimore:
106,000/56

Atlanta:
86,500/34

West Palm Beach–Boca Raton:
167,000/45

Houston–Galveston–Brazoria: 45,500/26

Miami–Ft. Lauderdale:
331,000/129

Experts point to four major reasons to explain this drop in numbers. First, the American Jewish community suffers from low fertility and is not reproducing itself. Each year more Jews die than are born. With the Jewish birthrate pegged at about 1.8 children per couple, below the 2.1 needed for replacement, the Jewish median age is rapidly rising and the number of Jewish children under the age of seventeen has fallen to historically low levels.[5]

In addition, Jewish immigration, which for years compensated for the low birthrate, has declined drastically. Whereas between 1970 and 1990 more than 200,000 Jews entered the United States from such countries as the Soviet Union, Iran, South Africa, and Israel, Jewish immigration dropped off in the late 1990s owing both to changes in American immigration law and to the collapse of Communism. No longer can the American Jewish community look across the ocean for demographic support.[6]

Third, conversions to Judaism have also plummeted. One survey finds that the total number of converts within the American Jewish community actually *fell* slightly between 1990 and 2001, from 174,000 to 170,000. Most observers blame this drop on the acceptance by Reform and Reconstructionist Judaism of the principle of patrilineal descent. Once these movements agreed to recognize children who identified as Jews to be Jews even if their mothers remain non-Jewish, a central incentive for conversion disappeared. Today, the number of annual conversions to Judaism has slowed to a trickle.[7]

Finally, and most important, intermarriage has cut into America's Jewish population totals. The National Jewish Population Survey of 1990 uncovered 1,325,000 individuals whose grandparents had been Jews but who now practice other religions, mostly as a result of marrying non-Jews. The more recent American Jewish Identity Survey ups that number to 2,345,000. These and other surveys demonstrate that the children of mixed Jewish-Christian marriages identify overwhelmingly either with Christianity or with no religion; only about 25 percent of them, in a 1999 national survey of incoming college freshmen, identified themselves as Jews. Had those descendants remained Jewish, the demography of the American Jewish community would look entirely different.[8]

INTERMARRIAGE

Because it affects Jewish numbers (what Jews have come to call "continuity") so greatly, and because it long represented a strong communal taboo, intermarriage became the focus of Jewish survey research during the last decades of the twentieth century. In some Jewish circles, the intermarriage rate is as widely followed and analyzed as the inflation rate, serving as a perennial subject for discussion and debate. To be sure, intermarriage has been a factor in American Jewish life since colonial days. But during the first half of the twentieth century, at least, intermarriage figures remained reassuringly low (below 7 percent). Most Jews, as we have seen, lived largely within a subculture of their own, where they met and married other Jews. The bulk of non-Jewish Americans, through the 1950s, likewise married people of their own background and faith. Notwithstanding the melting pot rhetoric, endogamy in America was the rule, with Jews being even more endogamous than their Protestant and Catholic neighbors.[9]

That rule changed during the last third of the twentieth century. Following the social upheavals of the 1960s, the decline of segregated neighborhoods, and the lessening of parental involvement in children's marital choices, mixed marriages of every kind proliferated in the United States, crossing ethnic, religious, and racial lines. Swedish, Norwegian, German, Italian, and Irish Americans—all, according to 1980 census data, experienced intermarriage rates in excess of 60 percent. Among Catholics, intermarriage rates among young people exceeded 50 percent. Comparable Protestant data would be meaningless given the movement's size, but in one cohort studied, 69 percent of young Methodists married non-Methodists, 70 percent of young Lutherans married non-Lutherans, and 75 percent of young Presbyterians married non-Presbyterians. In the much smaller Greek Orthodox Church, by the early 1990s, fully two-thirds of all marriages involved a partner who was not Greek Orthodox, leading the laity to proclaim that "the battle against intermarriage is over. The focus now must be on how to retain the non-Greek spouse and the children of the intermarried." Asian Americans and African Americans likewise witnessed dramatic upswings in intermarriage. "Nearly half of recent marriages for U.S. born Asian-Americans have been to non-Asian White Americans," according to an account published in 2002, while marriages between blacks and whites multiplied sevenfold between 1960 and 1993. Popular attitudes, meanwhile, kept pace with these changes. Acceptance of intermarriage on the part of Americans rose dramatically as the twentieth century wound down. To oppose marriages between men and women of different ethnicities, faiths, and races seems to many people to be un-American and racist.[10]

These developments soon made themselves felt within the Jewish community. In the 1950s, the norms and expectations of American society reinforced Jews' own traditional sense that out-marriage was wrong and in-marriage was right, but by the 1990s Jews who sought to promote in-group marriage faced a cultural mainstream (which included Jews) that legitimated and even celebrated intermarriage. Moreover, Jewish-Christian social interactions multiplied as prejudice declined, freeing young Jews living far from their parents in college dorms and singles' pads to follow their passions. The results were predictable: "In recent years," the 1990 National Jewish Population Survey reported, "just over half of Born Jews who married, at any age, whether for the first time or not, chose a spouse who was born a Gentile and has remained so." Since 1985, it calculated, "twice as many mixed couples (Born Jew with Gentile spouse) have been created as Jewish couples." Critics charged that the survey exaggerated the rate of inter-marriage. Instead of an intermarriage rate of 52 percent, they argued, the true rate was more like 41 percent. Even so, this represented a fivefold increase in thirty years and meant, as the twenty-first century dawned, that as many as one-third of all American Jews live in mixed Jewish-Gentile households.[11]

The effects of all this on twenty-first-century Judaism can scarcely be overestimated. As a result of intermarriage, the number of households containing at least one person of Jewish origin has multiplied—even, we have seen, as the total number of Jews in America declines. Some scholars now talk euphemistically about an "enlarged Jewish population" consisting not only of "core Jews" but also of those non-Jews with whom they share their lives. More non-Jewish Americans than ever before find themselves with Jewish relatives, and more Jews with Christian relatives, a phenomenon that contributes both to intra-familial tensions and to an improvement in inter-religious understanding. Yet what Judaism means to members of this "enlarged Jewish population" is anything but clear. According to various studies, between 70 and 82 percent of intermarried families in the United States raise their children in dual faith, no faith, or non-Jewish homes. Their "Jewish and something else" children, even if nominally raised as Jews, are ambiguous and ambivalent about their Jewish identification. Many grow up celebrating Christmas and Easter with non-Jewish relatives. Only about 25 percent of them, we have seen, identify themselves as Jews when they enter college, or later when they talk to survey researchers. Optimists hope to increase that number, contending that intermarriage represents an opportunity to win new recruits for Judaism. They encourage rabbis to perform mixed marriages (as growing numbers of liberal rabbis do), and they promote efforts to make the non-Jewish partners and children of Jews feel "wanted and accepted." Pessimists, by contrast, warn that intermarriage fosters "religious syncretism." They oppose any rabbinic involvement in mixed marriages and perceive intermarriage as the single greatest threat to American Judaism's demographic survival.[12]

Reform and Reconstructionist Judaism, the only Jewish movements willing to consider non-Jews for synagogue membership and honors, have experienced the greatest changes as a result of intermarriage. "More and more," one report discloses, "non-Jews—partners/spouses, grandparents, children, in-laws and siblings—are involved in the life of synagogues in some way." They attend and join synagogues, sometimes hold dual memberships in synagogues and churches, and even become active in synagogue life, taking on positions of leadership. In synagogues with large numbers of intermarried Jews among their members, non-Jews may constitute a quarter or more of those attending services. Some Jewish leaders glory in this development, seeing in it a fulfillment of Isaiah's biblical prophecy (56:7): "My House shall be called a house of prayer for all peoples." Others simply accept the new reality as a byproduct of contemporary life. Either way, the presence of non-Jewish members in synagogues has changed the demographics of Judaism's religious movements. For the first time in more than a century, Reform in the 1990s constituted the largest religious movement in American Judaism, while Reconstructionism promoted itself as Judaism's fastest-growing religious movement. Movements that refused to accept non-Jews as synagogue members attracted far fewer intermarried couples and experienced no similar spurts of growth.[13]

Yet within Reform and Reconstructionist Judaism, non-Jewish involvement in the life of the synagogue also poses agonizing boundary dilemmas. Should the synagogue treat Jewish and non-Jewish members as equals, or does being a Jew confer benefits that non-Jews can attain only through conversion? Should non-Jews be counted as part of the minyan? Should they be invited to lead the worship service? Should they be permitted to recite prayers (like the traditional blessings over the candles and the Torah) that are directed to the Jewish people alone? Should they be allowed to participate in synagogue governance and in planning the spiritual life of the congregation? These and related quandaries yield no easy solutions. The desire to be welcoming, liberal, and fair is difficult to reconcile with boundary maintenance and the demands of Jewish peoplehood.

Indeed, Jewish peoplehood—the traditional idea that all Jews, wherever they may live, are related to one another and responsible for one another —has declined as intermarriage rises. A survey in 1998 found that only a bare majority of American Jews still warmed to the concept. Just 52 percent, for example, agreed with the traditional statement "I look at the entire Jewish community as my extended family," and only 47 percent agreed that "I have a special responsibility to take care of Jews in need around the world." Intermarried Jews, the survey discloses, are the most likely of all to *disagree* with these statements, six times more likely than in-married ones. To many intermarried Jews, tribalistic notions of peoplehood (what one scholar calls "historical familism") seem uncomfortably alien, at odds with personal autonomy and America's universalistic and individualistic ethos. Jewish peoplehood, mutual responsibility, and the related ideas that Jews subsume under the rubric of *klal yisrael* ("Catholic Israel") have become, in those circles, endangered Jewish values.[14]

Support for in-group marriage as a value and religious norm seems endangered as well. A 1985 survey of Reform Jewish leaders found that only a minority of them considered it "essential" for a "good Jew" to marry a Jew, while 30 percent of those who had themselves intermarried thought that this made "no difference" at all. Converts to Judaism in the survey proved particularly unsympathetic to the idea that Jews should marry Jews. Only about 20 percent of these leaders (and presumably fewer still of their followers) signified that it would bother them "a great deal" if their own children married non-Jews, while more than half confessed that they would not even be greatly bothered if their children decided to convert to Christianity. A broader study, conducted in greater Boston in 1995, found that only one-third of the community's unmarried Jewish adults and 25 percent of those living in America four generations or more considered it "very important to marry someone Jewish"; the rest did not. A nationwide study of "moderately affiliated Jews" reveals the same "withering of opposition to intermarriage." Although 60 percent of respondents to that study did agree that "Jews should marry Jews," only 28 percent consider marrying a Jew or a convert to Judaism to be essential. Throughout much of the American Jewish community, in short, romantic love rather than religion or ethnicity has become the prime determinant of whom to marry; the same as among Americans generally. Opposition to intermarriage, once normative in American Jewish life, is fast becoming exceptional.[15]

A BIPOLAR MODEL

Even as intermarriage and fertility statistics seem to portend a gloomy future for Judaism in America, other indicators give reason for good cheer. We have already noted the late twentieth-century Jewish awakening that revitalized and transformed so many aspects of American Jewish religious life; it shows little sign of abating. In addition, Jewish culture in all of its manifold forms continues to boom—theater, art, dance, music, film, television, as well as all forms of print media. Jewish education too shows improvement at every level, from day care to all-day schools to university-based Jewish studies programs to adult Jewish education to distance learning. Jewish camps, community centers, retreat centers, cultural centers, and a wide range of other innovative projects, programs, and institutions—some community-based and others in cyberspace—all project the image of a vibrant and creative community, not one languishing in the throes of decline.

Synagogues likewise offer hope for the future. A census in 2001 enumerated 3,727 synagogues across the United States, a number at least as great as in the 1930s, when the last census was taken, and fully reflective of the enormous diversity of American Jewish life (including four types of Orthodox synagogues, as well as synagogues that labeled themselves Sephardic, Traditional, Conservative, Reconstructionist, Reform, Humanistic, Gay/ Lesbian, and Jewish Renewal). Other studies show that about two-thirds of American Jews belong to a synagogue at some point in their lives, more than affiliate with any other kind of Jewish institution. At least in Boston, both synagogue membership and synagogue attendance rose significantly between 1985 and 1995. An influential nationwide program entitled "Synagogue 2000" works to make synagogues even more enticing, promoting what it calls "synagogue transformation." By focusing on formal and informal learning, heightened spirituality, and programs directed at formerly neglected groups like single parents, childless couples, the unmarried, gays, lesbians, and Jews by choice, it seeks to help synagogues "become moral and spiritual centers responsive to the exciting demographic and religious realities of Jewish life." The program's optimism is palpable: synagogues, it believes, are "poised at an historic moment in time to play out the next and finest chapter in the saga of Jewish destiny."[16]

The nomination of Joseph Lieberman as the Democratic vice presidential candidate in 2000—he is the first Jew ever to be nominated for this post by a major political party—reinforced this sense of optimism. His selection demonstrated that a Jew need not abandon most of the practices of his faith in order to succeed. Even a practicing Orthodox Jew like Lieberman could win the respect of his countrymen and aspire to the highest office in the land.

At one and the same time, then, American Judaism seems to be experiencing both revitalization and assimilation; it radiates optimism concerning the future of American Jewish life, as well as bleak pessimism. Indeed, some scholars speak of a "bipolar community," with "certain parts of American Jewry . . . deepening their Jewishness" and "others . . . on an accelerated assimilatory course out of the Jewish community."[17] The most thorough-going assessment, by historian Jack Wertheimer writing in the *American Jewish Year Book,* finds more drift than recommitment but concludes on an appropriate note of uncertainty, recognizing the existence of both trends and seeing the future as far from preordained:

> In the religious sphere, a bipolar model is emerging, with a large population of Jews moving toward religious minimalism and a minority gravitating toward greater participation and deepened concern with religion. The latter include: newly committed Jews and converts to Judaism, whose conscious choice of religious involvement has infused all branches of American Judaism with new energy and passion; rabbinic and lay leaders of the official denominations, who continue to struggle with issues of continuity and change within their respective movements; and groups of Jews who are experimenting with traditional forms in order to reappropriate aspects of the Jewish past. These articulate and vocal Jews have virtually transformed American Judaism during the past two decades. At the same time, an even larger population of American Jews has drifted away from religious participation. Such Jews have not articulated the sources of their discontent but have "voted with their feet," by absenting themselves from synagogues and declining to observe religious rituals that require frequent and ongoing attention. To a great extent, their worrisome patterns of attrition have been obscured by the dynamism of the religiously involved. It remains to be seen, therefore, whether the transformation of American Judaism wrought by the committed minority during the past two decades will sustain its present energy and inspire greater numbers of Jews to commit themselves to a living Judaism.[18]

FOUR CHALLENGES

Amid all of these uncertainties, four issues confronting American Judaism appear particularly daunting. While by no means the only ones crying out for communal attention, all four cut across the full spectrum of American Jewish life and produce significant conflicts, and all four find analogues in the larger world of American religion. Whatever the future holds, these issues need to be addressed.

The issue of boundaries stands at the top of this list. Religious groups, like states and countries, are necessarily demarcated by boundaries that define who is in and who is out. Setting and patrolling these boundaries, even if unpleasant, is an essential task of group maintenance. For Jews, the boundary issues that matter most are those that separate Judaism from other religions, thereby defining "who is a Jew," and those that separate Jewish religious movements from one another—putting someone, for example, beyond the pale of Orthodoxy or distinguishing Conservative Judaism from Reform. Clamorous recent debates over conversion, patrilineal descent, and the place of unconverted non-Jews in the synagogue highlight boundary dilemmas within Judaism. In the absence of clearly demarcated lines, hundreds of thousands of individuals find themselves in the anomalous position of being considered Jewish by some Jews but not by others.

In the case of conversion, Orthodox and Reform Jews disagree over the rituals and obligations demanded of converts, and over who holds the authority to accept them into the Jewish fold. Many a convert, as a result, may be a member in good standing of a Reform temple but barred from marrying a Jew in the state of Israel (where standards are set by the established Orthodox rabbinate). Patrilineal Jews, recognized as Jewish only by the Reconstructionist and Reform movements since their fathers and not their mothers are Jewish, face similar problems.

Jews for Jesus and others who openly insist that they can simultaneously identify both as Jews and as Christians generate far less controversy. Jewish circles, we have seen, broadly agree that being a Jew means, at the very least, being "not Christian." There is also broad agreement that an identifying but totally non-believing and non-observant Jew remains a Jew, a member of the Jewish people if not a God-fearing adherent of its faith. Syncretistic behaviors, such as the practice by Jews of Buddhist rites, the worship of female divinities, Wiccan rituals, even the belief of some Lubavitch Jews that their rebbe is the long-awaited messiah, raise more difficult questions. Some consider these behaviors "over the line," others do not. The basic tension, a familiar one to students of religion, pits proponents of inclusivity against proponents of exclusivity, those who advocate a tolerant, broadly expansive view of Judaism against those who fear the dilution of its purity and spirit.

Similar tensions characterize boundary disputes *between* the different Jewish religious movements. Some define Orthodox, Conservative, Reform, and Reconstructionist Judaism so broadly as to embrace all Jews who self-identify with these movements or at least pay dues. Others insist that membership must be based on theological and ritual commitments that require policing. Still others look beyond the different movements, seeking to build bridges between them. They advocate what they call postdenominational or transdenominational Judaism. The problem of boundary maintenance is particularly acute in Orthodoxy, which represents itself as the guardian of Jewish law and tradition. Can someone who openly flouts Jewish law or contravenes traditional beliefs still be accepted as an Orthodox Jew? What about an Orthodox rabbi who admits that he is openly gay, or an Orthodox woman who challenges traditional Jewish gender roles?

Reform Judaism, while far more latitudinarian, faces boundary challenges as well. In early 1994, for example, the Board of Trustees of the Union of American Hebrew Congregations struggled with the issue of whether to admit a Humanistic Jewish congregation in Cincinnati named Beth Adam (House of Man) into the Reform congregational body. Beth Adam, following Humanistic teachings, asserts the "right and responsibility" of human beings to control their own destiny "based upon ethics and morals arising out of the human condition." It excludes God from its liturgy and recites neither the Shema nor the traditional kaddish prayer for mourners. Does this open rejection of God contravene Reform Jewish teachings? The answer, by an overwhelming vote of the lay trustees of the Union of American Hebrew Congregations, was yes. "Some common understanding is necessary to give us the kind of ideological cohesion which a religious movement . . . requires to retain its distinctiveness and to secure its continuity," UAHC President Rabbi Alexander Schindler asserted after the vote.[19] Yet many other boundary questions, including what distinguishes right-wing Reform Judaism from left-wing Conservatism Judaism, remain unanswered. Nor are the boundaries of Conservative Judaism any easier to define. Indeed, every movement in Judaism faces agonizing challenges to its boundaries. Competitive pressures and the nation's pluralistic ethos encourage all-embracing strategies that promote maximal inclusion, but as the case of Beth Adam demonstrates, each movement is also defined by its decisions —sometimes painful ones—on whom to exclude.

A second challenge of central importance to contemporary Judaism concerns the broad area of authority and leadership. Historically, the absence of any central religious authority helps to explain the oft-noted contentiousness of American Jewish life. No ultimate authority in American Judaism—no rabbi, no court, no lay body—makes religious decisions that are ever broadly accepted as final. Americans generally, to be sure, have long been wary of religious authority figures, as evidenced by the long history of anticlericalism in American life, and the nation's powerful tradition of lay religious governance, particularly within American Protestantism. With the decline of the Protestant establishment and the rebellion of young people against authority figures of every sort in the 1960s, religious authorities came under particular attack. American Judaism fit well within this tradition of ambivalence to religious authority—witness Jews' almost visceral resistance to the idea of a chief rabbi and the perennial tensions that flared between congregational rabbis and their lay board members. As the twentieth century waned, problems of authority only multiplied.

In Orthodoxy, a severe leadership crisis developed with the passing of its greatest twentieth-century leaders, such rabbis as Joseph B. Soloveitchik, Moshe Feinstein, and Menachem Schneerson. The last of the generation trained in prewar Europe, not one of these men could be replaced by someone commanding the same level of respectful awe. Rabbi Aharon Lichtenstein, Rabbi Soloveitchik's son-in-law who heads Yeshivat Har Etzion in Israel, has candidly acknowledged the problem, bemoaning "the current dearth of first-rank *gedolim* [rabbinic giants]" in America and lamenting that there is "no giant majestically bestriding the contemporary scene and securely moving American Orthodoxy into the future." Perhaps for this reason, young American Orthodox Jews look increasingly to Israeli rabbis and Talmudic sages for direction, a risky strategy since historically religious movements in America that cannot count on an indigenous leadership to direct them have not fared well. The problems faced by Yeshiva University's trustees in finding a successor to its longtime president, Rabbi Norman Lamm—they finally selected the respected Orthodox lawyer and organizational leader Richard Joel, who is not a rabbi—and the emergence of Orthodox rabbinical seminaries that seek to compete with Yeshiva on both the right (Touro College) and the left (Yeshiva Chovevei Torah) underscore the leadership vacuum in Orthodoxy's ranks. Without a commanding presence who exercises wide-ranging religious authority, American Orthodoxy seems to be fragmenting.[20]

Conservative Judaism likewise faces serious problems of religious authority. Organized from its inception as a stratified religious movement influenced by Anglicanism, it had once been governed from the top down, with authority residing in the leadership of the Jewish Theological Seminary and its Talmud faculty. As part of the battle over women's ordination, however, power became more diffused within the movement, and the authority of the seminary and its leadership declined—so much so that in 1996 the seminary's western branch, known as the University of Judaism, declared its independence and opened a competing Conservative rabbinical training seminary, the Ziegler School of Rabbinic Studies. On a host of important religious issues, from fidelity to Jewish law to the language of the liturgy to the question of whether to ordain gay rabbis, the Conservative movement too seems to be fragmenting. Well-respected rabbis continue to exercise substantial influence and authority within their own congregations, but a study of the movement as a whole finds it suffering "from a paucity of compelling leaders able to confront its problems and motivate others to respond to them." Almost two-thirds of Conservative synagogue members, in one survey, feel that religious authority has devolved into their own hands. "Conservative Judaism," they insist, "lets you choose those parts of Judaism you find meaningful."[21]

Generally within American Judaism there is a sense that traditional authority structures are breaking down. For example, the Conference of Presidents of Major American Jewish Organizations, organized in 1955 to speak and act "on the basis of consensus of its fifty-four member agencies on issues of national and international Jewish concern," finds consensus increasingly elusive and has failed to provide the kind of leadership, particularly on matters related to Israel, that once it did. The major Jewish religious seminaries likewise find their authority challenged. While particularly true among the Conservative and the Orthodox, growing numbers of liberal rabbis likewise boast private ordination, or ordination from the dissident Academy for Jewish Religion, a pluralistic New York seminary that is particularly accommodating to nontraditional students and distance learners. Much to the chagrin of the major seminaries and rabbinic associations, rabbis ordained in this way manage nevertheless to win recognition. In the Boston area, for example, two significant synagogues employ rabbis with these nontraditional forms of ordination, and a new pluralistic seminary independent of all of the religious movements has recently opened its doors.[22]

"It bothers me when people try to tell me that there's a right way to be Jewish," declare 83 percent of participants in one nationwide survey of American Jews. Continuing a trend toward personal autonomy begun centuries earlier, and paralleling the behavior of their non-Jewish neighbors, fewer and fewer American Jews view their religious leaders, movements, and communal institutions "as custodians of authority or as gatekeepers to personal authenticity." Instead, American Jews turn ever more inward, selecting their own religious authorities, spurning religious authorities with whom they disagree, and making a wide range of critical religious decisions on their own. This poses formidable challenges not only to the established Jewish religious movements but also to anyone concerned with the preservation of Jewish communal life. The question is whether American Jews can find some way to balance religious authority with personal autonomy, so that community may be preserved and religious fragmentation averted.[23]

A third challenge confronting American Judaism concerns contemporary culture. Sexual freedom, gender equality, personal autonomy, gay and lesbian rights, openness to intermarriage, and a host of other liberal twenty-first-century American values raise anew one of modern Judaism's perennial questions: accommodate to contemporary culture or resist it? Like the well-known tension between "Christ and Culture" in Christianity, the Jewish dilemma, at its core, involves a conflict of loyalties: faith pulls in one direction, America in the other.[24]

Rather than openly confronting this challenge, many Jews through the years have promoted the goal of synthesis, insisting that Americanism and Judaism can march happily hand in hand. Some go further, insisting that the two are "essentially" one and the same. "There is nothing incompatible between being a good Jew and a good American, or between Jewish and American standards of behavior," according to one analysis of what, based on their behavior, American Jews most deeply believe. "In fact, for a Jew, the better an American one is, the better Jew one is." Through what has been called "unconscious coalescence," many American Jews happily merge American and Jewish teachings, "incorporating American liberal values . . . into their understanding of Jewish identity."[25]

Beneath the surface, however, contradictions and tensions abound. The holiday of Christmas, for example, annually reminds American Jews just how far apart they stand from central aspects of contemporary American culture. Although they may attempt to magnify the relatively minor holiday of Hanukkah into a surrogate for Christmas, Christmas remains an awkward day for many American Jews. "On no other day during the year" do they "so deeply feel the clash between the country they love and the faith they cherish." Jewish baseball players, like Hank Greenberg, Sandy Koufax, and Shawn Green, have all experienced a similar clash when the Jewish High Holidays in the fall coincide with critical baseball games. Koufax became a latter-day hero for many Jews in 1965 when he refused to pitch the opening game of the World Series and observed Yom Kippur instead. Revealingly, this was an example neither of synthesis nor of coalescence: he was forced to make a stark choice (and the Dodgers lost the game). At a deeper level, as we have seen, issues like intermarriage and gay rights pose this same stark choice between traditional Jewish values and liberal American ones. The question, which Jews have unhappily confronted from the very beginning of their American sojourn but can neither fully admit nor finally resolve, is how to balance American culture and sacred religious teachings, when to compromise and when to stand firm?[26]

Finally, American Jews, living in a society that privileges individualism and gives no official recognition to religious group identity, face the challenge of preserving Jewish unity. With so many bitter divisions in Jewish life— between the different religious movements and among them; between Jews of different backgrounds and ideologies; between in-married Jews and inter-married Jews; between matrilineal Jews and patrilineal Jews; between straight Jews and gay Jews; between born Jews and converted Jews; between American Jews and Israeli Jews; between committed Jews and indifferent Jews— some have questioned whether Jews can remain a united people at all in the twenty-first century. Knowledgeable observers have foreseen "an unbridgeable schism" in Jewish life, "a cataclysmic split," "the bifurcation of Jewry." Well-regarded volumes on contemporary Judaism carry titles like *A People Divided* and *Jew vs. Jew.*[27]

Issues like patrilineal descent, the ordination of openly gay rabbis, the sanctioning of same-sex marriages, and the ordination of women feed the "culture wars" within American Judaism. Ugly local disputes, many of them involving Orthodox efforts to find accommodation for their religious needs and lifestyle choices, also publicly pit Jews against one another, sometimes even in court. Some Orthodox Jews, in response to these developments, question whether rabbis should perform marriages between Orthodox and Reform Jews. Some Reform Jews, in response to these same developments, question whether intermarriage with a liberal non-Jew is not preferable to marrying an Orthodox Jew. Even the Torah itself no longer provides a basis for Jewish unity. Synagogues across the spectrum of Jewish life once used the same text and commentary on the Torah, a volume edited in England by the American-trained Chief Rabbi Joseph H. Hertz. In the twenty-first century, Reform, Conservative, and Orthodox Judaism each offers members their own movement's text and commentary on the Torah, and each views with disdain those produced by the other movements.[28]

For all of these dangers, however, Jewish unity is far from dead. In fact, as America moves back to the center politically, signs within American Judaism suggest a parallel return to the "vital center" and a shift away from the divisive struggles of earlier decades. Independent day schools, trans-denominational high schools, nationwide programs of adult Jewish learning, the revitalized Hillel programs on college campuses, the Birthright Israel travel initiative, and an array of other local and national activities aimed at revitalizing American Judaism all look to bring together Jews of different religious persuasions. Threats to the state of Israel and fears of rising world-wide antisemitism likewise promote a sense among American Jews that they need to find ways to communicate and cooperate with one another across the various religious streams, distances and differences notwithstanding. The question, not so different from the one facing Jews on the eve of the Civil War, remains where to compromise for the sake of unity and where to stand firm for the sake of principle.

A recent book entitled *One People, Two Worlds: A Reform Rabbi and an Orthodox Rabbi Explore the Issues That Divide Them* (2002) captures this dilemma. Its two authors, rabbis who stand on opposite ends of the Jewish spectrum, prove by the very act of communicating with each other that "discourse among Jews can be civil even when disagreements exist." Yet the controversy generated by the book also demonstrates the fragility of these efforts, for the Orthodox coauthor, at the behest of his fervently Orthodox colleagues, withdrew from a seventeen-city speaking tour where he and his Reform counterpart were set to appear jointly on stage. This mixed message of communication and cleavage reflects, perhaps even more than the authors intended, the parlous tension between "compromise" and "principle," "one people" and "two worlds." The fate of American Judaism— whether its adherents will step back from the edge of schism or fall into it —hangs perilously in the balance.[29]

CONTEMPORARY DILEMMAS

With so many questions and issues and tensions confronting them, it comes as no surprise that as they approach their 350th anniversary on American soil, Jews feel bewildered and uncertain. Should they focus on quality to enhance Judaism or focus on quantity to increase the number of Jews? Embrace intermarriage as an opportunity for outreach or condemn it as a disaster for offspring? Build religious bridges or fortify religious boundaries? Strengthen religious authority or promote religious autonomy? Harmonize Judaism with contemporary culture or uphold Jewish tradition against contemporary culture? Compromise for the sake of Jewish unity or stand firm for cherished Jewish principles?

Simultaneously, indeed, Jews witness two contradictory trends operating in their community, assimilation and revitalization. Which will predominate and what the future holds nobody knows. That will be determined day by day, community by community, Jew by Jew.

Regularly, American Jews hear, as I did at the start of my career from a scholar at a distinguished rabbinical seminary—and as other Jews did in colonial times, and in the era of the American Revolution, and in the nineteenth century, and in the twentieth century—that Judaism in America is doomed, that assimilation and intermarriage are inevitable. Should high rates of intermarriage continue and the community grow complacent, that may yet prove true.

But history, as we have seen, also suggests another possibility: that today, as so often before, American Jews will find creative ways to maintain and revitalize American Judaism. With the help of visionary leaders, committed followers, and generous philanthropists, it may still be possible for the current "vanishing" generation of American Jews to be succeeded by another "vanishing" generation, and then still another.

"A nation dying for thousands of years," the great Jewish philosopher Simon Rawidowicz once observed, "means a living nation. Our incessant dying means uninterrupted living, rising, standing up, beginning anew." His message, delivered to Jews agonizing over the loss of 6 million of their compatriots, applies equally well today in the face of contemporary challenges to Jewish continuity. "If we are the last—let us be the last as our fathers and forefathers were. Let us prepare the ground for the last Jews who will come after us, and for the last Jews who will rise after them, and so on until the end of days."[30]

Appendix: American Jewish Population Estimates, 1660–2000

	ESTIMATED TOTALS (LOW–HIGH)	PERCENTAGE OF TOTAL POPULATION
1660	50	—
1700	200–300	—
1776	1,000–2,500	.04–.10
1790	1,300–3,000	.03–.08
1800	2,500	.04
1820	2,650–3,000	.03
1830	4,000–6,000	.03–.05
1840	15,000	.09
1850	50,000	.22
1860	125,000–200,000	.40–.63
1880	230,000–300,000	.46–.60
1890	400,000–475,000	.64–.75
1900	938,000–1,058,000	1.23–1.39
1910	1,508,000–2,044,000	1.63–2.22
1920	3,300,000–3,600,000	3.12–3.41
1930	4,228,000–4,400,000	3.44–3.58
1940	4,771,000–4,831,000	3.63–3.68
1950	4,500,000–5,000,000	2.98–3.31
1960	5,367,000–5,531,000	2.99–3.08
1970	5,370,000–6,000,000	2.64–2.95
1980	5,500,000–5,921,000	2.42–2.61
1990	5,515,000–5,981,000	2.24–2.43
2000	5,340,000–6,155,000	1.90–2.20

Sources: Jacob R. Marcus, *To Count a People: American Jewish Population Data, 1585–1984* (Lanham, Md.: University Press of America, 1990), 237–240. Jack J. Diamond, "A Reader in Demography," *American Jewish Year Book* 77 (1977): 251–319; 91 (1991): 209; 92 (1992): 143; 102 (2002): 255, 615.

Abbreviations

AHR	*American Historical Review*
AJA	American Jewish Archives, Cincinnati, Ohio
AJA	*American Jewish Archives* (publication)
AJH	*American Jewish History*
AJHQ	*American Jewish Historical Quarterly*
AJHS	American Jewish Historical Society, Waltham, Mass., and New York City
AJS	Association for Jewish Studies
AJYB	*American Jewish Year Book*
ANB	*American National Biography*
CCARYB	*Central Conference of American Rabbis Year Book*
CJ	*Conservative Judaism*
EJ	*Encyclopaedia Judaica*
HUCA	*Hebrew Union College Annual*
JPS	Jewish Publication Society
JSS	*Jewish Social Studies*
JTS	Jewish Theological Seminary
LTF	Leaders Training Fellowship
NFJC	National Foundation for Jewish Culture
PAAJR	*Proceedings of the American Academy for Jewish Research*
PAJHS	*Publications of the American Jewish Historical Society*
UAHC	Union of American Hebrew Congregations
YA	*YIVO Annual*

Notes

INTRODUCTION

1. J. Gordon Melton (ed.), *The Encyclopedia of American Religions* (New York: Gale, 1989), lists American religions with their memberships. For the Huguenots, see Butler, *Huguenots in America,* and Edwin S. Gaustad and Philip L. Barlow, *New Historical Atlas of Religion in America* (New York: Oxford, 2001), 48. Figures for denominational disappearance are from Reid et al., *Dictionary of Christianity in America,* 351.
2. *PAJHS* 18 (1909), 20; Blau and Baron, *Jews of the U.S.,* 8–11.
3. Silk, "Notes on the Judeo-Christian Tradition in America," 65–85; Herberg, *Protestant-Catholic-Jew.*
4. Sklare, *Conservative Judaism,* 35; Nahum M. Sarna, *Studies in Biblical Interpretation* (Philadelphia: Jewish Publication Society, 2000), 174.
5. Ahlstrom, *Religious History of the American People,* xiv.
6. Jon Butler, "Enthusiasm Described and Decried: The Great Awakening as Interpretive Fiction," *Journal of American History* 69 (1982): 305–325; "Symposium on Religious Awakenings," *Sociological Analysis* 44 (1983): 81–122; Michael Birchen, "The Awakening-Cycle Controversy," *Sociological Analysis* 46 (1985): 425–443.
7. William G. McLoughlin, "Timepieces and Butterflies: A Note on the Great-Awakening Construct and Its Critics," *Sociological Analysis* 44 (1983): esp. 108; William G. McLoughlin, *Revivals, Awakenings, and Reform* (Chicago: University of Chicago, 1978). Vytautas Kavolis, *History on Art's Side: Social Dynamics in Artistic Efflorescences* (Ithaca: Cornell University Press, 1972), offers a parallel analysis that I have found helpful. See Sarna, *Great Awakening,* for a more extensive discussion of the late nineteenth-century Jewish awakening.
8. Gerson D. Cohen, *The Blessing of Assimilation in Jewish History* (Boston: Hebrew Teachers College, 1966), 9; the posthumous reprint of the address in *Jewish History and Jewish Destiny,* ed. Gerson D. Cohen (New York: Jewish Theological Seminary,

1997), 155, deletes part of this passage. See also Milton M. Gordon, *Assimilation in American Life* (New York: Oxford University Press, 1964), 60–83.

9. D. O. Moberg, "Denominationalism," in Reid et al., *Dictionary of Christianity in America,* 350–352; Ahlstrom, *Religious History of the American People,* 381–382.

10. Quoted in Theodore C. Blegen, *Norwegian Migration to America* (New York: Haskell House, 1969 [1940]), 2: 596.

CHAPTER 1: COLONIAL BEGINNINGS

1. Other sources provide other names, including the *St. Charles.* See Marcus, *Colonial American Jew,* 1: 210.

2. "Letter and Narrative of Father Isaac Jogues, 1643, 1645," J. Franklin Jameson (ed.), *Narratives of New Netherland, 1609–1664* (New York, 1909), 235–254; Goodfriend, *Before the Melting Pot,* 8–21; Wiznitzer, "Exodus from Brazil," 80–98; Marcus, *Colonial American Jew,* 1: 209–211. Hershkowitz, "New Amsterdam's Twenty-Three Jews," 171–183, questions elements of the traditional story.

3. Lewis S. Feuer, *Jews in the Origins of Modern Science and Bacon's Scientific Utopia: The Life and Work of Joachim Gaunse, Mining Technologist and First Recorded Jew in English-Speaking North America,* Brochure Series of the American Jewish Archives VI (Cincinnati: American Jewish Archives, 1987); Smith, "Strangers and Sojourners," 23; Emmanuel, "New Light on Early American Jewry," 51.

4. Oliver A. Rink, "Private Interest and Godly Gain: The West India Company and the Dutch Reformed Church in New Netherland, 1624–1664," *New York History* 75 (July 1994): 245–264; Henry H. Kessler and Eugene Rachlis, *Peter Stuyvesant and His New York* (New York: Random House, 1959), 66; Bonomi, *Under the Cope of Heaven,* 25.

5. Oppenheim, "Early History of the Jews in New York," 4, 5, 20.

6. Ibid., 8–37; Goodfriend, *Before the Melting Pot,* 11, 84; James Homer Williams, "An Atlantic Perspective on the Jewish Struggle for Rights and Opportunities in Brazil, New Netherland, and New York," in Bernardini and Fiering (eds.), *Jews and the Expansion of Europe to the West,* 369–393.

7. E. T. Corwin (ed.), *Ecclesiastical Records of the State of New York* (Albany, N.Y., 1901), 1: 530.

8. Oliver A. Rink, *Holland on the Hudson: An Economic and Social History of Dutch New York* (Ithaca: Cornell University Press, 1986); David Sorkin, "The Port Jew: Notes Toward a Social Type," *Journal of Jewish Studies* 50 (1999): 87–97; Lois Dubin, *The Port Jews of Habsburg Trieste: Absolutist Politics and Enlightenment Culture* (Stanford: Stanford University Press, 1999); Kaplan, "Fictions of Privacy," 1031–1064.

9. Gerber, *Jews of Spain,* 115–144, 285–289; Beinart (ed.), *Moreshet Sepharad,* 2: 11–41.

10. Beinart (ed.), *Moreshet Sepharad,* 2: 43–67; Renée Levine Melammed, *Heretics or Daughters of Israel? The Crypto-Jewish Women of Castile* (New York: Oxford, 1999).

11. Yosef Kaplan, "The Sephardim in North-Western Europe and the New World," in Beinart (ed.), *Moreshet Sepharad,* 240–287.

12. *EJ* 14, col. 1171; H. J. Zimmels, *Ashkenazim and Sephardim* (London: Marla, 1976 [1958]); Martin A. Cohen, "The Sephardic Phenomenon: A Reappraisal," in Cohen and Peck (eds.), *Sephardim in the Americas*, 3–4.

13. The term, according to Haim Beinart, originated among the Portuguese, who employed it against Crypto-Jews "in a tone of hatred and contempt." Conversos transvalued the term. To belong to the "people of the nation" became for them a "sign of honor and distinction." See Beinart (ed.), *Moreshet Sepharad*, 58.

14. Kaplan, "Portuguese Community in Amsterdam in the 17th Century," 166–181; Swetschinski, *Reluctant Cosmopolitans*, 165–167; Miriam Bodian, *Hebrews of the Portuguese Nation: Conversos and Community in Early Modern Amsterdam* (Bloomington: Indiana University Press, 1997).

15. Swetschinski, *Reluctant Cosmopolitans;* Kaplan, "Portuguese Community in Amsterdam in the 17th Century"; Odette Vlessing, "New Light on the Earliest History of the Amsterdam Portuguese Jews," *Dutch Jewish History* 3 (1991): 62.

16. Wiznitzer, *Jews in Colonial Brazil*, esp. 57.

17. Ibid., 128–130; Isaac S. Emmanuel, "Seventeenth-Century Brazilian Jewry: A Critical Review," *AJA* 14 (April 1962): 41; Marcus, *Colonial American Jew*, 67–84; *PAJHS* 33 (1934): 103–105; and Emmanuel, "New Light on Early American Jewry," 43–46.

18. Yerushalmi, "Between Amsterdam and New Amsterdam," 172–192.

19. Jonathan Israel, "Menasseh Ben Israel and the Dutch Sephardic Colonization Movement of the Mid-Seventeenth Century (1645–1657)," in Yosef Kaplan et al. (eds.), *Menasseh Ben Israel and His World* (Leiden: Brill, 1989), 139–163; Ismar Schorsch, "From Messianism to Realpolitik: Menasseh Ben Israel and the Readmission of the Jews to England," *PAAJR* 45 (1978): 187–208; Yosef Kaplan, "The Jewish Profile of the Spanish-Portuguese Community of London During the Seventeenth Century," *Judaism* 41 (Summer 1992): 229–240.

20. *PAJHS* 16 (1907): 184; Yerushalmi, "Between Amsterdam and New Amsterdam," 184–189; Marcus, *Colonial American Jew*, 95–208; Bernardini and Fiering (eds.), *Jews and the Expansion of Europe to the West*.

21. Wiznitzer, "The Exodus from Brazil and Arrival in New Amsterdam of the Jewish Pilgrim Fathers, 1654," 80–98, esp. 92; Joseph Krauskopf, "The Jewish Pilgrim Fathers," *PAJHS* 14 (1906): 121–130.

22. Marcus, *Colonial American Jew*, 216–217, 1226.

23. *PAJHS* 18 (1909): 24, 25, 35, 36; Leon Huhner, "Asser Levy: A Noted Jewish Burgher of New Amsterdam," *PAJHS* 8 (1900): 9–23; Malcolm H. Stern, "Asser Levy—A New Look at Our Jewish Founding Father," *AJA* 26 (April 1974): 66–77; Leo Hershkowitz, "Asser Levy and the Inventories of Early New York Jews," *AJH* 80 (Autumn 1990): 21–55.

24. Pool, *Portraits Etched in Stone*, 7–12, 25.

25. Emmanuel, "New Light on Early American Jewry," 17–23, 56.

26. For evidence of privately held seventeenth-century Torah scrolls in New York, see *AJH* 80 (Autumn 1990): 22; and Pool, *Portraits Etched in Stone*, 188; for Savannah, see *AJHQ* 54 (March 1965): 247; for Lancaster, see Brener, "Lancaster's First Jewish Community," 232; and for Reading, see Trachtenberg, *Consider the Years*, 31; see also Smith, "Portraits of a Community," 14.

27. *PAJHS* 18 (1909): 33; Cecil Roth, *A History of the Jews in England* (Oxford:

Clarendon, 1978): 171; Schappes, *Documentary History,* 19; Kaplan, "Fictions of Privacy," 1042.

28. Leo Hershkowitz, "The Mill Street Synagogue Reconsidered," *AJHQ* 53 (1964): 408; Marcus, *Colonial American Jew,* 402.

29. Arnold Wiznitzer, "The Merger Agreement and Regulations of Congregation Talmud Torah of Amsterdam (1638–39)," *Historia Judaica* 20 (October 1958): 109–132; Swetschinski, *Reluctant Cosmopolitans,* 174–187; Miriam Bodian, "The Escamot of the Spanish-Portuguese Jewish Community of London, 1664," *Michael* 9 (1985): 12–13. The Ashkenazi community in Amsterdam established its own congregation in 1635; see Kaplan, "Portuguese Community in 17th-Century Amsterdam," 29.

30. Arnold Wiznitzer in *PAJHS* 46 (1956): 48 n.41 suggests that the name refers to the "remnant of Israel" that survived from Recife in 1654 and points to the use of this phrase in a depiction of Recife's fall by Isaac Aboab de Fonseca. Jacob R. Marcus, however, cites documents from the early 1720s suggesting that the congregation's original name was not Shearith Israel but Shearith Yaakob [Remnant of Jacob]; see Marcus, *Studies in American Jewish History,* 44–45.

31. Pool, *Old Faith;* Marcus, *Colonial American Jew,* 855–1110; quote is from Hershkowitz and Meyer, *Letters of the Franks Family,* 60.

32. Herman P. Salomon, "K. K. Shearith Israel's First Language: Portuguese," *Tradition* 30 (Fall 1995): 74–84; Denah Lida, "Language of the Sephardim in Anglo-America," in Cohen and Peck (eds.), *Sephardim in the Americas,* 309–329, esp. 312.

33. Barnett, *El Libro de los Acuerdos,* 3; Salomon, "Joseph Jesurun Pinto," 18–29.

34. *PAJHS* 27 (1920): 187–188.

35. Marcus, *Colonial American Jew,* 899–911.

36. *PAJHS* 21 (1913): 50–51, 84; John B. Kirby, "Early American Politics—The Search for Ideology: An Historiographical Analysis and Critique of the Concept of Deference," *Journal of Politics* 32 (1970): 808–838; J. A. Pocock, "The Classical Theory of Deference," *AHR* 81 (1976): 516–523.

37. Barnett, *El Libro de los Acuerdos,* 15; Zvi Loker, *Jews in the Caribbean* (Jerusalem: Misgav Yerushalayim, 1991), 41; Grinstein, *New York,* 469; Pointer, *Protestant Pluralism and the New York Experience,* 13–15.

38. Grinstein, *New York,* 84–87; Marcus, *American Jewry—Documents,* 132, 282; Marcus, *Colonial American Jew,* 928–934.

39. Emmanuel and Emmanuel, *History of the Jews of the Netherlands Antilles,* 544; Barnett, *El Libro de los Acuerdos,* 11. See also Judah Cohen, "Documents Concerning the Jews of the Virgin Islands" (private collection); Beinart, *Moreshet Sepharad,* 2: 348.

40. Yosef Kaplan, "Deviance and Excommunication in the Eighteenth Century: A Chapter in the Social History of the Sephardic Community of Amsterdam," *Dutch Jewish History* 3 (1993): 103–115; Marcus, *Colonial American Jew,* 924–926.

41. *PAJHS* 21 (1913): 74–76; Butler, *Awash in a Sea of Faith,* 173–174.

42. Butler, *Awash in a Sea of Faith,* 113–116; Wischnitzer, *Synagogue Architecture in the United States,* 11–19; Krinsky, *Synagogues of Europe,* 412–415; Kaplan, "Fictions of Privacy," 1031–1064.

43. Jonathan D. Sarna, "Seating and the American Synagogue," in Vandermeer and Swierenga (eds.), *Belief and Behavior,* 189–194; Wiznitzer, *Records of the Earliest*

Jewish Community in the New World, 17; Barnett, *El Libro de los Acuerdos,* 4; Pool, *Old Faith in the New World,* 44.

44. Marcus, *Studies in American Jewish History,* 50; Pool, *Portraits Etched in Stone,* 169–173; *PAJHS* 27 (1920): 4; Faber, *A Time for Planting,* 64; Malcolm H. Stern and Marc D. Angel, *New York's Early Jews: Some Myths and Misconceptions* (New York: Jewish Historical Society of New York, 1976); Marcus, *Colonial American Jew,* 1001–1006.

45. Marcus, *Colonial American Jew,* 351; Stern, "Sheftall Diaries," 247; Stern, "New Light on the Jewish Settlement of Savannah," 163–199; Snyder, "'We Have the World to Begin Againe,'" 122–132.

46. Marcus, *Colonial American Jew,* 314–325, 343–348; Gutstein, *Story of the Jews of Newport,* 114.

47. Chyet, *Lopez of Newport,* 173; Kaplan, "Portuguese Community in Amsterdam," 178–179.

48. Marcus, *Colonial American Jew,* 1023; Gutstein, *Story of the Jews of Newport,* 170–172.

49. Endelman, *Jews of Georgian England,* 132–165; Marcus, *Colonial American Jew,* 955–960.

50. Isaac Pinto (trans.), *Prayers for Shabbath, Rosh Hashanah and Kippur* (New York, 1765–66), preface.

51. Gutstein, *Story of the Jews of Newport,* 132; Chyet, *Lopez of Newport,* 158; Marcus, *American Jewry—Documents,* 265; Kalm reprinted in Handlin, *This Was America,* 32.

52. Grinstein, *New York,* 334; Marcus, *Colonial American Jew,* 956–957.

53. "Lancaster in 1772," *Journal of the Lancaster County Historical Society* 5 (1901): 108–109.

54. Godfrey and Godfrey, *Search Out the Land,* 77; Marcus, *Colonial American Jew,* 978–983.

55. Wolf and Whiteman, *Philadelphia,* 73–74.

56. Hershkowitz and Meyer (eds.), *Letters of the Franks Family,* 7–8; Wolf and Whiteman, *Philadelphia,* 64; Stern, "New Light on the Jewish Settlement of Savannah," 185; Handlin, *This Was America,* 32; Berman, *Shehitah,* 274–283.

57. Stern, "Two Jewish Functionaries in Colonial Pennsylvania," 24–35, 49–51; Aaron Lopez to Ab'm Abraham (September 6, 1767) and Aaron Lopez to Isaac Da Costa (September 17, 1767), reprinted in Broches, *Jews in New England,* 2: 61–62; Barbara Kirshenblatt-Gimblett, "The Cut that Binds: The Western Ashkenazi Torah Binder as Nexus Between Circumcision and Torah," *Celebration: Studies in Festivity and Ritual,* ed. Victor Turner (Washington, D.C.: Smithsonian, 1982).

58. Marcus, *American Jewry—Documents,* 15; Marcus, *Colonial American Jew,* 947, 954; *Essays in American Jewish History,* 115; *PAJHS* 34 (1937): 70; Franklin B. Dexter (ed.), *The Literary Diary of Ezra Stiles* (New York: Charles Scribner's Sons, 1901), 1: 19; Gershom Scholem, *Sabbatai Sevi: The Mystical Messiah* (Princeton: Princeton University Press, 1973), 594–595; Hershkowitz and Meyer (eds.), *Letters of the Franks Family,* 66; Hershkowitz, "Another Abigail Franks Letter," 224.

59. Marcus, *Colonial American Jew,* 397–515, 1113–1248.

60. Stern, "Function of Genealogy in American Jewish History," 85; Marcus, *Colonial American Jew,* 1232; Butler, *Huguenots in America,* 187.

61. Hershkowitz and Meyer (eds.), *Letters of the Franks Family,* 116–125.
62. Stern, "Function of Genealogy in American Jewish History," 94–97; Marcus, *Colonial American Jew,* 1225–1235; Godfrey and Godfrey, *Search Out the Land,* 294, n.14.
63. Marcus, *American Jewry—Documents,* 104; Schappes, *Documentary History,* 67.
64. Rosenwaike, "Estimate and Analysis," 23–67.
65. Marcus, *American Jewry—Documents,* 129–130.
66. Marcus, *Colonial American Jew,* 1222, notes "a young Jewish girl in Rhode Island" who was allegedly influenced by George Whitefield's revivalist preaching. For the Jewish sermon, see Haim Isaac Carigal, *A Sermon Preached at the Synagogue in Newport, Rhode-Island, called "The Salvation of Israel" . . . May 28, 1773* (Newport, 1773).

CHAPTER 2: THE REVOLUTION IN AMERICAN JUDAISM

1. *PAJHS* 27 (1920): 31–32.
2. *PAJHS* 6 (1897): 129; *AJYB* 6 (1904–5): 41; Marcus, *U.S. Jewry,* 1: 48.
3. Richard Morris, "The Jews, Minorities and Dissent in the American Revolution," *Migration and Settlement: Papers on Anglo-American Jewish History* (London: Jewish Historical Society of England, 1971), 152; Pointer, *Protestant Pluralism and the New York Experience,* 79–81.
4. Marcus, *U.S. Jewry,* 1: 54, 56, 66; Pool, *Old Faith,* 328. Marcus's survey and Rezneck, *Unrecognized Patriots,* are the most reliable accounts.
5. Marcus, *U.S. Jewry,* 1: 66–77; Laurens R. Schwartz, *Jews and the American Revolution: Haym Salomon and Others* (Jefferson, N.C.: McFarland, 1987); Emmanuel and Emmanuel, *History of the Jews of the Netherlands Antilles,* 1: 518–527; Marcus, *Colonial American Jew,* 1: 141–143.
6. *PAJHS* 6 (1897): 130; Pool, *Old Faith,* 168–169. Shearith Israel still had the use of at least two Torah scrolls during the British occupation (Pool, 47).
7. *AJHQ* 54 (March 1965): 251; *AJA* 27 (November 1975): 156–159; Chyet, *Lopez of Newport,* 157–162. Lopez died in 1782 while returning to Newport.
8. *AJA* 27 (November 1975): 164–165, 184–185, 189–190.
9. Ibid., 157–158, 168–171; Chyet, *Lopez of Newport,* 161.
10. *AJA* 27 (November 1975): 209–210; *PAJHS* 27 (1920): 32–37; cf. Butler, *Awash in a Sea of Faith,* 216–218.
11. Sarna and Dalin, *Religion and State,* 2–3, 63–71.
12. Ibid., 71–76; Sarna, "Impact of the American Revolution," 151–152.
13. Stanley F. Chyet, "The Political Rights of the Jews in the United States: 1776–1840," *AJA* 10 (1958): 14–75; Milton Borden, *Jews, Turks, and Infidels* (Chapel Hill: University of North Carolina Press, 1984); Sarna and Dalin, *Religion and State.*
14. Wolf and Whiteman, *Philadelphia,* 150–151; *AJA* 27 (November 1975): 246–250; Sarna, "Impact of the American Revolution," 154; Catherine L. Albanese, *Sons of the Fathers: The Civil Religion of the American Revolution* (Philadelphia: Temple University Press, 1976), 214–215; John M. Shaftesley, "Culinary Aspects of Anglo-Jewry," *Studies in the Cultural Life of the Jews in England: Folklore Research Studies,* vol. 5, ed. Dov Noy and Issachar Ben-Ami (Jerusalem: Magnes Press, 1975), 182.
15. Blau and Baron, *Jews of the U.S.,* 8–11; Sarna and Dalin, *Religion and State,* 79–82.

The editor of Jefferson's Papers suggests that Jefferson may even have drafted Washington's reply to the Jews of Newport; see Julian P. Boyd (ed.), *The Papers of Thomas Jefferson* (Princeton: Princeton University Press, 1974), 19: 610n. For Jefferson's views on toleration, see Charles B. Sanford, *The Religious Life of Thomas Jefferson* (Charlottesville: University of Virginia Press, 1984), 27.

16. Schappes, *Documentary History,* 77–84; Marcus, *American Jewry—Documents,* 167–170; Rubin, *Third to None,* 40–43.

17. Marcus, *U.S. Jewry,* 1: 310, 677.

18. Wolf and Whiteman, *Philadelphia,* 142–145; Marcus, *U.S. Jewry,* 1: 563–564; Nathan M. Goodman, ed., *A Benjamin Franklin Reader* (New York: Thomas Y. Crowell, 1945), 245.

19. Pool, *Portraits Etched in Stone,* 368–370; Pointer, *Protestant Pluralism and the New York Experience,* 104; Marcus, *Handsome Young Priest,* 23.

20. Hershkowitz, *Wills of Early New York Jews,* 177; Grinstein, *New York,* 85–86; Marcus, *Handsome Young Priest,* 26.

21. Pool, *Portraits Etched in Stone,* 72–74.

22. Robert M. Healey, "Jefferson on Judaism and the Jews: 'Divided We Stand, United, We Fall!'" *AJH* 73 (June 1984): see esp. 365–366; Sarna, "The 'Mythical Jew,'" 59–60.

23. Ahlstrom, *Religious History of the American People,* 379–384; Reid, *Dictionary of Christianity in America,* 1227.

24. Sarna, "Jewish Prayers for the United States Government," 206; Wolf and Whiteman, *Philadelphia,* 121; *PAJHS* 27 (1920): 126; Pool, *Old Faith,* 87; Salomon, "Joseph Jesurun Pinto," 26 n. 38.

25. Marcus, *American Jewry—Documents,* 149, 150, 154–155.

26. Ibid., 155.

27. Elazar, Sarna, and Monson, *Double Bond,* 113.

28. Hatch, *Democratization of American Christianity,* 6, 64.

29. Wolf and Whiteman, *Philadelphia,* 128–131.

30. Fish, "Problem of Intermarriage in Early America," 93–94.

31. *AJA* 19 (November 1967): 142–143.

32. Wolf and Whiteman, *Philadelphia,* 237–238; Berman, *Richmond Jewry,* 53–55; Moses, *Last Order of the Lost Cause,* 24–25.

33. Marcus, *American Jewry—Documents,* 52.

34. Ibid., 52–54; *AJA* 27 (November 1975): 212–213.

35. Berman, *Richmond Jewry,* 16; Wolf and Whiteman, *Philadelphia,* 123; Eleazar Levy to Aaron Hart (June 4, 1794), in Marcus, ed., *On Love, Marriage, Children,* 41; Ezekiel and Lichtenstein, *Richmond,* 131; Marcus, *U.S. Jewry,* 1: 177; Marcus, *Jew in the American World,* 137; cf. Cecil Roth, "Some Revolutionary Purims (1790–1801)," *Hebrew Union College Annual* 10 (1935): 451–483.

36. Marcus, *U.S. Jewry,* 1: 610–613.

37. Pool, *Old Faith,* 44; Sarna, "Seating and the American Synagogue," 192.

38. Pool, *Old Faith,* 50; Goldman, *Beyond the Synagogue Gallery,* 47, 51–52; Susan Tobin (archivist, Shearith Israel) to author, December 1, 1997.

39. Grinstein, *New York,* 193; Philipson, *Letters of Rebecca Gratz,* 74; Goldman, *Beyond the Synagogue Gallery,* 81–92.

40. Goldman, *Beyond the Synagogue Gallery,* 51–54; Pool, *Old Faith,* 453.

41. Terry D. Bilhartz, "Sex and the Second Great Awakening: The Feminization of American Religion Reconsidered," in Vandermeer and Swierenga, eds., *Belief and Behavior,* 117–135; Bruce Dorsey, "City of Brotherly Love: Religious Benevolence, Gender, and Reform in Philadelphia, 1780–1844" (Ph.D. diss., Brown University, 1993), 208–209; Pool, *Old Faith,* 50–51; Philipson, *Letters of Rebecca Gratz,* 75–76.

42. Ashton, *Unsubdued Spirits,* 93–120; Evelyn Bodek, "Making Do: Jewish Women and Philanthropy," in Friedman, *Jewish Life in Philadelphia,* 145–150.

43. Pool, *Old Faith,* 287–288; Berman, *Richmond Jewry,* 102–103.

44. Marcus, *American Jewry—Documents,* 134–136; Marcus, *Colonial American Jew,* 995; Wolf and Whiteman, *Philadelphia,* 140, 446 n. 11; Goldman, *Beyond the Synagogue Gallery,* 68–75.

45. Marcus, *American Jewry—Documents,* 135; Marcus, *Jew in the American World,* 137–138.

46. Mikveh Israel Minutes, September 10, 1826, as quoted in Jay M. Eidelman, "'In the Wilds of America': The Early Republican Origins of American Judaism, 1790–1830" (Ph.D. diss., Yale University, 1997), 134; Wolf and Whiteman, *Philadelphia,* 237.

47. Marcus, *American Jewry—Documents,* 135; Marcus, *U.S. Jewry,* 82, 584–585; Benjamin, *Three Years in America,* 62–63; Myer Moses, *An Oration Delivered Before the Hebrew Orphan Society on the 15th of October 1806* (Charleston: Apollo, 1807), 18, 32.

48. Hagy, *This Happy Land,* 64–68; Solomon Breibart, "Two Jewish Congregations in Charleston, S.C., Before 1791: A New Conclusion," *AJH* 69 (March 1980): 360–363.

49. Marcus, *U.S. Jewry,* 1: 222–223, 238; Fish, *Bernard and Michael Gratz,* 212–217; Wolf and Whiteman, *Philadelphia,* 225–228; Davis, *History of Rodeph Shalom,* 11–14.

50. Samuel Oppenheim, "The Question of the Kosher Meat Supply in New York in 1813: With a Sketch of Earlier Conditions," *PAJHS* 25 (1917): 54–57; Pool, *Old Faith,* 243–247; Berman, *Shehitah,* 286–287.

51. Elazar, Sarna, and Monson, *Double Bond,* 116; Hagy, *This Happy Land,* 63–64, 70–71; M. M. Noah to N. Phillips (10 May 1812), in Isaac Goldberg, "Mr. Noah, American," *Menorah Journal* 24 (Autumn 1936): 287–288.

52. Malcolm H. Stern, "The 1820s: American Jewry Comes of Age," in Korn, *Bicentennial Festschrift,* 539–549.

53. Blau and Baron, *Jews of the U.S.,* 547–548; Sarna, "American Jewish Response to Nineteenth-Century Christian Missions," 35–51.

54. W. Gunther Plaut, *The Rise of Reform Judaism: A Sourcebook of Its European Origins* (New York: World Union for Progressive Judaism, 1963), 31; Meyer, *Response to Modernity,* 53–61; Emmanuel and Emmanuel, *History of the Jews of the Netherlands Antilles,* 1: 306–327, esp. 319.

55. Blau and Baron, *Jews of the U.S.,* 541; Pool, *Old Faith,* 436; Grinstein, *New York,* 40–49.

56. [New York] *National Advocate,* December 5, 1825, p. 2; Blau and Baron, *Jews of the U.S.,* 542–545; *Christian Inquirer,* September 17, 1825, p. 151; Jick, *Americanization of the Synagogue,* 20–23.

57. Pool, *Old Faith,* 437; Goldstein, *Century of Judaism,* 54–55. The original spelling of the congregation's name was "B'nai Yeshiorun."
58. Goldstein, *Century of Judaism,* 55–56.
59. See Heller, *As Yesterday When It Is Past,* 26–27; Trachtenberg, *Consider the Years,* 237.
60. These average ages are based on incomplete data assembled by Solomon Breibart; see Robert Liberles, "Conflict over Reforms: The Case of Congregation Beth Elohim, Charleston, South Carolina," in Wertheimer, ed., *American Synagogue,* 282.
61. Moise, *Biography of Isaac Harby;* Lou H. Silberman, *American Impact: Judaism in the United States in the Early Nineteenth Century,* B. G. Rudolph Lectures in Judaic Studies (Syracuse: Syracuse University, 1964); Hagy, *This Happy Land,* 128–160; Meyer, *Response to Modernity,* 228–233; Zola, *Isaac Harby of Charleston,* 112–149.
62. Moise, *Biography of Isaac Harby,* 61, 72–73 (emphasis in the original).
63. Ibid., 101; Meyer, *Response to Modernity,* 231–233; Zola, *Isaac Harby,* 146–147.
64. Hatch, *Democratization of American Christianity,* 59.
65. Grinstein, *New York,* 472–474; Wolfe, *Synagogues of New York's Lower East Side,* 37.
66. Sarna, "Evolution of the American Synagogue," 219–221.
67. Pool, *Old Faith,* 264.

CHAPTER 3: UNION AND DISUNION

1. *Buffalo Patriot-Extra* (September 17, 1825), 1–2; Sarna, *Jacksonian Jew,* 65–66.
2. Blau and Baron, *Jews of the U.S.,* 894–900; *PAJHS* 21 (1913): 230–252; Michael Schuldiner and Daniel J. Kleinfeld, *The Selected Writings of Mordecai Noah* (Westport: Greenwood Press, 1999), 105–147; Sarna, *Jacksonian Jew,* 61–75.
3. Sarna, *Jacksonian Jew,* 61–62.
4. Sarna, *Jacksonian Jew,* 72–74; Marcus, *To Count a People,* 237–240.
5. Rosenwaike, *On the Edge of Greatness,* 40, 140–164.
6. Isaac Markens, *The Hebrews in America* (New York, 1888).
7. Baron, *Steeled by Adversity,* 277; but contrast Diner, *A Time for Gathering,* 53, 251 n.42.
8. Barkai, *Branching Out,* 17–24; Diner, *A Time for Gathering,* 43–44; Anny Bloch, "Mercy on Rude Streams: Jewish Emigrants from Alsace-Lorraine to the Lower Mississippi Region and the Concept of Fidelity," *Southern Jewish History* 2 (1999): 81–110.
9. Meyer, *German-Jewish History in Modern Times,* 2: 7–49, esp. 24, 29; Barkai, *Branching Out,* 1–2. While poor Christians also faced some restrictions on marriage in Bavaria, they responded with a high illegitimacy rate; see Mack Walker, *Germany and the Emigration, 1816–1885* (Cambridge: Harvard University Press, 1964), 54–55, 163–166.
10. Aaron Phillips to Parents (June 12, 1825), as translated and quoted in Mark I. Greenberg, "Creating Ethnic, Class, and Southern Identity in Nineteenth-Century America: The Jews of Savannah, Georgia, 1830–1880" (Ph.D. diss., University of Florida, 1997), 85.
11. Blau and Baron, *Jews of the U.S.,* 809–811.

12. Benjamin, *Three Years in America,* 1: 75.

13. Sarna and Klein, *Jews of Cincinnati,* 3; Gartner, *History of the Jews of Cleveland,* 8; Stefan Rohrbacher, "From Württemberg to America: A Nineteenth-Century German-Jewish Village on Its Way to the New World," *AJA* 41 (Fall–Winter 1989): 143–161.

14. Barkai, *Branching Out,* 9, 16; Walter D. Kamphoefner, Wolfgang Helbich, and Ulrike Sommer (eds.), *News from the Land of Freedom: German Immigrants Write Home* (Ithaca: Cornell University Press, 1991), 10–11.

15. Gartner, *History of the Jews of Cleveland,* iv, 8–9, 41; Marcus, *This I Believe,* 75–76.

16. Glanz, *Studies in Judaica Americana,* 29, 40.

17. Sellers, *The Market Revolution;* Stokes and Conway (eds.), *The Market Revolution in America,* quote is from 266.

18. Glanz, *Studies in Judaica Americana,* 105.

19. Jewish women peddlers who could not feed their children were assisted by the Female Hebrew Benevolent Society in 1858. See Ashton, *Rebecca Gratz,* 101.

20. Whiteman, "Notions, Dry Goods, and Clothing," 311–313.

21. Whiteman, "Notions, Dry Goods, and Clothing," 311; Barkai, *Branching Out,* 44–53; Diner, *A Time for Gathering,* 66–73.

22. Glanz, "Spread of Jewish Communities Through America Before the Civil War," 7–45; Glanz, "Where the Jewish Press Was Distributed in Pre-Civil War America," 1–14; Engelman, "Jewish Statistics," 130.

23. Goodman, "A Jewish Peddler's Diary," 97.

24. Marcus, *Memoirs of American Jews,* 1: 206.

25. Sefton D. Temkin, "Rabbi Max Lilienthal Views American Jewry in 1847," in Korn, *Bicentennial Festschrift,* 595–596.

26. James K. Gutheim, *Address Delivered at the Laying of the Corner Stone of the Synagogue of the Congregation "B'nai Yeshurun"* (Cincinnati, 1846), 1; Schappes, *Documentary History,* 177–179; Sarna and Goldman, "From Synagogue-Community to Citadel of Reform," 160; Marcus, *Memoirs of American Jews,* 1: 205.

27. Ahlstrom, *Religious History of the American People,* 470–471.

28. Ehrlich, *Zion in the Valley,* 54–59, 88–108.

29. Dolores Liptak, *Immigrants and Their Church* (New York: Macmillan, 1989), 114–115; Rosenbaum, *Visions of Reform,* 6–9.

30. Abraham J. Karp, "Overview: The Synagogue in America—A Historical Typology," in Wertheimer, *American Synagogue,* 5; Linda K. Pritchard, "The Spirit in the Flesh: Religion and Regional Economic Development," in Vandermeer and Swierenga, *Belief and Behavior,* 97; Blau and Baron, *Jews of the U.S.,* 810.

31. Mostov, "A 'Jerusalem' on the Ohio," 150; Engelman, "Jewish Statistics," 129.

32. Sarna, "American Jewish Response to Nineteenth-Century Christian Missions," 35–51; Sarna, *Jacksonian Jew,* 56–57; Shalom Goldman, "Joshua/James Seixas (1802–1874): Jewish Apostasy and Christian Hebraism in Early Nineteenth-Century America," *Jewish History* 7 (Spring 1993): 65–88; Bingham, *Mordecai,* 114–115, 179–180.

33. Simeon Abrahams, "Intermarrying with Gentiles," *Occident* 2 (March 1845), available online at www.jewish-history.com/Occident/volume2/mar1845/intermarry.html; Marcus, *U.S. Jewry,* 2: 68; Marcus, *Memoirs of American Jews,* 1: 247.

34. Grusd, *B'nai B'rith*, 20.

35. Mordecai M. Noah, *Discourse on the Evidences of the American Indians Being the Descendants of the Lost Tribes of Israel* (New York, 1837), 37, online at olivercowdery.com/texts/noah1837.htm.

36. Sellers, *The Market Revolution*, 29–31, 202–236; Stokes and Conway (eds.), *The Market Revolution in America*, 259–307; Reid, *Dictionary of Christianity in America*, 77–79.

37. Reid, *Dictionary of Christianity in America*, 992–993; Jay R. Berkovitz, *The Shaping of Jewish Identity in Nineteenth-Century France* (Detroit: Wayne State University Press, 1989), 14–17.

38. Sussman, *Isaac Leeser*, 61–62.

39. Ibid., 59–67; Singer, "Anglo-Jewish Ministry," 284–286; Friedenberg, *Hear O Israel*, 26–38 (quote from Leeser is on p. 38).

40. Leeser, *Discourses on the Jewish Religion*, 5: 77, 80; see also 7: 178–191, 8: 15–29.

41. Ibid., 3: ix–x.

42. Sussman, *Isaac Leeser*, 71–72, 234–235.

43. See ibid., 128.

44. Sorkin, *Transformation of German Jewry*, 15–21, 94–99; Meyer, *German-Jewish History in Modern Times*, 2: 200–204, 3: 307.

45. Sarna and Goldman, "From Synagogue-Community to Citadel of Reform," 169; Richard L. Bushman, *The Refinement of America: Persons, Houses, Cities* (New York: Knopf, 1992).

46. As quoted in Gartner, "Temples of Liberty Unpolluted," 172. For the treatment of Jews and Judaism in the schoolbooks of Leeser's day, see Ruth Miller Elson, *Guardians of Tradition: American Schoolbooks of the Nineteenth Century* (Lincoln: University of Nebraska Press, 1964), 81–87.

47. Rebecca Gratz to Maria G. Gratz (1838) as quoted in Sussman, *Isaac Leeser*, 97.

48. Much of this paragraph is drawn from Sarna and Sarna, "Jewish Bible Scholarship and Translations in the United States," 86–88. See also Bratt, "The Reorientation of American Protestantism," 64; and Paul C. Gutjahr, *An American Bible: A History of the Good Book in the United States, 1777–1880* (Stanford: Stanford University Press, 1999).

49. Paul Mendes-Flohr and Jehuda Reinharz, *The Jew in the Modern World: A Documentary History*, 2nd ed. (New York: Oxford, 1995), 461–463; Sarna, *JPS: The Americanization of Jewish Culture*, 1–4.

50. Bingham, *Mordecai*, 24.

51. Moise, *Biography of Isaac Harby*, 128–140; Zola, *Isaac Harby of Charleston*, 146–147; Meyer, *Response to Modernity*, 232–233.

52. *PAJHS* 21 (1913): 200; Sarna, *Jacksonian Jew*, 138. Noah subsequently backed away from his most far-reaching suggestions.

53. Blau and Baron, *Jews of the U.S.*, 3: 954–955.

54. Reid, *Dictionary of Christianity in America*, 790; Meir Benayahu, "Da'at Hakhme Italya Al Ha-Neginah B-Ogev Be-Tfilah," *Asufot* 1 (1987): 265–318.

55. For what follows, see Tarshish, "The Charleston Organ Case," 411–449; Hagy, *This Happy Land*, 240–256; Meyer, *Response to Modernity*, 233–235.

56. Breibart, *The Rev. Mr. Gustavus Poznanski*, 1–8.

57. Abraham Moise to Isaac Leeser (August 12, 1841) in Moise, *Isaac Harby,* 84; Meyer, *Response to Modernity,* 234; Kershen and Romain, *Tradition and Change,* 16; Tarshish, "Charleston Organ Case," 435, 438.

58. Meyer, *Response to Modernity,* 52; Kershen and Romain, *Tradition and Change,* 39–41.

59. Tarshish, "Charleston Organ Case," 439–445.

60. Abraham Moise to Isaac Leeser (August 12, 1841) in Moise, *Isaac Harby,* 87.

61. *Occident* 3 (April 1845), and 5 (May 1847). I have used the on-line version available at www.jewish-history.com/occident (search under "Orthodox," "Orthodoxy").

62. Rubenstein, *History of Har Sinai Congregation,* unpaginated; Greenberg, *Chronicle of Baltimore Hebrew Congregation,* 13–14; Wischnitzer, *Synagogue Architecture in the United States,* 41–42, 45.

63. Stern, *Rise and Progress of Reform Judaism,* 13–41; Grinstein, *New York,* 353–363; Meyer, *Response to Modernity,* 236–237; "Imanuel," *Encyclopaedia Biblica* 6 (1971): col. 291–295 [in Hebrew].

64. Jacob Rosenfeld, "Israel's Union," reprinted in Hagy, *This Happy Land,* 259.

65. Marcus, *Memoirs of American Jews,* 1: 249, 252; Marcus, *U.S. Jewry,* 1: 335–336; Ashkenazi, *Business of Jews in Louisiana,* 160–168.

66. Grusd, *B'nai B'rith,* 20.

67. Boris D. Bogen, "Historic Sketch of the B'nai B'rith," *B'nai B'rith Manual,* ed. Samuel Cohon (Cincinnati, 1926), 323.

68. Moore, *B'nai B'rith;* Grinstein, *New York,* 109–112, 154; Soyer, "Entering the 'Tent of Abraham,'" 159–182; Cornelia Wilhelm, "The Independent Order of True Sisters: Friendship, Fraternity, and a Model of Modernity for Nineteenth-Century American Jewish Womanhood," *AJA* 54: 1 (2002): 37–63.

69. Sussman, *Isaac Leeser,* 116–125, 172–178; Sidney E. Mead, "The Rise of the Evangelical Conception of the Ministry in America (1607–1850)," *The Ministry in Historical Perspective,* ed. H. Richard Niebuhr and Daniel D. Williams (New York, 1956), 217.

70. Sharfman, *The First Rabbi,* 25–39, 68–74; Davis, "Abraham I. Rice," 100; Tabak, "Rabbi Abraham Rice of Baltimore," 102–103.

71. Reissner, "German-American Jews," 104–107; Henry Illoway, *Sefer Milchamot Elohim* (Berlin, 1914), available on-line at www.jewish-history.com/Illoway/introduction.html; Isaac M. Wise, *Judaism and Christianity* (Cincinnati, 1883), 1: 126–127; Temkin, *Isaac Mayer Wise,* 23.

72. Wise, *Reminiscences,* 51; Grinstein, *New York,* 513–517; Bernard Cohn, "Leo Merzbacher," *AJA* 6 (1954): 22.

73. Wise, *Reminiscences,* 158.

74. Sharfman, *The First Rabbi,* 25–39, 68–74; Davis, "Abraham I. Rice," 100; Tabak, "Rabbi Abraham Rice of Baltimore," 102–103; Fein, *Making of an American Jewish Community,* 54–58; Jick, *Americanization of the Synagogue,* 70–73.

75. Tabak, "Rabbi Abraham Rice of Baltimore," 102, 108; Sharfman, *The First Rabbi,* 254, 711.

76. For what follows, see Korn, *Eventful Years and Experiences,* 40–42, 99–108; Goldstein, *A Century of Judaism in New York,* 110–153, esp. 126, 150; Morais, *Eminent Israelites of the Nineteenth Century,* 287–91; Wischnitzer, *Synagogue Architecture*

in the United States, 54–55; Wise, *Reminiscences*, 128, 131; Jick, *Americanization of the Synagogue*, 130–132.

77. In New England, the "top tier" of Protestant ministers at this time "made between $1200 and $2000." See Donald M. Scott, *From Office to Profession: The New England Ministry, 1750–1850* (Philadelphia: University of Pennsylvania Press, 1978), 113.

78. Wise, *Reminiscences*, 149; Temkin, *Isaac Mayer Wise*, 62–72.

79. Temkin, *Isaac Mayer Wise*, 1–76, esp. 56, 73; Wise, *Reminiscences*, 165; Meyer, *Response to Modernity*, 238–243.

80. *Asmonean* 7 (December 10, 1852): 91; (November 5, 1852): 30.

81. Sarna and Klein, *Jews of Cincinnati*, 14–15; Meyer, *Response to Modernity*, 240.

82. Philipson and Grossman, *Selected Writings of Isaac M. Wise*, 379; *American Israelite*, August 14, 1863, p. 52.

83. For what follows, see Kaufmann Kohler, "David Einhorn, the Uncompromising Champion of Reform Judaism," *CCARYB* 19 (1909): 215–270; Meyer, *Response to Modernity*, 244–250; Rubenstein, *History of Har Sinai Congregation*, unpaginated [22–42].

84. Heller, *As Yesterday When It Is Past*, 68–72.

85. Sherman, *Bernard Illowy;* Kalisch, *Studies in Ancient and Modern Judaism*, 40, 57.

86. Davis, *Emergence of Conservative Judaism*, 142.

87. Marcus, *Memoirs of American Jews*, 2: 283; Marcus, *Jew in the American World*, 175; Benjamin, *Three Years in America*, 1: 79–80.

88. Benjamin, *Three Years in America*, 1: 78.

89. Reissner, "German-American Jews," 104–107; Cohn, "Leo Merzbacher," 21–24; Meyer, *Response to Modernity*, 237.

90. Jonathan D. Sarna, "Max Lilienthal," *ANB*, 13: 653–654; Sarna and Goldman, "From Synagogue-Community to Citadel of Reform," 174.

91. Sharfman, *The First Rabbi*, 715–16; Dantowitz, *Generations and Reflections*, 35–38. Rice's adopted daughter, Caroline, was actually Leucht's first wife. After her untimely death in 1864, he remarried.

92. For what follows, see Eisenstein, *Ozar Zikhronothai*, esp. 246–251, 338–358; Eisenstein, "The History of the First Russian-American Jewish Congregation," 63–74; Sherman, "Struggle for Legitimacy," 63–74.

93. *AJYB* 2 (1900–1901): 185–490.

94. Buchler, "Struggle for Unity," 39–41; Blau and Baron, *Jews of the U.S.*, 930; Sarna, *Jacksonian Jew*, 123–125; Jonathan Frankel, *The Damascus Affair: "Ritual Murder," Politics, and the Jews in 1840* (New York: Cambridge University Press, 1997), 224–227.

95. Sussman, *Isaac Leeser*, 125–130; Moise, *Isaac Harby*, 83–89.

96. Steven Singer, "The Anglo-Jewish Ministry in Early Victorian London," *Modern Judaism* 5 (October 1985): 279–300; Cecil Roth, "Britain's Three Chief Rabbis," *Jewish Leaders*, ed. Leo Jung (New York: Bloch, 1953), 477–490; Isaac Leeser, "Spiritual Authority," *The Occident* 2 (March 1845): 571 available on-line at www.jewish-history.com/Occident/volume2/mar1845/authority.html.

97. Sharfman, *The First Rabbi*, 171–175; Isaac Leeser, "The Jews and Their Religion," *An Original History of the Religious Denominations at Present Existing in the United States*, ed. I. Daniel Rupp (Philadelphia, 1844), 368.

98. Rubenstein, *History of Har Sinai Congregation*, unpaginated [7, 14].

99. Gad Ben-Ami Sarfatti, "The Tablets of the Law as a Symbol of Judaism," in *The Ten Commandments in History and Tradition,* ed. Ben-Zion Segal and Gershon Levi (Jerusalem: Magnes, 1990), 383–418; Lewis, "Touro Synagogue," 286; Wischnitzer, *Synagogue Architecture in the United States,* 54 and s.v. "tablets of the law." For rabbis opposed to the placement of the Ten Commandments in the synagogue, see sources cited in Ovadia Yosef, *Sefer Yalkut Yosef* (Jerusalem, 1985), II, paragraphs 145–146: 12 [in Hebrew].

100. Gershom Scholem, "The Star of David: History of a Symbol," *The Messianic Idea in Judaism* (New York: Schocken, 1971), 257–281; Joaneath Spicer, "The Star of David and Jewish Culture in Prague around 1600, Reflected in Drawings of Roelandt Savery and Paulus van Vianen," *Journal of the Walters Art Gallery* 54 (1996): 203–224; Plaut, *Magen David;* Wischnitzer, *Synagogue Architecture in the United States,* 40–42.

101. Jeffrey H. Tigay, *Deuteronomy: The JPS Torah Commentary* (Philadelphia: Jewish Publication Society, 1996), 438–441; Louis Jacobs, "Shema, Reading of," *EJ* 14, 1370–1374; Sarna, *Jacksonian Jew,* 66; Dantowitz, *Generations and Reflections,* 36; Bratt, "Reorientation of American Protestantism," 81.

102. On this conference, see Plaut, *Growth of Reform Judaism,* 20; Davis, *Emergence of Conservative Judaism,* 130–134, 424; Sussman, *Isaac Leeser,* 196–201; Sherman, *Bernard Illowy,* 151–165; Meyer, *Response to Modernity,* 243–244.

103. David I. Kertzer, *The Kidnapping of Edgardo Mortara* (New York: Knopf, 1997), 127; Korn, *American Reaction to the Mortara Case.*

104. *Israelite,* January 27, 1860, p. 236; February 24, 1860, p. 268; *Occident,* February 16, 1860, p. 278; *Jewish Messenger,* January 2, 1860, p. 44; *Occident,* August 2, 1860, p. 113; August 16, 1860, p. 126; Tarshish, "Board of Delegates of American Israelites," 16–32; Sussman, *Isaac Leeser,* 215–218.

105. *Occident,* July 6, 1859, 88–89; Meyer, *The American Jew in the Civil War,* 277–280; Hertzberg, *Strangers Within the Gate City,* 231.

106. Korn, *American Jewry and the Civil War,* 15–31; Schappes, *Documentary History,* 405–428; Mark Noll, "The Bible and Slavery," *Religion and the American Civil War,* ed. Miller, Stout, and Wilson, 43–73.

107. Korn, *American Jewry and the Civil War,* 15; Hagy, *This Happy Land,* 91–106; Rosen, *Jewish Confederates,* 16, 383 n.23; Dale Rosengarten et al., *Between the Tracks: Charleston's East Side During the Nineteenth Century,* Charleston Museum Archeological Contributions 17 (Charleston: Charleston Museum, 1987), 47; Korn, "Jews and Negro Slavery in the Old South," 152–158.

108. Louis Ruchames, "The Abolitionists and the Jews: Some Further Thoughts," *Bicentennial Festschrift for Jacob Rader Marcus,* ed. Korn, 505–515; S. Yahalom, "Was There a Consensus on the Question of Slavery on the Eve of the Civil War?" *Divre Ha-Kongres Ha-Olami Ha-11 LeMadae Hayahadut* [in Hebrew] (Jerusalem, 1994), part 2, 2: 99–105. On the larger question of the Jewish role in the slave trade, see Eli Faber, *Jews, Slaves, and the Slave Trade* (New York: New York University Press, 1998); Seymour Drescher, "Jews and New Christians in the Atlantic Slave Trade," in *The Jews and the Expansion of Europe to the West,* ed. Bernardini and Fiering, 439–470; David Brion Davis, "The Slave Trade and the Jews," *New York Review of Books,* December 22, 1994, pp. 14–17.

109. Korn, *American Jewry and the Civil War*, xxii, 108, 119; Meyer, *The American Jew in the Civil War*, 303; Marcus, *Jew in the American World*, 223–224.

110. Eli Evans, *Judah P. Benjamin: The Jewish Confederate* (New York: Free Press, 1988).

111. Korn, *American Jewry and the Civil War*, 98–120, esp. 101.

112. Rosen, *Jewish Confederates*, 35–37.

113. Korn, *American Jewry and the Civil War*, 28; Rosen, *Jewish Confederates*, 43, 148–154; Marcus, *Memoirs*, 2: 35, 1: 265; Spiegel, *A Jewish Colonel in the Civil War*, 202.

114. Sussman, *Isaac Leeser*, 218–219; Dianne Ashton, "Shifting Veils: Religion, Politics and Womanhood in the Civil War Writings of American Jewish Women," *Women and American Judaism*, ed. Nadell and Sarna, 81–106.

115. Korn, *American Jewry and the Civil War*, 88–90; Rosen, *Jewish Confederates*, 211–212.

116. Korn, *American Jewry and the Civil War*, 36, 50; *Universal Jewish Encyclopedia* 5 (1941): 134; Davis, "Lincoln-Hart Correspondence," 142–145.

117. Spiegel, *A Jewish Colonel in the Civil War*, 163, 227; Miller, Stout, and Wilson, *Religion and the American Civil War*, 17.

118. Rosen, *Jewish Confederates*, 405.

119. This manuscript is found in the Rabbi Eliyahu Guttmacher collection of the YIVO Institute, Center for Jewish History, New York. I am grateful to Rabbi Victor Reinstein for drawing it to my attention and providing me with a copy.

120. Rosen, *Jewish Confederates*, 199, 233; Korn, *American Jewry and the Civil War*, 88, 97; Spiegel, *A Jewish Colonel in the Civil War*, 163; Young, *Where They Lie*, 124.

121. See www.jewish-history.com/seder.html; *Jewish Messenger*, March 30, 1866, reprinted in Meyer, *The American Jew in the Civil War*, 309–311.

122. Sussman, *Isaac Leeser*, 224–225.

123. Korn, *American Jewry and the Civil War*, 56–97, esp. 64; James Moorhead, *American Apocalypse: Yankee Protestants and the Civil War, 1860–1869* (New Haven, 1978); Randall Miller, "Catholic Religion, Irish Ethnicity, and the Civil War," *Religion and the American Civil War*, ed. Miller, Stout, and Wilson, 264–269.

124. From the copy of the order enclosed in a letter from Isaac M. Wise to Edward Stanton (December 30, 1862), AJA.

125. Ash, "Civil War Exodus," 505–523; John Y. Simon (ed.), *The Papers of Ulysses S. Grant* (Carbondale: Southern Illinois University Press, 1979), 7: 50–57; Korn, *American Jewry and the Civil War*, 121–155.

126. Korn, *American Jewry and the Civil War*, 125; Markens, "Lincoln and the Jews," 118.

127. Korn, *American Jewry and the Civil War*, 126, 156–188; Ash, "Civil War Exodus," 519.

128. Sussman, *Isaac Leeser*, 227 [misdated]; Korn, *American Jewry and the Civil War*, 206.

129. Korn, *American Jewry and the Civil War*, 206–216, 239–243; Emanuel Hertz, *Abraham Lincoln, the Tribute of the Synagogue* (New York, 1927); Meyer, *The American Jew in the Civil War*, frontispiece and 186.

130. Rosen, *Jewish Confederates*, 333; Kohut, *My Portion*, 21, 26–27; Charles Reagan Wilson, *Baptized in Blood: The Religion of the Lost Cause* (Athens: University of Georgia Press, 1980); *Religion and the American Civil War*, ed. Miller, Stout, and Wilson, s.v. "Lost Cause."

131. Rosen, *Jewish Confederates,* 339; see Rosengarten and Rosengarten, *A Portion of the People,* 134–135.

132. Rosen, *Jewish Confederates,* 338–340, 367–368; Moses Jacob Ezekiel, *Memoirs from the Baths of Diocletian,* ed. Joseph Gutmann and Stanley F. Chyet (Detroit: Wayne State University Press, 1975), 30–41, 71–73, 112–113.

133. Benny Kraut, "Judaism Triumphant," 179–230, esp. 192–196; *New Era* I (October 1870): 1–2, and 3 (1873): 2; Kalisch, *Studies in Ancient and Modern Judaism,* 61.

134. Engelman, "Jewish Statistics"; Wischnitzer, *Synagogue Architecture in the United States,* 70–73, 76; Heller, *As Yesterday When It Is Past;* Sarna, "A Sort of Paradise for the Hebrews," 152; Sarna and Goldman, "From Synagogue-Community to Citadel of Reform," 176.

135. Meyer, *Response to Modernity,* 251–252; Meyer, *Judaism Within Modernity,* 223–238; Sarna and Goldman, "From Synagogue-Community to Citadel of Reform," 177. For a brief history of praying without a head-covering, a practice that began in America in 1864 at Temple Emanu-El in New York and spread rapidly in the 1870s, see *CCARYB* 28 (1918): 122–123.

136. Sarna and Goldman, "From Synagogue-Community to Citadel of Reform," 178.

137. For what follows, see Sarna, "The Debate over Mixed Seating in the American Synagogue."

138. Davis, *Emergence of Conservative Judaism,* 162–165.

139. Kuznets, "Immigration of Russian Jews to the United States," 42; Zvi Hirsch Bernstein, "An Account of the Jews and Judaism 34 Years Ago in New York (circa 1870)," translated and annotated by Gary P. Zola, *American Jewish Archives* 50 (1998): 113; Ehrlich, *Zion in the Valley,* 248–250; Gutstein, *A Precious Heritage,* 202–205; Gurock, *American Jewish Orthodoxy in Historical Perspective,* 77; *Israelitische Wochenschrift* as quoted in Meyer, *Response to Modernity,* 252.

140. Fox, "On the Road to Unity," 145–193.

141. Meyer, *Response to Modernity,* 260–263; Meyer, "A Centennial History," 7–38; Fierstien, *A Different Spirit,* 13–14; Sarna, "A Sort of Paradise for the Hebrews," 152.

142. The discussion that follows is revised and condensed from Sarna, "Late Nineteenth-Century American Jewish Awakening," 1–25; also published in different form as *A Great Awakening: The Transformation That Shaped Twentieth-Century American Judaism and Its Implications for Today* (New York: Council for Initiatives in Jewish Education, 1995).

143. Kraut, *From Reform Judaism to Ethical Culture.* On the intermarriage of Helen Wise, see Anne C. Rose, *Beloved Strangers: Interfaith Families in Nineteenth-Century America* (Cambridge: Harvard University Press, 2001), 77–78, 115–118.

144. Paul A. Carter, *The Spiritual Crisis of the Gilded Age* (Dekalb: Northern Illinois University Press, 1971); Cohen, "Challenges of Darwinism and Biblical Criticism to American Judaism," 121–157; Swetlitz, "American Jewish Responses to Darwin and Evolutionary Theory," 209–245; Kraut, "Judaism Triumphant," 202–225; Kraut, "The Ambivalent Relations of American Reform Judaism with Unitarianism," 58–68.

145. Cohen, "American Jewish Reactions to Anti-Semitism in Western Europe," 29–65, esp. 31; Meyer, *Judaism Within Modernity,* 323–344; Dinnerstein, *Antisemitism in*

America, 39–41; Birmingham, *Our Crowd,* 169–180; *Coney Island and the Jews* (New York: G. W. Carleton, 1879); Michael Selzer (ed.), *Kike! A Documentary History of Anti-Semitism in America* (New York: Meridian, 1972), 56.

CHAPTER 4: TWO WORLDS OF AMERICAN JUDAISM

1. Max Cohen to Solomon Solis-Cohen (October 14, 1879, November 10, 1879) and Cyrus L. Sulzberger ("Yitzhak Aryeh") to Solomon Solis-Cohen (October 5, 1880), Solomon Solis-Cohen Papers, Collection of Helen Solis-Cohen Sax and Hays Solis-Cohen, Jr., National Museum of American Jewish History, Philadelphia. I am grateful to Helen Solis-Cohen Sax for granting me access to these papers.
2. Max Cohen to Solomon Solis-Cohen (November 10, 1879), Solis-Cohen Papers; "An Appeal to the Israelites of New York," June 21, 1868, reprinted in Abraham J. Karp, "American Jewish History Source Material," in author's possession.
3. Sarna, "Is Judaism Compatible with American Civil Religion?" 162–163; Max Cohen to Solomon Solis-Cohen (December 22, 1879), Solis-Cohen Papers. See also Joselit, "'Merry Chanukah,'" 103–129; and Joselit, *The Wonders of America,* 53–89.
4. Cowen, *Memories of an American Jew,* 40–56, esp. 49, 55; Max Cohen to Solomon Solis-Cohen (November 19, 1879), Solis-Cohen Papers.
5. Cowen, *Memories of an American Jew,* 40–111, esp. 42, 50; Wyszkowski, *A Community in Conflict,* xiii–xvii, 101; Max Cohen, "Some Memories of Alexander Kohut," in Kohut, *Ethics of the Fathers,* xcviii.
6. Cyrus L. Sulzberger to Solomon Solis-Cohen (October 5, 1880), Solis-Cohen Papers.
7. For an extended discussion of this theme, see Sarna, "The Late Nineteenth-Century American Jewish Awakening," from which this section is largely drawn.
8. *The Jewish Advance* 79 (December 12, 1879): 4; *Jewish Chronicle* [London], March 11, 1887, p. 13; *American Hebrew* 56 (1894): 22, 181.
9. Robert Singerman, *Judaica Americana: A Bibliography of Publications to 1900* (New York: Greenwood Press, 1990); Sarna, *JPS,* 34–44; Mitchell E. Panzer, "Gratz College: A Community's Involvement in Jewish Education," *Gratz College Anniversary Volume,* ed. Isidore D. Passow and Samuel T. Lachs (Philadelphia: Gratz College, 1971), 1–9; Peggy K. Pearlstein, "Understanding Through Education: One Hundred Years of the Jewish Chautauqua Society, 1893–1993" (Ph.D. diss., George Washington University, 1993); Rogow, *Gone to Another Meeting,* 23.
10. Higham, *Send These to Me,* 71–80; Joe Rooks Rapport, "The Lazarus Sisters: A Family Portrait" (Ph.D. diss., Washington University, 1988), 12–108; Lazarus, *Epistle to the Hebrews,* 8, 64, 73; Emma Lazarus, *Selections from Her Poetry and Prose,* ed. Morris U. Schappes (New York: Emma Lazarus Federation of Jewish Women's Clubs, 1978), 35–37.
11. Lazarus, *Epistle to the Hebrews,* 34–35, 77; Zieger, "Emma Lazarus and Pre-Herzlian Zionism," 77–108.
12. Cowen, *Memories of an American Jew,* 344.
13. Litman, *Ray Frank Litman;* Clar and Kramer, "The Girl Rabbi of the Golden West," 99–111, 223–236, 336–351. For the year of Ray Frank's birth, see Sarna, "The Late Nineteenth-Century American Jewish Awakening," n.46.
14. *Jewish Messenger,* May 23, 1890, reprinted in Marcus, *The American Jewish Woman,*

380; Litman, *Ray Frank Litman,* 8–9, 12–13; Umansky and Ashton, *Four Centuries of Jewish Women's Spirituality,* 128–129.

15. Litman, *Ray Frank Litman,* 68, 15, 43–45, 55–57.

16. Ibid., 50; *Papers of the Jewish Women's Congress* (Philadelphia: Jewish Publication Society of America, 1894), 8, cf. pp. 52–65; *Reform Advocate,* August 7, 1989, p. 412, as cited in Clar and Kramer, "Girl Rabbi of the Golden West," 231.

17. For her subsequent career and her contributions to the founding of Hillel, see Litman, *Ray Frank Litman,* 143–202; and Winton U. Solberg, "The Early Years of the Jewish Presence at the University of Illinois," *Religion and American Culture* 2 (Summer 1992): 215–245.

18. Rogow, *Gone to Another Meeting,* 43–78; Goldman, "The Ambivalence of Reform Judaism," 477–499.

19. Rogow, *Gone to Another Meeting,* 53, 76; Wenger, "Jewish Women and Voluntarism," 16–36, esp. 36.

20. Felicia Herman, "From Priestess to Hostess: Sisterhoods of Personal Service in New York City, 1887–1936," *Women and American Judaism,* ed. Nadell and Sarna, 148–181; William Toll, "From Domestic Judaism to Public Ritual," ibid., 138–140.

21. Pool, *An Old Faith in the New World,* 369–370.

22. Dash, *Life of Henrietta Szold;* Levin, *Szolds of Lombard Street;* Sarna, *JPS,* 23–135; *AJYB* 16 (1914–15): 284.

23. William R. Hutchison, *Errand to the World: American Protestant Thought and Foreign Missions* (Chicago: University of Chicago Press, 1987), 111; Carol B. Kutscher, "Hadassah," in Dobkowski (ed.), *Jewish American Voluntary Organizations,* 151–152; Carol B. Kutscher, "The Early Years of Hadassah, 1912–1922" (Ph.D. diss., Brandeis University, 1976); Henrietta Szold to Alice L. Seligsberg (October 10, 1913), in Marvin Lowenthal, *Henrietta Szold: Life and Letters* (New York: Viking Press, 1942), 82.

24. David Stern to Bernhard Felsenthal (April 24, 1884), Felsenthal Papers, AJHS; Sarna, "The Late Nineteenth-Century American Jewish Awakening," 7; Sarna, "The Making of an American Jewish Culture," 150–151.

25. Meyer, *Response to Modernity,* 263; Meyer, "A Centennial History," 37–38.

26. Fierstien, *A Different Spirit,* 20–23; John J. Appel, "The Treyfa Banquet," *Commentary* 41 (February 1966): 75–78; Meyer, "A Centennial History," 41–43.

27. Kohut, *My Portion,* 81, 93; Kohut, *Ethics of the Fathers,* liv; Waxman, *Tradition and Change,* 93; Nadell, *Conservative Judaism in America,* 165–168.

28. Kohut, *Ethics of the Fathers,* 7; Kaufmann Kohler, *Backwards or Forwards: A Series of Discourses on Reform Judaism* (New York, 1885), 7, 9; Davis, *Emergence of Conservative Judaism,* 225.

29. Kohut, *My Portion,* 80–84; Davis, *Emergence of Conservative Judaism,* 200–228; Fierstien, *A Different Spirit,* 37.

30. *Proceedings of the Pittsburgh Rabbinical Conference* (1923), reprinted in Jacob (ed.), *Changing World of Reform Judaism,* esp. 93, 94, 104 (emphasis in original); see Meyer, *Response to Modernity,* 265–270; Sarna, "New Light on the Pittsburgh Platform of 1885"; and Sefton D. Temkin, "The Pittsburgh Platform: A Centenary Assessment," *Journal of Reform Judaism* 32 (Fall 1985): 1–12.

31. Jacob, *Changing World of Reform Judaism,* 92–103.

32. The platform is reprinted in Meyer, *Response to Modernity,* 387–388.

33. Meyer, *Response to Modernity,* 269–270, 454 n.14; Sarna, "New Light on the Pittsburgh Platform of 1885," 367–368.

34. *Proceedings of the Union of American Hebrew Congregations* 2 (1879–85): 1573, 1618, 1629, 1639, 1641; "Authentic Report" in Jacob (ed.), *Changing World of Reform Judaism,* 92–102, 109.

35. Sarna, "The Late Nineteenth-Century American Jewish Awakening," 18, 25 n.69.

36. Ibid., 18–19, 25 n.72.

37. Kuznets, "Immigration of Russian Jews to the United States," esp. 39–40, 51, 63.

38. John D. Klier and Shlomo Lambroza (eds.), *Pogroms: Anti-Jewish Violence in Modern Russian History* (Cambridge, 1992), esp. 328; Gartner, "Jewish Migrants en Route from Europe to North America: Traditions and Realities," 49–61.

39. *AJYB* 3 (1901–2): 83, 86; Kuznets, "Immigration of Russian Jews to the United States," 51, 83.

40. *Ha-Melitz* 18 (April 27, 1882): 302, as quoted in *AJHQ* 59 (December 1969): 182–183.

41. Kuznets, "Immigration of Russian Jews to the United States," 49; Gur Alroey, "The Jewish Immigration at the Beginning of the Twentieth Century: The Case of Palestine" [in Hebrew] (Ph.D. diss., Hebrew University, 2001), 18. During the peak years of 1905–14, the disproportion in favor of America was even greater: a total of 1,089,000 East European Jews emigrated to the United States, but only 21,654 to Palestine (Alroey, 108).

42. Gartner, "Jewish Migrants en Route from Europe to North America," 54; Levi, *Memorial Volume,* 59; Rosengarten, *A Portion of the People,* 146; Rikoon, *Rachel Calof's Story,* esp. 105–133; Rischin, *Promised City,* 51, 94, 297 n.26.

43. Sarna, "Myth of No Return," 256–268; Kuznets, "Immigration of Russian Jews to the United States," 95–96.

44. Israel Meir Hacohen, *The Dispersed of Israel* (New York, 1951), 316–317; Rothkoff, "The American Sojourns of Ridbaz," 560; Hertzberg, "Treifene Medine," 7–30.

45. Akiva Ben Ezra, "Rabbi Pinchas Michael ZT"L" [in Hebrew], in *Antopol: Sefer Yizkor* (Tel Aviv, 1972), 49; Karp, "New York Chooses a Chief Rabbi," 137–141.

46. Bartal, "Heavenly America," 511–522 [in Hebrew], contains all of these quotations; translations mine.

47. Anatole Leroy-Beaulieu, "Jewish Immigrants and Judaism in the United States," *Judaean Addresses* 2 (1917): 35; Hertzberg, *Jews in America,* 161; Kuznets, "Immigration of Russian Jews to the United States," 104–112, 122. In addition, Jews from northwestern Russia were more likely to immigrate to America than were Jews from other regions; see Shaul Stampfer, "The Geographic Background of East European Jewish Migration to the United States before World War I," in *Migration Across Time and Nations,* ed. Ira A. Glazier and Luigi De Rosa (New York: Holmes & Meier, 1986), 227.

48. Caplan, "Rabbi Isaac Margolis," 225; Rothkoff, "American Sojourns of Ridbaz," 561. See Liebman, "Orthodoxy in American Jewish Life," 27–30; David Singer, "David Levinsky's Fall: A Note on the Liebman Thesis," *American Quarterly* 19 (Winter 1967): 696–706.

49. Lisitzky, *In the Grip of Cross-Currents,* 66–69.

50. Caplan, "Rabbi Isaac Margolis," 231 (translation from Hebrew mine); Rischin,

Promised City, 77; Marcus Ravage, *An American in the Making: The Life Story of an Immigrant* (1917; New York: Dover, 1971), 87; Jonathan D. Sarna, "From Immigrants to Ethnics: Toward a New Theory of 'Ethnicization,'" *Ethnicity* 5 (1978): 370–378.

51. This classification follows Dawidowicz, *On Equal Terms,* 47–49.

52. Weinberger, *People Walk on Their Heads,* 42, 59; *Yevreiski Mir,* February 4, 1910, as translated in Judith Zabarenko [Abrams], "The Image of America in the Russo-Jewish Press, 1881–1910" (Rabbinic Thesis, Hebrew Union College–Jewish Institute of Religion, 1985), 114.

53. Weinberger, *People Walk on Their Heads,* 59; Karp, *Jewish Continuity in America,* 52–53; Caplan, "In God We Trust," 89–93.

54. Weinberger, *People Walk on Their Heads,* 7–9, 25, 59; Caplan, "Rabbi Isaac Margolis," 229. Cf. Hapgood, *Spirit of the Ghetto,* 53–75. For evidence of anticlericalism among more established American Jews, see Sarna, "Making of an American Jewish Culture," 151; and Levi, *Memorial Volume,* 150–158.

55. *AJYB* 2 (1900–1901): 500; Engelman, "Jewish Statistics in the U.S. Census of Religious Bodies," 143, 152; *Yiddish Velt,* February 2, 1904, p. 1, as cited in David Weinberg, "The Jewish Theological Seminary and the 'Downtown' Jews of New York at the Turn of the Century," in Wertheimer (ed.), *Tradition Renewed,* 2: 13; *Jewish Communal Register,* 121; Howe, *World of Our Fathers,* 190–191.

56. Weinberger, *People Walk on Their Heads,* 15–16, 46–50; Goren, *New York Jews and the Quest for Community,* 79; Berman, *Shehitah,* 294–305; Gastwirt, *Fraud, Corruption, and Holiness,* 55–123.

57. Gurock, *American Jewish Orthodoxy,* 77; Heinze, *Adapting to Abundance,* 51–59.

58. Goldstein (ed.), *Forty Years of Struggle for a Principle,* 17–19. Joselit, *New York's Jewish Jews,* 12, describes this volume as "a combination fable and cautionary tale."

59. Rischin, *Promised City,* 146–147; *Shas Tehinah Hadashah* (New York: Hebrew Publishing Company, 1916), 38–41 (translation from Yiddish mine). In East European cities like Odessa and Lemberg, Sabbath violations also became common among Jews at this time; see Morawska, *Insecure Prosperity,* 22 and sources cited therein.

60. Hyman, *Gender and Assimilation in Modern Jewish History,* 93–133, esp. 97; Heinze, *Adapting to Abundance,* 51–85; Weinberger, *People Walk on Their Heads,* 75, 123.

61. Engelman, "Jewish Statistics in the U.S. Census of Religious Bodies," 151.

62. Swichkow and Gartner, *History of the Jews of Milwaukee,* 197; Gartner, *Jews of Cleveland,* 128, 133; Plaut, *Jews in Minnesota,* 129; Kula et al., *Writing Home,* 331–332.

63. For what follows, see Soyer, *Jewish Immigrant Associations,* esp. 49–112.

64. Bernheimer, *Russian Jew in the United States,* 162.

65. Soyer, *Jewish Immigrant Associations,* 58.

66. Ibid., 150; Kaufman, *Shul with a Pool,* 169–174.

67. *AJYB* 2 (1900–1901): 257, 313, 318, 497; Engelman, "Jewish Statistics in the U.S. Census of Religious Bodies," 139–154; *Jewish Communal Register,* 90, 122 and facing chart.

68. Howe, *World of Our Fathers,* 299; *Frayer Arbayter Shtime,* September 19, 1890, as translated and quoted in Antonovsky and Tcherikower (eds.), *Early Jewish Labor Movement in the United States,* 257.

69. Melech Epstein, *Profiles of Eleven* (Detroit: Wayne State University Press, 1965), 67.

70. Paula E. Hyman, "Immigrant Women and Consumer Protest," 91–105; Weinberger,

People Walk on Their Heads, 15–16, 46–50; Goren, *New York Jews and the Quest for Community,* 78.

71. *Yevreiski Mir,* February 4, 1910, as translated in Judith Zabarenko [Abrams], "The Image of America in the Russo-Jewish Press, 1881–1910" (Rabbinic Thesis, Hebrew Union College–Jewish Institute of Religion, 1985), 112–113; Rikoon, *Rachel Calof's Story,* 85–86; Howe, *World of Our Fathers,* 191–193; Goren, *New York Jews and the Quest for Community,* 78.

72. Metzker, *Bintel Brief,* 97–98. Concerning other holiday observances, see Heinze, *Adapting to Abundance,* 68–85.

73. Antonovsky and Tcherikower (eds.), *Early Jewish Labor Movement in the United States,* esp. 252–253; Howe, *World of Our Fathers,* 106; Metzker, *Bintel Brief,* 98.

74. Rikoon, *Rachel Calof's Story,* 47, 49; for other examples, see Kate Simon, *Bronx Primitive: Portraits in a Childhood* (New York: Harper, 1982), 14, 64, 114, 117, 176.

75. *New York Tribune* (August 16, 1903), in Schoener, *Portal to America,* 107; Weinberger, *People Walk on Their Heads,* 14–17, 76–83; Regina Stein, "The Road to Bat Mitzvah in America," in Nadell and Sarna (eds.), *Women and American Judaism,* 223–234.

76. Soyer, *Jewish Immigrant Associations,* 87–93; Arthur A. Goren, "Traditional Institutions Transplanted," 62–78; Gary P. Zola, "The People's Preacher: A Study of the Life and Writings of Zvi Hirsch Masliansky (1856–1943)" (Ordination thesis, Hebrew Union College–Jewish Institute of Religion, 1982), 116–117.

77. Weinberger, *People Walk on Their Heads,* 51–56; Mordecai M. Kaplan and Bernard Cronson, "First Community Survey of Jewish Education in New York City, 1909," *Jewish Education* 20 (1949): 113–116.

78. Gurock, *American Jewish Orthodoxy,* 78; Kaufman, *Shul with a Pool,* 175; Weinberger, *People Walk on Their Heads,* 12, 106.

79. Weinberger, *People Walk on Their Heads,* 12–14, 98–106; Gurock, *American Jewish Orthodoxy,* 78–79; Slobin, *Chosen Voices,* 51–77. For problems faced by cantors, see *Jewish Communal Register,* 301–305.

80. Weinberger, *People Walk on Their Heads,* 12; Kaufman, *Shul with a Pool,* 178.

81. Kaufman, *Shul with a Pool,* 183–184; Gurock, *American Jewish Orthodoxy,* 24.

82. Kaufman, *Shul with a Pool,* 174–193; Gurock, *American Jewish Orthodoxy,* 78.

83. Compare Joselit, *New York's Jewish Jews,* 25–53, esp. 26.

84. Weinberger, *People Walk on Their Heads,* 33, 55; Gurock, *American Jewish Orthodoxy,* 104–5; Klaperman, *Story of Yeshiva University,* 17–33.

85. On "accommodation" and "resistance" as themes in American Orthodoxy, see Gurock, *American Jewish Orthodoxy,* esp. xii–xxv, 1–62, 103–116.

86. Karp, "New York Chooses a Chief Rabbi," 132–133, 188.

87. Ibid., 135–137, 191.

88. Ibid., 129–187; Kimmy Caplan, "Rabbi Jacob Joseph, New York's Chief Rabbi: New Perspectives," *HUCA* 67 (1996): Hebrew Section, 1–43; Gurock, *American Jewish Orthodoxy,* 103–116; Menahem Glenn, *Israel Salanter: Religious Ethical Thinker* (New York: Bloch, 1953), 90–92.

89. Abraham Cahan, "A Back Number," in *Grandma Never Lived in America,* ed. Moses Rischin (Bloomington: Indiana University Press, 1985), 73.

90. Dinnerstein, "Funeral of Rabbi Jacob Joseph," 275–298.

91. Kohut, *My Portion,* 80–81; Kohut in *American Hebrew,* January 7, 1887, as quoted in

Scult, *Judaism Faces the Twentieth Century,* 39. On the founding of the Seminary, see Fierstien, *A Different Spirit,* and Diner, "Like the Antelope and the Badger," 3–42.

92. Fierstien, *A Different Spirit,* 46, 58; David Weinberg, "JTS and the 'Downtown' Jews of New York at the Turn of the Century," in Wertheimer (ed.), *Tradition Renewed,* 2: 15; Karp, "Solomon Schechter Comes to America," 61; Gurock, *American Jewish Orthodoxy,* 114.

93. Markovitz, "Henry Pereira Mendes," 377; *AJYB* 1 (1899–1900): 99–102; Fierstien, *A Different Spirit,* 110; Joselit, *New York's Jewish Jews,* 6–7; Saul Bernstein, *The Orthodox Union Story: A Centenary Portrayal* (Northvale, N.J.: Jason Aronson, 1997), 47–61.

94. Diner, "Like the Antelope and the Badger," 34–35; Gurock, *American Jewish Orthodoxy,* 83–86, 155–158, 285–297, esp. 287; Berman, "A New Spirit on the East Side," 60–75; Reid et al., *Dictionary of Christianity in America,* 256–257; William Shaw, *The Evolution of an Endeavorer: An Autobiography* (Boston: Christian Endeavor World, 1924).

95. Karp, "Solomon Schechter Comes to America," 54; Sarna, "Two Traditions of Seminary Scholarship," 55–61; *AJYB* 4 (1902–3): 15.

96. *Yiddishes Tageblatt,* English Department, November 24, 1902, reproduced in Wertheimer (ed.), *Tradition Renewed,* 2: 30; Sarna, *JPS,* 54–55; Norman Bentwich, *Solomon Schechter: A Biography* (Philadelphia, 1948).

97. Markovitz, "Henry Pereira Mendes," 380, n.51.

98. Mel Scult, "Schechter's Seminary," in Wertheimer (ed.), *Tradition Renewed,* 1: 45–102; Jenna Weissman Joselit, "By Design: Building the Campus of the Jewish Theological Seminary," ibid., esp. 275; Baila R. Shargel, "The Texture of Seminary Life During the Finkelstein Era," ibid., 518.

99. "Sermon Delivered at Temple Emanu-El, April 24, 1910," reprinted in Goren, *Dissenter in Zion,* 111.

100. Sarna, *JPS,* 55; Waxman, *Tradition and Change,* 111–127; Karla Goldman, "A Respectful Rivalry: The Hebrew Union College–Jewish Institute of Religion and JTS," in Wertheimer (ed.), *Tradition Renewed,* 2: 595–606.

101. *Constitution of the United Orthodox Rabbis of America, Organized 24th of Tamuz 5662* [in Hebrew] (New York, 1902); *Sefer Ha-Yovel Shel Agudath Ha-Rabbanim . . .* [in Hebrew] (New York, 1928); Gurock, *American Jewish Orthodoxy,* 16; Markovitz, "Henry Pereira Mendes," 381. The organization subsequently changed its English name to the Union of Orthodox Rabbis of the United States and Canada.

102. Gurock, *Men and Women of Yeshiva,* 18–42, esp. 19; Klaperman, *Story of Yeshiva University,* 48–72.

103. Gurock, *The Men and Women of Yeshiva,* 19, 33; Jeffrey S. Gurock, "Yeshiva Students at JTS," in Wertheimer (ed.), *Tradition Renewed,* 475–483.

104. Meyer, *Response to Modernity,* 264; Samuel Schulman, "American Judaism," *Twenty-Second Council Union of American Hebrew Congregations,* ed. Isidor Lewi (New York, 1911), 77–95.

105. Kaufmann Kohler, *The Mission of Israel and Its Application to Modern Times* (New York, 1919); Emil G. Hirsch, *My Religion* (New York, 1925), 263; Joseph Krauskopf, *Fifteenth Series of Sunday Lectures Before Reform Congregation Keneseth Israel, 1891–1892* (Philadelphia, 1892).

106. Meyer, *Response to Modernity,* 286–289; *CCARYB* 28 (1918): 102; Feldman, "Social Gospel and the Jews," 308–322; Mervis, "Social Justice Movement," 171–230.

107. Leo Franklin, "A New Congregational Policy," Beth El Scrapbook, Box X-201, AJA; Stephen S. Wise, "What Is a Free Synagogue?" *Free Synagogue Pulpit* (New York: Bloch, 1908), 1: 10–15; Sarna, "Seating and the American Synagogue," 195–200.

108. Berman, "A New Spirit on the East Side," esp. 79.

109. Goren, *Dissenter in Zion,* 112; *Judaean Addresses* 2 (1917): 189–192; Cohen, *Not Free to Desist,* 10, 17; Meyer, *Response to Modernity,* 293.

110. Meyer, "A Centennial History," 75.

111. For an elaboration of this theme, see my "Cult of Synthesis in American Jewish Culture," 52–79, where full documentation is provided.

112. *AJYB* 5 (1903–4): 39; Cyrus Adler, *The Voice of America on Kishineff* (Philadelphia, 1904); Philip E. Schoenberg, "The American Reaction to the Kishinev Pogrom of 1903," *AJHQ* 63 (March 1974): 262–283; Edward H. Judge, *Easter in Kishinev: Anatomy of a Pogrom* (New York, 1992).

113. Sarna, "The Twentieth Century Through American Jewish Eyes," 18–19; Cohen, "Abrogation of the Russo-American Treaty of 1832," 3–41; Goldstein, *Politics of Ethnic Pressure,* esp. 143–144.

114. Cohen, *Not Free to Desist,* 37–53; Panitz, "In Defense of the Jewish Immigrant," 57–97.

115. Goren, *New York Jews and the Quest for Community,* esp. 3, 251; *Report of the Executive Committee Presented at the Second Annual Convention of the Jewish Community (Kehillah) New York, February 25 and 26, 1911* (New York, 1911), 5.

116. *American Hebrew* 61 (May 7, 1897): 18; Friesel, *Zionist Movement in the United States;* and Urofsky, *American Zionism from Herzl to the Holocaust,* are standard works.

117. Israel Klausner, "Adam Rosenberg: One of the Earliest American Zionists," *Herzl Year Book* 1 (1958): 232–287; Gurock, *American Jewish Orthodoxy,* 117–133; Henrietta Szold to Elvira N. Solis (December 12, 1909), in Marvin Lowenthal, *Henrietta Szold: Life and Letters* (New York, 1942), 67; Halpern, "The Americanization of Zionism," 15–33; Ofer Shiff, "The Integrative Function of Early American Zionism," *The Journal of Israeli History* 15 (1994): 1–16; Sarna, "A Projection of America as It Ought to Be," 41.

118. *Proceedings of the Union of American Hebrew Congregations* 5 (1898–1903): 4002; Meyer, "American Reform Judaism and Zionism," 49–64.

119. Ava Kahn (ed.), *Jewish Life in the American West* (Seattle: University of Washington Press, 2002), 25.

120. Naomi W. Cohen, "Reaction of Reform Judaism in America to Political Zionism," esp. 380; Meyer, "A Centennial History," 66–67; Schechter, *Seminary Addresses and Other Papers,* 93; Sarna, "Converts to Zionism in the American Reform Movement," esp. 196–199.

121. Sarna, "Greatest Jew in the World Since Jesus Christ," 346–364; Bernard A. Rosenblatt, *Social Zionism* (New York: Public Publishing, 1919), 13; Sarna, "A Projection of America as It Ought to Be," 54–57.

122. Schechter, *Seminary Addresses,* xii.

123. Kaufman, *Shul with a Pool,* 196–200; Yosef Salmon, "The Mizrachi Movement in

America: A Belated but Sturdy Offshoot," *AJA* 48 (Fall–Winter 1996): 161–175; "Mizrachi," *EJ* 12, col. 175–180; Friesel, *Zionist Movement in the United States,* 135–137.

124. Calculated from *AJYB* 16 (1914–15): 358.

CHAPTER 5: AN ANXIOUS SUBCULTURE

1. *New York Times* (December 16, 1917), reprinted in *Jewish Communal Register,* 1485–1490; other quotes from 1470, 1472.
2. *Jewish Communal Register,* 1480; Rosenfelt, *This Thing of Giving.*
3. Jacob Schiff, "An Appeal," in *Jewish Communal Register,* 1479; Morris Lazaron in *CCARYB* 30 (1920): 258.
4. *AJYB* 17 (1915–16): 269, 226.
5. Bauer, *My Brother's Keeper,* 3–18; *Jewish Communal Register,* 1470, 1473–1478.
6. Szajkowski, *Jews, Wars, and Communism,* 1: 3, 10, 65–110; Zosa Szajkowski, *Catalogue of the Exhibition: Morris Rosenfeld (1863–1923) and His Time* (New York: YIVO, 1962), 21 #480; Scult (ed.), *Communings of the Spirit,* 1: 118; Goren, *Dissenter in Zion,* 24–27; Zosa Szajkowski, "The Pacifism of Judah Magnes," *Conservative Judaism* 22 (Spring 1968): 36–55; G. A. Dobbert, "The Ordeal of Gotthard Deutsch," *AJA* 20 (1968): 129–155.
7. *The War Record of American Jews* (New York, 1919); *AJYB* 20 (1918–19): 173–227; 21 (1919–20): 142–148. See Christopher M. Sterba, *Good Americans: Italian and Jewish Immigrants During the First World War* (New York: Oxford, 2003).
8. Charles J. Teller, "The Jewish Welfare Board," *AJYB* 20 (1918–19): 98–102; Janowsky, *JWB Survey,* 45–61.
9. *Abridged Prayer Book for Jews in the Army and Navy of the United States* (Philadelphia: Jewish Publication Society, 1917); *AJYB* 20 (1918–19): 95.
10. *AJYB* 20 (1918–19): 95; *CCARYB* 28 (1918): 77–84, 129.
11. *CCARYB* 28 (1918): 81, 83; Szajkowski, *Jews, Wars, and Communism,* 1: 352.
12. Scult (ed.), *Communings of the Spirit,* 1: 132–133; Morawska, *Insecure Prosperity,* 72–73 and works cited n.2; Moore, *At Home in America,* 22–23, 61.
13. Higham, *Strangers in the Land,* 264–299; Dinnerstein, *Antisemitism in America,* 78–127.
14. Szajkowski, *Jews, Wars, and Communism,* vol. 2, esp. 13.
15. Reznikoff (ed.), *Louis Marshall Champion of Liberty,* 1: 174–182, 204; *AJYB* 24 (1922–23): 355–356.
16. *CCARYB* 31 (1921): 107; Kuznets, "Immigration of Russian Jews to the United States," 46; Teller, *Strangers and Natives,* 98; Higham, *Strangers in the Land,* 300–330.
17. Dinnerstein, *Antisemitism in America,* 3–104; Dinnerstein, *The Leo Frank Case;* Dinnerstein, "The Fate of Leo Frank," 98–109; Stephen J. Goldfarb, "The Slaton Memorandum: A Governor Looks Back at His Decision to Commute the Death Sentence of Leo Frank," *AJH* 88 (September 2000): 325–339.
18. Dinnerstein, *Antisemitism in America,* 78; *CCARYB* 32 (1922): 101.
19. Henry Ford, *The International Jew* (4 vols.; New York, 1920–22), chs. 33, 47; Baldwin, *Henry Ford and the Jews,* 238–239; Ribuffo, "Henry Ford and *The International Jew,*" 437–477.

20. *CCARYB* 32 (1922): 20; *AJYB* 25 (1923–24): 192; Sarna and Golden, "The Twentieth Century Through American Jewish Eyes," 33–35. For Henry Ford's attack on Kol Nidre, see *Dearborn Independent* (November 5, 1921), available online at http://www .noontidepress.com/books/ford/ij71.html.

21. Sprecher, "Let Them Drink and Forget Our Poverty," 134–179, esp. 161; *AJYB* 25 (1923–24): 377–379, 401–425; Golinkin, *The Responsa of Professor Louis Ginzberg,* III–133 [English section], 1–77 [Hebrew section].

22. Alexander, *Jazz Age Jews,* esp. 52; Stember, *Jews in the Mind of America,* 54.

23. Dinnerstein, *Antisemitism in America,* 85–86.

24. Ibid., 92–93; Moore, *At Home in America,* 38.

25. Dinnerstein, *Antisemitism in America,* 96–99; Jenny Goldstein, "Transcending Boundaries: Boston's Catholics and Jews, 1929–1965" (Senior honors thesis, Brandeis University, 2001), available on-line, http//www.bc.edu/bc-org/research/cjl/articles/ goldstein.htm, esp. ch. 2; J. Stack, *International Conflict in an American City: Boston's Irish, Italians, and Jews, 1935–1944* (Westport, Conn., 1979), 134–139.

26. Hertzberg, *The Jews in America,* 217.

27. Babylonian Talmud, Tractate Shavuoth, p. 39a; Morawska, *Insecure Prosperity,* 20; Wenger, *New York Jews and the Great Depression,* 10–32; Morton Weinfeld, "The Ethnic Sub-Economy: Explication and Analysis of the Jews of Montreal," in *The Jews of Canada,* ed. Robert J. Brym, William Shaffir, and Morton Weinfeld (Toronto: Oxford University Press, 1993), 218–237.

28. Kahan, *Essays in Jewish Social and Economic History,* 135; *AJYB* 21 (1919–20): 334; Marianne Sanua, *Going Greek: Jewish College Fraternities in the United States, 1895–1945* (Detroit: Wayne State University Press, 2003); *Jewish Communal Register,* 562; *AJYB* 33 (1931–32): 148; Kanfer, *A Summer World,* 65–66, 77.

29. Moore, *At Home in America,* 30–32; Gartner, *Jews of Cleveland,* 270; Morawska, *Insecure Prosperity,* 77.

30. Seymour Leventman, "From Shtetl to Suburb," in *The Ghetto and Beyond,* ed. Peter I. Rose (New York: Random House, 1969), 43–44; Sorkin, *Transformation of German Jewry,* 122–123; cf. 5–8.

31. Julius Drachsler, *Intermarriage in New York City* (New York, 1921), 43; *AJYB* 60 (1959): 9; Joselit, *The Wonders of America,* 43–54.

32. *AJYB* 31 (1929–30): 175; Tina Levitan, *Islands of Compassion: A History of the Jewish Hospitals of New York* (New York, 1964), 19, notes that by 1964 there were "not less than seventy Jewish hospitals in 26 cities." Major libraries even kept Jewish books segregated from their general book collections; see Jonathan D. Sarna, "Jewish Culture Comes to America," *Gesher* 48 (Summer 2002): 52–60 [in Hebrew].

33. Vivian Gornick, "There Is No More Community," *Interchange* 2 (April 1977): 4; cf. Moore, *At Home in America,* 62–64.

34. Goodman (ed.), *The Faith of Secular Jews,* 54.

35. Ibid., esp. 10, 38, 54; on Zhitlowsky, see David H. Weinberg, *Between Tradition and Modernity* (New York: Holmes & Meier, 1996), 83–144, esp. 106.

36. Hoberman and Shandler, *Entertaining America,* 113–127; Donald Weber, "The Jewish-American World of Gertrude Berg," in Joyce Antler (ed.), *Talking Back: Images of Jewish Women in American Popular Culture* (Hanover, N.H.: Brandeis University Press, 1998), 85–99.

37. *AJYB* 21 (1919–20): 331; *Census of Religious Bodies 1926: Jewish Congregations— Statistics, History, Doctrine and Organization* (Washington, D.C., 1929), 6 [based on the same data, *AJYB* 30 (1928–29): 199 found "one permanent congregation to serve every 1386 Jewish men, women and children," while *AJYB* 31 (1929–30): 109 reduced this to "one congregation for 1356 Jews"]; Sherman, *The Jew Within American Society,* 208–209.

38. Moore, *At Home in America,* 126–127; McGill, "Some Characteristics of Jewish Youth in New York City," 253; Nettie P. McGill and Ellen N. Matthews, *The Youth of New York City* (New York, 1940), 241; Nathan Goldberg, "Religious and Social Attitudes of Jewish Youth in U.S.A.," *Jewish Review* 1 (December 1943): 135–168, esp. 148; U. Z. Engelman, "The Jewish Synagogue in the United States," *American Journal of Sociology* 41 (1935–36): 44; Wenger, *New York Jews and the Great Depression,* 184.

39. *CCARYB* 39 (1920): 255; *Census of Religious Bodies 1926,* 19; Rudavsky, "Trends in Jewish School Organization and Enrollment in New York City, 1917–1950," 45– 81, esp. 50; Morawska, *Insecure Prosperity,* 148 and 326 n.30; *AJYB* 31 (1929–30): 126–130, 149–151; *CCARYB* 34 (1924): 367; Sarna, *JPS,* 142.

40. *CCARYB* 33 (1923): 104; *Sefer Ha-Yovel Shel Agudath ha-Rabbanim Ha-Orthodoksim B'Amerika,* 114 (translation mine); *AJYB* 32 (1930–31), 72; *AJYB* 35 (1933–34): 162–163; for Stern's plan, see also Wenger, *New York Jews and the Great Depression,* 254, n.95.

41. Robert T. Handy, "The American Religious Depression, 1925–1935," *Church History* 29 (1960): 3–16; *AJYB* 35 (1933–34): 163; *CCARYB* 33 (1923): 103; Meyer, *Response to Modernity,* 296; Hoberman and Shandler, *Entertaining America,* 77–92.

42. Teller, *Strangers and Natives,* 133.

43. Mintz, *Hasidic People,* 21.

44. Gross and Kaminetsky, "Shraga Feivel Mendlowitz," 551–572; Parsons, "The Role of Shraga Feivel Mendlowitz"; Rosenblum, *Reb Shraga Feivel.*

45. *Jewish Communal Register,* 394–395; Kranzler, *Hasidic Williamsburg,* 62–63; William B. Helmreich, *The World of the Yeshiva,* 26–30, 356 n.20; Parsons, "The Role of Shraga Feivel Mendlowitz" (microfilm is unpaginated); Rosenblum, *Reb Shraga Feivel,* 302.

46. Mintz, *Hasidic People,* 21–26, 53–56; Sobel, "The M'lochim."

47. *Jewish Communal Register,* 341–346; Robinson, "The First Hasidic Rabbis in North America," 501–506; cf. Levi Y. Horowitz, *And the Angels Laughed* (New York: Mesorah, 1997), and Seth Farber, "Between Brooklyn and Brookline: American Hasidism and the Evolution of the Bostoner Hasidic Tradition," *AJA* 52 (2000): 35–53, for the origins of another Hasidic court that developed in America during these years.

48. Rothkoff, *Bernard Revel,* is the standard biography.

49. Ibid., 46.

50. *Jewish Communal Register,* 1201; Gurock, *The Men and Women of Yeshiva,* 43–66.

51. Rothkoff, *Bernard Revel,* 78, 81, 94; Moore, *At Home in America,* 185, 187.

52. Gurock, *The Men and Women of Yeshiva,* 78, 186–212; Gordis as excerpted in Waxman (ed.), *Tradition and Change,* 235.

53. Rothkoff, *Bernard Revel,* 154–156; Joselit, *New York's Jewish Jews,* xv, 2.

54. Gurock, *American Jewish Orthodoxy,* 88, 228, 243; Stein, *The Boundaries of Gender,* 38–39. Kaufman, *Shul with a Pool,* 200–205, untangles Young Israel's complex early history.

55. Breuer, *Modernity Within Tradition,* 43–44.

56. Joselit, *New York's Jewish Jews,* 26, 43.

57. Gurock, "Jewish Commitment and Continuity in Interwar Brooklyn," 237.

58. *Cantor on Trial [Khazn afn Probe]* (1931), National Center for Jewish Film, Brandeis University, Waltham, Mass.; J. Hoberman, *Bridge of Light: Yiddish Film Between Two Worlds* (New York: Schocken, 1991), 261–262; on Waldman, see *Proceedings: Cantors Assembly Thirty-Third Annual Convention* (New York, 1980), 11–18.

59. Robert Gordis, "A Program for American Judaism," in Waxman (ed.), *Tradition and Change,* 234, cf. 230; Wertheimer (ed.), *American Synagogue,* 300, 311, 383; Rothkoff, *Bernard Revel,* 102–113; Rakeffet-Rothkoff, "The Attempt to Merge the Jewish Theological Seminary and Yeshiva College," 254–280; Jeffrey S. Gurock, "Yeshiva Students at JTS," in Wertheimer (ed.), *Tradition Renewed,* 1: 473–513, esp. 473, 493.

60. Waxman (ed.), *Tradition and Change,* 173; Wertheimer (ed.), *American Synagogue,* 118; *United Synagogue Recorder* 6 (October 1926): 35 as cited in Stein, *The Boundaries of Gender,* 47.

61. Wertheimer (ed.), *American Synagogue,* 118.

62. Ibid., 116.

63. Karp, *A History of the United Synagogue of America;* Rosenblum, *The Founding of the United Synagogue of America,* 1913; Nadell, *Conservative Judaism in America,* 325–354; Rubenovitz, *The Waking Heart,* 35–54, 57–59, 124–135; Davis, *Emergence of Conservative Judaism,* 317–321.

64. *Sefer Le-dor Aharon* (Brooklyn, 1937), esp. 13, 14, 23, 90, 98 [in Hebrew]; Louis M. Epstein, *Li-She'elath ha-'Agunah* (New York, 1940), esp. 28–31 [in Hebrew]; Golinkin (ed.), *Proceedings of the Committee on Jewish Law and Standards,* 2: 619–711; cf. Rubenovitz, *The Waking Heart,* 61–67.

65. For the best English-language account, see Stein, *Boundaries of Gender,* 251–357.

66. Robinson (ed.), *Cyrus Adler: Selected Letters,* 319; Golinkin, *Responsa of Professor Louis Ginzberg,* 85–89; Rothkoff, *Bernard Revel,* 163–164.

67. Joseph Goldberg, "Twenty-Five Years of Brooklyn Jewish Center History," as quoted in Stein, *The Boundaries of Gender,* 149.

68. Stein, *Boundaries of Gender,* 155, 165 (emphasis in original); Golinkin (ed.), *Proceedings of the Committee on Jewish Law and Standards,* 3: 1061.

69. Stein, *Boundaries of Gender,* 179; Sarna, "Mixed Seating in the American Synagogue," 379–386.

70. Sarna, "Mixed Seating in the American Synagogue," 379–386.

71. Wertheimer (ed.), *American Synagogue,* 119–120, 200, 312–313; Golinkin (ed.), *Proceedings of the Committee on Jewish Law and Standards,* 3: 1085; Sklare, *Conservative Judaism,* 102–108.

72. Rubenovitz, *The Waking Heart,* esp. 73–84, illustrates the split in Conservative ranks.

73. Scult, *Judaism Faces the Twentieth Century;* Gurock and Schacter, *A Modern Heretic and a Traditional Community.*

74. Scult (ed.), *Communings of the Spirit,* 1: 61.

75. Kaplan, *Judaism as a Civilization,* xii; Scult (ed.), *Communings of the Spirit,* 1: 78, 98; Libowitz, *Mordecai M. Kaplan and the Development of Reconstructionism,* 30–41; Allen Lazaroff, "Kaplan and John Dewey," in *The American Judaism of Mordecai M. Kaplan,* ed. Emanuel S. Goldsmith, Mel Scult, and Robert Seltzer (New York: New York University Press, 1990), 173–197; Scult, *Judaism Faces the Twentieth Century,* 188–191; Gurock and Schacter, *A Modern Heretic and a Traditional Community,* 38–105; Mordecai M. Kaplan, "A Program for the Reconstruction of Judaism," *Menorah Journal* 6, no. 4 (August 1920): esp. 183, 195–196; cf. *Jewish Forum* 4 (1921): 645–646, 724–731, and 778–783, for replies by Rabbis Bernard Drachman and Leo Jung.

76. Scult, *Judaism Faces the Twentieth Century,* 197, 254, 257; see 409 n.1 for the claim that only twenty-two families founded the new congregation; Scult (ed.), *Communings of the Spirit,* 1: 159, 503; Gurock and Schacter, *A Modern Heretic and a Traditional Community,* 106–134.

77. Cited from an undated document in the Kaplan archive by Libowitz, *Mordecai M. Kaplan and the Development of Reconstructionism,* 200.

78. Kaplan, *Judaism as a Civilization,* esp. x, 513, 522.

79. Quotes from Liebman, "Reconstructionism in American Jewish Life," 9; [Reconstructionist] *Sabbath Prayer Book* (New York, 1945), as reprinted in Marc Lee Raphael, *Jews and Judaism in the United States: A Documentary History* (New York: Behrman, 1983), 230; Kaplan, *Judaism as a Civilization,* 438.

80. Scult, *Judaism Faces the Twentieth Century,* 256.

81. Gilman, *Conservative Judaism,* 78–79.

82. Liebman, "Reconstructionism in American Jewish Life," 68–71 (emphasis added).

83. Kaplan, *Judaism as a Civilization,* 180; see Jeffrey Shandler, "Producing the Future: The Impresario Culture of American Zionism Before 1948," *Divergent Jewish Cultures,* ed. Deborah Dash Moore and S. Ilan Troen (New Haven: Yale University Press, 2001), 53–71.

84. Kaufman, *Shul with a Pool,* 235.

85. Ibid., esp. 227; Reichel, *The Maverick Rabbi,* 107–135, 169–172, esp. 170–171.

86. Kaufman, *Shul with a Pool,* 239, 257; Deborah Dash Moore, "A Synagogue Center Grows in Brooklyn," in Wertheimer (ed.), *American Synagogue,* 304.

87. Kaplan, *Judaism as a Civilization,* 108–125; *Jewish Communal Register,* chart opposite p. 122; *CCARYB* 36 (1926): 317.

88. *CCARYB* 36 (1926): 320; Sarna and Goldman, "From Synagogue-Community to Citadel of Reform," 191; *AJYB* 31 (1929–30): 31; Meyer, *Response to Modernity,* 322; *Reform Judaism in the Large Cities—A Survey* (New York, 1931), 14–15, 26–29.

89. Michael A. Meyer, "American Reform Judaism and Zionism," 49–64; Polish, *Renew Our Days: The Zionist Issue in Reform Judaism,* 115–235; Greenstein, *Turning Point;* Meyer, *Response to Modernity,* 302; Philipson, *My Life as an American Jew,* 361–362.

90. Urofsky, *A Voice That Spoke for Justice,* 302–303.

91. Meyer, *Response to Modernity,* 298–301, esp. 299; Jonathan B. Krasner, "Representations of Self and Other in American Jewish History and Social Studies Schoolbooks: An Exploration of the Changing Shape of American Jewish Identity" (Ph.D.

diss., Brandeis University, 2002), 165–256, esp. 176; Harry L. Comins, *Arts-Crafts for the Jewish Club* (Cincinnati, 1934), 3.

92. Felicia Herman, "From Priestess to Hostess: Sisterhoods of Personal Service in New York City, 1887–1936," in Nadell and Sarna (eds.), *Women and American Judaism,* esp. 170–171; *AJYB* 29 (1927–28), 27.

93. *Proceedings of the National Federation of Temple Sisterhoods* (Cincinnati, 1941), 136, as quoted in Zollman, *Shopping for a Future,* 50; "Jane Evans: A Builder of Reform Judaism," *Reform Judaism* 12 (Fall 1983): 30–31, 36; Nadell, "National Federation of Temple Sisterhoods," 981–982; Ellen Umansky, "Evans, Jane," typescript in AJA; cf. Jenna Weissman Joselit, "The Special Sphere of the Middle-Class American Jewish Woman: The Synagogue Sisterhood, 1890–1940," in Wertheimer (ed.), *American Synagogue,* 206–230.

94. Meyer, *Response to Modernity,* 318–320, 332–334, 388–391; Thomas A. Kolsky, *Jews Against Zionism: The American Council for Judaism, 1942–1948* (Philadelphia: Temple University Press, 1990).

95. Marty, *Modern American Religion,* vol. 2: *The Noise of Conflict, 1919–1941,* 2–3, 145.

96. Wenger, *New York Jews and the Great Depression,* 10–15; Teller, *Strangers and Natives,* 113–117; Ron Chernow, *The House of Morgan* (New York: Atlantic Monthly Press, 1990), 326–327.

97. *AJYB* 33 (1931–32): 38–44.

98. Wenger, *New York Jews and the Great Depression,* 169, 171; Wertheimer (ed.), *American Synagogue,* 123; Kennedy, *Freedom from Fear,* 186; Pilch (ed.), *History of Jewish Education in the United States,* 83.

99. Interview with Solomon Skaist, September 17, 1979, as quoted in William B. Helmreich, "Old Wine in New Bottles: Advanced Yeshivot in the United States," *AJH* 92 (1979): 238–239.

100. Rothkoff, *Bernard Revel,* 181–203.

101. *AJYB* 33 (1931–32): 38–44; Sarna and Klein (eds.), *Jews of Cincinnati,* 135.

102. Morawska, *Insecure Prosperity,* 129; Wenger, *New York Jews and the Great Depression,* 9, 98.

103. Hunnicut, "The Jewish Sabbath Movement in the Early Twentieth Century," 196–225, esp. 205, 207; Benjamin Kline Hunnicutt, *Work Without End: Abandoning Shorter Hours for the Right to Work* (Philadelphia: Temple University Press, 1988), 70, 168, 246–247; *Sefer Ha-Yovel Shel Agudath Ha-Rabbanim Ha-Orthodoksim B'Amerika,* 105; *Historical Statistics of the United States, Colonial Times to 1970* (Washington, D.C., 1975), I: 169–170, 172.

104. *AJYB* 33 (1931–32): 23.

105. *AJYB* 33 (1931–32): 76; 35 (1933–34): iii, 21–39; 36 (1934–35): iii; 37 (1935–36): 135; 41 (1939–40): 261, 264, 268.

106. Lipstadt, *Beyond Belief.*

107. Breitman and Kraut, *American Refugee Policy and European Jewry, 1933–1945,* 9; Medoff, "New Evidence Concerning the Allies and Auschwitz," 98–99; Wyman, *Paper Walls,* 209.

108. Wyman, *Paper Walls,* 173; Feingold, "Who Shall Bear Guilt for the Holocaust," 261–282; Kennedy, *Freedom from Fear,* 412–415, 417; Feingold, *A Time for Searching,*

251; Breitman and Kraut, *American Refugee Policy and European Jewry, 1933–1945,* 73. For other evidence of American Jewish opposition to taking in German-Jewish refugees, see Arad, *America, Its Jews, and the Rise of Nazism,* 160–163, 199.

109. Herbert A. Strauss (ed.), *Jewish Immigrants of the Nazi Period in the USA* (6 vols., New York: K. G. Saur, 1978–) provides a comprehensive summary and bibliography.

110. For poll data, see Stember, *Jews in the Mind of America,* 121–123. For differing perspectives on what might have been done to save Jews, see Feingold, "Who Shall Bear Guilt for the Holocaust," 261–282, and Wyman, *The Abandonment of the Jews.* The War Refugee Board, established by Roosevelt in 1944, may have saved as many as 200,000 Jews, an indication of how much more might have been accomplished earlier had similar efforts been exerted.

111. Arad, *America, Its Jews, and the Rise of Nazism,* 215; Wyman, *The Abandonment of the Jews,* 42–55, esp. 51; Breitman and Kraut, *American Refugee Policy and European Jewry, 1933–1945,* 146–160.

112. Wyman, *The Abandonment of the Jews,* 71; Marty, *Modern American Religion,* vol. 3: *Under God Indivisible,* 59–60.

113. The Conservative rabbi Israel Goldstein, who was also president of the Synagogue Council of America, could not participate at the last minute; see Wyman, *The Abandonment of the Jews,* 72, and Zuroff, *The Response of Orthodox Jewry in the United States to the Holocaust,* 228–229.

114. Sarna, *JPS,* 186–187; Wyman, *The Abandonment of the Jews,* 91; Ben Hecht, *"We Will Never Die": A Memorial Dedicated to the 2,000,000 Jewish Dead of Europe* (New York, 1943), esp. 33–37; Moore, *To the Golden Cities,* 15–16.

115. Wyman, *The Abandonment of the Jews,* 120–121.

116. Ibid., 160–167; Kohanski (ed.), *The American Jewish Conference,* 178–181.

117. Zuroff, *The Response of Orthodox Jewry in the United States to the Holocaust,* 257–264, esp. 261.

118. *AJYB* 45 (1943–44): 180; *American Jews in World War II* (New York, 1947), 1: 348–356, and 2: 17–27; Barish (ed.), *Rabbis in Uniform: The Story of the American Jewish Military Chaplain,* 118, 156–157; *Prayer Book Abridged for Jews in the Armed Forces of the United States,* iv.

119. *Prayer Book Abridged for Jews in the Armed Forces of the United States,* 327; Dawidowicz, *On Equal Terms,* 110.

120. Dinnerstein, *Antisemitism in America,* 129, 132, 136.

121. Ibid., 128–149, esp. 129, 132, 141; Bendersky, *The "Jewish Threat": Anti-Semitic Politics of the U.S. Army,* 287–347, 350–364.

122. Sussman, "'Toward Better Understanding': The Rise of the Interfaith Movement in America and the Role of Rabbi Isaac Landman," 35–51; Kraut, "A Wary Collaboration," 193–230; Silk, *Spiritual Politics,* 40–53; Silk, "Notes on the Judeo-Christian Tradition in America," 65–85.

123. Ofer Shiff, *Assimilation in Pride: Anti-Semitism, Holocaust and Zionism as Challenges to Universalistic American Jewish Reform Ideology* [in Hebrew] (Tel Aviv: Am Oved, 2001), 179–180; Barish, *Rabbis in Uniform,* 237–238, 285–287; *American Jews in World War II,* 1: 306–309; Shapiro, *A Time for Healing,* 17; Silk, *Spiritual Politics,* 40; Deborah Dash Moore, "Jewish GIs and the Creation of the Judeo-Christian Tradition," *Religion and American Culture* 8 (Winter 1998): 31–53.

124. Kaplan, *Judaism as a Civilization,* 76; for Germany, see Michael Brenner, *The Renaissance of Jewish Culture in Weimar Germany* (New Haven: Yale University Press, 1996).

125. Alvin I. Schiff, *The Jewish Day School in America* (New York: Jewish Education Committee of New York, 1966), 37, 42, 44, 49; Jonathan D. Sarna, "The Crucial Decade in Jewish Camping," *The Beginnings of Reform Jewish Camping in America,* ed. Michael M. Lorge and Gary P. Zola (Tuscaloosa: University of Alabama Press, forthcoming); Moore, "Inventing Jewish Identity in California," 201–221; Sarna, *JPS,* 183–184; *AJYB* 47 (1945–46): 559.

126. Betty D. Greenberg and Althea O. Silverman, *The Jewish Home Beautiful* (New York, 1941), esp. 13, 14, 18, 37; Rose B. Goldstein, "Women's Share of Responsibilities for the Future of Judaism," *Women's League Outlook* 8, no. 4 (May 1938): 13, as quoted in Zollman, *Shopping for a Future,* 45; *Minutes of the 1940 Convention of the Women's League* (Atlantic City, N.J.: May 10–14, 1940) as quoted in ibid., 54; Joselit, *The Wonders of America,* 161–163; Barbara Kirshenblatt-Gimblett, *Destination Culture: Tourism, Museums, and Heritage* (Berkeley: University of California Press, 1998), 126–128.

127. Goodman, *The Faith of Secular Jews,* 19; Ruth Whitman (trans. and ed.), *The Selected Poems of Jacob Glatstein* (New York: Octagon, 1972), 59–60; Goodman (ed.), *Our First Fifty Years: The Sholem Aleichem Folk Institute,* 18–19, 64–66.

128. Goodman (ed.), *Our First Fifty Years,* 64–66.

129. *AJYB* 43 (1941–42): 28, 780, 789.

CHAPTER 6: RENEWAL

1. Liebman, *Peace of Mind,* esp. xiv, 143, 169–171; Andrew R. Heinze, "*Peace of Mind* (1946): Judaism and the Therapeutic Polemics of Postwar America," *Religion and American Culture* 12 (Winter 2002): 31–58; Rebecca T. Alpert, "Joshua Loth Liebman: The Peace of Mind Rabbi," *Faith and Freedom: A Tribute to Franklin H. Littell,* ed. Richard Libowitz (Oxford: Pergamon Press, 1987), 177–191; see Donald Meyer, *The Positive Thinkers: A Study of the American Quest for Health, Wealth and Personal Power from Mary Baker Eddy to Norman Vincent Peale* (Garden City, N.Y.: Doubleday, 1965).

2. Shapiro, *A Time for Healing,* 8–15, 18–19; Andrew Kopkind, "Best Bets," *Village Voice* (November 12, 1979), 19–20, as quoted by Shapiro.

3. Harap, *Creative Awakening,* 137–149; Harap, *In the Mainstream,* 1–26; Erens, *The Jew in American Cinema,* 179; *AJYB* 51 (1950): 554.

4. *Jewish Book Annual* 5 (1946–47): 3–4; Elliot E. Cohen, "An Act of Affirmation," *Commentary* 1 (November 1945): 1; Elliot E. Cohen, "Jewish Culture in America," *Commentary* 3 (May 1947): 414; Sarna, *JPS,* 205–208.

5. *AJYB* 50 (1948–49): 1, and 100 (2000): 46–47.

6. Quotes from Marty, *Modern American Religion,* 3: 285, 292–293; see also Whitfield, *The Culture of the Cold War,* 77–100.

7. Finkelstein (ed.), *The Jews,* xxvi; Sarna, "Two Traditions of Seminary Scholarship," 71–73.

8. Herberg, *Protestant-Catholic-Jew,* 256–257; Dalin, "Will Herberg in Retrospect,"

38–43; Marty, *Modern American Religion,* 3: 286–291; Sussman, "The Suburbanization of American Judaism," 36 (quoted); *Time,* October 15, 1951, and December 13, 1963.

9. *AJYB* 51 (1950): 110; Dinnerstein, *Antisemitism in America,* 151, 162, 170.

10. Nathan Glazer, "The American Jew and the Attainment of Middle-Class Rank: Some Trends and Explanations," in Sklare (ed.), *The Jews,* 138–142; Herberg in *AJYB* 53 (1952): 3–74; Goren, "A 'Golden Decade' for American Jews," 3–20.

11. *AJYB* 52 (1951): 86; 59 (1958): 115–116; and 64 (1963): 145. Kramer and Leventman, *Children of the Gilded Ghetto,* 46, 154.

12. Whitfield, *The Culture of the Cold War,* 86; Sklare (ed.), *The Jews,* 117, 334; Sklare and Vosk, *The Riverton Study,* 16.

13. Sherman, *The Jew Within American Society,* 211; Sklare and Vosk, *The Riverton Study,* 11; Teller, *Strangers and Natives,* 223.

14. Sklare and Greenblum, *Jewish Identity on the Suburban Frontier,* 57; cf. Sklare and Vosk, *The Riverton Study,* 11.

15. Sussman, "The Suburbanization of American Judaism," esp. 32.

16. Dushkin and Engelman, *Jewish Education in the United States,* 1: 45, 50; Pilch, *A History of Jewish Education in the United States,* 121–122, 141, 200; *AJYB* 47 (1945–46): 215, 234, 243.

17. *AJYB* 57 (1956): 189; Sarna, *JPS,* 233–247; Whitfield, *The Culture of the Cold War,* 84.

18. Goldy, *The Emergence of Jewish Theology in America,* esp. 3, 37, 43; Abraham J. Heschel, *The Insecurity of Freedom: Essays on Human Existence* (New York: Schocken, 1975), 133; Robert Gordis, "The Genesis of JUDAISM: A Chapter in Jewish Cultural History," *Judaism* 30 (1981): 392.

19. Sarna, *JPS,* 247–253; *AJYB* 70 (1969): 37–58.

20. Marty, *Modern American Religion,* 3: 280; Whitfield, *The Culture of the Cold War,* 77–100, 85; Liebman, *Peace of Mind,* 146–147; Janowsky, *The JWB Survey,* 269.

21. Pilch, *A History of Jewish Education in the United States,* 130; Sherman, *The Jew Within American Society,* 222.

22. *AJYB* 53 (1952): 157; Herbert J. Gans, "Park Forest: Birth of a Jewish Community," *Commentary on the American Scene,* ed. Elliot E. Cohen (New York: Knopf, 1953), 205–223; Gordon, *Jews in Suburbia,* xvii, xix; Goldstein and Goldscheider, *Jewish Americans,* 49; Hertzberg, *Jews in America,* 321.

23. Kenneth Jackson, *Crabgrass Frontier: The Suburbanization of the United States* (New York: Oxford University Press, 1985); Marty, *Modern American Religion,* 3: 403; Gordon, *Jews in Suburbia,* ix–xix.

24. Gans, "The Origin and Growth of a Jewish Community in the Suburbs," 209, 243; Gordon, *Jews in Suburbia,* 170; Prell, *Fighting to Become Americans,* 158–161.

25. Gordon, *Jews in Suburbia,* 96–97.

26. Ibid., 97–98, 101; Gurock, *The Men and Women of Yeshiva,* 146. See Litvin, *Sanctity of the Synagogue,* 243–250, 299–311, for Orthodox presentations in these debates.

27. The Conservative movement added about 450 synagogues, the Reform movement about 330, and the Orthodox about 100; Wertheimer, *A People Divided,* 5; Gurock, *The Men and Women of Yeshiva,* 148.

28. Sklare, *Conservative Judaism,* esp. 20, 253–255; Meyer, *Response to Modernity,* 358; Gordon, *Jews in Suburbia,* 97; Wertheimer, *A People Divided,* 9.

29. Golinkin (ed.), *Proceedings of the Committee on Jewish Law and Standards of the Conservative Movement, 1927–1970,* 3: 1118–1120.

30. Ibid., 3: 1168, 1173; Nadell, *Conservative Judaism in America,* 9–11; Gurock, *The Men and Women of Yeshiva,* 146–147; Litvin, *Sanctity of the Synagogue,* 244.

31. Gordon, *Jews in Suburbia,* 64; Gans, "The Origin and Growth of a Jewish Community in the Suburbs," 215; Michael Brown, "It's Off to Camp We Go: Ramah, LTF, and the Seminary in the Finkelstein Era," *Tradition Renewed,* ed. Jack Wertheimer, 1: 821–854.

32. Gans, "The Origin and Growth of a Jewish Community in the Suburbs," 62–63; Prell, *Fighting to Become Americans,* 173 (emphasis added).

33. Litvin, *Sanctity of the Synagogue,* 302; Sarna, "The Debate over Mixed Seating in the American Synagogue," 380–386; Sklare, *Conservative Judaism,* 88–89.

34. Golinkin, *Proceedings of the Committee on Jewish Law and Standards of the Conservative Movement, 1927–1970,* 1: 230, 377 and 3: 1086–1108.

35. Scult, *Judaism Faces the Twentieth Century,* 301–302, 415 n.31; Dov Sadan, "Bat Mitzvah," *Dat Umedinah* (Jerusalem, 1949), 59–61; David H. Wice, "Bar Mitzvah," and Isaac Landman, "Confirmation," in *Universal Jewish Encyclopedia,* 1940 ed.; Hyman, "The Introduction of Bat Mitzvah in Conservative Judaism in Postwar America," 133–146, esp. 135; Regina Stein, "The Road to Bat Mitzvah in America," *Women and American Judaism,* ed. Nadell and Sarna, 223–234, esp. 229; Wertheimer (ed.), *American Synagogue,* 120, 131; Joselit, *The Wonders of America,* 127–133; Sklare, *Conservative Judaism,* 154; Sklare and Greenblum, *Jewish Identity on the Suburban Frontier,* 296; Moore, *To the Golden Cities,* 101–102; Sara Friedland Ben Arza (ed.), *Bat Mitzvah: Collected Writings and Reflections* (Jerusalem: MaTaN-Sadie Rennert Women's Institute for Torah Studies, 2002).

36. Meyer, *Response to Modernity,* 353–360; Schulman, *Like a Raging Fire: A Biography of Maurice N. Eisendrath;* Meyer, "From Cincinnati to New York," 302–313; Siegel, "Reflections on Neo-Reform," 65.

37. Meyer, *Response to Modernity,* 353–360, 472 n.73; Gordon, *Jews in Suburbia,* 108; Sklare and Greenblum, *Jewish Identity on the Suburban Frontier,* 106–119.

38. Siegel, "Reflections on Neo-Reform," 63–84; American Council for Judaism, *An Interim Recommended Religious School Curriculum* (New York, 1952), quotes are from 4, 6 [in author's collection]; Sklare and Greenblum, *Jewish Identity on the Suburban Frontier,* 133–151.

39. *AJYB* 61 (1960): 55; Svonkin, *Jews Against Prejudice,* 16–18; Higham, *Send These to Me,* 155.

40. Gurock, *The Men and Women of Yeshiva,* 147–148; Liebman, "Religion and the Chaos of Modernity," 147–164, esp. 156–158.

41. Etan Diamond, *"And I Will Dwell in Their Midst."*

42. Sussman, "The Suburbanization of American Judaism," esp. 31; Gordon, *Jews in Suburbia,* 99; Shapiro, *A Time for Healing,* 168; George M. Goodwin, "The Design of a Modern Synagogue: Percival Goodman's Beth-El in Providence, Rhode Island," *AJA* 45 (Spring–Summer 1993): 31–71; Kimberly J. Elman and Angela Giral (eds.), *Percival Goodman: Architect, Planner, Teacher, Painter* (New York: Columbia University Press, 2001); Bernstein, "The Emergence of the English-Speaking Orthodox Rabbinate," 82–85, 107–112, 565–568; Bernstein, *Challenge and Mission,* 37–41.

43. Miami data is for "persons in Jewish households including snowbirds." I am grateful to demographer Ira Sheskin for this information (personal communication, November 25, 2002). Moore, *To the Golden Cities,* 23–26, 265; Marcus, *To Count a People,* 24, 46. Regional data calculated from *AJYB* 42 (1940–41): 222, 227–228; *AJYB* 101 (2001): 256–257, 280. See also Goldstein and Goldstein, *Jews on the Move,* 37–47.

44. Moore, *To the Golden Cities,* esp. 95, 270.

45. *Jewish Immigrants of the Nazi Period in the USA,* 6 vols., ed. Herbert A. Strauss (New York: K. G. Saur, 1978–86).

46. Lowenstein, *Frankfurt on the Hudson,* esp. 25, 68, 115; Benny Kraut, *German-Jewish Orthodoxy in an Immigrant Synagogue: Cincinnati's New Hope Congregation and the Ambiguities of Ethnic Religion* (New York: Markus Wiener, 1988).

47. Mortimer J. Cohen, *Pathways Through the Bible,* illustrated by Arthur Szyk (Philadelphia: Jewish Publication Society, 1946), viii; Sarna, *JPS,* 207; Abraham J. Heschel, *The Earth Is the Lord's: The Inner World of the Jew in East Europe* (New York: H. Schuman, 1950); Heschel, undated circular [late 1950s] in the possession of Dr. David Assaf; Jacob Robinson and Philip Friedman, *Guide to Jewish History Under Nazi Impact* (New York: YIVO, 1960); Elie Wiesel, *Night* (New York: Hill and Wang, 1960).

48. Sarna, *JPS,* 272–273; Young, *Texture of Memory,* 287–294; *Seder Ritual of Remembrance* (New York: Seder Ritual Committee, n.d.); Novick, *The Holocaust in American Life;* Bialystok, *Delayed Impact.*

49. Mintz, *Hasidic People,* esp. 3, 30; Kranzler, *Williamsburg,* 61, 178, 218; Mayer, *From Suburb to Shtetl.*

50. Mintz, *Hasidic People,* 29, 85–90; Rubin, *Satmar.*

51. Mintz, *Hasidic People,* 198–207; Poll, *The Hasidic Community of Williamsburg.*

52. Michael Beizer, "The Leningrad Jewish Religious Community: From the NEP Through Its Liquidation," *Jews in Eastern Europe* 3 (Winter 1995): 24–36; Kortick, "Transformation and Rejuvenation," 29, 72; Avrum M. Ehrlich, "Leadership in the Habad Movement" (Ph.D. diss., University of Sydney, 1997), 174ff; Mintz, *Hasidic People,* 43–53.

53. Kortick, "Transformation and Rejuvenation," 79; Shaul Shimon Deutsch, *Larger Than Life: The Life and Times of the Lubavitcher Rebbe, Rabbi Menachem Mendel Schneerson,* 2 vols., (New York: Chasidic Historical Productions, 1995, 1997).

54. Gershon Greenberg, "Redemption After Holocaust According to Mahane Israel-Lubavitch, 1940–1945," *Modern Judaism* 12 (1992): 61–84, esp. 70; Edward Hoffman, *Despite All Odds: The Story of Lubavitch* (New York: Simon & Schuster, 1991).

55. David Berger, *The Rebbe, the Messiah, and the Scandal of Orthodox Indifference* (London: Littman, 2001); Sue Fishkoff, "Black Hat Blitz," *Moment* 25 (August 2000): 46–53, 85; www.lubavitch.com/lubavitch_today.html.

56. Finkelman, "Haredi Isolation in Changing Environments," 62.

57. Bomzer, *The Kollel in America;* Helmreich, *The World of the Yeshiva;* Liebman, "Orthodoxy in American Jewish Life," 49–53, 75–79; "Telsiai," *EJ* 15, p. 938.

58. Sorsky, *Marbitse Torah Umusar,* 3: 215–266, esp. 247–248; Finkelman, "Haredi Isolation in Changing Environments," 61–82; Moshe Sherman, "Kotler, Aaron," *ANB* 12, p. 889.

59. Sorsky, *Marbitse Torah Umusar,* vol. 3, esp. 254; Bunim, *A Fire in His Soul,* 173–247; Helmreich, *The World of the Yeshiva,* 40–45; Bomzer, *The Kollel in America,* 26–34; *Kol Hayovel: Celebrating 50 Years of Torah Scholarship in America* (Lakewood, N.J., 1992) [copy in Hebrew University library]. I rely on this official source for the number of students in different eras; Finkelman supplies slightly different numbers.

60. Bunim, *A Fire in His Soul,* 227–231, 338; Bernstein, "Emergence of the English-Speaking Rabbinate," 297–331, 556; Bernstein, *Challenge and Mission,* 141–156; see Chayim Dalfin (ed.), *Conversations with the Rebbe* (Los Angeles: JEC Publishing, 1996), 71–89.

61. Shulamith Soloveitchik Meiselman, *The Soloveitchik Heritage: A Daughter's Memoir* (Hoboken: Ktav, 1995), 214–217; Shaul [Seth] Farber, "Community, Schooling, and Leadership: Rabbi Joseph B. Soloveitchik's Maimonides School and the Development of Boston's Orthodox Community" (Ph.D. diss., Hebrew University, 2000), 53–98; Aaron Rakeffet-Rothkoff, *The Rav: The World of Rabbi Joseph B. Soloveitchik* (New York: Ktav, 1999), 21–78.

62. Joseph B. Soloveitchik, *Halakhic Man,* translated by Lawrence Kaplan (Philadelphia: Jewish Publication Society, 1983), esp. 3, 141–142; Singer and Sokol, "Joseph Soloveitchik: Lonely Man of Faith," 227–272; Jonathan Sacks, *Tradition in an Untraditional Age* (London: Vallentine, Mitchell, 1990), 35–55, 267–285.

63. Soloveitchik, "Rupture and Reconstruction," 64–130; idem, "Migration, Acculturation, and the New Role of Texts in the Haredi World," 197–235; see also his exchange with Isaac Chavel in *The Torah U-Madda Journal* 7 (1997): 122–149.

64. *Commentary* 31 (April 1961): 311–359, esp. 312, 329; Rubin-Dorsky and Fishkin (eds.), *People of the Book,* 129–30, 332.

65. *AJYB* 52 (1951): 92; 53 (1952): 163; 54 (1953): 106. Albert Vorspan and Eugene J. Lipman, *Justice and Judaism: The Work of Social Action* (New York: UAHC, 1956), 24; Staub, *Torn at the Roots,* 57; *Where We Stand,* 78; Joint Commission on Social Action, *Justice, Justice Shalt Thou Pursue: Resolutions on Social Action Adopted by the Constituent Bodies of the Conservative Movement in Judaism* (New York: United Synagogue of America, 1955); Meyer, *Response to Modernity,* 366; Richard G. Hirsch, *From the Hill to the Mount* (New York: Geffen, 2000), 34–39; www.rac.org.

66. Weiss, "Long-Distance Runners of the Civil Rights Movement," 126; *Where We Stand,* 8; Diner, *In the Almost Promised Land.*

67. *AJYB* 50 (1948–49): 826; Svonkin, *Jews Against Prejudice,* esp. 18; Staub, *Torn at the Roots,* 48–49; Michael B. Friedland, *Lift Up Your Voice Like a Trumpet,* 38.

68. Blumberg, *One Voice,* 68; Bauman and Kalin (eds.), *The Quiet Voices;* Greene, *The Temple Bombing,* 1, 6.

69. www.joachimprinz.com contains a biography and the text of his speech; Staub, *Torn at the Roots,* 45–57, esp. 47.

70. Kaplan and Dresner, *Abraham Joshua Heschel;* Abraham Joshua Heschel, *Between God and Man: An Interpretation of Judaism,* ed. Fritz A. Rothschild (New York: Harper, 1959); Heschel, *Moral Grandeur and Spiritual Audacity.*

71. Abraham J. Heschel, "Religion and Race," *The Insecurity of Freedom: Essays on Human Existence* (New York: Farrar Straus and Giroux, 1966), 85.

72. Heschel, "Theological Affinities in the Writings of Abraham Joshua Heschel and Martin Luther King, Jr.," 168–186, esp. 168–69, 175–177; Friedland, *Lift Up Your Voice Like a Trumpet,* 71–72, 131; Reuven Kimelman, "In Memoriam: Abraham Joshua Heschel," *Response* 6 (Winter 1972–73): 17.

73. Wigoder, *Jewish-Christian Relations Since the Second World War;* "Aggiornamento," *Dictionary of Christianity in America* (1990): 31. *AJYB* 66 (1965): 99–136; 67 (1966): 45–77; 74 (1973): 534–536.

74. *AJYB* 67 (1966): 59, 46; 74 (1973): 536.

75. Abraham J. Heschel, "No Religion Is an Island" (1966), in Heschel, *Moral Grandeur and Spiritual Audacity,* 235–250, esp. 237, 249; see also Abraham J. Heschel, "What Ecumenism Is," *Face to Face: A Primer in Dialogue,* ed. Lily Edelman (New York: B'nai B'rith, 1967).

76. Ellenson, "A Jewish Legal Authority Addresses Jewish-Christian Dialogue," 113–128; Joseph B. Soloveitchik, "Confrontation," *A Treasury of Tradition,* ed. Norman Lamm and Walter Wurzberger (New York: Hebrew Publishing Company, 1967), 55–80, esp. 73, 79.

77. Friedland, *Lift Up Your Voice Like a Trumpet,* 159–235, esp. 185; Heschel, *Moral Grandeur and Spiritual Audacity,* 219–229; Staub, *Torn at the Roots,* 118–128, 175–179; Eisendrath as quoted in Meyer, *Response to Modernity,* 366; *AJYB* 68 (1967): 79–81; D. Granberg, "Jewish–Non-Jewish Differences on the Vietnam War," *American Sociologist* 8:3 (August 1973): 105, cites various studies demonstrating "greater dovishness of Jews on the Vietnam issue."

78. Staub, *Torn at the Roots,* 128; Abraham J. Heschel, *Israel: An Echo of Eternity* (New York: Farrar Straus, 1969), 196–197; Emil Fackenheim, *The Jewish Return into History* (New York: Schocken, 1978), 38–39, 185; *AJYB* 69 (1968): 218–227.

79. Kaufman, "From Philanthropy to Commitment," 176.

80. Urofsky, *We Are One,* 356; Sergio Della Pergola et al., "The Six-Day War and Israel-Diaspora Relations: An Analysis of Quantitative Indicators," *The Six-Day War and World Jewry,* ed. Eli Lederhendler, 40; Deborah Dash Moore, "From David to Goliath: American Representations of Jews around the Six-Day War," *The Six-Day War and World Jewry,* ed. Eli Lederhendler, 79–80.

81. *AJYB* 70 (1969): 172; Della Pergola et al., "The Six-Day War and Israel-Diaspora Relations," 23, 31; Avruch, *American Immigrants in Israel;* Solotaroff and Rapoport (eds.), *The Schocken Book of Contemporary Jewish Fiction,* xv; cf. Nessa Rapoport, "Jewish Cultural Confidence in American Letters: A Writer's Thoughts," *The Six-Day War and American Jewry,* ed. Eli Lederhendler, 117–123.

82. See the works cited in Haim Avni and Jeffrey Mandl, "The Six-Day War and Communal Dynamics in the Diaspora: An Annotated Bibliography," *The Six-Day War and World Jewry,* ed. Eli Lederhendler, 311–332.

83. For what follows, see Orbach, *The American Movement to Aid Soviet Jews;* Appelbaum, "The Soviet Jewry Movement in the United States," 613–638; and Friedman and Chernin (eds.), *A Second Exodus.*

84. As quoted in Appelbaum, "The Soviet Jewry Movement in the United States," 623.

85. Wertheimer, *A People Divided,* 29.

86. Margolis, "Seeds of Community," 319–364.

87. These two paragraphs draw heavily upon an unpublished paper by Meredith L.

Woocher, "Radical Tradition: The Ideological Underpinnings of the Early Havurah Movement" (Seminar paper, Brandeis University, 1997), esp. 6, 14–15, 19, 20, 27; see also James A. Sleeper and Alan L. Mintz (eds.), *The New Jews* (New York: Vintage, 1971); and Prell, *Prayer and Community,* 92–93, 103. The term "commune congregation" is from Danzger, *Returning to Tradition,* 99.

88. Richard Siegel, Michael Strassfeld, and Sharon Strassfeld, *The Jewish Catalog* (Philadelphia: Jewish Publication Society, 1973); Sarna, *JPS,* 281–285.

89. Harold M. Schulweis, "Restructuring the Synagogue," *Conservative Judaism* 27 (Summer 1973): 18–19; Prell, *Prayer and Community,* esp. 24; John Ruskay as quoted in Woocher, "Radical Tradition," 63; see also Bernard Reisman, *The Chavurah: A Contemporary Jewish Experience* (New York: Union of American Hebrew Congregations, 1977); Gerry Bubis et al., *Synagogue Havurot: A Comparative Study* (Washington, D.C.: University Press of America, 1983).

90. Charles Liebman, "The Training of American Rabbis," 3–112; Ira Eisenstein, *Reconstructing Judaism: An Autobiography* (New York: Reconstructionist Press, 1986), 230–231; Alpert and Staub, *Exploring Judaism,* 66.

91. Wertheimer, *A People Divided,* 163; Alpert and Staub, *Exploring Judaism,* 57–59.

92. Wertheimer, *A People Divided,* 160–169.

93. *Highlights of the 1996 Demographic Study of the Reconstructionist Movement* [1996], 2, 11.

94. Sarna, "The Great American Jewish Awakening," 30.

95. Ibid.; *Reform Judaism* 27 (Winter 1998): 23–24; Sanford Seltzer, *Worship and Ritual Patterns of Reform Congregations: An Interim Report* (Brookline, n.d. [1990]), 9.

96. Meyer, *Response to Modernity,* 392; "A Statement of Principles for Reform Judaism Adopted at the 1999 Pittsburgh Convention Central Conference of American Rabbis" (www.ccarnet.org/platforms/principles.html); Kaplan (ed.), *Contemporary Debates in American Reform Judaism.*

97. Isaac Klein, *A Guide to Jewish Religious Practice* (New York: Jewish Theological Seminary, 1979); *Emet Ve-Emunah: Statement of Principles of Conservative Judaism* (New York, 1988), 23–25; Nancy T. Ammerman, "Conservative Jews Within the Landscape of American Religion," in Wertheimer (ed.), *Jews in the Center,* 371; Steven M. Cohen, "Assessing the Vitality of Conservative Judaism in North America: Evidence from a Survey of Synagogue Members," in Wertheimer (ed.), *Jews in the Center,* 35–38.

98. Freedman, *Jew vs. Jew,* 338; Sarna, "The Great American Jewish Awakening," 31–32; Danzger, *Returning to Tradition,* 89, 232–233; Davidman, *Tradition in a Rootless World,* 13–23; Kaufman, *Rachel's Daughters;* Aviad, *Return to Judaism;* Della Pergola and Rebhun, "American Orthodox Jews," 31.

99. Joselit, *New York's Jewish Jews,* 21; *New York Times,* August 7, 2000 (ad for "Abuzz"), and September 6, 1992 (obituary page).

100. Cohen and Eisen, *The Jew Within,* esp. pp. 73, 91, 97.

101. Ibid., 2, 42; see Horowitz, *Connections and Journeys.*

102. Jonathan Woocher, Foreword to Joseph Reimer, *Succeeding at Jewish Education* (Philadelphia: Jewish Publication Society, 1997), xi; Wertheimer, "Jewish Education in the United States," esp. 4.

103. Marvin Schick, *A Census of Jewish Day Schools in the United States* (New York:

Avi Chai Foundation, 2000), 3, 8, 20; Wertheimer, "Jewish Education in the United States," 43, 52–56; *Jewish Advocate,* April 16–22, 2002, p. B12; Sylvia Barack Fishman, *Jewish Education and Jewish Identity Among Contemporary American Jews: Suggestions from Current Research* (Boston: Bureau of Jewish Education, 1995), 5–6.

104. Moshe Davis (ed.), *Teaching Jewish Civilization: A Global Approach to Higher Education* (New York: NYU Press, 1995), 260–328; www.brandeis.edu/ajs/ajsmission .html; Arnold J. Band, "Jewish Studies in American Liberal-Arts Colleges and Universities," *AJYB* 67 (1966): 3–30; Irving Greenberg, "The Jewish College Youth," in Gilbert Rosenthal (ed.), *The Jewish Family in a Changing World* (New York: Thomas Yoseloff, 1970), 202; Sarna, "The Road to Jewish Leadership," 39–41; www.hillel.org. For background, see Paul Ritterband and Harold S. Wechsler, *Jewish Learning in American Universities: The First Century* (Bloomington: Indiana University Press, 1994).

105. Woocher, *Texts in Tension;* Jonathan D. Sarna, "The Cyclical History of Adult Jewish Learning in the United States," *Seymour Fox Festschrift* (forthcoming).

106. Shapiro, *A Time for Healing,* 29; Neil Gabler, *An Empire of Their Own: How the Jews Invented Hollywood* (New York: Doubleday, 1988); Brando as quoted in Whitfield, *In Search of American Jewish Culture,* xi–xii.

107. See the foundation's website, www.jewishculture.org, esp. the section "about NFJC."

108. Fishman, "American Jewish Fiction Turns Inward," 35–69; Solotaroff and Rapoport (eds.), *The Schocken Book of Contemporary Jewish Fiction,* xiii–xxx.

109. Dan Schifrin, "Conflicts and Challenges of Jewish Culture," www.jewishculture .org/docs/about_nfjc_articles_conflictsandchallenges.html; Berel Lang, "Jewish Culture," *AJYB* 99 (1999): 199.

110. Berel Lang, "Jewish Culture," *AJYB* 99 (1999): 205; Rabbi Dan Freelander as quoted on www.jewishtanglewood.com/about.shtml; Seldin, "American Jewish Museums," esp. 77; Nessa Rapoport, "Cultural Confidence," in Abraham J. Karp (ed.), *The Jews in America: A Treasury of Art and Literature* (New York: Hugh Lauter Levin Associates, 1994), 370.

111. Dan Schifrin, "Conflicts and Challenges of Jewish Culture"; Seldin, "American Jewish Museums," 112.

112. *1999 Annual Survey of American Jewish Opinion Conducted for the American Jewish Committee by Market Facts, Inc.* (New York: American Jewish Committee, 2000), esp. 13, 17.

113. Novick, *The Holocaust in American Culture,* 127–145; Shandler, *While America Watches,* 81–132, 155–178; Lipstadt, "America and the Memory of the Holocaust, 1950–1965," 195–214.

114. *AJYB* 50 (1948–49): 107; 100 (2000): 48, 50, 59.

115. *AJYB* 53 (1952): 552, 564–568; Liebman, *Pressure Without Sanctions,* 118–131.

116. Dushkin and Engelman, *Jewish Education in the United States,* 194; Raphael Patai, "Literature on Israel, 1948–1950," *Jewish Quarterly Review* 41 (April 1951): 437.

117. Abraham G. Duker, "Impact of Zionism on American Jewish Life," in *Jewish Life in America,* ed. Theodore Friedman and Robert Gordis (New York: Horizon, 1955), 316; Sklare (ed.), *The Jews,* 437–450; Sklare and Greenblum, *Jewish Identity on the Suburban Frontier,* 214–249, esp. 229.

118. Moore, *To the Golden Cities,* 227–261, esp. 253; Whitfield, "Israel as Reel," 293–316; Murray Blackman, *A Guide to Jewish Themes in American Fiction, 1940–1980* (Metuchen, N.J.: Scarecrow, 1981).

119. Kaufman, "Envisioning Israel," 228–231; Raphael, *A History of the United Jewish Appeal,* 66–71.

120. Sarna, *JPS,* 276–278; Deborah Lipstadt, "From Noblesse Oblige to Personal Redemption," 306; Hillel Halkin, *Letters to an American Jewish Friend* (Philadelphia: JPS, 1977), esp. 25, 71, 246; Hillel Halkin, "After Zionism, Reflections on Israel and the Diaspora," *Commentary* 103 (June 1997): 25–31.

121. Neusner, *Stranger at Home,* 1; Ellenson, "Envisioning Israel in the Liturgies of North American Liberal Judaism," 117–148, esp. 126.

122. Woocher, *Sacred Survival,* 135–136.

123. Peter S. Knobel (ed.), *Gates of the Seasons: A Guide to the Jewish Year* (New York: Central Conference of American Rabbis, 1983), 6, 102. The National Jewish Community Relations Advisory Council adopted formal guidelines for Holocaust commemoration in 1974, and the Central Conference of American Rabbis resolved in favor of annual commemorations in 1977; see Goldberg, *Jewish Power,* 191; *Gates of the Seasons,* 103.

124. Sheramy, *Defining Lessons,* 122–155, esp. 122; Stier, "Lunchtime at Majdanek," 57–66.

125. Gerda Lerner, *The Creation of Feminist Consciousness* (New York: Oxford University Press, 1993), 14, cf. 274; Ruth Rosen, *The World Split Open: How the Modern Women's Movement Changed America* (New York: Penguin, 2001), 141; Nadell and Sarna (eds.), *Women and American Judaism,* 11.

126. Antler, *The Journey Home,* 259; see also Katharina von Kellenbach, *Anti-Judaism in Feminist Religious Writings* (Atlanta: Scholars Press, 1994).

127. Marcus, *The American Jewish Woman: A Documentary History,* 896; Hyman, "Ezrat Nashim and the Emergence of a New Jewish Feminism," 284–295; Silverstein, "The Evolution of Ezrat Nashim," 41–51.

128. Simon Schwartzfuchs, *A Concise History of the Rabbinate* (Cambridge, Mass.: Blackwell, 1993); Sondra Henry and Emily Taitz, *Written Out of History: Our Jewish Foremothers* (Sunnyside, N.Y.: Biblio Press, 1988); Schwartz, "We Married What We Wanted to Be," 223–246.

129. Nadell, *Women Who Would Be Rabbis,* esp. 71, 93; Jacob (ed.), *American Reform Responsa,* 25–31; Sarna, "From Antoinette Brown Blackwell to Sally Priesand," 43–53.

130. Nadell, *Women Who Would Be Rabbis,* esp. 132–135, 141; Zola (ed.), *Women Rabbis: Exploration and Celebration;* Nadell and Sarna (eds.), *Women and American Judaism,* 305, n.2.

131. *Tomeikh KaHalakhah: Responsa of the Panel of Halakhic Inquiry,* ed. Wayne R. Allen (Mount Vernon, N.Y.: Union of Traditional Conservative Judaism, 1986), 22; Greenberg (ed.), *The Ordination of Women as Rabbis,* 65; Wenger, "The Politics of Women's Ordination," 488–489.

132. Nadell, *Women Who Would Be Rabbis,* 193; Lerner, "Who Hast Not Made Me a Man," 21–22; Hyman, "Feminism in the Conservative Movement," 379, n.3; for a different survey, see Wertheimer, *A People Divided,* 153.

133. Lerner, "Who Hast Not Made Me a Man," 25; Wenger, "The Politics of Women's Ordination," 499; Greenberg (ed.), *The Ordination of Women as Rabbis,* 2.

134. Wenger, "The Politics of Women's Ordination," 514; Wertheimer, *A People Divided,* 152.

135. Fishman, *A Breath of Life,* esp. 121–141; Laura Geller, "From Equality to Transformation: The Challenge of Women's Rabbinic Leadership," in Zola (ed.), *Women Rabbis: Exploration and Celebration,* 69–80; Umansky and Ashton (eds.), *Four Centuries of Jewish Women's Spirituality,* 23–24; 191–334; Penina V. Adelman, *Miriam's Well: Rituals for Jewish Women Around the Year* (New York: Biblio Press, 1986).

136. E. M. Broner, *The Telling* (San Francisco: HarperSanFrancisco, 1993); *Women and Water: Menstruation in Jewish Life and Law,* ed. Rahel Wasserfall (Hanover, N.H.: Brandeis University Press, 1999).

137. Sarna, "Future of American Orthodoxy," 1–3; *Jewish Action* 59 (Fall 1998): 35.

138. Fishman, *Changing Minds: Feminism in Contemporary Orthodox Jewish Life,* esp. 26, 74.

139. Arthur Green, "Spirituality," *Contemporary Jewish Religious Thought,* ed. Arthur A. Cohen and Paul Mendes Flohr (New York: Free Press, 1987), 903–907; Green, *Jewish Spirituality,* 1: xiii, xv; Porterfield, *The Transformation of American Religion,* 40.

140. Mandelbaum, *Holy Brother;* Kligman, "Contemporary Jewish Music in America," 99–104; Kalman Serkez, *The Holy Beggars' Banquet* (Northvale, N.J.: Jason Aronson, 1998), xiii–xvii; *Kol Chevra* 6 (November 1999); Shlomo Carlebach, *L'maan Achai V'reai: An In-Depth Explanation of the Jewish Way of Life, Shabbat, and Festivals* [in Hebrew] (Jerusalem, 1998).

141. Mandelbaum, *Holy Brother,* 52; "Carlebach, Joseph," *EJ,* vol. 5, col. 182–183; Naphtali Carlebach, *Joseph Carlebach and His Generation* (New York, 1959); *Toldois Chabad B'Artzois Ha'Bris* [History of Chabad in the United States of America] (New York: Kehot, 1988), 280.

142. "Chasidic Guitar," *Young Israel Viewpoint* 48 (September–October 1958): 10–11, as quoted in Stein, *The Boundaries of Gender,* 59.

143. Kligman, "Contemporary Jewish Music in America," 99–104; *Jewish Week,* November 22, 1996, p. 6; Mandelbaum, *Holy Brother,* xviii.

144. Polner, *American Jewish Biographies,* 58; cf. Yaakov Ariel, "Counterculture and Mission," 245.

145. Sarah Blustain, "A Paradoxical Legacy: Rabbi Shlomo Carlebach's Shadow Side," *Lilith* 23 (March 31, 1998): 10.

146. Mandelbaum, *Holy Brother,* xxxiii, 72; Porterfield, *The Transformation of American Religion,* 158; *Jewish Week,* October 25, 1996, pp. 8–9; *Jerusalem Report,* October 2, 1997, pp. 50–51; *Haaretz* [English edition], August 14, 2001, p. 10; Avraham A. Trugman, "Probing the Carlebach Phenomenon," *Jewish Action* 63 (Winter 2002): 9–12.

147. Diane Winston, "Participatory Judaism: A Look at the Jewish Renewal Movement and Its Attractiveness to Lots of People," *Long Island Jewish World,* August 27–September 2, 1993, p. 3; Kamenetz, *Stalking Elijah,* 17–18; *Elat Chayyim: A Center for Healing and Renewal* [brochure] (1997), 2.

148. Kamenetz, *Stalking Elijah,* 58; Shira Dicker, "Spiritual Renewal in the Catskills," *Long Island Jewish World,* October 30–November 5, 1992, p. 16; Debra Nussbaum Cohen, "Renewal's Struggle for Acceptance," *Jewish Week,* April 21, 2000, pp. 1, 14–15.

149. Robert Michael Esformes, "Introduction," *Worlds of Jewish Prayer: A Festschrift in Honor of Rabbi Zalman M. Schachter-Shalomi* (Northvale, N.J.: Jason Aronson, 1993), xvii; Kamenetz, *Stalking Elijah,* esp. 21–23; Zalman Schachter, "A First Step: A Devotional Guide," *The [First] Jewish Catalog* (Philadelphia: Jewish Publication Society, 1973), 296–317.

150. Kamenetz, *Stalking Elijah,* 21; *AJYB* 101 (2001): 602; *Elat Chayyim: A Center for Healing and Renewal* [brochure] (1997).

151. Jungreis, *Jewish Soul on Fire,* esp. 16, 21; Jungreis as quoted in Mandelbaum, *Holy Brother,* 39; Schwartz, "Ambassadors Without Portfolio," 244–253.

152. Isaiah 6:8.

153. Mandelbaum, *Holy Brother,* 39; Jungreis, *The Jewish Soul on Fire,* 33–34; Roy S. Neuberger, *From Central Park to Sinai: How I Found My Lost Jewish Soul* (Middle Village, N.Y.: Jonathan David Publishers, 2000), [5], 82, 150; www.hineni.org.

154. Debra Nussbaum Cohen, "Crossover Dreams: Can Folksinger Debbie Friedman Cure Our Spiritual Blues?" *Moment* 21 (June 1996): 50–53, 68–71; Jennifer Lapidus, "The Joan Baez of Jewish Song," *Forward,* December 29, 1995; Kligman, "Contemporary Jewish Music in America," 121–123; "Debbie Friedman Home Page," www.soundswrite.com/swdf.html.

155. Nancy Flam, "Healing of Body; Healing of Spirit," *Sh'ma* 28 (October 3, 1997): 4; E. J. Kessler, "Baby Boomers Start to Pray for Healing," *Forward,* April 30, 1999; Lesley Sussman, "Finding Wellness in Angels, Auras, and the Healing Touch," *Forward,* June 30, 1995.

CONCLUSION

1. Others count the people present using the ten Hebrew words from Psalms 28:9; see *Kitzur Shulhan Aruch* 15:3.

2. Babylonian Talmud, Tractate Yoma 22B; I Samuel 11:18; 2 Samuel 28; Nahum M. Sarna, *Exodus: The JPS Torah Commentary* (Philadelphia: JPS, 1991), 195; Patricia Cline Cohen, *A Calculating People* (Chicago: University of Chicago Press, 1982), 225.

3. The National Jewish Population Survey data may be found on www.ujc.org/njps; the American Jewish Identity Survey is at www.egonmayer.com.

4. Edwin Scott Gaustad and Philip L. Barlow, *New Historical Atlas of Religion in America* (New York: Oxford University Press, 2001), 98, 100, 177; Marlena Schmool and Frances Cohen, *A Profile of British Jewry: Patterns and Trends at the Turn of the Century* (London, 1998); *AJYB* 102 (2002): 621, 632, 641. One researcher challenged reports that the American Jewish population is shrinking, but his own study was roundly condemned; see Sidney Goldstein and Ira Sheskin, "Two Studies, Only One Authentic," *Jewish Week,* October 18, 2002, p. 26.

5. United Jewish Communities, Press Release, October 8, 2002, pp. 2–3; Erich Rosenthal, "Jewish Fertility in the United States," *AJYB* 62 (1961): 3–27, discusses earlier trends.

6. *AJYB* 102 (2002): 614–615.

7. Egon Mayer et al., *American Jewish Identity Survey 2001* (New York: Graduate Center of the City University of New York, 2002), 25 [available at www.egonmayer.com].

8. Linda J. Sax, *America's Jewish Freshmen* (Los Angeles: Higher Education Research Institute, UCLA, 2002), 52–54.

9. Sarna and Golden, "The Twentieth Century Through American Jewish Eyes," 66; Stanley Lieberson and Mary C. Waters, *From Many Strands: Ethnic and Racial Groups in Contemporary America* (New York: Russell Sage Foundation, 1988), 232–235.

10. Jonathan D. Sarna, "Interreligious Marriage in America," *The Intermarriage Crisis* (New York: William Petschek National Jewish Family Center of the American Jewish Committee, 1991), 1–6; Paul R. Spickard, *Mixed Blood: Intermarriage and Ethnic Identity in Twentieth-Century America* (Madison: University of Wisconsin Press, 1989), 59ff, 344; Lieberson and Waters, *From Many Strands*, 173, 225; Robert Wuthnow, *The Restructuring of American Religion: Society and Faith Since World War II* (Princeton: Princeton University Press, 1988), 333 n.58; "Intermarriage," Orthodox Christian Laity, www.ocl.org/intermar.htm; Statistical Assessment Service, www.stats.org/newsletters/9708/interrace2.htm; Michael Rosenfeld and Byung-Soo Kim, "Between Families: On the Independence and Intermarriage of Young Adults in the US," available as preprint on www.stanford.edumrosenfe/Rosenfeld +Kim%20November%202002.pdf; "Intermarriage and Homogamy: Causes, Patterns, Trends," www.sistahspace.com/nommo/ir25.html.

11. Mik Moore, "Sex, Miscegenation, and the Intermarriage Debate," *New Voices: National Jewish Student Magazine* 6 (November 1997): 4; Barry A. Kosmin et al., *Highlights of the CJF 1990 National Jewish Population Survey* (New York: Council of Jewish Federations, 1991), 13–14; Steven M. Cohen, "Why Intermarriage May Not Threaten Jewish Continuity," *Moment* 19 (December 1994): 95 (see the responses in the April 1995 issue); *Jerusalem Report*, September 5, 1996, pp. 26–27.

12. Sergio Della Pergola, "World Jewish Population," *AJYB* 101 (2001): 536 n.7; Sylvia Barack Fishman, *Jewish and Something Else: A Study of Mixed-Married Families* (New York: American Jewish Committee, 2001); Sylvia Barack Fishman, *Double or Nothing: Jewish Families and Mixed Marriage* (Hanover: Brandeis University Press, 2004); see also the debate between Edmund Case and Jack Wertheimer in *Jerusalem Report*, December 16, 2002, p. 56.

13. Michael A. Meyer, "The Role and Identity of Non-Jews in Reform Temples," *Gesher* 48 (Winter 2002): 66–74 [in Hebrew]; *Jerusalem Report*, September 5, 1996, p. 27; for Reconstructionst deliberations on this issue, see www.jrf.org/cong/rolenonjew -sum.html.

14. Steven M. Cohen, *Religious Stability and Ethnic Decline: Emerging Patterns of Jewish Identity in the United States* (New York: Florence G. Helier–Jewish Community Centers Association Research Center, 1998), esp. 19–20, 44; Jonathan D. Sarna, "Reform Jewish Leaders, Intermarriage and Conversion," *Journal of Reform Judaism* 37 (Winter 1990): 5–6; Cohen and Eisen, *The Jew Within*, 29–30, 103–105.

15. Mark L. Winer et al., *Leaders of Reform Judaism* (New York: Union of American Hebrew Congregations, 1987), 106–112; Sarna, "Reform Jewish Leaders, Intermarriage and Conversion," 7; Israel, *Comprehensive Report on the 1995 Demographic Study*, 94; Cohen and Eisen, *The Jew Within*, 132–133.

16. Jim Schwartz et al., "Census of U.S. Synagogues, 2001," *AJYB* 102 (2002): 112–150; Bernard Lazerwitz et al., *Jewish Choices: American Jewish Denominationalism* (Albany: SUNY Press, 1998), 125; Israel, *Comprehensive Report on the 1995 Demographic Study*, 40, 48; Isa Aron, *Becoming a Congregation of Learners* (Woodstock, Vt.: Jewish Lights, 2000), xiii–x, 10–13.

17. *AJYB* 88 (1988): 203.

18. *AJYB* 89 (1989): 162.

19. Kaplan, *American Reform Judaism*, 54–58.

20. *Jewish Action* 59 (Fall 1998): 52; Sarna, "The Future of American Orthodoxy," 1–3.

21. Elazar and Geffen, *The Conservative Movement in Judaism*, 117–118; Wertheimer, *Jews in the Center*, 58, 353.

22. *AJYB* 102 (2002): 221–222, 647; "A Most Unorthodox Rabbi," *Boston Globe*, October 22, 1996; Walter Ruby, "Saturday, The Rabbi Stayed Home," *Moment*, October 1997, pp. 39–44, 81–84.

23. Cohen and Eisen, *The Jew Within*, 91–92, 192.

24. H. Richard Niebuhr, *Christ and Culture* (New York: Harper, 1951); Jay P. Dolan, *In Search of an American Catholicism: A History of Religion and Culture in Tension* (New York: Oxford University Press, 2002).

25. Sarna, "The Cult of Synthesis in American Jewish Culture," 52–79; Liebman, "Reconstructionism in American Jewish Life," 68; Fishman, *Jewish Life and American Culture*, 1.

26. Jonathan D. Sarna, "Is Judaism Compatible with American Civil Religion? The Problem of Christmas and the 'National Faith,'" 153; Jane Leavy, *Sandy Koufax: A Lefty's Legacy* (New York: HarperCollins, 2002), 169–195.

27. Wertheimer, *A People Divided*, xiii; Reuven Bulka, *The Coming Cataclysm: The Orthodox-Reform Rift and the Future of the Jewish People* (Oakville, Ontario: Mosaic, 1984), 13; Irving Greenberg, *Will There Be One Jewish People in the Year 2000?* (New York: National Jewish Resource Center, 1985); David Vital, *The Future of the Jews: A People at the Crossroads?* (Cambridge: Harvard University Press, 1990), 101; Freedman, *Jew vs. Jew*.

28. Freedman, *Jew vs. Jew*; Debra Nussbaum Cohen, "Are the Jewish People Splitting Apart?" available online at www.jewishaz.com/jewishnews/971003/split-sb.html.

29. Ammiel Hirsch and Yosef Reinman, *One People, Two Worlds: A Reform Rabbi and an Orthodox Rabbi Explore the Issues That Divide Them* (New York: Schocken, 2002); Samuel G. Freedman, "They Canceled Dialogue," *Jerusalem Report*, December 16, 2002, p. 54.

30. Simon Rawidowicz, *Studies in Jewish Thought*, ed. Nahum N. Glatzer (Philadelphia: Jewish Publication Society of America, 1964), 223; Marshall Sklare, *Observing America's Jews* (Hanover, N.H.: University Press of New England, 1993), 262–274.

Glossary

Adjunta Spanish for the standing committee (council, *mahamad*) of the synagogue; typically comprises men of wealth and substance.

Agunah (plural, *agunot*) Hebrew for an "anchored" or "deserted" woman who cannot remarry, either because her husband has denied her a divorce or because it is not known whether he is alive.

Aliyah (plural, *aliyot*) Hebrew for "ascent"; used in connection with one who is called up to the Torah, or who immigrates ("makes *aliyah*") to settle in the Land of Israel.

Ashkenazi/Ashkenazic (plural, *Ashkenazim*) From the biblical word associated with Germany *(Ashkenaz);* refers to Jews who trace their roots to the Germanic lands.

Ba'al teshuva (plural, *baale teshuva*) Hebrew for penitent Jew(s) who "return" to the path of traditional Judaism (akin to being "born again").

Bar mitzvah The initiation of a Jewish boy, aged thirteen, into full-fledged membership in the Jewish community.

Bat mitzvah The initiation of a Jewish girl, aged twelve or older, into adult membership in the Jewish community. This ceremony developed only in the twentieth century.

B'nai B'rith Hebrew for "Sons of the Covenant." A fraternal organization founded in 1843 to strengthen the bonds of brotherhood among Jewish men in the United States and later around the world.

Chabad See *Lubavitch*

Converso(s) Jew(s) who converted to Christianity in fourteenth- or fifteenth-century Spain, either forcibly or voluntarily. Prohibited by church law from ever returning to Judaism, many conversos practiced Judaism in secret as Crypto-Jews, called by their opponents *marranos*.

Davvenen   Yiddish for "to worship" or "to pray."

Ezrat-nashim   Hebrew for the women's section of the synagogue.

Glatt kosher   A more stringent standard of what is deemed to be kosher. While originally based on whether the lungs of the animal were "smooth" (glatt), the term later came to mean kosher beyond any shadow of a doubt.

Haftarah   Literally "conclusion"; refers to the reading from the biblical Prophets that follows the conclusion of the Torah-reading on Sabbaths and holidays.

Haham   Hebrew for "sage," the title given to a rabbi in the Sephardic community.

Halakhah   Jewish law.

Hanukkah   Eight-day post-biblical Jewish holiday commemorating the rededication of the temple in Jerusalem in the year 165 BCE, following its defilement by Greek worship. Marked by the lighting of candles.

Hasid (plural, *Hasidim*)   Adherents of the movement known as Hasidism (from a Hebrew word meaning "piety"), which spread through Eastern Europe beginning in the second half of the eighteenth century. Fervor, ecstasy, close-knit fellowship, and charismatic leadership characterize the Hasidic movement. Many of its adherents wear distinctive clothing to distinguish themselves both from other Jews and from non-Jews.

Haskamah (plural, *Haskamot;* also *Askamah/Askamot*)   Hebrew for "agreement" or "covenant," referring to the constitution and by-laws of the community.

Havurah (plural, *Havurot*)   Hebrew for "fellowship." Groups that gather periodically for worship, study, celebration, mutual support, and social action, echoing the separatist religious fellowships of the late Second Temple era.

Hazzan   Hebrew for "cantor." In early America, the hazzan not only chanted the prayers but frequently functioned as the minister of the congregation as well.

Herem   Hebrew for "excommunication."

Hillel   Jewish campus organization founded in 1923 and reorganized in 1988. Named for one of the greatest of the ancient Jewish sages, Hillel the Elder (first century BCE).

Kabbalah   Jewish mysticism.

Kaddish   A liturgical doxology recited by mourners as well as during the regular worship service.

Kahal   See *Kehillah*

Kahal Kadosh   Hebrew for "holy community." Often abbreviated as "K. K." before the name of a synagogue.

Kashrut   Literally, "lawfulness"; the term refers to the system of Jewish dietary laws that governs whether food is "kosher"—fit to be eaten by observant Jews.

Kehillah (plural *Kehillot*)   Hebrew for "community." Though it harks back to the distinctive form of communal self-government that characterized Jewish life in the Middle Ages, the term came to apply to any Jewish community ("the kehillah of Philadelphia"), as well as to the community of members in any particular synagogue.

Kippah   Head covering, skullcap; known in Yiddish as a *yarmulke*. While customs vary, Jewish tradition views the covering of the head by men as a sign of humility before God, and as an identifying marker of Judaism.

K'lal Yisrael   The entire community of Israel; the Jewish people ("Catholic Israel").

Kolel (plural, *Kolelim*)   Institutions of advanced Talmudic studies for married yeshivah students.

Kosher   See *Kashrut*

Landsmanshaftn   Associations of immigrants from the same home town (Yiddish).

Lubavitch (also spelled Lubavitz or Lubavich)   A late eighteenth-century Hasidic movement dedicated to "wisdom, understanding, and knowledge" (the acronym for which, in Hebrew, transliterates as *Chabad*). Centered until World War I in the Belorussian city of Lubavitch. The sixth rebbe of Lubavitch settled in America in 1940.

Magen David   Literally "shield of David," the name is used for the hexagram (six-pointed star), that came to be known as the "Jewish star" or "star of David."

Mahamad   See *Adjunta*

Matzah   Unleavened bread; the only bread permitted during Passover.

Mehizah   Hebrew for the partition separating male and female worshippers in the synagogue.

Mezuzah (plural, *Mezuzot*)   Hebrew for "doorpost." The handwritten parchment scroll containing passages from Deutcronomy 6:4–9 and 11:13–21 that is affixed to the doorpost, in compliance with Deuteronomy 6:9 "Inscribe them on the doorposts of your house and on your gates."

Mikveh   A pool of water used for ritual immersion and purification.

Minhag   Hebrew for a custom or ritual practice, often specific to a family or community.

Minyan   Hebrew for the prayer quorum required for Jewish group worship, traditionally consisting of ten males over the age of thirteen.

Mitzvah (plural, *Mitzvot*)   Hebrew for "commandments." According to Jewish tradition there are 613 commandments: 365 negative and 248 affirmative. In common parlance, the term *mitzvah* often refers merely to a "good deed" or an act of charity.

M'lochim   Literally "angels," a Hasidic sect developed in America in the 1930s by followers of the charismatic Rabbi Chaim Avraham Dov Ber Levine HaCohen, known as the "Malach" (angel).

Mohel (plural, *mohalim*)   Hebrew for the ritual expert who performs the rite of circumcision, traditionally carried out on the eighth day of a baby boy's life, following God's commandment to Abraham (Genesis 17:10) "every male among you shall be circumcised."

Neshamah (plural, *neshamot;* in Yiddish, *neshomas*)   Hebrew for "soul."

Nigun (plural, *nigunnim*)   Hebrew word meaning melody, tune, or chant. Hasidim punctuate their prayers and ritual meals with wordless nigunnim.

Parnas   President; the head of the kehillah.

Purim   Feast of Lots, celebrated on the fourteenth day of the Hebrew month of Adar in commemoration of the events that saved the ancient Jewish community of Persia, as recounted in the Bible in the Book of Esther.

Rebbe   Hasidic term (Hebrew and Yiddish) for the leader of the sect, the "grand rabbi."

Rebbetzin   The Yiddish term for the wife of a rabbi.

Rosh Hashanah   The Jewish New Year, known as the Day of Judgment, celebrated on the first and second days of the Hebrew month of Tishre in the fall.

Rosh Hodesh   The new moon; the beginning of a new month according to the Jewish lunar calendar.

Sefer Torah   Hebrew for "book of the Pentateuch." A handwritten parchment scroll containing the Hebrew text of the first five books of the Bible (the Pentateuch), known by Jews as the Torah.

Sephardi/Sephardic (plural, *Sephardim*)   From the biblical name associated with Spain *(Sepharad)*. Refers to Jews who trace their roots back to the Iberian peninsula.

Shammash   The synagogue sexton or beadle, responsible for everything that the rabbi and cantor do *not* do, from secretarial and janitorial duties to carrying out minor religious functions.

Shavuot   Pentecost, the Feast of Weeks, celebrated on the fiftieth day after the second night of Passover. Originally celebrated as harvest festival, it also commemorates the giving of the Torah on Mount Sinai.

Shema   Judaism's preeminent expression of monotheism and quintessential expression of belief and commitment (Deuteronomy 6:4–9), beginning with the words "Hear (in Hebrew, *Shema*) O Israel, the Lord is our God, the Lord alone."

Shivah   Hebrew for "seven," a reference to the seven-day "memorial week" that Jews observe following the death of a close relative.

Shluchim   Emissaries; the rabbinic Hebrew term used by the rebbe of Lubavitch for those whom he dispatched to set up institutions and promote
his mission around the world.

Shoah   Catastrophe; the Hebrew term for what became known in English
as the Holocaust.

Shofar   The ram's horn, used in ancient Israel to signal important events,
and sounded in the synagogue on Rosh Hashanah and at the conclusion of Yom Kippur.

Shohet   A ritual slaughterer, necessary for kosher meat and poultry.

Shul   Yiddish for "synagogue"; also means "school."

Shvitser   Yiddish for "hustler," from a word meaning "to perspire."

Siddur   Hebrew for "prayer book," from a word meaning to "order" or
"arrange."

Simhat Torah   Rejoicing of the Torah, the fall holiday that marks the completion of the annual cycle of Pentateuchal readings. After reading
aloud the last chapter of Deuteronomy, Jews immediately begin again
with the first chapter of Genesis.

Takkanah (plural, *takkanot*)   A rabbinic enactment or ordinance.

Tallit   Prayer shawl. Traditionally, men wear the rectangular fringed tallit
over their shoulders or heads during morning prayers.

Tallit-katan   Literally, small prayer shawl. A four-cornered garment with
fringes that rests on the shoulders and is worn under the shirt by observant Jewish males during daylight hours. This fulfills the biblical commandment in Numbers 15:38–39: "Speak to the Israelite people and
instruct them to make for themselves fringes on the corners of their
garments throughout the ages. . . . Look at it and recall all the commandments of the LORD and observe them."

Talmud   The foundational document of Rabbinic Judaism. The Talmud
(from a Hebrew word that means "learning") is a vast compilation of
Jewish oral law divided into six orders and sixty-three tractates. The
Babylonian Talmud, which dates to the end of the sixth century, is more
complete and more widely studied than its counterpart from the Land
of Israel, and it forms the basis for Jewish law and practice.

Tefillin   Often translated as "phylacteries." Two boxes containing handwritten
Scriptural quotations, bound with leather straps to the forehead and
left arm during daily morning prayers, in fulfillment of Deuteronomy
6:8: "Bind them as a sign on your hand and let them serve as a symbol
on your forehead."

Tisha B'Av   The fast of the ninth day of the Jewish month of Av, which falls
in the summer. Traditionally the saddest day in the Jewish calendar,
the fast commemorates the destruction of both ancient temples, as well
as many subsequent catastrophes.

Torah   Refers narrowly to the Five Books of Moses (Pentateuch) and broadly to the whole body of Jewish learning and literature, written and oral.

Trefa   All forbidden or unkosher foods, derived from Exodus 22:30, where it refers to "flesh torn by beasts in the field."

Yahid (plural, *yehidim*)   First-class or full members of a Sephardic congregation.

Yarmulke   See *Kippah*

Yeshivah   A traditional Jewish Talmudic academy; a school of higher Jewish learning.

Yiddishkeit (Yehudishkeit)   Jewishness; a Yiddish term for the feelings, practices, and values that all Jews, religious and secular alike, are supposed to share.

Yom HaShoah   Holocaust Memorial Day; the annual day of mourning for the victims of the Holocaust, commemorated on the twenty-seventh day of the Hebrew month of Nisan, five days after Passover concludes.

Yom Kippur   The Day of Atonement, a twenty-five-hour fast day that climaxes the ten-day period of repentance beginning on *Rosh Hashanah*.

Zaddik   A righteous person, outstanding for his faith and piety. Often applied to the Hasidic rebbe.

Critical Dates in the
History of American Judaism

1492   Expulsion of Jews from Spain. Christopher Columbus "discovers" America.

1585   Joachim Gaunse arrives at Roanoke Island; a year later he departs.

1630   Holland captures Pernambuco, Brazil, from the Portuguese and invites Jewish settlement. A significant Jewish community develops in Recife.

1654   Portugal recaptures Brazil and expels Jews and Protestants. While most Jews return to Holland, a boatload of twenty-three Jews sails into New Amsterdam.

1655   Jews win the right to settle in New Amsterdam and establish a Jewish community.

1678   Jewish cemetery set up in Newport, Rhode Island.

c. 1695–1704   New York Jews experience transition from covert worship in a private home to public worship in a rented house.

1730   New York Jews build North America's first synagogue, Shearith Israel, on Mill Street.

1730s–50s   Jewish communities established in Savannah, Georgia; Charleston, South Carolina; Philadelphia; and Newport, Rhode Island.

1763   Newport Jews dedicate synagogue, later known as Touro Synagogue— the only surviving colonial synagogue structure.

1776   Jews divide in the face of the American Revolution; majority favors new nation.

1788   Ratification of the Constitution permits Jews to hold federal office.

1790   George Washington visits Newport and, in response to an address from its Jews, describes religious liberty as an inherent natural right.

1791   First Amendment to the Constitution forbids Congress from making any laws "respecting an establishment of religion or prohibiting the free exercise thereof."

1802   Rodeph Shalom, America's first Ashkenazic synagogue, founded in Philadelphia.

1819   Female Hebrew Benevolent Society, the first Jewish women's benevolent organization and the first non-synagogal Jewish charitable society of any kind, established in Philadelphia.

1823   Solomon H. Jackson establishes the first American Jewish periodical, *The Jew,* to combat Christian missionaries.

1825   Collapse of synagogue-community in Charleston and New York. Dissident Charleston Jews organize the Reformed Society of Israelites; dissident New York Jews form B'nai Jeshurun, the city's first Ashkenazic congregation.

1825   Mordecai M. Noah proclaims Grand Island, New York, to be "Ararat," a "city of refuge" for the Jews. The plan fails.

1829   Isaac Leeser appointed hazan of Mikveh Israel in Philadelphia. He soon introduces English-language sermons and other innovations designed to educate and reinvigorate his community within the parameters of traditional Jewish law and practice.

1838   Rebecca Gratz in Philadelphia establishes America's first Jewish Sunday School.

1840   Abraham Rice, America's first ordained rabbi, immigrates to America from Bavaria and assumes pulpit in Baltimore. Other rabbis follow, most of whom, unlike Rice, come to advocate religious reforms.

1840–46   Dispute over the installation of a synagogue organ rocks Charleston Jewry, dividing "Reform" Jews from those who begin to call themselves "Orthodox." The courts refuse to intervene, thereby setting an important precedent.

1843   Establishment of the Jewish fraternal organization B'nai B'rith, which aims to preserve Jewish life on the basis of peoplehood rather than through the practice of faith.

1851   Congregation Anshe Emeth in Albany becomes the first synagogue to seat men and women together in mixed pews.

1852   Immigrants from Lithuania and Poland establish New York's first East European Orthodox synagogue, the Beth Hamidrash.

1853   Isaac Leeser publishes his translation of the Bible into English. It is the first complete Anglo-Jewish translation of the Bible.

1854   Isaac Mayer Wise, who immigrated to America in 1846, moves to Cincinnati with a lifetime contract, promising to shape an American form of Judaism. He begins to publish the *Israelite* (later *American Israelite*).

1855   A rabbinical conference in Cleveland aimed at promoting a united

American Judaism ends in failure, underscoring American Judaism's deepening ideological divisions.

1859   Board of Delegates of American Israelites founded "to keep a watchful eye on all occurrences at home and abroad" and to collect statistics. It represents less than a fifth of America's synagogues.

1860   Rabbi Morris Raphall becomes the first Jewish clergyman to deliver a prayer at the opening of a session of Congress.

1862   Military chaplaincy law amended, following Jewish protests, allowing ministers ordained by non-Christian denominations to serve as chaplains in the Union army.

1862   General U. S. Grant, blaming "Jews as a class" for cotton speculation and smuggling, expels all Jews from his war zone, the most sweeping anti-Jewish act in American history. Cesar Kaskel, one of those expelled, appeals directly to President Abraham Lincoln, who overturns the order.

1867   Isaac Leeser founds Maimonides College, a short-lived rabbinical seminary.

1867   Rabbi Max Lilienthal exchanges pulpits with the Unitarian minister of Cincinnati. The widely publicized innovation is emulated around the country.

1873   Union of American Hebrew Congregations established in Cincinnati. It aims to create a rabbinical seminary, strengthen Jewish education, and preserve Jewish identity. Rather than embracing all American synagogues, as its founders hoped, it soon becomes the Reform Jewish congregational union.

1875   Hebrew Union College founded in Cincinnati under the presidency of Isaac Mayer Wise. Its graduates promote Reform Judaism.

1876   Felix Adler publicly renounces Judaism in favor of Ethical Culture, a universalistic faith focused on ethics and the teachings of world religions.

1877   Joseph Seligman, a prominent banker, is refused admission to the Grand Union Hotel in Saratoga Springs allegedly because he is a Jew. The incident highlights the growth of social antisemitism in America. The social status of Jews declines.

1879   The *American Hebrew,* a highbrow Jewish newspaper, established in New York by idealistic young Jews who seek to perpetuate and elevate the spirit of Judaism.

1881   Pogroms and anti-Jewish legislation in Russia following the assassination of Alexander II propel thousands of Jews to leave for the United States, marking the onset of mass East European Jewish immigration.

1883   Tenth anniversary of Union of American Hebrew Congregations and first ordination from Hebrew Union College marked by a non-kosher *(trefa)* banquet. Resulting uproar leads to calls for a more religiously traditional seminary.

1885   Public controversy in New York between Rabbis Kaufmann Kohler and Alexander Kohut highlights key differences between reformers and traditionalists.

1885   Eight-point "Pittsburgh Platform," promulgated by Reform rabbis called together by Kaufmann Kohler, seeks to demonstrate "what Reform Judaism means and aims at."

1886   Etz Chaim Yeshiva established in New York by Orthodox lay leaders. It places Talmud at the core of its curriculum and teaches secular studies after 4 P.M.

1887   Jewish Theological Seminary opens in New York to serve "Jews of America faithful to Mosaic law and ancestral tradition." Over time it becomes the training ground for Conservative rabbis.

1888   Jacob Joseph arrives in New York from Vilna to serve as the city's first chief rabbi. Finding himself powerless, he accomplishes little. No subsequent chief rabbi is ever appointed.

1888   The Jewish Publication Society is founded as part of a renaissance of American Jewish life.

1889   The Central Conference of American Rabbis is founded, under the presidency of Isaac Mayer Wise. Designed initially as a regional rabbinical association, it soon becomes the rabbinical arm of the Reform movement.

1893   National Council of Jewish Women founded in Chicago.

1897   Rabbi Isaac Elchanan Theological Seminary established in New York, the first advanced Talmudical academy in the United States. It aims to be an "American counterpart of the finest yeshivas of Eastern Europe."

1898   Orthodox Jewish Congregational Union of America founded, forerunner of the Orthodox Union. Its platform seeks to refute the Reform movement's Pittsburgh Platform, and it stands in opposition to the Union of American Hebrew Congregations.

1898   Federation of American Zionists established in New York City.

1901   First volume of *Jewish Encyclopedia* published in New York. The encyclopedia signifies that Jewish cultural authority is passing to the new world and that the language of Jewish scholarly discourse is shifting to English.

1902   Solomon Schechter, greatest English-speaking Jewish scholar of his day, arrives in New York from England to lead the reorganized Jewish Theological Seminary of America. He promises to transform it into a center of Jewish scholarship.

1902   Agudath ha-Rabbanim (Union of Orthodox Rabbis) founded to strengthen the authority of European-trained Orthodox rabbis and to resist Americanization.

1903　Emma Lazarus's poem "The New Colossus" (1883) added to the pedestal of the Statue of Liberty. It welcomes all immigrants with the words: "Give me your tired, your poor, / Your huddled masses yearning to breathe free."

1904　Temple Beth El in Detroit replaces assigned seats with a system of free seating, allowing all to sit where they choose. "In God's house," its rabbi declares, "all must be equal. There must be no aristocracy and no snobocracy."

1906　The American Jewish Committee established by Jewish patricians "to prevent infringement of the civil and religious rights of Jews, and to alleviate the consequences of persecution."

1909　The Kehillah, the organized Jewish community of New York, estab- lished to unite the community's many segments. Owing to financial, organizational, and political problems, it lasts only thirteen years.

1912　Henrietta Szold founds Hadassah, the Women's Zionist Organization of America.

1913　United Synagogue of America founded as the congregational arm of the Jewish Theological Seminary, signaling growing tensions between "Conservative" congregations and the Orthodox Union.

1913　Young Israel movement established, backed by students at the Jewish Theological Seminary, to "bring about a revival of Judaism among the thousands of young Jews and Jewesses . . . whose Judaism is at present dormant."

1914　First national convention of Mizrachi, the religious Zionist organiza- tion founded in Vilna in 1902. It takes as its English motto: "The Land of Israel for the people of Israel according to the Torah of Israel."

1914　American Jewish Joint Distribution Committee formed as organiza- tions representing different segments of the American Jewish commu- nity pool their funds and cooperate to apportion and send money and supplies abroad for Jewish war relief.

1915　Leo Frank, wrongly convicted of the murder of a young employee in Atlanta in a trial tainted by media frenzy and antisemitism, has his sentence commuted by Governor John Slaton. A mob that includes leading local citizens kidnaps Frank and lynches him.

1915　Bernard Revel assumes the leadership of the newly merged Etz Chaim yeshiva and Rabbi Isaac Elchanan Theological Seminary. In time he develops them into Yeshiva College, forerunner of Yeshiva University.

1916　Louis Brandeis, the "people's lawyer" and, since 1914, the leader of the Zionist movement, becomes America's first Jewish Supreme Court justice.

1917 Jewish Welfare Board established to meet the religious needs of Jewish soldiers serving in the World War. It represents fourteen different Jewish organizations and religious bodies and declares itself "Jewishly nonpartisan."

1917 Jewish Publication Society publishes a new English translation of the Hebrew Bible that wins broad acceptance throughout the Anglo-Jewish world.

1918 President Woodrow Wilson announces America's approval of the Balfour Declaration issued by Great Britain in 1917 favoring the establishment of a Jewish homeland in Palestine.

1920 Henry Ford's *Dearborn Independent* begins the publication of ninety-one articles purporting to describe an international Jewish conspiracy based on the notorious antisemitic forgery known as *The Protocols of the Elders of Zion.*

1920 The National Prohibition (Volstead) Act provides an exemption to those, like Jews, who use wine for "sacramental purposes." Following widespread abuses, many Jewish religious leaders advocate the use of grape juice in place of wine.

1922 Having published "A Program for the Reconstruction of Judaism" in 1920, Mordecai Kaplan resigns from his Orthodox congregation, the Jewish Center, and founds the Society for the Advancement of Judaism, a forerunner of Reconstructionism. There he performs a bat mitzvah for his daughter, Judith, the first known bat mitzvah on American soil.

1922 Stephen S. Wise founds the Jewish Institute of Religion in New York, a rabbinical seminary open to all Jews, and committed to Zionism, social justice, and the task of serving the Jewish people as a whole. In 1949 it merges into Hebrew Union College.

1927 Henry Ford, under intense pressure, publicly apologizes for publishing antisemitic canards. The text of his apology is drafted by Louis Marshall, president of the American Jewish Committee.

1927 National Conference of Christians and Jews established. It popularizes a religiously pluralistic image of America and sends ministers, priests, and rabbis to barnstorm the country in an effort to rout religious prejudice.

1928 Dedication of Yeshiva College's Washington Square campus in New York seen to symbolize the "successful arrival of Orthodoxy in the mainstream of American Jewry."

1930 The failure of the Jewish-owned Bank of the United States brings losses to countless Jewish individuals and businesses, aggravating Depression-era hardships.

1933 The American Jewish Congress leads a boycott of German goods to protest Germany's anti-Jewish boycott and antisemitic policies. The American Jewish Committee opposes the boycott, fearing that Jews in Germany will suffer on its account.

1934 Mordecai Kaplan publishes *Judaism as a Civilization: Toward a Reconstruction of American-Jewish Life,* one of the most widely discussed and influential Jewish books of the twentieth century.

1935 The Rabbinical Assembly tentatively approves Louis M. Epstein's proposal for solving the plight of the agunah. The plan faces withering attacks from the Agudath ha-Rabbanim, widening the breach between Conservative and Orthodox Jews.

1935 Rabbinical Council of America, a merger of the Rabbinical Association of the Rabbi Isaac Elchanan Theological Seminary and the Rabbinical Council of the Orthodox Union, becomes the central organization of American-trained Orthodox rabbis.

1937 The Columbus Platform provides a new set of guiding principles for Reform Jews, placing new emphasis on Jewish peoplehood, religious practices, and the building up of Palestine as a "Jewish homeland."

1938 The Fair Labor Standards Act enforces the five-day, forty-hour week in many industries. Instead of having to choose between the American pattern of work and the Jewish day of rest, increasing numbers of Jews can now embrace both.

1938 Father Charles Coughlin denounces Jews on his popular radio program and in his widely read magazine, *Social Justice.*

1940 Joseph I. Schneersohn, sixth Lubavitcher rebbe, receives presidential visa and settles in Crown Heights, Brooklyn. He establishes schools and other institutions aimed at transforming America into the "new center for Torah and Judaism," replacing Europe.

1941 Aharon Kotler, champion of fervent Orthodoxy, immigrates to America on a presidential visa. In 1943 he founds the Beth Medrash Govoha in Lakewood, New Jersey, now the leading academy of advanced Talmudic education in the United States.

1941 Opening of Camp Massad and Brandeis Camp Institute inaugurate an era of rapid growth for Jewish educational camps, including the creation of the Conservative (Ramah) and Reform camping movements in 1947 and 1952.

1941 Rabbi Joseph Soloveitchik succeeds his father as the senior Talmudic scholar at Yeshiva College. Through his teachings and writings he comes to embody the modern Orthodox quest to combine a commitment to traditional Jewish law with an openness to modern secular culture and society.

1942 Nazi plans to annihilate European Jewry reach Stephen Wise and are confirmed by the State Department. Wise announces that 2 million

Jews have been killed by the Nazis in an "extermination campaign."
Day of mourning held on December 2.

1942   Anti-Zionists in the Reform movement organize the American Council
for Judaism, which opposes a Jewish state and seeks to restore Reform
Judaism to its classical moorings.

1943   American Jewish Conference, a short-lived parliament of Jewish organizations, endorses American Zionism's Biltmore Platform, which calls
for the re-creation of the Jewish commonwealth in Palestine.

1943   Hundreds of Orthodox rabbis march on Washington seeking immediate
rescue efforts to save the Jews of Europe. President Roosevelt declines
to meet with the rabbis, whose march is later recalled as the only one of
its kind on behalf of Europe's Jews.

1944   Shraga Feivel Mendlowitz founds Torah Umesorah, the National
Society for Hebrew Day Schools, "to disseminate the true Torah spirit
by establishing yeshivas . . . throughout the United States of America."
It calls for "a day school in every community."

1945   *Commentary* magazine begins publication under the sponsorship of the
American Jewish Committee.

1946   Rabbi Joshua Loth Liebman's *Peace of Mind* tops the bestseller list.
Never before have so many Americans of diverse faiths turned to a
contemporary rabbi for help in meeting their own spiritual and psychological needs.

1948   Brandeis University established as America's first Jewish-sponsored
nonsectarian university. It provides a haven for refugee scholars and
admits students on the basis of merit, without quotas and without
regard to religion or race.

1948   The state of Israel declares its independence and is recognized by the
United States. Increasingly, Israel becomes central to American Jewish
identity.

1950   Israel's Prime Minister, David Ben Gurion, and the president of the
American Jewish Committee, Jacob Blaustein, exchange statements
concerning the relationship between American Jews and Israel, affirm-
ing American Jewry's independence.

1950   Breaking with Orthodoxy, the Conservative movement permits Jews
to use electricity and drive to the synagogue on the Sabbath, thereby
providing rabbinic sanction for the basic lifestyle changes adopted by
most suburban Jews.

1951   Union of American Hebrew Congregations relocates from Cincinnati
to New York in a bid to achieve closer proximity to the "vibrant multitudes of our people."

1953   Execution of Julius and Ethel Rosenberg, convicted of delivering atomic secrets to the Soviet Union, contributes to climate of fear in Jewish secularist circles. In the ensuing decade, many Yiddishist and secularist institutions collapse.

1954 Tercentenary of Jewish settlement in the United States displays communal optimism, reinforcing group consciousness and pride.

1955 Will Herberg's bestselling *Protestant-Catholic-Jew* elevates Jews to insider status in American religion, introducing the concept of a religious "triple melting pot."

1955 Rabbinical Assembly's Committee on Jewish Law and Standards accepts as a legitimate minority view the calling of women to the Torah (aliyot) on a regular basis.

1956 Leaders of fervent Orthodoxy ban official contacts between Orthodox rabbis and their Reform and Conservative counterparts through such organizations as the New York Board of Rabbis and the Synagogue Council of America.

1958 The bombing of Atlanta's oldest and most prestigious Reform temple in response to its rabbi's call for racial justice caps a series of violent attacks by extreme segregationists against Jewish institutions in the South.

1959 Shlomo Carlebach releases his first record album. It becomes an instant hit and creates a new genre: neo-Hasidic Orthodox folk music.

1960 Elie Wiesel publishes an English-language edition of his memoir, *Night,* the first of his many books written to keep the memory of the Holocaust alive.

1960 Release of the film *Exodus,* based on Leon Uris's novel, fosters identification with the state of Israel among Jews and Christians alike.

1962 The Reform Movement opens the Religious Action Center in Washington, D.C., dedicated to the pursuit of social justice and religious liberty.

1963 Joachim Prinz, speaking as an American Jew, proclaims that "the issue is silence" in a celebrated address at the civil rights march on Washington.

1963 Zalman Schachter founds B'nai Or, forerunner of the Jewish Renewal Movement, in an effort to renew Jewish prayer.

1964 The American Jewish Conference on Soviet Jewry and the Student Struggle for Soviet Jewry established, initiating a successful campaign to release Jews from Soviet bondage. Over 1.5 million Soviet Jews eventually emigrate to Israel, the United States, and Western Europe.

1965 Abraham Joshua Heschel walks arm in arm with Martin Luther King and other black leaders on the civil rights march from Selma to Montgomery, Alabama. A photo of the event becomes an icon of Jewish involvement in the civil rights movement.

1965 *Nostra Aetate,* an official Catholic statement on the Jews issued as part of Vatican II, marks a turning point in Catholic-Jewish relations as the church decries hatred, persecution, and displays of antisemitism.

1967 Six Day War between Israel and its Arab neighbors thrusts the fate of the Jewish state to the forefront of American Jewish consciousness. Amid fears of another Holocaust, American Jews raise $430 million for Israel and, in the war's wake, both tourism and emigration to Israel rise dramatically.

1968 Students in Massachusetts form Havurat Shalom, devoted to fellowship, peace, community, and a "new model of serious Jewish study." It serves as a forerunner of the Jewish counterculture and the havurah movement, and seeks to promote Jewish renewal.

1968 Reconstructionist Rabbinical College in Philadelphia opens, signaling Reconstructionism's willingness to institutionalize itself as an independent force in Jewish life. It is the first rabbinical seminary to admit women as students.

1969 Association for Jewish Studies founded, marking the growth of Jewish studies on college campuses across the country. By 2003, it boasts 1,600 members.

1971 Ezrat Nashim, founded by young, well-educated Conservative Jewish women, begins to agitate "for an end to the second-class status of women in Jewish life."

1972 Sally Priesand, America's first woman rabbi, ordained by Hebrew Union College. Sandy Eisenberg Sasso is ordained by the Reconstructionist Rabbinical College two years later.

1973 *The Jewish Catalog* published. The bestselling volume (later expanded to three) serves as the vehicle for transmitting the innovations pioneered by the Jewish counterculture to Jews throughout North America and beyond.

1973 Thousands throng Madison Square Garden's Felt Forum for Rebbetzin Esther Jungreis's first great "awakening." Her Hineni movement, modeled, in part, on the techniques of Billy Graham, wins numerous Jews back to Judaism.

1976 Centenary Perspective of the Reform Movement describes "diversity within unity" as the hallmark of Reform, thereby legitimating new religious currents within the movement, including the reclamation of once-abandoned rituals.

1983 The Reform movement adopts the principle of "patrilineal descent," accepted by Reconstructionism in 1968. Both movements recognize the offspring of a Jewish father as Jewish, even if the mother is not, so long as the child is raised as a Jew. Critics warn against two different definitions of who is a Jew.

1983 The Jewish Theological Seminary votes to ordain women as Conservative rabbis, following more than a decade of debate. Traditionalists break away and form the Union for Traditional Conservative Judaism. The first Conservative woman rabbi, Amy Eilberg, is ordained in 1985.

1985 The Wexner Heritage Program is established to promote high-level adult Jewish education. The Florence Melton Adult Mini Schools (1986), the Me'ah Program (1994), and other initiatives build on the rising nationwide interest in adult Jewish learning.

1985 The Union of American Hebrew Congregations votes to support the establishment of Reform Jewish day schools, setting aside objections from those who support public school education for Jews.

1993 The opening of the United States Holocaust Memorial Museum in Washington, and the release of the popular film *Schindler's List* by Steven Spielberg, heighten public awareness of the Holocaust throughout the United States.

1994 Death of Menahem Mendel Schneerson, seventh Lubavitcher rebbe, who spread his movement across the United States and the world. His demise heightens messianic fervor among some of his followers, while the Lubavitch movement continues to grow.

1999 New "Statement of Principles for Reform Judaism" invites Reform Jews to engage in a dialogue with tradition and calls for renewed attention to mitzvot, sacred obligations.

2000 Senator Joseph Lieberman nominated for the vice presidency on the Democratic Party ticket, the first Jew ever to be nominated for this post by a major political party. The ticket wins a plurality of the votes but loses the election.

2001 September 11 terrorist attacks on New York and Washington, D.C., spread fear through the Jewish community, leading to heightened security and a renewed sense of patriotism.

2002 Surveys point to a decline in America's Jewish population, the first since the colonial era.

2004 Jews celebrate 350 years of American Jewish history.

Selected Bibliography

Ahlstrom, Sydney E. *A Religious History of the American People.* New Haven: Yale University Press, 1972.

Alexander, Michael. *Jazz Age Jews.* Princeton: Princeton University Press, 2001.

Alpert, Rebecca T., and Jacob J. Staub. *Exploring Judaism: A Reconstructionist Approach.* New York: Reconstructionist Press, 1985.

American Jewish Committee. War Records Office. *The War Record of American Jews.* New York, 1919.

Antler, Joyce. *The Journey Home: Jewish Women and the American Century.* New York: Free Press, 1997.

Antonovsky, Aaron, and Elias Tcherikower, editors. *The Early Jewish Labor Movement in the United States.* New York: YIVO Institute, 1961.

Appelbaum, Paul S. "The Soviet Jewry Movement in the United States." In *Jewish American Voluntary Organizations,* edited by Michael N. Dobkowski. Westport, Conn.: Greenwood, 1986.

Arad, Gulie Ne'eman. *America, Its Jews, and the Rise of Nazism.* Bloomington: Indiana University Press, 2000.

Ariel, Yaakov. "Counterculture and Mission: Jews for Jesus and the Vietnam Era Missionary Campaigns, 1970–1975." *Religion and American Culture* 9 (Summer 1999): 233–257.

Ash, Stephen V. "Civil War Exodus: The Jews and Grant's General Order No. 11." *Historian* 44 (August 1982): 505–523.

Ashkenazi, Elliot. *Business of Jews in Louisiana, 1840–1875.* Tuscaloosa: University of Alabama Press, 1998.

Ashton, Dianne. "Shifting Veils: Religion, Politics, and Womanhood in the Civil War Writings of American Jewish Women." In *Women and American Judaism: Historical Perspectives,* edited by Pamela S. Nadell and Jonathan D. Sarna. Hanover, N.H.: Brandeis University Press, 2001.

Ashton, Dianne. *Unsubdued Spirits: Rebecca Gratz and Women's Judaism in America.* Detroit: Wayne State University Press, 1997.

Aviad, Janet O. *Return to Judaism: Religious Renewal in Israel.* Chicago: University of Chicago Press, 1983.

Avruch, Kevin. *American Immigrants in Israel: Social Identities and Change.* Chicago: University of Chicago Press, 1981.

Baldwin, Neil. *Henry Ford and the Jews: The Mass Production of Hate.* New York: Public Affairs, 2001.

Barish, Louis, editor. *Rabbis in Uniform: The Story of the American Jewish Military Chaplain.* New York: J. David, 1962.

Barkai, Avraham. *Branching Out: German-Jewish Immigration to the United States, 1820–1914.* New York: Holmes & Meier, 1994.

Barnett, Lionel D., editor and translator. *El Libro de los Acuerdos.* Oxford: Oxford University Press, 1931.

Baron, Salo W. *Steeled by Adversity: Essays and Addresses on American Jewish Life.* Philadelphia: Jewish Publication Society of America, 1971.

Bartal, Israel. "Heavenly America: The USA as an Ideal Model for Nineteenth-Century East European Jews" [in Hebrew]. In *Following Columbus: America, 1492–1992,* edited by Miriam Eliav-Felton. Jerusalem: Merkaz Shazar, 1996.

Bauer, Yehuda. *My Brother's Keeper: A History of the American Joint Distribution Committee, 1929–1939.* Philadelphia: Jewish Publication Society of America, 1974.

Bauman, Mark K., and Berkley Kalin, editors. *The Quiet Voices: Southern Rabbis and Black Civil Rights, 1880s to 1990s.* Tuscaloosa: University of Alabama Press, 1997.

Beinart, Haim, editor. *Moreshet Sepharad: The Sephardi Legacy.* Jerusalem: Magnes, 1992.

Bendersky, Joseph. *The "Jewish Threat": Anti-Semitic Politics of the U.S. Army.* New York: Basic Books, 2000.

Benjamin, I. J. *Three Years in America.* Translated by Charles Reznikoff. Philadelphia: Jewish Publication Society of America, 1956.

Berman, Jeremiah J. *Shehitah.* New York: Bloch, 1941.

Berman, Myron. "A New Spirit on the East Side: The Early History of the Emanu-El Brotherhood, 1903–1920." *American Jewish Historical Quarterly* 54 (1964): 53–81.

Berman, Myron. *Richmond's Jewry, 1769–1976: Shabbat in Shockoe.* Charlottesville: University of Virginia Press, 1979.

Bernardini, Paolo, and Norman Fiering, editors. *The Jews and the Expansion of Europe to the West, 1450–1800.* New York: Berghahn, 2001.

Bernheimer, Charles S. *The Russian Jew in the United States.* Philadelphia: John C. Winston, 1905.

Bernstein, Louis. *Challenge and Mission.* New York: Shengold, 1982.

Bernstein, Louis. "The Emergence of the English-Speaking Orthodox Rabbinate." Ph.D. diss., Yeshiva University, 1977.

Bialystok, Franklin. *Delayed Impact: The Holocaust and the Canadian Jewish Community.* Montreal: McGill–Queen's University Press, 2000.

Bingham, Emily. *Mordecai: An Early American Family.* New York: Hill and Wang, 2003.

Bingham, Emily. "Mordecai: Three Generations of a Southern Jewish Family, 1780–1865." Ph.D. diss., University of North Carolina at Chapel Hill, 1998.

Birmingham, Stephen. *Our Crowd.* New York: Dell, 1967.

Blau, Joseph L., and Salo W. Baron, editors. *The Jews of the United States: A Documentary History, 1790–1840.* New York: Columbia University Press, 1963.

Blumberg, Janice Rothschild. *One Voice: Rabbi Jacob M. Rothschild and the Troubled South.* Macon, Ga.: Mercer University Press, 1985.

Bomzer, Herbert W. *The Kollel in America.* New York: Shengold, 1985.

Bonomi, Patricia U. *Under the Cope of Heaven: Religion, Society and Politics in Colonial New York.* New York: Oxford University Press, 1986.

Bratt, James D. "The Reorientation of American Protestantism, 1835–1845." *Church History* 67 (1998): 58–82.

Breibart, Solomon. *The Rev. Mr. Gustavus Poznanski: First Jewish Reformist.* Charleston, S.C.: Kahal Kadosh Beth Elohim, 1979.

Breitman, Richard, and Alan M. Kraut. *American Refugee Policy and European Jewry, 1933–1945.* Bloomington: Indiana University Press, 1987.

Brener, David. *The Jews of Lancaster, Pennsylvania: A Story with Two Beginnings.* Lancaster, Pa.: Congregation Shaarai Shomayim in association with the Lancaster County Historical Society, 1979.

Brener, David. "Lancaster's First Jewish Community, 1715–1804: The Era of Joseph Simon." *Journal of the Lancaster County Historical Society* 80:4 (Michaelmas [September] 1976): 211–322.

Breuer, Mordechai. *Modernity Within Tradition: The Social History of Orthodox Jewry in Imperial Germany.* New York: Columbia University Press, 1992.

Broches, S. *Jews in New England: Six Monographs.* New York: Bloch, 1942.

Buchler, Joseph. "The Struggle for Unity: Attempts at Union in American Jewish Life, 1654–1868." *American Jewish Archives* 2 (June 1949): 2–27.

Bunim, Amos. *A Fire in His Soul.* New York: Feldheim, 1989.

Butler, Jon. *Awash in a Sea of Faith: Christianizing the American People.* Cambridge: Harvard University Press, 1990.

Butler, Jon. *Huguenots in America.* Cambridge: Harvard University Press, 1983.

Cahan, Abraham. "A Back Number." In *Grandma Never Lived in America,* edited by Moses Rischin. Bloomington: Indiana University Press, 1985.

Caplan, Kimmy. "In God We Trust: Salaries and Income of American Orthodox Rabbis, 1881–1924." *American Jewish History* 86 (1998): 89–93.

Caplan, Kimmy. *Orthodoxy in the New World: Immigrant Rabbis and Preaching in America (1881–1924)* [in Hebrew]. Jerusalem: Merkaz Shazar, 2002.

Caplan, Kimmy. "Rabbi Isaac Margolis: From Eastern Europe to America" [in Hebrew]. *Zion* 58 (1992–93): 215–240.

Chyet, Stanley F. *Lopez of Newport.* Detroit: Wayne State University Press, 1980.

Clar, Reva, and William M. Kramer. "The Girl Rabbi of the Golden West: The Adventurous Life of Ray Frank in Nevada, California, and the Northwest." *Western States Jewish History* 18 (1986): 99–111, 223–236, 336–351.

Cohen, Martin A., and Abraham J. Peck, editors. *Sephardim in the Americas: Studies in Culture and History.* Tuscaloosa: University of Alabama Press, 1993.

Cohen, Naomi W. "The Abrogation of the Russo-American Treaty of 1832." *Jewish Social Studies* 25 (1963): 3–41.

Cohen, Naomi W. "American Jewish Reactions to Anti-Semitism in Western Europe,

1875–1900." *Proceedings of the American Academy of Jewish Research* 45 (1978): 29–65.

Cohen, Naomi W. "The Challenges of Darwinism and Biblical Criticism to American Judaism." *Modern Judaism* 4 (May 1984): 121–157.

Cohen, Naomi W. *Encounter with Emancipation: The German Jews in the United States, 1830–1914.* Philadelphia: Jewish Publication Society, 1984.

Cohen, Naomi W. *Not Free to Desist: The American Jewish Committee, 1906–1966.* Philadelphia: Jewish Publication Society of America, 1972.

Cohen, Naomi W. "The Reaction of Reform Judaism in America to Political Zionism (1897–1922)." *Publications of the American Jewish Historical Society* 40 (1951): 361–394.

Cohen, Steven M., and Arnold M. Eisen. *The Jew Within: Self, Family, and Community in America.* Bloomington: Indiana University Press, 2001.

Cohn, Bernard. "Leo Merzbacher." *American Jewish Archives* 6 (1954): 21–24.

Coney Island and the Jews. New York: G. W. Carleton, 1879.

Cowen, Philip. *Memories of an American Jew.* New York: International Press, 1932.

Dalin, David G. "Will Herberg in Retrospect." *Commentary* 86 (July 1988): 38–43.

Dantowitz, Faith Joy. *Generations and Reflections: A History of Congregation B'nai Jeshurun, Short Hills, New Jersey.* Short Hills, N.J.: B'nai Jeshurun, 1998.

Danzger, Herbert. *Returning to Tradition: The Contemporary Revival of Orthodox Judaism.* New Haven: Yale University Press, 1989.

Dash, Joan. *The Life of Henrietta Szold.* New York: Harper & Row, 1979.

Davidman, Lynn. *Tradition in a Rootless World: Women Turn to Orthodox Judaism.* Berkeley: University of California Press, 1991.

Davis, Edward. *The History of Rodeph Shalom Congregation Philadelphia, 1802–1926.* Philadelphia: Edward Stern, 1926.

Davis, Moshe. *The Emergence of Conservative Judaism: The Historical School in Nineteenth-Century America.* Philadelphia: Jewish Publication Society of America, 1965.

Davis, Moshe. "The Lincoln-Hart Correspondence." *Publications of the American Jewish Historical Society* 38 (1948–49): 142–145.

Dawidowicz, Lucy S. *On Equal Terms: Jews in America, 1881–1981.* New York: Holt, Rinehart & Winston, 1984.

Della Pergola, Sergio, and Uzi Rebhun. "American Orthodox Jews: Demographic Trends and Scenarios." *Jewish Action* 59 (Fall 1998): 30–33.

Diamond, Etan. *"And I Will Dwell in Their Midst": Orthodox Jews in Suburbia.* Chapel Hill: University of North Carolina Press, 2000.

Diner, Hasia R. *In the Almost Promised Land: American Blacks and Jews, 1915–1935.* 2nd ed. Baltimore: Johns Hopkins University Press, 1995.

Diner, Hasia R. "Like the Antelope and the Badger: The Founding and Early Years of the Jewish Theological Seminary, 1886–1902." In *Tradition Renewed: A History of the Jewish Theological Seminary of America,* edited by Jack Wertheimer. 2 vols. New York: Jewish Theological Seminary, 1997.

Diner, Hasia R. *A Time for Gathering: The Second Migration, 1820–1880.* Baltimore: Johns Hopkins University Press, 1992.

Dinnerstein, Leonard. *Antisemitism in America.* New York: Oxford University Press, 1994.

Dinnerstein, Leonard. "The Fate of Leo Frank." *American Heritage* 47 (October 1996): 98–109.

Dinnerstein, Leonard. "The Funeral of Rabbi Jacob Joseph." In *Anti-Semitism in American History,* edited by David A. Gerber. Urbana: University of Illinois Press, 1986.

Dinnerstein, Leonard. *The Leo Frank Case.* New York: Columbia University Press, 1968.

Dobkowski, Michael N., editor. *Jewish American Voluntary Organizations.* Westport, Conn.: Greenwood, 1986.

Drachsler, Julius. *Intermarriage in New York.* New York, 1921.

Dushkin, Alexander M., and Uriah Z. Engelman. *Jewish Education in the United States.* New York: American Association for Jewish Education, 1959.

Ehrlich, Walter. *Zion in the Valley: The Jewish Community of St. Louis.* Columbia: University of Missouri Press, 1997.

Eisenstein, Judah D. "The History of the First Russian-American Jewish Congregation." *Publications of the American Jewish Historical Society* 9 (1901): 63–74.

Eisenstein, Judah D. *Ozar Zikhronothai: Autobiography and Memoirs* [in Hebrew]. New York, 1929.

Elazar, Daniel J., and Rela Mintz Geffen. *The Conservative Movement in Judaism: Dilemmas and Opportunities.* Albany: SUNY Press, 2000.

Elazar, Daniel J., Jonathan D. Sarna, and Rela G. Monson. *A Double Bond: The Constitutional Documents of American Jewry.* Lanham, Md.: University Press of America, 1992.

Ellenson, David. "Envisioning Israel in the Liturgies of North American Liberal Judaism." In *Envisioning Israel,* edited by Allon Gal. Detroit: Wayne State University Press/Magnes, 1996.

Ellenson, David. "A Jewish Legal Authority Addresses Jewish-Christian Dialogue: The Responsa of Rabbi Moshe Feinstein." *American Jewish Archives* 52 (2000): 112–128.

Emmanuel, Isaac S. "New Light on Early American Jewry." *American Jewish Archives* 7 (January 1955): 3–64.

Emmanuel, Isaac S., and Suzanne A. Emmanuel. *History of the Jews of the Netherlands Antilles.* Cincinnati: American Jewish Archives, 1970.

Encyclopedia Judaica. Jerusalem: Keter, 1972.

Endelman, Todd. *The Jews of Georgian England, 1714–1830.* Philadelphia: Jewish Publication Society, 1979.

Engelman, Uriah Zvi. "Jewish Statistics in the U.S. Census of Religious Bodies (1850–1935)." *Jewish Social Studies* 9 (1947): 127–174.

Erens, Patricia. *The Jew in American Cinema.* Bloomington: Indiana University Press, 1984.

Essays in American Jewish History to Commemorate the Tenth Anniversary of the Founding of the American Jewish Archives Under the Direction of Jacob Rader Marcus. Cincinnati: American Jewish Archives, 1958.

Ezekiel, Herbert T., and Gaston Lichtenstein. *The History of the Jews of Richmond from 1769 to 1917.* Richmond, Va.: Ezekiel, 1917.

Faber, Eli. *A Time for Planting: The First Migration.* Baltimore: Johns Hopkins University Press, 1992.

Fein, Isaac M. *The Making of an American Jewish Community: The History of Baltimore Jewry from 1773 to 1920.* Philadelphia: Jewish Publication Society of America, 1971.

Feingold, Henry L. *A Time for Searching: Entering the Mainstream, 1920–1945.* Baltimore: Johns Hopkins University Press, 1992.

Feingold, Henry L. "Who Shall Bear Guilt for the Holocaust: The Human Dilemma." *American Jewish History* 68 (March 1979): 261–282.

Feldman, Egal. "The Social Gospel and the Jews." *American Jewish Historical Quarterly* 58 (March 1969): 308–322.

Fierstien, Robert E. *A Different Spirit: The Jewish Theological Seminary of America, 1886–1902.* New York: Jewish Theological Seminary, 1990.

Finkelman, Yoel. "Haredi Isolation in Changing Environments: A Case Study in Yeshiva Immigration." *Modern Judaism* 22 (February 2002): 61–82.

Finkelstein, Louis, editor. *The Jews.* New York: Harper & Brothers, 1949.

Fish, Sydney M. *Bernard and Michael Gratz: Their Lives and Times.* Lanham, Md.: University Press of America, 1994.

Fish, Sydney M. "The Problem of Intermarriage in Early America." *Gratz College Annual of Jewish Studies* 4 (1975): 85–94.

Fishman, Sylvia Barack. "American Jewish Fiction Turns Inward, 1960–1990." *American Jewish Year Book* 91 (1991): 35–69.

Fishman, Sylvia Barack. *A Breath of Life: Feminism in the American Jewish Community.* New York: Free Press, 1993.

Fishman, Sylvia Barack. *Changing Minds: Feminism in Contemporary Orthodox Jewish Life.* New York: William Petschek National Jewish Family Center of the American Jewish Committee, 2000.

Fishman, Sylvia Barack. *Jewish Life and American Culture.* Albany: SUNY Press, 2000.

Fox, Steven A. "On the Road to Unity: The Union of American Hebrew Congregations and American Jewry, 1873–1903." *American Jewish Archives* 32 (1980): 145–193.

Freedman, Samuel G. *Jew vs. Jew: The Struggle for the Soul of American Jewry.* New York: Simon & Schuster, 2000.

Friedenberg, Robert V. *"Hear O Israel": The History of American Jewish Preaching, 1654–1970.* Tuscaloosa: University of Alabama Press, 1989.

Friedland, Michael B. *Lift Up Your Voice Like a Trumpet: White Clergy and the Civil Rights and Antiwar Movements, 1954–1973.* Chapel Hill: University of North Carolina Press, 1998.

Friedman, Murray, editor. *Jewish Life in Philadelphia.* Philadelphia: ISHI, 1983.

Friedman, Murray, and Albert D. Chernin, editors. *A Second Exodus: The American Movement to Free Soviet Jews.* Hanover, N.H.: Brandeis University Press, 1999.

Friesel, Evyatar. *The Zionist Movement in the United States, 1897–1914* [in Hebrew]. Tel Aviv: Kibbutz-Ha-Meuchad, 1970.

Gans, Herbert J. "The Origin and Growth of a Jewish Community in the Suburbs: A Study of the Jews of Park Forest." In *The Jews,* edited by Marshall Sklare. New York: Free Press, 1958.

Gartner, Lloyd P. "The Great Jewish Migration—Its East European Background." *Tel Aviver Jahrbuch fuer deutsche Geschichte* 27 (1998): 107–133.

Gartner, Lloyd P. *History of the Jews of Cleveland.* Cleveland: Western Reserve Historical Society, 1978.

Gartner, Lloyd, P. "Jewish Migrants en Route from Europe to North America: Traditions and Realities." In *The Jews of North America,* edited by Moses Rischin. Detroit: Wayne State University Press, 1987.

Gartner, Lloyd P. "Temples of Liberty Unpolluted: American Jews and Public Schools,

1840–1875." In *A Bicentennial Festschrift for Jacob Rader Marcus,* edited by Bertram W. Korn. New York: Ktav, 1976.

Gastwirt, Harold P. *Fraud, Corruption, and Holiness.* New York: Kennikat, 1974.

Gehring, Charles T., editor. *Council Minutes, 1655–1656.* Vol. 6 of New Netherland Documents Series. New York: Syracuse University Press, 1995.

Gerber, Jane S. *The Jews of Spain.* New York: Free Press, 1992.

Glanz, Rudolf. "The Spread of Jewish Communities Through America Before the Civil War." *YIVO Annual* 15 (1974): 7–45.

Glanz, Rudolf. *Studies in Judaica Americana.* New York: Ktav, 1970.

Glanz, Rudolf. "Where the Jewish Press Was Distributed in Pre-Civil War America." *Western States Jewish Historical Quarterly* 5 (1972): 1–14.

Glazer, Nathan. *American Judaism.* Chicago: University of Chicago Press, 1972.

Godfrey, Sheldon J., and Judith C. Godfrey. *Search Out the Land: The Jews and the Growth of Equality in British Colonial America, 1740–1867.* Montreal: McGill–Queen's University Press, 1995.

Goldberg, J. J. *Jewish Power.* Reading, Mass.: Addison-Wesley, 1996.

Goldman, Karla A. "The Ambivalence of Reform Judaism: Kaufmann Kohler and the Ideal Jewish Woman." *American Jewish History* 79 (Summer 1990): 477–499.

Goldman, Karla A. "Beyond the Gallery: The Place of Women in the Development of American Judaism." Ph.D. diss., Harvard University, 1993.

Goldman, Karla A. *Beyond the Synagogue Gallery: Finding a Place for Women in American Judaism.* Cambridge: Harvard University Press, 2000.

Goldstein, Herbert S., editor. *Forty Years of Struggle for a Principle: The Biography of Harry Fischel.* New York: Bloch, 1928.

Goldstein, Israel. *A Century of Judaism in New York: B'nai Jeshurun, 1825–1925.* New York: Congregation B'nai Jeshurun, 1930.

Goldstein, Judith. *The Politics of Ethnic Pressure: The American Jewish Committee Fight Against Immigration Restriction, 1906–1917.* New York: Garland, 1990.

Goldstein, Sidney, and Calvin Goldscheider. *Jewish Americans: Three Generations in a Jewish Community.* Englewood, N.J.: Prentice Hall, 1968.

Goldstein, Sidney, and Alice Goldstein. *Jews on the Move.* New York: SUNY Press, 1996.

Goldy, Robert G. *The Emergence of Jewish Theology in America.* Bloomington: Indiana University Press, 1990.

Golinkin, David, editor. *Proceedings of the Committee on Jewish Law and Standards of the Conservative Movement, 1927–1970.* 3 vols. Jerusalem: Rabbinical Assembly and Institute of Applied Halakhah, 1997.

Golinkin, David. *Responsa of Professor Louis Ginzberg.* Jerusalem: Jewish Theological Seminary of America, 1996.

Goodfriend, Joyce D. *Before the Melting Pot: Society and Culture in Colonial New York City, 1664–1730.* Princeton: Princeton University Press, 1992.

Goodman, Abram V., editor. "A Jewish Peddler's Diary, 1842–1843." *American Jewish Archives* 3 (June 1951): 81–109.

Goodman, Saul L., editor. *The Faith of Secular Jews.* New York: Ktav, 1976.

Goodman, Saul L., editor. *Our First Fifty Years: The Sholem Aleichem Folk Institute.* New York: Sholem Aleichem Folk Institute, 1972.

Gordon, Albert I. *Jews in Suburbia.* Boston: Beacon, 1959.

Goren, Arthur A., editor. *Dissenter in Zion: From the Writings of Judah L. Magnes.* Cambridge: Harvard University Press, 1982.

Goren, Arthur A. "A 'Golden Decade' for American Jews: 1945–1955." *Studies in Contemporary Jewry* 8 (1993): 3–20.

Goren, Arthur A. *New York Jews and the Quest for Community: The Kehillah Experiment, 1908–1922.* New York: Columbia University Press, 1970.

Goren, Arthur A. "Traditional Institutions Transplanted: The Hevra Kadisha in Europe and in America." In *The Jews of North America,* edited by Moses Rischin. Detroit: Wayne State University Press, 1987.

Green, Arthur. *Jewish Spirituality.* New York: Crossroads, 1976.

Greenberg, Rose. *The Chronicle of Baltimore Hebrew Congregation, 1830–1975.* Baltimore: The Congregation, 1976.

Greenberg, Simon, editor. *The Ordination of Women as Rabbis: Studies and Responsa.* New York: Jewish Theological Seminary, 1988.

Greene, Melissa Fay. *The Temple Bombing.* Reading, Mass.: Addison-Wesley, 1996.

Greenstein, Howard. *Turning Point: Zionism and Reform Judaism.* Chico, Calif.: Scholars Press, 1981.

Grinstein, Hyman B. *The Rise of the Jewish Community of New York.* Philadelphia: Jewish Publication Society of America, 1945.

Gross, Alexander S., and Joseph Kaminetsky. "Shraga Feivel Mendlowitz." In *Men of the Spirit,* edited by Leo Jung. New York: Kymson, 1964.

Grusd, Edward E. *B'nai B'rith: The Story of a Covenant.* New York: Appleton-Century, 1966.

Gurock, Jeffrey S. *American Jewish Orthodoxy in Historical Perspective.* Hoboken, N.J.: Ktav, 1996.

Gurock, Jeffrey S. "Jewish Commitment and Continuity in Interwar Brooklyn." In *Jews of Brooklyn,* edited by Ilana Abramovitch and Sean Galvin. Hanover, N.H.: University Press of New England, 2002.

Gurock, Jeffrey S. *The Men and Women of Yeshiva University: Higher Education, Orthodoxy, and American Judaism.* New York: Columbia University Press, 1988.

Gurock, Jeffrey S., and Jacob J. Schacter. *A Modern Heretic and a Traditional Community: Mordecai M. Kaplan, Orthodoxy, and American Judaism.* New York: Columbia University Press, 1997.

Gutstein, Morris A. *A Priceless Heritage: The Epic Growth of Nineteenth-Century Chicago Jewry.* New York: Bloch, 1953.

Gutstein, Morris A. *The Story of the Jews of Newport.* New York: Bloch, 1936.

Hagy, James William. *This Happy Land: The Jews of Colonial and Antebellum Charleston.* Tuscaloosa: University of Alabama Press, 1993.

Halpern, Ben. "The Americanization of Zionism, 1880–1930." *American Jewish History* 69 (1979): 15–33.

Handlin, Oscar. *This Was America.* New York: Harper Torchbooks, 1964.

Hapgood, Hutchins. *The Spirit of the Ghetto.* Cambridge: Belknap Press of Harvard University, 1967.

Harap, Louis. *Creative Awakening: The Jewish Presence in Twentieth-Century American Literature, 1900–1940s.* New York: Greenwood, 1987.

Harap, Louis. *In the Mainstream: The Jewish Presence in Twentieth-Century American Literature, 1950–1980s.* New York: Greenwood, 1987.

Hatch, Nathan O. *The Democratization of American Christianity.* New Haven: Yale University Press, 1989.

Heilbut, Anthony. *Exiled in Paradise: German Refugee Artists and Intellectuals in America from the 1930s to the Present.* Berkeley: University of California Press, 1983.

Heinze, Andrew R. *Adapting to Abundance: Jewish Immigrants, Mass Consumption, and the Search for American Identity.* New York: Columbia University Press, 1990.

Heller, James G. *As Yesterday When It Is Past: A History of the Isaac M. Wise Temple, K. K. B'nai Yeshurun of Cincinnati, in Commemoration of the Centenary of Its Founding.* Cincinnati: Isaac M. Wise Temple, 1942.

Helmreich, William B. "Old Wine in New Bottles: Advanced Yeshivot in the United States." *American Jewish History* 69 (December 1979): 234–256.

Helmreich, William B. *The World of the Yeshiva: An Intimate Portrait of Orthodox Jewry.* New York: Free Press, 1982.

Herberg, Will. *Protestant-Catholic-Jew: An Essay in American Religious Sociology.* Rev. ed. New York: Anchor, 1960.

Hershkowitz, Leo. "Another Abigail Franks Letter and a Genealogical Note." *American Jewish Historical Quarterly* 59 (1969): 223–226.

Hershkowitz, Leo. "New Amsterdam's Twenty-Three Jews—Myth or Reality?" In *Hebrew and the Bible in America,* edited by Shalom Goldman. Hanover, N.H.: University Press of New England, 1993.

Hershkowitz, Leo. *Wills of Early New York Jews (1704–1799).* New York: American Jewish Historical Society, 1967.

Hershkowitz, Leo, and Isidore S. Meyer, editors. *The Lee Max Friedman Collection of American Jewish Colonial Correspondence: Letters of the Franks Family (1733–1748).* Waltham, Mass.: American Jewish Historical Society, 1968.

Hertzberg, Arthur. *The Jews in America: Four Centuries of an Uneasy Encounter.* New York: Simon & Schuster, 1989.

Hertzberg, Arthur. "Treifene Medine: Learned Opposition to Emigration to the United States." *Proceedings of the Eighth World Congress of Jewish Studies, 1981, Panel Sessions, Jewish History.* Jerusalem: World Union of Jewish Studies, 1984.

Hertzberg, Steven. *Strangers Within the Gate City: The Jews of Atlanta, 1845–1915.* Philadelphia: Jewish Publication Society of America, 1978.

Heschel, Abraham J. *Moral Grandeur and Spiritual Audacity: Essays.* Edited by Susannah Heschel. New York: Farrar, Straus & Giroux, 1996.

Heschel, Susannah. "Theological Affinities in the Writings of Abraham Joshua Heschel and Martin Luther King, Jr." In *Black Zion: African American Religious Encounters with Judaism,* edited by Yvonne Chireau and Nathaniel Deutsch. New York: Oxford University Press, 2000.

Higham, John. *Send These to Me: Immigrants in Urban America.* Baltimore: Johns Hopkins University Press, 1984.

Higham, John. *Strangers in the Land: Patterns of American Nativism, 1860–1925.* New York: Atheneum, 1963.

Hoberman, J., and Jeffrey Shandler. *Entertaining America: Jews, Movies, and Broadcasting.* Princeton: Princeton University Press, 2003.

Hoffman, Edward. *Despite All Odds: The Story of the Lubavitch.* New York: Simon & Schuster, 1991.

Horowitz, Bethamie. *Connections and Journeys: Assessing Critical Opportunities for Enhancing Jewish Identity.* New York: UJA–Federation of Jewish Philanthropies of New York, 2000.

Howe, Irving. *World of Our Fathers.* New York: Harcourt, Brace and Jovanovich, 1976.

Hunnicut, Benjamin Kline. "The Jewish Sabbath Movement in the Early Twentieth Century." *American Jewish History* 79 (December 1979): 196–225.

Hyman, Paula. "Ezrat Nashim and the Emergence of a New Jewish Feminism." In *The Americanization of the Jews,* edited by Robert M. Seltzer and Norman J. Cohen. New York: New York University Press, 1995.

Hyman, Paula. "Feminism in the Conservative Movement." In *The Seminary at 100: Reflections on the Jewish Theological Seminary and the Conservative Movement,* edited by Nina Beth Cardin and David Wolf Silverman. New York: Rabbinical Assembly and Jewish Theological Seminary of America, 1987.

Hyman, Paula. *Gender and Assimilation in Modern Jewish History: The Roles and Representation of Women.* Seattle: University of Washington Press, 1995.

Hyman, Paula. "Immigrant Women and Consumer Protest: The New York City Kosher Meat Boycott of 1902." *American Jewish History* 70 (September 1980): 91–105.

Hyman, Paula. "The Introduction of Bat Mitzvah in Conservative Judaism in Postwar America." *YIVO Annual* 19 (1990): 133–146.

Israel, Sherry R. *Comprehensive Report on the 1995 Demographic Study.* Boston: Combined Jewish Philanthropies, 1997.

Jacob, Walter, editor. *American Reform Responsa.* New York: Central Conference of American Rabbis, 1983.

Jacob, Walter, editor. *The Changing World of Reform Judaism: The Pittsburgh Platform in Retrospect.* Pittsburgh: Rodef Shalom Congregation, 1985.

Janowsky, Oscar. *The JWB Survey.* New York: Dial, 1948.

Jewish Communal Register of New York City, 1917–1918. New York: Kehillah, 1918.

Jick, Leon. *The Americanization of the Synagogue, 1820–1870.* Hanover, N.H.: Brandeis University Press, 1976.

Joselit, Jenna W. "Merry Chanukah: The Changing Holiday Practices of American Jews, 1880–1950." In *The Uses of Tradition: Jewish Continuity in the Modern Era,* edited by Jack Wertheimer. New York: Jewish Theological Seminary and Harvard University Press, 1993.

Joselit, Jenna W. *New York's Jewish Jews: The Orthodox Community in the Interwar Years.* Bloomington: Indiana University Press, 1990.

Joselit, Jenna W. *The Wonders of America: Reinventing Jewish Culture, 1880–1950.* New York: Hill and Wang, 1994.

Jungreis, Esther. *The Jewish Soul on Fire.* New York: William Morrow, 1982.

Kahan, Arcadius. *Essays in Jewish Social and Economic History.* Chicago: University of Chicago Press, 1986.

Kalisch, Isidor. *Studies in Ancient and Modern Judaism.* New York: Dobsevage, 1928.

Kamenetz, Rodger. *Stalking Elijah: Adventures with Today's Jewish Mystical Masters.* New York: Harper San Francisco, 1997.

Kanfer, Stefan. *A Summer World.* New York: Farrar, Straus & Giroux, 1989.

Kaplan, Benjamin J. "Fictions of Privacy: House Chapels and the Spatial Accommodation of Religious Dissent in Early Modern Europe." *American Historical Review* 107 (October 2002): 1031–1064.

Kaplan, Dana Evan. *American Reform Judaism: An Introduction.* New Brunswick, N.J.: Rutgers University Press, 2003.

Kaplan, Dana Evan, editor. *Contemporary Debates in American Reform Judaism: Conflicting Visions.* New York: Routledge, 2001.

Kaplan, Edward K., and Samuel H. Dresner, editors. *Abraham Joshua Heschel: Prophetic Witness.* New Haven: Yale University Press, 1998.

Kaplan, Mordecai M. *Judaism as a Civilization.* Philadelphia: Jewish Publication Society, 1994.

Kaplan, Yosef. "The Portuguese Community in Amsterdam in the Seventeenth Century: Between Tradition and Change." *Divre-Ha-Akademya Ha-Leumit Ha-Yisraelit Le-Mada'im* 7 (1986): 161–181.

Karff, Samuel, editor. *Hebrew Union College–Jewish Institute of Religion at One Hundred Years.* Cincinnati: Hebrew Union College Press, 1976.

Karp, Abraham J. *A History of the United Synagogue of America, 1913–1963.* New York: United Synagogue of America, 1964.

Karp, Abraham J. *Jewish Continuity in America: Creative Survival in a Free Society.* Tuscaloosa: University of Alabama Press, 1998.

Karp, Abraham J. "New York Chooses a Chief Rabbi." *Publications of the American Jewish Historical Society* 44 (1955): 129–198.

Karp, Abraham J. "Solomon Schechter Comes to America." *American Jewish Historical Quarterly* 53 (1963): 44–62.

Kaufman, David. *Shul with a Pool: The "Synagogue Center" in American Jewish History.* Hanover, N.H.: Brandeis University Press, 1999.

Kaufman, Debra R. *Rachel's Daughters: Newly Orthodox Women.* New Brunswick, N.J.: Rutgers University Press, 1991.

Kaufman, Isidor. *American Jews in World War II.* New York: Dial Press, 1947.

Kaufman, Menahem. "Envisioning Israel: The Case of the United Jewish Appeal." In *Envisioning Israel,* edited by Allon Gal. Detroit: Wayne State University Press/Magnes, 1996.

Kaufman, Menahem. "From Philanthropy to Commitment: The Six Day War and the United Jewish Appeal." *Journal of Israeli History* 15 (Summer 1994): 161–191.

Kennedy, David M. *Freedom from Fear: The American People in Depression and War, 1929–1945.* New York: Oxford University Press, 1999.

Kershen, Anne J., and Jonathan A. Romain. *Tradition and Change: A History of Reform Judaism in Great Britain, 1840–1995.* London: Vallentine Mitchell, 1995.

Klaperman, Gilbert. *The Story of Yeshiva University: The First Jewish University in America.* New York: Macmillan, 1969.

Kligman, Mark. "Contemporary Jewish Music in America." *American Jewish Year Book* 101 (2001): 99–104.

Kohanski, Alexander S., editor. *The American Jewish Conference: Its Organization and Proceedings of the First Session.* New York: American Jewish Conference, 1944.

Kohler, Kaufmann. "David Einhorn, the Uncompromising Champion of Reform Judaism." *Central Conference of American Rabbis Yearbook* 19 (1909): 215–270.

Kohut, Alexander. *The Ethics of the Fathers.* Edited and revised by Barnett A. Elzas. New York, 1920.

Kohut, Rebekah. *My Portion: An Autobiography.* New York: Thomas Seltzer, 1925.

Korn, Bertram Wallace. *American Jewry and the Civil War.* New York: Atheneum, 1970.

Korn, Bertram Wallace. *The American Reaction to the Mortara Case: 1858–1859.* Cincinnati: American Jewish Archives, 1957.

Korn, Bertram Wallace, editor. *A Bicentennial Festschrift for Jacob Rader Marcus.* New York: Ktav, 1976.

Korn, Bertram Wallace. *Eventful Years and Experiences: Studies in Nineteenth-Century American Jewish History.* Cincinnati: American Jewish Archives, 1954.

Korn, Bertram Wallace. "Jews and Negro Slavery in the Old South, 1789–1865." *Publications of the American Jewish Historical Society* 50 (1961): 151–201.

Kortick, Joel. "Transformation and Rejuvenation: The Arrival in America of Habad and Other Orthodox Jewish Communities: 1940–1950." Master's thesis, Hebrew University, 1996.

Kramer, Judith R., and Seymour Leventman. *Children of the Gilded Ghetto: Conflict Resolutions of Three Generations of American Jews.* New Haven: Yale University Press, 1961.

Kranzler, George. *Hasidic Williamsburg.* Northvale, N.J.: Jason Aronson, 1995.

Kranzler, George. *Williamsburg: A Jewish Community in Transition.* New York: Feldheim, 1961.

Krauskopf, Joseph. "The Jewish Pilgrim Fathers." *Publications of the American Jewish Historical Society* 14 (1906): 121–130.

Kraut, Benny. "The Ambivalent Relations of American Reform Judaism with Unitarianism in the Last Third of the Nineteenth Century." *Journal of Ecumenical Studies* 23 (Winter 1986): 58–68.

Kraut, Benny. *From Reform Judaism to Ethical Culture: The Religious Evolution of Felix Adler.* Cincinnati: Hebrew Union College Press, 1979.

Kraut, Benny. "Judaism Triumphant: Isaac Mayer Wise on Unitarianism and Liberal Christianity." *AJS Review* 7–8 (1982–83): 179–230.

Kraut, Benny. "A Wary Collaboration: Jews, Catholics, and the Protestant Goodwill Movement." In *Between the Times: The Travail of the Protestant Establishment in America, 1900–1960,* edited by William R. Hutchison. New York: Cambridge University Press, 1989.

Krinsky, Carol Herselle. *Synagogues of Europe: Architecture, History, Meaning.* Cambridge: MIT Press, 1985.

Kula, Witold, Nina Assorodobraj-Kula, and Marcin Kula. *Writing Home: Immigrants in Brazil and the United States, 1890–1891.* Edited and translated by Josephine Wtulich. New York: Columbia University Press, 1986.

Kuznets, Simon. "Immigration of Russian Jews to the United States." *Perspectives in American History* 9 (1975): 35–124.

Lazarus, Emma. *An Epistle to the Hebrews.* With an introduction and notes by Morris U. Schappes. New York: Jewish Historical Society of New York, 1987.

Lederhendler, Eli, editor. *The Six Day War and World Jewry.* Bethesda: University Press of Maryland, 2000.

Leeser, Isaac. *Discourses on the Jewish Religion.* Philadelphia: Sherman, 1867.

Leeser, Isaac. "The Jews and Their Religion." In *An Original History of the Religious Denominations at Present Existing in the United States,* edited by I. Daniel Rupp. Philadelphia, 1844.

Lerner, Anne Lapidus. "'Who Hast Not Made Me a Man': The Movement for Equal Rights for Women in American Jewry." *American Jewish Year Book* 77 (1977): 3–38.

Levi, Leo N. *Memorial Volume.* Chicago, 1905.

Levin, Alexandra Lee. *The Szolds of Lombard Street.* Philadelphia: Jewish Publication Society of America, 1960.

Levitan, Tina. *Islands of Compassion: A History of the Jewish Hospitals of New York.* New York: Bloch, 1964.

Lewis, Theodore. "Touro Synagogue—National Historic Site." *Newport History* 48 (Summer 1975): 281–320.

Libowitz, Richard. *Mordecai M. Kaplan and the Development of Reconstructionism.* New York: Edward Mellen, 1983.

Liebman, Charles S. "Orthodoxy in American Jewish Life." *American Jewish Year Book* 66 (1965): 21–97.

Liebman, Charles S. *Pressure Without Sanctions.* Cranbury, N.J.: Associated University Presses, 1977.

Liebman, Charles S. "Reconstructionism in American Jewish Life." *American Jewish Year Book* 71 (1970): 3–99.

Liebman, Charles S. "Religion and the Chaos of Modernity: The Case of Contemporary Judaism." In *Take Judaism for Example,* edited by Jacob Neusner. Chicago: University of Chicago Press, 1983.

Liebman, Charles S. "The Training of American Rabbis." *American Jewish Year Book* 69 (1968): 2–112.

Liebman, Joshua Loth. *Peace of Mind.* New York: Simon & Schuster, 1946.

Lipstadt, Deborah E. "America and the Memory of the Holocaust, 1950–1965." *Modern Judaism* 16 (1996): 195–214.

Lipstadt, Deborah E. *Beyond Belief: The American Press and the Coming of the Holocaust, 1933–1945.* New York: Free Press, 1986.

Lipstadt, Deborah E. "From Noblesse Oblige to Personal Redemption: The Changing Profile and Agenda of American Jewish Leaders." *Modern Judaism* 4 (1984): 306.

Lisitzky, Ephraim E. *In the Grip of Cross-Currents.* New York: Bloch, 1959.

Litman, Simon. *Ray Frank Litman: A Memoir.* New York: American Jewish Historical Society, 1957.

Litvin, Baruch, editor. *The Sanctity of the Synagogue.* 3rd ed. New York: Ktav, 1987.

Loker, Zvi. *Jews in the Caribbean.* Jerusalem: Misgav Yerushalayim, 1991.

Lowenstein, Steven M. *Frankfurt on the Hudson: The German-Jewish Community of Washington Heights, 1933–1983, Its Structure and Culture.* Detroit: Wayne State University Press, 1989.

Mandelbaum, Yitta Halberstam. *Holy Brother: Inspiring Stories and Enchanted Tales About Shlomo Carlebach.* Northvale, N.J.: Jason Aronson, 1997.

Marcus, Jacob R. *The American Jewish Woman, 1654–1980.* Cincinnati: American Jewish Archives, 1981.

Marcus, Jacob R. *The American Jewish Woman: A Documentary History.* Cincinnati: American Jewish Archives, 1981.

Marcus, Jacob R. *American Jewry—Documents—Eighteenth Century.* Cincinnati: Hebrew Union College Press, 1959.

Marcus, Jacob R. *The Colonial American Jew, 1492–1776.* Detroit: Wayne State University Press, 1970.

Marcus, Jacob R. *The Handsome Young Priest in the Black Gown: The Personal World of Gershom Seixas.* Cincinnati: American Jewish Archives, 1970.

Marcus, Jacob R., editor. *The Jew in the American World: A Sourcebook.* Detroit: Wayne State University Press, 1996.

Marcus, Jacob R. *Memoirs of American Jews, 1775–1865.* Philadelphia: Jewish Publication Society of America, 1955.

Marcus, Jacob R., editor. *On Love, Marriage, Children . . . and Death, Too.* Cincinnati: Society of Jewish Bibliophiles, 1965.

Marcus, Jacob R. *Studies in American Jewish History.* Cincinnati: Hebrew Union College Press, 1969.

Marcus, Jacob R. *This I Believe: Documents of American Jewish Life.* Northvale, N.J.: Jason Aronson, 1990.

Marcus, Jacob R. *To Count a People: American Jewish Population Data, 1585–1984.* Lanham, Md.: University Press of America, 1990.

Marcus, Jacob R. *United States Jewry, 1776–1985.* 4 vols. Detroit: Wayne State University Press, 1989–93.

Margolis, Peter. "Seeds of Community: The Role of the Reconstructionist Movement in Creating Havurot in America." *YIVO Annual* 23 (1996): 319–364.

Markens, Isaac. "Lincoln and the Jews." *Publications of the American Jewish Historical Society* 17 (1909): 109–165.

Markovitz, Eugene. "Henry Pereira Mendes: Architect of the Union of Orthodox Jewish Congregations of America." *American Jewish Historical Quarterly* 55 (1966): 364–383.

Marty, Martin E. *Modern American Religion.* Vol. 2: *The Noise of Conflict, 1919–1941.* Chicago: University of Chicago Press, 1986.

Marty, Martin E. *Modern American Religion.* Vol. 3: *Under God Indivisible, 1941–1960.* Chicago: University of Chicago Press, 1996.

Mayer, Egon. *From Suburb to Shtetl: The Jews of Boro Park.* Philadelphia: Temple University Press, 1979.

McGill, Nettie P. "Some Characteristics of Jewish Youth in New York City." *Jewish Social Service Quarterly* 14 (September 1937): 251–272.

Mead, Sidney E. "The Rise of the Evangelical Conception of the Ministry in America (1607–1850)." In *The Ministry in Historical Perspective,* edited by H. Richard Niebuhr and Daniel D. Williams. New York, 1956.

Medoff, Rafael. "New Evidence Concerning the Allies and Auschwitz." *American Jewish History* 89 (March 2001): 91–104.

Mendes-Flohr, Paul, and Jehuda Reinharz. *The Jew in the Modern World: A Documentary History.* 2nd ed. New York: Oxford University Press, 1995.

Mervis, Leonard J. "The Social Justice Movement and the American Reform Rabbi." *American Jewish Archives* 7 (1955): 171–230.

Metzker, Isaac, editor. *A Bintel Brief.* New York: Doubleday, 1971.

Meyer, Michael A. "American Reform Judaism and Zionism: Early Efforts at Ideological Rapprochement." *Studies in Zionism* 7 (Spring 1982): 49–64.

Meyer, Michael A. "A Centennial History." In *Hebrew Union College–Jewish Institute of Religion at One Hundred Years,* edited by Samuel E. Karff. Cincinnati: Hebrew Union College Press, 1976.

Meyer, Michael A. "From Cincinnati to New York: A Symbolic Move. In *The Jewish Condition: Essays on Contemporary Judaism Honoring Rabbi Alexander Schindler,* edited by Aron Hirt-Mannheimer. New York: UAHC, 1995.

Meyer, Michael A., editor. *German-Jewish History in Modern Times.* 4 vols. New York: Columbia University Press, 1996.

Meyer, Michael A. "German-Jewish Identity in Nineteenth-Century America." In *Toward Modernity: The European Jewish Model,* edited by Jacob Katz. New Brunswick, N.J.: Transaction, 1987.

Meyer, Michael A. *Judaism Within Modernity: Essays on Jewish History and Religion.* Detroit: Wayne State University Press, 2001.

Meyer, Michael A. *Response to Modernity: A History of the Reform Movement in Judaism.* New York: Oxford University Press, 1988.

Miller, Randall M., Harry S. Stout, and Charles Reagan Wilson. *Religion and the American Civil War.* New York: Oxford University Press, 1998.

Mintz, Jerome R. *Hasidic People: A Place in the New World.* Cambridge: Harvard University Press, 1992.

Moise, L. C. *Biography of Isaac Harby.* Columbia, S.C.: R. L. Bryan, 1931.

Moore, Deborah Dash. *At Home in America: Second Generation New York Jews.* New York: Columbia University Press, 1981.

Moore, Deborah Dash. *B'nai B'rith and the Challenge of Ethnic Leadership.* Albany: SUNY Press, 1981.

Moore, Deborah Dash. "Inventing Jewish Identity in California: Shlomo Bardin, Zionism, and the Brandeis Camp Institute." In *National Variations in Jewish Identity: Implications for Jewish Education,* edited by Steven M. Cohen and Gabriel Horenczyk. Albany: SUNY Press, 1999.

Moore, Deborah Dash. *To the Golden Cities: Pursuing the American Dream in Miami and L.A.* Cambridge: Harvard University Press, 1996.

Morais, Henry Samuel. *Eminent Israelites of the Nineteenth Century.* Philadelphia: E. Stern, 1880.

Morawska, Eva. *Insecure Prosperity: Small-Town Jews in Industrial America, 1890–1940.* Princeton: Princeton University Press, 1996.

Moses, Raphael J. *Last Order of the Lost Cause: The Civil War Memoirs of a Jewish Family from the "Old South."* Edited by Mel Young. Lanham, Md.: University Press of America, 1995.

Mostov, Steven G. "A 'Jerusalem' on the Ohio: The Social and Economic History of Cincinnati's Jewish Community, 1840–1875." Ph.D. diss., Brandeis University, 1981.

Nadell, Pamela S. *Conservative Judaism in America: A Biographical Dictionary and Sourcebook.* New York: Greenwood, 1988.

Nadell, Pamela S. "National Federation of Temple Sisterhoods." In *Jewish Women in America: An Historical Encyclopedia,* edited by Paula Hyman and Deborah Dash Moore. New York: Routledge, 1997.

Nadell, Pamela S., *Women Who Would Be Rabbis: A History of Women's Ordination, 1889–1985.* Boston: Beacon, 1998.

Nadell, Pamela S., and Jonathan D. Sarna, editors. *Women and American Judaism: Historical Perspectives.* Hanover, N.H.: University Press of New England, 2001.

Neusner, Jacob. *Stranger at Home.* Chicago: University of Chicago Press, 1981.

Noll, Mark. "The Bible and Slavery." In *Religion and the American Civil War,* edited by Randall Miller, Harry S. Stout, and Charles Reagan Wilson. New York: Oxford University Press, 1998.

Novick, Peter. *The Holocaust in American Life.* Boston: Houghton Mifflin, 1999.

Oppenheim, Samuel. "The Early History of the Jews in New York, 1654–1664. Some New Matter on the Subject." *PAJHS* 18 (1909): 1–91.

Orbach, William W. *The American Movement to Aid Soviet Jews.* Amherst: University of Massachusetts Press, 1979.

Panitz, Esther. "In Defense of the Jewish Immigrant." *American Jewish Historical Quarterly* 55 (September 1965): 57–97.

Parsons, Sanford B. "The Role of Shraga Feivel Mendlowitz in the Founding and Development of Hebrew Day Schools in the United States." Ph.D. diss., New York University, 1983.

Philipson, David. *Letters of Rebecca Gratz.* Philadelphia: Jewish Publication Society of America, 1929.

Philipson, David. *My Life as an American Jew.* Cincinnati: John G. Kidd, 1941.

Philipson, David, and Louis Grossman, editors. *Selected Writings of Isaac M. Wise.* Cincinnati, 1900.

Pilch, Judah, editor. *A History of Jewish Education in America.* New York: National Curriculum Research Institute of the American Association for Jewish Education, 1969.

Plaut, W. Gunther. *The Jews in Minnesota: The First Seventy-Five Years.* New York: American Jewish Historical Society, 1959.

Plaut, W. Gunther. *The Magen David.* Washington, D.C.: B'nai B'rith Books, 1991.

Pointer, Richard W. *Protestant Pluralism and the New York Experience: A Study of Eighteenth-Century Religious Diversity.* Bloomington: Indiana University Press, 1988.

Polish, David. *Renew Our Days: The Zionist Issue in Reform Judaism.* Jerusalem: World Zionist Organization, 1976.

Poll, Solomon. *The Hasidic Community of Williamsburg.* New York: Free Press, 1962.

Polner, Murray. *American Jewish Biographies.* New York: Facts on File, 1982.

Pool, David de Sola. *Portraits Etched in Stone.* New York: Columbia University Press, 1952.

Pool, David de Sola, and Tamar de Sola Pool. *An Old Faith in the New World: Portrait of Shearith Israel, 1654–1954.* New York: Columbia University Press, 1955.

Porterfield, Amanda. *The Transformation of American Religion,* New York: Oxford University Press, 2001.

Prayer Book Abridged for Jews in the Armed Forces of the United States. Rev. ed. New York: National Jewish Welfare Board, 1945.

Prell, Riv-Ellen. *Fighting to Become Americans: Jews, Gender, and the Anxiety of Assimilation.* Boston: Beacon, 1999.

Prell, Riv-Ellen. *Prayer and Community: The Havurah in American Judaism.* Detroit: Wayne State University Press, 1989.

Proceedings of the National Federation of Temple Sisterhoods. Cincinnati, 1941.

Rakeffet-Rothkoff, Aaron. "The Attempt to Merge the Jewish Theological Seminary and Yeshiva College." *Michael* 3 (1975): 254–280.

Raphael, Marc Lee. *A History of the United Jewish Appeal, 1939–1982.* Providence, R.I.: Brown University Press/Scholars Press, 1982.

Rapoport, Nessa. "Cultural Confidence." In *The Jews in America: A Treasury of Art and Literature,* edited by Abraham J. Karp. New York: Hugh Lauter Levin Associates, 1994.

Rapoport, Nessa. "Jewish Cultural Confidence in American Letters: A Writer's Thoughts." In *The Six-Day War and World Jewry,* edited by Eli Lederhendler. Bethesda: University of Maryland Press, 2000.

Reichel, Aaron I. *The Maverick Rabbi: Rabbi Herbert S. Goldstein and the Institutional Synagogue—"A New Organizational Form."* 2nd ed. Norfolk, Va.: Donning, 1986.

Reid, Daniel, et al. *Dictionary of Christianity in America.* Downers Grove, Ill.: Inter-Varsity Press, 1990.

Reform Judaism in the Large Cities—A Survey. New York, 1931.

Report of the Executive Committee Presented at the Second Annual Convention of the Jewish Community (Kehillah) New York, February 25 and 26, 1911. New York, 1911.

Rezneck, Samuel. *Unrecognized Patriots: The Jews in the American Revolution.* Westport, Conn.: Greenwood, 1975.

Reznikoff, Charles, editor. *Louis Marshall Champion of Liberty: Selected Papers and Addresses.* Philadelphia: Jewish Publication Society of America, 1957.

Ribuffo, Leo P. "Henry Ford and the International Jew." *American Jewish History* 69 (June 1980): 437–477.

Rikoon, J. Stanford., editor. *Rachel Calof's Story: Jewish Homesteader on the Northern Plains.* Bloomington: Indiana University Press, 1995.

Rischin, Moses. *The Promised City: New York's Jews, 1870–1914.* New York: Harper Torchbooks, 1970.

Robinson, Ira. "The First Hasidic Rabbis in North America." *American Jewish Archives* 44 (1992): 501–506.

Rogow, Faith. *"Gone to Another Meeting": The National Council of Jewish Women, 1893–1993.* Tuscaloosa: University of Alabama Press, 1993.

Rosen, Robert N. *The Jewish Confederates.* Columbia: University of South Carolina Press, 2000.

Rosenbaum, Fred. *Visions of Reform: Congregation Emanu-El and the Jews of San Francisco, 1849–1999.* Berkeley, Calif.: Judah L. Magnes Museum, 2000.

Rosenblum, Herbert. "The Founding of the United Synagogue of America, 1913." Ph.D. diss., Brandeis University, 1970.

Rosenblum, Yonoson. *Reb Shraga Feivel.* New York: Mesorah, 2001.

Rosenfelt, Henry. *This Thing of Giving.* New York: Plymouth Press, 1924.

Rosengarten, Theodore, and Dale Rosengarten, editors. *A Portion of the People: Three Hundred Years of Southern Jewish Life.* Columbia: University of South Carolina Press, 2002.

Rosenwaike, Ira. "An Estimate and Analysis of the Jewish Population of the United States in 1790." *Publications of the American Jewish Historical Society* 50 (1960): 23–67.

Rosenwaike, Ira. *On the Edge of Greatness: A Portrait of American Jewry in the Early National Period.* Cincinnati: American Jewish Archives, 1985.

Rothkoff, Aaron. "The American Sojourns of Ridbaz: Religious Problems within the Immigrant Community." *American Jewish Historical Quarterly* 57 (1968): 557–572.

Rothkoff, Aaron. *Bernard Revel: Builder of American Jewish Orthodoxy.* Philadelphia: Jewish Publication Society of America, 1972.

Rubenovitz, Herman H., and Mignon L. Rubenovitz. *The Waking Heart.* Cambridge: Nathaniel Dame, 1967.

Rubenstein, Charles A. *History of Har Sinai Congregation of the City of Baltimore.* Baltimore: Har Sinai Congregation, 1918.

Rubin, Israel. *Satmar: Two Generations of an Urban Island.* 2nd ed. New York: Peter Lang, 1997.

Rubin, Saul J. *Third to None: The Saga of Savannah Jewry.* Savannah, Ga.: Mickve Israel, 1983.

Rubin-Dorsky, Jeffrey, and Shelley Fisher Fishkin, editors. *People of the Book: Thirty Scholars Reflect on Their Jewish Identity.* Madison: University of Wisconsin Press, 1996.

Rudavsky, David. "Trends in Jewish School Organization and Enrollment in New York City, 1917–1950." *YIVO Annual* 10 (1955): 45–81.

Salomon, Herman P. "Joseph Jesurun Pinto (1729–1782): A Dutch Hazan in Colonial New York." *Studia Rosenthaliana* 13 (January 1979): 18–29.

Sarna, Jonathan D. "The American Jewish Response to Nineteenth-Century Christian Missions." *Journal of American History* 68 (June 1981): 35–51.

Sarna, Jonathan D. "Converts to Zionism in the American Reform Movement." In *Zionism and Religion,* edited by Shmuel Almog et al. Hanover, N.H.: Brandeis University Press, 1998.

Sarna, Jonathan D. "The Cult of Synthesis in American Jewish Culture." *Jewish Social Studies,* n.s., 5 (Fall–Winter 1999): 52–79.

Sarna, Jonathan D. "The Cyclical History of Adult Jewish Learning in the United States: Peer's Law and Its Implications." *Seymour Fox Festschrift* (forthcoming).

Sarna, Jonathan D. "The Debate over Mixed Seating in the American Synagogue." In *The American Synagogue: A Sanctuary Transformed,* edited by Jack Wertheimer. New York: Cambridge University Press, 1987.

Sarna, Jonathan D. "The Evolution of the American Synagogue." In *The Americanization of the Jews,* edited by Robert M. Seltzer and Norman J. Cohen. New York: New York University Press, 1995.

Sarna, Jonathan D. "From Antoinette Brown Blackwell to Sally Priesand: An Historical Perspective on the Emergence of Women in the American Rabbinate." In *Women Rabbis: Exploration and Celebration,* edited by Gary Phillip Zola. Cincinnati: HUC-JIR Alumni Association, 1996.

Sarna, Jonathan D. "The Future of American Orthodoxy." *Sh'ma* 31 (February 2001): 1–3.

Sarna, Jonathan D. "The Great American Jewish Awakening." *Midstream* 28 (October 1982): 30–34.

Sarna, Jonathan D. *A Great Awakening: The Transformation That Shaped Twentieth Century American Judaism and Its Implications for Today.* New York: Council for Initiatives in Jewish Education, 1995.

Sarna, Jonathan D. "'The Greatest Jew in the World Since Jesus Christ': The Jewish Legacy of Louis D. Brandeis." *American Jewish History* 81 (1984): 346–364.

Sarna, Jonathan D. "The Impact of the American Revolution on American Jews." *Modern Judaism* 1 (1981): 149–160.

Sarna, Jonathan D. "Is Judaism Compatible with American Civil Religion? The Problem of Christmas and the 'National Faith.'" In *Religion and the Life of the Nation,* edited by Rowland A. Sherill. Urbana: University of Illinois Press, 1990.

Sarna, Jonathan D. *Jacksonian Jew: The Two Worlds of Mordecai Noah.* New York: Holmes & Meier, 1980.

Sarna, Jonathan D. "Jewish Prayers for the United States Government: A Study in the Liturgy of Politics and the Politics of Liturgy." In *Moral Problems in American Life: New Perspectives on Cultural History,* edited by Karen Halttunen and Lewis Perry. Ithaca: Cornell University Press, 1998.

Sarna, Jonathan D. *JPS: The Americanization of Jewish Culture.* Philadelphia: Jewish Publication Society, 1989.

Sarna, Jonathan D. "The Late Nineteenth-Century American Jewish Awakening." In *Religious Diversity and American Religious History: Studies in Traditions and Cultures,* edited by Walter H. Conser and Sumner B. Twiss. Athens, Georgia: University of Georgia Press, 1997.

Sarna, Jonathan D. "The Making of an American Jewish Culture." In *When Philadelphia Was the Capital of Jewish America,* edited by Murray Friedman. Philadelphia: Balch Institute Press, 1993.

Sarna, Jonathan D. "The 'Mythical Jew' and the 'Jew Next Door' in Nineteenth-Century America." In *Anti-Semitism in American History,* edited by David A. Gerber. Urbana: University of Illinois Press, 1986.

Sarna, Jonathan D. "The Myth of No Return: Jewish Return Migration to Eastern Europe, 1881–1914." *American Jewish History* 71 (December 1981): 256–268.

Sarna, Jonathan D. "New Light on the Pittsburgh Platform of 1885." *American Jewish History* 76 (March 1987): 358–368.

Sarna, Jonathan D. "A Projection of America as It Ought to Be: Zion in the Mind's Eye of American Jews." In *Envisioning Israel: The Changing Ideals and Images of North American Jews,* edited by Allon Gal. Detroit: Wayne State University Press, 1996.

Sarna, Jonathan D. "The Road to Jewish Leadership." In *Expectations, Education, and Experience of Jewish Professional Leaders: Report of the Wexner Foundation Research Project on Contemporary Jewish Professional Leadership,* edited by Charles Liebman. Waltham, Mass., and Ramat Gan, Israel: Cohen Center for Modern Jewish Studies and Argov Center for the Study of Israel and the Jewish People, 1995.

Sarna, Jonathan D. "Seating and the American Synagogue." In *Belief and Behavior: Essays in the New Religious History,* edited by Philip R. Vandermeer and Robert P. Swierenga. New Brunswick, N.J.: Rutgers University Press, 1991.

Sarna, Jonathan D. "Two Traditions of Seminary Scholarship." In *Tradition Renewed: A History of the Jewish Theological Seminary of America,* edited by Jack Wertheimer. 2 vols. New York: Jewish Theological Seminary, 1997.

Sarna, Jonathan D., and David G. Dalin. *Religion and State in the American Jewish Experience.* Notre Dame: University of Notre Dame Press, 1997.

Sarna, Jonathan D., and Jonathan J. Golden. "The Twentieth Century Through American Jewish Eyes: A History of the *American Jewish Year Book,* 1899–1999." *American Jewish Year Book* 100 (2000): 3–102.

Sarna, Jonathan D., and Karla Goldman. "From Synagogue-Community to Citadel of Reform." In *American Congregations,* edited by James Lewis and James Wind. Chicago: University of Chicago Press, 1994.

Sarna, Jonathan D., and Nancy H. Klein. *The Jews of Cincinnati.* Cincinnati: Center of the Study of the American Jewish Experience, 1989.

Sarna, Jonathan D., and Pamela S. Nadell. *Women and American Judaism.* Hanover, N.H.: University Press of New England, 2001.

Sarna, Jonathan D., and Nahum M. Sarna. "Jewish Bible Scholarship and Translations in the United States." In *The Bible and Bibles in America,* edited by Ernest S. Frerichs. Atlanta: Scholars Press, 1988.

Sarna, Jonathan D., and Ellen Smith. *The Jews of Boston.* Boston: Combined Jewish Philanthropies, 1995.

Schachter, Zalman. "A First Step: A Devotional Guide." In *The [First] Jewish Catalog,* edited by Richard Siegel et al. Philadelphia: Jewish Publication Society of America, 1973.

Schappes, Morris U. *A Documentary History of the Jews of the United States, 1654–1875.* New York: Schocken, 1971.

Schechter, Solomon. *Seminary Addresses and Other Papers.* Cincinnati: Ark, 1915.

Schoener, Allon. *Portal to America: The Lower East Side, 1870–1925.* New York: Holt, Rinehart & Winston, 1967.

Schulman, Avi M. *Like a Raging Fire: A Biography of Maurice N. Eisendrath.* New York: UAHC, 1993.

Schwartz, Laurens R. *Jews and the American Revolution: Haym Salomon and Others.* Jefferson, N.C.: McFarland, 1987.

Schwartz, Shuly Rubin. "Ambassadors Without Portfolio? The Religious Leadership of *Rebbetzins* in Late-Twentieth-Century American Jewish Life." In *Women and American Judaism: Historical Perspectives,* edited by Pamela S. Nadell and Jonathan D. Sarna. Hanover, N.H.: University Press of New England, 2001.

Schwartz, Shuly Rubin. "We Married What We Wanted to Be: The *Rebbetzin* in Twentieth-Century America." *American Jewish History* 83 (June 1995): 223–246.

Scult, Mel, editor. *Communings of the Spirit: The Journals of Mordecai M. Kaplan.* Detroit: Wayne State University Press, 2001.

Scult, Mel. *Judaism Faces the Twentieth Century: A Biography of Mordecai M. Kaplan.* Detroit: Wayne State University Press, 1993.

Sefer Ha-Yovel Shel Agudath Ha-Rabbanim Ha-Orthodoksim B'Amerika. New York, 1928.

Seldin, Ruth R. "American Jewish Museums: Trends and Issues." *American Jewish Year Book* 91 (1991): 71–117.

Sellers, Charles G. *The Market Revolution: Jacksonian America, 1815–1846.* New York: Oxford University Press, 1991.

Shandler, Jeffrey. *While America Watches: Televising the Holocaust.* New York: Oxford University Press, 1999.

Shapiro, Edward S. *A Time for Healing: American Jewry Since World War II.* Baltimore: Johns Hopkins University Press, 1992.

Sharfman, I. Harold. *The First Rabbi: Origins of Conflict Between Orthodox and Reform: Jewish Polemic Warfare in Pre-Civil War America: A Biographical History.* Malibu, Calif.: Pangloss, 1988.

Sheramy, Rona. "Defining Lessons: The Holocaust in American Jewish Education." Ph.D. diss., Brandeis University, 2001.

Sherman, Charles. *The Jew Within American Society.* Detroit: Wayne State University Press, 1961.

Sherman, Moshe. "Bernard Illowy and Nineteenth Century American Orthodoxy." Ph.D. diss., Yeshiva University, 1991.

Sherman, Moshe. "Struggle for Legitimacy: The Orthodox Rabbinate in Mid-Nineteenth Century America." *Jewish History* 10 (Spring 1996): 63–74.

Siegel, Lawrence. "Reflections on Neo-Reform in the Central Conference of American Rabbis." *American Jewish Archives* 20 (April 1968): 63–84.

Silk, Mark. "Notes on the Judeo-Christian Tradition in America." *American Quarterly* 36 (Spring 1984): 65–85.

Silk, Mark. *Spiritual Politics: Religion and America Since World War I.* New York: Simon & Schuster, 1988.

Silverstein, Alan. *Alternatives to Assimilation: The Response of Reform Judaism to American Culture, 1840–1930.* Hanover, N.H.: University Press of New England, 1994.

Silverstein, Alan. "The Evolution of Ezrat Nashim." *Conservative Judaism* 30 (Fall 1975): 41–51.

Singer, David, and Moshe Sokol. "Joseph Soloveitchik: Lonely Man of Faith." *Modern Judaism* 2 (October 1982): 227–272.

Sklare, Marshall. *Conservative Judaism: An American Religious Movement.* New York: Schocken, 1972.

Sklare, Marshall, and Joseph Greenblum. *Jewish Identity on the Suburban Frontier: A Study of Group Survival in an Open Society.* Chicago: University of Chicago Press, 1979.

Sklare, Marshall, and Mark Vosk. *The Riverton Study.* New York: American Jewish Committee, 1957.

Slobin, Mark. *Chosen Voices: The Story of the American Cantorate.* Urbana: University of Illinois Press, 1989.

Smith, Ellen. "Portraits of a Community: The Image and Experience of Early American Jews." In *Facing the New World: Jewish Portraits in Colonial and Federal America,* edited by Richard Brilliant. New York: Jewish Museum, 1997.

Smith, Ellen. "Strangers and Sojourners: The Jews of Colonial Boston." In *The Jews of Boston,* edited by Jonathan D. Sarna and Ellen Smith. Boston: Combined Jewish Philanthropies, 1995.

Snyder, Holly. "'We Have the World to Begin Againe': Jewish Life in Colonial Savannah, 1733–1783." *Proceedings of the Middle Atlantic Historical Association of Catholic Colleges and Universities* 6 (1991): 122–132.

Sobel, Bernard Zvi. "The M'lochim: A Study of a Religious Community." Master's thesis, New School for Social Research, 1956. Microfilm copy found at the Jewish National Library, Jerusalem.

Solotaroff, Ted, and Nessa Rapoport, editors. *The Schocken Book of Contemporary Jewish Fiction.* New York: Schocken, 1992.

Soloveitchik, Haym. "Migration, Acculturation, and the New Role of Texts in the Haredi World." In *Accounting for Fundamentalism,* edited by Martin E. Marty and R. Scott Appleby. Chicago: University of Chicago Press, 1994.

Soloveitchik, Haym. "Rupture and Reconstruction: The Transformation of Contemporary Orthodoxy." *Tradition* 28 (1994): 64–130.

Sorkin, David. *The Transformation of German Jewry, 1780–1840.* Detroit: Wayne State University Press, 1999.

Sorsky, Aaron. *Marbitse Torah Umusar* [in Hebrew]. Brooklyn, 1977.

Soyer, Daniel. "Entering the 'Tent of Abraham': Fraternal Ritual and American-Jewish Identity, 1880–1920." *Religion and American Culture* 9 (Summer 1999): 159–182.

Soyer, Daniel. *Jewish Immigrant Associations and American Identity in New York, 1880–1939.* Cambridge: Harvard University Press, 1997.

Spiegel, Marcus M. *A Jewish Colonel in the Civil War: Marcus M. Spiegel of the Ohio Volunteers.* Lincoln: University of Nebraska Press, 1995.

Sprecher, Hannah. "'Let Them Drink and Forget Our Poverty': Orthodox Rabbis React to Prohibition." *American Jewish Archives* 43 (Fall–Winter 1991): 134–179.

Staub, Jacob J., and Rebecca T. Alpert. *Exploring Judaism: A Reconstructionist Approach.* New York: Reconstructionist Press, 1995.

Staub, Michael E. *Torn at the Roots: The Crisis of Jewish Liberalism in Postwar America.* New York: Columbia University Press, 2002.

Stein, Regina. "The Boundaries of Gender: The Role of Gender Issues in Forming American Jewish Denominational Identity, 1913–1963." Ph.D. diss., Jewish Theological Seminary of America, 1998.

Stember, Charles H. *Jews in the Mind of America.* New York: Basic Books, 1966.

Stern, Malcolm H. "The Function of Genealogy in American Jewish History." In *Essays in Jewish History.* Cincinnati: American Jewish Archives, 1958.

Stern, Malcolm H. "New Light on the Jewish Settlement of Savannah." *American Jewish Historical Quarterly* 54 (March 1963): 163–199.

Stern, Malcolm H. "The Sheftall Diaries: Vital Records of Savannah Jewry (1733–1808)." *American Jewish Historical Quarterly* 54 (1965): 243–277.

Stern, Malcolm H. "Two Jewish Functionaries in Colonial Pennsylvania." *American Jewish Historical Quarterly* 57 (1967): 24–51.

Stern, Malcolm H., and Marc D. Angel. *New York's Early Jews: Some Myths and Misconceptions.* New York: Jewish Historical Society of New York, 1976.

Stern, Myer. *The Rise and Progress of Reform Judaism.* New York: Myer Stern, 1895.

Stier, Oren. "Lunchtime at Majdanek: The March of the Living as a Contemporary Pilgrimage of Memory." *Jewish Folklore and Ethnology Review* 17 (1995): 57–66.

Stokes, Melvin, and Stephen Conway, editors. *The Market Revolution in America: Social, Political, and Religious Expressions, 1800–1880.* Charlottesville: University of Virginia Press, 1996.

Strauss, Herbert A., editor. *Jewish Immigrants of the Nazi Period in the USA.* 6 vols. New York: K. G. Saur, 1978–86.

Sussman, Lance Jonathan. *Isaac Leeser and the Making of American Jewry.* Detroit: Wayne State University Press, 1995.

Sussman, Lance Jonathan. "The Suburbanization of American Judaism." *American Jewish History* 75 (1985): 31–47.

Sussman, Lance Jonathan. "'Toward Better Understanding': The Rise of the Interfaith Movement in America and the Role of Rabbi Isaac Landman." *American Jewish Archives* 34 (April 1982): 35–51.

Svonkin, Stuart. *Jews Against Prejudice: American Jews and the Fight for Civil Liberties.* New York: Columbia University Press, 1997.

Swetlitz, Marc. "American Jewish Responses to Darwin and Evolutionary Theory." In *Disseminating Darwinism: The Role of Place, Race, Religion, and Gender,* edited by Ronald L. Numbers and John Stenhouse. New York: Cambridge University Press, 1999.

Swetschinski, Daniel. *Reluctant Cosmopolitans: The Portuguese Jews of Seventeenth-Century Amsterdam.* London: Littman Library, 2000.

Swichkow, Louis J., and Lloyd P. Gartner. *History of the Jews of Milwaukee.* Philadelphia: Jewish Publication Society of America, 1963.

Szajkowski, Zosa. *Jews, Wars and Communism.* 2 vols. New York: Ktav, 1972–74.

Tabak, Israel. "Rabbi Abraham Rice of Baltimore." *Tradition* 7 (Summer 1965): 100–120.

Tarshish, Allan. "The Board of Delegates of American Israelites (1859–1878)." *Publications of the American Jewish Historical Society* 49 (1959): 16–32.

Tarshish, Allan. "The Charleston Organ Case." *American Jewish Historical Quarterly* 54 (1965): 411–449.

Tcherikover, Elias, and Aaron Antonovsky, editors. *The Early Jewish Labor Movement in the United States.* New York: YIVO, 1961.

Teller, Charles J. "The Jewish Welfare Board." *American Jewish Year Book* 20 (1918–19): 173–227.

Teller, Judd L. *Strangers and Natives: The Evolution of the American Jew from 1921 to the Present.* New York: Delacorte, 1968.

Temkin, Sefton D. *Isaac Mayer Wise, Shaping American Judaism.* Oxford: Published for the Littman Library by Oxford University Press, 1992.

Trachtenberg, Joshua. *Consider the Years: The Story of the Jewish Community of Easton, 1752–1942.* Easton, Pa.: Centennial Committee of Temple Brith Sholom, 1944.

Umansky, Ellen M., and Dianne Ashton. *Four Centuries of Jewish Women's Spirituality: A Sourcebook.* Boston: Beacon, 1992.

Urofsky, Melvin I. *American Zionism from Herzl to the Holocaust.* New York: Doubleday, 1975.

Urofsky, Melvin I. *A Voice that Spoke for Justice: The Life and Times of Stephen S. Wise.* Albany: SUNY Press, 1982.

Urofsky, Melvin I. *We Are One! American Jewry and Israel.* Garden City, N.Y.: Anchor, 1978.

Vandermeer, Philip R., and Robert Swierenga, editors. *Belief and Behavior: Essays in the New Religious History.* New Brunswick, N.J.: Rutgers University Press, 1991.

Waxman, Mordecai, editor. *Tradition and Change: The Development of Conservative Judaism.* New York: Burning Bush, 1958.

Weinberger, Moses. *People Walk on Their Heads: Moses Weinberger's Jews and Judaism in New York.* Translated and edited by Jonathan D. Sarna. New York: Holmes & Meier, 1982.

Weiss, Nancy J. "Long-Distance Runners of the Civil Rights Movement: The Contribution of Jews to the NAACP and the National Urban League in the Early Twentieth Century." In *Struggles in the Promised Land: Toward a History of Black-Jewish Relations in the United States,* edited by Jack Salzman and Cornel West. New York: Oxford University Press, 1997.

Wenger, Beth S. "Jewish Women and Voluntarism: Beyond the Myth of Enablers." *American Jewish History* 79 (Autumn 1989): 16–36.

Wenger, Beth S. *New York Jews and the Great Depression: Uncertain Promise.* New Haven: Yale University Press, 1996.

Wenger, Beth S. "The Politics of Women's Ordination: Jewish Law, Institutional Power, and the Debate over Women in the Rabbinate." In *Tradition Renewed: A History of the Jewish Theological Seminary of America,* edited by Jack Wertheimer. 2 vols. New York: Jewish Theological Seminary, 1997.

Wertheimer, Jack, editor. *The American Synagogue: A Sanctuary Transformed.* Cambridge: Cambridge University Press, 1987.

Wertheimer, Jack. "Jewish Education in the United States: Recent Trends and Issues." *American Jewish Year Book* 99 (1999): 3–115.

Wertheimer, Jack, editor. *Jews in the Center: Conservative Synagogues and Their Members.* New Brunswick, N.J.: Rutgers University Press, 2000.

Wertheimer, Jack. *A People Divided: Judaism in Contemporary America.* New York: Basic, 1993.

Wertheimer, Jack. "Recent Trends in American Judaism." *American Jewish Year Book* 89 (1989): 63–162.

Wertheimer, Jack, editor. *Tradition Renewed: A History of the Jewish Theological Seminary of America.* 2 vols. New York: Jewish Theological Seminary, 1997.

Where We Stand: Social Action Resolutions by the Union of American Hebrew Congregations. New York: Commission on Social Action of Reform Judaism, 1960.

Whiteman, Maxwell. "Notions, Dry Goods, and Clothing: An Introduction to the Study of the Cincinnati Peddler." *Jewish Quarterly Review* 53 (1947): 306–321.

Whitfield, Stephen J. *The Culture of the Cold War.* Baltimore: Johns Hopkins University Press, 1996.

Whitfield, Stephen J. *In Search of American Jewish Culture.* Hanover, N.H.: Brandeis University Press, 1999.

Whitfield, Stephen J. "Israel as Reel: The Depiction of Israel in Mainstream American Films." In *Envisioning Israel,* edited by Allon Gal. Detroit: Wayne State University Press/Magnes, 1996.

Wigoder, Geoffrey. *Jewish-Christian Relations Since the Second World War.* Manchester, Eng.: Manchester University Press, 1988.

Wischnitzer, Rachel. *Synagogue Architecture in the United States.* Philadelphia: Jewish Publication Society of America, 1955.

Wise, Isaac Mayer. *Reminiscences.* New York: Central Synagogue, 1973.

Wiznitzer, Arnold. "The Exodus from Brazil and Arrival in New Amsterdam of the Jewish Pilgrim Fathers, 1654." *Publications of the American Jewish Historical Society* 44 (1954): 80–98.

Wiznitzer, Arnold. *Jews in Colonial Brazil.* New York: Columbia University Press, 1960.

Wiznitzer, Arnold. *The Records of the Earliest Jewish Community in the New World.* New York: American Jewish Historical Society, 1954.

Wolf, Edwin II, and Maxwell Whiteman. *The History of the Jews of Philadelphia from Colonial Times to the Age of Jackson.* Philadelphia: Jewish Publication Society of America, 1975.

Wolfe, Gerard R. *The Synagogues of New York's Lower East Side.* New York: New York University Press, 1978.

Woocher, Jonathan. *Sacred Survival: The Civil Religion of American Jews.* Bloomington: Indiana University Press, 1986.

Woocher, Meredith L. "Texts in Tension: Negotiating Jewish Values in the Adult Jewish Learning Classroom." Ph.D. diss., Brandeis University, 2003.

Wyman, David S., *The Abandonment of the Jews: America and the Holocaust, 1941–1945.* New York: Pantheon, 1984.

Wyman, David S. *Paper Walls: America and the Refugee Crisis, 1938–1941.* New York: Pantheon, 1985.

Wyszkowski, Charles. *A Community in Conflict: American Jewry During the Great European Immigration.* Lanham, Md.: University Press of America, 1991.

Yerushalmi, Yosef Hayim. "Between Amsterdam and New Amsterdam: The Place of Curaçao and the Caribbean in Early Modern Jewish History." *American Jewish History* 72 (December 1982): 172–192.

Young, James. *The Texture of Memory: Holocaust Memorials and Meaning.* New Haven: Yale University Press, 1993.

Young, Mel. *Where They Lie.* Lanham, Md.: University Press of America, 1991.

Zieger, Arthur. "Emma Lazarus and Pre-Herzlian Zionism." In *Early History of Zionism in America,* edited by I. S. Meyer. New York: American Jewish Historical Society, 1958.

Zola, Gary Phillip. *Isaac Harby of Charleston, 1788–1828.* Tuscaloosa: University of Alabama Press, 1994.

Zola, Gary P., editor. *Women Rabbis: Exploration and Celebration.* Cincinnati: HUC-JIR Rabbinic Alumni Association Press, 1996.

Zollman, Joellyn Wallen. "Shopping for a Future: A History of the American Synagogue Gift Shop." Ph.D. diss., Brandeis University, 2002.

Zuroff, Efraim. *The Response of Orthodox Jewry in the United States to the Holocaust.* Hoboken, N.J.: Ktav, 2000.

Index